L. R. Gay

Florida International University

Educational Evaluation & Measurement

Competencies for Analysis and Application

Charles E. Merrill Publishing Company
A Bell & Howell Company
Columbus   Toronto   London   Sydney

Published by Charles E. Merrill Publishing Co.
A Bell & Howell Company
Columbus, Ohio 43216

This book was set in Palatino.
Production Editor: Martha Morss
Cover Design Coordination: Will Chenoweth

Photo Credits:
p. 2—Courtesy of Twentieth Century-Fox. Copyright©1979 Twentieth
Century-Fox Film Corp. All rights reserved.
p. 34—*New York Daily News*.
p. 104, 106, 296—Norman Rockwell, *Saturday Evening Post*.
p. 160—*St. Jerome Studying in His Cell* by George de la Tour. The Louvre.
p. 210—*Faith and Confidence* by William C. Beall.
p. 310—*The Lesson* by Jean Baptiste Simeon Chardin. The National Gallery,
London.
p. 380—From the television series "THE HULK." Courtesy of Universal City
Studios, Inc. THE HULK is a trademark and copyright©1978 of the Marvel
Comics Group, a division of Cadence Industries Corporation. All rights reserved.
p. 474—*The Gleaners* by Jean Francois Millet. The Louvre.

Library of Congress Catalog Card Number: 79-90705
International Standard Book Number: 0–675–08143-2

Printed in the United States of America
1   2   3   4   5   6   7   8   9   10—85   84   83   82   81   80

TO MY SISTERS

Pat, Dot and Debbie Hines

Contents

List of tables

List of figures

Preface

Traditionally, schools and colleges of education have acknowledged that professionals in all areas of education need to possess measurement knowledge and skills. A measurement course may be a basic requirement for undergraduate education majors, or it may be a requirement for a graduate degree, but at some point most education students must take such a course. Increasingly, however, the need for instruction, the broader field of *evaluation* is being recognized. Some schools and colleges are attempting to meet this need by offering a separate course in evaluation. Others are supplementing existing measurement or research courses with evaluation topics.

The philosophy which guided the development of this text is that measurement and evaluation are not separate disciplines. Measurement is an integral part of the evaluation process. The purpose of this text is to present measurement concepts within the framework of contemporary evaluation. This book is designed primarily for use in either an introductory-level graduate course or a senior-level undergraduate course. Since the topic coverage is relatively comprehensive, however, this text may easily be adapted for use in either a more advanced graduate course or a lower-level undergraduate course.

The instructional philosophy behind this text is that an introductory course in measurement and evaluation should be skill oriented rather than knowledge oriented, and application oriented rather than theory oriented. Thus, the purpose of this book is *not* simply to have students become familiar with evaluation procedures or acquire a body of knowledge. The purpose of this book is *not* to mystify students with theoretical and statistical jargon. The purpose of this book is *not* simply to have students acquire in-depth understanding of theory. The purpose of this book *is* to help students acquire the skills and knowledge needed to be a competent consumer and producer of measurement and evaluation tools and techniques. The emphasis is not on what the student knows but rather on what the student can do with what he or she knows. Expertise involves more than the acquisition of skills and knowledge; through experience one acquires insights, intuitions, and strategies related to measurement and evaluation. Experience has meaning, however, only if it is related to a foundation of basic skills and knowledge. Another basic assumption of this text is that there is considerable overlap in the skills and knowledge needed to be a competent consumer of measurement and evaluation tools and techniques and those needed to be a competent producer of same. A person is in a much better position to assess the efforts of others *after* she or he has personally performed the major tasks involved. The instructional strategy of the text, then, is to help students acquire a knowledge of concepts and procedures *and* to involve them in processes of measurement and evaluation.

Two of the most important points about evaluation are made in Part 1. First, although the emphasis of the text is on student evaluation, the basic evaluation process is the same regardless of what is being evaluated, and the basic concepts of measurement are the same regardless of what is being measured. Many people believe that program or project evaluation and evaluation of instruction, for example, involve entirely different processes. The current proliferation of "different" evaluation models has reinforced this assumption. All systems and models for evaluation involve the same essential components, namely: specification of goals and objectives; selection and/or development of measurement tools; delineation and execution of strategies for obtainment; and analysis and interpretation of results. Second, evaluation should not be an afterthought; it should be planned for at the beginning of an endeavor, not at the end.

In part 1, each student identifies and describes an evaluation situation of interest which has relevance to his or her professional life. In each succeeding part, the student simulates the procedures involved in the planning, process, and product phases of the evaluation. Specifically, the student specifies objectives (part 2), specifies the measurement techniques most appropriate for determining achievement of the objectives (part 3), selects standardized instruments (part 4), designs and develops an instrument, and performs an item analysis (part 5), describes implementation strategies (part 6), analyzes and interprets the results of testing (part 7), and reports results (part 8).

This book is more than just a textbook to be read as part of a course; it is actually a total instructional system which includes stated objectives, or competencies, instruction, and procedures for assessment of each competency. The system emphasizes demonstration of skills and individualization within a basic structure. The format for each part is essentially the same. Following an introduction, the task to be performed for that part is described. Tasks require students to show that they can perform particular evaluation functions. Since each student works with a different set of objectives (as specified in part 2), each student demonstrates the competency required by a task as it applies to her or his objectives. Each chapter within a part begins with a list of student performance outcomes. These outcomes entail knowledge and skills which should facilitate students' ability to perform the task for a given part. In many instances, these expected outcomes may be assessed by using written exercises submitted by students or by using criterion-referenced tests, whichever the instructor prefers. For some outcomes the first option is clearly preferable. Each part is directed toward the accomplishment of a task.

Discussion of concepts and procedures in the text is as simple and straightforward as possible. Whenever feasible, procedures are presented as a series of steps, and concepts are illustrated with examples. In a number of cases, relatively complex topics beyond the scope of the text are presented at a very elementary level, and students are directed to other sources for in-depth discussion. There is also a degree of intentional repetition. A number of concepts are discussed at different points in the text in different contexts and from different perspectives. Also, at the risk of eliciting more than a few groans, I have sprinkled the text with humorous comments and notes. Each part includes a rather lengthy summary with headings and subheadings which directly parallel those in the chapters. The summaries are designed to facilitate both review and location of topics in the running text. Each part concludes with Performance Criteria associated with the part task.

Each part in the text corresponds to a section in the student manual, *Educational Evaluation and Measurement: Models of Performance*. The primary purpose of the student manual is to provide the student with model examples of tasks based on work submitted by previous students, supplementary examples, and self-test exercises. In combination, the text and student manual permit implementation of a variety of instructional approaches.

I express my sincere appreciation to all the EDU 517 students whose feedback and performance stimulated constant revision and refinement of the content and presentation of this text. I am grateful to the Literary Executor of the late Sir Ronald A. Fisher, F.R.S., to Dr. Frank Yates, F.R.S., and to Longman Group Ltd., London, for permission to reprint Table VII (abridged) from their book *Statistical Tables for Biological, Agricultural and Medical Research* (6th edition, 1974). I also thank Professors Charles Dzuiban, Larry Henricksen, David Krus, Darrell Sabers, Terry

Schurr, Patricia Simun, Roy Sommerfield, and Wilbur Williams for their conscientious and helpful reviews of portions of earlier drafts of the manuscript. I especially thank Professor Joan Michael, who carefully reviewed the entire manuscript, Nick Maruhnich, who assisted in the preparation of the section on Title I models, and Ron Visco, who made many constructive suggestions regarding chapter 14. Thanks are also extended to Professors Mervin Lynch, Carlton Lemkuhl, and Al Kuolmos for their participation in class testing this manuscript.

Once again, appreciation beyond words is due to my better half for continuous and total understanding, encouragement, and support during the time that "Magnum Opus II" was being written.

L. R. Gay

For students only

If you are anything like students I have taught in the past, you are quite a diverse group. Many of you are teachers, some of you are school administrators or counselors, and some of you are involved with state or local education agencies. A few of you are not associated with the public schools at all, but are involved in fields such as nursing, banking, and homemaking. Most of you are using this text in a course required (Ugh!) for a degree.

The fact that you are in the course indicates that *somebody* thought it involved concepts important for you to know. While there is general agreement that measurement and evaluation skills are important, there is considerable disagreement about exactly what you need to know or should be able to do. Your own feelings about what you need and want to know also vary widely. Regardless of this, all of you are involved in evaluation activities every day, whether you realize it or not. Each concept presented in this book represents an aspect of evaluation in which you are involved personally and professionally, directly or indirectly, as an interested participant in or as an interested consumer of evaluation. If you are a teacher, for example, you may see the value of knowing how to develop a classroom test, but may not see the need for being familiar with standardized tests; after all, *you* never give any. As a teacher, however, you are really at the center of all educational evaluation activities. No matter at what level an activity occurs, ultimately you and your students are the participants. Even if you do not administer standardized tests, your students take them and you receive the results.

Years of classroom experience have shown me that students in a measurement and evaluation course *want* to know a lot of things that other people don't think they *need* to know. Teachers, for example, want to be informed about concepts such as competency testing and standardized testing. There would probably be a lot less resistance to many of the evaluation activities that go on in the schools, for example, if all participants were "let in on it," that is, if they had a general understanding of the purpose and nature of the activities. This book represents a combination of what most instructors agree you need to know and what I think you need to know and believe you want to know.

Some of you may find the contents of this text as exciting as an unexpected promotion (well, almost!), and some of you may find them about as exciting as a Friday afternoon staff meeting. While admittedly some topics are inherently more interesting than others, the important thing is how you approach the content. The stock market report can be engrossing or irrelevant depending upon whether you own any stock. All of you have some "stock" in evaluation since you all constantly evaluate and are in turn evaluated. Therefore, it is in your best interest to be as skilled and knowledgeable in this area as possible.

It would be next to impossible for you to achieve the objectives of this text and not be a more informed consumer of evaluation information and a more capable conductor of evaluation activities. The basic format of the text goes like this. The task given at the beginning of each part represents measurement and evaluation activity that you should be able to perform after reading the part. The Performance Criteria at the end of each part give you additional guidance as to how each part is to be done. At the beginning of each chapter a number of subtasks are listed; these are activities you should be able to do after reading the chapter. If you can do these subtasks, you shouldn't have any trouble doing the task. If you are still not sure how the tasks work, read the preface. In fact, it wouldn't be a bad idea to read the preface anyway (you've never read a preface in your whole life, right?!).

One final note. I love fan mail. I wrote this book for *you*, not for the instructors—they already know the stuff. So I would really appreciate any feedback (positive or negative!) concerning the format or structure of this text. Tell me what you liked and didn't like, and I'll use the information to improve the book.

The study of evaluation, as Professor Kingsfield might say, is "something new and unfamiliar to most of you, unlike any other schooling that you have ever known before."

part one
introduction to educational evaluation

The study of educational evaluation, as Professor Kingsfield might say, is "something new and unfamiliar to most of you, unlike any other schooling that you have ever known before." Therefore, in order to meaningfully learn about and perform components of the evaluation process, it is first necessary for you to develop a cognitive structure into which such experiences can be integrated. The purpose of chapters 1-3 is to provide an overview of the evaluation process and of the various types and phases of evaluation. In succeeding chapters specific components of the evaluation process will be systematically studied and executed.

The goal of part 1 is for you to acquire an understanding of the evaluation process and evaluation methodology which will facilitate acquisition of specific evaluation knowledge and skills. After you have read part 1, you should be able to perform the following task.

task one
Select the type of evaluation of most relevance and interest to you. Briefly describe a specific instance of this type, real or hypothetical, in which you are, will be, or could be involved (e.g. a unit of instruction or a specific program). Briefly describe the factors of interest giving specific examples, which would be involved in the planning phase of evaluation of the above-described endeavor.

(See Performance Criteria, p. 53.)

1 the nature of evaluation

After reading chapter 1, you should be able to:

1 Define or describe evaluation.
2 Describe the major steps in the evaluation process.
3 Define or describe measurement.
4 List at least three ways in which data can be collected.
5 Describe the major benefit to be derived from increased demands for accountability.

Definition and purpose

Evaluation is the systematic process of collecting and analyzing data. If you are thinking that that is not much of a definition, you are correct; it is only part of a definition. It is, however, the only part of the definition of evaluation on which everyone agrees. Examination of evaluation literature makes it very evident, very quickly, that there are almost as many definitions of evaluation as there are evaluation "experts." With minor variations, most of the definitions basically represent one of two philosophical viewpoints, as illustrated by the following two definitions:

1 Evaluation is the systematic process of collecting and analyzing data in order to determine whether, and to what degree, objectives have been, or are being, achieved.
2 Evaluation is the systematic process of collecting and analyzing data in order to make decisions.

A systematic process of data collection, that is, measurement and the analysis of collected data, is common to both definitions. Although some definitions seem to equate measurement with evaluation, most recognize that measurement is but one essential component of evaluation.[1]

The basic difference between the two definitions is the issue of whether decisions, or judgments, are an integral component of evaluation. Proponents of definition 1 agree that the *results* of evaluation may be used for decision making; proponents of definition 2 consider decision making to be *a part of* evaluation. For two major reasons, the second definition would seem to be the preferable of the two. First of all, definition 2 does not preclude the process described in definition 1; in other words, definition 2 is more inclusive. The decisions of definition 2, for example, may be based on determination of the status of objective achievement. Second, the notion that evaluation can be conducted for strictly descriptive purposes, as definition 1 implies, is naive at best. Perhaps, ideally, the sole purpose of evaluation should be to provide feedback in order to improve the object of the evaluation, as the first definition suggests. If that were the case, evaluation would involve determining the difference (if any) between where we are and where we would like to be (our objectives) and if necessary, devising ways to eliminate or lessen the difference.

Realistically speaking, however, provision of feedback is only one aspect of evaluation. Even by dictionary definition, evaluation typically involves some degree of valuing. Questions such as the following are posed:

1 Is this special program *worth* what it costs?
2 Is the new, experimental reading curriculum *better* than the former curriculum?
3 *Should* Fenster be placed in a program for the gifted?

Answers to these questions require the collection and analysis of data and interpretation of that data with respect to one or more criteria. The more objective the

---

[1] For a discussion of the various definitions of evaluation, see Gephart, W. J. Three definitions of evaluation. *SRIS Quarterly*, 1973, 6(2), 4–7.

criteria, the better, although some degree of subjectivity is unavoidable since people determine the criteria. For example, whether a new, experimental curriculum is "better" depends upon the criteria for success. One obvious criterion would be student achievement. Other criteria might include student attitudes and teacher attitudes. Examination of test scores might reveal that students averaged two points higher with the new curriculum. Objectively, and strictly speaking, the new curriculum was "better" with respect to student achievement. School administrators, however, may have decided that an achievement difference of at least ten points would be necessary in order to justify the time, effort, and cost required to change over to the new curriculum. Similarly, determining whether Fenster meets the criteria for admittance to the program for the gifted (e.g. has a specific IQ score and grade point average) would be an objective process; setting the criteria themselves would be a more subjective process.

Deciding whether a special program is "worth" what it costs is even more complex and typically involves serious value judgments. If a special program cost a school system $100,000 per school year but reduced school vandalism by the amount of $150,000, there would not be much disagreement concerning whether the program was worth what it cost. But what if a program cost $100,000 per school year and reduced the ninth grade dropout rate by 5%? How much is an education worth? How much is it worth to have a child increasing his or her knowledge instead of roaming the streets or attempting to enter an already crowded job market? Opinion on this issue varies greatly. The philosophy of the current school board would probably determine whether or not the program continued.

Notice that in none of the examples was the purpose of the evaluation to determine whether something was "good," or worthwhile, as opposed to "bad," or worthless, per se. That is not the function of evaluation. The purpose of evaluation is to determine the current status of the object of the evaluation, to compare that status with a set of standards, or criteria, and to select an alternative in order to make a decision. There may be only two alternatives (e.g. continue the program or not, adopt the new curriculum or keep the current one) or there may be several alternatives (e.g. many textbooks may be available for adoption). Further, every effort is based on one or more objectives, whether they are stated (as they should be) or not, and the purpose of evaluation is the same regardless of the type of evaluation or the nature of the objectives, be they instructional, curricular, or project objectives, explicit or implicit, process oriented or product oriented, short-term or long-term. In all cases the evaluation process is basically the same and involves determination of the types of data which need to be collected, determination of the individual, group, or groups from whom the data will be obtained, collection of the data, analysis of the data, interpretation of the data and decision making.

As the previous examples illustrated, the persons responsible for data collection may or may not be the persons who make the subsequent decisions. The director of a special program or an external evaluator, for example, may collect data concerning the program's accomplishments, but probably does not make the decision to continue or discontinue the program.[2] Decisions such as these are usually made by administrators or funding sources. Decisions are made, however, by persons at all levels of the educational community—by students, parents, teachers, principals, school boards, state departments, and legislators, to name a few. For example: students decide what courses to take; parents decide whether to send

---

[2] An external evaluator is a person with evaluation skills, who is not associated with the program being evaluated, who collects and analyzes appropriate data or verifies existing data.

their children to a private school; teachers decide what grades to assign to students; principals decide who will be chairperson of the English department; school boards decide which special programs to fund; state departments decide what the requirements for high school graduation will be; and legislators decide how much money to appropriate for education. All of these decisions represent the evaluation process, conducted either formally or informally. Of course, the validity of such decisions is a function of the validity of the data collection and analysis procedures.

Measurement

Basing decisions on valid procedures is critical because although all decisions are not equally important, each one has a consequence which directly or indirectly affects students. The more serious the consequences, the more important the decision. Clearly, the decision to place a child in a special education class requires more care with respect to the evaluation process than the decision to appoint a child as hall monitor. Every educational decision, however, should be made on a rational, objective basis to the greatest degree possible and should be based on the best data available. Too many decisions are based on either visceral "data" (gut-level reactions) or the "cardiac principle" (in my heart I feel it's right).

The data collected during the evaluation process are only as good as the measurements upon which they are based. *Measurement* is the process of quantifying the degree to which someone or something possesses a given trait, i.e., quality, characteristic, or feature. Measurement permits more objective description concerning traits and facilitates comparisons. Thus, instead of saying that Minnie is underweight for her age and height, we can say that Minnie is 16 years old, 5' 8" tall, and only weighs 85 pounds. Further, instead of saying that Minnie is more intelligent than Ziggie, we can say that Minnie has a measured IQ of 125 and Ziggie has a measured IQ of 88. In each case, the numerical statement is more precise, more objective, and less open to interpretation than the corresponding verbal statement. To further clarify the advantages of measurement, study the following set of scores:

Student	IQ Score
Suzy Smart	140
Bobby Bright	139
Annie Average	100
Nigel Notso	90
Lester Lesso	82

In each case, it can be said that the student listed is more intelligent than any student below him or her. Yet the *meaning* of that phrase varies considerably depending upon which two students we compare. It can mean that they are both very intelligent and have essentially the same IQ score (Suzy and Bobby). It can mean that one of them is considerably more intelligent than the other (Suzy versus Lester). It can also mean that although one of them is more intelligent than the other, neither of them has a very high IQ score. Thus, we see that expressing their intelligence numerically considerably reduces ambiguity and provides much more useful information.

There is some professional disagreement about whether all traits of interest can be measured. Can you *really* measure elusive qualities such as empathy, appreciation, motivation, and interest? Can you really measure values and attitudes? The answer is yes, but it is not easy. Supporters of this position basically put forth the following argument: If something exists, it exists in quantities, or amounts; if it exists in quantities, it can be measured. If you accept this logic, any trait of interest to educators can be measured. Thus, the purpose of educational measurement is to represent how much of "something" is possessed by a person or entity—very little, some, a great deal—in a numerical way.

Agreeing that at least theoretically all things can be measured and measuring them are two quite different processes. Valid measurement in education is not easy. The major problem is that, with the exception of measurement of physical characteristics such as height and weight, all measurement is indirect; there are no yardsticks or scales for measuring traits like intelligence, achievement, or attitude. Even if you cut open skulls and removed and dissected brains, you would not be able to locate and measure intelligence. Assessment of such traits must of necessity be based upon inference. The problem is further complicated by the lack of well validated instruments. In some areas the problem is not as serious as in others, as we shall see in chapter 6. Achievement tests, as an example, are generally of higher quality than attitude and personality measures such as self-concept scales.

The term measurement is not synonymous with the administration of a test. Data may also be collected via processes such as observation and analysis and rating of a product (such as a science project). In some cases, since they were collected for some purpose other than evaluation, required data may already be available and retrievable from records. A program aimed at improving student behavior, for example, might use data such as number of days absent, number of referrals for disciplinary action, and number of suspensions and expulsions. In many cases, however, some combination of standardized and/or self-developed tests is required. The word "test" has an unduly narrow connotation for many people. A test is not necessarily a written set of questions to which an individual responds in order to determine whether he or she "passes". A more inclusive definition of a *test* is a means of measuring the knowledge, skills, feelings, intelligence, or aptitude of an individual or group.

A number of people object to the use of tests (and in some cases to evaluations in general!) on the grounds that they are demeaning, not very valid indices of traits anyway, and in general do more harm than good. While this point of view has some validity, the conclusion that because testing has some problems we should do away with it appears to be an overreaction. There is no question that there are a lot of poor tests around, both standardized and "homemade," but especially the latter. There are also some very good ones. Whose fault is it if a poor one is used or a good one is misused—the test's? Of course not. It is the responsibility of the persons selecting or developing tests to use the very best instrument possible and to interpret the results with appropriate caution.[3] Also, good evaluation usually involves decisions based on data obtained from a number of sources, not just on the results of a single test. Besides, what is the alternative? If we had no measuring instruments, what would we have to base decisions on other than intuition? It is clearly better to base judgments and decisions on the best data avail-

---

[3] In chapter 7 we will discuss the characteristics which distinguish "good" tests from "bad" ones.

able rather than on subjective impressions. In addition, there is research evidence which indicates that testing does indeed enhance retention of learned concepts.[4]

As suggested earlier, the key is to base decisions on the best data possible, and all instruments administered should have evidence of sufficient validity and reliability. The evaluation process and the resulting decisions are only as good as the data upon which they are based. This concept is especially critical when we consider that the lives of persons involved in the educational process may be seriously affected by decisions. In fact, the whole notion of accountability requires the availability *and use* of valid indices of performance.

Evaluation and accountability

In everyday English, *accountability* means being answerable, or responsible, for one's own actions. Thus, we may speak of one being accountable for his or her behavior, i.e., subject to consequences, good or bad, for actions, good or bad. In education, accountability means essentially the same thing. To varying degrees, any person or program which receives funds from one or more sources is accountable to each source. This means that each is responsible for providing evidence of its accomplishments and successes. To put it bluntly, the people who pay the bills want to know, and feel they have a right to know, how their money was spent and what they got for it.

The accountability concept applies to school personnel, such as teachers, whose salaries are ultimately paid by the American taxpayer, as well as to programs and projects which receive direct funding from local, state, or national governmental agencies or from private foundations. What they are accountable for depends upon their agreed-upon functions and objectives. A teacher, at least to some degree, is accountable for the achievement of her or his students. A program or project may be accountable for producing a set of materials which meet certain criteria, for increasing student achievement in a given content area, for improving student behavior, or for developing and field-testing some type of management technique. Even nonprofit governmental agencies are accountable. Volunteer agencies, such as the Lighthouse for the Blind, are responsible for giving an accounting of how their funds were spent and with what results.

The manner in which the accountability principle is implemented depends upon who is demanding accountability and from whom. There is scarcely any school system which does not require some type of annual evaluation of teachers. In some cases, a program or project may simply be required to submit a report detailing expenditures and accomplishments. In other words, data collection and analysis are done internally. In other cases, an external evaluator may be required. Federally funded programs, for example, typically require that a certain percent of a budget be allocated for evaluation and that an external auditor or evaluator be involved at one or more points in time. Program personnel may collect and analyze the data, but an external person is responsible at the very least for verifying the accuracy and validity of the data collection and analysis procedures.

The increased interest in, and demand for, accountability is not difficult to understand. The education enterprise is requiring, or at least requesting, a progressively larger budget year after year. The persons supplying the funding, both

[4] Gay, L. R., & Gallagher, P.D. The comparative effectiveness of tests versus written exercises. *Journal of Educational Research*, 1976, 70(2), 59–61.

directly and indirectly, want to know what is happening to the money. The revelation that across the nation high school students' scores are progressively declining on tests such as the Scholastic Aptitude Test (SAT) and the American College Testing Program (ACT) has intensified the demand for accountability in the schools.[5] The causes of the test score decline are multiple and complex, and it is certainly an oversimplification to say it is the fault of the schools. Further, test score decline appears to be a worldwide phenomenon rather than a problem peculiar to the United States.[6] But be that as it may, the general public has cried out in indignation and has aimed its criticisms primarily at the public education system. The pressure for accountability has come from inside the school system as well as from outside. School budgets are getting increasingly tight and therefore competition for available dollars is understandably stiff. As a consequence, any course or program not considered to be absolutely necessary must justify its existence in terms of dollars and results. This "no-frills" approach, coupled with the concern over student performance, has resulted in the elimination of a number of activities considered desirable but too expensive and an increased investment in the so-called basics.

Understandably but irrationally, the word *accountability* strikes terror in the hearts of many. It is a very scary word to a number of people. Almost everyone and everything is accountable to someone and engages in evaluation activities. Even persons who express negative attitudes about objectives, evaluation, and accountability engage in evaluation all the time and demand accountability in their everyday activities. Suppose, as an example, you are in the process of selecting a bank at which to open an account. The first thing you do is to identify banks in your neighborhood and collect data as to the convenience of the various banks' hours, their services, and perhaps even their assets. Then you analyze the "data" by identifying which ones meet your needs (your objectives) and comparing the positive and negative features of each. Finally, you make your decision and choose a bank. The process you engaged is called evaluation. Surprised? Now that is not necessarily the end of it. Suppose you find that you have to stand in line for 30 minutes every Friday in order to deposit your paycheck. You may decide to complain or you may change banks. You may decide to trade off an extra ¼% interest on your savings (which only amount to $23.92 anyway!) for shorter lines at another bank. This is still not necessarily the end of your evaluation. As your needs change so may the criteria by which you select a bank. Enough about banks.

Let's look at another example which illustrates the point from a different angle. Suppose you want to buy a pair of white tennis shoes that are sturdy but not too expensive (the criteria for your objective are defined in your own terms; i.e., "not too expensive" may mean under $20.). You do some comparison shopping and purchase your shoes. Two days later, after a spirited tennis match, you notice that the rubber sole of your left shoe is split in half and flapping in the breeze. What do you do? Do you shake your head woefully and say, "Oh well, I've been had again." Probably not. Instead you march back to the store where you purchased the shoes and demand either your money back or a new pair of shoes. Why? Because you want your money's worth. That is accountability. Everyone wants it and most see to it that they get it with respect to purchased goods and

---

[5] For a discussion concerning the test score decline, see Harnischfeger, A., & Wiley, D. E. Achievement test score drop. So what? *Educational Researcher*, 1976, *5*(3), 5–12.
[6] Rudman, H. C. The superintendent and testing: Implications for the curriculum. *NCME: Measurement in Education*, 1977, *8*(4), 1–8.

services. Thus, it is perfectly natural that parents should indicate their desire for more accountability with respect to the progress of their children.[7]

It is precisely because of the consumer demand for accountability that businesses offer warranties, guarantees, refunds, and replacements. It is the nature of accountability that it leads to increased efforts to produce quality products and efficient procedures. And so it is with education. Increased demands for accountability should result in increased efforts to improve the educational experiences of all children. Or, as Leon Lessinger, the "father" of the accountability movement in education, expresses it, the goal of accountability is to make "every kid a winner."[8] Most people recognize the value and potential benefits of accountability and think that it is a great idea—unless they are the ones being evaluated! It is not that they don't think they are doing a good job; there is just a natural anxiety associated with any type of evaluation. The feeling is similar to the one you get when you find out that you are going to be audited by the Internal Revenue Service—even if you were totally honest when you filed your tax return. Some people fail to realize the personal benefits that can result from an evaluation of their performance. If they are doing an excellent job, this fact will be validated and everyone will know. But nobody is perfect. Everyone can benefit from feedback. The evaluation process can provide the feedback which will identify those things that we are doing right and those things that need improvement, what is working and what is not. Thus, the evaluation process is a mechanism for improvement, a process which helps us to get closer to our objectives. It provides us with feedback which helps us to make decisions about our objectives, strategies, and activities.

Evaluation and accountability are worthwhile concepts only if related procedures are competently conducted and results are interpreted with proper care. As mentioned previously, any evaluation is only as good as the data upon which it is based. Whether we are evaluating student progress or the effectiveness of a Title I program, it is imperative that valid indices be used in data collection. Further, it is critical to the whole process that people be evaluated on, and be held accountable for, only those things over which they have control and only to the degree that they do. It seems obvious that a student cannot be held responsible for being able to solve quadratic equations if quadratic equations were never taught. It is not always so easy, however, to determine who is accountable for what. For example, how accountable is a teacher for the achievement of her or his students? Not at all? Totally? Somewhat? How much control does the teacher actually have over the factors which lead to a given achievement outcome? Teachers do not have control over the ability level, aptitudes, or experiences which students bring to the classroom. Nor do they have much control over the facilities, curriculum, or instructional materials. Teachers do have control, however, over how they deal with students, over how well they adapt the curriculum to meet the needs of the students, and over how well available resources are utilized. Thus, teachers are at least partially responsible for the achievement of students. The point is that in any evaluation situation the persons being evaluated, whether students, teachers, administrators, or project directors, can only be held accountable for outcomes to the degree to which they had control over factors which brought them about.

---

[7] The results of a Gallup survey indicated that 67% of adults were in favor of an accountability system with respect to student progress. See Gallup, G. The public's attitude toward the public schools. *Phi Delta Kappan*, 1970, *52*, 100.

[8] Lessinger, L. M. *Every kid a winner: Accountability in education.* Palo Alto: Science Research Associates, 1970.

2 types of evaluation

After reading chapter 2, you should be able to:

1 Define or describe what is meant by "types" of evaluation.
2 List the components which are common to all valid models of evaluation.
3 List at least five variables of interest in student evaluation.
4 List at least three kinds of decisions which are made based on the results of student evaluation.
5 State two major variables which are measured in curriculum evaluation.
6 Describe three ways in which a new program can be cost-effective.
7 State the major kinds of decisions which result from school evaluation.
8 List four variables which should be measured as part of a school testing program.
9 Define or describe evaluation of large populations.
10 Define or describe evaluation of special projects and programs.
11 Define or describe evaluation of personnel.

Types versus models

When we speak of "types" of evaluation, we are referring to the different processes, products, and persons *subject to* evaluation. These include students, curricula, schools, school systems, large populations, special programs and projects, and personnel. The fact that we speak of different types of evaluation does not mean that there are a number of different evaluation processes. The basic evaluation process is the same regardless of what is being evaluated. What differs is what is being evaluated, how the evaluation process is applied, and the types of decisions made. Depending upon what is being evaluated, different kinds of data will be collected, different criteria will be applied to the data, and different kinds of decisions will be made. But the basic evaluation process is the same and the same general concepts and principles of measurement and evaluation are applicable.

A false dichotomy has been fostered in the minds of many to the effect that classroom, or pupil, evaluation and other types of evaluation, such as project evaluation, involve entirely different processes. Further, it is incorrectly believed by a number of people that each type of evaluation requires a different process or model. The current proliferation of "different" evaluation models only serves to reinforce this erroneous belief. Gephart expressed the situation well:

> We have reached a point of absurdity! In a recent conversation 27 "different" models of the evaluation process were delineated. . . . To present just a partial list, we have the formative model; the summative model; the measurement model; the accreditation model; the CIPP, Discrepancy, CSE, Hammond, Fortune-Hutchinson, Countenance, Responsive, Legal, advocate team, adversary, and Hincle-McElhinney models and the OTT Taxonomy; the goal-free model; the consumer product model; the ethno-evaluation model; the multiple method model; and the Organizational Policy Evaluation (OPE) model. This sorry state of affairs is made even worse by our tendency to refer to the Stake, or Stufflebeam, or Scriven, or Alkin, or Scriven #2, or Provus models, or. . . .[1]

Probably the two most widely known and used models are CIPP and DEM. CIPP, which was developed by Stufflebeam, stands for Context, Input, Process, and Product.[2] Context evaluation refers to the processes involved in selecting objectives; Input evaluation refers to evaluation of, and selection from, a number of alternative strategies for achieving objectives; Process evaluation involves evaluating the implementation of selected strategies; and Product evaluation deals primarily with whether, and to what degree, objectives are being achieved. DEM, developed by Provus, stands for Discrepancy Evaluation Model.[3] Under this model, evaluation basically involves making decisions based on a determination of the differences, or discrepancies, which exist between standards and actual performance. In other words, evaluation involves a comparison of the way things are with how they should be. There is nothing wrong with either one of these models. If you followed one of them, or one of the many others available, you would have

---

[1] Gephart, W. J. Editorial. *The CEDR Quarterly*, Summer, 1976, *9*(2), 2.
[2] Stufflebeam, D. L., et al. *Educational evaluation and decision making*. Itaska, Ill.: F. E. Peacock, 1971.
[3] Provus, M. *Discrepancy evaluation*. Berkeley: McCutchan, 1971.

valid guidelines for conducting an evaluation.[4] The point is, however, that all valid systems and models for evaluation involve the same essential components, namely: specification of goals and objectives; selection and/or development of measurement tools; delineation of strategies for objective attainment; process and product procedures (to be discussed in the next section); and analysis and interpretation of results. The terms used to describe these processes may vary, and the level of specificity at which they are described may vary, but the basic processes are the same.

A major point of disagreement among evaluators is the issue of whether evaluation efforts should be based on research design, particularly when group comparisons are involved such as, Does curriculum A lead to higher achievement than curriculum B? Some argue that educational research and educational evaluation have distinctly different purposes, that research seeks control while evaluation assesses what is, and that the natural settings characteristic of evaluation essentially preclude that control. In reality, however, there is often a fine line between research and evaluation, and an evaluation may very easily utilize a research design. Both research and evaluation involve decision making and both are based on the scientific method. In research one states hypotheses, and the researcher's *objective* is to test these hypotheses. The researcher also selects or develops measurement tools, delineates strategies for testing the hypotheses, engages in process and product activities, and analyzes and interprets results. Further, many research studies are conducted in natural, real-world settings and are subject to the same control problems which are faced by evaluators. The same maxim applies in conducting evaluation as in conducting research: Do the very best you can. After all, that is all you can do! If it is feasible to use a good experimental design in an evaluation, do so. If not, do the next best thing that is feasible.[5]

Now that we have all of that straight, let us look at some of the various types of evaluation.

Student evaluation

When you think of student evaluation, you probably think of achievement. Achievement, however, is but one of many variables on which a student is assessed. Other variables include: aptitude, intelligence, personality, attitudes and interests, to name a few of the major ones. Many different kinds of data are collected on each student in order to make a variety of decisions. Tests, both standardized and teacher made, are administered, projects, procedures, and oral presentations are rated, and formal and informal observations are made. The data obtained are recorded on teachers' records and in guidance files, which include, of course, the ever-popular cumulative folder. Not all of the subsequent decisions relate directly to the student. A teacher uses performance data not only to evaluate student progress but also to evaluate her or his own instruction. In other words, the process of evaluating students provides feedback to the teacher. If only a small number of students seem to experience difficulty in achieving a given objective,

[4] For additional information on these and other models, see Popham, W. J. (Ed.). *Evaluation in education.* Berkeley: McCutchan, 1974, *and* Anderson, S.B., Murphy, R.T., & Associates. *Encyclopedia of educational evaluation.* San Francisco: Jossey-Bass, 1976.
[5] Evaluation designs will be discussed further in chapter 14.

the teacher may conclude that the original instructional strategy was successful. If many students have trouble with a given objective, the teacher may decide that the original instructional strategy was inadequate. In either case, the teacher will probably devise an alternate strategy (or strategies) for some or all of the students.

Feedback on current student progress also gives direction to future instructional activities. The teacher may decide, for example, that the rate of presentation should be slowed down (or sped up); in other words, the teacher may realize that he or she has been "going too fast." Testing may also reveal that a number of students are lacking certain skills or concepts which are prerequisites to current learnings. Thus, lesson plans may be revised to deal with these deficiencies *before* further work is attempted with the current objectives. Of course in certain systems of individualized instruction many of these procedures are built into the system, greatly facilitating the job of the teacher. These systems include instruments which permit continuous assessment on an individual student basis. They provide tests of entry behavior (prerequisites), pretests on given sets of objectives, posttests, and cumulative, or milestone, tests. Students in such systems typically progress at their own rate. In any event, it should be clear that evaluation of student performance provides valuable feedback on past instruction which gives direction to current and future efforts.

There are all kinds of decisions made which do directly affect the student; not all of these decisions are made by the teacher. The teacher determines whether the student has achieved objectives, or to what degree, and provides either appropriate remediation or the next set of objectives. The teacher also makes judgments as to whether a student is working up to potential and if not, may attempt to find out why. Results of intelligence tests and aptitude tests, as well as records of previous performance, provide the teacher with a general level of expectation concerning each student's ability. It is a teacher's responsibility to deal with apparent underachievement and to attempt to provide motivating experiences. In certain instances, a teacher may decide that a child has special needs which cannot be met in a regular classroom and may recommend that the child be placed in a special environment, be it a special education class for learning disabled children, a program for gifted children, or a school for emotionally disturbed children.

The teacher also makes cumulative decisions about students based on their performance over an extended period of time. At certain intervals grades must usually be assigned, be they letter grades, numerical indices, or pass-fail judgments, which indicate level of student achievement. An effort grade may be assigned separately, or one grade may be used which reflects both actual performance *and* effort. Thus, low-ability students may receive A's indicating that they are achieving very well *at their level*.[6] Finally, at the end of the school year, many teachers must make a decision on each child whether or not to recommend promotion to the next grade. Such decisions are often based on a variety of academic and personal-social data. A first grader's lack of achievement may be linked with a lack of social maturity, for example, indicating that the child was not ready for the first grade. Since first grade skills form the foundation for all subsequent learning, it might be decided that repeating the first grade would be very beneficial to the student.

There are numerous decisions that are made concerning students in which the teacher is either not involved or only makes recommendations. The decision to place a child in a special program may be made by a school psychologist based on

[6] Advantages and disadvantages of various grading systems will be discussed in chapter 19.

a combination of teacher input, test results, eligibility requirements, and parental approval. Promotion decisions usually involve more data than that supplied by the teacher. Also, following graduation from high school, students are evaluated by employers and higher education entrance personnel based on previous performance, recommendations, and a variety of measures which they themselves administer to applicants.

This brief look at the evaluation life of a child should make it clear that the number of educational decisions that are made concerning each one is staggering. Many of these decisions have powerful effects on the child's life and future. Such decisions should not be made lightly or based on insufficient or invalid data. Of all the types of evaluation discussed, student evaluation is probably the most critical, with the possible exception of evaluation of personnel. The reason is that decisions made affect individuals as individuals, as opposed to curricular decisions for example, which affect groups. This is not to say that group decisions are not important. In one sense they are more important in that the consequences are multiplied by the number of persons in the group. Decisions about individuals, however, such as decisions to promote or not promote, often have consequences of a more serious nature.

Curriculum evaluation

Curriculum evaluation involves the evaluation of any instructional program or instructional materials, and includes evaluation of such factors as instructional strategies, textbooks, audiovisual materials, and physical and organizational arrangements. Curriculum evaluation may involve evaluation of a total package or evaluation of one small aspect of a total curriculum, such as use of films. Although ongoing programs are subject to evaluation, curriculum evaluation is usually associated with innovation, a new or different approach. The approach may be general, i.e., applicable to many curriculum areas, or specific to a given subject area. Examples of general approaches include: programmed instruction, individualized instruction, the open-space concept, computer-assisted instruction, computer-managed instruction, and multimedia instruction. The characteristics of these various innovations are not necessarily mutually exclusive; individualization strategies of one kind or another, for example, are inherent in a number of recent curriculum innovations. There is scarcely a subject area which has not been introduced to a new approach to instruction within recent history. Some of these are by now familiar to almost everyone; they include the "new" math, BSCS biology, PSSC physics, and the inquiry approach to social studies. Others, such as the ITA (Initial Teaching Alphabet) reading method, are known mostly to persons within a particular field. Given the large number of curriculum packages, strategies, and materials which have been developed and proposed during the last 20 years, their accompanying costs, and increased attention to accountability, it is not surprising that curriculum evaluation has received progressively more attention.

Curriculum evaluation usually involves both internal and external criteria and comparisons. Internally, evaluation is concerned with whether the new process or product achieves its own stated objectives, that is, whether it does what it purports to do, as well as with evaluation of the objectives themselves. Externally, evaluation is concerned with whether the process or product does whatever it does better than some other process or product. The "other" may be what is currently being used or it may be a different innovation. The difference between internal and external evaluation can best be illustrated through a concrete example.[7] ISIS (Individualized Science Instructional System) is a modularized, multidisciplinary, high school science curriculum consisting of a number of minicourses in such areas as life science, physics, chemistry, and a multidisciplinary app ɔach to science. Each minicourse has 12 to 18 specific instructional objectives and accompanying tests. Students receive feedback on their test performance and remedial instruction when necessary.[8] The major question with regard to internal evaluation for any system such as this one would be whether, or to what degree, students do indeed achieve the specified objectives. The major question with regard to external evaluation would be how students in this system compare in achievement with students in other systems of instruction, being taught essentially the same concepts.[9] Thus, we see that student evaluation is almost always a part of curriculum evaluation. When we speak of student evaluation we are concerned with how each student is performing; when we speak of curriculum evaluation our concern is with group, not individual, performance.

Although we will discuss this point further in chapter 4, it should at least be mentioned here that there are persons who hold the view that evaluating a curriculum in terms of objectives is restrictive and nonproductive. These persons advocate what is called "goal-free" evaluation, and suggest that the focus of attention should be on actual outcomes, not on prespecified outcomes.[10] But more on that later.

In addition to student achievement, there are a number of other factors which are generally recommended for inclusion in curriculum evaluation. Attitudes are one such factor. How do teachers feel about it? How do students react? Are they learning more but liking school less? What about parents, administrators, and the community at large? These are important considerations. How a teacher feels about a curriculum change, for example, may significantly affect its ultimate effectiveness. Anecdotal evidence supporting this assertion is found in the following true story. A number of schools in a particular county, let us call it Wynot County, had adopted a new curricular approach to reading instruction. The results of yearly achievement testing revealed that some of these schools showed marked increases in reading achievement since the adoption of the new approach while others showed marked decreases. A number of school and university persons were discussing possible reasons for this paradoxical finding. One of the discussants, who was at that time a reading specialist in Wynot County, made a revealing observation. She said that in her role as reading specialist she had interacted with every reading teacher in the county and that the only significant variable which she could discern related to the effectiveness (or lack of it) of the new approach was the attitude of the teacher implementing it. If the teacher liked it, it worked swell; if not, it did not work at all.

There is also research evidence to support this contention. Brownell, for

[7] To avoid possible confusion, it should be noted that the terms "internal evaluation" and "external evaluation" are sometimes used in a different context, with an internal evaluation being one conducted by program or project personnel and an external evaluation being one conducted by one or more external evaluators, as previously defined.

[8] Evaluation Staff. Individualized Science Instructional System Project (ISIS). Tallahassee: College of Education, Florida State University, 1977.

[9] The concepts of internal and external evaluation are considered aspects of formative and summative evaluation which will be discussed later in the chapter.

[10] Scriven, M. Prose and cons about goal-free evaluation. *Evaluation Comment*, 1972, 3(4), 1–4.

example, tested the hypothesis that differences are due to the enthusiasm of teach-ers.[11] To test this hypothesis, he studied two approaches to arithmetic instruction in both Scotland and England—use of cuisenaire rods and use of traditional methods and materials. Cuisenaire rods were viewed as "new" in Scotland, but in England, where teachers had been exposed to one new system of instruction after another, they were viewed as just one more innovation. In Scotland, apparently due to teacher enthusiasm, the cuisenaire approach was found to be more effective than traditional methods whereas in England the traditional approach was found to be more effective.

Clearly, it is foolhardy to attempt to evaluate a curriculum without collect-ing data on teacher attitudes. Further, determining the reasons for any teacher dis-satisfaction may suggest remedies which when implemented will bring about a change of teacher attitude and subsequently increase the effectiveness of the cur-riculum. Frequently, the complaint is not with the curriculum per se but with some related factor such as management. As an example, many teachers express the feeling that individualized instruction is a very effective approach to student learning but that it is very difficult to manage. Systems involving individualiza-tion require a great deal of record keeping and numerous other clerical tasks such as grading many pretests and posttests. As a consequence, efforts have been ini-tiated—such as the development of computer management systems, the provision of automatic scoring devices, and an increased use of paraprofessionals—in order to relieve the teacher of these nonteaching duties. Such remedies not only improve teacher attitudes, but they also result in increased time being available for direct instruction.

Attitudes of other involved groups are also important. In the short run, for example, students may achieve under a system they do not like, but it is doubtful that they will cooperate for very long with an approach they find distasteful. Again, inquiring as to *why* they do not like something may provide feedback which will result in curricular revision and a subsequent improvement in student attitude. Administrators may object to a new program because it involves what they consider to be an inefficient utilization of space. Parents may object for a vari-ety of reasons. They may not like the idea of their children being in a class of 100 students (they may not realize that there are four teachers working with those 100 children). Or, they may feel that computers are going to replace teachers and their children will be talking to a machine all day! As these latter examples illustrate, objections are sometimes based upon misinformation or lack of information. By surveying involved groups we can identify specific objections and determine whether they are correctable.

A final, major factor to be considered in curriculum evaluation is cost. As discussed with respect to accountability, education dollars are not plentiful and any new program has to be able to justify itself in terms of cost. Other factors being equal, a new program is usually considered to be cost-effective if one of the following is true: (1) it costs essentially the same as other programs but results in greater achievement (if achievement is the same, why bother?!); (2) it costs less and results in equal or greater (unlikely!) achievement; (3) it costs more but results in significantly greater achievement (assuming it is affordable to the group inves-tigating its effectiveness). Unless the difference is minimal, anything that costs more usually must be demonstrably, and practically unequivocally, better. Even then it may still be judged to be not sufficiently cost-effective. Having a private

[11] Brownell, W. A. *Arithmetic abstractions: The movement toward conceptual maturity under differing sys-tems of instruction.* Berkeley: University of California Press, 1967.

tutor for each and every child could probably be shown to be very effective, but the chances of this strategy being adopted by the public school system are essentially zero.

Curriculum evaluation has one major well-known problem associated with it. It is very difficult to compare fairly the effectiveness of one program or approach with another. Even if two programs deal with the same subject area, they may involve objectives which are very different. As a consequence, it may be next to impossible to find a test or other measure which is equally fair, or valid, for both programs. If it is not equally fair, then by definition one group will have an advantage over the other. In some cases this problem is obvious and in others not so obvious, although most people are at least aware of the potential difficulty. A classic case which illustrates this phenomenon is the early studies which compared the "new" math with the "old" math. These studies invariably found no achievement differences between students taught under the two approaches. The problem was that, while the same content area was involved in both, the "new" math was emphasizing concepts and principles while the achievement tests were emphasizing computational skill. When tests were developed which contained an adequate sampling of items measuring concepts and principles, studies began to find that the two approaches to teaching math resulted in essentially equal computational ability, but that the "new" math resulted in greater conceptual understanding. The moral of the story is clear. If one curriculum is to be compared to another, the objectives of each must be examined carefully; if no test can be located which is equally appropriate to both, then one must be developed which is.

One final point. As mentioned previously, curriculum evaluation differs from student evaluation in that it is concerned with group, rather than individual, performance. In some cases, group sizes are very large; the evaluation of the ISIS curriculum discussed previously, for example, involves several thousand students from coast to coast. In such cases, administering a number of complete tests to each and every student (and scoring them) can be very time-consuming and costly. A relatively new technique which has been developed to deal with this problem is referred to as *matrix sampling*. Matrix sampling basically involves dividing a test into a number of subtests, using random sampling techniques on the items, and administering each subtest to a subgroup of students, also randomly selected from a total group.[12] Thus, no student takes the total test. Using statistical procedures, one can estimate rather well what the results would have been if all students had been tested on all items. This procedure results in a considerable reduction in both testing time and cost. With the exception of evaluation of personnel, matrix sampling is also very useful for each of the remaining types of evaluation to be discussed, as they also are concerned with group, rather than individual, performance.

School evaluation

Evaluation of a school involves evaluation of the total educational program of the school and entails the collection of data on all aspects of its functioning. The purpose of school evaluation is to determine the degree to which school objectives are

---

[12] Shoemaker, D. M. Matrix sampling in a nutshell. *The CEDR Quarterly*, Fall, 1976, 9(3), 4–6.

being met and to identify areas of strength and weakness in the total program. This information provides feedback which gives direction to the future activities of the school and results in decisions concerning the allocation of school resources. Based upon a school evaluation, for example, the decision might be made to eliminate the pen pal program and to redirect the resulting resources to the reading program. Such decisions do not come easily, but they are often necessary nonetheless. The processes leading to the outcomes, as well as the outcomes themselves, are evaluated. If student performance is lower in one area than in any other, then all school-based factors related to achievement in that area must be evaluated. Thus, all aspects of the total curriculum must be evaluated as well as student performance, and we see that curriculum evaluation is part of school evaluation.

One major component of school evaluation is the school testing program. The more comprehensive the testing program, the more valuable are the resulting data. Achievement is, of course, the single most important testing area since the main objectives of any school center on student learning. And no one would deny that measures of aptitude are also valuable. But there is more, much more. Factors which are *not* measured may in fact represent the key variables which are related to given achievement patterns. Evaluation of the curriculum will not reveal this, nor will all the achievement and aptitude tests in the world. A profile of results on various personality and interest variables can be very enlightening. Self-concept, for example, is a variable which has been theoretically and empirically linked to achievement, and children classified as disadvantaged tend to have lower self-concepts.[13] Administration of a self-concept scale in a school located in a low socio-economic neighborhood might very well reveal a prevalence of low self-concept. Subsequent discussions of strategies for improving achievement might include consideration of strategies which could be implemented that are aimed at raising the self-concept level of the student population. There are numerous other variables related to achievement which can be assessed. These include measures of aggression, anxiety, aspiration, and motivation, as well as measures of attitude, such as attitude toward school.

Tests selected for a school evaluation must match the objectives of the school and be appropriate for the students to be tested. In addition to reviewing information concerning the validity and reliability of a test, factors such as the characteristics of the norm group and the readibility of the test must be considered. If validity data, reliability data, and norms (such as percentiles) are based on administration of the test to a group of students distinctly different from those in your school, then the applicability of such data to your situation is very questionable. If such a test is administered anyway, then results must be interpreted with extreme caution. It is highly questionable, for example, whether a test normed on a group of upper-middle–class midwestern students is appropriate for a group of inner-city students in Boston. Relatedly, factors such as readibility are important. If a test contains vocabulary and terms that are not familiar to your students, then the test is not appropriate.

The question of the appropriateness of norms is a critical issue since most schools are very concerned (perhaps overly so) with how well their students perform compared to the national norm. It is sadly amusing how upset some con-

[13] See, for example, Brookover, W. B., Le Pere, J. M., Hamachek, D. E., Thomas, S., & Erickson, E. L. *Self-concept of ability and school achievement, II* (USOE Cooperative Research Report, Project No. 1636). East Lansing: Michigan State University, 1965, *and* Stenner, A. J., & Katzenmeyer, W. G. Self concept, ability, and achievement in a sample of sixth grade students. *The Journal of Educational Research*, 1976, *69*(7), 270–273.

cerned parents and school personnel get when they learn that 45% of a school's students, for example, are below average. By definition, half of the students in the country have to be below average; every child cannot be above average. If the skills and knowledge of every student in the United States increased 100%, half of them would still be below average because the performance associated with average would increase. Of course, national norms can be useful as a very general standard, and it is helpful to know that 70% of the students in a given school score at or below the 20th percentile in reading. Given, however, the range of variables that affect achievement, many of which the school has no control over, the tendency to overreact to national norm comparisons should be avoided (recall our discussion of accountability). When available, as is often the case with larger school systems, county or system norms are more useful as a basis for comparison than national norms. Local system norms at least take into account factors such as the size, location, and resources of the system, and all schools within that system are subject to the same school board policies and regulations.

Do not get the mistaken impression that school evaluation and school testing programs are synonymous terms. School evaluation involves more than the administration of tests to students. It may require any combination of questionnaires, interviews, and observations, with data being collected from all persons in the school community, including administrators, teachers and counselors. School evaluation is a *total* effort and all relevant groups must be involved in all phases— planning, execution, interpretation of results, and subsequent decision making.

One last word on school evaluation. You may encounter discourse on "institutional evaluation," probably in relation to evaluation of institutions of higher education. Institutional evaluation, however, is concerned with the objectives, processes, and outcomes of any institution; the concepts are equally applicable to all educational or training institutions, including schools.

Evaluation of large populations

Evaluation of large populations involves assessing the current status and the educational progress of large numbers of students, typically distributed over a large geographic region. This type of evaluation includes statewide assessment programs as well as efforts involving national samples. Statewide assessment programs have developed primarily in response to the increased demands for accountability. Florida, for example, was one of the first states to pass legislation requiring accountability in the form of a uniform statewide assessment system designed to permit the comparison of school districts with each other and the comparison of Florida with other states and regions. The program is based on the premises that the state system of education is responsible for student achievement of certain basic skills required for effective functioning in our society, and that programs designed to promote achievement of the basic skills should be as effective and economical as possible. The Florida program focuses on the assessment of student achievement of specified minimum objectives, that is, objectives which virtually all students should be able to achieve by certain times in their school career. Thus there are minimum objectives for various grade levels and for various subjects. One of the major purposes of the assessment is to provide information to state and local decision makers about the adequacy of the basic educational program, the goal being "to provide the incentive for establishing a basic educational program for all Florida students which will minimize the frequency of societal rejection of individuals for their lack of certain basic skills."[14]

The Florida plan involves measurement of minimum educational objectives and selected optional objectives using both criterion-referenced and norm-referenced tests. The program strives for economy and efficiency of testing, with regard to both cost and student time. Thus, all students are tested on some objectives while samples of students are tested on other objectives (using matrix sampling techniques). The plan involves a multi-year sequence with different subject matter areas being tested in order of their assigned priority. Accordingly, student performance in the area of reading was assessed during the 1971–72 school year and in the areas of writing and mathematics during the 1972–73 school year, with other areas scheduled for subsequent years.[15] Thus, the Florida assessment program is based on the assumption that the state is accountable to some degree for the education of its students. It involves collecting and analyzing data on the degree of achievement of prespecified minimum objectives and the provision of feedback to both local- and state-level decision makers.

National assessment efforts have also been prompted by the accountability movement. Perhaps the largest and best known of these endeavors is the National Assessment of Educational Progress (NAEP) program. NAEP is a "national, census-like survey of the knowledge, skills, understandings, and attitudes of certain groups of young Americans," and its stated rationale clearly shows its relationship to accountability.[16] Its stated purpose is to determine what benefit has been derived from the billions of dollars spent yearly on education, in terms of what Americans know and can do. The major goal of NAEP is to measure growth or decline in performance, with respect to selected learning areas, which is evidenced over time. Implementation of NAEP required the identification of objectives representative of the outcomes which the educational system is attempting to achieve, and the development of exercises to measure those objectives.

Each year a selected group of exercises are administered to a randomly selected group numbering approximately 80,000, located in various parts of the country, and representing the ages 9, 13, 17, and 26–35. As with Florida's statewide assessment, different subject areas are assessed each year, with assessment of a given area repeated at different times. These areas include citizenship, science, writing, music, mathematics, literature, social studies, reading, art, and career and occupational development, with others being considered. Responses are reported in terms of the percentage of responders who answered each exercise correctly and are presented by category, i.e., age, geographic region, size of community, type of community, sex, color, and socio-economic background.

The exercises represent very basic objectives of the type required for adequate functioning in a democratic society. They measure such fundamentals as the ability to balance a checkbook. The results of the exercises give evidence of continuous growth in certain areas. Citizenship exercises, for example, revealed that more people 26–35 years old (90%) are aware that the President does not have the right to do anything affecting the United States that she or he wants to than are 17-year-olds (80%), 13-year-olds (70%), or 9-year-olds (50%). Further, the per-

---

[14] Impara, J. C. A system of educational assessment in the state of Florida. Tallahassee: Statewide Assessment Program, Evaluation Section, Florida Department of Education, 1972.

[15] Impara, J. C., Daniel, K. F., & Haynes, J. L. Statewide assessment in Florida. *Florida Reading Quarterly*, 1972, 4–7.

[16] National Assessment of Educational Progress. *Questions and answers about the National Assessment of Educational Progress*, June, 1971.

centage of respondents able to give an appropriate reason for this also increased with age, from 20% (9-year-olds) to 80% (26–35-year-olds).[17]

Reactions to NAEP have not all been positive as evidenced by this quote from Stake:

> The way I see it, National Assessment is Ralph Tyler's baby. Some folks call it Frank Keppel's baby. Some folks call it Wendell Pierce's baby. Some people think its Rosemary's baby.[18]

A number of educators question the program's potential for improving the educational system. The major objection is its perceived overemphasis on factual knowledge and corresponding lack of sufficient attention to higher-order learnings. In any event, NAEP does represent a major attempt to provide data indicative of the effectiveness of American education.[19]

Evaluation of special projects and programs

Special projects and programs include all those organized efforts which are not, strictly speaking, part of the regular school program. They are typically innovative in nature and the duration of their existence is dependent upon their success. They may be school specific or nationwide in scope. Many forms of curriculum evaluation can be assigned to this category. Funding is rarely, if ever, permanently guaranteed for such efforts and many of them are federally funded. If their success is sufficiently demonstrated, they are frequently incorporated into the regular school program following termination of external funding. Demonstrating success requires evaluation.

If federally funded, a special project or program is generally required to conduct at least a yearly evaluation. Even if not required, however, conducting evaluation is in the best interest of the project since it is the only valid way to verify its effectiveness. Project evaluation involves some unique problems. By its very nature it is likely to be concerned with objectives for which there are no corresponding standardized instruments. For example, "Evaluating–Diagnosing–Prescribing for Staff Improvement" was an ESEA Title IV-C (Innovation) project designed to develop and field test a county-wide system of staff evaluation. The scope of the project included evaluation of all personnel in the county school system, including teachers and administrators. The plan involved having all groups evaluated by all other relevant groups, including both subordinates and superordinates. Thus, for example, teachers were to be evaluated by students, other teachers, and administrators. Results were to be anonymous and known only to the individual, the intent being to provide constructive feedback which would result in subsequent self-improvement. This effort required numerous evaluation instruments; the student-evaluates-teacher component alone required several instruments, one for each of several grade-level ranges. A review of the state of the

---

[17] Womer, F. B. National Assessment says. *NCME*, 1970, 2(1), 1–8.
[18] Stake, R. E. National Assessment. *Proceedings of the 1970 Invitational Conference on Testing Problems — The Promise and Perils of Educational Information Systems.* Princeton, N.J.: Educational Testing Service, 1971.
[19] For further information, write to: NAEP, 300 Lincoln Tower, 1860 Lincoln Street, Denver, CO 80203.

art revealed the lack of availability of appropriate instruments. Thus, each one had to be developed, validated, field-tested, and revised until acceptability criteria were met. This process alone consumed the better part of two years.[20] Thus, we see that in this type of evaluation, as in any type of evaluation, lack of appropriate standardized tests greatly complicates matters. It must be reemphasized at this point that the validity of evaluation decisions is very much dependent on the validity of data-gathering instruments; if they must be developed, proper attention must be paid to establishing their validity and reliability.

Evaluation of personnel

Evaluation of personnel (staff evaluation) includes evaluation of all persons responsible, either directly or indirectly, for educational outcomes. Thus, the term includes not just teachers but also other groups such as counselors and administrators. The very fact that the staff evaluation project described in the previous section was considered to be "innovative" tells you something about the state of affairs in this area of evaluation. Until fairly recently, far too little attention was paid to the development of valid procedures and instruments for such evaluation. In the increased interest in this area we once again see the influence of the accountability movement.

One of the major reasons that this area of evaluation has been so slow to progress is that it is so complicated. Since teacher evaluation of one form or another is a relatively universal phenomenon, we will use it as an example. Typically, teacher evaluation is based on observation of the teacher in the classroom by some administrator, usually the principal, and completion of a rating form by that administrator. In some cases, the teacher may be asked to complete a self-report rating form or students may be requested to rate their teacher on a number of factors; the later procedure is more likely to occur at the college level. The validity of the observation approach, as typically used, is questionable on a number of dimensions. For one thing, the number of observations made per teacher is very small (one per year is not uncommon) and therefore a very small sample of behavior is observed. Second, there are certain reactive effects related to observation which are well known to the research community. People have a tendency to act differently than they usually do just because they are being observed, because they are "on stage," as it were. Thus, teachers may perform better than usual or they may become nervous and perform uncharacteristically poorly. Even worse, there is rarely any evidence regarding the validity or reliability of the rating form; the problem is even greater when forms are completed some time after the actual observation.

OK, so what is the alternative? Before we work on how to evaluate behavior, we need to decide what our objectives are and what behaviors are to be evaluated. What distinguishes a "good" teacher from a "poor" one? What does it mean to be a "good" teacher? Does it mean that the teacher is popular, or loved by his or her students? Does it mean that the teacher's students learn? In other words, for what should the teacher be accountable? These are ve-ry tricky questions. Ideally, we would like to evaluate teacher effectiveness in terms of student performance

---

[20] For further information regarding this project, write to: John E. Arena, Project Director, Evaluating–Diagnosing–Prescribing for Staff Development Project, Walker Annex, 1001 NW 4 Street, Ft. Lauderdale, FL 33312.

rather than teacher performance. After all, while a teacher's actions are certainly important, and it is nice to be popular, in the final analysis what the educational system is all about is bringing about student learning, not teaching per se. Unfortunately, this ideal is a lot easier to discuss than to implement. Recall our earlier discussion concerning all the variables that are related to student achievement, many of which a teacher has no control over. It is very difficult to determine to what degree a teacher can be held accountable for the achievement of students. One approach to this problem taken by educational researchers has been to look for relationships between identified teacher behaviors and student achievement. Questions such as the following have been investigated: Other factors being equal, is the frequency with which teachers ask higher-order questions related to student achievement; that is, are more questions associated with more learning? While some studies have demonstrated empirical relationships between certain teacher behaviors and student achievement, so far this line of research has not been very productive. While some relationships appear to be very promising, such relationships are typically weak and no firm conclusions have been established to date.[21] In other words, there are no teacher behaviors which have been shown to be sufficiently related to student achievement to allow us to hold teachers accountable for exhibiting them.

Clearly, this is a very challenging area of evaluation, not because we do not know *how* to evaluate, but because we are not sure *what* to evaluate; that is, we do not know what our objectives are. It is impossible to evaluate anything without valid criteria against which to compare actual performance. Thus, until we have validated indicators of success, we will have to do the best we can. Although the degree of responsibility is debatable, no one would disagree with the basic premise that teachers are accountable for the achievement of their students. Further, there are a number of variables which, at least logically, would seem to be related to teacher effectiveness. These include such factors as intellectual competence, classroom organization, and enthusiasm. And in fact research has been conducted which has found relationships between a number of such variables and teacher effectiveness *as perceived by students*.[22] So, given that teacher evaluation is here to stay, the least we can do is to improve on our current system of evaluation. If teachers are to be observed, then variables such as those previously identified should be observed and rated and valid instruments for recording observations should be employed. Further, multiple observations should be made in order to acquire a more adequate sampling of behavior. Lastly, ratings should be obtained from other groups such as peers and, at the very least, students; they are, after all, the consumers.

Although the above discussion concerned only the evaluation of teachers, the same general problems apply to evaluation of other types of personnel, only more so. Even less effort has been expended in relation to evaluation of principals,

---

[21] See, for example, Aspy, D. N., & Roebuck, F. N. An investigation of the relationship between student levels of cognitive functioning and the teacher's classroom behavior. *The Journal of Educational Research*, 1972, 65(8), 365–368; Rosenshine, B. Classroom instruction. In N. L. Gage (Ed.), *The Psychology of teaching methods: Seventy-fifth yearbook of the National Society for the Study of Education*. Chicago: University of Chicago Press, 1976; *and* Solomon, D., Rosenburg, L., & Bizdik, W. E. Teacher behavior and student learning. *Journal of Educational Psychology*, 1964, 55, 23–30.

[22] See, for example, Baird, L. L. Teaching styles: An exploratory study of dimensions and effects. *Journal of Educational Psychology*, 1973, 64(1), 15–21; Denton, J. J., Calarco, J. F., & Johnson, C. M. Pupil perception of a student teacher's competence. *The Journal of Educational Research*, 1977, 70(4), 180–185; *and* Sherman, B. R., & Blackburn, R. T. Personal characteristics and teaching effectiveness of college faculty. *Journal of Educational Psychology*, 1975, 67(1), 124–131.

Type of Evaluation	Major Variables Measured	Major Types of Decisions
Student	1. Achievement 2. Aptitude 3. Personality	1. Grading and promotion 2. Selection and placement 3. Future instructional activities
Curriculum	1. Achievement 2. Attitude 3. Cost	1. Objectives-referenced effectiveness of approach, strategy or materials 2. Comparative effectiveness 3. Cost-effectiveness
School	1. Achievement 2. Aptitude 3. Personality	1. Future instructional and noninstructional activities 2. Allocation of resources
Large Populations	1. Achievement	1. Objectives-referenced effectiveness of educational systems 2. Comparative effectiveness of various subsystems
Special Projects and Programs	1. Project/program specific	1. Objectives-referenced effectiveness 2. Comparative effectiveness
Personnel	1. Performance, e.g., classroom behavior of teachers and students 2. Attitudes and opinions of persons evaluated, e.g., teachers 3. Attitudes and opinions of relevant others, e.g., students	1. Retention 2. Promotion 3. Salary

figure 2.1
Summary of variables and decisions involved in the major types of evaluation

for example, and again the major problem is one of defining criteria. The solution, at least for the present, involves collecting the best data possible, from as many sources as possible, as often as possible.

Figure 2.1 summarizes the variables and decisions involved in the major types of evaluation.

3 phases of evaluation

After reading chapter 3, you should be able to:

1 List five problems associated with "at-the-end" evaluation.
2 Define or describe the planning phase of evaluation.
3 List two activities involved in situation analysis.
4 Define or describe an objective.
5 Describe how prerequisites are determined.
6 State the minimum type of measurement required in an evaluation.
7 Define or describe "strategy."
8 State the factors which differentiate a "good" design from a "poor" design.
9 List the major steps involved in the process phase.
10 List three ways in which the results of the product phase of evaluation are used.

The continuity of evaluation

Evaluation is a continuous process; contrary to public opinion, it is not what you do "at the end"! Evaluation should be planned for prior to execution of any effort and should be involved throughout the duration—that's right, at the beginning, in the middle, and at the end (if there is an end). There are typically a series of temporary "ends" in a continuous cycle. Take student evaluation, for example. We start with a set of instructional objectives. Then we implement instructional strategies to facilitate their achievement. Then we measure achievement—a temporary end in the instructional cycle. Based on the results, we reassess our objectives and strategies and proceed. Thus, the process is cyclic with feedback from one cycle guiding the next. As the above discussion illustrates, we do not just evaluate the outcomes; every stage of the process is subject to evaluation, beginning with the objectives.

The notion that evaluation must be planned for before execution is a critical one. There was a time, not too long ago, when evaluation was almost an afterthought. A program would be implemented and allegedly do all sorts of wonderful things. Then, after some period of time, perhaps at the end of the school year, participants would start thinking about how they were going to evaluate the program. Typically, an evaluator would be hired as a consultant to "do" the evaluation and "show" that the program was "good." Take it from the voice of experience, evaluation after the fact is tough, not to mention extremely unwise. The program may very well have done some very good things; providing valid evidence to that effect was very difficult, however. Further, by ignoring evaluation until the end, the program missed out on feedback which would have come from ongoing evaluation and might well have resulted in even more positive results.

To examine some of the major problems associated with at-the-end evaluation, let us look at a hypothetical (but typical) example. School X petitions the school board for funds with which to conduct a series of human relations workshops for teachers during the school year. Funds are granted. Beginning October 1, and every week thereafter, teachers participate for one hour per week in a human relations workshop. In June the teachers are asked to put their reactions to the program in writing and to put them in the program director's mailbox. About 40% of them do and all reactions are positive. Teachers express satisfaction with the program; some say they liked it, some say they think it helped them to understand their students better, and so forth. Enter the evaluator. The first question the evaluator asks is "What were your objectives?" Response—"To make our teachers more humane." Evaluator inwardly cringes. The objective is vague, unclear, and unmeasurable as stated. For one thing, there is no indication of the desired behavior. If a teacher did become "more humane," how would we know? What does "more humane" *mean*? It is the same old problem—you have to know what you are going to measure before you can determine how to measure it. So, the evaluator works with the program director, and they translate the original vague objective into several specific objectives, one dealing with knowledge of human relations concepts, one concerned with observable classroom behavior, and one dealing with teacher attitudes. Unfortunately, no data were collected on any of these variables. Yes, there are the reaction sheets which are an indication of attitude. But, in the first place, no standard information was collected. Only some of the teachers, for example, indicated that they thought the workshops had

helped them to understand their students better; what about the rest of the teachers? Further, only 40% of the teachers turned in reaction sheets; we have no idea
how the remaining 60% of the teachers felt—a majority, incidentally. They may
have considered the whole program a bore and a waste of time. Also, the evaluator
knows of a good instrument available for measuring knowledge of human relations concepts but it usually takes six weeks after you order it to receive it, and
school will be out for the summer in two weeks, and it is a little late to think about
developing an instrument. Et cetera, et cetera, et cetera.

The above example illustrates some basic problems with at-the-end evaluation. Objectives are frequently worthy ones but unmeasurable as stated. Data are
likely to be insufficient and inappropriate. There may have been too few participants (e.g. students) or data may have been collected on too few of them. What
data were collected may not be the data needed for determining achievement of
the objectives. It is often too late to develop or obtain appropriate measures or to
conduct reasonable observations. Careful planning certainly does not guarantee
that you will have no problems but it certainly does increase your chances. And
when a problem does arise, you generally have time to work out a solution. Planning ahead not only increases your chances of success, it also eliminates a lot of
unnecessary weeping and gnashing of teeth!

The evaluation process, as we have discussed before, entails decision
making. Any educational endeavor involves a whole host of decisions which must
be made—decisions about objectives, decisions about strategies, decisions about
measurement, and so forth. These various decisions can be classified in terms of
when they are made, that is, during what stage of the activity under study. Thus
each phase of evaluation involves different kinds of decisions. Logically, we can
identify three phases: the planning phase, the process phase, and the product
phase.[1] That is a lot of *p*'s! The planning phase deals with "What *will* we do" questions; the process phase asks "How *are* we doing?"; and the product phase is concerned with "How *did* we do?" at least so far. By now you have a pretty good idea
what evaluation is all about. A discussion of the events in each of the three phases
of evaluation should further clarify the concepts. Keep in mind that the evaluation
process is basically the same regardless of what is being evaluated.

The planning phase

This initial phase of evaluation takes place prior to actual implementation and involves making decisions about what course of action will be taken and toward
what ends. The *planning phase* involves the following processes: analysis of the
situation, specification of goals and objectives, selection and/or development of
instruments, delineation of strategies and activities for attainment of the objectives, selection of a research design, (if appropriate and feasible), and preparation
of a time schedule.

---

[1] At this point, there is definitely an almost overwhelming urge to refer to these phases as PPP or P³, or
to use some other nifty handle. Given the current overabundance of acronyms and such, however, we
will resist.

Situation analysis

The first step is to analyze the situation as it presently exists in order to establish the parameters of the effort. This step includes activities such as the collection of background information and assessment of existing constraints. For a teacher this may involve examination of the cumulative records of his or her students in order to get a frame of reference based on their abilities and histories. For a program director, a review of related literature may very well be called for. Such a review will indicate, for example, what approaches have and have not been found to be successful. The director of the hypothetical program previously discussed, designed to improve the human relations skills of teachers, for example, might find that role playing has been shown to be an effective technique in other similar efforts. Such a review may also reveal instruments which may be appropriate for collecting relevant data. Constraints and resources need to be carefully assessed in order to make reasonable decisions concerning the feasibility of alternative courses of action. You do not want to plan for something you either cannot afford or cannot obtain. A math teacher, for example, cannot plan to use pocket calculators if the school cannot afford them; a football coach cannot plan Saturday morning practice sessions if the school is closed on weekends; a program director cannot plan to use videotapes in teacher workshops if videotape equipment is not available or obtainable within the given budget. And so forth. After the parameters of the situation have been established, more realistic goals and objectives can be formulated.

Specification of objectives

Goals are general statements of purpose, or desired outcomes, and are not as such directly measurable. Each goal must be translated into one or more specific objectives which are measurable. Thus, *objectives* are specific statements of what is to be accomplished and how well, and are expressed in terms of quantifiable, measurable outcomes. The desire "to improve arithmetic achievement level" is more of a goal, whereas the statement "All students will be able to add correctly three two-digit numbers" is an objective. Similarly, the statement "The Whooper reading system will result in greater reading achievement" is a program goal whereas "All students participating in the Whooper reading system during the school year will increase their reading level by two years" is an objective.

Objectives may be process oriented or product oriented. *Process objectives* describe outcomes desired during the execution of the effort; in other words, they relate to development and execution; *product objectives* describe outcomes intended as a result of the effort. These terms are useful primarily for program and project evaluation, although a teacher may well have process objectives. Process objectives do not typically involve student behavior; desired student outcomes are almost always product oriented. Process objectives deal with strategies and activities which are intended to result in achievement of the product objectives. Thus, achievement of process objectives is intended to result in achievement of product objectives. For example, a product objective might state that "attendance will be increased by 20%," attendance being defined as the number of days students are present during the school year. A corresponding process objective might state that "the home of every student will be visited at least twice during the school year, once prior to the December holidays." The assumption indicated here is that closer contact with the home will result in improved student attendance.

Thus, the objectives give direction to all subsequent activities and achievement of objectives is ultimately measured. Objectives, whether instructional objectives or program objectives, form the foundation of all subsequent evaluation activities, and therefore it is critical that they themselves be evaluated in terms of both relevance, measurability, substance, and technical accuracy. Objectives serve as the "guiding light" for students and teachers as well as for program directors. They let students in on exactly what is expected of them, thus allowing them to focus their efforts appropriately. They give direction to all instruction and to subsequent measurement.

Specification of prerequisites

Objectives entail a unique procedure with respect to student evaluation. In most cases, specification of a given set of instructional objectives is based on the assumption that students have already acquired certain skills and knowledge. If the assumption is incorrect, then the objectives are not appropriate. These assumed behaviors are referred to as *prerequisites,* or *entry behaviors.* Systematic instruction and evaluation require that these prerequisites be specified and measured. Assessment of entry behavior is especially important at the beginning of the school year or at the beginning of any new unit of instruction, when the teacher does not have firsthand knowledge concerning the present capabilities of his or her students. Knowing what students were allegedly taught last year is not good enough. Even if they really did learn everything they were supposed to, there is no guarantee that they retained it. There is substantial research evidence which indicates that there is considerable forgetting over periods of time such as summer vacation.[2] Layton, for example, found that up to 66% of first-year algebra material may be nonretrievable after one year.[3]

To arrive at prerequisites, you simply ask yourself the following question: What must my students know or be able to do prior to instruction in order that they may benefit from instruction and achieve my objectives? You can *teach* division, for example, from September to June, but students will never *learn* how to divide if they do not know how to add, subtract, and multiply. If you are planning to teach division, you are probably pretty safe in assuming that your students can add and subtract; multiplication is another story. If it is found that a number of students do not possess one or more specified prerequisite capabilities, then objectives must be revised; more than likely, new ones will be added which must be achieved before instruction on the original set begins. Whether or not students possess the necessary prerequisites is generally determined by administration of a test of entry behavior.

[2] See, for example, Pressey, S. L., Robinson, F. P., & Horrocks, J. E. *Psychology in Education.* New York: Harper & Row, 1959; Schrepel, M., & Laslett, H. R. On the loss of knowledge by junior high pupils over the summer vacation. *Journal of Educational Psychology,* 1936, *27,* 299–303; *and* Sterrett, M. D. & Davis, R. A. The permanence of school learning: A review of studies. *Educational Administration and Supervision,* 1954, *40*(8), 449–460.
[3] Layton, E. T. The persistence of learning in elementary algebra. *Journal of Educational Psychology,* 1932, *23,* 46–55.

Selection and development of measuring instruments

More often than not, collection of data to determine degree of achievement of objectives requires administration of one or more instruments. But not always. Data are always needed, but they may be naturally available. If, for example, the objective deals with improving rate of attendance, such figures will be a matter of record. When an instrument is required, be it an achievement test, an attitude scale, or an observation form, it must either be selected or developed. Selection of an instrument is not simply a matter of locating a test that appears to measure what you want to measure; it involves examining those that are available and selecting the best one, "best" being defined in terms of being most appropriate for your objectives and your user group.[4] If an acceptable test cannot be located, then one must be developed.

Instrument development is not a task which should be taken lightly. It may not take much to develop a test, but it does take considerable time, effort, and skill to develop a "good" test! Training at least equivalent to a course in measurement is necessary in order to acquire the skills that are needed for good instrument development. The mere fact that thousands of tests are developed each year by thousands of persons without such training, does not alter that premise. True, a teacher must of necessity develop a myriad of tests during a school year, each suited to his or her particular needs and objectives. But the value of the results of such tests is questionable at best when they are developed by persons without proper training. It is more than a little unnerving to think of all those decisions about all those students based on the results of all those poor tests. Whose responsibility it is to ensure that a teacher receives such training is debatable, but it seems safe to say that the obligation is shared by teacher training institutions, inservice education programs of school systems, and teachers themselves. You, of course, have nothing to worry about since you are receiving proper training now!

At a very minimum, posttests of desired behavior are required. After some appropriate period of time has elapsed, following some unit of instruction or implementation of a given program, achievement of objectives must be assessed. Thus, normally such a test will include no more or no less than the objectives dictate. Also, it is almost always a good idea to administer a pretest of the same material prior to instruction or implementation. Unless you are very sure that students have no knowledge or skill related to your objectives, it is a good idea to assess what they may already know, both as a group and as individuals. It gives you a baseline with which to compare posttest results. You may also find that most of your students have already achieved a given objective. Also, as previously indicated, assessment of entry behavior is recommended. Such a test must measure any skill or knowledge which is prerequisite to understanding forthcoming instruction and which cannot be safely assumed to be possessed by students. The assumption is that they have it; the test of entry behavior confirms or disconfirms the assumption. Again, future activities will depend upon how many students do or do not possess the necessary prerequisites. While all needed instruments are identified during the planning phase, they are not necessarily all available prior to the process phase, especially if one or more must be developed. Posttests, for example, may be developed during the process phase.

---

[4] As mentioned previously, the literature in a given area can be a source of suitable tests. In chapter 7 other sources of tests and test information will be discussed.

Delineation of strategies

Strategies are general approaches to promoting achievement of one or more objectives. We may speak of instructional strategies, curriculum strategies, program strategies, and the like. Each strategy generally entails a number of specific activities. There are typically a number of strategies to choose from and one may be selected as being the one most likely to succeed, given available information such as that reviewed during situation analysis. Or there may be two (or more) strategies which appear promising and the decision may be made to try them both, at different times with the same students, for example, or at the same time with different students. Or, a combination of strategies may be called for. Execution of these strategies must be planned for to ensure the availability of necessary resources.

In case you are still not clear about what a strategy is, we will look at two examples, one instructional and one program related. Suppose Mr. Al Gebra is planning a unit on polynomials. His objectives include: knowledge of the concepts of monomial, binomial, and polynomial; determining the degree of a monomial, binomial, and polynomial; and addition of monomials, binomials, and polynomials.[5] The first strategy decision that must be made is to determine the optimal sequence for presenting these topics. The question is, which sequence will best facilitate learning? This decision is always the first, regardless of what is being taught. Obviously, presenting topics in random order generally will not work; you cannot teach degree of a monomial before your students even know what a monomial is. Some of these skills are prerequisite to others, i.e., must be learned first. One possibility would be to teach all about monomials first (starting with the concept of a monomial, then the degree of a monomial, and lastly, addition of monomials) and then all about binomials, and finally, all about polynomials. A second reasonable strategy would be to teach all the concepts first (i.e., what a monomial is, what a binomial is, what a polynomial is), then teach how to determine the degree of each, and last how to add monomials, and so forth. The latter strategy would probably be preferable since it involves going from the less complex (definitions and concepts) to the more complex (addition of polynomials), whereas the first strategy seesaws back and forth.

There is a process for determining the order in which objectives should be taught which also facilitates the translation of goals into objectives. It is called *task analysis* and involves ordering a set of knowledge and skills into a hierarchy in terms of which are subordinate, or prerequisite, to which others. To perform a task analysis, you start with a terminal, or cumulative, objective at the top of the hierarchy; you then move down the hierarchy by determining what capabilities students need in order to achieve that objective following instruction. For those prerequisite capabilities identified, the process is repeated. The process continues until a point is reached at which the necessary prerequisite capabilities are considered to be entry behaviors—skills and knowledge which students have already acquired. The sequence of instruction is then determined by the hierarchy, with those at the bottom being presented first since they are prerequisite to all the rest. Of course, the process could be carried on almost indefinitely, but at some point identified capabilities are classified as entry behavior. Thus, in our example, the

[5] Remember? A monomial is one term with a coefficient and an exponent (not necessarily greater than 1), such as $2x^2$, y^3, or $7z$; a binomial is two such terms, such as $4x + 6y^2$; and a polynomial is more than two terms.

concepts (e. g. monomial) would be taught first, since this knowledge is prerequisite to learning the skill of determining the degree of each which, in turn, is prerequisite to learning the skill of addition. Knowledge and skills related to coefficients and exponents would probably be considered entry behavior.[6]

Review is another instructional strategy which is applicable to virtually all areas of instruction. There is considerable research evidence which indicates that systematic review of concepts promotes retention.[7] Provision of practice and feedback are also variables which have been shown to promote learning and which most teachers include in their instruction, either systematically or informally. Depending upon the objectives, there are any number of other factors which may be considered. The teacher, for example, is not the only medium of instruction. There are many types of media available (e.g., films, audio cassettes, videotapes) which may facilitate student learning of an objective. Thus, the planning phase involves analyzing each objective to determine which type of medium might be appropriate. Learning to speak a foreign language, for example, can be aided by the use of audiotapes which contain dialogue between native speakers.[8] We can see that Mr. Gebra has a number of decisions to make. He might decide to have a brief review at the beginning of every period, an oral quiz at the end of each period, and to use the overhead projector frequently.

Now that you are getting the idea, we will look at a program-related example more briefly. Suppose the Big Brothers, Big Sisters Program in Chicago is planning its activities for the coming year. The goal of this agency is to supply male or female models for fatherless boys and motherless girls. Thus, one of its specific objectives for the year might be "to increase the number of big brothers in Chicago by 10% (from 400 to 440) during a six-month period beginning September 1." Three major strategies for achieving this objective might be broad public exposure (use of mass media), group contact, and individual contact. Each strategy would then entail one or more specific activities. Broad public exposure could be implemented by placing newspaper ads and sponsoring 30-second messages on radio and television. Group contact might be achieved in at least two different ways: (1) presentations to civic organizations such as the Elks and the Lions (by agency members and children needing big brothers); and (2) informal, social gatherings at which children could meet members of such organizations. Individual contact could be accomplished by arranging private, one-to-one meetings between children and potential big brothers. Got the idea?

Thus, delineation of strategies involves identifying general approaches and translating each into specific activities (much like the process of translating goals into objectives). There are a number of instructional strategies, such as sequencing, review, feedback, and practice, which are generalizable across subject

---

[6] For further discussion of the rationale and process of task analysis, see: Briggs, L. J. *Sequencing of instruction in relation to hierarchies of competencies.* Pittsburgh: American Institutes for Research, 1968; Gagné, R. M. Abilities and learning sets in knowledge acquisition. *Psychological Monographs,* 1961, *75*(14, whole no. 518); *and* Gagné, R. M. The acquisition of knowledge. *Psychological Review,* 1962, *69,* 355–365.

[7] See, for example: Ausubel, D. P. & Youssef, M. The effect of spaced repetition on meaningful retention. *The Journal of General Psychology,* 1965, *73,* 147–150; Gibson, J. T. The effects on retention of programmed classroom reviews. *The Journal of Educational Research,* 1965, *58*(10), 449–452; Spitzer, H. F. Studies in retention. *Journal of Educational Psychology,* 1939, *30*(9), 641–656; *and* Tiedeman, H. R. A study of classroom learning. *The Journal of Educational Research,* 1948, *41,* 516–531.

[8] For further discussion concerning the use of media instruction, see: Briggs, L. J., Campeau, P. L., Gagné, R. M., & May, M. A. *Instructional media: A procedure for the design of multi-media instruction, a critical review of research, and suggestions for future research.* Pittsburgh: American Institutes for Research, 1967.

areas and objectives. Other strategies, such as grouping, role playing, and use of a given medium, are appropriate only for certain objectives.

Selection of a design

As discussed previously, use of a research design is not always appropriate, necessary, or feasible. When called for, however, the very best one that is feasible should be selected. While some would argue the point, it seems clear that many evaluation efforts could benefit from the application of an experimental or quasi-experimental design to their procedures.[9] *Experimental design* refers to the basic structure of a process. Its purpose is to assist in making valid decisions concerning the effectiveness of an approach (or product) and usually involves comparisons between or among groups using different approaches. Evaluation of a new reading curriculum, for example, would involve determining (1) whether students achieved intended objectives and (2) whether students using the new curriculum achieved significantly more reading skills than students using the regular (or some other) curriculum. The answer to question 2 could only be validly determined through the application of an experimental design. The essence of experimentation is the concept that if you start with two (or more) groups who are essentially equal on relevant variables (such as ability) and treat them the same, controlling for all factors which might affect one group differently than the other—*except* that each group is receiving a different treatment (e.g. curriculum)—then, if the groups perform differently after some reasonable period of time, the difference is probably due to the differential effectiveness of the treatments.

Now, what differentiates a "good" design from a "poor" design is the degree to which the design assures initial group equivalency and controls for unwanted factors. Application of a good design permits us to conclude that one curriculum was superior to another and that the results are probably generalizable to other groups of similar students. Almost all of the good designs involve a comparison group, a group to compare "your" group with. This comparison is only valid to the degree to which the groups are equivalent to begin with. If one group has a much higher level of reading ability, for example, it will be difficult to determine how much of their final performance is due to curriculum differences and how much is due to initial group differences. The best single way to insure group equality is to take one large group (randomly selected if possible) and randomly divide them in half, each half receiving a different treatment, e.g., curriculum. The very best designs, called true experimental designs, all require this procedure.

If random assignment is not feasible (and sometimes even when it is), then at least pretest data should be collected; such data allow us to see how similar the groups actually are. In many evaluation studies, randomization is not feasible because they are conducted in real-world settings, such as schools, where students are already in classes. When existing groups are compared, a quasi-experimental design is required. Such designs are not as good as true experimental designs but they do a reasonable job of controlling extraneous factors. And remember, we always do the best we can. In selecting a design, you first determine which designs

[9] Stanley, J. C. Controlled experimentation: Why seldom used in evaluation? In *Toward a theory of achievement measurement. Proceedings of the 1969 Invitational Conference on Testing Problems.* Princeton, N.J.: Educational Testing Service, 1970, 104–108.

are appropriate for your situation. Then you determine which of those are feasible, given any constraints under which you may be operating. From the designs which are both appropriate and feasible, you select the one which controls for the most extraneous factors (referred to as sources of internal and external invalidity). In other words, you select the best design you possibly can which will yield the data you need, given the constraints under which you are operating.[10]

Unless experimenting with a new approach in her or his classes, a teacher is not concerned with design; student evaluation, per se, does not require it. Other types of evaluation, such as curriculum evaluation, benefit from its application. Without carefully controlled comparisons, it is almost impossible to make valid decisions concerning the relative effectiveness of two or more alternatives.

Preparation of a time schedule

Preparation of a realistic time schedule is important for all types of evaluation. It is an infrequent event when one has as long as one pleases to conduct an evaluation. Students must be evaluated prior to report card time, and most programs and projects must be evaluated periodically in order to receive further support, financial or otherwise. The existence of deadlines typically necessitates careful budgeting of time. Basically, a time schedule includes a listing of the major activities of the proposed evaluation effort and corresponding expected initiation and completion times for each activity. Such a schedule helps the evaluator to assess the feasibility of various alternative plans. It also helps the evaluator to stay on schedule. In developing a time frame, do not make the mistake of "cutting it too thin" by allowing a minimum amount of time for each activity. Allow yourself enough time so that if an unforeseen, minor delay occurs, you can still meet your final deadline. You should also plan to make the completion date for your final activity a date sometime in advance of your actual deadline. Your schedule will not necessarily be a series of sequential steps such that one activity must be completed before another is begun. Instrument development, for example, may be going on at the same time the program is being implemented.

A very useful approach for constructing a time schedule is to use what is called the Gantt chart method.[11] A Gantt chart lists the activities to be completed down the left-hand side of the page and the time span of the entire project across the top of the page. A bar graph format is used to indicate the beginning and ending date for each activity. Such a chart permits the evaluator or evaluation team to easily see the "big picture" and to identify concurrent activities.

The process phase

The *process phase* involves making decisions based upon events which occur during actual implementation of the planned instruction, program, or project. The first step is to administer pretests, if such are appropriate, and in the case of student evaluation, tests of entry behavior. Based on the results, decisions may be made concerning the appropriateness of the already specified objectives. In indi-

---

[10] Sampling and design will be discussed further in chapter 14.
[11] Archibald, R. D., & Villoria, R. L. *Network-based management systems (PERT/CPM)*. New York: John Wiley, 1967.

vidualized instruction programs, the results of such tests are used to make decisions concerning optimal placement of each student; different students start at different points in the curriculum depending upon their entering level of proficiency. Following initial testing, planned strategies and activities are executed in the predetermined sequence. Data collected during this phase provide feedback concerning whether execution is taking place as planned and whether strategies and activities are being effective. In other words, questions such as the following are raised: Are we doing what we said we were going to do? If we are, is it working? If it is not, what can we do about it—what can we do differently from now on? Thus, the basic purposes of this phase are to determine whether the effort is being executed as intended, to determine the degree of achievement of process objectives, and to identify ways in which improvements can be made. If several strategies are being used simultaneously, then at various points in time decisions will be made as to which ones are working and which are not. The Big Brothers, Big Sisters program, for example, might conclude after two months that television and radio spots are not bringing very many new big brothers; since such spots are so expensive, it might be decided to stop them and to concentrate efforts on group contact activities—a strategy which does seem to be working.

Very few efforts work out exactly as planned. There is nothing wrong with making changes in midstream if the end result will be improved because of them. If a teacher sees (based on test results, for example) that her or his instructional strategy is not working, it is her or his responsibility to make some revisions in method or material. After all, the goal is student learning, not a perfectly executed plan. The whole purpose of evaluation during this phase is to guide future activities for the sake of improvement. Further, the same data that provide feedback to the teacher also provide feedback to the students. Each student can evaluate his or her own progress in various areas and make decisions as to how, and how much, energy will be expended in each area. Feedback also provides reinforcement.

The relative degree of emphasis given to individual student achievement (as opposed to group achievement) during this phase depends upon the type of evaluation involved. In student evaluation the teacher is concerned with providing feedback, reinforcement, and prescriptive actions for each child; in curriculum, program, and project evaluation, the emphasis is on improving strategies which apply to total groups. It should be noted that reinforcement and feedback have been shown to be factors which do lead to greater learning and retention.[12]

The process phase of evaluation is often referred to as *formative evaluation* and is typically defined in discrepancy terms. In other words, it is concerned with analyzing differences between intended and actual outcomes in terms of content and procedures.[13] As with models of evaluation, however, there is no scarcity of descriptive terms in the field of evaluation, many of which represent the same basic processes. Do not get lost in the verbiage or confused by differences of opinion regarding minor points. What matters are the basic procedures and decisions involved, not what they are called. So, if you would prefer to call the "process phase" the "aardvark phase," go ahead! It does not matter as long as you understand that this phase involves decisions concerning the implementation process itself and attempts to make needed changes.

[12] See, for example, O'Neill, M., Rasor, R. A., & Bartz, W. R. Immediate retention of objective test answers as a function of feedback complexity. *The Journal of Educational Research*, 1972, 66(3), 72–74, and Wexley, K. N., & Thornton, C. L. Effect of verbal feedback of test results upon learning. *The Journal of Educational Research*, 1972, 66(3), 119–121.

[13] Singer, R. N., & Dick, W. *Teaching physical education: A systems approach*. Boston: Houghton Mifflin, 1974.

The product phase

The *product phase* involves making decisions at *the* end or, more likely, at the end of one cycle of instruction (e.g. a unit), a program or project. For programs or projects, whether or not the product phase marks *the* end may well depend upon the findings of the product phase! Decisions made during this phase are based on the results of posttests (of achievement, attitude, behavior, and the like) and on other cumulative types of data. The major purpose of this phase is to collect data in order to make decisions concerning the overall effectiveness of instruction, a program, or a project (or whatever). During this phase it is determined whether and/or to what degree intended product objectives were achieved. Unanticipated outcomes are also analyzed. It might be found, for example, that a program designed to improve self-concept also appears to have affected a significant increase in attendance. Planned for or not, this outcome warrants reporting and further investigation. If an experimental or quasi-experimental design involving group comparisons was applied to the evaluation, final group performance is now compared to determine if differences are significant, that is, whether they are due to chance factors or probably due to differential treatments.[14]

A by-product of the whole accountability movement has been a rapid rise in the number of independent, external evaluators, or auditors, involved in the product phase of evaluation. As previously defined, an independent evaluator is a person with evaluation skills who is not connected with the program being evaluated. While such a person may very well be (and should be) involved during the planning and process phases, her or his involvement is more likely during the product phase. The independent evaluator (or evaluation team) either verifies procedures and results as reported by program personnel or actually collects and analyzes appropriate data. This individual, for example, assesses the adequacy of measuring instruments, the equality of groups, and the appropriateness of analysis procedures. The presence of outside evaluators does not indicate a lack of trust; they are not there to "check up" on anyone. Their major function is to provide skills and knowledge related to evaluation which are often not possessed by program or project personnel.

Data analysis and interpretation is almost always followed by the preparation of a report which describes the objectives, procedures, and outcomes of the effort. Of course, in the case of student evaluation, this may not involve much more than the assignment and reporting of grades to parents and students or the awarding of a diploma. Whether a report goes to parents, the school board, or an outside funding agency, it should be written understandably—it should communicate as clearly and concisely as possible. There is no need to overwhelm people with technical terms and jargon.

The results of the product phase of evaluation are used in at least three major ways. First, they provide feedback and direction to all who were involved, e.g., students, teachers, program directors; and thus each cycle of an activity benefits from analysis of the outcomes of the previous cycle. Second, they provide feedback to outside decision makers such as parents, principals, school board members, and funding sources. The decision to continue or discontinue an effort, at the same or a different (greater or lesser) level of funding, is justified primarily on the basis of the results of the product phase of evaluation. Third, depending

---

[14] The concept of significance will be discussed further in chapter 17.

upon the type of evaluation involved, there are a number of groups who can utilize the results. Knowledge of student performance, for example, is useful information for guidance and counseling personnel; the results of curriculum evaluation are utilized by school administrators; and often results are very useful to educational researchers and other evaluators.

Results of the product phase need to be interpreted with care. Failure to meet objectives, for example, is not necessarily fatal; degree of achievement needs to be considered. If at the end of six months, for example, the Big Brothers, Big

When Executed	Types of Decisions	Specific Activities
Planning Phase		
Prior to actual implementation of the instruction, program or project (or whatever)	1. Outcomes to be achieved. 2. Courses of action to be taken.	1. Situation analysis. 2. Specification of objectives 3. Specification of prerequisites. 4. Selection/development of measuring instruments. 5. Delineation of strategies. 6. Selection of a design. 7. Preparation of a time schedule.
Process Phase		
During implementation	1. Degree to which execution is taking place as planned. 2. Changes needed for the sake of improvement.	1. Administration of pretests. 2. Administration of tests of entry behavior. 3. Assessment of appropriateness of objectives. 4. Periodic data collection, e.g. testing. 5. Analysis of effectiveness of strategies.
Product Phase		
Following implementation	1. Overall effectiveness of the instruction, project or program (or whatever). 2. Future courses of action.	1. Collection of data pertinent to the objectives, e.g., administration of posttests. 2. Collection of data related to unanticipated outcomes. 3. Analysis and interpretation of the data. 4. Reporting.

figure 3.1

Summary of the decisions and activities involved in the three phases of evaluation.

Sisters program had increased the number of big brothers by 8%, and not 10% as intended, that would still be good. Personnel could further analyze their strategies and activities in cost-effectiveness terms and determine how to proceed in similar future efforts. Similarly, if 95% of a teacher's students achieved a set of objectives, the teacher could consider that he or she had done a good job. It is pretty safe to say that all students are not likely to achieve all objectives, unless they are very low-level objectives. We will have more to say on this subject in part 2. Suffice it to say for now that there are objectives which should be achieved by virtually all students and others for which this expectation is unreasonable.

Just as the process phase is often referred to as formative evaluation, so also the product phase is frequently referred to as *summative evaluation*. Again, the terms are not important—the concepts are. Thus, during the product phase of evaluation, decisions are made concerning the effectiveness and comparative effectiveness of the endeavor being evaluated. The results provide feedback to persons inside and outside the system and form the bases for decisions concerning future courses of action.

Figure 3.1 summarizes the decisions and activities involved in the three phases of evaluation.

part one **summary**

1 the nature of evaluation

Definition and purpose

1 Evaluation is the systematic process of collecting and analyzing data in order to make decisions.

2 Although some definitions seem to equate measurement with evaluation, most recognize that measurement is but one essential component of evaluation.

3 Answers to questions regarding degree of objective achievement and relative worth require the collection and analysis of data and interpretation of that data with respect to one or more criteria.

4 The purpose of evaluation is *not* to determine whether something is "good," or worthwhile, as opposed to "bad," or worthless, *per se*.

5 The purpose of evaluation *is* to determine the current status of the object of the evaluation, to compare that status with a set of standards, or criteria, and to select an alternative from among two or more to make a decision.

6 The purpose of evaluation is the same regardless of the type of evaluation or the nature of the objectives, whether instructional, curriculum, or project objectives, explicit or implicit, process oriented or product oriented, short-term or long-term.

7 In all cases the evaluation process is basically the same and involves determination of the types of data which need to be collected, determination of the individual, group, or groups from whom data will be obtained, collection of the data, analysis of the data, interpretation of the data, and decision making.

8 The person or persons responsible for data collection may or may not be the persons who make the subsequent decisions.

9 An external evaluator is a person with evaluation skills, who is not associated with the program being evaluated, who collects and analyzes appropriate data or verifies existing data.

10 The validity of decisions is a function of the validity of the data collection and analysis procedures.

Measurement

11 Basing decisions on valid procedures is critical because although all decisions are not equally important, each one has a consequence which directly or indirectly affects students.

12 The data collected during the evaluation process are only as good as the measurement upon which they are based.

13 *Measurement* is the process of quantifying the degree to which someone or something possesses a given trait, i.e., quality, characteristic, or feature.

14 Measurement permits more objective description concerning traits and facilitates comparisons.

15 Expressing a trait numerically considerably reduces ambiguity and provides much more useful information.

16 Although, theoretically, all traits of interest can be measured, educational measurement is complicated by the fact that almost all measurement is indirect; there are no yardsticks for measuring traits such as intelligence.

17 The term measurement is not synonymous with the administration of a test; data may also be collected via processes such as observation or may already be available and retrievable from records.

18 A *test* is a means of measuring the knowledge, skills, feelings, intelligence, or aptitude of an individual or group.

19 The very best instruments available should be used and results should be interpreted with appropriate caution.

20 Good evaluation usually involves decisions based on data obtained from a number of sources, not just on the results of a single test.

21 It is clearly better to base judgments and decisions on the best data available rather than on subjective impressions.

22 The whole notion of accountability requires the availability *and use* of valid indices of performance.

Evaluation and accountability

23 To varying degrees, any person or program which receives funds from one or more sources is accountable to each source; this means that each is responsible for providing evidence related to accomplishments and successes.

24 What a person or program is accountable for depends upon agreed-upon functions and objectives.

25 The manner in which the accountability principle is implemented depends upon who is demanding accountability and from whom.

26 The increased interest in, and demand for, accountability is not difficult to understand given the rising costs of the education enterprise and the apparently declining test scores of high school students.

27 Even persons who express negative attitudes about objectives, evaluation, and accountability engage in evaluation all the time and demand accountability in their everyday activities with respect to purchased goods and services.

28 It is the nature of accountability, e.g., in business, that it leads to increased efforts to produce quality products and efficient procedures; likewise, increased demands for accountability in education should result in increased efforts to improve the educational experiences of all children.

29 Everyone can benefit from feedback; the evaluation process can provide the feedback which will identify those things that we are doing right and those things that need improvement, and helps us to make decisions about our objectives, strategies, and activities.

30 Evaluation and accountability are worthwhile concepts only if related procedures are competently conducted and results are interpreted carefully.

31 It is critical to the whole process that people be evaluated on, and be held accountable for, only those things over which they have control and only to the degree that they do.

32 A teacher is only partially responsible for the achievement of students.

2 types of evaluation

Types versus models

33 When we speak of "types" of evaluation, we are referring to the different processes, products, and persons subject to evaluation—students, curricula, schools, school systems, large populations, special programs and projects, and personnel.

34 The basic evaluation process is the same regardless of what is being evaluated; what differs is what is being evaluated, how the evaluation process is applied, and the types of decisions made.

35 All valid systems and models for evaluation involve the same essential components, namely: specification of goals and objectives; selection and/or development of measurement tools; delineation of strategies for objective attainment; process and product procedures; and analysis and interpretation of results.

36 There is often a fine line between research and evaluation, and an evaluation may very easily utilize a research design; both research and evaluation involve decision making and both are based on the scientific method.

Student evaluation

37 Achievement is but one of many variables on which a student is assessed; other major variables include aptitude, intelligence, personality, attitudes, and interests.

38 In order to assess achievement, tests, both standardized and teacher made, are administered; projects, procedures, and oral presentations are rated; and formal and informal observations are made.

39 A teacher uses performance data not only to evaluate student progress but also to evaluate his or her own instruction.

40 Feedback on current student progress also gives direction to current and future instructional activities.

41 Teachers make both short-term and cumulative decisions concerning students, based on a variety of academic and personal-social data.

42 There are numerous other decisions that are made concerning students in which the teacher is either not involved or only makes recommendations.

43 Of all the types of evaluation, student evaluation is probably the most critical (with the possible exception of evaluation of personnel) because decisions made affect individuals as individuals, as opposed to, for example, curricular decisions, which affect groups.

Curriculum evaluation

44 Curriculum evaluation involves the evaluation of any instructional program or instructional materials, and includes evaluation of such factors as instructional strategies, textbooks, audiovisual materials, and physical and organizational arrangements.

45 Curriculum evaluation may involve evaluation of a total package or evaluation of one small aspect of a total curriculum, such as a film.

46 Although ongoing programs are subject to evaluation, curriculum evaluation is usually associated with innovation, a new or different approach; the approach may be general, i.e., applicable to many curriculum areas, or specific to a given subject area.

47 Curriculum evaluation usually involves both internal and external criteria and comparisons.

48 Internal evaluation is concerned with whether the new process or product achieves its stated objectives, that is, whether it does what it purports to do, as well as with evaluation of the objectives themselves.

49 External evaluation is concerned with whether the process or product does whatever it does better than some other process or product.

50 Student evaluation is almost always a part of curriculum evaluation, but we are concerned with *group*, not individual, performance.

51 Some persons advocate what is called "goal-free" evaluation, and suggest that attention should be focused on actual outcomes, not on prespecified outcomes.

52 In addition to student achievement, there are a number of other factors which are generally recommended for inclusion in curriculum evaluation; attitudes are one such factor.

53 Research has demonstrated a relationship between teacher attitude toward a curriculum and its ultimate effectiveness.

54 Determining the reasons for any teacher dissatisfaction may suggest remedies which when implemented will bring about a change of teacher attitude and subsequently increase the effectiveness of the curriculum.

55 For similar reasons, attitudes of other involved groups, such as students, administrators, and parents, are also important.

56 Other factors being equal, a new program is usually considered to be cost-effective if one of the following is true: (1) it costs essentially the same as other programs but results in greater achievement (if achievement is the same, why bother?!); (2) it costs less and results in equal or greater (unlikely!) achievement; (3) it costs more but results in significantly greater achievement (assuming it is affordable to the group investigating its effectiveness).

57 Curriculum evaluation has one major well-known problem associated with it: it is very difficult to compare fairly the effectiveness of one program or approach with another. Even if two programs deal with the same subject area, they may deal with objectives which are very different, and it is very difficult to find a test or other measure which is equally fair, or valid, for both programs.

58 If one curriculum is to be compared to another, the objectives of each must be examined carefully; if no measure can be located which is equally appropriate to both, than one must be developed that is.

59 Matrix sampling basically involves dividing a test into a number of subtests, using random sampling techniques on the items, and administering each subtest to a subgroup of students, also randomly selected from a total group.

60 Matrix sampling considerably reduces both testing time and cost.

School evaluation

61 Evaluation of a school involves evaluation of the total educational program of the school and entails the collection of data on all aspects of its functioning.

62 The purpose of school evaluation is to determine the degree to which school objectives are being met and to identify areas of strength and weakness in the total program.

63 Information from school evaluation provides feedback which gives direction to the future activities of the school and results in decisions concerning the allocation of school resources.

64 One major component of school evaluation is the school testing program; the more comprehensive the testing program, the more valuable are the resulting data.

65 A school testing program should include measurement of achievement, aptitude, personality, and interest.

66 Tests selected for a school evaluation must match the objectives of the school and be appropriate for the students to be tested.

67 The question of the appropriateness of norms is a critical issue; when available, county or system norms are more useful as a basis of comparison than national norms.
68 A school evaluation involves more than the administration of tests to students; it may require any combination of questionnaires, interviews and observations, with data being collected from all persons in the school community, including administrators, teachers, and counselors.
69 School evaluation is a *total* effort and all relevant groups must be involved in all phases—planning, execution, interpretation of results, and subsequent decision making.

Evaluation of large populations

70 Evaluation of large populations involves assessing the current status and the educational progress of large numbers of students, typically distributed over a large geographic region.
71 Statewide assessment programs are generally based on the premises that the state system of education is responsible for student achievement of certain basic skills required for effective functioning in our society, and that programs designed to promote achievement of the basic skills should be as effective and economical as possible.
72 One of the major purposes of state assessment is to provide information to state and local decision makers about the adequacy of the basic educational program.
73 Statewide assessment typically involves measurement of minimum educational objectives and selected optional objectives using both criterion-referenced and norm-referenced tests.
74 The largest and best known of assessment efforts at the national level is the National Assessment of Educational Progress (NAEP) program.
75 NAEP is a national, census-like survey of the knowledge, skills, understandings, and attitudes of certain groups of young Americans.
76 NAEP's purpose is to determine what benefit has been derived from the billions of dollars spent yearly on education, in terms of what Americans know and can do.
77 The major goal of NAEP is to measure growth or decline in performance over time with respect to selected learning areas.
78 Each year NAEP administers a selected group of exercises to a randomly selected group numbering approximately 80,000, located in various parts of the country, and representing the ages 9, 13, 17, and 26–35.
79 NAEP exercises represent very basic objectives of the type required for adequate functioning in a democratic society.
80 The major objection to NAEP is its perceived overemphasis on factual knowledge and corresponding lack of sufficient attention to higher-order learnings.

Evaluation of special projects and programs

81 Special projects and programs include all those organized efforts which are not, strictly speaking, part of the regular school program; they are typically innovative in nature and the duration of their existence is dependent upon their success.
82 Whether it is required or not, conduct of evaluation is in the best interest of a project since it is the only valid way to verify its effectiveness.

83 One problem unique to project evaluation is that by its very nature it is likely to be concerned with objectives for which there are no corresponding standardized instruments; all needed instruments must be developed, validated, field-tested, and revised until acceptability criteria are met.

Evaluation of personnel

84 Evaluation of personnel (staff evaluation) includes evaluation of all persons responsible, either directly or indirectly, for educational outcomes, i.e., teachers, administrators, counselors, and so forth.

85 One of the major reasons that this area of evaluation has been so slow to progress is that it is so complicated; it is difficult to determine *what* behaviors are to be evaluated.

86 Although the *degree* of responsibility is debatable, teachers are in some way accountable for the achievement of their students.

87 The solution to the personnel evaluation problem, at least for the present, involves collecting the best data possible, from as many sources as possible.

3 phases of evaluation

The continuity of evaluation

88 Evaluation is a continuous process; contrary to public opinion, it is not what you do "at the end."

89 Evaluation should be planned for prior to execution of any effort and should be involved throughout the duration—at the beginning, in the middle, and at the end, if there is an end; there are typically a series of temporary "ends" in a continuous cycle.

90 Every stage of every process is subject to evaluation, beginning with the objectives.

91 Evaluation must be planned for *before* execution of any effort.

92 When evaluation is put off until the end, it is very difficult to provide valid evidence concerning effectiveness; also, valuable feedback, which would have come from ongoing evaluation and might well have resulted in more positive results, is missed.

93 Some basic problems with "at the end" evaluation include the following: objectives are frequently worthy ones but unmeasurable as stated; data are likely to be insufficient and inappropriate; there may have been too few participants or data may have been collected on too few of them; what data were collected may not be the data needed for determining achievement of the objectives; and it is often too late to develop or obtain appropriate measures or to conduct reasonable observations.

94 Careful planning for evaluation does not guarantee that you will have no problems but it certainly does increase your chances.

95 The evaluation process entails decision making (decisions about objectives, strategies, measurement, and so forth); these various decisions can be classified in terms of when they are made, that is, during what stage of the effort of interest.

96 Each of the three phases of evaluation involves different kinds of decisions: the planning phase deals with "What *will* we do?"; the process phase asks

"How *are* we doing?"; and the product phase is concerned with "How *did* we do, at least *so far?*"

The planning phase

97 The planning phase of evaluation takes place prior to actual implementation and involves making decisions about what courses of action will be taken and toward what ends.

Situation analysis

98 The first step in the planning phase is to analyze the present situation in order to establish the parameters of the effort.

99 Situation analysis includes activities such as the collection of background information and assessment of existing constraints.

100 After the parameters of the situation have been established, more realistic goals and objectives can be formulated.

Specification of objectives

101 *Goals* are general statements of purpose, or desired outcomes, and are not as such directly measurable; each goal must be translated into one or more specific objectives.

102 *Objectives* are specific statements of what is to be accomplished and how well, and are expressed in terms of quantifiable, measurable outcomes.

103 *Process objectives* describe outcomes desired during the execution of the effort, in other words, they relate to development and execution.

104 *Product objectives* describe outcomes intended as a result of the effort.

105 Process objectives do not typically involve student behavior; they deal with those strategies and activities which are intended to result in achievement of the product objectives.

106 Objectives give direction to all subsequent activities and achievement of objectives is ultimately measured.

107 It is critical that objectives themselves be evaluated in terms of both relevance and measurability, substance, and technical accuracy.

Specification of prerequisites

108 Specification of a given set of instructional objectives is based on the assumption that students have already acquired certain skills and knowledge; if the assumption is incorrect, then the objectives are not appropriate.

109 These assumed behaviors are referred to as *prerequisites*, or *entry behaviors*.

110 Systematic instruction and evaluation require that prerequisites be specified and measured (with a test of entry behavior), especially at the beginning of a school year or a new unit of study.

111 To arrive at prerequisites, you simply ask yourself: What must my students know or be able to do prior to instruction in order that they may benefit from instruction and achieve my objectives?

Selection and development of measuring instruments

112 More often than not, collection of data to determine the degree of achievement of objectives requires administration of one or more instruments, but

not always; certain data, such as attendance figures, will normally be a matter of record.

113 Selection of an instrument is not simply a matter of locating a test which appears to measure what you want to measure; it involves examination of those that are available and selection of the best one available, best being defined in terms of being most appropriate for your objectives and your user group.

114 If an acceptable test cannot be located, then one must be developed; training at least equivalent to a course in measurement is necessary in order to acquire the skills needed for good instrument development.

115 At a very minimum, posttests of desired behavior are required in order to measure achievement of product objectives.

116 It is also almost always a good idea to administer a pretest of the same material prior to instruction or implementation; assessment of entry behavior is also recommended.

117 While all needed instruments are identified during the planning phase, they are not necessarily all available prior to the process phase, especially if one or more must be developed.

Delineation of strategies

118 *Strategies* are general approaches to promoting achievement of one or more objectives; we may speak of instructional strategies, curriculum strategies, program strategies, and the like.

119 Each strategy generally entails a number of specific activities, and there are typically a number of strategies to choose from.

120 Execution of these strategies must be planned for, to ensure the availability of necessary resources.

121 *Task analysis* is a process for determining the order (sequence) in which objectives should be taught which also facilitates the translation of goals into objectives.

122 Task analysis involves ordering a set of knowledge and skills into a hierarchy in terms of which are subordinate, or prerequisite, to which others.

123 To perform a task analysis, you start with a terminal, or cumulative, objective at the top of the hierarchy; you then move down the hierarchy by determining what capabilities students need in order to achieve that objective following instruction; this process is repeated for each identified objective until a point is reached at which the necessary prerequisite capabilities are considered to be entry behaviors.

124 There is considerable research evidence which indicates that systematic review of concepts promotes retention; provision of practice and feedback are also variables which have been shown to promote learning.

125 There are a number of instructional strategies, such as sequencing, review, feedback, and practice, which are generalizable across subject areas and objectives.

126 Other instructional strategies, such as grouping, role playing, and use of a given medium, will be appropriate only for certain objectives.

Selection of a design

127 Use of a research design is not always appropriate, necessary, or feasible; when called for, however, the very best one that is feasible should be selected.

128 *Experimental design* refers to the basic structure of a process; its purpose is to assist in making valid decisions concerning the effectiveness of an approach (or product) and usually involves comparisons between or among groups using different approaches.

129 What differentiates a "good" design from a "poor" design is the degree to which the design assures initial group equivalency and controls for unwanted factors.

130 The best single way to insure initial group equality is to take one large group (randomly selected if possible) and randomly divide them in half, each half receiving a different treatment, e.g., curriculum.

131 If random assignment is not feasible (and sometimes even when it is), at least pretest data should be collected; such data allow us to see how similar the groups actually are.

132 In many evaluation studies, randomization is not feasible because they are conducted in real-world settings such as schools, where students are already in classes.

133 When existing groups are compared, a quasi-experimental design is required; such designs are not as good as true experimental designs (which require randomly formed groups) but they do a reasonable job of controlling extraneous factors (and remember, we always do the best we can).

134 You select the best design you possibly can which will yield the data you need, given the constraints under which you are operating.

135 Student evaluation, per se, does not require application of an experimental design.

136 Without carefully controlled comparisons, it is almost impossible to make valid decisions concerning the relative effectiveness of two or more alternatives.

Preparation of a time schedule

137 Preparation of a realistic time schedule is important for all types of evaluation; rarely do we have as long as we please to conduct an evaluation.

138 Basically, a time schedule includes a listing of the major activities of the proposed evaluation effort and corresponding expected initiation and completion times for each activity.

139 You should allow yourself enough time so that if an unforeseen minor delay occurs, you can still meet your final deadline.

140 The Gantt chart method is a very useful approach for constructing a time schedule. A Gantt chart lists the activities to be completed down the left-hand side of the page and the time to be covered by the entire project across the top of the page; a bar graph format is used to indicate the beginning and ending date for each activity.

The process phase

141 The *process phase* involves making decisions based upon events which occur during actual implementation of the planned instruction, program, or project.

142 The first step in the process phase is to administer pretests, if such are appropriate, and in the case of pupil evaluation, tests of entry behavior.

143 Based on the pretest results, decisions may be made concerning the appropriateness of the already specified objectives.

144 Following initial testing, planned strategies and activities are executed in the predetermined sequence.

145 The basic purposes of this phase are to determine whether the effort is being executed as intended, to determine the degree of achievement of process objectives, and to identify ways in which improvements can be made.

146 If several strategies are being used simultaneously, then at various points in time decisions will be made as to which ones are working and which are not.

147 Very few efforts work out exactly as planned; there is nothing wrong with making changes in midstream if the end result will be improved because of them.

148 The process phase of evaluation is often referred to as *formative evaluation* and is typically defined in discrepancy terms, that is, differences between intended and actual outcomes.

The product phase

149 The *product phase* involves making decisions at *the* end or, more likely, at the end of one cycle of instruction (e.g., a unit), a program, or project.

150 Decisions made during the product phase are based on the results of posttests (of achievement, attitude, behavior, and the like) and on other cumulative types of data.

151 The major purpose of the product is to collect data in order to make decisions concerning the overall effectiveness of instruction, a program, or project (or whatever).

152 During this phase it is determined whether and/or to what degree intended product objectives were achieved; unanticipated outcomes are also analyzed.

153 If an experimental or quasi-experimental design involving group comparisons was applied to the evaluation, final group performance is now compared to determine if differences are significant, i.e., probably due to chance factors or probably due to differential treatments.

154 An independent evaluator (or evaluation team) either verifies procedures and results as reported by program personnel or actually collects and analyzes appropriate data.

155 The major function of an independent evaluator is not to "check up" on anyone but rather to provide skills and knowledge related to evaluation which are often not possessed by program or project personnel.

156 Data analysis and interpretation is almost always followed by the preparation of a report which describes the objectives, procedures and outcomes of the effort.

157 Whether a report goes to parents, the school board, or an outside funding agency, it should be written understandably—it should communicate as clearly and concisely as possible.

158 The results of the product phase of evaluation are used in at least three major ways: (1) they provide feedback and direction to all who were involved in the effort, e.g., students, teachers, program directors, and thus, each cycle (of instruction, for example) can benefit from analysis of the outcomes of the previous cycle; (2) they provide feedback to outside decision makers, such as parents, principals, school board members, and funding sources; and (3) depending upon the type of evaluation involved, there are a number of groups who can utilize the results, i.e., guidance and counseling personnel, school administrators, educational researchers, and other evaluators.

159 Results of the product phase need to be interpreted with care. Failure to meet objectives, for example, is not necessarily fatal; degree of achievement needs to be considered.

160 Just as the process phase is often referred to as formative evaluation, so also the product phase is frequently referred to as *summative evaluation*.

task one **performance criteria**

Your description should include the following:

a The type of background information which needs to be collected.

b Any major constraints which might be operating.

c The kinds of objectives which will be developed and at least one specific example.

d The kind of prerequisites which are involved (if appropriate) and at least one specific example.

e The types of measurement which will be involved (e.g., an algebra achievement test) and how measures will be obtained (e.g., a standardized test will be selected from those available).

f Basic strategies (and related activities) for objective attainment.

g The type of design which will be utilized (if appropriate).

h A time schedule for the major events in all three phases of the evaluation (the planning phase, the process phase, and the product phase).

NOTE: You are not expected to produce a plan which is technically accurate. In chapter 5, for example, you will learn the correct way to state an objective. For now it is sufficient that you demonstrate comprehension of the activities involved in the planning phase of evaluation and the ability to apply that knowledge to a specific situation.

Because of unforeseen circumstances, a traffic jam for instance, drivers may not get to their destination, or they may take longer than they expected, but they know where they are headed.

part two
specification of objectives

Specification of objectives, or intended outcomes, occurs early in the evaluation process, prior to the execution of an effort, regardless of the type of evaluation involved. Objectives suggest strategies and give direction to all subsequent activities, permit assessment of degree of progress at any point in time, facilitate communication concerning an effort's purposes and procedures, and form the basis for assessment of an effort's achievements. Thus, it is critical that the best possible objectives, both technically and in terms of content, be selected or developed.

The goal of part 2 is for you to understand and appreciate the role of objectives and to be able to formulate or select appropriate objectives for any educational endeavor. After reading part 2, you should be able to do the following task.

task two

For the evaluation situation which you described in task 1, specify two intermediate objectives and for *one* of them formulate a set of at least ten specific objectives. If learning objectives are involved, the intermediate objectives should represent two different domains (i.e. one cognitive and one affective, one affective and one psychomotor, or one cognitive and one psychomotor).

(See Performance Criteria, p. 103.)

4 the nature of objectives

After reading chapter 4, you should be able to:

1 Defend or refute the position "Objectives are an important component of the evaluation process," giving at least three reasons.
2 Discuss the pros and cons of goal-free evaluation.
3 List the basic components of any valid needs assessment model.
4 List three factors to be considered when assigning priorities to identified needs.

Definition and purpose

In this and subsequent chapters we will discuss in depth various components of the evaluation process introduced in chapter 3. Further discussion of some topics, such as the review of related literature which may be involved in situation analysis, is beyond the scope of this text. For the most part, however, topics such as these will normally be included in an introductory educational research text.[1]

As we saw in chapter 3, specification of objectives occurs early in the evaluation process, regardless of the type of evaluation involved. Initial impetus for the current recognition of the importance of objectives can probably be credited to the writings of Ralph Tyler in the early 1930s.[2] The objectives movement was further fostered by the popularity of programmed instruction in the early 1960s. While interest in programmed instruction declined, interest in objectives increased, due at least in part to a short but effective book by Robert Mager entitled *Preparing Instructional Objectives.*[3] While the book was originally written with specific reference to programmed instruction, the concepts it presented are obviously and easily generalizable to any type of instruction and, perhaps more importantly, to any educational activity.

Definition

In general, objectives are the desired outcomes of an effort, the results intended at the end of a series of activities. As stated in chapter 3, objectives are specific statements of what is to be accomplished and how well, and are expressed in terms of quantifiable, measurable outcomes. In this sense we are talking about product objectives because we are concerned with results. In some instances, as discussed in chapter 3, we may specify process objectives which indicate what will be done in order to bring about the desired results. In all cases, however, objectives are stated prior to execution of an effort and are subject to technical and substantive review. While more will be said on the subject later in the chapter, it should be noted that the fact that an objective is quantifiable and measurable does not necessarily mean that it deals with a trivial outcome. Some educators are of the opinion that some of the "truly important" objectives of instruction, for example, cannot be expressed in specific, measurable terms. This is simply not true, although nobody said it was necessarily easy. Even elusive outcomes such as music appreciation and good citizenship can be measured *if* you can specify what you mean. In other words, you have to know what *you* mean when you say you want students to appreciate music. What exactly would a student have to do to demonstrate music appreciation? Buy longhair records? Watch "Previn and the Pittsburgh" on PBS? If a desired outcome cannot be expressed as a measurable behavior, it is probably not because it is unmeasurable; it is probably because the desired outcome has not been sufficiently thought through.

Instructional objectives, outcomes desired of students, are a little trickier than some other types simply because we are dealing with indirect measurement.

[1] See, for example, Gay, L. R. *Educational research: Competencies for analysis and application.* Columbus: Merrill, 1976.
[2] See, for example, Tyler, R. W. *Constructing achievement tests.* Columbus: Ohio State University, 1934.
[3] Mager, R. F. *Preparing instructional objectives.* Palo Alto, Calif.: Fearon, 1962.

As defined by Mager, an *instructional objective* is "an intent communicated by a statement describing a proposed change in a learner—a statement of what the learner is to be like when he has successfully completed a learning experience."[4] Learning, however, is an inferred event, not a directly observable phenomenon. If a pep club has an objective "to sell $500 worth of candy turtles by November 15," it is a very straightforward process to determine whether the objective is achieved. Money is directly observable and someone needs only to count the money collected. In contrast, if a teacher has an objective to the effect that students "will be able to write complete sentences," the process of determining objective achievement is more complex. The actual *ability* to write a complete sentence is not directly observable because learning takes place inside of students' heads. In fact, there are two factors involved—whether students can write complete sentences and whether they acquired this ability as a result of instruction. Thus, first it must be determined what behavior, or performance, will constitute sufficient evidence that the desired ability exists. In the case of writing complete sentences, there are virtually an infinite number of such sentences which exist; it might be decided, however, that if a student can write five complete sentences it will be accepted (inferred) that she or he has the desired capability. Whether a capability is acquired, or learned, as a result of instruction can only be determined by observing performance at two different points in time, before and after instruction, and seeing if performance has changed; a positive change in performance implies that learning has taken place. Thus, while learning per se cannot be directly observed or measured, changes in performance can.[5]

Pros and cons

Based on what you have read thus far in this book about objectives, you probably have concluded that objectives are a given, a universally accepted component of any educational endeavor. This, unfortunately, does not happen to be the case. There are some educators (and noneducators) who are opposed to objectives on a variety of grounds; some objections are related to the nature and purpose of objectives themselves, while others stem from strong skepticism as to whether their alleged benefits are ever really actualized.

Pros

Supporters of objectives argue that their main advantage is that they give direction to, or guide the activities of, an effort. Without objectives activities are haphazard at worst and loosely directed at best; with objectives activities are focused and organized. At the very least this argument has a good deal of commonsense appeal. As with accountability, even persons who express negative attitudes toward objectives, utilize them in their everyday activities, albeit informally, whether they realize it or not.

Very few rational individuals, for example, get into their cars in the morning and drive for 50 minutes with no particular destination in mind or a

---

[4] See footnote 3.
[5] Burns, R. W. The theory of expressing objectives. *Educational Technology*, 1968, 8(18), 13–14.

vague destination such as "wherever I happen to be after driving south for 50 minutes." People tend to have very definite intended destinations, be it school, the office, or the 7–11 grocery store. Because of unforeseen circumstances, such as an automobile accident or a traffic jam, they may not get there or they may take longer than they expected, but they know where they are headed. Further, they probably have determined the most efficient route to take. The analogies to educational activities are obvious and numerous. It is as irrational to teach for 50 minutes without a definite destination in mind, for example, as it is to drive for 50 minutes without a definite destination. It certainly does not seem logical to say that a teacher will teach for 50 minutes per day for 180 days and whatever the students happen to know at the end will be OK. Nor does it make much sense to fund a special project for ten months to the tune of $100,000 and then in the eleventh month decide to find out what it "came up with" in the way of results.

Objectives provide direction in a number of ways. First, they suggest general strategies and specific activities for their attainment. Different sets of objectives will usually generate different strategies. As an example, suppose that there are three French teachers, teacher A, teacher B, and teacher C. Teacher A has no specific objectives; she is simply "teaching French." Teacher B has a set of objectives related to students being able to speak conversational French. Teacher C has a set of objectives related to students being able to read and write French. Can you see how their classroom activities probably differ? Almost anything teacher A does, even if she or he just reads a French textbook out loud every day, is appropriate, i.e. constitutes "teaching French." Teacher B, on the other hand, probably spends a lot of time speaking French, playing records of conversations in French, and having students converse in French. Teacher C probably devotes a lot of time to having students translate written passages from French into English, either orally or in writing. Instructional objectives also give direction to the students themselves. They know what is expected of them and can utilize their study time efficiently. Pity the students of teacher A! What should they study? Should they memorize the text, or what? Telling students precisely what you want them to know and be able to do is not "teaching to the test." If you tell students that you want them to be able to translate a simple sentence in English into French, using vocabulary acquired to date, that is not the same as telling them that you want them to be able to translate "I love Paris in the springtime" into French.

Objectives also serve a diagnostic-prescriptive function. If we know where we were when we started and where we want to be (the difference being our objectives), then at any point in time we can assess where we are, that is, how much progress has been made, and act accordingly. This is equally true with respect to a project designed to reduce vandalism as it is with respect to desired student learning. Further, regardless of when we assess our status, or progress (during the effort or at the end), our objectives dictate to a great extent the way in which we collect status data. If an objective deals with student achievement, an appropriate achievement test is probably called for. If, on the other hand, an objective deals with decreased instances of disruptive behavior, observation is probably required. The existence of objectives does not necessarily mean that an undertaking will be more successful than it otherwise would have been, but they do allow determination of what has been accomplished. In fact, without objectives it is questionable whether it is even possible to evaluate an effort at all. How can it be said that an effort did or did not "do the job" if "the job" was never specified?

Last, objectives serve a communication function. Personnel can communicate to interested groups not only what is being done but also to what end. Teachers can communicate to students and parents not only their objectives, but also where students are, as a group or as individuals, with respect to those objectives. Administrators can communicate similar information to school boards and the community at large. Special project and program personnel can communicate to funding sources. And so forth. Communication is enhanced primarily because discussion can deal with specifics, not vague generalities. As an example, a parent wishing to help her child at home with arithmetic would not benefit much from a statement to the effect that "Horatio cannot do fractions." In contrast, the message that "Horatio is having difficulty multiplying and dividing improper fractions" would provide more direction to home help sessions.

Cons

Opponents of objectives believe that they produce rigid, conforming procedures, standards, and behavior which discourage creativity and spontaneity and fail to take into consideration individual differences. They also question seriously whether all important educational outcomes can be objectified. With respect to instruction, for example, they feel that at best objectives are suitable for a limited number of cut-and-dry areas, such as arithmetic, and totally inappropriate for all other areas. Opponents also contend that there is a natural tendency to select objectives which are easy to measure, not necessarily important. The result is often a set of easy-to-measure objectives representing outcomes of trivial importance. It is easier to measure acquisition of facts, for example, than ability to synthesize; consequently, chances are that, given a choice, teachers will select objectives which describe what students "will know." Furthermore, opponents claim that the really important outcomes of any effort are long-term results, not short-term accomplishments, and therefore objectives dealing with here-and-now achievement are largely irrelevant. After all, what difference does it make if a student can identify the cause of a significant event in a reading selection? What we really want is for students to be able to successfully function in society after graduation.

In support of their position, opponents cite the fact that there is very little evidence that the existence of objectives actually results in greater achievement. Even those who agree with the concept of objectives on a theoretical level argue that in reality their use is impractical because any given effort can spawn an unmanageable multiplicity of objectives. This is especially true with respect to areas of instruction. Reading comprehension, for example, may entail close to 100 separate objectives, such as "given a work which conveys a moral, the learner will identify the moral," or "given a significant event from a reading selection, the learner will identify its cause."[6]

Rebuttal

There is obviously a great deal of truth in the above objections, but they represent mostly potential dangers, not flaws inherent in objectives. In other words, analysis of the alleged cons of objectives will reveal that they deal at least in part with problems that may arise from their *misuse*. Several of the objections

[6] Patalino, M., & Stangel, G. *Structure of Reading Skills.* Los Angeles: Center for the Study of Education, UCLA Graduate School of Education, 1971.

could easily be translated into suggestions, or caveats, for writing objectives; for example: "Avoid selecting objectives simply because they are easy to measure." Many people get killed in automobile accidents as a result of speeding, reckless driving, and driving while drinking. The logical conclusion is not that cars per se are dangerous but that they can be dangerous when misused. We do not say, "Down with cars!" Instead we say, "Slow down," "Drive carefully," and "If you drink, don't drive." While some specific responses to each objection have been discussed earlier within a different context, let us briefly look at each one.

First, objectives are not restrictive in and of themselves. For any objective there are invariably alternative strategies which can be utilized to promote achievement. If your objective is to get to work at 44 East Drudgery Street, there are probably any number of reasonable routes that you can take. One route may be a few miles longer but have less traffic and thus take less time. Another route may be the shortest in terms of both miles and time but require a 50-cent toll. Based on your priorities, you will select the route best suited to you. Similarly, a teacher will utilize a strategy that is best suited to her or his students, given available resources. There is plenty of room for creativity in terms of putting to best use what is available. Further, the use of objectives by no means negates the existence of individual differences. Different students, for example, may be working on different objectives at different times; each student may take a different length of time to achieve a given objective; different instructional strategies may be used with different students. All students may or may not have the same objectives; there may be a set of minimum objectives to be achieved by all and a number of optional or enrichment objectives. In other words, objectives are not inherently restrictive.

The issue of the "objectifiability" of all desired educational outcomes was addressed earlier. There is a degree of consensus among educators regarding the appropriateness of objectives in basic skills areas such as reading and math. The lack of consensus regarding other, more elusive, areas such as music appreciation stems not from the immeasurability of the outcomes but from the inability of people to specify what they really *mean* by music appreciation. And, if you cannot say what music appreciation means, i.e. if you cannot translate it into observable behavior, how then can you teach it, and more critically, how can you know whether students "have" it? With enough thought, even the fuzziest of outcomes can be operationally defined and translated into observable, measurable behaviors.

As pointed out before, the fact that people may tend to select trivial, easy to measure objectives, is their fault, not an inherent characteristic of objectives. All *important* desired outcomes can be expressed in observable, measurable terms. This is not to say that the task is always an easy one. With a reasonable amount of serious effort, however, it can be done. As for the alleged irrelevance of short-term outcomes, most people would agree that long-term outcomes are the real concern of educational efforts. The point is, however, that long-term outcomes do not just happen; they require a proper foundation and systematic development. As shall be seen later when the relationship between goals and objectives is discussed, all objectives are, at least theoretically, related to some long-term outcome, or goal. As an example, a basic goal of public school education, a desired long-term outcome, is economic self-sufficiency. This goal can be analyzed into component abilities such as literacy, preparedness for future training, and vocational skill. Each of these can be further analyzed into a greater number of abilities such as the ability to read and comprehend, the ability to write coherently, the ability to compute, the ability to make intelligent vocational choices, and so on and so on and so on.

Each of these discrete, prerequisite skills and knowledge can be developed over a period of years in different courses at different times. In isolation, any given objective may appear to be of little consequence. When looked at in combination with other related objectives—past, present and future—however, their relevance is much more evident.

With respect to the lack of evidence supporting the effectiveness of objectives, it is true that, anecdotal data aside, there is very little conclusive research data. This is due at least in part to the fact that related studies are typically conducted in real-world environments such as classrooms. In such situations there are a myriad of controllable and uncontrollable variables operating, and it is very difficult to determine the effect of any one variable of interest. In any event, objectives make sense logically, and even if they do not directly result in greater achievement, they do permit assessment of exactly what has been accomplished. Further, there are many other organizational activities, such as lesson planning, which are accepted as good practice despite the absence of evidence regarding their effectiveness.

It is difficult to refute the charge that any effort can spawn an unmanageable multiplicity of objectives. The basic assertion is true, although the "unmanageable" part is debatable. When a general desired outcome such as reading comprehension, computational skill, or coherent writing is translated into a set of observable, measurable behaviors which cover all aspects of the desired outcome, the result is likely to be a large number of specific objectives. It must be emphasized, however, that the component behaviors exist regardless of whether or not they are identified. Not specifying objectives does not decrease the number of relevant behaviors. To purposely not identify them because the result might be somewhat overwhelming is an "ostrichy" response to say the least. In fact, the reality that there are so many component behaviors involved in any major outcome constitutes a good argument for identifying them. Without a list of such behaviors it is much more likely that a number of them will be overlooked, thereby decreasing the chances of achieving the general desired outcome. Thus, while it is true that a given area may spawn a large number of specific objectives, the benefits to be derived from specifying them makes the effort worthwhile. As to the manageability issue, logically it would seem to be easier to organize and manage day-to-day activities when they are directed toward the achievement of specific outcomes. On the other hand, in certain situations, especially those involving individualized instruction, keeping track of objectives achievement and related clerical activities may well require more organization and time. This problem, however, is due more to the nature of the system (e.g. individualization) than to the objectives per se. If anything, it would seem that having objectives would facilitate organization in such a system.

In conclusion, opposition to objectives is based more on their possible misuse than on the nature of objectives per se. There are poorly written objectives dealing with important outcomes and well written objectives dealing with trivial outcomes. But the existence of such objectives does not diminish in any way the potential advantages.to be derived from well written, relevant objectives. The above discussion is not intended to suggest that objectives are always required for every activity. Just as there are times when one may take a ride for pure enjoyment, with no particular destination in mind, there is a place in education for minimally directed exploratory activities. In one sense such activities do have an objective, for example, increased awareness or self-expression, but the intent is not the achievement of any specific, measurable skill or knowledge. Activities like these, however, comprise a very small percentage of the total educational enterprise. For the vast majority of educational endeavors, objectives are highly appropriate and useful.

Needs assessment

It would be virtually impossible for the educational system to attempt to foster achievement of all possible objectives; there are just too many of them, both theoretically and in reality. Formally or informally, each educational endeavor must select the goals and objectives with which it will be concerned. Further, unless the number is small, priorities must be established for any given set of objectives. A general term for this process is "needs assessment."

Definition and purpose

Conceptually, if there is a gap between the way things are (current status) and the way we would like them to be (desired outcomes), a *need* exists. Depending upon how specifically a need has been defined, it can be translated into either a goal or an objective, the intent being to eliminate the need. Thus, *needs assessment* is the process of identifying needs and (usually) establishing the relative priorities of those needs. Before the term "needs assessment" came into vogue, the process still occurred but typically in a less systematic way. As we shall discuss shortly, the basic goals and objectives of the educational system have remained relatively stable but the emphases, or priorities, have shifted over time.

Following the launching of Sputnik, for example, American education for a time became very math-science oriented. This period was followed by a predictable shift in emphasis to humanistic education. Today we are in the middle of an also predictable "back to basics" movement. These shifts in priorities are at least to some degree necessary. Times change, needs change, and priorities change. For example, "command of the fundamental skills (reading, writing, arithmetic)" and "worthy use of leisure time" have always been basic educational goals. The former, however, has always been given a much higher priority than the latter. While the priorities will probably never reverse, use of leisure time has been given progressively more attention as the prospects for a shorter work week have increased. An even more relevant example is the recent priority given to objectives related to the metric system of measurement. Such objectives are no longer considered just desirable; they have become a necessity. In fact, minimum testing programs typically include assessment of such objectives. The educational system cannot be static; it must be sensitive to, and responsive to, the ever-changing needs of society. Even so, change does not come rapidly, and there is generally a sizable lag between the emergence of a national priority change and the reflection of that change in the public school system. This lag has been humorously satirized in *The Saber-Tooth Curriculum*, in which instruction in areas such as dealing with saber-tooth tigers persisted in the curriculum long after the tigers were gone![7]

A by-product of the accountability movement has been the formalization of needs assessment and the development of empirical, systematic procedures for

[7] Peddiwell, J. A. *The saber-tooth curriculum.* New York: McGraw-Hill, 1939.

determining and ordering needs. As concern for resource allocation has grown, so has the importance of establishing priorities. Clearly, the choice of objectives and the determination of relative importance involves value judgments; there is no objective truth (no pun intended!) concerning *the* best objectives. Thus the needs assessment process is based on consensus and involves gathering input from a variety of educational and community groups such as teachers and parents. It is interesting to note that inclusion of the community in the decision-making process, in the spirit of accountability, is not considered to be an extension of a courtesy, or a polite gesture, but rather the recognition of a right. The results of a needs assessment are used to justify decisions concerning the allocation of both personnel and financial resources.

Applications

Application of needs assessment procedures is not limited to curriculum decisions at the school level although it is most often used for this purpose. Special projects, for example, are typically funded, at least initially, for a fixed amount of money for a fixed time period. In the interest of both optimal resource use and fair evaluation, it is imperative that such projects focus their attention on a manageable number of high-priority objectives which are agreed upon by all relevant groups (including the funding agency). In other words, it is preferable to have a smaller number of more important objectives. It is more likely that these objectives will be achieved than if resources are diluted to include a larger number of objectives of varying priority. Needs assessment can be applied to, and used by, all levels and components of the educational system, including classrooms, programs, projects, schools, school systems, states, a-a-and countries. As an example, district-level needs assessment has been mandated by a number of states, including Florida and Iowa. Such needs assessment may be conducted by a variety of personnel such as teachers, principals, superintendents, and department of education personnel. As with the formulation of objectives, the utility of the needs assessment process depends to a great degree on the intelligence with which it is applied. If done too carelessly or informally, it will not be of much value; in such cases the results may differ little from what plain common sense would dictate. It can also be "overdone," in which case it is neither practical nor cost-effective.

Models

As with models of evaluation, the literature is rampant with needs assessment models. Most of them are reasonable and provide useful guidelines, but often their differences are superficial. All valid needs assessment models involve the same essential components, namely: compilation of a comprehensive list of appropriate objectives; ordering of the objectives in terms of perceived importance; determination of the degree of discrepancy between actual and desired levels of performance on high-priority objectives, that is, identification of needs; and ranking of the identified needs. The terms used to describe these processes may vary, the level of specificity at which they are described may vary, and the context within which they are described may vary, but the basic processes are the same.

The type of objectives involved and their level of specificity depends on

the level and context of the needs assessment, although they are typically intermediate objectives (a concept to be discussed in chapter 5). For example, an elementary school–level needs assessment might include an objective such as "compre-
hends written materials." The ordering of objectives is based on the combined
ratings of all persons involved in their ranking. At this point the various models
diverge in terms of how needs are identified, that is, how the discrepancy
between actual and desired levels of performance is determined.

Subjective versus objective models

So-called subjective models for needs assessment identify discrepancies
by asking judges to give their opinions as to degree of need in given areas.[8] Objective models determine discrepancies by collecting performance data to assess current status and comparing data to acceptable levels of performance. Of course both
approaches involve both subjectivity and objectivity. Subjective models may collect judgmental data in an objective manner and judgments may be made based on
objective data; objective models involve subjectivity in setting desired standards.
The Center for the Study of Evaluation (CSE) at UCLA has developed a comprehensive set of materials for use in conducting an objective needs assessment. The
CSE kit, which includes a large collection of objectives, has been extensively field-
tested and is widely used.[9] A number of states have also developed guidelines and
materials for needs assessment. Such states typically provide support, financial
and otherwise, for districts implementing a needs assessment.

Components

A brief look at Ohio's guidelines supports the previous contention that
while they vary in particulars, valid needs assessment models involve the same
essential components:

1 Form a needs assessment committee.
2 Identify goals and subgoals.
3 Develop and administer a survey instrument to determine perceived educational needs.
4 Achieve an acceptable response rate and analyze the data.
5 Determine weighting procedures, rank perceived needs, and select areas
for further assessment; i.e. assign priorities to the perceived needs.
6 Determine desired performance standards for high priority needs.
7 Select and administer instruments for assessing actual performance levels.
8 Compare actual and desired performance levels.
9 Put identified needs in priority order.[10]

[8] See, for example, Rose, B. K. *Phi Delta Kappa model.* Chico, Calif.: Northern California Program Development Center, 1973.
[9] For further information write to: Center for the Study of Evaluation, UCLA Graduate School of Education, Los Angeles, CA 90024; or telephone 213-825-4711. See also, Hoepfner, R., Bradley, P. A., Klein,
S. P., & Alkin, M. C. *CSE Elementary school evaluation kit: Needs assessment.* Center for the Study of
Evaluation, University of California at Los Angeles. Boston: Allyn and Bacon, 1972.
[10] See, Ohio Department of Education, *Needs Assessment guidelines.* Columbus: Division of Planning
and Evaluation, 1973, *and* Lewis, J. L. Problems encountered in conducting an assessment of educational needs in selected Ohio school districts. Paper presented at the American Educational Research
Association Convention, Toronto, 1978.

Thus we see that even in objective needs assessment there is a large subjective component as group opinion is relied upon heavily. In this connection the Delphi technique should at least be mentioned since it is a method for achieving group consensus which is occasionally used in needs assessment. It can be used whenever consensus is desired from a relatively large, diverse group and thus is applicable to group selection of goals and objectives, determination of perceived needs, the assignment of priorities to perceived needs, the setting of standards for desirable performance, and the assignment of priority to identified needs. The Delphi technique typically involves mailing questionnaires to participants, providing them with feedback on actual responses, and giving them opportunities to revise their responses. This process is repeated until consensus is reached. Of course the process results in consensus only, not necessarily in the best decisions. It is also a costly, time-consuming procedure. While at one time it was the "in" technique, the novelty seems to have worn off and it is currently used much less frequently than it once was.

The last step in the needs assessment process, assigning priorities to identified needs, is considerably more complex than it may appear. As a simplistic example, suppose testing reveals discrepancies between desired and actual performance for objective A and objective B. The discrepancy for A is larger than for B, but B represents a more important objective. Which should receive higher priority in terms of further action, A or B, the larger discrepancy or the more critical area? Another factor to be considered is the number of students exhibiting various discrepancies. Should resources be directed at improving the very poor scores of a small number of students or at raising the general performance level of the majority of students? Other considerations include the costs involved and the probability of success. Performance is easier to increase in some areas than in others. Thus decisions at this stage are difficult and complex, and reflect the combined biases of the decision makers.

Problems

A number of problems are associated with needs assessment. Some of these are unique to needs assessment, most are not. In a recent study, Lewis reported problems identified by school districts in Ohio which had expressed interest in conducting a needs assessment and which had received grants from the Ohio Department of Education to do so.[11] Activities most frequently considered to be problem areas were: (1) obtaining a satisfactory response rate when surveying parents and community members, (2) identifying educational goals, (3) determining subgoals, and (4) preparing the survey instrument. Difficulty was also reported in setting desired levels of student performance and selecting appropriate instruments for measuring the actual level of student performance. Based on his experiences, Lewis made a number of observations regarding the needs assessment process. First, schools usually need the assistance of consultants and/or financial support; the districts in his study received from $10,000 to $24,000 and had a quarter- to half-time coordinator. Second, key personnel involved require training. Third, successful execution of the process requires the cooperation of a great many people, and getting their cooperation is not easy. Further, the process tends to take a lot longer than one might imagine; districts in his study were funded for 13

[11] See footnote 10.

months and yet 2 of them only completed about two-thirds of the activities. Also, as alluded to earlier, the results may end up differing little from what common sense would dictate. And, as with the Delphi technique, a number of components produce consensus only, not necessarily the best or most valid decisions; at the very worst, the needs assessment process may represent the pooling of ignorance and misinformation.

All in all, in too many instances needs assessment appears to be another classic example of overkill. It is a conceptually good idea that has been strangled in overly complex and detailed procedures. As Lewis has expressed it, even under the near ideal conditions present in the participating Ohio school districts, i.e. provision of financial and consultant assistance and expressed interest in the endeavor, "school personnel encountered numerous and severe problems in conducting the needs assessment. The findings indicate that a systematic assessment of student educational needs is a difficult, expensive, and time-consuming process. It seems likely that this type of needs assessment will not be a part of the planning process in most school districts." Of course, as it is, very similar types of needs assessment are being applied by mandate in a number of states. Further, as typically implemented, the process does not appear to be cost-effective. Unless a hard look is taken at the process and a serious attempt is made to make it more efficient and manageable, it is very likely this basically good idea will be discarded because it is too much trouble.

Goal-free evaluation

As mentioned in chapter 2, there are some educators who advocate what is called "goal-free" evaluation, a concept proposed by Michael Scriven.

Definition and rationale

Goal-free evaluation is the assessment of *actual* outcomes, or effects, not *intended* outcomes as specified in an effort's objectives. It is not that Scriven is opposed to objectives, per se; he does not dispute their usefulness in earlier phases of evaluation. He does feel, however, that the assessment of the effectiveness of a curriculum, program, or project should not be contaminated, or biased, by knowledge of intended effects. The basic premise is the notion that the really important outcomes of an effort may or may not be the ones intended. If attention is focused only on intended outcomes, some really important effects may be overlooked. Scriven is concerned with outcomes period—good or bad, anticipated or not. He claims that some programs achieve all their objectives but have some very negative, unanticipated side effects, for example, the students learned but hated every minute of it. Other programs fail to achieve their objectives but produce very positive, unanticipated outcomes, for example, students did not learn any more than usual but attendance improved 30%. Of course these examples represent the extremes. In Scriven's view most programs involve a combination of anticipated and unanticipated outcomes. The evaluator should collect data related to a broad spectrum of actual outcomes before examining program objectives. The evaluator's resulting report may well include suggestions for revision of objectives and/or strategies and activities in order to heighten positive outcomes and eliminate negative outcomes.

An example

While much has been written on the subject, actual applications of goal-free evaluation have been limited in both number and scope. The following example should give you a better understanding of the nature of, and problems associated with, goal-free evaluation. In 1975 a federally funded, product-oriented project was completing its first year of operation. The evaluator felt that the project was a good candidate for an experimental goal-free evaluation because: (1) he had very little knowledge concerning the project's objectives, (2) the project staff was interested in possible side effects of the materials, and (3) trial versions of a number of products were available for review. The evaluator viewed the situation as an opportunity to learn more about how the goal-free approach actually works in practice. Data were collected in two major ways. First, an external review panel rated the products. Second, an intermediary interviewed key project personnel and was in turn questioned by the evaluator, being careful not to mention project objectives.

The resulting evaluation report was mainly a summary of the judges' comments and ratings for each product. It also included the evaluator's general impressions and a summary of the intermediary's interviews. The evaluator's observations concerning the approach were very enlightening. Among them were the following:

1 The anxiety level of the staff was very high during the process, probably because of a lack of opportunity for the development of mutual trust to be established between the staff and himself.
2 Selecting a fair standard for evaluation is difficult in the absence of knowledge of intended outcomes.
3 Care must be taken not to become too "infatuated" by occasional unanticipated or negative outcomes.
4 The approach is most appropriate when the development of products is the major focus of the program.
5 The approach is probably best used in conjunction with other kinds of evaluation; it heightens the need for objectivity even if it does not guarantee it.
6 The approach is in need of improved methodology.

All in all, the evaluator felt that the pluses of the approach slightly outweighed the minuses. He did, however, place his reflections within the context that his experimental application of goal-free evaluation was limited and that more applications are needed in order to refine the approach and to give it a fair and adequate test.[12]

Thus, the basic concept of looking for unanticipated outcomes makes sense, but assessing outcomes "in the dark" does not. In all fairness, an effort should only be held accountable for the degree to which it achieved whatever it intended to achieve. Further, if an effort is carefully conceived and planned, the chances that some startling, unanticipated outcome will occur are slim. There will always be, however, unanticipated outcomes of one kind or another. The most rational course of action is to identify and analyze them and to make appropriate program revisions based on them.

---

[12] Welch, W. W. Goal-free formative evaluation—An example. Paper presented at the American Educational Research Association Convention, Toronto, 1978.

5 classification and statement of objectives

After reading chapter 5, you should be able to:

1 Explain how the concepts of "time" and "degree of learning" differ in a mastery learning system as compared to a traditional system.
2 Explain how a group objective differs from an individual objective.
3 State two major issues, or problems, associated with minimum competency testing.
4 List three examples of goals.
5 List three examples of intermediate objectives.
6 List three examples of specific objectives.
7 State whether you think objectives should, in general, be developed or selected and give your reasons.
8 State a guiding principle for determining the degree of specificity required for an objective.
9 State two examples for each of the three strategies for setting a group criterion.
10 Select an area of interest and write one related objective for each major category of the cognitive taxonomy.
11 Select an area of interest and write one related objective for each major category of the affective taxonomy.
12 State any objective of your choice and identify the cognitive component, the affective component, and the psychomotor component.

Types of objectives

Types of evaluation, as discussed in chapter 2, refers to the different processes, products, and persons subject to evaluation, i.e. students, curricula, schools, school systems, large populations, special programs and projects, and personnel. Just as the basic evaluation process is the same regardless of what is being evaluated so also objectives look basically the same regardless of the type of evaluation. All objectives indicate intended outcomes; there are differences, however, in terms of the nature of the intended outcomes. One basic difference is that certain types of evaluation, and their corresponding objectives, are primarily concerned with the performance of individuals whereas others are primarily concerned with the performance of groups.

Objectives for individuals

As mentioned previously, student evaluation and personnel evaluation are concerned mainly with individual performance. Interestingly, these two types of evaluation are on opposite ends of the continuum with respect to the degree to which intended outcomes have been objectified. Literally thousands and thousands of objectives covering virtually every area of instruction have been written to express desired student behaviors. In contrast, very little exists in terms of performance objectives for teachers, even less for administrators, and essentially nothing for special program and project personnel. It has thus far simply not been possible to justify evaluating personnel even on a small number of objective behaviors. As pointed out before, this is due mainly to the lack of empirical evidence linking given behaviors with job success. For example, no teacher behaviors have been shown to be sufficiently related to student achievement to allow us to hold teachers accountable for exhibiting them.

Competency-based education

A number of schools and colleges of education across the country have taken the position that, given the lack of empirical evidence, professional and community consensus is a reasonable way of determining skills and knowledge required of school personnel. Such schools of education have developed what are commonly called *competency-based,* or performance-based, *training programs* for preservice teachers, administrators, counselors, and others. The objectives, or competencies, to be achieved by students in the various programs are typically developed by university or college instructors, experts in their respective fields (early childhood education, for example), and reviewed by appropriate public school and community groups. The intent is to identify behaviors *believed* to be required for successful job performance (as a first grade teacher, for example), and to have students demonstrate these behaviors prior to graduation. As a specific example, most such programs agree that the "ability to interpret the results of a reading readiness test" is a necessary competency for first grade teachers. This approach really represents a limited form of job analysis.[1] Of course, we are talking about objectives for people preparing to be teachers, administrators, counselors, and so forth. Thus they are instructional objectives, not personnel objectives. While any number of such objectives might be quite valid for evaluating the performance of in-service personnel, it is not likely that they will be accepted for this purpose without empirical, supporting evidence.

Mastery objectives

Instructional objectives are concerned with changes in student performance, or behavior, which indicate that learning has taken place as a result of instruction. They are variously referred to as performance objectives, behavioral objectives, learning objectives, and classroom objectives. There are other terms which are occasionally referred to (recall that there is no scarcity of descriptive terms in the field of evaluation!) but the ones above are the ones most commonly used. Certain instructional objectives are considered to be required, minimum essentials, i.e. objectives which should be achieved by virtually all students, regardless of ability or background; these are referred to as *mastery*, or minimum skills, *objectives*. The concept is not a new one to education but it has gained prominence and widespread adoption as a result of the accountability movement. The idea is that there are certain skills and knowledge which are essential prerequisites to the learning of subsequent skills and knowledge which are essential prerequisites to the learning of further subsequent skills and knowledge, and so forth. The culminating skills and knowledge are required for effective functioning in a Democratic society; students are entitled to instruction that will help them achieve these. Thus, various mastery objectives may be identified at all grade levels.

Traditionally, time spent on instruction has been a constant, with degree of learning among students varying considerably. In a mastery system, amount learned, as evidenced by objectives achieved, is the constant and time required to achieve objectives varies among students.[2] The basic premise of a mastery system is that, due to differential aptitudes among students, all students do not achieve all objectives in the same amount of time—some need more time than others.[3] But if students are given sufficient time and appropriate instruction, then most students, probably 90–95%, will be able to "master" what is taught and achieve the objectives.[4] Some educators agree with Benjamin Bloom that all instruction should be based on the mastery learning model. But primarily for cost-effectiveness reasons, the model is probably most appropriate for minimum skills objectives. As you may have deduced, mastery learning involves individualized instruction and all that goes with it, e.g. much testing and retesting on an individual basis. Standards of achievement accepted as evidence of mastery are specified in advance,

[1] Job analysis is a technique borrowed from industry and the military and involves analyzing a job, or position, in order to determine what skills and knowledge are required for that job. Data are collected using a variety of survey and observational techniques. The results indicate what training is necessary and the degree of proficiency to be required of trainees.
[2] Mayo, S. T. Mastery learning and mastery testing. *NCME*, 1970 *1* (3), 1–4.
[3] Carroll, J. B. A model of school learning. *Teachers College Record*, 1963, *64*, 723–733.
[4] Bloom, B. S. Learning for mastery. *Evaluation Comment* 1968, *1*(2); Bloom, B. S., Hastings, J. T., & Madaus, G. F. *Handbook on formative and summative evaluation of student learning.* New York: McGraw-Hill, 1971, chapter 3.

i.e. achievement is determined on an individual basis, not by comparison with group performance. Thus, mastery tests represent one form of criterion-referenced measurement, about which we will have more to say in chapter 6.

Objectives for groups

Objectives for the remaining types of evaluation—curriculum evaluation, school-level evaluation, evaluation of large populations, and evaluation of specific projects and programs—express outcomes intended for groups, not individuals. The groups involved may very well be students or teachers, but the primary interest is in their performance as a whole, not as individuals.

An example

An example will help to clarify the distinction between individual and group objectives. Suppose the area of interest is reading comprehension. Specific instructional objectives might include

1 Given passages written at an appropriate difficulty level, the student will correctly answer related factual questions, with 80% accuracy.
2 Given passages written at an appropriate difficulty level, the student will select the main idea for each from among four choices, with 80% accuracy.
3 Given passages written at an appropriate difficulty level, the student will select the best title for each among four choices, with 80% accuracy.

As noted earlier, reading comprehension might entail in the neighborhood of 100 specific objectives. For each student it could easily be determined at any time whether and which objectives had been achieved.

A teacher might also be interested in the progress of the class as a whole; that is, he or she might want to know what percent of the class had achieved what percent of the objectives at any given point in time. The intent might be, for example, to have 90% of the class achieve a certain set of mastery objectives. This type of question, however, as opposed to "How is Ziggy doing?" would be of prime interest in curriculum evaluation, and the emphasis would be on clusters of objectives. Recall the distinction between internal and external evaluation. Internal evaluation would be concerned with whether students in the curriculum under study achieved the curriculum's objectives. Curriculum objectives might include:

1 Ninety percent of the students will reach criterion (achieve successfully) on objectives 1–27.
2 Seventy-five percent of the students will reach criterion on objectives 28–92.

External evaluation would be concerned with whether students under the curriculum of interest performed better, that is, displayed higher levels of reading comprehension, than students under some other curriculum. It might seem logical to say that "students under curriculum A will achieve significantly *more objectives* than students under curriculum B." As pointed out previously, however, this will not generally be appropriate since different curricula may involve different objectives. The trick would be to identify or to develop a measure equally appropriate for assessing the reading comprehension of students in each curriculum. The resulting objective might be:

> Students under curriculum A will achieve significantly higher scores on the Gates-MacGinitie reading comprehension test than students under curriculum B.

Minimum competency testing

Since the types of objectives characteristic of the other types of evaluation have been illustrated previously in this chapter and in part 1, we will not belabor the point further except to discuss the concept of mastery objectives as they are involved in the evaluation of large populations. Statewide assessment programs focus on the assessment of student achievement of specified minimum objectives, that is, objectives which virtually all students should be able to achieve by certain times in their school career. Thus there are minimum objectives for various grades and for various subjects. Since the purpose of state assessment is to provide information to state and local decision makers about the adequacy of the basic educational program, the interest is clearly in group, not individual, achievement.

An outgrowth of state assessment, however, has been the minimum competency testing movement. *Minimum competency testing* involves assessing whether students have met state-mandated standards for grade promotion or high school graduation. In just a few short years, upwards of 30 states have mandated such standards. Florida, for example, passed such an accountability law in 1976. In the words of Thomas H. Fisher, then Director of the Student Assessment Section, Florida State Department of Education:

> The 1976 act mandated new minimum graduation standards for the class of 1978–79—namely, the accumulation of a minimum number of course credits as required by the local district, mastery of the basic skills, and satisfactory performance on functional literacy tests. It was decided that the Florida Statewide Assessment Program would become the focal point for determining student mastery of the basic skills and functional literacy. The program had previously tested all public school students in grades 3 and 5, but the new act expanded it to grades 3, 5, 8, and 11.[5]

The Florida plan also makes provisions for remedial instruction for students who do poorly on the eleventh grade test. Any student who fails to pass the state exam three times will receive a certificate of attendance, not a high school diploma.

Now comes the troublesome aspect of minimum competency testing. When the results of state tests are to be also used to make competence decisions concerning *individual* students, several critical issues emerge. It is not that these issues are not important in any mastery system, it is just that in the case of minimum competency testing the resulting decisions are more serious. Among them are the questions "Which objectives should be measured?" and "What should be

---

[5] Fisher, T. H. Florida's approach to competency testing. *Phi Delta Kappan*, 1978, *59*(9), 599–602.

the minimum passing score?'' These are not easy questions and the alternative answers are numerous. Brickell, for example, has identified three different types of objectives which could be tested: basic skills objectives (e.g. reading, writing and arithmetic), school subject objectives (e.g. art, science and social studies), and life objectives (e.g. citizenship, vocations and family). And of course there are objectives which combine these areas such as those involving the application of basic skills in a given school subject.[6] The issue of which objectives are required minimums for being promoted to the next higher grade or for graduation, and the related issue of how well a student needs to perform on a test of such objectives, have not yet been satisfactorily resolved. In the meantime, each state is making its own decisions based mainly on the consensus of qualified, involved groups.

The taxonomies of educational objectives

In science, a *taxonomy* is an orderly classification of plants and animals according to their presumed natural relationships.[7] The term has been "borrowed" by education to describe a comprehensive classification scheme for instructional objectives. The taxonomies classify all objectives into a hierarchy of categories based on presumed complexity. Each succeeding category involves behavior believed to be more complex than the one previous and each is considered to be prerequisite to the next; in other words, performance of objectives at a higher level implies the ability to perform related objectives at lower levels. The stated purpose of the taxonomies is to facilitate communication.[8] The identification, naming, and description of categories of behavioral outcomes permits educators to use the same terms to describe the same behaviors in the same way. The existence of the taxonomies also focuses attention on a wide range of behavioral outcomes, thus making it less likely that all the objectives for a given effort will involve lower-level behaviors only. The actual taxonomies are very helpful in that in addition to describing behaviors in each of the categories and subcategories, they also provide illustrative examples.

Three taxonomies have been proposed, corresponding to three domains of learning—the cognitive domain, the affective domain, and the psychomotor domain. Although there is overlap, it is believed that all instructional outcomes can be classified as belonging primarily to one of the three domains. The *cognitive domain* deals with, as the name implies, cognitive processes, and the taxonomic categories range from simple recall of facts to the making of evaluative judgments. The *affective domain* involves feelings, attitudes, interests, and values, and the categories range from willingness to receive or attend to characterization by a value. The *psychomotor domain* is concerned with physical abilities, such as muscular or motor skills, manipulation, and neuromuscular coordination. The taxonomies of cognitive and affective outcomes have been generally accepted. While several taxonomies of the psychomotor domain have been developed, none of them has achieved the degree of acceptance of the other two.

---

[6] Brickell, H. M. Seven key notes on minimum competency testing, *Phi Delta Kappan*, 1978, 59(9), 589–592.
[7] This definition is courtesy of Webster.
[8] Bloom, B. S. (Ed.). *Taxonomy of educational objectives, Handbook I: Cognitive domain.* New York: David McKay, 1956.

The cognitive domain

The taxonomy of cognitive objectives, developed by Bloom and his associates, has definitely made educators aware of the wide range of abilities involved in cognitive learning. Each of the six major categories represents a different kind of learning process. By being given descriptions and examples of the kind of behaviors involved in each category, educators have been able to insure that higher order kinds of learning are considered and planned for. It would be a reasonable conjecture to say that since publication of the cognitive taxonomy in 1956, emphasis has shifted considerably from memorization tasks to more meaningful outcomes. Below is a brief description of each of the major categories of the cognitive taxonomy of educational objectives. The topic "inflation" has been used to illustrate how the intended behavior changes and becomes progressively more complex at each level of the taxonomy.

1.00 Knowledge. This category includes memorization behaviors, that is, the recall or recognition of previously encountered information, for example, the ability to define the term inflation from memory.

2.00 Comprehension. Behaviors in this category are those that show understanding, not just memorization. Being able to explain or interpret is an indication of comprehension, for example, the ability to explain ways in which inflation affects an economy.

3.00 Application. Application involves being able to use, or apply, an abstract concept to a specific situation, for example, the ability to apply general principles of inflation to the current United States economy.

4.00 Analysis. Analysis involves the ability to break down a communication into its component parts and to identify the relationships which exist between them, for example the ability to determine the common elements in three different plans for reducing inflation in the United States.

5.00 Synthesis. Synthesis refers to the ability to combine elements and parts to form a unique whole, a new communication, for example, the ability to develop an original plan for reducing inflation in the United States.

6.00 Evaluation. Evaluation is the making of judgments about the value of some communication (work, solution, method) for a given purpose, for example, the ability to critique a proposed plan for reducing inflation in the United States.

Classification of the types of learning has been approached from a different angle by Robert Gagné. He believes that types, or classes, of learning can be categorized based on the conditions of instruction necessary to facilitate learning of each type. As Gagné explains it, "The external events that are called instruction need to have different characteristics, depending on the particular class of performance change that is the focus of interest."[9] He has distinguished eight classes of learning and corresponding instructional conditions for learning that are associated with them: signal learning, stimulus-response learning, chaining, verbal

[9] Gagné, R. M. *The conditions of learning* (2nd ed.). Holt, Rinehart, and Winston, 1970.

association, discrimination learning, concept learning, rule learning, and problem solving.

In the past, education has been criticized for paying too much attention to cognitive outcomes and not being concerned enough with the feelings and attitudes of students. The affective domain deals with such outcomes.

The affective domain

The taxonomy of affective objectives, developed by Krathwohl and his associates, deals with outcomes that are much more difficult to promote and to measure.[10] Objectives in this domain relate to such intangibles as feelings, attitudes, interests and values. The categories represent a hierarchy of acceptance which ranges from willingness to receive, or attend, to characterization by a value. As one moves up the hierarchy an internalization process is evident, a process that begins with total rejection of an entity and culminates in total acceptance. All educational efforts have affective objectives, though not necessarily in a formal sense. All teachers, for example, certainly want students to feel positively toward their particular subject areas but they do not often have specific affective objectives. Thus, there are frequently no organized efforts made to foster achievement of such objectives or to assess affective outcomes. The last 10-20 years have seen a great increase in interest in affective outcomes, and in fact, a large number of programs have been funded whose objectives were exclusively affective. Even endeavors with primarily cognitive outcomes have been concerned with the affective impact of their curriculum, program, or project.

As with all objectives, the intent is to identify observable, measurable behaviors from which we can infer learning. This is clearly more difficult for affective outcomes. Too often, achievement of affective objectives is determined through administration of self-report measures. Such measures typically ask people to indicate how they feel about the topic of interest and entail a number of problems. It has been shown, for example, that people frequently give what they perceive to be socially acceptable responses rather than their true feelings. It is much better, when feasible, to have objectives which involve actions rather than self-report. It would be a more valid assessment of whether a student enjoys reading, for example, to find out if the student has voluntarily checked any books out of the library rather than to ask "Do you enjoy reading?" Typical action verbs for affective objectives include: respond, choose, prefer, volunteer and participate. In practice, assessment of affective outcomes too frequently involves little more than asking for written reactions or opinions on an open-ended questionnaire with questions such as "Do you feel that you benefited from participation in the program? Why?"

There is a feeling among certain educators and noneducators that the school has no right to attempt to shape, or to interfere with, students' values. They believe that affective outcomes should be the concern of a student's family or religious group. However, most people recognize that a basic function of the school in a democratic society is to assist students in achieving independence in judgments and actions, not to advocate particular political or sectarian views. Further, the school should strongly refrain from encouraging conformity to some arbitrary group norm of behavior. It is generally agreed, however, that objectives based on

[10] Krathwohl, D. R., Bloom, B. S., & Masia, B. B. *Taxonomy of educational objectives, Handbook II: Affective domain.* New York: David McKay, 1964.

"the belief in the dignity and worth of the individual without regard to race, religion, income or ethnic background" are acceptable since these are basic values of our country as established by the constitution. Thus objectives related to respect for others, support for the law, and freedom of religion, for example, are perfectly legitimate in the school curriculum.[11]

Below is a brief description of each of the major categories of the affective taxonomy of educational objectives. The general outcome "values poetry" has been used to illustrate how degree of acceptance of a value progressively increases at each level of the taxonomy.

> **1.00 Receiving.** At this level the individual is sensitized to the phenomenon of interest to the extent that he or she is willing to receive or to attend (pay attention) to it, for example, listens attentively when the teacher reads a poem to the class.
>
> **2.00 Responding.** At this level the individual is sufficiently motivated or interested to the extent that she or he makes an active response for example, answers questions related to a poem which has been read to the class.
>
> **3.00 Valuing.** At this level the individual acknowledges, or recognizes, that something has value and is worthwhile, for example, chooses reading poetry as a free-period activity.
>
> **4.00 Organization.** At this level the individual incorporates values into an organized, hierarchic value system such that some are more important, or internalized, than others, for example, checks a book of poetry out of the library to read on her or his own time.
>
> **5.00 Characterization by a value or Value complex.** At this level the individual has so completely internalized a value that it is a dominant characteristic which affects behavior in a consistent way. It is at this level that it would be widely recognized that "Percy loves poetry," or "Percy reads poetry every chance he gets."

Concerning characterization, the authors of the affective taxonomy point out:

> Rarely, if ever, are the sights of educational objectives set to this level of the *Affective Taxonomy*. Realistically, formal education generally cannot reach this level, at least in our society.

The psychomotor domain

According to the authors of the affective taxonomy, the psychomotor domain entails physical abilities, those involving muscular or motor skills, manipulation of objects, or neuromuscular coordination. As mentioned earlier, several serious attempts have been made at developing a taxonomy for the psychomotor domain, none of which has been given the degree of acceptance of the other two taxonomies.

The problem is that the task of taxonomy development is considerably more complex in the psychomotor domain because of the large cognitive compo-

[11] Based on a discussion by Typer, R. W. Assessing educational achievement in the affective domain. *NCME*, Spring, 1973, 4(3).

nent involved in many psychomotor outcomes. Actually, all learnings involve all three domains to varying degrees. For example, the objective "writes a complete sentence" clearly has a cognitive component (e.g. knowledge of the parts of a sentence), an affective component (e.g. willingness to respond), and a psychomotor component (e.g. neuromuscular coordination). The domains tend to complement each other. How a student *feels* about learning and the learning environment, for example, influences the student's actual learning. A student who enjoys learning probably achieves more, and conversely, success in a certain area encourages positive attitudes about that area. Further, there is a psychomotor component in many cognitive outcomes and a cognitive component in many psychomotor outcomes. When we classify an objective as being in one of the three domains we do so on the basis of its primary focus and intent. Thus, while reading involves an affective and a psychomotor component, the *intent* is cognitive; in music appreciation the intent is affective; and in gymnastics the intent is psychomotor. Psychomotor objectives, however, involve such a large cognitive component that it is difficult to identify the strictly physical aspects of such skills.

It may be that it is not even possible to classify psychomotor outcomes into a hierarchy of categories using a classification system that is generally acceptable to most educators. Or it may be that *the* approach just has not been conceived of as yet. In any event, several valiant attempts have been made at developing a taxonomy in this difficult area. The best known is probably the work of Anita Harrow. She has classified psychomotor outcomes into six major categories: reflex movements, basic-fundamental movements, perceptual abilities, physical abilities, skilled movements, and nondiscursive communication (e.g. expressive and interpretive movements).[12] In contrast is the work of Elizabeth Simpson, who has proposed the following categories: perception, set, guided response, mechanism, complex overt response, adaptation, and origination.[13] Thus, while there is disagreement as to the categories, the intent is the same—to develop a hierarchy for the classification of psychomotor objectives into a lower-order to higher-order continuum.

Levels of specificity

Objectives can be written at varying levels of specificity. At one end of the continuum we have very broad statements of long-term outcomes; these are generally referred to as goals, or general objectives. At the other end of the spectrum we have very precise statements of more immediate outcomes, each representing only one behavior or result; these are generally referred to as specific objectives. In the dictionary definition sense, there is virtually no difference between a goal and an objective; a goal is defined as "the end toward which effort is directed," and an objective is defined as "something toward which effort is directed."[14] Traditionally, however, the terms have been used to make the distinctions described above. And, of course, there are a variety of intermediate levels of specificity. We may, for example, speak of course objectives, terminal objectives, or milestone objectives;

[12] Harrow, A. J. A. *A taxonomy of the psychomotor domain*. New York: David McKay, 1972.
[13] Simpson, E. J. The classification of educational objectives, psychomotor domain. *Illinois Teacher of Home Economics*, 1966–1967, *10*, 110–144. Simpson added "adaption" and "origination" a few years after the original scheme was formulated.
[14] *Webster's new collegiate dictionary*. Springfield, Mass.: G. & C. Merriam, 1977.

Level	Definition	Related Terms
General objectives	Broad statements of long-term outcomes.	Goals
Intermediate objectives	More precise statements of more short-term outcomes.	Second-Level objectives Unit objectives Course objectives Terminal objectives Milestone objectives
Specific objectives	Precise statements of immediate outcomes.	Instructional objectives

figure 5.1
Summary of terminology associated with levels of specificity of objectives.

in each case we are indicating a level of specificity somewhere between a broad goal and a specific objective.

Figure 5.1 provides a summary of the terminology associated with the levels of specificity of objectives.

General objectives—goals

Goals, as we said, are global statements of long-term outcomes. Of course the definition of "long-term" varies somewhat depending upon the activity. Project goals, for example, typically involve outcomes of a more immediate nature than the goals of public education in general. The goal of the National School Volunteer Program is "to increase the quantity and quality of volunteerism in order to improve education" whereas a goal of public education is that its graduates will be economically self-sufficient. These examples also illustrate another characteristic of goals, namely, that achievement of goals is not measured directly. Although educational goals do represent *the* important outcomes of the educational system, it cannot be held directly accountable for their achievement. Rather, as noted previously, achievement of more short-term objectives believed to be prerequisite are measured. Thus, goals do not deal with definite skills, related specific objectives do. The notion of "economic self-sufficiency," for example, entails any number of basic skills and/or vocational skills.

There is a reasonable degree of consensus concerning the overall purpose of education and what the goals of the educational system should be. The purpose of education is to provide individuals with experiences which will result in their acquisition of the knowledge, skills, and attitudes which will allow them to meet their individual needs as well as the needs of society. Of course many of these needs tend to overlap; it is to the benefit of society and the individual if the individual is economically self-sufficient. True, there is no way in our "future shock" society to know in advance with certainty what students will "need" in the future; it is possible, however, to make very reasonable projections. Further, while in earlier times it was literally possible to teach all known knowledge, this is clearly no longer even remotely feasible. Therefore, the emphasis today is on search skills, that is, information retrieval skills, whereby students learn how to locate desired information.

Goals tend to be established at the national level, by groups such as the National Education Association (NEA) and more recently NAEP, adopted at the state level, and ultimately have an impact at the classroom level. Interestin ;ly, the Seven Cardinal Principles of Secondary Education, put forth by a commission of the NEA, represent goals that are as appropriate today as they apparently were in 1918 when they were written. They are concerned with the individual's health, role as a family member, basic skills (referred to as "fundamental processes"), vocational skills, citizenship, use of leisure time, and moral behavior. The words change and emphases shift, but the basic goals of education remain the same. Any specific objective should relate to one of those goals. Music appreciation objectives, for example, would relate to worthy use of leisure time.

Intermediate objectives

Prior to the delineation of specific objectives, goals are frequently translated into what are typically referred to as intermediate objectives. In practice, objectives at this level are also referred to as goals since they do represent relatively global outcomes. Objectives at this level are more precise than general objectives but not as detailed as specific objectives. They are, in various situations, referred to as cumulative objectives, terminal objectives, milestone objectives, course objectives, and tasks. Such objectives are usually measurable and typically represent more complex behaviors expected as a result of achievement of a number of prerequisite specific objectives. An end-of-course objective for a typing course, for example, might be that students will be able to type a dictated, one-page letter in proper form, in a given number of minutes, with no more than a specified number of errors. Such an objective would clearly be cumulative in nature, requiring prior achievement of any number of specific objectives.

Recall that educational efforts usually do not have *one* end but a series of temporary ends in a continuous cycle. Thus, intermediate objectives specify outcomes intended at the end of a given cycle, "cycle" being defined in such terms as a unit, a course, or a time span. Public agencies such as Big Brothers, Big Sisters, for example, might very well set objectives on a yearly basis and one of its objectives might be "to increase the number of big brothers in Chicago by 10% (from 400–440) during the six-month period beginning September 1." This objective follows naturally from the agency's major goal and in turn would entail any number of specific objectives to be achieved during the six-month period. Clearly, there may well be cycles within cycles and therefore intermediate objectives represent varying degrees of specificity and comprehensiveness. Thus, for example, we have units within courses and unit objectives leading to course objectives.

Specific objectives

Specific objectives deal with the most discrete intended outcomes. They are the measurable outcomes upon which day-to-day activities such as instruction are based. The task analysis and job analysis procedures described earlier are two methods of translating cumulative objectives into specific objectives. There are literally thousands and thousands of specific instructional objectives which have been written for virtually any curriculum area you can think of. Many professional organizations, especially those concerned with specific curriculum areas (e.g. the National Council of Teachers of Mathematics) have published lists of such objectives. A number of state departments of education and local education agencies have initiated any number of objectives development efforts. Teachers themselves have generated an incredible number of objectives. In addition, several major efforts have been made to collect objectives and/or related test items from a variety of sources and to develop comprehensive, computerized objectives banks. Probably the largest and best known is the Instructional Objectives Exchange (IOX) developed at the Center for the Study of Evaluation at UCLA.[15] The IOX bank contains thousands of objectives and corresponding test items representing a myriad of subject areas and grade levels.[16] Of course if you obtained available sets of objectives in a given area (e.g. tenth grade biology) from a number of different sources, the objectives in the various sets would not be exactly the same. While there is a great deal of similarity in the objectives of different collections, they do vary as to the level of specificity, depth and breadth of content area represented, and degree of communicability (i.e. how well they communicate the specific behavior intended).

There is a difference of opinion among educators concerning whether instructional objectives should be selected or developed by users. Proponents of selection argue that objective development should be left to the experts and that sufficient objectives are already available to meet most anybody's needs. Supporters of user development believe that the process of determining objectives has value in and of itself. Objectives are more meaningful when time is taken to think through and specify intended outcomes as opposed to merely picking them from somebody else's list. While both positions have merit, it would seem that the average educator has better things to do with her or his time than to reinvent the wheel. If suitable objectives are already available, or if there are objectives which would be suitable with slight modification, there does not seem to be much point in starting from scratch. Of course there may be times when appropriate objectives are simply not available. This may be the case, for example, for unusual course offerings such as "Introduction to Psychic Phenomena." And really there is no correct position on the matter. If an instructor prefers to develop his or her own objectives and is willing to take the time necessary to do a creditable job, there are certainly benefits to be realized.

Degree of specificity

So far we have discussed three general levels at which objectives can be written, each level representing a progressively finer degree of specificity with respect to the intended performance. Specific objectives represent the most discrete intended outcomes. The question which arises is "How specific is specific?" In other words, in order to effectively communicate the intended performance, how detailed does the objective need to be, how exact does the description of intended performance need to be? An objective can be so vague that it is ambiguous or so detailed that it is trivial and impractical. Compare the following two objectives:

[15] Popham, W. J. The instructional objectives exchange: New support for criterion-referenced instruction. *Phi Delta Kappan*, 1970, 52(3), 174–175.
[16] For further information, write to: Instructional Objectives Exchange, Box 24095, Los Angeles, CA 90024.

A Use a calculator.

B Given a hand-held calculator which performs the operations of addition, subtraction, multiplication and division, and given the oral command to find the product of two one-digit numbers, the student will turn on the calculator, push the button corresponding to the first digit, push the multiplication button, push the button corresponding to the second digit, push the equal-sign button, read the response on the display portion of the calculator, and record the response in writing on a separate sheet of paper.

Which objective do you think is written at an effective level of specificity? A? B? All of the above? None of the above? If you picked "none of the above," you are beginning to think like an evaluator. Objective A is clearly too fuzzy to be of much use. The person who wrote it probably knows what performance is intended but the intent is not clearly communicated. If you cannot tell what is intended, it is impossible to know when it has been achieved. The outcome "use a calculator" could mean any number of things, including objective B. The intent of objective B, on the other hand, is pretty clear, and almost anyone would probably be able to determine whether a student had achieved objective B. But is all that detail really necessary? Probably not. If all objectives related to using a calculator were spelled out in such gory detail, it would take many moons and sheets of paper. Further, the first given, i.e. "given a hand-held calculator which performs the operations of addition, subtraction, multiplication and division," would be repeated in every one. Not only would that be very boring, it would also not be necessary. If it were a necessary given, it could be stated one time, prior to the list of objectives. As it is, it is not necessary because virtually all calculators perform those operations. There are other obvious redundancies in the objective which make it unnecessarily lengthy and clumsy.

There is clearly some reasonable middle ground between A and B. A sensible, guiding principle, which was proposed by Robert Gagné in the mid-1960s, suggests that each objective should represent a distinct task, a *task* being defined as "the smallest component of performance which has a distinct and independent purpose."[17] Applying this guideline, objective A is too broad because it involves more than one task and objective B is too detailed because it involves activities extraneous to the basic purpose. An appropriate objective might read "performs multiplication problems involving two one-digit numbers." The phrase "uses the calculator to" at the beginning of the objective would probably not be necessary since this objective would be one of a set, all dealing with use of the calculator. Gagné's suggestion is also useful because it eliminates objectives with no obvious purpose, objectives which prompt the feeling "What does anyone want to do *that* for?" Within this context, to use his example, we are unlikely to see the purpose of "identifies the infinitive form of irregular French verbs."

You might argue that while the basic objective might well be that the student "performs multiplication problems involving two one-digit numbers," it certainly cannot be achieved if the student does not know how to turn on a calculator and use the appropriate buttons. This is certainly true. A concept which has been applied to deal with such performances is that of *enablers,* or enabling objectives. When such are used, they accompany a task, or major objective. A task represents

---

[17] Gagné, R. M. Educational objectives and human performance. In J. D. Krumboltz (Ed.). *Learning and the educational process.* Chicago: Rand McNally, 1965.

an important outcome, a performance with a clear purpose. Enablers represent knowledge and skills which facilitate students' ability to perform a task. Thus, for our calculator-multiplication objective, an enabler might be that the student "demonstrates the ability to use each button appropriately."

As with definitions of evaluations and evaluation models, it seems as if there are as many guidelines for developing objectives as there are experts. Many of these are so prescriptive and result in such overly detailed objectives that they do more harm than good. Instead of being helpful guides for writing objectives, they make a relatively simple process appear to be terribly complicated. The over-kill scares some people, who then shy away from objectives altogether. Those who defend their "44 components of a good objective," or whatever, believe that it is a cop-out to say that objectives do not have to be super specific, that it is the time and trouble that are objected to, not the process. Au contraire! The more simply worded objective is clearly more functional. To use an analogy, think of giving someone directions to a restaurant. The key to good directions is communication. Now, which set of directions below do you think would be more helpful and less confusing:

A From your house go to Fourth and Main, turn right, drive two blocks, and it is the first building on the right.
B From your house (401 Elm) go past 403 Elm, the blue house with white shutters; go past 405 Elm, the brick house with the white picket fence; go past 407 Elm . . . etc., etc., etc.

Got the idea?!

Stating objectives

Selection or development of the objectives is really the most important aspect of any educational endeavor, be it instruction or execution of a special program. The objectives give direction to every remaining activity. Fuzzy objectives tend to lead to fuzzy efforts; trivial objectives tend to lead to a waste of time and money. For example, if a project had the objective "to reduce the number of dropouts" and if the project spent $450,000 and reduced the number of dropouts during a given year from an expected number of 167 to an actual number of 166, that would surely be an example of a project that achieved its objectives! Thus, prior to execution of the effort, general intended outcomes must be translated into specific, measurable, meaningful outcomes. It is not enough to have a general idea what you are all about; you must determine precisely what you want to achieve or what you want students to achieve, or whatever, and when. You may have enabling objectives, major objectives, and cumulative objectives; these will obviously not all be anticipated to be completed at the same time.

Criteria

Whether you develop objectives or select them, the same basic criteria of "goodness" should be applied in evaluating each objective. First, as previously discussed, the appropriateness of the level of specificity must be evaluated. Is it too vague? Too detailed? Is it functional; that is does it convey a distinct purpose? Closely related is the issue of the objective's communicability. An objective should communicate the intended outcome well enough that any evaluator would assess it in essentially the same way and be able to tell whether it had been achieved. In other words, all qualified persons would measure the objective in basically the same way and all would agree that it had or had not been achieved. A well-written objective to a great extent dictates the method of measurement and tells you how you will know if it is achieved. Consider the following objectives:

A Given a reprint of a research report, the student will identify the hypothesis and corresponding conclusion.

B The student will recite from memory any poem of his or her choice which is at least 100 words in length.

Both of these objectives suggest how achievement of the objectives will be determined, and any qualified person would probably be able to determine whether or not it had been achieved. True, the word "identify" in objective A is a little fuzzy in that there are several ways in which this could be done; the student could underline the hypothesis and conclusion, or tell someone what they were, or write them on a sheet of paper, and so forth. But the point is that it really does not make any difference. The intent of the objective is that students be able to recognize hypotheses and related conclusions; there are a number of equally acceptable ways in which this ability can be demonstrated. Objective B clearly specifies that the student will *recite*; thus, writing a poem from memory would not be acceptable. In this case the *method* of showing knowledge of a poem is important. The intent of the objective is in the recitation, not in the knowledge of a poem per se.

There is a false hierarchy in the minds of many people to the effect that an objective that calls for a paper-and-pencil response is somehow inferior to one that calls for an actual performance. Within this framework an instructional objective which can be measured with a multiple-choice test, for example, it is not as "important" or as "good" as one that requires a student to do something—adjust a microscope, for example. This belief is based on the assumption that paper-and-pencil tests measure only lower-order learnings such as recall of facts whereas actual performance entails higher-order learnings such as application or problem solving. In practice this assumption is often borne out; in theory the assumption is groundless. There are many higher-order outcomes which can be measured with some form of written test, yes, even with a multiple-choice test. Conversely, a performance can represent a very trivial outcome. After all, which represents the more important outcome, the ability to identify a complete sentence or the ability to draw a straight line with a ruler? While this will be discussed further in subsequent sections, the concept is an important one to keep in mind.

Components

By now you have probably deduced the components of a well-written specific objective, usually referred to as the behavior, the conditions, and the criterion. Briefly, the behavior component speaks for itself, the conditions are the "givens," and the criterion is the "how well" part.

The behavior

The *behavior component* describes what will happen, for example, "the number of big brothers will be increased," or, as in the case of instructional objectives, what observable, measurable performance will constitute satisfactory evidence that the desired learning has occurred. Note that the behavior is stated in terms of the *learner*, not the teacher or the content area. Alas, occasionally one encounters alleged objectives such as the following:

A Explain how to take a blood pressure reading.
B Supreme court decisions affecting education, 1950–1975.

Neither **A** nor **B** indicates what the result of instruction will be. **A** says what the teacher will do, not the student; **B** simply states an area to be covered. Theoretically, both of these objectives could be achieved without anybody learning anything!

As all of the previous examples have illustrated, an objective should state the intended outcome using an action verb that represents an observable outcome. Thus, an objective that states that "students will *learn* French" is inadequate. We must determine what a student must do to indicate that French has been learned; one objective might be that "students will *translate* French passages into English." Thus, verbs such as "understand," "know," and "appreciate" are to be avoided whereas verbs such as "translate," "compute," "select," "identify," "list," and "solve" are appropriate. This discussion should make sense given the previous statement that if an objective is well written, all qualified persons will measure it in essentially the same way and agree on whether it has been achieved. It is doubtful whether all evaluators would agree on how to measure "knows fractions." Of course the same principle applies to all objectives, not just instructional objectives. Thus a program objective "to make teachers more humane in their interactions with students" would not be acceptable whereas an objective "to increase instances of positive verbal reinforcement in the classroom" would be.

As our previous examples have also illustrated, each objective should entail achievement of one and only one behavior; otherwise measurement of achievement is confounded. A student may achieve one part of an objective, but not another. You will note that all the acceptable objectives discussed earlier did this while the unacceptable ones did not. The objective "knows fractions" is not well written for a variety of reasons, but note that it involves any number of behaviors, whereas the objective "reduces fractions to lowest terms" deals with one capability. Similarly, "gives a patient a checkup" involves many skills whereas "takes a pulse" involves one. Such objectives as "gives a patient a checkup" are fine as intermediate objectives, but are not adequate specific objectives. On the other side of the coin we have objectives which appear to be trivial because they deal with one instance, or one application, of a behavior, not the behavior itself. Thus "takes the pulse of a 22-year-old woman" and "reduces the fraction 25/60 to lowest terms" are too specific.

One final word on the behavior component. In most objectives, the statement of the intended outcome is preceded by a phrase indicating who will perform the action, for example, "The *student* will identify the main character in a short story." Usually this is not necessary since the person who is to exhibit the behavior is obvious. While it is repetitious and boring, it really does not hurt anything and it does make for complete sentences. Some people feel more comfortable with objectives such as "The student will correctly record the pinfall for each of ten frames of bowling" than with "correctly records the pinfall for each of ten frames of bowling." Either way, it is no big deal.

The conditions

The *conditions component* of an objective is the "givens," the context within which the behavior will be exhibited. Conditions usually specify necessary materials, allowable resources, or imposed restrictions, and the word "given" is not necessarily used, although it often is. Thus we might say, "Given a map of the United States, the student will. . . ." or "Using any standard reference materials. . ." or "Without the aid of a dictionary. . ." The use of conditions is greatly overdone and they are often inserted when they are obvious. If an objective for teachers is to increase instances of positive verbal reinforcement, it is certainly not necessary to say, "Given a class of students. . . ." Similarly, if students are to construct geometric figures, e.g. a circle, it is not necessary to say, "Given a piece of paper and a pencil. . . " although it may be necessary to specify, "Given a protractor. . . ."

Of course there are instances in which the presence or absence of a condition changes the whole meaning of an objective. It certainly makes a difference whether a scout is supposed to be able to start a fire with or without matches! Similarly, if students are supposed to be able to apply a certain statistical technique (e.g. analysis of variance) to a given set of data, it makes a big difference whether or not the objective says "given the formula. . ." Thus, conditions should be stated only if they clarify the intent of the objective. There is no law that says an objective has to have a condition. If conditions are fairly obvious, or if there are several equally acceptable conditions (e.g. "given a piece of paper and a pencil" versus "given a blackboard and chalk"), do not take the time, energy, or space to include them.

The criterion

When stated, the *criterion component* of an objective is the part that tells us how well the behavior must be performed. It is the standard against which actual performance is compared. If the criterion is obvious or 100%, as for "Identify three natural sources of vitamin E," it is generally not stated. The criterion may be expressed in terms such as percentage of correct answers, percentage of increase, time to completion, or distance. If the criterion is complex or dependent upon the group involved (the criterion for a written book report, for example), it may be stated separately. The basic issue is to establish how well or how often a performance must be exhibited in order to constitute sufficient evidence that the objective has been achieved. Thus a program may have an objective "to decrease absenteeism *by 25% within a six-month period.*" A project may have an objective "to increase the number of parent volunteers *by 25%.*" It is fairly easy to determine whether or to what degree these objectives have been achieved.

Instructional objectives are a little trickier. For example, suppose the objective is that students be able to formulate the past tense form of any regular verb. The question is, How many times and for how many verbs does the student have to do it correctly before we are reasonably convinced that he or she "knows" how to do it for all such verbs? One time for one verb certainly would not be sufficient. Fifty times for fifty different verbs probably would be very convincing but also very time-consuming. Thus, given that it is a relatively simple skill, we might be satisfied if, given five verbs, the student stated the past tense form for all of them. For certain objectives the criterion must take into consideration the human error factor. For example, even players who definitely have the ability to serve a tennis ball into the proper service court miss more than occasionally. Thus a high school physical education teacher might be satisfied if a student could correctly serve six balls out of ten attempts. Similarly, on a set of arithmetic problems we might settle for 80% accuracy. The stringency of the criterion really depends on the nature of the objective.

As you have probably gathered, there is no scientific formula for setting a criterion of achievement. There is a great deal of judgment involved. Further, unless one is involved in some type of individualized instruction, objectives are not generally assessed one at a time. One test may include items representing ten objectives, thereby complicating the task of determining objective achievement. Further, with the exception of mastery systems, even if all the students have not achieved all of the objectives, there comes a time when the teacher must move on. While objectives guide the instructional process, they should not bog it down. There are several possible strategies which can be applied. One involves setting a criterion which takes into consideration the performance of both the class and the individual; for a given set of objectives a teacher might decide that if the class averages 80% achievement, and no individual scores less than 60%, she or he will be satisfied. Another strategy involves setting a class standard; for example, 80% of the class will achieve 80% of the objectives. A third strategy, the one probably most often used in practice, is to simply assess the level of achievement, whatever it may be, without formally comparing it to any predetermined standard, and to make an existential decision. Thus, if the class as a whole does "reasonably well" on a test of the metric system, that is that. If a sizable number of students do poorly, more instruction may follow, perhaps using a different instructional strategy. For certain kinds of objectives, criteria of performance may not be numerical at all. This is especially likely when complex behaviors are involved. If the objective is that the student be able to develop a weekly budget based on a given amount of money, for example, the criterion might specify certain items (e. g. food) which must be included in order for the budget to be acceptable. Also, in many training programs partial, or percent, performance is not acceptable. In a small-appliance repair class, for example, the criterion might be that a previously broken electric toothbrush operate properly.

Standards of instructional objective attainment for other than student and personnel evaluation always involve group criteria. A curriculum, for example, may be judged to be sufficiently developed when 90% of the students are achieving 90% of the objectives. Such fixed standards are feasible only when there is ample time for revision and reassessment cycles. Most projects must report their degree of success at certain fixed periods of time. A state-funded project might report that by the end of the funding period the number of parent volunteers had been increased by 20%, not 25% as specified by the objective. The project's report would probably also include recommendations for further project activities, should additional funds be forthcoming.

Some evaluators advocate what are referred to as experiential standards. They feel that it is sometimes unfair to judge the merits of a program strictly on the basis of objective achievement. *Experiential standards,* according to Dryden, are "those standards of worth inherent in the value structure of those persons involved in, or affected by, the program to be evaluated . . . and represent the summative judgments that people make about the overall program or some component of it."[18] Dryden further notes that such standards are comparative in nature and based on experience, and that judgments can be made about both intended and unintended outcomes. While some are considerably more enthusiastic about the notion of experiential standards than others, the concept is a reasonable one and resulting judgments may provide useful insights.

Concluding remarks

The use of objectives in the planning, execution, and assessment of an effort is probably one of the best things that ever happened to education. True, there are a lot of lousy objectives floating around. But in most cases even less than adequate objectives are better than no objectives at all. The basic concept is that intended outcomes should be stated in advance in language that communicates. In a well-intentioned effort to standardize objective writing, however, a number of sets of overly prescriptive guidelines have been disseminated by a variety of individuals and groups. A suggested, reasonably short, set of guidelines for writing objectives is as follows:

1 Specify the intended outcome in objective, measurable terms: avoid including more than one behavior in one objective, and avoid specifying an instance of a behavior rather than the behavior itself.
2 Specify any conditions affecting performance that are not obvious or that significantly alter the intent of the objective.
3 If necessary, specify the criterion of acceptable performance.

[18] Dryden, J. A model for evaluating compensatory education programs at the local school level. Paper presented at the American Educational Research Association Convention, Toronto, 1978.

part two **summary**

4 the nature of objectives

Definition and purpose

Definition

1 Objectives are specific statements of what is to be accomplished and how well, and are expressed in terms of quantifiable, measurable outcomes.
2 Objectives are stated prior to execution of an effort and are subject to technical and substantive review.
3 An *instructional objective* is an intent communicated by a statement describing a proposed change in a learner—a statement of what the learner is to be like when he has successfully completed a learning experience.
4 Learning is an inferred event, not a directly observable one; thus it must be determined what behavior, or performance, will constitute sufficient evidence that the desired ability exists.
5 Whether a capability is acquired, or learned, as a result of instruction can only be determined by observing performance at two different points in time, before and after instruction, and seeing whether performance has changed.
6 Learning per se cannot be directly observed or measured, changes in performance can.

Pros and cons

Pros

7 Supporters of objectives argue that their main advantage is that they give direction to, or guide the activities of, an effort.
8 Objectives suggest general strategies and specific activities for their attainment; different sets of objectives will usually generate different strategies.
9 Instructional objectives give direction to students as well as teachers.
10 Telling students precisely what you want them to know and be able to do is not "teaching to the test."
11 Objectives also serve a diagnostic-prescriptive function; at any point in time we can assess where we are, how much progress has been made, and act accordingly.
12 Objectives dictate to a great extent the way in which we collect status data.
13 The existence of objectives does not necessarily mean that an undertaking will be more successful than it otherwise would have been, but they do allow determination of what has been accomplished.
14 Without objectives it is questionable whether it is even possible to evaluate an effort at all.
15 Objectives serve a communication function; personnel can communicate to interested groups not only what is being done but also to what end.

Cons

16 Opponents of objectives believe that they produce rigid, conforming procedures, standards, and behavior which discourage creativity and spontaneity and fail to take into consideration individual differences.

17 Opponents question seriously whether all important educational outcomes can be objectified.

18 There is a natural tendency to select objectives which are easy to measure, not necessarily important.

19 Opponents maintain that the really important outcomes of any effort are long-term results, not short-term accomplishments, and therefore objectives dealing with here-and-now achievement are largely irrelevant.

20 There is very little evidence that the existence of objectives actually results in greater achievement.

21 Opponents say objectives are impractical because any given effort can spawn an unmanageable multiplicity of objectives.

Rebuttal

22 Analysis of the alleged cons of objectives will reveal that they deal at least in part with problems that may arise from their misuse.

23 Objectives are not restrictive in and of themselves; for any objective there are invariably alternative strategies which can be utilized to promote achievement.

24 The use of objectives by no means negates the existence of individual differences; different students, for example, may be working on different objectives at different times.

25 The lack of consensus on the appropriateness of objectives in nonbasic skills areas such as music appreciation stems not from the immeasurability of the outcomes but from the inability of people to specify what they really mean by music appreciation.

26 All *important* desired outcomes can be expressed in observable, measurable terms.

27 Long-term outcomes do not just happen; all objectives are, at least theoretically, related to some long-term outcome, or goal.

28 Objectives make sense logically, and even if they do not directly result in greater achievement, they do permit assessment of exactly what has been accomplished.

29 Component behaviors for an objective exist whether or not they are identified; without a list of such behaviors it is much more likely that a number of them will be overlooked, thereby decreasing the chances of achieving the general desired outcome.

30 Opposition to objectives is based more on their possible misuse than on the nature of objectives per se.

31 There is a place in education for minimally directed exploratory activities; such activities, however, comprise a very small percentage of the total educational enterprise.

Needs assessment

32 It would be virtually impossible for the educational system to attempt to foster achievement of all possible objectives; formally or informally, each educa-

tional endeavor must select, and put in priority order, the goals and objectives with which it will be concerned.

Definition and purpose

33 Conceptually, if there is a gap between the way things are (current status) and the way we would like them to be (desired outcomes), a *need* exists.
34 Depending upon how specifically a need has been defined, it can be translated into either a goal or an objective, the intent being to eliminate the need.
35 *Needs assessment* is the process of identifying needs and (usually) establishing the relative priorities of those needs.
36 The basic goals and objectives of the educational system have remained relatively stable but the emphases, or priorities, have shifted over time.
37 The educational system cannot be static; it must be sensitive to, and responsive to, the ever-changing needs of society.
38 Change does not come rapidly, and there is generally a sizable lag between the emergence of a national priority change and the reflection of that change in the public school system.
39 A by-product of the accountability movement has been the formalization of needs assessment and the development of empirical, systematic procedures for determining and ordering needs.
40 The needs assessment process is based mainly on consensus and involves gathering input from a variety of educational and community groups such as teachers and parents.
41 The results of needs assessment are used to justify decisions concerning the allocation of both personnel and financial resources.

Applications

42 Application of needs assessment procedures is not limited to curriculum decisions at the school level although it is most often used for this purpose.
43 In the interest of both optimal resource use and fair evaluation, it is imperative that special projects focus their attention on a manageable number of high-priority objectives which are agreed upon by all relevant groups.
44 Needs assessment can be applied to, and used by, all levels and components of the educational system, including classrooms, programs, projects, schools, school systems, states, and countries.
45 The utility of the needs assessment process depends to a great degree on the intelligence with which it is applied; it can be done too carelessly or it can be overdone.

Models

46 All valid needs assessment models involve the same essential components: compilation of a comprehensive list of appropriate objectives; ordering of the objectives in terms of perceived importance; determination of the degree of discrepancy between actual and desired levels of performance on high priority objectives; and ranking of the identified needs.
47 The type of objectives involved and their level of specificity depends on the level and context of the needs assessment, although they are typically intermediate objectives.

Subjective versus objective models

48 Subjective models of needs assessment identify discrepancies by asking judges to give their opinions as to degree of need in given areas.
49 Objective models determine discrepancies by collecting performance data to assess current status and comparing data to acceptable levels of performance.
50 Both models involve both subjectivity and objectivity.

Components

51 The Delphi technique is a method for achieving group consensus which is occasionally used in needs assessment.
52 The Delphi technique can be used whenever consensus is desired from a relatively large, diverse group.
53 The Delphi technique involves multiple mailings and is a costly, time-consuming procedure.
54 The last step in the needs assessment process, assigning priorities to identified needs, is considerably more complex than it may appear; factors to be considered include: the size and importance of the need, the number of students exhibiting the need, cost, and probability of success.

Problems

55 Most of the problems associated with needs assessment are not unique to needs assessment.
56 In an important study, activities most frequently considered to be problem areas were: (1) obtaining a satisfactory response rate, (2) identifying educational goals, (3) determining subgoals, and (4) preparing the survey instrument.
57 Schools usually need consultant and financial assistance; key personnel involved require training; the cooperation of a great many people is required; the process takes longer than one would expect.
58 A number of components produce consensus only, not necessarily the best or most valid decisions.
59 All in all, in too many instances needs assessment appears to be another classic example of overkill.
60 Even under ideal conditions needs assessment has numerous serious problems.
61 As typically implemented, the process does not appear to be cost-effective.
62 A serious attempt must be made to make it more efficient and manageable.

Goal-free evaluation

Definition and rationale

63 *Goal-free evaluation* is the assessment of *actual* outcomes, or effects, not *intended* outcomes as specified in an effort's objectives.
64 Objectives per se are not generally objected to; their usefulness in earlier phases of evaluation is not disputed.
65 Proponents of goal-free evaluation feel that the assessment of the effectiveness of a curriculum, program, or project should not be contaminated, or biased, by knowledge of intended effects.
66 The basic premise of goal-free evaluation is the notion that the really

important outcomes of an effort may or may not be those intended; if attention is focused only on intended outcomes, some really important effects may be overlooked.

67 Most programs involve a combination of anticipated and unanticipated outcomes; the evaluator should collect data related to a broad spectrum of actual outcomes before examining program objectives.

An example

68 Goal-free evaluation is most appropriate when the development of products is the major focus of the program.

69 The approach is probably best used in conjunction with other kinds of evaluation.

70 The approach is in need of improved methodology.

71 All in all, the pluses of the goal-free approach probably slightly outweigh the minuses.

72 The basic concept of looking for unanticipated outcomes makes sense, but assessing outcomes "in the dark" does not.

5 classification and statement of objectives

Types of objectives

73 Objectives look basically the same regardless of the type of evaluation; all objectives indicate intended outcomes.

74 One basic difference is that certain types of evaluation, and their corresponding objectives, are primarily concerned with the performance of individuals whereas others are primarily concerned with the performance of groups.

Objectives for individuals

75 Literally thousands and thousands of objectives, covering virtually every area of instruction, have been written to express desired student behaviors.

76 In contrast, very little exists in terms of performance objectives for teachers, even less for administrators, and essentially nothing for special program and project personnel; this is due mainly to the lack of empirical evidence linking given behaviors with job success.

Competency-based education

77 The objectives, or competencies to be achieved by students in various programs are typically developed by university or college instructors, experts in their respective fields, and reviewed by appropriate public school and community groups.

78 The intent of competency-based education is to identify behaviors *believed* to be required for successful job performance and to have students demonstrate these behaviors prior to graduation.

Mastery objectives

79 Instructional objectives are variously referred to as performance objectives, behavioral objectives, learning objectives, and classroom objectives.

80 Certain instructional objectives are considered to be required, minimum essentials, i. e. objectives which should be achieved by virtually all students, regardless of ability or background; these are referred to as *mastery*, or minimum skills, *objectives*.

81 Various mastery objectives may be identified at all grade levels.

82 In a mastery system, amount learned, as shown by objectives achieved, is the constant and time required to achieve objectives varies among students.

83 If students are given sufficient time and appropriate instruction, then most students, probably 90–95%, will be able to "master" what is taught and achieve the objectives.

84 Primarily for reasons of cost-effectiveness, mastery learning is probably most appropriate for minimum skills objectives.

85 Mastery learning involves individualized instruction and all that goes with it.

Objectives for groups

An example

86 A group instructional objective might be to have 90% of a class achieve a certain set of mastery objectives; this type of question, however, as opposed to "How is Ziggy doing?" would be of prime interest in curriculum evaluation, and the emphasis would be on clusters of objectives.

87 Curriculum objectives might include: Ninety percent of the students will reach criterion (achieve successfully) on objectives 1–27.

88 It might seem logical to say that "students under curriculum A will achieve significantly *more objectives* than students under curriculum B"; this will not generally be appropriate, however, since different curricula may involve different objectives.

89 A more appropriate objective might be: "Students under curriculum A will achieve significantly higher scores on the Gates-MacGinitie reading comprehension test than students under curriculum B."

Minimum competency testing

90 An outgrowth of state assessment has been minimum competency testing, which involves assessing whether students have met state-mandated standards for grade promotion or high school graduation.

91 Minimum competency testing programs typically require students to demonstrate mastery of the basic skills and functional literacy on state developed tests.

92 Minimum competency programs usually include provisions for remedial instruction.

93 When the results of state tests are to be also used to make competence decisions concerning individual students, several critical issues emerge; among them are the questions "Which objectives should be measured?" and "What should be the minimum passing score?"

94 Three different types of objectives which could be tested for minimum competency are basic skills objectives, school subject objectives, and life objectives; and there are objectives which combine these areas such as those involving the application of basic skills in a given school subject.

The taxonomies of educational objectives

95 The taxonomies classify all objectives into a hierarchy of categories based on presumed complexity.

96 Each succeeding category involves behavior believed to be more complex than the one previous and each is considered to be prerequisite to the next.

97 The stated purpose of the taxonomies is to facilitate communication.

98 The existence of the taxonomies also focuses attention on a wide range of behavioral outcomes, thus making it less likely that all the objectives for a given effort will involve lower-level behaviors only.

99 It is believed that all instructional outcomes can be classified as belonging primarily to one of the three domains of learning—cognitive, affective, and psychomotor.

The cognitive domain

100 The taxonomy of cognitive objectives has definitely made educators aware of the wide range of abilities involved in cognitive learning.

101 Each of the six major categories represents a different kind of learning process.

102 The major categories of the cognitive taxonomy of educational objectives are as follows:

1.00 Knowledge. Memorization; recall or recognition of information.

2.00 Comprehension. Understanding; ability to explain or interpret.

3.00 Application. Ability to use, or apply, an abstract concept to a specific situation.

4.00 Analysis. Ability to break down a communication into its component parts and to identify the relationships which exist between them.

5.00 Synthesis. Ability to combine elements and parts so as to form a unique whole, a new communication.

6.00 Evaluation. Ability to make judgments about the value of some communication for a given purpose.

103 Gagné believes that types, or classes, of learning can be categorized based on the conditions of instruction necessary to facilitate learning of each type.

104 He has distinguished eight classes of learning: signal learning, stimulus-response learning, chaining, verbal associations, discrimination learning, concept learning, rule learning, and problem solving.

105 In the past, education has been criticized for paying too much attention to cognitive outcomes and not being concerned enough with the feelings and attitudes of students.

The affective domain

106 The taxonomy of affective objectives deals with outcomes that are much more difficult to promote and to measure, intangibles such as feelings, attitudes, interests, and values.

107 The affective categories represent a hierarchy of acceptance which ranges from willingness to receive, or attend, to characterization by a value.

108 The last 10–20 years have seen a great increase in interest in affective outcomes.

109 As with all objectives, the intent is to identify observable, measurable behav-

iors from which we can infer learning; this is clearly more difficult for affective outcomes.

110 Too often, achievement of affective objectives is determined through administration of self-report measures which entail a number of problems; people frequently give what they perceive to be socially acceptable responses rather than their true feelings.

111 It is much better, when feasible, to have objectives which involve actions rather than self-report.

112 Most people recognize that a basic function of the school in a democratic society is to assist students in achieving independence in judgments and actions, not to advocate particular political or sectarian views.

113 The school should strongly refrain from encouraging conformity to some arbitrary group norm of behavior.

114 It is generally agreed that objectives related to respect for others, support for the law, and freedom of religion are perfectly legitimate in the school curriculum.

115 The major categories of the affective taxonomy of educational objectives are as follows:

 1.00 Receiving. Being sensitized to a phenomenon; being willing to receive or to attend to it.

 2.00 Responding. Being sufficiently motivated to make an active response, to take an action.

 3.00 Valuing. Acknowledging or recognizing that something has value and is worthwhile.

 4.00 Organization. Incorporating values into a hierarchic value system.

 5.00 Characterization by a value. Completely internalizing a value such that it is a dominant characteristic which consistently affects behavior.

The psychomotor domain

116 The psychomotor domain entails physical abilities, those involving muscular or motor skills, manipulation of objects, or neuromuscular coordination.

117 Several serious attempts have been made at developing a taxonomy for the psychomotor domain, none of which has been given the degree of acceptance of the other two taxonomies.

118 The task of taxonomy development is considerably more complex in the psychomotor domain because of the large cognitive component involved in many psychomotor outcomes.

119 All learnings involve all three domains to varying degrees.

120 Psychomotor objectives involve such a large cognitive component that it is difficult to identify the strictly physical aspects of such skills.

121 Of the several valiant attempts that have been made at developing a taxonomy in this difficult area, probably the best known work in this area is that of Harrow.

122 Harrow has classified psychomotor outcomes into six major categories: reflex movements, basic-fundamental movements, perceptual abilities, physical abilities, skilled movements, and nondiscursive communication.

123 In contrast is the work of Simpson who has proposed the following categories: perception, set, guided response, mechanism, complex overt response, adaptation, and origination.

124 While there is disagreement as to the categories, the intent is the same, to de-

velop a hierarchy for classification of psychomotor objectives into a lower-order to higher-order continuum.

Levels of specificity

125 At one end of the objectives continuum we have very broad statements of long-term outcomes; these are generally referred to as goals, or general objectives.

126 At the other end of the spectrum we have very precise statements of more immediate outcomes, each representing only one behavior or result; these are generally referred to as specific objectives.

127 There are a variety of intermediate levels of specificity; we may, for example, speak of course objectives, terminal objectives, or milestone objectives; in each case we are indicating a level of specificity somewhere between a broad goal and a specific objective.

General objectives—goals

128 Goals are global statements of long-term outcomes; the definition of "long-term" varies somewhat depending upon the effort.

129 Achievement of goals is not measured directly; although educational goals do represent *the* important outcomes of the educational system, it cannot be held directly accountable for their achievement; rather, achievement of more short-term objectives believed to be prerequisite is measured.

130 Goals do not deal with definite skills; related specific objectives do.

131 The overall purpose of education is to provide individuals with experiences which will allow them to acquire the knowledge, skills, and attitudes which will allow them to meet their individual needs as well as the needs of society; many of these needs tend to overlap.

132 There is no way in our "future shock" society to know in advance with certainty what students will "need" in the future; it is possible, however, to make very reasonable projections.

133 The emphasis today is on search skills, information retrieval skills, whereby students learn how to locate desired information.

134 Goals tend to be established at the national level by groups such as the NEA and NAEP, adopted at the state level, and ultimately have an impact at the classroom level.

135 The words change and emphases shift, but the basic goals of education remain the same.

Intermediate objectives

136 In practice, intermediate objectives are also referred to as goals since they do represent relatively global outcomes.

137 Intermediate objectives are more precise than general objectives but not as detailed as specific objectives.

138 They are, in various situations, referred to as cumulative objectives, terminal objectives, milestone objectives, course objectives and, tasks.

139 Such objectives are usually measurable and typically represent more complex behaviors expected as a result of achievement of a number of prerequisite specific objectives.

140 Intermediate objectives specify outcomes intended at the end of a given cycle, "cycle" being defined in such terms as a unit, a course, or a time span.

141 There may well be cycles within cycles, and therefore intermediate objectives represent varying degrees of specificity and comprehensiveness.

Specific objectives

142 Specific objectives deal with the most discrete intended outcomes; they are the measurable outcomes upon which day-to-day activities such as instruction are based.

143 Task analysis and job analysis procedures are two methods of translating cumulative objectives into specific objectives.

144 Objectives have been developed by professional organizations (especially those related to curriculum areas), state departments of education, local education agencies, and teachers.

145 There have been several major efforts to collect objectives and/or related test items from a variety of sources and to develop comprehensive, computerized objectives banks; probably the largest and best known is the IOX developed at the Center for the Study of Evaluation at UCLA.

146 While there is a great deal of similarity in the objectives of different collections, they do vary as to the level of specificity, depth and breadth of content area represented, and degree of communicability.

147 Proponents of objective selection argue that objective development should be left to the experts and that sufficient objectives are already available to meet most anybody's needs.

148 Supporters of user development believe that the process of determining objectives has value in and of itself, that objectives are more meaningful when time is taken to think through and specify intended outcomes as opposed to merely picking them from somebody else's list.

149 If suitable objectives are already available, or if there are objectives which would be suitable with slight modification, there does not seem to be much point in starting from scratch.

Degree of specificity

150 An objective can be so vague that it is ambiguous or detailed that it is trivial and impractical.

151 A sensible, guiding principle suggests that each objective should represent a distinct task, a *task* being defined as "the smallest component of performance which has a distinct and independent purpose."

152 A *task*, or major objective, represents an important outcome, a performance with a clear purpose; *enablers*, or enabling objectives, represent knowledge and skills which facilitate students' ability to perform a task.

153 The more simply worded objective is clearly more functional.

Stating objectives

154 Selection or development of the objectives is really the most important aspect of any educational endeavor.

155 The objectives give direction to every remaining activity; fuzzy objectives tend to lead to fuzzy efforts, trivial objectives tend to lead to a waste of time and money.

Criteria

156 The appropriateness of the level of specificity of objectives must be evaluated.

157 An objective should communicate the intended outcome well enough that any evaluator would assess it in essentially the same way and be able to tell whether it had been achieved.

158 There is a false hierarchy in the minds of many to the effect that an objective that entails a paper-and-pencil response is somehow inferior to one that calls for an actual performance.

159 The assumption that paper-and-pencil tests only measure lower-order learnings is false.

Components

The behavior

160 The *behavior component* indicates what will happen or, as in the case of instructional objectives, what observable, measurable performance will constitute satisfactory evidence that the desired learning has occurred.

161 An objective should state the intended outcome using an action verb that represents an observable outcome.

162 Verbs such as "understand," "know," and "appreciate" are to be avoided whereas verbs such as "translate," "compute," "select," "identify," "list," and "solve" are appropriate.

163 Each objective should entail achievement of one and only one behavior; otherwise measurement of achievement becomes confounded.

164 Some objectives appear to be trivial because they deal with one instance, or one application, of a behavior, not the behavior itself.

165 It is usually not necessary to begin an objective with a phrase that indicates who will perform the intended outcome, (e.g. "The *student* will . . .").

The conditions

166 The *conditions component* of an objective is the "givens," the context within which the behavior will be exhibited.

167 Conditions usually specify necessary materials, allowable resources, or imposed restrictions, and the word "given" is not necessarily used.

168 The use of conditions is greatly overdone and they are often inserted even when they are obvious.

169 There are instances in which the presence or absence of a condition changes the whole meaning of an objective.

170 Stated conditions should be included only if they clarify the intent of the objective.

The criterion

171 When stated, the *criterion component* of an objective is the part that tells us how well the behavior must be performed; it is the standard against which actual performance is compared.

172 If the criterion is obvious or 100%, it is generally not stated.

173 The criterion may be expressed in terms such as percentage correct, percentage of increase, time to completion, or distance.

174 If the criterion is complex or dependent upon the group involved, it may be stated separately.

175 The basic issue is to establish how well or how often a performance must be exhibited in order to constitute sufficient evidence that the objective has been achieved.

176 For certain objectives the criterion must take into consideration the human error factor.

177 There is no scientific formula for setting a criterion of achievement; there is a great deal of judgment involved.

178 Unless one is involved in some type of individualized instruction, objectives are not generally assessed one at a time; one test may include items representing several objectives.

179 With the exception of mastery systems, even if all the students have not achieved all of the objectives, there comes a time when the teacher must move on.

180 One strategy involves setting a criterion which takes into consideration the performance of both the class and the individual.

181 Another strategy involves setting a class standard.

182 A third strategy, the one probably most often used in practice, is to simply assess the level of achievement, whatever it may be, without formally comparing it to any predetermined standard, and to make an existential decision.

183 For certain kinds of objectives, criteria of performance may not be numerical at all, especially when complex behaviors are involved.

184 Standards of instructional objective attainment other than student and personnel evaluation always involve group criteria.

185 A curriculum, for example, may be judged to be sufficiently developed when 90% of the students are achieving 90% of the objectives.

186 Fixed standards are feasible only when there is ample time for revision and reassessment cycles; most projects must report their degree of success at certain fixed periods of time.

187 *Experiential standards* refer to those standards of worth inherent in the value structure of those persons involved in, or affected by, the program to be evaluated and represent the summative judgments that people make about the overall program or some component of it.

188 Experiential standards are comparative in nature and based on experience, and judgments can be made about both intended and unintended outcomes.

Concluding remarks

189 In most cases even less than adequate objectives are better than no objectives at all.

190 The key point is that intended Outcomes should be stated in advance in language that communicates.

191 A suggested, reasonably short, set of guidelines for writing objectives is as follows: (1) specify the intended outcome in objective, measurable terms; (2) specify any conditions affecting performance that are not obvious or that significantly alter the intent of the objective; and (3) if necessary, specify the criterion of acceptable performance.

task four **performance criteria**

The specific instance of a type of evaluation which you described in task 1 will probably suggest one primary domain of learning. For example, if you described a project designed to improve reading comprehension you would obviously be most concerned with the cognitive domain. You would probably state a cognitive intermediate objective and an affective intermediate objective. Of course if learning objectives are not involved, as may be the case with certain projects, this criterion will not apply.

In reality, the actual number of specific objectives would depend upon the situation. Rarely, however, would less than ten be appropriate. Therefore, unless the number is staggering (12 is not staggering!), try to specify all of the appropriate objectives for the selected intermediate objective.

Each of your objectives should include a behavior component, conditions if necessary, and a criterion if not obvious. If appropriate, you should also state a group criterion.

Finally, if learning objectives are involved, your objectives should represent more higher-order outcomes than lower-order outcomes. If, for example, your objectives are cognitive, most of them should represent categories above the knowledge level.

You may recall how you and your class were on your best behavior. Suddenly you had a class full of little angels.

part three
tests

Measurement is a critical component of the evaluation process. Evaluation involves decision making, and rational decision making requires valid data; decisions are only as good as the measurement upon which they are based. The major method for collecting necessary information is the administration of a test. A test, however, is not necessarily a paper-and-pencil instrument. The term "test" includes a wide variety of measurement approaches. In order to select the most appropriate measurement techniques(s) for a given evaluation situation, it is necessary to be knowledgeable concerning the alternatives.

The goal of part 3 is for you to be knowledgeable concerning a wide range of measurement options and to be able to determine which are most appropriate for a given evaluation situation. After reading part 3, you should be able to do the following task.

task three

For the evaluation situation which you described in task 1, and the objectives you formulated in task 2, specify the measurement technique(s) which would be most appropriate for determining the status of individuals with respect to the objectives. (see Performance Criteria, p. 159.)

You could ask students about their sportsmanship, but more objective information would probably be obtained by actually *observing* students at a sporting event.

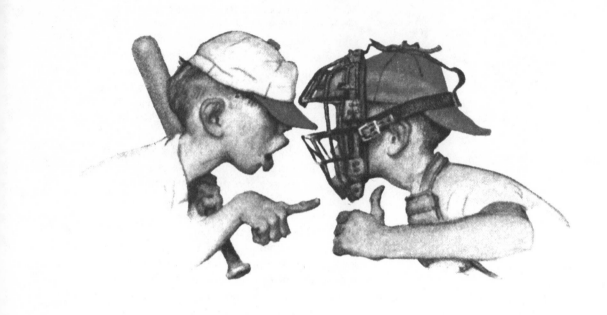

6 classification of tests

After reading chapter 6, you should be able to:

1 State three major ways to collect data and identify one situation for which each is appropriate.

2 In terms of item difficulty and test time, describe the difference between a speed test, a power test, and a mastery test.

3 List four major differences between a standardized test and a locally-developed test.

4 State the information which should be available concerning a norm group.

5 Describe the type of situation for which a locally developed test is more appropriate than a standardized test.

6 State two objectives, achievement of which could appropriately be determined with a written test, and two objectives which would require a performance test.

7 Briefly describe five self-report measurement techniques and state one situation for which each would be appropriate.

8 Briefly describe three types of observation and state one situation for which each would be appropriate.

9 List two objectives, achievement of which could be determined using a rating scale, and for each give one sample item.

10 State one purpose for which a standardized achievement test is more appropriate and one purpose for which a locally developed achievement test is more appropriate.

11 State how the results of a personality inventory can be used by (a) teachers and (b) counselors.

12 Give two examples of items which might appear on (a) a teacher-developed Likert attitude scale and (b) a teacher-developed semantic differential scale.

13 Describe how the results of a genetic aptitude test can be used by (a) teachers, (b) counselors, and (c) administrators.

14 State the purpose of a specific aptitude test and how the results of a multi–aptitude battery are used.

15 Describe the type of information which results from administration of a norm-referenced test and from a criterion-referenced test.

16 State three situations for which use of a norm-referenced test is more appropriate and three situations for which a criterion-referenced test is more appropriate.

Purpose and process

As discussed earlier, measurement is but one essential component of the evaluation process. It is, however, a critical one since resulting decisions are only as good as the data upon which they are based. In a general sense, data collection is involved in all phases of evaluation—the planning phase, the process phase, and the product phase. *Measurement,* however, the process of quantifying the degree to which someone or something possesses a given trait, normally occurs in the process and product phases.

Uses of measurement

Testing is necessary at certain points and useful at others. As a bare minimum, testing is conducted at the end of an evaluation cycle, for example, at the conclusion of the first year of operation of a special project. Such posttesting is for the purpose of determining the degree to which objectives (formal or informal) have been achieved, be they instructional, curriculum, or program objectives. Frequently, pretest or baseline data are collected at the beginning of a cycle. Pretests serve several purposes; knowledge of the current status of a group may provide guidance for future activities as well as a basis of comparison for posttest results (a pretest should of course measure the same behaviors as its corresponding posttest). September testing in a junior high school, for example, will reveal areas in which there have been substantial retention losses since spring testing, both on an individual and group basis. As another example, if a school parent volunteer program has as an objective "to increase the number of parent volunteers by 25%," then it is obviously necessary to know how many there are at the beginning of the effort.

There are many other purposes for which testing is conducted. As mentioned previously, a teacher may very well administer tests of entry behavior to determine whether assumed prerequisites have indeed been achieved. A special project designed to reduce dropouts may administer attitude tests and tests of personality variables such as introversion, aggression and anxiety in an attempt to identify potential dropouts or to better understand students having difficulties. A school may administer tests of scholastic aptitude in order to determine realistic achievement goals for students and to assist in the guidance process. There are many more examples which could be given. In this chapter various kinds of tests will be discussed, some of which may be totally unfamiliar to you. Although some kinds are more suitable for certain types of evaluation than others and some are more often used in research studies, any of them *may* be used in a given evaluation effort.

In many situations there are any number of tests which could be administered to collect useful information. A project designed to reduce dropouts, for example, would probably find data on all of the following variables helpful: achievement, aptitudes (general and specific), personality, attitudes, creativity, and interests. Such information on students would also be useful to classroom teachers. One cannot, however, spend all one's time collecting data and testing. As you increase testing time you of necessity decrease instructional time or program intervention time. On the other hand, collecting too little data makes it difficult, if not impossible, to take needed action or to make valid decisions concerning the success of an effort. Thus decisions must be made in the planning phase as to what will be measured, when, and how much total time will be allotted to testing. A reasonable guideline is to collect enough relevant data to validly make intended decisions and not to collect extraneous data which would be "nice to have" but not necessary. Another consideration is the fact that testing is a very anxiety-producing experience for some students. Unnecessary and excessive testing may cause undue unhappiness or depression and therefore do more harm than good.

Recall that while all needed instruments are determined during the planning phase, they are not necessarily available prior to the process phase, especially if one or more must be developed. Posttests, for instance, may be developed during the process phase. If instruments are to be selected from those available, however, selections should be made during the planning phase, mainly to insure that they will be on hand at the appropriate time. A standardized test, for example, might involve a six-week interval between the ordering date and the delivery date.

Data collection

There are three major ways to collect data: (1) administer a standardized instrument, (2) administer a locally-developed instrument, or (3) record naturally available data (such as grade point averages and absenteeism rates). Depending upon the situation, one of these ways may be most appropriate or a combination may be required. Collection of available data, requiring a minimum of effort, sounds very attractive. There are not very many situations, however, for which this type of data is appropriate. Even when it is appropriate, that is, will facilitate intended decision making, there are problems inherent in this type of data. For example, the same letter grade does not necessarily represent the same level of achievement, even in two different classes in the same school or two different schools in the same system. Further, the records from which the data are taken may be incomplete or disorganized. Developing an instrument for a particular purpose also has several major drawbacks. The development of a "good" instrument requires considerable time, effort, and skill. Training at least equivalent to a course in measurement is necessary in order to acquire the skills needed for good instrument development.

In contrast, the time it takes to select an appropriate instrument (usually from among standardized, commercially available instruments) is inevitably less than the time it takes to develop an instrument which measures the same thing. Further, standardized instruments are typically developed by experts who possess the necessary skills. Thousands of standardized instruments are available which yield a wide variety of data for a wide variety of purposes. Major areas for which numerous measuring instruments have been developed include achievement, personality, and aptitude. Each of these can in turn be further divided into many subcategories. Personality instruments, for example, can be classified as nonprojective or projective; nonprojective instruments include measures of attitude and interest.

In general, it is usually a good idea to find out whether a suitable instrument is already available before jumping into instrument development. There are situations, however, for which use of available instruments is impractical, inappropriate, or both. A teacher-made achievement test, for example, is invariably more appropriate, or valid, for assessing the degree to which students have achieved the objectives of a given unit. It would also be highly impractical for a teacher to administer a standardized test every time she or he wanted to determine the degree of progress of a class of students.[1]

As was discussed in chapter 1, the use of tests is criticized by a number of people. The alternative, however, is to make many decisions "in the dark," based on intuition and subjective impressions. It is clearly better to base judgments and decisions on the best data available. Just about any variable that one might want information on *can* be measured by a test, albeit indirectly. True, we cannot measure psychological traits such as intelligence with the same precision that we can measure physical traits such as length (there is no "yardstick" for intelligence). On the other hand, the expected accuracy of measurement varies with the trait being measured. The ability to perform addition of two-digit numbers, for instance, can be fairly accurately determined. Even measurement of fuzzier traits such as intelligence, however, can be reasonably accurate, and the estimate of ability indicated by the results of a well-validated intelligence test will invariably be better than our best guess. If an intelligence test score indicates that Horatio has an IQ of 120, his true IQ may be somewhat higher or lower, but it is probably safe to assume that he has above average ability.

Selection or development of instruments is critical to the whole evaluation process. It does not matter how carefully planned or well executed an effort is if inadequate instruments are involved. Poor instruments can only lead to poor decisions. Contrary to the beliefs of some, selection of an instrument is not simply a matter of locating any test which appears to measure what you want to measure; it involves careful examination of those that are available and selection of the best one, "best" being defined in terms of being most appropriate for your purpose and your user group. Of course if no appropriate test is available, then one must be developed. The selection process involves determination of the type of instrument needed (e. g. a reading comprehension test) and than a comparative analysis of available tests of that type. Therefore, in order to intelligently select an instrument, one must be familiar with the wide variety of types of instruments that exist and must also be knowledgeable concerning the criteria which should be applied in selecting one from among alternatives. The major purpose of this chapter is to provide you with a brief overview of the various classification schemes used in describing tests.

Classification schemes

At this point it must be reemphasized that a test is not necessarily a written set of questions to which an individual responds in order to determine whether he or she "passes." A more inclusive definition of a *test* is a means of measuring the knowledge, skill, feeling, intelligence, or aptitude of an individual or group. Tests produce numerical scores which can be used to identify, classify, or otherwise evaluate test takers. While in practice the majority of tests are paper-and-pencil achievement tests, there are many different kinds of tests and many different ways

---

[1] In this chapter we will discuss the various types of tests which can be selected or developed. In part 4, the variables relevant to instrument selection will be discussed, as well as the procedures for selecting an instrument. In part 5, guidelines for test development will be presented.

to classify them. The various classification schemes overlap considerably, and categories are by no means mutually exclusive. Any test can be classified on more than one dimension; a test, for example, might be described as being a standardized, norm-referenced aptitude test or as a locally-developed criterion-referenced achievement test.

As mentioned, there are many different ways to classify tests. We can, for example, classify tests according to variables related to test administration. In such a scheme tests can be classified as individual tests or group tests, depending upon whether they are administered to one person at a time or to more than one person. They can also be classified as written or oral, depending upon whether test questions are in written form or are given orally. We can also classify tests according to difficulty-versus-time variables. Tests vary in difficulty and the time allotted for test completion varies. In such a scheme we can classify tests as speed, power, or mastery tests. A *speed test* is one in which the time limit is fixed and the items, or tasks, are of low difficulty. The idea is to see how many items are done correctly in a limited period of time, for example, how many addition problems involving two one-digit numbers are done in five minutes. A *power test* is one in which the items vary in difficulty, usually being arranged in order of increasing difficulty from very easy to very difficult, and the time limit is generous. Theoretically, there is no time limit, but in reality we do not give test takers six months to do the test. The intent is to see how many items are done correctly given as much time as is reasonably needed. An example of a power test is a spelling test in which the words become increasingly difficult, beginning with "duck" and "soup" and ending with "hysteria" and "neurosis." A *mastery test* has characteristics of speed tests and power tests. It is one in which the items are of a low level of difficulty and the time limit is generous. Mastery tests are typically used for measuring achievement of minimum essentials, while power tests are used to measure achievement beyond the minimums. Question: What do you call a test in which the items are all very difficult and the time limit is short? Answer: A downer!

The classification schemes presented in this chapter have been selected because they illustrate the myriad of measurement options available to the evaluator. The first, response behaviors, refers to the way in which the behaviors to be measured are exhibited, primarily in written form or as a performance. The second, data collection methods, describes various methods and instruments for recording behavior. The third, behaviors measured, classifies tests according to the type of behavior measured, such as achievement, character and personality, or aptitude. The last, performance standards, refers to the standards or criteria to which the exhibited behavior is compared when results are interpreted. Figure 6.1 summarizes the various classification schemes to be discussed.

Response behaviors

The term *response behaviors* refers to the way in which behaviors to be measured are exhibited. While in some cases responses to questions or other stimuli are given orally, usually they are either written or take the form of an actual performance. The term "written" is used loosely here to include both constructed responses and the selection and marking of responses chosen from among alternatives (e.g. a multiple-choice test).

Response Behaviors	Written tests	Essay/objective Standardized/Locally-developed
	Performance tests	Procedures Products
Data Collection Methods	Self-report	Questionnaires and Interviews Sociometric techniques Diary techniques Q sorts
	Observation	Natural observation Simulation observation Content analysis
Behaviors Measured	Achievement	Achievement batteries Individual area tests Diagnostic tests
	Character and Personality	Personality Attitudes Creativity Interest
	Aptitude	General Specific Readiness
Performance Standards	Norm-referenced	
	Criterion-referenced	

figure 6.1
Summary of classification schemes for tests

Written responses

Written tests can be further classified as either essay or objective and as standardized or locally-developed.

Essay versus objective tests

An *essay test* is one in which the number of questions is limited and responders must compose answers, typically lengthy, e.g. "Identify and discuss supreme court decisions from 1955 to the present which have had an impact on public education in the United States." Determining the "goodness" or correctness of answers to such questions involves a certain amount of subjectivity. An *objective test* is one for which subjectivity in scoring is eliminated, at least theoretically. In other words, anyone scoring a given test should come up with the same score. Examples of objective tests are multiple-choice tests, true-false tests, matching tests, and short-answer tests. On a multiple-choice item, for example, if the answer is C, either the responder selected C or not; there is no subjectivity involved in determining whether someone answered the question correctly.

Things get a little trickier, however, with respect to short-answer tests. If the items require completion of a sentence by filling in one word (or phrase), and only one word is correct, there is usually no problem; for example, "The capital of Tennessee is _____." Things get a little more complicated with items like "In the story, the main character was _____." Answers such as "Jerry," "the little boy," and "Alice's brother" might all be correct if they represent the same person. Thus, in questions such as this all acceptable answers must be identified. Things really get tough with an item like "Define accountability." Unless the response is a regurgitated, verbatim, textbook definition, some subjectivity is likely to creep into the scoring. There is a fine line between an essay question requiring a brief response and a short-answer question requiring a multiple-word response.[2]

Standardized tests

Most of you are probably familiar with the concept of a standardized test. A *standardized test* is one that is: (1) developed by subject matter and measurement specialists, (2) field-tested under uniform administration procedures, (3) revised to meet certain criteria, and (4) scored and interpreted using uniform procedures and standards. Standardization permeates all aspects of the test to the degree that it can be administered and scored exactly the same way every time it is given. Although other measurement instruments, (e. g. observation instruments), can be standardized, most standardized tests are objective, written tests requiring written responses.

Standardized tests are big business. Hundreds of thousands of standardized tests are administered each year. Largely because of the competition among companies for various markets, considerable time and money is typically invested in the development and revision of standardized tests. Measurement experts and experts in the area of the behavior to be measured determine the content and format of the test. Fixed directions and time limits are developed so that the test can be administered in exactly the same way (as much as that is humanly possible) every time it is given. Scoring procedures are developed to insure objectivity and uniformity of scoring. While a standardized test may contain essay questions, this is not typical. Although there are exceptions, the vast majority of standardized tests have been administered to groups referred to as "norm groups." The performance of the norm group for a given test serves as the basis of comparison and interpretation for other groups to whom the test is administered. The scores of the norm group are called norms and are presented in norms tables.

Ideally, the *norm group* is a large, well-defined group which is representative of the group and subgroups for whom the test is intended. Since most standardized tests are intended for use virtually anywhere, norms should ideally be based on a national sample which is geographically representative. For example, if a test is supposed to measure reading achievement and be appropriate for grades

---

[2] In part 5 we will discuss guidelines for construction of the various types of tests.

one to six, then the norm group should include a number of first graders at various locations, and likewise for the other grades, and norms should be presented by grade level. The description of the norm group should include all pertinent information such as size, location, and major characteristics. The time of testing (e.g. March 1980) should also be given. Time of testing is important; results for students at the end of the ninth grade, for example, would not be applicable to students just beginning the ninth grade.

Of course norm groups are not always what they should be (what an understatement!). Unfortunately, it is not too unusual to find statements such as the following:

> The Ding-Dong Algebra Test was administered to 30 ninth grade students in Nomansland, USA; the results are presented in Table 4.

Well whoopee. The performance of such a norm group would hardly qualify as national norms. Descriptions of norm groups for the Stanford Achievement Test are more like it and typically read as follows:

> The norm group was selected to duplicate the distribution according to region and size of system for students in public, private nonsectarian, and private sectarian schools throughout the country. Eight-hundred and fifty thousand students, representing two-hundred and sixty-four school systems in fifty states, were tested between February 25, 1976, and March 15, 1976.

A relatively recent innovation with respect to norms is that they are more and more being presented for different kinds of populations to permit more valid comparisons. The Stanford Achievement Test, for example, presents norms for given age groups which do not include the scores of accelerated or retarded students, as well as norms for the total group which include the scores of all students tested. Some test publishers are reporting separate norms for special groups such as learning disabled students. Another relatively recent phenomenon is the development of system norms. Some large school systems have formulated norms tables for various subgroups in the system based on the results of tests such as the Stanford Achievement Test. When available, such norms provide a more valid basis of comparison for certain purposes, analysis of achievement patterns in the system over time, for example.

Norms tables typically include the distribution of raw scores as well as a number of score equivalents such as percentiles and stanines. The lowest raw scores correspond to the 1st percentile and the highest scores correspond to the 99th percentile. The average raw scores correspond to the 50th percentile, and so forth. Thus norms tables permit what are referred to as norm-referenced interpretations. A given student's score is compared to the scores of the norm group. If his or her score corresponds to the average score of the norm group, then the interpretation is that he or she is average with respect to the variables measured. Strictly speaking, there is no indication of whether the score is "good," only whether it is better (or worse) than the average performance of the norm group. There is also no interpretation which tells us exactly what a given student knows or can do, only whether what she or he knows or can do is more or less than "average."

Locally-developed tests

The opposite of a standardized test is obviously a nonstandardized test. Such tests are usually developed locally for a special purpose. Tests developed by teachers for use in the classroom are examples of locally-developed tests. Such tests do not have the characteristics of standardized tests. They are not typically developed by measurement experts, for example, they are not fieldtested and revised, and they are not administered to a norm group. They are developed for a specific situation, a specific set of objectives, and a specific group, and they may only be administered once. A locally-developed test *may* be as good as a standardized test, but the probability is that it is not. Of course there is considerable variability in the quality of such tests. A three-year experimental project, for example, may develop some very good instruments, especially if they are intended to be used after the termination of the project. Recall the ESEA Title IV-C project described in chapter 2. Its purpose was to develop a county-wide system of staff evaluation. A review of the state of the art revealed the lack of availability of appropriate instruments. The resulting instrument development process used in this project closely resembled that used in the development of standardized tests. Measurement experts were heavily involved and instruments were validated, fieldtested and revised until acceptability criteria were met.[3]

As mentioned earlier, use of locally-developed tests is often more practical and more appropriate. Although there are thousands of different standardized tests, there is certainly not one for every possible measurement need. A locally-developed achievement test would likely reflect what was actually taught to a greater degree than would a standardized test which aims at a wider audience. Also, it would obviously be impractical to have standardized "pop quizzes"! Further, there are a number of situations for which standardized test development would not be financially feasible. Commercial test producers make their money by selling a lot of tests. It is not worth the effort to develop a test for which the market is very small. Thus, if a school system instituted a course on psychic phenomena, it would probably have to rely on a locally-developed test to measure achievement.

Performance tests

For many objectives and areas of learning, use of written tests is an inappropriate way of measuring behavior. You cannot determine how well a student can type a letter, for example, with a multiple-choice test. There are other objectives achievement of which *can* be measured with a paper-and-pencil test but not as well as by using other approaches. Attitudes, for example, can be assessed by asking persons to respond to a number of questions, but observation of actual behavior is normally a more valid way of determining attitude—I *say* I am a good sport but do I *act* like one? I say I like poetry but do I ever check a poetry book out of the library? Clearly, in many situations it is necessary or preferable to assess a performance.

---

[3] You are probably wondering what these "acceptability criteria" are. In Part 4 we will discuss desirable characteristics of tests and things should be clearer. An acceptable level of reliability, for example, is a major concern in any test development effort.

Performance can take the form of a procedure or a product. In either case the performance is observed and rated in some way. Thus, a performance test is one which requires the execution of an act or the development of a product in order to determine whether or to what degree a given ability or trait exists. It should be noted that for aptitude tests (to be discussed later in the chapter) performance tests are frequently used in an attempt to eliminate the language factor from the assessment of aptitude. The results of a written IQ test, for example, can be contaminated and misleading if administered to persons with a poor command of the English language. In an attempt to eliminate this problem, certain IQ tests involve nonverbal tasks such as making indicated designs with colored blocks and putting together picture puzzles.

As we said, a performance can take the form of execution of a procedure or the development of a product. A *procedure* is a series of steps, usually in a definite order, executed in performing an act or task. While the procedure may involve one step or action, usually several are involved. Examples of procedures are adjusting a microscope, passing a football, setting margins on a typewriter, drawing geometric figures with a protractor, taking blood pressure, and changing the spark plugs in a car. A *product* is a tangible outcome or result. Examples of products are a typed letter, a painting, a poem, a science project, a blueprint, and batch of peanut butter cookies. As the above examples illustrate, a performance may be in writing, e.g. a poem. Such performances are not, however, written tests in the sense that they do not represent a series of answers to a series of questions. Also, you can generally not obtain the same degree of objectivity of scoring as you can with, for example, a multiple-choice test. If you know what you are looking for, however, that is, if you have clearly specified the intended behavior, a high degree of objectivity can be obtained in many cases. A typed letter, for example, can be examined to determine such things as the number of typographical errors. It can be determined whether a football was thrown a specific number of yards, and so forth.

As you have probably deduced, procedures frequently precede products. You might be interested in determining, for example, whether students can properly thread a sewing machine (a procedure) and in whether they can stitch a straight hem (a product). Notice that procedures typically involve verbs (adjusting, setting, passing, drawing, taking, changing) while products involve nouns (letter, painting, poem, project, blueprint, cookies). The distinction between procedures and products, however, is not always so easy to make. Is a gymnastic routine, for example, a procedure or a product? The answer would probably depend upon the nature of the objective or intended behavior, i.e. whether it involved performing a specified set of moves or the creation of a unique routine.

Although measurement of intended behavior must sometimes, of necessity, given the nature of the behavior, involve procedures or products, they are usually avoided if there is another option, even if it is an inferior one. The reason is that such measurement is very time-consuming and may require resources not readily available. Those of you who are teachers know how long it takes to read 35 notebooks or to evaluate 35 science projects. You also know what a frustrating experience it is to try to have 35 students all equipped on a given day with a piece of material and a pattern, or a protractor and a compass (not to mention a pencil!).[4]

---

[4] For those of you who would like to pursue this subject further, there are a number of tests and measurement texts which contain numerous examples of procedures and products. See, for example, Ahmann, J. S. & Glock, M. D. *Evaluating pupil growth*. Boston: Allyn and Bacon, 1978

Data collection methods

There are many different ways to collect data and classifying data collection methods is not easy. However, a logical way to categorize them initially is in terms of whether the data are obtained through self-report or observation. Self-report data are data solicited from individuals using instruments such as written achievement tests, questionnaires, or attitude scales. Observation data are data obtained not by asking individuals for information but through other means such as direct observation of procedures.

Self-report versus observation

There are frequently alternative methods available for collecting desired data, one of which is generally more appropriate. Suppose, for example, you wish to determine how elementary-school teachers spend their time during the school day, before and after a series of workshops dealing with behavior modification techniques. A major objective of the workshops might be to decrease significantly the amount of time teachers spend in disciplinary activities. Your first thought might be to mail a questionnaire to the principals of the schools at which the participating teachers are employed. This procedure, however, would be based on the assumption that principals *know* how teachers spend their time. While principals would of course be familiar with the duties and responsibilities of their teachers, it is likely that teacher reports concerning time devoted to various activities would differ, perhaps significantly, from principal reports. Thus, directly asking the teachers themselves would probably result in more accurate information. On the other hand, it is possible that teachers might not be totally objective in estimating the amount of time devoted to various activities; it is possible, for example, that they might tend to subconsciously exaggerate the amount of time they spend on activities they consider to be distasteful, activities such as clerical operations (grading papers, for example) and discipline. Thus, further thought might indicate that direct observation would probably yield the most objective, accurate data.

Self-report methods

With the exception of Q sorts (which are not used very often anyway), self-report data consist of the oral or written responses of individuals. An obvious type of self-report data is that resulting from the administration of standardized or locally-developed written tests, including certain achievement, personality, and aptitude tests. Another type of self-report measure used in certain evaluation efforts is the questionnaire, an instrument with which you are probably familiar. Also, interviews are sometimes used. An interview is essentially the oral, in-person administration of a questionnaire to each person in the group of interest. There are several other techniques which are occasionally used in evaluation efforts—sociometry, diary techniques, and Q sorts.

Questionnaires and interviews

Questionnaires are usually objective, containing multiple-choice and/or short-answer questions. Questionnaires are frequently used in evaluation efforts, to assess the attitudes of program participants, for example. As compared to questionnaires, interviews have a number of unique advantages and disadvantages. When well conducted, an interview can produce in-depth data not obtainable with a questionnaire. On the other hand, interviews are expensive and time-consuming, generally involve smaller groups, and require training of interviewers. The interview is most appropriate for asking questions which cannot effectively be structured into a multiple-choice format, such as questions of a personal nature. While questionnaires typically are objective, interviews often involve a combination of objective items and subjective, open-ended questions. Program and project personnel, for example, are frequently interviewed in order to determine their impressions concerning the objectives, procedures, and outcomes of the program or project.

In contrast to the questionnaire, the interview is flexible; the interviewer can adapt the situation to each subject. By establishing rapport and a trust relationship, the interviewer can often obtain data that subjects would not give on a questionnaire. The interview may also result in more accurate and honest responses since the interviewer can explain and clarify both the purpose of the interview and individual questions. Another advantage of the interview is that the interviewer can follow up on incomplete or unclear responses by asking additional probing questions. Reasons for particular responses can also be determined. On the other hand, direct interviewer-interviewee contact also has its disadvantages. The responses given by a person may be biased and affected by her or his reaction to the interviewer, either positive or negative. For example, a person may become hostile or uncooperative if the interviewer reminds him of his not-too-beloved boss!

Telephone interviews are occasionally used to collect data. They have some of the advantages of interviews and are not as costly. Of course data may be affected because not everyone has a phone and because some people are hesitant to reveal their true feelings or give personal information on the phone; it is very difficult to establish rapport on the telephone.[5]

Use of questionnaires and interviews entails a number of problems. Lack of response is one of them; many people do not return mailed questionnaires or attend scheduled interviews. In these situations it is very difficult to interpret findings since people who do not respond may feel differently from those who do. Twenty percent of a group of parents, for example, might feel very negatively about the experimental peer tutoring program being conducted in some of the schools and might avail themselves of every opportunity to express their unhappiness, such as on your questionnaire. The other 80%, who feel neutrally or positively, might not be as motivated to respond. Thus, if decisions concerning the continuation of the program were based only on those who responded, the wrong decisions might be made.

---

[5] Fink, A., & Kosecoff, J. (Eds.). How to collect evaluation information. *How to Evaluate Education Programs*, 1978, 2(1), 1–8.

As the above example illustrates, both questionnaires and interviews are used to collect survey data. A *survey* is an attempt to collect data from members of a population in order to determine the current status of that population with respect to one or more variables. Populations may be broadly defined, such as the American tax-paying public, or narrowly defined, such as tax payers in Teenytown, USA. Determining "current status . . . with respect to some variable" may involve assessment of a variety of types of information such as attitudes, opinions, characteristics, and demographic information. One type of survey which is unique to education is the school survey which may involve the study of an individual school or of all the schools in a particular system. School surveys are generally conducted for the purpose of internal or external evaluation or for the assessment and projection of needs, and usually are conducted as a cooperative effort between local school personnel and a visiting team of experts, typically from local educational agencies and institutions. Resulting recommendations and/or projections are based upon the collection of data concerning status of variables such as community characteristics, institutional and administrative personnel, curriculum and instruction, finances, and physical facilities. School surveys can provide necessary and valuable input for decision making to both the schools studied and to other agencies and groups (such as boards of public instruction) whose operations are school related.

Sociometry

Sociometry is the assessment and analysis of the interpersonal relationships within a group of individuals. By analyzing the expressed choices or preferences of group members for other members of the group, degree of acceptance or rejection for members of the group can be determined. The basic sociometric process involves asking each member to indicate with which other members she or he would most like to engage in a particular activity. For example, you might ask students to list in order of preference the three individuals they would most like to work with on a cooperative project. As you well know, choices will vary depending upon the activity; the person you would most enjoy going to a party with is not necessarily the same person with whom you would like to write a joint term paper. The choices made by the group members are graphically depicted in a diagram which is called a *sociogram*. A sociogram may take many forms and use a variety of symbols, but basically it shows who chose whom. A sociogram will clearly identify "stars" (members chosen quite frequently), "isolates" (members not chosen), and "cliques" (small subgroups of individuals who mutually select each other).

Sociometric techniques are utilized by evaluators, researchers, and practitioners. A human relations project, for example, might involve assessment of initial interpersonal relationship patterns, introduction of an approach designed to change the existing patterns, and postassessment to determine pattern changes. A similar procedure might be utilized by teachers in an attempt to bring isolates into the group. If Clancy Clutz were identified as being an isolate, his teacher could make a special effort to provide opportunities for Clancy to interact with other members of the group. Thus, the sociometric process is one which is relatively simple to apply and can provide useful data.

Diary techniques

Another technique, which is not very precise but may be useful in certain situations, is the *diary technique.* Basically it involves asking people to keep a record of specified behaviors, attitudes, thoughts, or ideas. Closely related, the critical incident technique asks people to record and describe only things of special interest. You could, for example, have high school students keep a record of acts of violence which occurred in television shows which they viewed. Of course the value of such data for evaluation purposes is highly questionable. People are not very good about keeping up diaries and the results are typically very difficult to score and interpret.[6]

The Q sort

The *Q Sort* technique basically involves what it sounds like it involves— sorting. An individual is given a set of items or statements, usually on cards, and asked to place them into specified categories so that each category contains some minimum number of cards. For example, a principal might be given a set of 20 budget items, such as media, teacher salaries, and intramurals, and be asked to place each one into 1 of 5 categories representing varying degrees of priority; category 1 might be labeled "top priority," for example. The principal might be instructed to place at least two items in each category. The Q sort has a lot of problems. It often forces people to make tough distinctions and complex analysis methods may be required for the resulting data.[7]

Observation

When observation is used, data are collected not by asking but by observing. A person being observed usually does not write anything; he or she *does* something and the behavior is observed and recorded. For certain evaluation questions, observation is clearly the most appropriate approach. To use previous examples, you could ask students about their sportsmanship and you could ask teachers how they handle discipline in their classrooms, but more objective information would probably be obtained by actually observing students at a sporting event and teachers in their classrooms. The value of observation is illustrated by a study which was conducted in the Southwest on the classroom interaction between teachers and Mexican-American students.[8] Many teachers claimed that Mexican-American children are difficult to teach because of their lack of participation in classroom activities, their failure to ask or answer questions, and the like. Systematic observation, however, revealed that the main reason they did not answer questions, for example, was that they were not asked very many! Observation revealed that teachers tended to talk less often and less favorably to Mexican-

---

[6] See footnote 5.
[7] See footnote 5.
[8] Jackson, G., & Cosca, C. The inequality of educational opportunity in the Southwest: An observational study of ethnically mixed classrooms. *American Educational Research Journal*, 1974, 11(3), 219–229.

American children, and to ask them fewer questions. Thus, observation not only provided more accurate information than teacher reports but also made the teachers aware that they were unintentionally part of the problem.

Observational techniques may also be used in experimental efforts. A special project, for example, might have as its major objective "to significantly increase positive interactions between students of different ethnic backgrounds." Students could be observed prior to and following implementation of the project's strategies in order to determine if instances of positive interactions were increased in number. Observational data can be collected on inanimate objects such as books as well as human beings.

The major types of observation which are used in evaluation efforts are natural observation, observation of simulation, and content analysis.

Natural observation

Certain kinds of behavior can only be (or can best be) observed as they occur naturally. In such situations the observer purposely does not control or manipulate anything, and in fact works very hard at not affecting the observed situation in any way. As an example, classroom behavior—behavior of the teacher, behavior of the students, and the interactions between teachers and students—can best be assessed through natural observation.

Simulation observation

In simulation observation the evaluator creates the situation to be observed and tells participants what activities they are to engage in. This technique allows the evaluator to observe behavior which occurs infrequently in natural situations or not at all (for example, having a teacher trainee role play a teacher-parent conference). The major disadvantage of this type of observation is, of course, that it is not natural, and the behavior exhibited by people may not be the behavior that would occur in a natural setting. People may behave the way they think they should behave rather than the way they really would behave. In reality, this potential problem is not as serious as it may sound. People tend to get carried away with their roles and often exhibit very true-to-life emotions. Besides, even if people "fake it" at least they show that they are aware of the correct way to behave. A student who demonstrates the correct way to interact with an irate parent at least *knows* what should be done.

Two major types of simulation are individual role playing and team role playing. In individual role playing the observer is interested in the behavior of one person, although other "players" are involved. The individual is given a role, a situation, and a problem to solve. The observer then records and scores the individual's solution to the problem and the way in which she or he executed it. As an example, a teacher trainee might be told:

> Yesterday you caught Sammy Shifty cheating on a history test. You tore up his paper and gave him a zero. The principal has just informed you that an extremely irate Mrs. Shifty is on her way to see you. What will you say to Mrs. Shifty?

In a team role playing situation, a small group is presented with a situation and a problem and solutions are recorded and scored. Qualities such as leadership ability may also be studied. As an example, a group might be told:

> The faculty has appointed you a committee of six. Your charge is to come up with possible solutions to the problem of student fights in the halls, an occurrence which has been increasing.

Content analysis

Content analysis is the systematic, quantitative description of the composition of an object. Typical subjects for content analysis include books, instructional materials, notebooks, typed pages, documents, and creative productions such as musical compositions, works of art, and photographs. Project personnel might, for example, develop written instructional materials designed to present vocational information to handicapped students. Content analysis may be quite simple, involving primarily frequency counts (counting the number of typographical errors, for example), or very sophisticated and complex, involving investigation of the existence of bias or prejudice in a textbook.

Additional data collection instruments

As the previous discussions indicated, there are a variety of instruments which can be used to collect data. Many of these have already been described in connection with a corresponding data collection method, e.g. collection of survey data often involves a questionnaire. There are several additional instruments which are frequently used, rating scales and checklists, and observation recording forms. They are being discussed separately since they can be utilized in a number of different measurement situations.

Rating scales and checklists

A rating scale is typically an instrument with a number of items related to a given variable, each item representing a continuum of categories between two extremes; persons responding to the items place a mark to indicate their position on each item. There are a minimum of two categories per item, although usually two categories will be insufficient. Theoretically there is no maximum number of categories, although in practice more than seven categories require overly difficult discrimination. The following items should illustrate the above points:

Place an X at that point on the continuum which best represents your feelings.

1. The topic "evaluation" is very boring/totally fascinating.

2. The topic "evaluation" is

1	2	3	4	5	6	7	8	9	10	11	12	13	14	15
Very														Totally
boring														fascinating

In item 1 you are forced to express an extreme position. If you think evaluation is "fairly interesting," you would probably choose "totally fascinating" as best representing your attitude, given the two choices, but your choice would not really reflect your true feeling. In item 2, you really have too many choices. If we assume that 8 represents a neutral point, then "fairly interesting" would fall somewhere between 8 and 15, but where? Furthermore, is there really any reliable difference in the feelings of persons who mark 12 and those who mark 13? The results would be very difficult to interpret. The following item would probably be more than sufficient:

The topic "evaluation" is

1	2	3	4	5	6	7
Very boring						Totally fascinating

If you think evaluation is "fairly interesting," you would probably mark 5.

Rating scales can be self-report instruments or observation instruments depending upon how they are used. As the previous example illustrated, they can be used for self-report of attitudes and opinions (toward self, others, and a variety of other activities, institutions, and situations). They can also be used in the observation of procedures and products. When procedures are observed, the observer is required to assess the behavior and give it a rating, say from 1 to 3. For example, an observer might rate a teacher's explanations as 1—not very clear, 2—clear, or 3—very clear. In procedures observation as many as five categories (infrequently more than five) are used, with three probably being the ideal number. The more categories there are, the more difficult it becomes to correctly classify. An observer could probably discriminate between "not very clear" and "clear" fairly easily; deciding between "very unclear" and "not very clear" would not be as simple. When products are rated, as many as seven categories may be manageable. You might, for example, use the following item in observing a student's cookies:

1	2	3	4	5	6	7
Shapeless Globs		Not Well Shaped		Well Shaped		Perfectly Shaped

Because they are fairly easy to develop, score, and interpret, rating scales can be very useful in many types of evaluation. One major problem with rating scales is rater bias, or response set. When used as a self-report instrument, there are situations in which persons may not report their true feelings but rather what they perceive to be socially acceptable or desired feelings. To please a teacher, for example, certain students might indicate that they feel evaluation is totally fascinating when in reality the whole topic gives them a headache. Whether rater bias results from conscious or unconscious motivations, it can seriously affect interpretation of results. A similar problem occurs when an observer rates a procedure or product. Ratings may be influenced by factors other than those actually being observed. Two such factors are the "halo effect" and the "generosity error." The *halo effect* is the tendency of a rater to let overall feelings toward a person affect responses to individual items. A student who thinks a professor is a "terrific teacher" may rate that professor high on all items even though in reality the professor may not, for example, always be "well prepared" for class. The *generosity error* is the tendency of a rater to give the person being rated the benefit of the doubt whenever the rater does not have sufficient knowledge to make an objective rating. Both the halo effect and the generosity error can work in reverse of course. Again, such factors can seriously hamper interpretation of results.

Whenever rating scales are used in observation, it is important to ensure that raters have sufficient opportunity to observe the behaviors to be rated. When you ask people to rate items for which they have little or no first-hand knowledge, you are inviting problems such as the generosity error. Also, whenever feasible, it is a good idea to have both raters and ratees (those being rated) participate in the design and development of the rating scale. If teachers, for example, are to be evaluated using a scale which rates their classroom behavior, they will be a lot more cooperative and positive about the evaluation if they have a say as to what behaviors are to be observed. Teachers may agree that "degree of preparation" is a reasonable variable for inclusion but may object to being rated on their style of dress.

Occasionally, a ranking scale may be used. Basically, a ranking scale involves having responders put a set of items in order according to some criterion. You might ask students to rank a number of books in terms of the order in which they would like to read them. As with rating scales, they are easy to develop but entail a number of similar problems, especially if there are an excessive number of items to be ordered.

A checklist is an enumeration of a number of behaviors or features that constitute a procedure or product. When a procedure is involved, the steps are typically listed in the desired order. The person completing the checklist indicates whether a given behavior or feature occurred, or is present, or not. In some cases, an indication may be made as to the order in which the steps were executed. You might, for example, use a checklist in determining the adequacy of a student teacher's lesson plan. Items such as the following might be included:

	Yes	No
Objectives defined	_____	_____
Instructional strategy described	_____	_____
Materials listed	_____	_____

Observation recording forms

It is important for a person observing behavior to have a well-thought-out, efficient recording instrument. It would obviously be inefficient and impractical to have an observer simply write down everything that occurs. Observers should spend their time thinking about what is occurring rather than how to record it. Thus, an observation form should include all events of interest, and the observer should simply have to indicate which ones occurred, in what order, and how often.

Rating scales and checklists are frequently used as observation instruments, especially by classroom teachers for assessing achievement of students. More formal, systematic observations typically utilize a category or coding system which is often standardized. A form reflecting a category system involves a relatively small number of categories, representing all events of interest. The observer simply records each event that occurs, using the appropriate code; recordings are made at predetermined intervals, every five seconds for example. The Flanders System, for example, which is widely used for the observation of verbal behavior in the classroom, classifies all teacher behaviors and all student behaviors into one of ten categories, each of which is represented by a number.[9] Categories 1–7 reflect different types of teacher behavior, 8 and 9 deal with student behavior, and 10 indicates silence or confusion. Thus, for example, if a teacher praises a student, the observer records that "2" occurred. The Flanders System has been used in a number of efforts such as the one previously described dealing with the class participation of Mexican-American children. Sometimes, especially when complex behaviors are being observed, the behavior to be observed is recorded on an audiotape or videotape and transferred to a recording form at a later date. This permits the observer to replay the tape as many times as necessary to assure accurate categorizations.

As with rating scales, observation involves its own types of bias—observer bias and observee bias.[10] Observer bias refers to invalid observations which result from the way in which the observer observes. Observee bias refers to invalid observations which result from the fact that observees may behave differently simply because they are being observed. A response set is the tendency of an observer to rate the majority of observees as above average, average, or below average regardless of the observees' actual behavior. A related problem is the old "halo effect" whereby initial impressions concerning an observee (positive or negative) affect subsequent observations. A final major source of observer bias occurs when the observer's knowledge concerning observees affects observations. A teacher, for example, may rate Suzy Shiningstar's science project higher than it should be because he knows that Suzy is an excellent student.

The other side of the problem, observee bias, refers to the phenomenon whereby persons being observed behave atypically simply because they are being observed. If you are a teacher, you probably served an internship prior to graduation. You may recall how you and your class were on your best behavior whenever your supervising teacher came to observe. Suddenly you had a class full of little angels. The best way to handle the problem is to make observers aware of it so that they can attempt to be as unobtrusive (inconspicuous) as possible. Observees apparently tend to ignore the presence of an observer after a few sessions. Thus, simply observing a few sessions prior to recording any data is an effective technique. Another approach to the problem of observee bias is to eliminate observees. If the same information can be obtained by observing inanimate objects (referred to as unobtrusive measures), use them. School suspension lists, for instance, have never been known to act differently because they were being observed. Such lists might be one unobtrusive measure of the disruptive behavior of students.

Behaviors measured

Amazing as it may seem, virtually all possible behaviors that can be measured fall into one of three categories: achievement, character and personality, and aptitude. Although all of these can be standardized or self-developed, written or perform-

[9] Flanders, N. A. *Interaction analysis in the classroom: A manual for observers.* Minneapolis: University of Minnesota, College of Education, 1960.
[10] Observee is a term used by the author (with apologies to Webster) meaning "a person being observed." You are the observ*er*; the person being observed is the observ*ee*.

ance tests, most tests of character and personality and aptitude are written, standardized tests. Therefore, the discussions which follow will be primarily within this framework. The categories to be discussed apply equally well to cognitive, affective, and psychomotor outcomes.

Achievement

Achievement tests measure the currect status of individuals with respect to proficiency in given areas of knowledge or skill. Achievement tests are appropriate for many types of evaluation besides individual student evaluation. Many evaluation studies, for example, are designed to compare the effectiveness of two or more curriculum approaches; effectiveness is usually defined in terms of student achievement.

Individual achievement tests and batteries

Locally-developed tests generally measure achievement in one specific subject matter or content area, such as reading, science, social studies, language, art, music, or physical education. Standardized achievement tests are available for individual curriculum areas such as reading and math, and also in the form of comprehensive batteries which measure achievement in several different areas. The California Achievement Test Battery, for example, is a commonly used battery which measures achievement in reading, language, and arithmetic. Since locally-developed tests are developed with different intents, which is appropriate in a given situation depends largely upon the purpose for which it is being administered. In addition to the characteristics already described which differentiate standardized and locally-developed tests, there is another major difference which applies to achievement tests. Standardized tests are designed to measure what *most* teachers cover, that is, content common to many classes of a certain kind (e.g. Algebra I classes). The specialists who develop such tests analyze texts and other instructional materials used throughout the country and derive the objectives to be sampled by the test. They are carefully developed to include measurement of objectives common to many school systems. There is no way a standardized test could include items to measure everything that any teacher might include in instruction. Thus, there will be certain facts, concepts, and principles on a standardized high school biology test, for example, which some students have never encountered, and there will be other facts, concepts, and principles which they have learned which will not be measured. A locally-developed test, on the other hand, is designed to measure a particular set of learning outcomes, precisely those intended by a teacher, for example. Such a test should be based solely on texts and materials involved in instruction and therefore more accurately reflect achievement of what was actually taught.

There are a number of purposes for which a standardized test is more appropriate than a locally-developed test. First of all, it is important to know how well Ziggy is doing compared to other students of a similar age or grade level. Ziggy may be doing swell in Ms. Chalk's class but Ms. Chalk's class may contain only remedial students or Ms. Chalk may be an "easy" teacher. For guidance purposes, for instance, it would be helpful to know that Ziggy is actually performing way below the "national" norm, or average score. Moreover, the overall performance of a group of students says something about the effectiveness of instruction. If many students (not just Ziggy) do poorly on a standardized test, the reasons should be investigated (assuming that the students are similar on relevant variables to those in the norm group). There are any number of factors which could be involved, such as the curriculum (it might be woefully outdated) or the instruction itself. An interesting debate question is: Should teachers be held accountable for the performance of their students on standardized tests? Actually, the answer is yes and no. The teacher cannot be held accountable to the degree that students in their classes differ from the norm group or to the degree that what was actually taught differs from what the standardized test measures. On the other hand, there should be some overlap between a given teacher's objectives and most teachers' objectives. If you took a standardized test on facts, concepts, and principles of educational evaluation after finishing this book and did terribly, you would be upset. If I told you not to worry because this book does not cover any of the topics that other evaluation books do, you would want to know why. The point is, there is considerable room for individual variation beyond a common core; *all* elementary students, for example, should be taught how to multiply two two-digit numbers.

Standardized tests are also preferable when large-scale comparisons are to be made between performance at two different points in time. A principal, a superintendent, and a director of a curriculum evaluation project, for example, may all be interested in comparing September results with May results for the same test. Also, since such results are normally part of a student's file, teachers can use them as one input in the planning phase. Finally, standardized tests are usually more appropriate when the achievement of a large population is being measured. By the nature of the way in which they are designed, they are more likely to measure what most of the students have learned.

As was mentioned earlier, standardized achievement tests are available for individual curriculum areas such as reading and math, and also in the form of comprehensive batteries which measure achievement in several different areas. If an evaluation effort is only interested in one area of achievement, such as reading, then either an individual reading test or a subtest of a battery can be administered. Which is preferable depends again upon the purpose and the seriousness of the decisions. A subtest tends to be shorter and thus provide less coverage than an individual test. On the other hand, there are several batteries which have very good subtests. The Stanford Achievement Test: Reading, for example, measures word meaning and paragraph meaning and is generally considered to be a good test.[11]

When assessment of achievement in a number of areas is needed, it is better to administer a battery than a number of individual tests. Besides being more convenient and efficient in terms of time and money, a battery allows comparisons which are not possible or risky when a number of individual tests are given. Since all subtests of the battery were normed on the same group, one can compare a student's relative achievement in the various areas tested and identify areas in which he or she performs better than others (although objectively the student may not excel in any area). We might, for example, determine that Esmeralda's best subject is arithmetic, even though she may be somewhat below average in arithmetic achievement. Depending upon such factors as the number of

[11] The term "good" refers mainly to validity and reliability, concepts which will be discussed in chapter 7.

achievement areas included, batteries take from one hour to several days to ad-
minister. Several commonly used achievement batteries include: California
Achievement Test, Comprehensive Tests of Basic Skills, Iowa Tests of Basic Skills,
Metropolitan Achievement Test, and Stanford Achievement Test. The Stanford
Achievement Test, for example, is a fairly good test designed to measure word
meaning, paragraph meaning, spelling, language, arithmetic computation, arithmetic concepts, arithmetic applications, social studies and science. The Stanford
Achievement Test was designed to provide information for longitudinal studies of
achievement, e.g. in a school system, and has six level tests, each appropriate for a
different grade range.

In closing, it should be reemphasized that for many purposes locally-developed tests are preferable. Only a teacher-made test, for example, can precisely
determine whether students have learned what the teacher taught and exactly
what they have learned, i.e. whether and to what degree objectives have been attained by the group and by each individual. Also, such tests can be administered
frequently, providing feedback to students and to teachers or project personnel.
Indicated changes in strategy can be made as they are needed thereby enhancing
the effectiveness of further instruction or other activities. Further, since standardized tests are primarily written, objective tests, locally-developed instruments
permit considerably more flexibility with respect to measurement alternatives. A
teacher, for example, can use observation of procedures and products.

Diagnostic tests

A *diagnostic test* is a type of achievement test which yields multiple scores
for each area of achievement; these scores facilitate identification of specific areas
of deficiency or learning difficulty. Diagnostic tests may be standardized or locally
developed and are administered after a given unit of instruction. Total scores are
of very little value since the purpose is to identify precisely what a particular student can and cannot do. Indirectly, of course, diagnostic tests also identify problems with instruction. Standardized and locally-developed diagnostic tests each
have their own advantages and disadvantages.

Standardized diagnostic tests are developed in cooperation with experts
in the area of learning difficulties and are based on research findings concerning
common sources of learning difficulty. They include measurement of essential
skills in a given area; for those skills that are measured a number of different types
of items are included so that areas of difficulty can be precisely pinpointed. Since a
standardized diagnostic test is developed by a cadre of experts, it provides most
teachers with much more valid results than they could obtain themselves using
more informal techniques.

Diagnostic tests are administered mainly to identify individual strengths
and weaknesses and to identify students in need of remediation. Items in a diagnostic test represent skills that virtually all students should have achieved at a
given point in their education. The nature of the appropriate remediation depends
of course on the reasons for the identified deficiencies. Scholastic aptitude test
scores are frequently used in conjunction with diagnostic test results in determining the nature of the problem. It may be that a student is performing as well as
could be expected, and the decision might be made to either provide the student
with supplementary instruction or to place the student in a special class. On the

other hand, the student might have above average ability and be underachieving for personal reasons, in which case counseling might be indicated.

Although not primarily developed for that purpose, subtests of batteries *can* be used for diagnostic purposes. Although they only provide one score per subtest, performance on individual test items can be analyzed. The advantage is that they can be group administered (saving considerable time) whereas more comprehensive diagnostic tests are individually administered. The disadvantage is that they were not designed for the purpose of diagnosis, are typically shorter, and do not provide the depth of analysis possible with a diagnostic test. Because of the time and skill involved in administering, scoring, and interpreting diagnostic tests, as well as the fact that they are intended to identify specific deficiencies, it is neither desirable nor necessary to administer them to all students. They should be used as any other tool, as needed, for students apparently having learning problems. One frequently used diagnostic instrument is the Stanford Diagnostic Reading Test, which has different forms for different grade levels and is appropriate for use in elementary and junior high school. It is designed to identify specific difficulties and to facilitate the grouping of students according to their identified deficiencies. The skill areas measured include rate of reading, vocabulary, and word recognition skills. This test has generally received good reviews and appears to be a fairly valid and reliable instrument.

Standardized tests are appropriate for determining the exact nature of the problem when a student is having serious difficulty. Diagnosis should, however, be an ongoing process. In addition to administering a number of informal diagnostic instruments, the teacher should constantly be on the alert for signs of physical problems or learning difficulty. For example informal screening devices can be useful in detecting visual or hearing problems which may be the real reason for a student's low achievement. It is rather difficult to read, for example, when the words are fuzzy or drawkcab. Further, for the same reasons that teacher-made achievement tests are more valid indicators of achievement of what was actually taught, teacher-made diagnostic instruments may be more effective in identifying deficiencies following instruction. An informal reading diagnostic test, for example, can clarify which objectives or applications of objectives were not fully achieved. This information is especially important in hierarchic subjects such as mathematics where the learning of new skills is very much dependent on the achievement of previous skills. In addition to administering instruments, the teacher should be alert for early signs of difficulty. The earlier a problem can be detected, the easier it is to correct and the less cumulative damage is done.

Character and personality

Tests of character and personality are designed to measure characteristics of individuals along a number of dimensions and to assess feelings and attitudes toward self, others, and a variety of other activities, institutions, and situations. Such tests take many different forms—(written versus performance, individual versus group) although certain types are almost exclusively standardized (e.g. tests of certain personality variables such as aggression, anxiety, and introversion). As the above statements suggest, there are standardized tests to measure almost any aspect of personality you can think of. A brief perusal of Buros' *Mental Measurement*

Yearbooks should convince you of this.[12] Test titles such as the following appear in the various volumes (italics added): A–S Reaction Study: A Scale for Measuring *Ascendance-Submission* in Personality; The Cassel Group Level of *Aspiration* Test; the *Ego Strength* Q-Sort Test; *Human Relations* Inventory; the IPAT *Anxiety* Scale; and Vineland *Social Maturity* Scale. This is not to say that all such tests are developed to the point where they are appropriate for use in the schools—many are useful mainly for research—but they do exist.

A school testing program may well contain standardized tests of one or more character and personality variables such as a test of personal-social adjustment. While a teacher will not normally administer such a test, the results may be very useful to teachers and counselors in better understanding and working with students. Teachers, of course, may very well administer "home-made" tests of certain variables such as attitudes toward subject matter. Locally-developed instruments may also be used by personnel involved in other than student evaluation, e.g. curriculum evaluation and school-level evaluation. If an effort is designed to evaluate the Whoopee Reading System, a "new" curriculum, there obviously cannot be a standardized test available which measures attitudes toward the Whoopee Reading System.

Most tests of character and personality are nonprojective, or self-report, measures; such tests ask an individual to respond to a series of questions or statements. There is another category of such instruments referred to as projective tests. Projective tests were developed in an attempt to eliminate some of the major problems inherent in the use of self-report measures, such as the tendency of some respondents to give "socially acceptable" responses. The purposes of such tests are usually not obvious to respondents; the individual is typically asked to respond to ambiguous items. Since the intent of the test is not clear, conscious dishonesty of responses is reduced and respondents "project" their true feelings.

The most commonly used projective technique is the method of association. This technique asks the respondent to react to a stimulus such as a picture, inkblot, or word. Word-association tests are probably the most well known of the association techniques (tell me the first thing that comes to your mind!). Two of the most commonly used association tests are the Rorschach Ink Blot Test and the Thematic Apperception Test. The Rorschach Test presents the respondent with a series of inkblots and the respondent is asked to tell what he or she "sees." The Thematic Apperception Test presents the individual with a series of pictures; the respondent is then asked to tell a story about each picture.

Projective tests are utilized mainly by clinical psychologists and very infrequently in educational evaluation. They are not recommended for use in evaluation efforts partly because of their questionable validity and partly because the administration, scoring, and interpretation of projective tests require highly specialized training.

Personality

Measurement of personality traits is much more imprecise than measurement of other variables such as achievement. Still, information on such traits can be useful, especially for identifying students with severe problems. Personality

[12] Buros, O. K. (Ed.). *The eighth mental measurement yearbook.* Highland Park, N. J.: Gryphon, 1979. (This is the latest publication in a series which began in 1933).

measures are used much more frequently in research studies, but they do have a place in certain types of evaluation. School evaluation, for example, often includes administration of a personality inventory, the results being of interest to counselors and teachers. Although care should always be exercised in interpreting test results, this is especially important with personality measures. Serious decisions should not be made based on the results of one test; instead results should be considered together with other types of data. Their best use is as an initial screening device which indicates students who may have problems. This application is important because a student's mental condition may affect other aspects of her or his life including achievement and social relations with others. In fact many personality tests can be thought of as coping measures, i.e. measures designed to determine how well a person copes with, or adjusts to, his or her environment. A person who cannot cope with people may become introverted, a person who cannot cope with stress may exhibit high anxiety, and a person who cannot cope with frustration may score high on an aggression scale. Thus results of such measures may provide valuable insights into the behavior of certain individuals and suggest ways of dealing with it.

Personality inventories typically present lists of questions or statements which describe behaviors characteristic of certain personality traits, and the individual is asked to indicate (yes, no, undecided) whether the statement describes her or him. Some inventories are presented as simple checklists; the individual simply checks items which characterize her or him. An individual's score is based on the number of responses which are characteristic of the trait being measured. An introvert, for example, would be expected to respond "yes" to the statement "Playing solitaire is one of my favorite pastimes" and "no" to the statement "I love large parties." Inventories may be specific and measure only one trait, such as introversion-extroversion, or may be general and measure a number of traits. Since general inventories measure more than one trait at the same time, they are typically relatively long and take at least an hour to complete.

General inventories frequently used in education include the following: Adjective Check List; California Psychological Inventory; California Test of Personality; Edwards Personal Preference Schedule; Minnesota Multiphasic Personality Inventory, and Mooney Problem Check List. The California Test of Personality is a self-report inventory which has five series covering kindergarten to adult. Its primary purpose is to determine the extent to which a person is adjusting to her or his environment and is developing a normal, happy and socially effective personality. This test is considered to be one of the best of its kind. The Mooney Problem Check List is useful for identifying general problem areas; it is not designed for analyzing the depth and breadth of a problem. It is appropriate mainly for determining the major concerns of a group and secondarily for identifying the problems of individuals within the group.

One serious problem involved with the use of self-report inventories is the problem of accurate responses. Personality scores are only valid to the degree that the respondent is honest and selects responses which truly characterize him or her. A common phenomenon is the concept of a response set, which you may recall refers to the tendency of an individual to continually respond in a given way. A common response set is the tendency of an individual to select responses which she or he believes are the most socially acceptable. Whether response sets result from conscious or unconscious motives, they can seriously distort an appraisal of the individual's personality structure. Therefore, in utilizing such tests, every effort must be made to increase the honesty of responses.

Attitudes

Attitude scales attempt to determine what an individual believes, perceives, or feels. Attitudes toward self, others, and a variety of activities, institutions, and situations can be measured. Since attitudes are related to achievement (recall the discussion concerning the relationship between cognitive, affective and psychomotor outcomes), and since one of the basic goals of public education is the promotion of certain attitudes believed to be desirable in a democratic society, measurement of attitudes is a major concern in the public schools. Personnel at all levels are involved in assessing attitudes and providing activities conducive to the formation of desirable attitudes. Curriculum evaluation, for example, may be just as concerned with attitudes toward a curriculum as they are with resulting achievement levels. At the classroom level objectives related to attitudes and assessment of their achievement may be less formal, but the concern is there. It would be very surprising, for example, to find any teachers who would say that they could care less whether students hate their course. Teachers, of course, are more likely to assess attitudes with informal instruments, observation and sociometric techniques than with standardized attitude scales.

There are four basic types of attitude scales: Likert scales, semantic differential scales, Thurstone scales, and Guttman scales. The first two are used more often but you should at least be aware of the existence of the other two.

A *Likert scale* asks an individual to respond to a series of statements by indicating whether she or he strongly agrees (SA), agrees (A), is undecided (U), disagrees (D), or strongly disagrees (SD) with the statement.[13] Each response is associated with a point value and an individual's score is determined by summing the point values for each statement. For example, the following point values might be assigned to responses to positive statements: SA = 5, A = 4, U = 3, D = 2, SD = 1. For negative statements, the point values would be reversed, i.e., SA = 1, A = 2, and so on. An example of a positive statement might be "Short people are entitled to the same job opportunities as tall people." A high point value on a positively stated item would indicate a positive attitude, and a high total score on the test would be indicative of a positive attitude.

A *semantic differential scale* asks an individual to give a quantitative rating to the subject of the attitude scale on a number of bipolar adjectives such as good-bad, friendly-unfriendly, positive-negative. The respondent indicates the point on the continuum between the extremes which represents her or his attitude. Based on their research, the original developers of this approach reported that most adjective pairs represent one of three dimensions which they labeled evaluation (e.g. good-bad), potency (e.g. strong-weak), and activity (e.g. active-passive).[14] For example, on a scale concerning attitudes toward property taxes, the following items might be included:

Necessary ___ ___ ___ ___ ___ ___ ___ Unnecessary

Fair ___ ___ ___ ___ ___ ___ ___ Unfair

---

[13] Likert, R. A technique for the measurement of attitudes. *Archives of Psychology*, 1932, No. 140.
[14] Osgood, C. E., Suci, G. J., & Tannenbaum, P. H. *The measurement of meaning.* Urbana: University of Illinois Press, 1957.

In practice, however, these dimensions are frequently ignored and/or replaced by other dimensions thought to be more appropriate in a particular evaluation situation.

Each position on a continuum has an associated score value; by totalling score values for all items, it can be determined whether the respondent's attitude is positive or negative. Semantic differential scales usually have 5 to 7 intervals with a neutral attitude being assigned a score value of 0.[15] For the above items, the score values would be as follows:

Necessary   ___ ___ ___ ___ ___ ___ ___   Unnecessary
             3   2   1   0   -1   -2   -3

Fair   ___ ___ ___ ___ ___ ___ ___   Unfair
        3   2   1   0   -1   -2   -3

A person who checked the first interval (i.e. 3) on both of these items would be indicating a very positive attitude toward property taxes (fat chance!).

A Thurstone scale asks an individual to select from a list of statements which represent different points of view those with which he or she is in agreement. Each item has an associated point value between 1 and 11; point values for each item are determined by averaging the values of the items assigned by a number of "judges." An individual's attitude score is the average point value of all the statements checked by that individual.[16] A Guttman scale also asks respondents to agree or disagree with a number of statements. A Guttman scale, however, attempts to determine whether an attitude is unidimensional; it is unidimensional if it produces a cumulative scale. In a cumulative scale, an individual who agrees with a given statement also agrees with all related preceding statements, i.e. if you agree with statement 3, you also agree with statements 2 and 1.[17]

Measures of "attitude toward self" are referred to as measures of self-concept. Measures of self-concept are used in both educational research studies and educational evaluations, especially those designed to investigate the effects of self-concept on variables such as achievement and, conversely, the effects of various curricula and teaching methods on self-concept. Entire curricula, for example, have been developed with the major theme of enhancing students' self-concepts, in the belief that how students feel about themselves affects their achievement. One measure of self-concept which is frequently used is the Piers-Harris Children's Self Concept Scale (How I Feel About Myself). It is considered to be a reasonably good measure of self-concept.

Rating scales are also used to measure attitudes toward others. Such scales ask an individual to rate another individual on a number of behavioral dimensions. There are two basic types of such rating scales. One type is composed of items which ask an individual to rate another on a continuum (good to bad, excellent to poor). The second type asks the individual to rate another on a number of items by selecting the most appropriate response category (for example, excellent, above average, average, below average, poor). Two problems associated with the use of such scales have already been discussed—the halo effect and the generosity

[15] For further discussion of this approach, see: Snider, J. G., & Osgood, C. E. *Semantic differential technique: A sourcebook.* Chicago: Aldine, 1969.
[16] Thurstone, L. L., & Chave, E. J. *The measurement of attitude.* Chicago: The University of Chicago Press, 1929.
[17] Guttman, L. The basis for scaleogram analysis. In S. Stouffer, et al. (Eds.), *Measurement and prediction.* Princeton: Princeton University Press, 1950.

error. Of course attitude scales in general suffer from the same problems as personality inventories. One can never be sure that individuals are expressing their true attitude rather than, for example, a "socially acceptable" attitude. Again, the validity of decisions is directly related to the truthfulness of the responses made by individuals. Thus, whenever attitude scales are used, every effort must be made to reduce potential problems by giving appropriate directions to those completing the instruments.

Creativity

Measures of creativity are more often used in research studies than in evaluation efforts. Because they may be used in certain types of evaluation (e.g. those involved with curriculum areas such as art and music), and because they are so interesting, they are included in this section.

Tests of creativity are really tests designed to measure those personality characteristics that are related to creative behavior. One trait measured is referred to as divergent thinking. Unlike convergent thinkers, who tend to look for one right answer, divergent thinkers tend to seek alternatives. J. P. Guilford, probably the most well-known researcher in this area, has developed a number of widely used tests of divergent thinking. One such test asks the individual to list as many uses as he or she can think of for an ordinary brick. Think about it and list a few. If you listed uses such as build a school, build a house, build a library, etc., then you are not very creative; all of those uses are really the same, namely, you can use a brick to build something. Now, if you are creative, you listed different uses such as break a window, drown a rat, and hit a robber on the head. Another test asks individuals to compose plot titles for brief stories. The titles are then rated for their originality. One of the stories concerns a missionary in Africa who is captured by cannibals. He is given a choice of being boiled alive or marrying a princess of the tribe. He chooses death. Take a few minutes and think of some possible titles. Perhaps you came up with a title like "Missionary in Africa," "The Cannibal and the Missionary," or "Boiled in Africa." If you are especially clever, you may have come up with a title like "Better Boil Than Goil" (my favorite!), "A Mate Worse Than Death," or "He Left a Dish for a Pot." The more clever titles a person comes up with, the higher the score on originality, which is one aspect of divergent thinking.[18]

Another well-known research in this area is E. P. Torrance. The Torrance Tests of Creativity include graphic, or pictorial, items as well as verbal items. Tests are scored in terms of four factors: fluency, flexibility, originality, and elaboration.[19] The Torrance tests involve tasks such as listing as many uses as possible for an object and coming up with titles for pictures.

Interest

Interest can be assessed informally in the classroom in the same ways that attitude can, through the use of informal, teacher-made measures (checklists and rating scales) and through observation. Knowing students' interests can be of

---

[18] Guilford, J. P. *The nature of human intelligence.* New York: McGraw-Hill, 1967, *and* Guilford, J. P. Three faces of intellect. *American Psychologist,* 1959, 14(8), 469–479.
[19] Torrance, E. P. *Torrance Tests of Creative Thinking.* Princeton, N. J.: Personnel Press, 1966.

value to the teacher in promoting motivation and in making learning activities more relevant to students. At the school level, an ideal testing program includes a standardized interest inventory. The results of such tests are of interest to all school personnel, especially counselors. A standardized interest inventory asks an individual to indicate personal likes and dislikes, such as the kinds of activities she or he prefers to engage in. Responses are generally compared to known interest patterns. The most widely used type of standardized interest measure is the vocational interest inventory. Such inventories typically ask the respondent to indicate preferences with respect to leisure activities such as hobbies. The respondent's pattern of interest is then compared to the patterns of interest which are typical of successful persons in various occupational fields. The individual can then be counseled as to the fields in which he or she is likely to be happy and successful.

Two frequently used inventories are the Strong Vocational Interest Blank (SVIB) and the Kuder Preference Record—Vocational. The SVIB measures interest in a number of professional and business fields. It presents numerous activities and the respondent indicates whether she or he likes, dislikes, or has no opinion regarding each activity. These responses are then compared to those of persons in various professional and business occupations. The Kuder Preference Record—Vocational measures interest in broad occupational areas such as mechanical, scientific, persuasive, and social science. Each item lists three activities and respondents indicate which activity they would most like to engage in and which activity they would least like to engage in.

Aptitude

Aptitude tests are measures of potential. They are used to predict how well someone is likely to perform in a future situation. Tests of general aptitude are variously referred to as scholastic aptitude tests, intelligence tests, and tests of general mental ability. Since intelligence tests have developed a bad reputation in recent years, the term "scholastic aptitude" has become more popular. The intents of all such tests, however, are basically the same. Aptitude tests are also available to predict a person's likely level of performance following some specific future instruction or training. Aptitude tests are available in the form of individual tests in specific areas, such as algebra, and in the form of batteries which measure aptitude in several related areas. While virtually all aptitude tests are standardized and are administered as part of a school testing program, the results are useful to teachers, counselors, and administrators.

There is a difference of opinion among educators concerning whether teachers should have knowledge of students' general aptitude. Some feel that such knowledge is apt to bias a teacher and result in stereotyping of students. Others feel that such information can (1) help the teacher to set more realistic expectations for students, (2) assist the teacher in planning objectives and activities appropriate to students' abilities, and (3) facilitate the identification of underachievers. While both points of view have merit, it would seem that all in all the benefits to be derived from having such knowledge outweigh the potential problems. Counselors, of course, use such information to better understand individual students and to provide better guidance concerning, for example, career aspirations. Administrative decisions are also facilitated by knowledge of the general aptitude levels of students. Such data may be input, for example, for a decision to place a child in a special class, e.g. a class for the gifted or a class for the educable mentally retarded. It must be reemphasized, however, that serious decisions such as those noted above should be based on many different kinds of data, not just on the results of an aptitude test.

General aptitude

There are a variety of tests which fall into this category representing a variety of different definitions of general aptitude (or scholastic aptitude, or intelligence, or what have you). While the basic purpose of all such tests is to predict future academic performance, there is disagreement as to the factors which are being measured and are serving as the predictors. The term is variously defined to include variables such as abstract reasoning, problem solving, and verbal fluency. General aptitude tests typically ask the individual to perform a variety of verbal and nonverbal tasks which measure the individual's ability to apply knowledge and solve problems. Such tests generally yield three scores—an overall score, a verbal score, and a quantitative score—representing, for example, a total IQ, a verbal IQ, and a quantitative IQ. While general aptitude tests are intended to be measures of innate ability or potential, they appear actually to measure current ability; there is also some evidence to suggest that scores are to some degree affected by an individual's past and present environment. However, since they seem to do a reasonable job of predicting future academic success, and are in that sense measures of "potential," they are very useful to educators.

General aptitide tests may be group tests or individually administered tests. Each type has its relative advantages and disadvantages. Group tests are more convenient to administer, save considerable time, and provide an estimate of academic potential that is adequate for many purposes. Batteries are also available which comprise a number of tests suitable for different grade and age levels. Since tests in a battery are similarly structured, they permit the study of intellectual growth over time and comparisons among different levels. A commonly used group-administered battery is the California Test of Mental Maturity (CTMM). The CTMM has six levels and can be administered to all school-age children, college students, and adults. It includes 12 subtests representing 5 factors: logical reasoning, spatial relations, numerical reasoning, verbal concepts, and memory. The results include a language IQ, a nonlanguage IQ, and a total IQ. While some of the subtests are not as good as they might be, overall the test is considered to be a respectable measure of potential. Another frequently administered group test is the Otis-Lennon Mental Ability Test, which also has six levels and is designed for school-age children in grades K–12. The Otis-Lennon Mental Ability Test measures four factors—verbal comprehension, verbal reasoning, figurative reasoning, and quantitative reasoning—and is also considered to be a respectable measure of potential.

A serious disadvantage of group tests is that they require a great deal of reading. Thus, students with poor reading ability are at a disadvantage and may receive scores which reflect, for example, an IQ level lower than their true level. Individual tests, on the other hand, require much less reading. Another advantage of individual tests is that since they are administered one-on-one, the examiner is aware of factors such as illness or anxiety which might be adversely affecting the individual's ability to respond. The main disadvantage of individual tests is that they are considerably more difficult to administer and score; trained personnel are required to administer them and to score them. However, if there is any reason to question the validity of group tests for a particular group, very young children for example, an indiuidal test should be used. Probably the most well known of the individually administered tests is the Stanford-Binet Intelligence Scale; it has been used extensively, and there is considerable data concerning its validity. More and more, however, the Wechsler scales are being utilized. While the Stanford-Binet is appropriate only for older adolescents and adults, Wechsler scales are available to measure the intelligence of persons from the age of 4 to adulthood: the Wechsler Preschool and Primary Scale of Intelligence (WPPSI)—ages 4–61/2; the Wechsler Intelligence Scale for Children (WISC)—ages 5–15; and the Wechsler Adult Intelligence Scale (WAIS)—older adolescents and adults. As an example, the WISC is a scholastic aptitude test which includes verbal tests (e.g. general information, vocabulary) and performance tests (e.g. picture completion, object assembly). While the Stanford-Binet yields one IQ score, the Wechsler scales also yield a number of subscores.

As mentioned previously, there is evidence to indicate that IQ scores are affected by the individual's past and present environment. The validity of IQ tests for certain minority groups has been questioned, and such tests have been accused of being culturally biased. This criticism has prompted the development of "culture-fair" IQ tests. Culture-fair tests attempt to exclude culturally related items, such as items which include words that might not be familiar to certain groups of individuals. In fact, most of these tests do not require the use of language. Interestingly, however, there is some recent evidence which suggests that such tests may not be as culture-fair as originally believed; nonverbal tests may in fact be less culture-fair than verbal tests. The Culture-Fair Intelligence Test (ages 4 to adult) is probably the most frequently used culture-fair test.

Specific aptitude

As the term is generally used, aptitude tests attempt to predict the level of performance which can be expected of an individual following future instruction or training in a specific area or areas. Aptitude tests are available for a wide variety of academic and nonacademic areas such as mathematics and mechanical reasoning. As with tests of general aptitude, they are used by teachers, counselors, and administrators, and for the same reasons. They are also used as a basis for grouping, in math classes for example. Specific aptitude tests are also frequently used in research and evaluation studies. Their most common use in this regard is probably to equate groups which are going to be compared on achievement after receiving different treatments or curricula. If groups are different in aptitude to begin with, then final achievement differences might be attributable to this initial difference rather than to differences in treatment or curriculum. While most aptitude tests are standardized, written tests, some are performance tests. The latter are appropriate when the students taking the test have an English language difficulty, foreign students for example.

Aptitude tests are available for a number of specific areas such as algebra, music, and mechanical ability. Multi-aptitude batteries, which measure aptitudes in several related areas, are available for the assessment of both academic and non-academic aptitudes. Multi-aptitude batteries include a number of subtests which have been normed on the same group. This permits comparisons across subtest scores in order to determine a student's relative strengths and weaknesses. The Sequential Tests of Educational Progress (STEP) battery, an academic aptitude battery, includes tests on reading, writing, mathematics, and science, among others. The Differential Aptitude Tests (DAT), on the other hand, include tests on space relations, mechanical reasoning, and clerical speed and accuracy, among others, and is designed to predict success in various job areas.

Readiness tests

Readiness, or prognostic, tests are sometimes classified as aptitude tests, sometimes as achievement tests. Aptitude does seem to be a more appropriate categorization, however, since a readiness test is administered prior to instruction or training in a specific area in order to determine whether and to what degree a student is ready for, or will profit from, instruction. Due to increased interest in the basic skills, reading readiness tests have been given more attention than other types. Reading readiness tests typically include measurement of variables such as auditory discrimination, visual discrimination, and motor ability. The results of such a test are used to identify students who, for example, are not ready for formal reading instruction due to physical immaturity. This information can be applied in working with individual students and gives direction for grouping. Readiness batteries have also been developed to assess readiness in a number of areas. The Metropolitan Readiness Test, for example, was designed to measure the degree to which students starting school have developed the skills and abilities that contribute to readiness for first grade instruction in areas such as reading, arithmetic, and writing. Given the state of the art, i.e. the relative newness of readiness tests, the Metropolitan Readiness Test is considered to be a good test of its type.[20]

Performance standards

Performance standards are the criteria to which the results of measurement are compared in order to interpret them. The term "standard" is used here to mean "basis of comparison," not "model," or "ideal performance." A test score in and of itself means nothing. If I tell you that Hermie got 18 correct, what does that tell you about Hermie's performance? Absolutely nothing. Now if I tell you that the average score on the test was 15, at least you know that he did better than average. If instead I tell you that a score of 17 was required for a mastery classification, you don't know anything about the performance of the rest of the class, but you do know that Hermie attained mastery. The above "ifs" actually illustrate the two basic ways in which results can be interpreted: with norm-referenced standards and criterion-referenced standards. When the former are used, we use the term

[20] For a detailed description of a number of achievement, character and personality, and aptitude tests, see: Mehrens, W. A., & Lehmann, I. J. *Standardized tests in education.* New York: Holt, Rinehart and Winston, 1975.

norm-referenced measurement (NRM) or refer to a norm-referenced test (NRT); when the latter are used, we use the term criterion-referenced measurement (CRM) or refer to a criterion-referenced test (CRT). Basically, an NRT interprets a person's score by comparing it to the scores of others who took the same test. A CRT interprets a person's score by comparing it to a predetermined criterion.

Norm-referenced standards

Any test, standardized or locally-developed, which reports and interprets each score in terms of its relative position with respect to other scores on the same test, is *norm-referenced*. If your total IQ score based on the Wechsler Adult Intelligence Scale is 100, for example, the interpretation is that your measured intelligence is average, average *compared to* scores of persons in the norm group. The raw scores resulting from administration of a standardized NRT are typically converted to some other index which indicates relative position. One such equivalent probably familiar to you is a percentile. A given *percentile* indicates the percentage of the scores that were lower than the percentile's corresponding score. For example, a raw score of 42 on an achievement test might be equivalent to the 54th percentile, which would mean that 54 percent of the raw scores were lower than 42. Thus, if you scored at the 95th percentile, your score was higher than 95 percent of the scores. If your score was "average" what do you think your percentile would be? Right! The 50th percentile. Of course, none of these figures says anything about your absolute achievement. There is no indication of what you know and can do or do not know and cannot do. The only interpretations are in terms of your achievement compared to the achievement of others; you know more than average, a lot less than average, and so forth.

The normal curve concept

Norm-referenced standards are based on the assumption that measured traits involve normal curve properties. While the normal curve and its characteristics will be discussed in a later chapter, the basic concept can be explained here in folksy terms. The idea is that a measured trait, let us say math aptitude, exists in different amounts in different people. Some people have a lot of it, some have a little of it, and most have some amount called an "average" amount. Now, if you gave a math aptitude test to lots and lots of people, and plotted their scores, you would get a normal curve, sometimes referred to as a bell curve (see Figure 6.2). As Figure 6.2 illustrates, most of the scores (the highest frequency) are average, fewer scores are above or below average, and very few are way above or way below average. If a trait forms a normal curve, then the percentages in each section, or division, are constant. The average group always contains approximately 65% of the scores (68.26 to be exact); the above average group and below average group each contain approximately 15% of the scores; and the way above and way below groups each contain approximately 2.5% of the scores. Some of you may be familiar with "grading on the curve." In its extreme form the above percentages are applied to scores in order to determine grades. Thus the top 2–3% of the scores become A's the next 15% B's the next 65% C's and so forth. The grades are assigned irrespec-

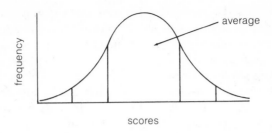

figure 6.2
A normal curve

tive of actual performance levels. If everyone does lousy, there are still some A's, and if everyone does swell, there are still failures. If 88 (out of 100) is the lowest score on the test, it is a failing grade! Boooo!

Thus we can see one problem with norm-referenced standards. Some people can get wonderful grades, or high percentiles, without necessarily exhibiting a high level of performance. Conversely, some can get poor grades or low percentiles without necessarily exhibiting a very low level of performance. This is less likely to be a problem when a large comparison group is involved because the odds are good that a wide range of performance is actually present. It is more of a problem in a more homogeneous group. Applying norm-referenced standards within a very homogeneous group, for example, could result in a student in an honors English class getting an F and a student in a remedial reading class getting an A. Now there may be good reasons why we would want to do this (motivation, for example), but the problem is that such equivalents are virtually impossible to interpret in terms of actual achievement or level of performance.

Score variability

With few exceptions, standardized tests are norm-referenced. Norm groups are selected with the intention of having a representative group with a wide spread of scores with respect to the trait being measured. As mentioned previously, to the degree that students taking a test are different from those in the norm group, to that degree are results subject to misinterpretation. The need for a lot of score variation, that is, a wide spread of scores, is further emphasized by the fact that most of our present-day techniques for analyzing scores require score variability. As we shall see in the next chapter, for example, all classical approaches to computing test reliability require score variability. Thus, when standardized tests are designed and developed, the intent is to include items that will "spread people out." If, for example, a tryout of a new test reveals a group of items that almost everyone gets correct (or incorrect), they will probably be eliminated; if everyone answers the same, the variability of scores is decreased and variability is the objective.

While this may not sound "fair," it does serve a purpose. The results of standardized tests are frequently used for classification or selection purposes; a good spread of scores facilitates the decision-making process. To use an example which may be painfully familiar to you, scores on The Graduate Record Exam

(GRE) are frequently used as a criterion for admission to graduate school. *Everyone* who wants to cannot go to graduate school because there is not enough room and there are not enough resources. Scores on the GRE have been shown to be related to some degree to performance in graduate school. Using GRE scores for selection is better than having students draw straws (probably!). Therefore, a high score on the GRE increases the probability of admission and a low score decreases the probability of admission. If the GRE did not discriminate between people, that is, if scores were very homogeneous, it could not be used for selection purposes. Similarly, the results of standardized tests are used for purposes such as grouping according to aptitude, determining who will receive scholarships, and counseling students with respect to career decisions. These uses of the results are only possible because the tests do a good job of ordering students on a wide continuum of performance.

Applications of NRTs

Due to some of the problems discussed, there is opposition to the use of norm-referenced standards. However, while they should not be used exclusively, they do serve several useful purposes in addition to those described above. People *are* different. They *do* possess different traits to varying degrees. It is helpful to both the individual and society to know where an individual's relative strengths and weaknesses lie. Furthermore, the "real world" is norm-referenced and students should learn to adjust to that fact. Employers, for example, do not say, "If you do X amount of work, or just do your best, you will get a nice raise." Rather, those who do the best work get the best raises (at least theoretically!).

Some of you with good memories may be wondering how norm-referenced standards fit into mastery systems. In such a system, theoretically at least, nearly everyone achieves mastery; they just take different amounts of time to get there. The mastery concept is a good one for certain "essentials." But even in such a system there is variability. If a mastery score is 16 out of 20, then some students will score 20, some 19, some 18, some 17, and some 16; and the amount of time taken to achieve mastery will vary tremendously. Further, knowing the performance of students in a given class, even if all students are achieving all objectives, does not tell us how well those students are doing compared to the rest of the world (figuratively speaking!). This information is valuable feedback for teachers and other school personnel, and it is information that individual students have a right to know. Thus, while the results of an NRT do not tell us much about actual performance, they do provide information regarding relative performance which is of value to individuals for personal reasons and for decision-making.

Criterion-referenced standards

Any test which reports and interprets each score in terms of an absolute standard is *criterion-referenced*. In other words, interpretation of one person's score has nothing to do with anybody else's score. A score is compared with a standard of performance, not with scores of other persons. When criterion-referenced standards are used, everyone taking the test may do "well" or everyone may do "poorly."

The definition problem

In a 1978 review of the literature on criterion-referenced standards, the following was noted:

> According to the most recent count, there are more than 600 references on the topic of criterion-referenced testing. Unfortunately, it seems that there are almost as many ideas about what a criterion-referenced test is as there are contributors to the field.[21]

How true. And, in fact, if you were to read any 50 references on the topic in an attempt to deduce a definition, you would probably come up with one that was "incorrect," given the intent of the original writers on the subject. In other words, there are some definitions of criterion-referenced measurement which match the theoretical or ideal definition as set forth by the originators of the term, but there are a host of definitions which basically agree with each other but not with the theoretically correct definition.

As originally defined by Glaser in 1963, criterion-referenced measures are those which "depend upon an absolute standard of quality" as contrasted with norm-referenced measures which "depend upon a relative standard."[22] In 1970 he expanded on his original definition by defining a criterion-referenced test as "one that is deliberately constructed to yield measurement that is directly interpretable in terms of specified performance standards."[23] According to this definition, criterion-referenced measurement is essentially the same as what is referred to as domain-referenced measurement, and in fact, a CRT is used to compare a person's performance with a well-defined behavior domain.[24] A well-defined behavior domain, according to Popham, refers to a class of learner behaviors (such as the ability to multiply correctly any pair of single-digit numbers) rather than a specific behavior (such as can multiply correctly 5×7). And therein lies the basis of the confusion that has arisen concerning criterion-referenced measurement. If all objectives were expressed in terms of clearly-defined *classes* of behavior, then criterion-referenced measurement would be, in essence, objectives-referenced measurement. But such is not the case. In all too many instances, objectives have been overly specific, of the "can multiply 5×7" variety.

In many cases this distinction has been ignored in discussing CRM and it has been defined as measurement in which test items are keyed to objectives. Whether such definitions have been due to misconceptions about CRM or whether they are based implicitly on a "class" definition of objectives (no pun intended!) is hard to say. In any case, measurement keyed to objectives is objectives-referenced measurement (ORM); whether ORM = CRM depends mostly on the nature and description of the objectives. It should be pointed out that there are

---

[21]Hambleton, R. K., Swaminathan, H., Algina, J., & Coulson, D. B. Criterion-referenced testing and measurement: A review of technical issues and developments. *Review of Educational Research*, Winter, 1978, *48*(1), 1–47.

[22] Glaser, R. Instructional technology and the measurement of learning outcomes. *American Psychologist*, 1963, *18*, 519–521.

[23] Glaser, R., & Nitko, A. J. Measurement in learning and instruction. In R. L. Thorndike (Ed.), *Educational measurement*. Washington, D.C.: American Council on Education, 1971.

[24] Millman, J. Criterion-referenced measurement. In W. J. Popham (Ed.), *Evaluation in education: Current applications*. Berkeley, Calif.: McCutchan, 1974 *and* Popham, W. J. *Educational evaluation*. Englewood Cliffs, N. J.: Prentice-Hall, 1975.

highly respected evaluation specialists (Popham, for example) who hold the view that no objective can include all the features that a good domain description includes without being unnecessarily long and cumbersome. This, of course, is a matter for discussion as is the need for highly defined behavioral domains. The fact remains, however, that most of the tests that are called criterion-referenced are technically objectives-referenced. Again, whether this represents (1) misconceptions about CRM, (2) a "class" definition of objectives, or perhaps (3) gradual evolution of the meaning of CRM, is hard to say. To further confuse you (you really want to hear this, right?), the term "content-referenced measurement" is occasionally used; it is closer to CRM in intent and involves analysis of objectives in order to define the appropriate content area, and the development of the appropriate number of items that are required to measure achievement of that area.

You may be thinking, what is the big deal? What difference does it make? Well, it does not make any difference what we call a test, but it does make a difference how the test was developed. The difference is in the interpretation of results. If a test contains items based on objectives of the "can multiply 5 × 7" variety, then the results are very limited in generalizability in terms of what behaviors have been achieved. On the other hand, if a test contains items which represent a class of behaviors (e.g., "can multiply any pair of one-digit numbers), the results are generalizable to the whole class. For a number of reasons, the second type of test is clearly preferable. Keeping in mind that differences, if any, between CRTs and NRTs are really differences in the objectives' descriptions upon which they are based, we will henceforth use the term criterion-referenced to include all situations in which the results are interpreted in terms of an absolute standard.

Definition of criterion

Another common apparent misconception about CRTs concerns the definition of the term "criterion," as in criterion-referenced measurement. Many have interpreted it to mean some required, minimum level of performance or cut-off score, e.g. pass = 75%. Livingston, for example, referred to a CRT as a test for which each person's score is compared to a specified criterion *score* (italics added).[25] However, the intent of the original writers on the topic was for "criterion" to refer to a domain of behaviors measuring an objective, not to a number. Actually, a CRT may or may not have a cut-off score. A CRT with a cut-off score is a mastery test. Thus, we may say that Homer has or has not achieved mastery. Of course, as was discussed with respect to minimum competency testing, setting a minimum cut-off score is a tricky business. If it is set too low (or too high), you run the risk of classifying some individuals as "masters" when in reality they are not—false positives, (or of classifying some as "nonmasters" when in reality they are—false negatives).

Interestingly, there is experimental evidence which suggests that increasing the required cut-off score, increases performance as measured by achievement tests, retention tests, and transfer tests.[26] On the other hand, a high cut-off score for mastery requires more time and resources in order to bring students up to that

---

[25] Livingston, S. A. A classical test-theory approach to criterion-referenced tests. Paper presented at the American Educational Research Association Convention, Chicago, 1972.
[26] Block, J. H. Student learning and the setting of mastery performance standards. *Educational Horizons*, 1972, *50*, 183–190.

level. Thus Millman has suggested that a lower cut-off score be set when remediation costs are high. Millman has also suggested a number of methods for determining what the cut-off score should be.[27] Ideally, for example, one could have a group of experts determine the minimum number of items that must be correct for mastery and for indicating that a student is ready for the next objective. In reality, of course, the teacher typically makes such decisions based on professional judgment. As Hambleton, Swaminathan, Algina, and Coulson have pointed out, there are a variety of proposed methods for determining cut-off scores and application of different methods results in different cut-off scores.[28] Since which approach is the most valid has not yet been determined, such decisions must for the time being continue to be made on logical bases.

An interesting question was raised by Airasian and Madaus: If test scores range from 0-100 and Ziggy averages 75 and gets a "C", is this percentage grading approach an example of criterion-referenced measurement?[29] Strictly speaking, the answer is no. You might think yes since Ziggy's score is not related to the scores of other students. But the key phrase is standards of comparison for interpretation. The tests, for example, may not be based on objectives at all but rather on some vaguely defined content area. Thus, we would not be able to interpret Ziggy's score in terms of any class of behaviors.

Criterion-referenced tests are not necessarily mastery tests and, in fact, many are not. CRTs can be used to assess various levels of proficiency. One of those levels is typically defined as a minimally acceptable performance as indicated by the corresponding objective. For example, an objective may indicate that students will be able to state the past tense of all regular verbs and that a score of 7 out of 10 is required to say that a student has achieved the objective. In a nonmastery system actual scores on the CRT may vary from 0–10, representing a wide range of achievement. Depending on the proportion of the students that does achieve satisfactorily, a decision is made either to "move on" or to devote additional instructional time to the objective. Thus, in a nonmastery CRM system the emphasis is on the performance of the group with respect to the criterion instead of the performance of each student.

Applications of CRTs

While the basic concept of criterion-referenced measurement is not new, interest in, and use of, CRTs grew steadily following Glaser's 1963 article. The growth in use of CRTs understandably paralleled the increased interest in objectives. Their popularity was also fostered as a result of rising criticism of the use of norm-referenced measures, especially standardized ones, for making judgments about people. Even critics of testing, however, concede that for certain purposes they are necessary—licensing of physicians, for example, based on demonstration that they can perform the required tasks. For those purposes, CRM is more appropriate than NRM. It matters little, for example, if a doctor was "above average" in surgery if she or he cannot correctly remove a ruptured appendix.

---

[27] Millman, J. Passing scores and test lengths for domain-referenced measures. *Review of Educational Research*, 1973, 43, 205–216.
[28] See footnote 20.
[29] Airasian, P. W., & Madaus, G. F. Criterion-referenced testing in the classroom. *NCME: Measurement in Education*, Fall, 1972, 3(4), 1–8.

Enthusiasm for CRTs varies widely. Of all nationally known evaluation specialists, Ebel is probably the least intrigued with the whole concept. His position is probably best summarized by the following quote:

> Criterion-referenced measurement may be practical in those few areas of achievement that focus on cultivation of a high degree of skill in the exercise of a limited number of abilities. Where the emphasis is on knowledge and understanding, effective use of criterion-referenced measurements seem much less likely, for knowledge and understanding consist of a complex fabric that owes its strength and beauty to an infinity of tiny fibers of relationship. Knowledge does not come in discrete chunks that can be defined and identified separately.[30]

The majority opinion, however, is that CRTs are useful and perhaps even more appropriate than NRTs in a number of situations. If nothing else, objectives and CRTs give direction to instruction and measurement. CRTs are probably most appropriate as locally-developed measures since they are developed to measure exactly what was taught. For certain instructional systems (e.g., mastery, individualized) CRTs are the only appropriate measurement devices since attention is focused on what each student can or cannot do. The results of CRTs also provide valuable input for program revision. Since CRTs permit pinpointing of areas of difficulty with respect to specific objectives, corresponding instructional strategies and materials can be readily identified and modified.

Theoretically, if properly developed, CRTs can be very useful in evaluating educational programs, either individually or comparatively.

Standardized CRTs are a relatively new phenomenon. Instead of giving raw score equivalents such as percentiles, standardized CRTs typically report results in terms of the number of items correct or as a percentage of the possible total. In general, however, development and validation information has been inadequate or not available, thus making meaningful interpretation of results difficult or impossible. In other words, procedures for determining content and for field-testing developed tests are fuzzy in many cases. In a 1978 issue of *How To Evaluate Educational Programs*, the editors described a detailed analysis of standardized tests.[31] A large number of publishers was contacted and information was solicited concerning reading and math CRTs. Information requested included sample tests at available grade levels; corresponding directions for administering and scoring the tests; all documentation data, such as manuals, field-test reports, and expert reviews; information on any special features such as cassette recorded directions; and cost information. Based on responses, 28 CRTs were identified for which there was adequate data for review purposes. Whenever necessary, publishers were contacted by telephone for clarification. As a result of their analysis, they were unable to find a single available CRT suitable for use in large-scale evaluation. One basic reason for this is that many of them were designed for classroom use, not for program evaluation. As a consequence, they yield much more data and take much more time to administer than is necessary or manageable in program evaluation. While standardized tests are usually more appropriate for levels of evaluation beyond the classroom, standardized CRTs do not seem to have

[30] Ebel, R. L. *Essentials of educational measurement.* Englewood Cliffs, N. J.: Prentice-Hall, 1979.
[31] Fink, A., & Kosecoff, J. (Eds.). How to consider criterion referenced tests for evaluation. *How To Evaluate Education Programs,* 1978, 2(5), 1–7.

evolved to the point where they can be considered a viable alternative to norm-referenced measures.

CRTs have come a long way and they still have a long way to go. The concept is a good one with many potential applications. While much theorizing and experimentation has taken place, there are still many fuzzy areas. As you have probably figured out by now, this book contains criterion-referenced measurement. The "task" at the beginning of each part represents a major objective and the "performance criteria" at the end of each part represent the criterion, or domain of expected behaviors. While the description of the criterion may not be detailed enough to satisfy some, it does represent a level of specificity that is practical, manageable, and sufficient for instructional evaluation purposes.

NRTs versus CRTs: summary

You have just digested (or choked on!) a lot of information. A brief review seems in order. The basic difference between an NRT and a CRT is in the interpretations of results—an NRT uses a relative standard and a CRT uses an absolute standard. On a CRT, one's performance is judged on its own merits, not in relation to the performance of others. Since the purpose of an NRT is to differentiate among individuals, score variability is very important. On the other hand, since the purpose of a CRT is to determine level of proficiency with respect to knowledge or skill, variability is irrelevant or even undesirable; considerable variability typically indicates a number of persons who are not achieving the intended objectives. Relatedly, an NRT contains items that discriminate, that is, items that are neither too easy nor too difficult. A CRT contains whatever items are necessary to measure achievement of the intended objective. Also, an NRT is more concerned with the performance of groups than with the performance of individuals. A CRT is more concerned with the performance of individuals.

Interestingly, NRTs and CRTs *look* alike. You probably could not tell by looking at a test whether it was an NRT or a CRT. The differences are in the purposes for which each is constructed and in the interpretation of results. Neither one is to be preferred in all situations. NRT versus CRT debates are not very productive. Which is more appropriate depends upon the situation and the decisions to be made. CRTs are more appropriate for student evaluation conducted by the teacher since it focuses on exactly what was taught. The results are also useful for ongoing revision of instructional procedures. NRTs are more appropriate for assessing the performance of larger groups such as are involved in school-level evaluation. The results of NRTs are useful for student guidance purposes and for classification or grouping decisions. NRTs, however, are appropriate at fewer stages than are CRTs. NRTs are typically given at the beginning and the end of an effort, e.g., the beginning and end of a school year. Certain NRTs, such as diagnostic instruments, may be used during the process phase. CRTs, on the other hand, can be used as pretests and posttests, as well as tests of entry behavior and progress tests (tests which can be administered as often as deemed necessary).

Anderson has suggested that almost all measurement has a norm-referenced base since even criterion-referenced standards are based on norm-referenced information.[32] To use Anderson's example, 50 words per minute (WPM)

---

[32] Anderson, S. B. Criterion-referenced measurement. In Anderson, S. B., Ball, S., Murphy, R. T., & Associates, *Encyclopedia of educational evaluation*. San Francisco: Jossey-Bass, 1976.

with no more than 2 errors may be set as the minimum standard for students to receive credit in a typing course. Sounds criterion-referenced, right? But, the reason we set these standards instead of 10 or 150 WPM is because these speeds do not reflect typical or average performance. Further, we *are* interested in variability recognizing that a person who types 80 WPM is a better typist than one who types 51 WPM. The point is well taken, interesting, and food for thought.

part 3 **summary**

6 classification of tests

Purpose and process

Uses of measurement

1 Posttesting is for the purpose of determining the degree to which objectives (formal or informal) have been achieved.
2 Pretests provide guidance for future activities as well as a basis of comparison for posttest results.
3 There are many other purposes for which testing is conducted, e.g. to determine if assumed prerequisites have indeed been achieved.
4 Decisions must be made in the planning phase concerning what will be measured, when, and how much total time will be allotted to testing.
5 A reasonable guideline is to collect enough relevant data to validly make intended decisions and not to collect extraneous data which would be "nice to have" but not necessary.
6 If instruments are to be selected from among those available, selections should be made during the planning phase, mainly to insure that they will be on hand at the appropriate time.

Data collection

7 There are three major ways to collect data: (1) administer a standardized instrument, (2) administer a locally-developed instrument, or (3) record naturally available data.
8 The time it takes to select an appropriate instrument, (usually from among standardized, commercially available instruments) is inevitably less than the time it takes to develop an instrument which measures the same thing.
9 There are thousands of standardized instruments available which yield a wide variety of data for a wide variety of purposes.
10 In general, it is usually a good idea to determine whether there is a suitable instrument already available before jumping into instrument development.
11 There are situations, however, for which use of available instruments is impractical, inappropriate, or both.
12 Just about any variable that one might want information on *can* be measured by a test, albeit indirectly.
13 Even measurement of fuzzier traits such as intelligence can be reasonably accurate, and the estimate of ability indicated by the results of a well-validated test will invariably be better than our "best guess."
14 Selection or development of instruments is critical to the whole evaluation process. It does not matter how carefully planned or well executed an effort is if inadequate instruments are involved; poor instruments can only lead to poor decisions.
15 The test selection process involves determination of the type of instrument needed, e.g. a reading comprehension test, and then a comparative analysis of available tests of that type.

Classification schemes

16   A *test* is a means of measuring the knowledge, skill, feeling, intelligence, or aptitude of an individual or group.

17   Any test can be classified on more than one dimension.

18   Tests can be classified as individual tests or group tests depending upon whether they are administered to one person at a time or to more than one person.

19   Tests can be classified as written or oral depending upon whether test questions are in written form or are given orally.

20   Tests can also be classified according to difficulty versus time variables.

21   A *speed test* is one in which the time limit is fixed and the items, or tasks, are of low difficulty.

22   A *power test* is one in which the items vary in difficulty, usually being arranged in order of increasing difficulty from very easy to very difficult, and the time limit is generous.

23   A *mastery test* has characteristics of speed tests and power tests; the items are of a low level of difficulty and the time limit is generous.

Response behaviors

24   The term "response behaviors" refers to the way in which behaviors to be measured are exhibited.

Written responses

Essay versus objective tests

25   An *essay test* is one in which the number of questions is limited and responders must compose answers, typically lengthy.

26   An objective test is one for which subjectivity in scoring is eliminated, at least theoretically and anyone scoring a given test should come up with the same score; examples are multiple-choice tests, true-false tests, matching tests, and short-answer tests.

Standardized tests

27   A standardized test is one that is: (1) developed by subject matter and measurement specialists, (2) field-tested under uniform administration procedures, (3) revised to meet certain criteria, and (4) scored and interpreted using uniform procedures and standards.

28   Although other measurement instruments (e.g. observation instruments) can be standardized, most standardized tests are objective, written tests requiring written responses.

29   The vast majority of standardized tests have been administered to groups referred to as "norm groups."

30   Ideally, a *norm group* is a large, well-defined group which is representative of the group and subgroups for whom the test is intended.

31   Norms should ideally be based on a national sample which is geographically representative.

32   The description of the norm group should include all pertinent information such as size, location, and major characteristics; time of testing should also be given.

33 A relatively recent innovation with respect to norms is that they are more and more being presented for different kinds of populations to permit more valid comparisons.

34 Another relatively recent phenomenon is the development of systems norms, e.g. norms for various subgroups in a school system.

35 Norms tables typically include the distribution of raw scores as well as a number of score equivalents, such as percentiles and stanines.

36 When norms are used for score interpretation, strictly speaking there is no indication of whether a given score is "good," only whether it is better (or worse) than the average performance of the norm group; there is also no interpretation which tells us exactly *what* a given student knows or can do, only whether what she or he knows or can do is more or less than "average."

Locally-developed tests

37 Locally-developed tests do not have the characteristics of standardized tests.

38 Local tests are developed for a specific situation, a specific set of objectives, and a specific group, and they may only be administered once.

Performance tests

39 For many objectives and areas of learning, use of written tests is an inappropriate way of measuring behavior; there are other objectives, achievement of which *can* be measured with a paper-and-pencil test but not as well.

40 Performance can take the form of a procedure or a product; in either case the performance is observed and rated in the same way.

41 A performance test is one which requires the execution of an act or the development of a product in order to determine whether or to what degree a given ability or trait exists.

42 For aptitude tests performance tests are frequently used in an attempt to eliminate the language factor from the assessment of aptitude.

43 A *procedure* is a series of steps, usually in a definite order, executed in performing an act or task, such as adjusting a microscope.

44 A *product* is a tangible outcome or result, such as a science project.

Data collection methods

Self-report versus observation

Self-report methods

45 With the exception of Q sorts, self-report data consist of the oral or written responses of individuals.

46 An obvious type of self-report data is that resulting from the administration of standardized or locally-developed written tests, including certain achievement, personality, and aptitude tests.

47 Another type of self-report measure used in certain evaluations is the questionnaire.

48 Relatedly, interviews are sometimes used; an *interview* is essentially the oral, in-person administration of a questionnaire to each person in the group of interest.

Questionnaires and interviews

49 *Questionnaires* are usually objective, containing multiple-choice and/or short-answer questions.
50 When well conducted, an interview can produce in-depth data not obtainable with a questionnaire, on the other hand, interviews are expensive and time-consuming, generally involve smaller groups, and require training of interviewers.
51 The interview may also result in more accurate and honest responses since the interviewer can explain and clarify both the purpose of the interview and individual questions.
52 On the other hand, direct interviewer-interviewee contact also has its disadvantages; the responses given by a subject, for example, may be biased or affected by her or his reaction to the interviewer, either positive or negative.
53 Telephone interviews are occasionally used to collect data.
54 Use of questionnaires and interviews entails a number of problems. Lack of response is one of them, as many people do not return mailed questionnaires or attend scheduled interviews.
55 When response is low, interpreting the findings is very difficult since people who do not respond may feel differently from those who do.
56 Both questionnaires and interviews are used to collect survey data; a *survey* is an attempt to collect data from members of a population in order to determine the current status of that population with respect to one or more variables.
57 One type of survey which is unique to education is the school survey, which may involve the study of an individual school or of all the schools in a particular system.

Sociometry

58 *Sociometry* is the assessment and analysis of the interpersonal relationships within a group of individuals.
59 The basic sociometric process involves asking each member to indicate with which other members she or he would most like to engage in a particular activity.
60 The choices made by the group members are graphically depicted in a diagram which is called a *sociogram*.

Diary techniques

61 The *diary technique* involves asking people to keep a record of specified behaviors, attitudes, thoughts, or ideas.
62 The critical incident technique asks people to record and describe only things of special interest.

The Q sort

63 The *Q sort* technique basically involves sorting; an individual is given a set of items or statements, usually on cards, and asked to place them into specified categories so that each category contains some minimum number of cards.

Observation

64 When observation is used, data are collected not by *asking* but by *observing*.
65 A person being observed usually does not write anything; he or she *does* something and the behavior is observed and recorded.

Natural observation

66 When observing in a natural situation, the observer purposely does not control or manipulate anything, and in fact works very hard at not affecting the observed situation in any way.

Simulation observation

67 In simulation observation the evaluator creates the situation to be observed and tells participants what activities they are to engage in.
68 Simulation observation allows the evaluator to observe behavior which occurs infrequently or not at all in natural situations.
69 Two major types of simulation are individual role playing and team role playing.

Content analysis

70 Content analysis is the systematic, quantitative description of the composition of an object.
71 Typical subjects for content analysis include books, instructional materials, notebooks, typed pages, documents, and creative productions such as musical compositions, works of art, and photographs.

Additional data collection instruments

Rating scales and checklists

72 A rating scale is typically an instrument with a number of items related to a given variable, each item representing a continuum of categories between two extremes; persons responding to the items place a mark to indicate their position on each item.
73 Rating scales can be self-report instruments or observation instruments, depending upon how they are used.
74 One major problem with rating scales is rater bias, or response set.
75 The *halo effect* is the tendency of a rater to let overall feelings toward a person affect responses to individual items.
76 The *generosity error* is the tendency of a rater to give the person being rated the benefit of the doubt whenever the rater does not have sufficient knowledge to make an objective rating.
77 Basically, a ranking scale is a type of scale which involves having responders put a set of items in order according to some criterion.
78 A checklist is an enumeration of a number of behaviors or features that constitute a procedure or product.
79 The person completing the checklist indicates whether or not a given behavior or feature occurred or is present.

Observation recording forms

80 Observers should spend their time thinking about what is occurring rather than how to record it.
81 Thus, an observation form should include all events of interest, and the observer should simply have to indicate which ones occurred, in what order, and how often.
82 Rating scales and checklists are frequently used as observation instruments.

83 A recording form reflecting a category system involves a relatively small number of categories, representing all events of interest.
84 Observer bias refers to invalid observations which result from the way in which the observer observes.
85 A response set is the tendency of an observer to rate the majority of observees as above average, average, or below average, regardless of the observees' actual behavior.
86 Observee bias refers to invalid observations which result from the fact that observees may behave differently simply because they are being observed.
87 If the same information can be obtained by observing inanimate objects (referred to as unobtrusive measures) use them.

Behaviors measured

Achievement

88 Achievement tests measure the current status of individuals with respect to proficiency in given areas of knowledge or skill.

Individual achievement tests and batteries

89 Locally-developed tests generally measure achievement in one specific subject matter or content area, such as reading, science, social studies, language, art, music, or physical education.
90 Standardized achievement tests are available for individual curriculum areas such as reading and math, and also in the form of comprehensive batteries which measure achievement in several different areas.
91 Standardized tests are designed to measure what *most* teachers cover, that is, content common to many classes of a certain kind (e.g. Algebra I classes).
92 A locally-developed test, on the other hand, is designed to measure a particular set of learning outcomes, precisely those intended by a teacher, for example.
93 It is important to know how well a student is doing compared to other students of a similar age or grade level.
94 Standardized tests are preferable when large-scale comparisons are to be made between performance at two different points in time.
95 Standardized tests are usually more appropriate when the achievement of a large population is being measured.
96 If an evaluation is only interested in one area of achievement such as reading, then either an individual reading test can be administered or a subtest of a battery.
97 When assessment of achievement in a number of areas is needed, it is better to administer a battery than a number of individual tests.

Diagnostic tests

98 A *diagnostic test* is a type of achievement test which yields multiple scores for each area of achievement; these scores facilitate identification of specific areas of deficiency or learning difficulty.
99 Since a standardized diagnostic test is developed by a cadre of experts, it provides most teachers with much more valid results than they could obtain themselves using more informal techniques.

100 Items in a diagnostic test represent skills that virtually all students should have achieved at a given point in their education.

101 Although not primarily developed for that purpose, battery subtests *can* be used for diagnostic purposes.

102 Diagnosis should be an ongoing process; in addition to administering a number of informal diagnostic instruments, the teacher should constantly be on the alert for signs of physical problems or learning difficulty.

Character and personality

103 Tests of character and personality are designed to measure characteristics of individuals along a number of dimensions and to assess feelings and attitudes toward self, others, and a variety of other activities, institutions, and situations.

104 Most tests of character and personality are nonprojective, or self-report, measures; such tests ask an individual to respond to a series of questions or statements.

Personality

105 Measurement of personality traits is much more imprecise than measurement of other variables such as achievement.

106 School evaluation often includes administration of a personality inventory, the results of which are of interest to counselors and teachers.

107 Serious decisions should not be made based on the results of one test; instead results should be considered together with other types of data.

108 Many personality tests can be thought of as coping measures, i.e. measures designed to determine how well a person copes with, or adjusts to, his or her environment.

109 Personality inventories typically present lists of questions or statements which describe behaviors characteristic of certain personality traits, and the individual is asked to indicate (yes, no, undecided) whether the statement describes her or him.

110 Personality scores are only valid to the degree that the respondent is honest and selects responses which truly characterize him or her.

Attitudes

111 Attitude scales attempt to determine what an individual believes, perceives, or feels.

112 Attitudes toward self, others, and a variety of activities, institutions and situations can be measured.

113 The four basic types of attitude scales are: Likert scales, semantic differential scales, Thurstone scales, and Guttman scales.

114 A *Likert scale* asks an individual to respond to a series of statements by indicating whether she or he strongly agrees (SA), agrees (A), is undecided (U), disagrees (D), or strongly disagrees (SD) with a statement.

115 A *semantic differential scale* asks an individual to give a quantitative rating to a subject on a number of bipolar adjectives such as good-bad, friendly-unfriendly, positive-negative.

116 Measures of "attitude toward self" are referred to as measures of self-concept.

117 Rating scales are also used to measure attitudes toward others; such scales ask

an individual to rate another individual on a number of behavioral dimensions.

Creativity

118 Tests of creativity are really tests designed to measure those personality characteristics that are related to creative behavior.

119 One trait measured is referred to as divergent thinking; unlike convergent thinkers, who tend to look for one right answer, divergent thinkers tend to seek alternatives.

Interest

120 A standardized interest inventory asks an individual to indicate personal likes and dislikes, such as the kinds of activities she or he prefers to engage in.

121 Responses are generally compared to known interest patterns.

122 The most widely used type of standardized interest measure is the vocational interest inventory.

Aptitude

123 Aptitude tests are measures of potential, used to predict how well someone is likely to perform in a future situation.

124 Tests of general aptitude are variously referred to as scholastic aptitude tests, intelligence tests, and tests of general mental ability.

General aptitude

125 While the basic purpose of all such tests is to predict future academic performance, there is disagreement as to the factors which are being measured and are serving as the predictors.

126 While general aptitude tests are intended to be measures of innate ability or potential, they appear actually to measure current ability; there is also some evidence to suggest that scores are to some degree affected by an individual's past and present environment.

127 However, since intelligence tests seem to do a reasonable job of predicting future academic success, and are in that sense measures of "potential," they are very useful to educators.

128 Culture-fair tests attempt to exclude culturally related items, such as items which include words that might not be familiar to certain groups of individuals.

Specific aptitude

129 As the term is generally used, aptitude tests attempt to predict the level of performance which can be expected of an individual following future instruction or training in a specific area.

130 Aptitude tests are available for a wide variety of academic and nonacademic areas such as mathematics and mechanical reasoning.

Readiness tests

131 A readiness, or prognostic, test is administered prior to instruction or train-

ing in a specific area in order to determine whether and to what degree a student is ready for, or will profit from, instruction.

132 The results of such a test are used to identify students who, for example, are not ready for formal reading instruction due to physical immaturity.

Performance standards

133 Performance standards are the criteria to which the results of measurement are compared in order to interpret them.

Norm-referenced standards

134 Any test, standardized or locally-developed, which reports and interprets each score in terms of its relative position with respect to other scores on the same test, is *norm-referenced*.

135 Norm-referenced tests do not indicate what a person knows and can do, or does not know and cannot do.

The normal curve concept

136 Norm-referenced standards are based on the assumption that measured traits involve normal curve properties.

137 The idea is that a measured trait, say math aptitude, exists in different amounts in different people; some people have a lot of it, some have a little of it, and most have some amount called an "average" amount.

Score variability

138 Norm groups are selected with the intention of having a representative group with a wide spread of scores with respect to the trait being measured.

139 Most of our present-day techniques for analyzing scores require score variability.

140 The results of standardized tests are frequently used for classification or selection purposes; a good spread of scores facilitates the decision-making process.

Application of NRTs

141 It is helpful to both the individual and to society to know where an individual's relative strengths and weaknesses lie; furthermore the "real world" is norm-referenced and students should learn to adjust to that fact.

Criterion-referenced standards

142 Any test which reports and interprets each score in terms of an absolute standard is *criterion-referenced*.

143 Interpretation of one person's score has nothing to do with anybody else's score; the comparison is with the standard of performance, not scores of other persons.

The definition problem

144 A criterion-referenced test (CRT) is "one that is deliberately constructed to yield measurement that is directly interpretable in terms of specified performance standards."

145 According to this definition, criterion-referenced measurement is essentially the same as what is referred to as domain-referenced measurement, and in fact, a CRT is used to compare a person's performance with a well-defined behavior domain.

146 A well-defined behavior domain refers to a class of learner behaviors (such as the ability to multiply correctly any pair of single-digit numbers) rather than a specific behavior, such as the ability to multiply correctly 5 × 7).

147 Measurement keyed to objectives is objectives-referenced measurement; whether objectives-referenced measurement equals criterion-referenced measurement depends mostly on the nature and description of the objectives.

148 If a test contains items which represent a class of behaviors, the results are generalizable to the whole class, i.e. "can multiply any pair of one-digit numbers."

Definition of criterion

149 The term "criterion" refers to a domain of behaviors measuring an objective, not to a number, e.g. 75%.

150 A CRT may or may not have a cut-off score; a CRT with a cut-off score is a mastery test.

151 CRTs are not necessarily mastery tests and, in fact, many are not; CRTs can be used to assess various levels of proficiency.

Application of CRTs

152 If nothing else, objectives and CRTs give direction to instruction and measurement.

153 CRTs are probably most appropriate as locally-developed measures since they are developed to measure exactly what was taught.

154 For certain instructional systems (e.g. mastery, individualized) CRTs are the only appropriate measurement devices since attention is focused on what each student can or cannot do.

155 The results of CRTs also provide valuable input for program revision.

156 While standardized tests are usually more appropriate for levels of evaluation beyond the classroom, standardized CRTs do not seem to have evolved sufficiently to be considered a viable alternative to norm-referenced measures.

NRTs versus CRTs: summary

157 The basic difference between a norm-referenced test (NRT) and a CRT is in the interpretations of results—an NRT test uses a relative standard and a CRT uses an absolute standard.

158 Since the purpose of an NRT is to differentiate among individuals, score variability is very important.

159 On the other hand, since the purpose of a CRT is to determine level of proficiency with respect to knowledge or skill, variability is irrelevant or even undesirable; considerable variability typically indicates a number of persons who are not achieving the intended objectives.

160 An NRT contains items that discriminate, that is, items that are neither too easy nor too difficult; a CRT contains whatever items are necessary to measure achievement of the intended objective.

161 An NRT is more concerned with the performance of groups than with the per-

formance of individuals whereas a CRT is more concerned with the performance of individuals.

162 NRTs and CRTs *look* alike; the differences are in the purposes for which each
is constructed and in the interpretation of results.

163 CRTs are more appropriate for student evaluation conducted by the teacher
since they focus on exactly what was taught; the results are also useful for ongoing revision of instructional procedures.

164 NRTs are more appropriate for assessing the performance of larger groups
such as are involved in school-level evaluation; the results of NRTs are useful
for guidance purposes and classification or grouping decisions.

task 3 **performance criteria**

Depending upon your objectives, one type of measurement may be appropriate
for all of them or they may naturally form clusters such that two or more different
measurement techniques are required. For each cluster, be specific in describing
the selected measurement approach, e.g. "a standardized, written, norm-referenced, reading achievement test," or "a locally-developed, observation, criterion-referenced, rating scale."

You should discuss each measurement approach selected in terms of the
classifications used in this chapter and indicate why a given category is more appropriate, e.g. "a locally-developed test is more appropriate than a standardized
test because. . ." The alternatives which should minimally be discussed include:

a Standardized versus locally-developed instruments
b Self-report versus observation instruments
c Norm-referenced versus criterion-referenced instruments

Whether the test is an achievement test, a test of character or personality,
or an aptitude test should be obvious; if not, specify which it is and why.

For each category selected, the appropriate subcategory should be discussed, if applicable. For example, if you indicate that a self-report instrument is
needed, you should specify what kind, e.g. a questionnaire, and why.

Content validity is determined by expert judgment.

part four
selecting a
test

Regardless of the purposes of the evaluation, the objectives to be assessed, and the
decisions to be made, you must have valid,
reliable instruments for collecting your
data. Acquiring needed instruments may
involve selecting the best instruments for
your purpose from those available, developing instruments tailored to your
needs, or both. Whichever is the case, you
must administer an instrument that will
yield precisely the data you wish to collect
in a quantifiable form.

When selecting a test, a number of
factors must be considered; some of these
are more crucial than others. The major
point to remember, however, is that one
does not select *an* instrument appropriate
for a given purpose but rather select *the
best* instrument available.

The goal of part 4 is for you to be
able to select the best instrument for a
given purpose from those that are available
and appropriate. After reading part 2, you
should be able to do the following task.

task four
If at least one of the measurement techniques which you specified in task 3 is a
standardized instrument, do task **a**; if not,
do task **b**.

a For each type of standardized instrument
specified, identify and describe three appropriate tests. Give all relevant data for
each test, e.g. validity and reliability
data, and based on your descriptions,
indicate which test is more acceptable
for your purpose and why.

b Identify a situation in which you are involved (either directly, indirectly or
hypothetically) which uses standardized
tests, e.g., a school testing program. Identify the types of tests that are required

and for each type describe three appropriate tests. Give all relevant data for each test, e.g. validity and reliability data, and based on your descriptions, indicate which test is most acceptable for your purpose and why.

(See Performance Criteria, p. 209.)

7 selection of measuring instruments

After reading chapter 7, you should be able to:

1 Identify the two major aspects of validity.
2 Define or describe content validity.
3 Define or describe construct validity.
4 Define or describe concurrent validity.
5 List the steps for determining concurrent validity by establishing relationship.
6 Define or describe predictive validity.
7 List the steps for determining predictive validity.
8 Describe how an expectancy table is developed.
9 Define or describe reliability.
10 Explain the concept of "true" score.
11 List the steps for determining test-retest reliability.
12 List the steps for determining equivalent-forms reliability.
13 List the steps for determining split-half reliability.
14 Define or describe rationale equivalence reliability.
15 State the major purpose of estimating the standard error of measurement.
16 Describe how SE_m confidence intervals are formed.
17 Identify and describe three factors which affect reliability.
18 Explain how the acceptability of a predictive validity coefficient varies with the purpose for which it is computed.
19 Explain how the acceptability of a reliability coefficient varies depending on the variable being measured.
20 Identify factors which influence selection of measurement methods.
21 State the most important guidelines for test selection.
22 List in order of importance the factors which should be considered in selecting a test from a number of alternatives.

Characteristics of a test

There are a number of characteristics shared by standardized tests. While these characteristics are desirable for all tests, they are much more likely to be in evidence for standardized tests than for locally-developed tests. Regardless of the type of standardized test being sought, certain kinds of descriptive information should be available. This information, or lack of it, forms the basis for test selection.

Recall that standardized tests are typically developed by experts and are therefore carefully constructed. Individual test items are analyzed and revised until they meet established standards of quality. Directions for administering, scoring, and interpreting a standardized test are carefully specified. One resulting characteristic of a standardized test is referred to as objectivity. In essence, test objectivity means that an individual's score is the same, or essentially the same, regardless of who is doing the scoring. Another major characteristic of standardized tests is the existence of validity and reliability data.

Validity is the most important quality of any test. Validity is concerned with what a test measures and for whom it is appropriate. Reliability refers to the consistency with which a test measures whatever it measures. Many types of validity and reliability can be estimated from score data using statistical techniques which typically result in a correlation coefficient. To explain it simply, for the moment, a correlation coefficient is a decimal number between zero and one; a number near .00 indicates low validity or reliability and a number near 1.00 indicates high validity or reliability. Proper interpretation of a traditional correlation coefficient, however, requires that scores have considerable variability. Since criterion-referenced tests may or may not involve score variability, traditional methods for estimating validity and reliability may not be appropriate for certain CRTs. Of course the validity and reliability of both NRTs and CRTs are a function of the care that is taken in test construction. Developing the appropriate kind and number of items is the key to producing valid, reliable instruments. It is precisely because they are developed systematically by persons with the necessary expertise that standardized tests are more likely to be characterized by satisfactory validity and reliability.

Specification of conditions for administering the test is also a very important characteristic of a standardized test. This insures that if directions are carefully followed, the test will always be administered in essentially the same way and will always yield the same kind of data. If directions are carefully spelled out, most educators should be able to properly administer most tests. The directions usually include instructions to be read to test takers, restrictions on time, if any, and guidelines concerning the amount and nature of communication permitted between the test administrator and the test takers. Last, and very importantly, standardized tests generally include directions for scoring and interpreting scores. Directions for scoring include specifications such as the criteria for acceptable responses, when such are appropriate, the number of points to be assigned to various responses, and the procedure for computing total scores. Guidelines for test score interpretation generally include a table of norms. In fact, the availability of normative data is part of the essence of standardization. Typically, a test is administered to a large number of appropriately defined individuals (a norm group) and resulting test scores are analyzed. A table of norms presents raw scores and one or more equivalent transformations, such as corresponding percentile ranks, which facilitate interpretation of an individual's score with respect to the perform-ance of the group.

To repeat then, the most important characteristic of a standardized test (or any test), is validity. Validity is indispensable; there is no quality or virtue of a test that can compensate for inadequate validity.

Validity

The most simplistic definition of validity is that it is the degree to which a test measures what it is supposed to measure. A common misconception is that a test *is* or *is not* valid. A test is not valid per se; it is valid for a particular purpose and for a particular group. The question is not "valid or invalid" but rather "valid for what and for whom." A valid test of biology achievement is not very likely to be a valid personality test. It would be obvious to almost anyone looking at a test of biology achievement that the test did not measure any aspect of personality. Whether the test was a valid measure of biology facts or principles, if either, would not be so easy to detect. With respect to the "for whom" aspect of validity, a test which is valid measure of vocabulary for high school students is certainly not a valid measure for second graders. Again, this would undoubtedly be self-evident to anyone examining a high school–level vocabulary test. Whether the test were valid for both ninth graders and seniors, if either, would not be so obvious. To further clarify the concept of "valid for what and for whom," let's apply the concept of validity to teaching. In general, "valid" teaching occurs when a teacher teaches whatever he or she is supposed to teach (or, if you prefer, when students learn what they are supposed to learn!). But a way of teaching, no matter how outstanding, is not valid per se. Teaching is valid for a particular purpose, that is, a particular area of instruction, and a particular age or grade level. Valid kindergarten teaching is not very likely to also be valid high school teaching, and valid high school trigonometry teaching is not very likely to also be valid high school physical education teaching. While the above analogy is admittedly loose, the concept it illustrates is important.

It is the "valid for whom" concern that makes the description of the norm group so important. Only to the degree that persons in the norm group are like the persons to whom we wish to administer the test can proper interpretation of re-sults be made. Twenty-year-old achievement norms are not likely to be appropri-ate for students in the 1980s. The usefulness of norms based on a sample of 50,000 upper-middle-class high school students in the Midwest is certainly questionable if the test is to be administered to inner-city students in Boston. And so forth. Of course even an "ideal" norm group with a cast of thousands is not going to be *entirely* appropriate in any situation. There are just too many variables and stu-dent characteristics which might affect results. Thus care must always be taken in selecting a test and interpreting results. But if information concerning the norm group is insufficient or if the information given indicates any major way in which the norm group is inappropriate, then every effort must be made to locate a more suitable test. If none is available, then the shortcomings must be seriously consid-ered when results are interpreted.

It is the "valid for whom" concern that is at the heart of the test bias issue. To the degree that a test is not appropriate for any reason for a given group, to that degree is it invalid for that group. If a test is invalid, it is by definition biased. If a test is biased, so are the results, and false conclusions are likely to be drawn concerning the status of individuals or groups with respect to the variable measured. While bias may result from improper test administration, scoring, or interpretation, the major source of bias is the test itself. The required reading level may be too high, for example, or the items may contain unfamiliar vocabulary. When a standardized test is developed, every effort is made to include items which are equally "fair" to all students. Certain terms and expressions, however, are bound to be more familiar to certain groups than to others. For example, IQ tests frequently include analogy items such as *"Black* is to *white* as *open* is to _____." If unfamiliar terms are used, some individuals may miss an item not because they don't understand the concept but because they don't understand the terms. A student living in Florida might very well miss the item *"Ignition key* is to *motor* as *kindling* is to _____" because of unfamiliarity with the term "kindling." (The answer is "fire"!) Therefore, test designers attempt to balance items so that some items will be more familiar to urbanites and others will be more familiar to suburbanites or ruralites, some will be more familiar to northerners and others to southerners, and so forth.[1] Certain individuals (e.g. geographical isolates) are so atypical that few tests are really appropriate for them. A well-developed test, however, should be reasonably valid for most test takers.

It has been said jokingly that achievement tests are biased against students who do not know much. While we may find the concept amusing, there is a tendency sometimes to blame low scores on biased tests. If a group of students does poorly, some educators and lay people are quick to find fault with the test rather than determine and face the real cause of low performance. There are any number of factors besides test bias which can lead to poor performance on a test. For example, the students' curriculum may be woefully outdated or otherwise inadequate. The point is that low scores do not automatically imply test bias. They do imply that the group tested does not possess a high degree of whatever the test measures—for whatever reason.

Any type of measure must have validity. This is as true for observation instruments as it is for self-report measures. As noted previously, a test is not valid, per se; it is valid for a particular purpose and for a particular group. Actually, even that statement is not entirely correct. A test is not strictly valid or invalid even for a particular purpose or group. Validity is a matter of degree, not a characteristic that is present or absent. A test may have low validity, satisfactory validity, or unusually high validity, for example. Thus, if we speak of a test as being a valid measure of X, we are implying that it has at least a satisfactory degree of validity. Further, validity is a somewhat temporal quality in that a test that once had adequate validity may no longer, and a test that currently has adequate validity will not necessarily in the future. For example, inclusion of items dealing with the metric system is increasingly becoming a prerequisite for the validity of certain math achievement tests. Ten years ago such items were not called for. Also, it is often said that it is not really the test itself which has validity but rather the interpretations of the results of the test. Actually, both are true and one is necessary for the other. If a test does what it alleges to do for a specified group, then correct interpretations are possible. On the other hand, poor test result interpretation, of course, does not necessarily imply an invalid test. Thus, it seems less confusing to speak of the validity of the test itself since it is present whether or not the test is used or interpreted correctly.

---

[1] Lyman, H. B. Talking test scores. *NCME Measurement News,* 1978, 21(2), 7.

Since tests are designed for a variety of purposes, and since validity can be evaluated only in terms of purpose, it is not surprising that there are several different types of validity: content, construct, concurrent, and predictive. Because of the different ways in which they are determined, they are classified as either logical or empirical validity. Logical validity includes content validity and is so named because validity is determined primarily through judgment. Empirical validity includes concurrent and predictive validity and is so named because in each case validity is determined by relating performance on a test to performance on another criterion. Empirical validity is determined in a more objective manner. Assessment of construct validity involves both judgment and external criteria. The term criterion-related validity is also often used to refer to concurrent and predictive validity. For any test it is important to seek evidence concerning the appropriate type of validity, given the intended purpose or purposes of the test.

Norm-referenced tests

The terms "content," "construct," "concurrent," and "predictive" are somewhat more appropriate for discussing the validity of norm-referenced tests. While the same basic concepts are applicable to criterion-referenced tests, different terms are often used to express them.

Content validity

Content validity is the degree to which a test measures an intended content area. It is of prime importance for achievement tests. Content validity requires both item validity and sampling validity. *Item validity* is concerned with whether the test items represent measurement in the intended content area, and *sampling validity* is concerned with how well the test samples the total content area. A test designed to measure knowledge of biology facts might have good item validity, because all the items do indeed deal with biology facts, but might have poor sampling validity, e.g. if all the items deal only with vertebrates. A test with good content validity adequately samples the appropriate content area. This is important because we cannot possibly measure each and every aspect of a certain content area; the required test would be "humongously" long. And yet we do wish to make inferences about performance in the entire content area based on performance on the items included in the test. Such inferences are only possible if the test items adequately sample the domain of possible items. This sampling is of course easier for well-defined areas such as spelling than for fuzzier content areas such as social studies.

The term "face validity" is sometimes used in describing tests. While its meaning is somewhat ambiguous, basically *face validity* refers to the degree to which a test *appears* to measure what it purports to measure. While determining face validity is not a psychometrically sound way of estimating validity, the process is sometimes used as an initial screening procedure in test selection.

As mentioned earlier, content validity is of prime importance for achievement tests. Test scores cannot accurately reflect student achievement if the test does not measure what the students were supposed to learn. While this may seem obvious, content validity is a problem in many evaluations. Many evaluation studies, for example, are designed to compare the effectiveness of two (or more) different curricula. Effectiveness is often defined in terms of final achievement of two groups as measured by a test. Sometimes the test used is more content valid for one of the groups than for the other. When this happens, final achievement differences may be at least partially attributable to the test used and not just curriculum differences. This phenomenon frequently occurs when an "innovative" approach is compared to a traditional approach. The different approaches often emphasize different areas of content. A classic case is the early studies which compared the "new" math with the "old" math. These studies invariably found no achievement differences between students learning under the two approaches. The problem was that the "new" math was emphasizing concepts and principles while the achievement tests were emphasizing computational skill. When tests were developed which contained an adequate sampling of items measuring concepts and principles, studies began to find that the two approaches to teaching math resulted in essentially equal computational ability, but that the "new" math resulted in better conceptual understanding. The moral of the story is: take care that a test measures what students actually learned. In an evaluation comparing curricula or instructional materials, be sure that the test is valid *for your purposes* and *for your participants*.

Content validity is determined by expert judgment. There is no formula for computing it and there is no way to express it quantitatively. Usually experts in the area covered by the test are asked to assess its content validity. These experts carefully examine all items on the test and make a judgment concerning how well they represent the intended content area. This judgment is based on whether all subareas have been included, and in the correct proportions. In other words, a comparison is made between what ought to be included in the test, given its intended purpose, and what is actually included. When selecting a test for an evaluation, the evaluator assumes the role of "expert" and assesses whether the test is content valid for the situation involved. The evaluator compares the content of the actual instruction or training with what is measured by the test.

Construct validity

Construct validity is the degree to which a test measures an intended hypothetical construct. A construct is a nonobservable trait, such as intelligence, which explains behavior. You cannot see a construct, you can only observe its effect. In fact, constructs were "invented" to explain behavior. We cannot prove they exist; we cannot perform brain surgery on a person and see his intelligence. Constructs, however, do an amazingly good job of explaining certain differences between individuals. For example, it was always observed that some students learn faster than others, learn more, and retain longer. To explain these differences a theory of intelligence was developed which hypothesized that there is something called intelligence which is related to learning and which everyone possesses to a greater or lesser degree. Tests were developed designed to measure how much of it a person has. As it happens, students whose scores indicate that they have a "lot" of it, i.e., students who have high IQs, tend to do better in school and other learning environments. Other constructs which have been hypothesized to exist and for which tests have been developed include anxiety, creativity, and curiosity.

Decisions based totally or partially on the measurement of constructs are only valid to the extent that the measure of the construct involved is valid. For example, the selection criteria for a program for gifted students might include: a specified minimum score on an intelligence test (116 for example), a specified minimum score on a test of creativity, a specified minimum grade point average for the previous academic year, teacher recommendations, and parental consent. If recent, appropriate scores were not available, tests of intelligence and creativity would need to be administered to likely candidates (perhaps those students who met the grade point average requirement). The validity of the resulting selection decisions would be a direct function of the validity of the intelligence test and creativity test administered. If the intelligence test did not really measure intelligence or the creativity test did not really measure creativity, decisions based on test results would probably be wrong for the most part. When selecting a test of a given construct, the evaluator must look for and critically analyze evidence presented related to the construct validity of the instrument.

Validating a test of a construct is by no means an easy task. Basically, it involves testing hypotheses deduced from a theory concerning the construct. If, for example, a theory of creativity hypothesized that more-creative people will come up with more alternative solutions to a given problem than less-creative people, then if persons who scored high on the test under consideration did subsequently come up with more alternative solutions to a set of tasks, this would be evidence to support the construct validity of the test. Of course, if people who scored high on the test did not, as hypothesized, produce more solutions, it would not necessarily mean that the test did not measure creativity. The hypothesis related to the behavior of more-creative persons might be incorrect. Generally, a number of independent studies are required to establish the credibility of a test of a construct.

Concurrent validity

Concurrent validity is the degree to which the scores on a test are related to the scores on another, already established test administered at the same time or to some other valid criterion available at the same time. Often, a test is developed which claims to do the same job as some other tests more easily or faster. If this is shown to be the case, then the concurrent validity of the new test is established, and in most cases the new test will be utilized instead of the other tests. A paper-and-pencil test which does the same job as a performance test, or a short test which measures the same behaviors as a longer test, will certainly be preferred in many situations.

Concurrent validity is determined by establishing relationship or discrimination. The relationship method involves determining the relationship between scores on the test and scores on some other established test or criterion (e.g. grade point average). In this case, the steps involved in determining concurrent validity are as follows:

1 Administer the new test to a defined group of individuals.
2 Administer a previously established, valid test (or acquire such scores if already available).
3 Correlate the two sets of scores.

The resulting number, or validity coefficient, indicates the concurrent validity of the new test. If the coefficient is high, the test has good concurrent validity. We will discuss the meaning and interpretation of correlation coefficients later in the chapter. But to facilitate understanding of the above-described process, a brief explanation is presented here.

Degree of relationship between two variables is expressed as a correlation coefficient. If a relationship exists between two variables, it means that scores within a certain range on one measure are associated with scores within a certain range on another measure. For example, there is a relationship between intelligence and academic achievement; persons who score high on intelligence tests tend to have higher grade point averages and persons who score low on intelligence tests tend to have lower grade point averages. Using the scores from the two measures, a correlation coefficient is computed. The coefficient indicates the degree of relationship between the two sets of scores. If the relationship is high it may be used to make predictions. The more highly related two variables are, the more accurate are predictions based on their relationship. For example, if we know that there is a high relationship between scores on an algebra aptitude test and achievement in algebra, we can use aptitude test scores to predict likely level of achievement in algebra. If two variables are highly related, a correlation coefficient near $+1.00$ (or -1.00) will be obtained; if two variables are not related, a coefficient near .00 will be obtained. Suppose, for example, that Professor Jeenyus developed a group test of intelligence for children which took only five minutes to administer. If scores on this test did indeed correlate highly (say .80) with scores on the Wechsler Intelligence Scale for Children, which must be administered to one child at a time and takes at least an hour, then Professor Jeenyus's test would definitely be preferable in many situations. On the other hand, if the correlation was low (say .18), this would indicate that the new test was not measuring the same things as the Wechsler test. It would have low concurrent validity, and it would not be considered an acceptable substitute.

The discrimination method of establishing concurrent validity involves determining whether test scores can be used to discriminate between persons who possess a certain characteristic and those who do not, or between those who possess more of it and those who possess less. For example, a test of mental adjustment would have concurrent validity if scores resulting from it could be used to classify correctly institutionalized and noninstitutionalized persons.

When selecting a test for a given evaluation purpose, you will usually be seeking a test that measures what you wish in the most efficient manner. If you select a shorter or more convenient test which allegedly measures the desired behavior, be careful that concurrent validity has been established using a valid criterion.

Predictive validity

Predictive validity is the degree to which a test can predict how well an individual will do in a future situation. An algebra aptitude test which has high predictive validity will fairly accurately predict which students will do well in algebra and which students will not. Predictive validity is extremely important for tests which are used to classify or select individuals. An example which may be all too familiar to you is the Graduate Record Examination (GRE) which is used to select students for admission to graduate school. Many graduate schools require a certain minimum score for admission, often 1000, in the belief that students who achieve that score have a higher probability of succeeding in graduate school. The predictive validity of the GRE has been the subject of many research studies. Results seem to indicate that the GRE has higher predictive validity for certain areas of graduate study than for others. For example, while it appears to have satisfactory predictive validity for predicting success in graduate studies in English, its validity in predicting success in an art education program appears to be questionable. Another example which illustrates the critical importance of predictive validity is the use of tests to determine which students should be assigned to special education classes. The decisions to remove a child from the normal educational environment and to place him or her in a special class is a serious one. In this situation it is imperative that the decision be based on the results of valid measures.

As the GRE example illustrates, the predictive validity of a given instrument varies with a number of factors. The predictive validity of an instrument may vary depending upon such factors as the curriculum involved, textbooks used, and geographic location. The Mindboggling Algebra Aptitude Test, for example, may predict achievement better in courses using the Brainscrambling Algebra I text than in courses using other texts. Thus, if a test is to be used for prediction, it is important to compare the description of the manner in which it was validated with the situation in which it is to be used.

No test, of course, has perfect predictive validity. Therefore, predictions based on the scores of any test will be imperfect. However, prediction based on a valid predictor test will invariably be more accurate than predictions based on hunches or subjective speculation. Further, predictions based on a combination of several test scores will invariably be more accurate than predictions based on the scores of any one test. Therefore, when important classification or selection decisions are to be made, they should be based on data from more than one indicator. For example, we can use high school GPA to predict college GPA at the end of the freshman year. We can also use scholastic aptitude score or rank in graduating class to predict college GPA. A prediction based on all three variables, however, will be more accurate than a prediction based on any one or two of them.

The predictive validity of a test is determined by establishing the relationship between scores on the test and some measure of success in the situation of interest. The test which is used to predict success is referred to as the *predictor*, and the behavior which is predicted is referred to as the *criterion*. In establishing the predictive validity of a test, the first step is to identify and carefully define the criterion. The criterion selected must be a valid measure of the behavior to be predicted. For example, if we wished to establish the predictive validity of an algebra aptitude test, final examination scores at the completion of a course in algebra might be considered a valid criterion, but number of days absent during the course probably would not. As another example, if we were interested in establishing the predictive validity of a given test for predicting success in college, grade point average at the end of the first year would probably be considered a valid criterion, but number of extracurricular activities in which the student participated probably would not. The proportion of individuals who can be expected to meet a certain criterion is referred to as the base rate. Here a word of caution is in order. You should avoid trying to predict a criterion for which the base rate is very high or very low. For example, suppose we wished to establish the predictive validity of a test designed to predict who will graduate summa cum laude. Since a very, very small percentage of students do so, all we would have to do is predict that no one would reach this criterion and we would be correct in almost every case! A test could hardly predict any better and would therefore be of very limited value.

Once the criterion has been identified and defined, the procedure for determining predictive validity is as follows:

1 Administer the test (the predictor variable).
2 Wait until the predicted behavior (the criterion variable) occurs.
3 Obtain measures of the criterion.
4 Correlate the two sets of scores.

The resulting number, or validity coefficient, indicates the predictive validity of the test; if the validity coefficient is high, the test has good predictive validity. For example, suppose we wished to determine the predictive validity of a physics aptitude test. First we would administer the test to a large group of potential physics students. Then we would wait until the students had completed a course in physics and would obtain a measure of their success, such as final exam scores. The correlation between the two sets of scores would determine the predictive validity of the test; if the resulting correlation coefficient was high, the test would have high predictive validity.

Often a combination of predictors is used to predict a criterion. In this case a prediction equation may be developed. A person's scores on each of a number of tests are inserted into the equation and her or his future performance is predicted. In this case the validity of the equation should be reestablished through cross-validation. *Cross-validation* involves administering the predictor tests to a different sample from the same population and developing a new equation. Of course, even if only one predictor test is involved, it is a good idea to determine predictive validity for more than just one sample of individuals. In other words, the predictive validity of a test should be reconfirmed.

You may have noticed (if you had a high score on the SAT or GRE!) that the procedures for determining concurrent validity and predictive validity are very similar. The major difference is when the criterion measure is administered. In establishing concurrent validity it is administered at the same time as the predictor or within a relatively short period of time. In establishing predictive validity, one usually has to wait for a much longer period of time to pass before criterion data can be collected. Occasionally, concurrent validity is substituted for predictive validity in order to save time and to eliminate the problems of keeping track of the test group. For example, we might administer a mechanical aptitude test to a group of mechanics and correlate scores on the test with some measure of their skill. The problem with this approach is that we would be dealing only with those who "made it"! Persons for whom the test would have predicted a low probability of success would not become mechanics. In other words, most of the persons in the sample would be persons for whom the test would have predicted success. Therefore, the resulting validity coefficient would probably be an underestimate of the predictive validity of the test.

In discussing both concurrent and predictive validity we said that if the resulting coefficient is high, the test has good validity. You may have wondered, How high is high? The question of how high the coefficient must be in order to be considered "good" is not easy to answer. There is not magic number that a coefficient should reach. In general, it is relative matter. A coefficient of .50 might be acceptable if there is only one test available designed to predict a given criterion. On the other hand, a coefficient of .50 might be inadequate if there are other tests available with higher coefficients. This subject will be discussed further later in the chapter.

Criterion-referenced tests

Methods for determining certain types of validity are not as refined for CRTs as they are for NRTs. The major problem is that many of the traditional approaches involve correlation which in turn requires score variability. Since score variability is typically lower for CRTs than for NRTs, traditional approaches may be inappropriate in certain situations involving CRTs.

Since CRTs are designed primarily to measure achievement of one or more specific objectives, content validity is the major concern with such measures. Performance on CRTs is occasionally used for prediction purposes, and in these situations predictive validity is a concern.

Content validity

The content validity of a CRT involves the degree to which the test measures the achievement of the intended objectives. As with NRTs, we are interested in both item validity and sampling validity, that is, whether the items measure only the intended objectives and how adequately the test samples the objectives. The content validity of CRTs is generally expected to be higher than for NRTs, mainly because the domain of behaviors to be measured, i.e. those described by the objectives, is usually more precisely defined. In fact, according to some evaluation specialists, a well-defined behavior domain includes item-generating rules.

Popham and others prefer the term "descriptive validity" which refers to the degree to which a test accurately measures the class of behaviors described in a domain description.[2] They prefer this term because validity is a function of the accuracy of a test's descriptive ability, that is, whether performance can be accurately interpreted according to the domain description, and because the term content validity *sounds* cognitive whereas affective and psychomotor outcomes are also of interest.

The content validity of CRTs is determined in essentially the same manner as for NRTs. The procedure is somewhat easier, however, since the description of intended behaviors is more detailed. The content validity of CRTs is determined by expert judgment. These experts carefully examine all items on the test and make a judgment concerning how well they represent the intended behavior domain. Of course for many classroom CRTs, the role of expert is assumed by the teacher. Actually, it is pretty hard to construct a CRT that does not have at least adequate content validity. If the objectives are reasonably specific and the items measure the objectives, some degree of content validity is practically automatic. Of course the more carefully the test is designed, the higher the content validity is likely to be. While this is true for NRTs also, all things being equal (preparation time, for example), a CRT will have higher content validity than an NRT.

While CRTs are designed primarily to measure achievement, they may be

---

[2] Popham, W. J. *Educational evaluation*, Englewood Cliffs, N.J.: Prentice-Hall, 1975.

used for other purposes, such as prediction. But unless a CRT has content validity it is virtually useless for any purpose.

Predictive validity

As with NRTs, the predictive validity of a CRT involves the ability of the test to predict future performance. While prediction is not really the purpose for which a CRT is developed, there are situations in which we might want to use a CRT in this way. For instance, suppose we wanted to validate an eighth grade competency test and that a score of 75 was required for promotion to the ninth grade. We would of course be concerned with content validity; we would want the test to adequately sample concepts taught in the eighth grade. We would also be interested in whether students who achieved a score of 75 or higher performed better in the ninth grade than those who did not (predictive validity). If the relationship between scores on the competency test and, say, grades in the ninth grade was low, then using the test as a prerequisite for promotion would be questionable. Another example of the predictive use of CRTs would be to validate a criterion-referenced final exam in a small appliance repair course to see if persons achieving mastery actually perform well "on the job."

Popham and others prefer to use the term "functional validity" instead of criterion-related or predictive validity.[3] *Functional validity* refers to the degree to which a CRT serves the purpose for which it is being used. Thus, one *function* of a test may be to make predictions. If it does so reasonably well, it is said to have functional validity. The term "functional" is preferred since there are a number of functions we may wish a test to perform and prediction is but one of them.

When NRTs are involved, determining predictive validity involves correlating predictor and criterion scores to determine degree of relationship. However, since correlation requires score variability, and since scores on a CRT may or may not involve variability, use of correlational techniques is more or less appropriate depending upon the actual spread of scores involved. If everyone achieved essentially the same score on some predictor test (e.g. mastery), there would obviously be no relationship between scores on the predictor and scores on the criterion. Thus, when correlational techniques are used with CRTs, the results must be interpreted intelligently and cautiously.

One relatively simple way to determine relationship between a predictor and a criterion is to develop an "expectancy table." An *expectancy table* is basically a two-way table that lists predictor scores or categories down the left side and criterion scores or categories across the top. Entries in the table represent the number or percentage of persons at each intersection. Table 7.1 represents a hypothetical example of what the results might be if we attempted to validate the predictive validity of the eighth grade competency test mentioned earlier. The left-hand column describes the predictor and indicates the number of students who passed (achieved a score of 75 or better) and the number who did not. Across the top are categories of the criterion variable (ninth grade achievement). The symbol n indicates the number of students in each category, and (%) indicates the percentage of the total that figure represents. Thus, Table 7.1 indicates, for example, that only 1% of the students in the "pass" group achieved a GPA less than 1 (.00 − .99)

---

[3] See footnote 2.

table 7.1
Simplified expectancy table

Competency Test	GPA at End of the Ninth Grade							
	.00–.99		1.00–1.99		2.00–2.99		3.00–4.00	
	n	(%)	n	(%)	n	(%)	n	(%)
Pass (n = 350)	5	(01)	30	(09)	225	(64)	90	(26)
Fail (n = 150)	20	(13)	45	(30)	75	(50)	10	(07)

whereas 13% of the "fail" group achieved that GPA. On the other hand, 26% of the pass group achieved a GPA of 3.00 or greater whereas only 7% of the fail group did. These results would provide some evidence of the predictive validity of the competency test and would indicate that as a group students who passed did better in the ninth grade. It must be kept in mind, however, that (1) these results are for just one group and should be verified with another group, and (2) all individuals do not match the general pattern. Some of the students who failed the competency test, for example, did achieve a GPA of at least 3.00. Of course the fact that the results are based on the performance of 500 students gives us more confidence in the pattern than if they were based on say 50 students. While expectancy tables are often based on norm-referenced scores, they are especially useful for criterion-referenced test scores, especially when low score variability is a factor.

While CRTs may be used for prediction, their primary purpose is to determine achievement of objectives. A CRT with wonderful content validity may not be very useful for prediction purposes. It does not make much sense to revise a CRT in an attempt to improve predictive validity if the result is a decrease in content validity. If prediction is your main interest, it is more rational to use an NRT than to sabotage a CRT.

Closely related to the concept of validity is the concept of reliability, which deals with score consistency.

Reliability

In everyday English, reliability means dependability, or trustworthiness. The term means essentially the same thing with respect to measurement. Basically, *reliability* is the degree to which a test consistently measures whatever it measures. The more reliable a test is, the more confidence we can have that the scores obtained from the administration of the test are essentially the same scores that would be obtained if the test were readministered to the same group. An unreliable test is essentially useless. If a test were unreliable then scores for a given group would be expected to be quite different every time the test was administered. If an intelligence test were unreliable, a student scoring an IQ of 120 today might score 140 tomorrow, and 95 the day after tomorrow. If the test were highly reliable and if the student's IQ were 110, then we would not expect that score to fluctuate too greatly from testing to testing. A score of 105 would not be unusual, but a score of 145 would be very unlikely. As with validity, any type of measurement must have reliability. This applies to self-report measures as well as observation instruments, criterion-referenced tests as well as norm-referenced tests. The reliability of a rating form, for example, is just as important as the reliability of a multiple-choice achievement test. Anyone using the same rating form to rate the same behavior should come up with essentially the same rating.

Any type of measurement involves some kind of error. There are many factors which affect a score besides the degree to which a person possesses the trait being measured. Some sources of error are related to temporary and permanent characteristics of the persons taking the test. A person's IQ score, for example, may be in error due to illness at the time the test was taken. Other sources of error are related to characteristics of the test itself or to the way in which it is administered, scored, or interpreted. A student's achievement score, for example, may be in error due to a large number of inappropriate items. Errors of measurement may be random or systematic. Random errors affect reliability whereas systematic, or constant, errors affect validity.

If an achievement test were too difficult for a certain group of students, all scores would be systematically lowered and the test would have low validity for that group (remember "valid for whom"). The same test, however, might yield consistent scores, that is, might be reliable. In other words, the scores might be systematically lowered in the same way every time. A student whose "true" achievement score was 80 and who scored 60 on the test (invalidity) might score 60 every time he or she took the test (reliability). This case illustrates an interesting relationship between validity and reliability: A valid test is always reliable, but a reliable test is not necessarily valid. If a test is measuring what it is supposed to be measuring, it will be reliable and do so every time, but a reliable test can consistently measure the wrong thing and be invalid! Suppose a test that purported to measure social studies concepts really measured facts. It would not be a valid measure of concepts but it could certainly measure the facts very consistently.

Because of the many sources of measurement error which are beyond the test developer's control, random errors of measurement can never be completely eliminated, though every effort should be made to minimize them. To the extent that random errors are minimal, a test will be reliable. Classical test theory is based on the assumption that each person's score on a test really represents the result of a combination of two factors—the person's "true" score and errors of measurement.

$$X = T + E$$

where

X = score actually obtained on the test
T = true score
E = errors of measurement score

It is also assumed that the errors of measurement are random, that some persons' scores are affected positively (their obtained score is higher than their true score) and some negatively (their obtained score is lower than their true score), and that overall the positive and negative errors average out, i.e. equal zero. Thus, a person's true score is the score which, theoretically, a person would obtain *if* there were no errors of measurement and the test were totally reliable.

Another way of thinking about true scores relates to the fact that any given test is but one of many possible tests that *could* have been constructed to measure the same behaviors. Any achievement test, for example, contains one set of items selected from a very large pool of possible items. If we could construct all possible tests (or even a very large number of them), administer them all to an individual, and score each test, the person's *average* score would theoretically be his or her true score for that test. This assumes of course that all the tests would be identical in every way (number of items, for example) and that taking one test would not affect performance on any other test (no advantages from practice). Thus, the scores for any given test really represent an estimate of the individual's status with respect to the variable being measured, an estimate which is affected by many factors.

When we discuss score consistency, we may be concerned with the score consistency of a group as a group or with the accuracy, or preciseness, of individual scores. When we speak of reliability, we usually are referring to the score consistency of a group. Estimates of such consistency typically involve correlation coefficients. When we speak of the accuracy of an individual's score, i.e. how much confidence we can have in any individual's score, then we are interested in the standard error of measurement. Both of these concepts are important and are frequently discussed when information about tests is presented. Knowledge of them promotes intelligent test selection and score interpretation.

All this talk about error might lead you to believe that measurement in education is pretty sloppy and imprecise to say the least. Actually it's not as bad as it may sound. There are many tests that measure intended traits quite accurately. In fact, as Nunnally has pointed out, measurement in other areas of science often involves as much, if not more, random error.[4] To use his example, the measurement of blood pressure, a physiological trait, is far less reliable than most phychological measures. There are any number of "conditions of the moment" which may temporarily affect blood pressure—joy, anger, fear, and anxiety, to name a few. Thus, a person's blood pressure reading is also the result of a combination of "true" blood pressure and error.

At least for norm-referenced measures, reliability is easier to assess than validity. There are a number of different types of reliability. Each is determined in a different manner and each deals with a different kind of consistency. Test-retest, equivalent-forms, and split-half reliability are all determined through correlation. Rationale equivalence reliability is established by determining how each item on a test relates to all other items on the test and to the total test.

Norm-referenced tests

Scores can be reliable, or consistent, in several different ways. They can be categorized according to whether they involve one test administered once, one test administered twice, or two tests administered once. When one test is administered once, estimates of internal consistency reliability are calculated. Methods for determining internal consistency reliability include the *split-half* and *rationale equivalence* techniques. When one test is administered twice, we are interested in score stability over time and *test-retest reliability* is calculated. When two tests are administered once, we are concerned with whether the two tests measure essentially the same behaviors and *equivalent-forms reliability* is calculated. Excepting rationale equivalence, reliability estimates are calculated using correlational

[4] Nunnally, J. C. *Psychometric theory.* New York: McGraw-Hill, 1967.

techniques; in all cases, however, reliability is expressed as a decimal number between .00 and 1.00.

Test-retest reliability

Test-retest reliability is the degree to which scores are consistent over time. It indicates score variation that occurs from testing session to testing session as a result of errors of measurement. In other words, we are interested in evidence that the score a person obtains on a test at some moment in time is the same score, or close to the same score, that the person would get if the test were administered some other time. We want to know how consistently the test measures whatever it measures. This type of reliability is especially important for tests used as predictors, aptitude tests for example. Such a test would not really be too helpful if it indicated a different aptitude level each time it was given.

Determination of test-retest reliability is appropriate when alternate (equivalent) forms of a test are not available, and when it is unlikely that persons taking the test the second time will remember responses made on the test the first time. Test takers are more likely to remember items from a test with a lot of history facts, for example, than from a test with algebra problems. The procedure for determining test-retest reliability is basically quite simple:

1 Administer the test to an appropriate group.
2 After some time has passed, say a week, administer the *same test* to the *same group*.
3 Correlate the two sets of scores.

If the resulting coefficient, referred to as the *coefficient of stability*, is high, the test has good test-retest reliability. A major problem with this type of reliability is the difficulty of knowing how much time should elapse between the two testing sessions. If the interval is too short, the chances of students' remembering responses made on the test the first time are increased and the estimate of reliability tends to be artificially high. If the interval is too long, students' ability to do well on the test may increase due to intervening learning or maturation and the estimate of reliability tends to be artificially low.

Thus, when test-retest information is given concerning a test, the time interval between testings should be given as well as the actual coefficient. While it is difficult to say precisely what, in general, the ideal time interval should be, one day will generally be too short and one month too long. The problems associated with test-retest reliability are taken care of by equivalent-forms reliability.

Equivalent-forms reliability

Equivalent forms of a test are two tests which are identical in every way except for the actual items included. The two forms measure the same variable, have the same number of items, the same structure, the same difficulty level, and the same directions for administration, scoring, and interpretation. In fact, if the same group takes both tests, the average score as well as the degree of score variability should be essentially the same on both tests. Only the specific items are not the same, although they do measure the same trait, or objectives. In essence, we are selecting, or sampling, different items from the same behavior domain. We are interested in whether scores depend upon the particular set of items selected or whether performance on one set of items is generalizable to other sets. If items are well selected, and if each set adequately represents the domain of interest, the latter should be true.

Equivalent-forms reliability, also referred to as alternate-forms reliability, indicates score variation that occurs from form to form, and is appropriate when it is likely that test takers will recall responses made during the first session and, of course, when two different forms of a test are available. When alternate forms are available, it is important to know the equivalent-forms reliability; it is reassuring to know that a person's score will not be greatly affected by which form is administered. Also, sometimes in formal evaluations two forms of a test are administered to the same group, one as a pretest and the other as a posttest. It is crucial, if the effects of the intervening activities are to be validly assessed, that the two tests be measuring essentially the same things. In addition, using equivalent forms eliminates any inadvertent "teaching to the test."

The procedure for determining equivalent-forms reliability is very similar to that for determining test-retest reliability:

1 Administer one form of the test to an appropriate group.
2 At the same session, or shortly thereafter, administer the *second form* of the test to the *same group*.
3 Correlate the two sets of scores.

If the resulting coefficient (referred to as the *coefficient of equivalence*) is high, the test has good equivalent-forms reliability. If the two forms of the test are administered at two different times (the best of all possible worlds!), the resulting coefficient is referred to as the *coefficient of stability and equivalence*. In essence, this approach represents a combination of test-retest and equivalent-forms reliability and thus assesses stability of scores over time as well as the generalizability of the sets of items. Since more sources of measurement error are possible than with either method alone, the resulting coefficient is likely to be somewhat lower. Thus the coefficient of stability and equivalence represents a conservative estimate of reliability.

Equivalent-forms reliability is the single most acceptable and most commonly used estimate of reliability for most tests used in evaluation and research. The major problem involved with this method of estimating reliability is the difficulty of constructing two forms that are essentially equivalent. Lack of equivalence is a source of measurement error. Even though equivalent-forms reliability is considered to be the best estimate of reliability, it is not always feasible to administer two different forms of the same test, or even the same test twice. Imagine telling your students that they had to take two final examinations! Imagine someone telling *you* to take the GRE or SAT twice! Fortunately, there are other methods of estimating reliability which require administering a test only once.

Split-half reliability

Internal consistency reliability, as the name implies, is a type of reliability which is based on the internal consistency of the test. A common type of internal consistency reliability is referred to as *split-half reliability*. Since split-half reliability procedures require only one administration of a test, certain sources of errors of measurement are eliminated, such as differences in testing conditions, which can occur in establishing test-retest reliability for example. Split-half reliability is especially appropriate when a test is very long.

The procedure for determining split-half reliability is as follows:

1 Administer the *total test to one group*.
2 *Divide the test* into two comparable halves, or subtests; the most common approach is to include all odd-numbered items in one half and all even-numbered items in the other half.
3 Compute each person's score on the two halves (each person will subsequently have two scores, a score for the odd-numbered items and a score for the even-numbered items).
4 Correlate the two sets of scores.

If the coefficient is high, the test has good split-half reliability. A number of logical and statistical methods can be used to divide a test in half, random selection of half of the items for example. In reality, the odd-even strategy, however, is most often used. Actually, this approach works out rather well regardless of how a test is organized. Suppose, for example, a test is a 20-item power test and the items get progressively more difficult. Items 1, 3, 5, 7, 11, 13, 15, 17, and 19 as a group should be approximately as difficult as items 2, 4, 6, 8, 10, 12, 14, 16, 18, and 20. Items 1 and 2 will be easy, 3 and 4 will be more difficult, and so forth. Or, suppose a test is organized by topic so that items 1–10 deal with circles and items 11–20 deal with quadrilaterals. In this case the odd items will contain items on circles and quadrilaterals and so will the even items. Thus, regardless of how the test is organized, an odd-even split should produce essentially equivalent halves. In fact, in essence what we are doing is artificially creating two equivalent forms of a test and computing equivalent-forms reliability; the two equivalent forms just happen to be in the same test. Thus the label "internal consistency reliability."

Since longer tests tend to be more reliable, and since split-half reliability actually represents the reliability of a test only half as long as the actual test, a correction formula must be applied to the reliability coefficient. The correction formula which is used is the Spearman-Brown prophecy formula. For example, suppose the split-half reliability coefficient for a 50-item test were .80. The .80 would be based on the correlation between scores on 25 odd items and 25 even items and would therefore be an estimate of the reliability of a 25-item test, not a 50-item test. The Spearman-Brown formula would need to be applied to estimate the reliability (*r*) of the 50-item test. The formula is a very simple one, even for those of you who are not mathematically inclined:

$$r_{\text{total test}} = \frac{2r_{\text{split half}}}{1 + r_{\text{split half}}}$$

Applying the formula to our example:

$$r_{\text{total test}} = \frac{2(.80)}{1 + .80} = \frac{1.60}{1.80} = .89$$

Thus, the split-half estimate of .80 was corrected to an estimate of .89. One problem with the correction formula is that it tends to give a higher estimate of reliability than would be obtained using other procedures. Another approach to estimating internal consistency is the method of rationale equivalence.

Rationale equivalence reliability

Rationale equivalence reliability is not established through a single correlation but rather estimates internal consistency by determining how all items on a test relate to all other items and to the total test. Rationale equivalence reliability is determined through application of one of the Kuder-Richardson formulas, usually formula 20 or 21 (KR=20 or KR=21). Application of a Kuder-Richardson formula results in an estimate of reliability which is essentially equivalent to the average of the split-half reliabilities computed for all possible halves. Use of formula 21 requires less time and is easier to compute than any other method of estimating reliability. Its application also usually results in a more conservative estimate of reliability, especially if more than one trait is being measured. The formula is as follows:

$$r_{\text{total test}} = \frac{K(SD^2) - \overline{X}(K - \overline{X})}{(SD^2)(K - 1)}$$

where

K = the number of items in the test
SD = the standard deviation of the scores
$\overline{X}$ = the mean of the scores

In a later chapter you will learn how to compute the mean and standard deviation of a set of scores. For the moment, let it suffice to say that the mean $(\overline{X})$ is the average score on the test for the group that took it and the standard deviation (SD) is an indication of the amount of score variability, or how spread out the scores are. For example, assume that you have administered a 50-item test and have calculated the mean to be 40 $(\overline{X} = 40)$ and the standard deviation to be 4 (SD = 4). The reliability of the test (which in this example turns out to be not too hot!) would be calculated as follows:

$$r_{\text{total test}} = \frac{50(4^2) - 40(50 - 40)}{(4^2)(50 - 1)}$$

$$= \frac{50(16) - 40(10)}{(16)(49)}$$

$$= \frac{800 - 400}{784} = \frac{400}{784} = .51$$

This formula should be more comprehensible to you after you have completed chapter 17 on analysis and interpretation of results, but even at this stage the ease of applying the formula should be evident.

Figure 7.1 summarizes the methods for estimating test reliability. One (1) test administration indicates either that only one test is administered (split-half and KR-21 reliability) or that two tests are administered at essentially the same time (equivalent-forms reliability). Two (2) administration times indicates a time interval exists (say a week) between the two administrations (test-retest and stability and equivalence reliability). You should keep in mind when reviewing test information that while the size of the reliability coefficient is of prime importance, the method used to calculate it should also be considered.

Number of different tests

		1	2
Number of administration times	1	Split-half KR-21	Equivalent-forms
	2	Test-retest	Stability and equivalence

figure 7.1
Summary of methods for estimating reliability

Scorer/rater reliability

There are other situations for which reliability must be investigated. Such situations usually occur when the scoring of tests involves subjectivity, such as with essay tests, short-answer tests involving more than a one-word response, rating scales, and observation instruments. In such situations we are concerned with interjudge (interscorer, interrater, interobserver) reliability and/or intrajudge reliability. Interjudge reliability refers to the reliability of two (or more) independent scorers; intrajudge reliability refers to the reliability of the scoring of individual scorers. Scoring and rating are sources of errors of measurement and it is important to estimate the consistency of scorers' assessments. Estimates of interjudge or intrajudge reliability are usually obtained using correlational techniques, as have already been discussed, but can also be expressed simply as percent agreement. While such reliabilities are unfortunately usually not very good, a number of standardized instruments have been developed to the point where interjudge and intrajudge reliability appear to be relatively quite good. Validation studies involving the Flanders system for the observation of classroom verbal behavior, for example, have reported interrater and intrarater reliabilities ranging from the mid eighties (e.g. .85) to the low nineties.

Criterion-referenced tests

As with NRTs, the reliability of a CRT refers to the consistency with which a test measures whatever it measures. All of the types of reliability discussed with respect to NRTs are relevant to CRTs. However, if CRTs are properly constructed, internal consistency should be virtually assured. Thus, our major concern with CRTs is the assessment of degree of stability or equivalence (test-retest and equivalent forms reliability). Traditional methods for estimating these types of consistency require a degree of variability which is not necessarily present in the results of CRT, particularly with mastery CRTs. Thus, nonmastery CRTs and mastery CRTs involve the same problems with respect to estimation of reliability but to different degrees.

Nonmastery CRTs

While score variability is not a desirable characteristic of a CRT, it is none-theless usually present. If a CRT is administered and individual levels of performance are recorded, there will almost always be score variability. The degree of variability will of course vary from test to test and group to group, but it will be present. When sufficient variability is present, traditional measures for computing reliability may be used. In such situations test-retest and equivalent-forms reliability may be estimated as described for NRTs. Of course in most cases the degree of variability will be lower than for NRTs and the reliability coefficient (r) will tend to be lower, that is, will be a conservative estimate, or underestimate, of reliability. Thus, if a reliability coefficient is satisfactorily high we will be happy, but if it is low we should not necessarily be unhappy. Such coefficients should be interpreted realistically, not pessimistically or optimistically.

You may be wondering why we ever apply a basically inapporpriate technique in the first place. The reason is that presently there is no approach to the calculation of the reliability of CRTs which is generally accepted as being appropriate. Many alternatives have been suggested, much work has been done in the area, and some promising efforts are under way. For the time being, however, we must get by the best we can.

Mastery CRTs

Probably the most well known of the approaches suggested for estimating the reliability of CRTs is that proposed by Livingston.[5] Livingston's formula is essentially a generalization of classical reliability theory. In essence, his formula computes the reliability of a CRT by first computing a traditional measure of reliability (appropriate for NRTs), then adjusting it based on the criterion, or cut-off, score of the CRT. Thus, any type of reliability can be calculated by converting a traditional estimate. Of course, because of its reliance on a criterion or cut-off score, the formula is really only appropriate for mastery tests. Calculation using his formula is really quite simple:

$$r_{CR} = \frac{r_{NR}(SD^2) + (\overline{X} - C)^2}{(SD^2) + (\overline{X} - C)^2}$$

where

r_{CR} = the reliability of the criterion-referenced test
r_{NR} = any traditional estimate of reliability
SD = the standard deviation of the scores (SD^2 is referred to as the variance of the scores)
$\overline{X}$ = the mean (average) of the scores
C = the criterion or cutoff score

Note that if $\overline{X} = C$ (the average score *is* the criterion score), then $\overline{X} - C = 0$, the formula reduces to $r_{CR} = r_{NR}$, and the estimates are the same. When the average

[5] Livingston, S. A. Criterion-referenced applications of classical test theory. *Journal of Educational Measurement*, 1972, *9*(1), 13–26.

score is not the same as the criterion score, then r_{CR} is always greater than r_{NR}. Recall that simply applying a traditional technique to the results of a CRT typically results in an underestimate of reliability. Thus, Livingston's adjustment increases the reliability estimate, presumably to more accurately reflect reliability. As an example, suppose we administer a 100-item CRT with a criterion score of 80 ($C = 80$). And suppose we calculate the average score to be 75 ($\overline{X} = 75$), the variance to be 25 ($SD^2 = 25$), and the test-retest reliability to be .60 ($r_{NR} = .60$). Substituting this information into Livingston's formula, we would get the following:

$$r_{CR} = \frac{r_{NR}(SD^2) + (\overline{X} - C)^2}{(SD^2) + (\overline{X} - C)^2} = \frac{.60(25) + (75 - 80)^2}{25 + (75 - 80)^2}$$

$$= \frac{15 + 25}{25 + 25}$$

$$= \frac{40}{50}$$

$$= .80$$

In this case, Livingston's estimate would be considerably higher than that obtained using only the traditional test-retest formula. Note that if the average score were 85 (and the criterion score 80), or if the criterion score were 70 (and the average score 75), the estimate of reliability would still be .80. Thus Livingston's estimate of the reliability of a CRT will usually be higher, but in no case lower, than estimates using traditional approaches.

Some have criticized Livingston's formula on the grounds that since his reliability estimate is a function of the criterion score, you can manipulate reliability by simply raising or lowering the criterion. Livingston agrees that this is possible but points out that traditional estimates can also be manipulated—for example, by purposely including students who will get very high or very low scores thus increasing score variability and calculated reliability. It has also been stated that while Livingston's reliability coefficient may be numerically higher, the standard error of measurement is the same regardless of whether his approach or a traditional approach is used.[6] Again, Livingston agrees that the standard error of measurement is the same but points out that the standard error of measurement is concerned with the true scores of individuals whereas reliability is concerned with the score consistency of a group. And the larger reliability coefficient produced using his formula "*does* imply a more dependable overall determination of whether each test score falls above or below the criterion level when this decision is to be made for every individual score in the distribution."

An alternate approach to the reliability of mastery CRTs, one that appears promising, is that proposed by Brennan and Kane.[7] While discussion of their approach is beyond the scope of this text, it is similar in many ways to Livingston's, differing mainly in the theoretical framework within which it is developed. Brenner and Kane prefer the term "index of dependability" to "reliability coefficient."

[6]Harris, C. W. An interpretation of Livingston's reliability coefficient for criterion-refernced tests. *Journal of Educational Measurement*, 1972, 9(1), 27–29.
[7] Brennan, R. L. & Kane, M. T. An index of dependability for mastery tests. *Journal of Educational Measurement*, 1977, 14, 277–289.

Popham has suggested several informal approaches for getting a rough indication of degree of reliability.[8] One suggestion is to compare the scores of a group on a test on two different occasions and determine the percentage of scores that were different by given percentages. For example, we might determine that 68% of the scores were different by as much as 10% (10% might represent a 5 point difference either higher or lower). Another suggestion is to compare decisions made on two separate occasions based on test results. For example, based on scores we might classify 22 students as having achieved mastery (perhaps defined as a score of 16 out of 20) and 6 students as not having achieved mastery. We might administer the same test at another date and independently classify the students again. We could then determine the percentage of students for whom the same decision was made both times, e.g. they were classified as having achieved mastery on both occasions. In this case the variability of the individual scores would not be as important as the consistency of the decisions.

Standard error of measurement

Reliability can also be expressed in terms of the standard error of measurement. This is a concept which you should be familiar with since such data are often reported for a test. It is information which is useful to teachers and counselors in interpreting individual scores and can be computed for both NRTs and CRTs. Basically, the *standard error of measurement* is an estimate of how often you can expect errors of a given size. Thus, a small standard error of measurement indicates high reliability, and a large standard error of measurement indicates low reliability. If a test were perfectly reliable (which no test is), a person's obtained score would be his or her true score. As it is, an obtained score is an estimate of a true score. If you administered the same test over and over to the same group, the score of each individual would vary. How much variability would be present in individual scores would be a function of the test's reliability. The variability would be small for a highly reliable test (zero if the test were perfectly reliable) and large for a test with low reliability. If we could administer the test many times we could see how much variation actually occurred. Of course, realistically we can't do this; administering the same test twice to the same group is tough enough. Fortunately, it is possible to estimate this degree of variation (the standard error of measurement) using the data from the administration of a test once to a group. In other words, the standard error of measurement allows us to estimate how much difference there probably is between a person's obtained score and true score, the size of this difference being a function of the reliability of the test. We can estimate the standard error of measurement using the following simple formula:

$$SE_m = SD\sqrt{1 - r}$$

where

SE_m = standard error of measurement
SD = the standard deviation of the test scores
r = the reliability coefficient

[8] See footnote 2.

For example, for a 25-item test we might calculate the standard deviation of a set of scores to be 5 (SD = 5) and the split-half reliability to be .84 (r = .84). In this case the standard error of measurement would be calculated as follows:

$$SE_m = SD\sqrt{1 - r} = 5\sqrt{1 - .84}$$
$$= 5\sqrt{.16}$$
$$= 5(.4)$$
$$= 2.0$$

As the above example illustrates, the size of the SE_m is a function of both the SD and r. Higher reliability is associated with a smaller SE_m and a smaller SD is associated with a smaller SE_m. If in the above example r = .64, would you expect SE_m to be larger or smaller? Right, larger, and in fact it would be 3.0. Also, if in the above example SD = 10, what would you expect to happen to SE_m? Right, it would be larger, 4.0 to be exact. While we prefer the SE_m to be small, indicating less error, it is impossible to say how small is "good." This is because SE_m is expressed in the same units as the test and how small is "small" is relative to the size of the test. Thus SE_m = 5 would be large for a 20-item test but small for a 200-item test. In our example, SE_m = 2.0 would be considered small.

SE_m estimates are frequently used to construct what are called *confidence intervals*, or bands, around individual scores. If Winston Whizkid, for example, gets a score of 84 on a test with SE_m = 3, then we can add 3 and subtract 3 from 84 to form an interval (84 + 3 = 87 and 84 − 3 = 81) so 81–87 is our interval. What we just said is that $X \pm 1\ SE_m$ = 84 ± 3 = 81–87. Using normal curve properties, we would say that we are approximately 68% confident that Winston's *true* score falls within the interval 81–87. Of course we could be wrong, but we are *probably* correct. We might also calculate $X \pm 2\ SE_m$ which in Winston's case would be 84 ± 2(3) = 84 ± 6 = 78–90. In this case, we would say that we are approximately 95% confident that Winston's true score falls within the interval 78–90. And similarly, we can be 99% confident (almost positive!) that Winston's true score is within the interval $X \pm 3\ SE_m$ = 84 ± 3(3) = 84 ± 9 = 75–93. In practice, $X \pm 1\ SE_m$ is usually used. You should understand that SE_m = 3 does *not* mean that a person's true score absolutely does not differ from his or her true score by more than 3, but it does mean that 68% of the time a person's observed score will be within +3 of his or her true score.

Differences in the obtained scores of different students may be due to measurement error and not real differences in true scores. SE_m bands can be used to make such determinations. Overlapping intervals suggest that the true scores on the test are not really different whereas intervals that do not overlap suggest true score differences. Suppose that SE_m = 4, and that Ziggy's obtained score = 70, Lulu's = 72, and Hornrim's = 82. We can compute $X \pm 1\ SE_m$ for each student and we get: Ziggy = 70 ± 4 = 66–74; Lulu = 72 ± 4 = 68–76; and Hornrim = 82 ± 4 = 78–86. Ziggy's interval overlaps with Lulu's (they both include the score 72, for example), but neither overlaps with Hornrim's. Thus we would say that Ziggy's and Lulu's true scores are essentially the same but Hornrim's is really higher than theirs.

To facilitate better interpretation of scores, some test publishers do not just present the SE_m for the total group but also give a separate SE_m for each of a number of identified subgroups.

The procedure above described is somewhat simplified and therefore not entirely correct. In reality, for example, confidence intervals are not symmetrical around the obtained score. There are more precise techniques which can be used. We can, for example, estimate true scores and place them in SE_m confidence intervals. In practice, however, SE_m bands based on obtained scores are the ones most commonly used and reported. Further, if the test has high reliability the SE_m bands for obtained scores and estimated true scores are very similar anyway. Therefore, knowledge of the above approach should be sufficient for most of you since you are only going to administer highly reliable tests (!). If additional information is desired on some alternative approaches, however, there are a number of sources which can be consulted.[9]

Factors affecting reliability

A number of factors can affect the reliability coefficient of a test. Some of these factors are related to the test itself, some to the group taking the test, and some to the environment in which the test is administered, including factors such as test administration and scoring procedures. Knowledge of these factors improves test development procedures, test usage, and analysis of test information. It is important, for example, to be aware that there are certain factors which can artificially increase the computed reliability. In other words, increasing the reliability coefficient is not necessarily the same thing as increasing the reliability of the test. For example, suppose we compute the split-half reliability of a speed test. A speed test, you will recall, is one in which the items are easy and testing time is limited. Thus, if a student completes 20 problems in 5 minutes, chances are all 20 are correct. If we compute odd and even scores, the student's score will be the same on both halves, i.e. 10 and 10, and similarly all students' odd and even scores will be the same or very close. In this case, the reliability coefficient will be very, very high. Obviously, internal consistency measures are not appropriate for speed tests.

Reliability can be increased in several major ways. Although it will be apparent from some of the discussion, it should be noted that some of the factors to be described pertain mainly to traditional methods of estimating reliability.

Test length

Probably the most rational way to increase reliability is to increase the length of the test. This does not mean putting the test on longer sheets of paper! It refers to the fact that (other factors being equal) adding items to a test, items that are as good as the items already in the test, increases the reliability. The reason is that adding items improves the sampling of the intended behavior domain. Improved sampling results in higher validity and reduces chance factors. This is as true for CRTs as it is for NRTs, perhaps more so. Think of it this way. Suppose you wanted to know what the student body was like at Crossexen University. Suppose you met one student and he happened to be a male Indian. If you stopped there,

[9] See, for example, Stanley, J. C. Reliability. In R. L. Thorndike (Ed.), *Educational measurement.* Washington, D.C.: American Council on Education, 1971.

your best evidence would be that students at Crossexen University are all male Indians. Clearly one student would not be representative of the whole university. In fact, he might be the only Indian at the university. Suppose you met two students, one male Indian and one female Caucasian—that would be better but not by much. Obviously the more students you met, the more accurate your conclusions would be. The same applies to tests. The more items that are included, the better the sampling and the more representative the test becomes of the total domain of behaviors.

Of course, from other standpoints tests can be too long. Unwanted factors such as student fatigue may occur. In most cases, especially with classroom tests, a balance must be struck such that the test is long enough but not too long. For certain situations, such as when important decisions are going to be made based on test results, very long tests are necessary. The GRE, you may recall, was not exactly a shortie. In general, however, lengthening a test to improve reliability does have reasonable limits. Further, an increase in test length is not accompanied by an equal increase in reliability. If you double the length of a test, for example, you do not double the reliability. This makes sense since the theoretical maximum is 1.00. If a test has a reliability coefficient of .70 to begin with, no matter how many items you add, the reliability is never going to be 1.01! In fact, the higher the reliability is to begin with, the less is to be gained by increasing the length of the test.

To verify this concept we need to look at a method for estimating the gain in reliability to be achieved by increasing the length of a test by a certain factor. Recall that when we discussed split-half reliability, we used the Spearman-Brown formula to estimate the reliability of the total test. Actually, we used a special case of the formula, the situation where we are estimating the reliability of a test twice as long as the original. The formula is

$$r_2 = \frac{2r}{1 + r}$$

where

r = current reliability of the test
r_2 = the reliability of a test twice as long

Applying the formula, we can estimate the reliability of a test twice as long as a test which has a reliability of .70:

$$r_2 = \frac{2r}{1 + r} = \frac{2(.70)}{1 + .70} = \frac{1.40}{1.70} = .82$$

Similarly, we can estimate the following reliability increases resulting from doubling the length of a test:

r	r_2
.90	.95
.80	.89
.70	.82
.60	.75
.50	.66

Thus we see that larger increases are expected from lower initial reliabilities.

The more general formula for estimating the change in reliability resulting from a change in test length is as follows:

$$r_n = \frac{nr}{1 + (n - 1)r}$$

We can see this formula for estimating the reliability of a test increased or decreased by any factor; that is, n may equal 3, or 4, or even ½. If we triple the length of a test ($n = 3$) where $r = .70$, we have:

$$r_3 = \frac{3r}{1 + (3 - 1)r} = \frac{3(.70)}{1 + (2).70} = \frac{2.10}{2.40} = .88$$

If we reduce the length of a test with $r = .86$ by a half, that is, remove half of the items, we have:

$$r_{1/2} = \frac{\frac{1}{2}r}{1 + (\frac{1}{2} - 1)r} = \frac{\frac{1}{2}(.86)}{1 + (-\frac{1}{2}).86} = \frac{.43}{1 - .43} = \frac{.43}{.57} = .75$$

We can also rearrange the formula a little bit and solve for n to estimate by what factor a test has to be lengthened in order to achieve a desired reliability coefficient. For example, suppose we have an achievement test with $r = .80$ and we would like the r to be at least .90. We can use the following formula to determine how much we have to lengthen the test (n):

$$n = \frac{r_n(1 - r)}{r(1 - r_n)}$$

where

r_n = the desired reliability coefficient
r = the present reliability coefficient

To compute n for our example:

$$n = \frac{r_n(1 - r)}{r(1 - r_n)} = \frac{.90(1 - .80)}{.80(1 - .90)} = \frac{.90(.20)}{.80(.10)} = \frac{.18}{.08} = 2.25$$

Thus $n = 2.25$, which means that to increase the reliability coefficient to .90 we have to make the test 2.25 times as long. If for our example, the present test with $r = .80$ has 20 items, the new test has to have 2.25 (20) = 45 items. Of course we have to keep in mind that the new items have to be as *good* as the existing ones.

Score variability

Traditional correlational methods for estimating reliability require score variability. If variability is reduced, as may be the case with CRTs, the reliability coefficient is lowered. Correspondingly, if variability is increased, the reliability coefficient is increased. So, by increasing score variability, or the spread of scores, we can increase the reliability coefficient. This can be accomplished in different ways. One major way involves the difficulty of the test itself and another involves the range of ability of the test takers. First, what kind of a test, other factors being equal, do you think would result in more score variability—(a) a test with all easy items, (b) a test with all average-difficulty items, or (c) a test with all very difficult items? Think about it. If you reasoned that the answer is (b) a test with all average-difficulty items, even if it was only a hunch, you deserve a gold star. If all the items are easy (as with a mastery test), there will be little variability since most test takers will get a high score. Likewise, if all the items are very difficult, there will be little variability because most test takers will get a low score.[10] Of course if either one of these actually happens, it does not necessarily mean that the test is unreliable, but it does mean that traditional methods for estimating reliability are inappropriate and will result in underestimates to the degree that variability is reduced.

Now here's another thought question for you: What kind of a group do you think will have a wider spread of scores, that is, more score variability—(a) a group in which all the persons have approximately the same ability (low, average, or high), or (b) a group in which the persons represent a wide range of ability (from very low to very high)? If you concluded that the answer is (b) wide range of ability, you're really beginning to see the light. The more homogeneous the group is, the more homogeneous their responses will be. The more heterogeneous a group is, the more heterogeneous, or variable, their scores will be. An important implication of this concept is the fact that the scores for any given grade or age level will tend to be more homogeneous than the combined scores of several grade or age levels. As an example, the reliability coefficient of a test for the fourth, fifth and sixth grades will be an overestimate of the reliability for any one of the grades. Therefore, separate reliability coefficients should be presented for each level, even if the test is appropriate for several levels.

When a group is homogeneous with respect to the variable being measured, there is said to be a restriction in range. A correction formula for restriction in range can be applied to obtain an estimate of what the coefficient *would be* if the range of scores were not restricted. If such a correction is reported it must be interpreted with caution; keep in mind that the resulting coefficient does not represent what was actually found.

Score objectivity

You will recall that an objective test is one for which subjectivity in scoring is, at least theoretically, eliminated; anyone scoring a particular test should come up with the same score. Multiple-choice tests and true-false tests are examples of objective tests. Score objectivity is therefore a given with most objective tests. Recall that short-answer tests, however, may involve some subjectivity in scoring. Essay tests are very likely to involve subjectivity as are instruments used in the assessment of procedures and products, though to a lesser degree. The reason is that a test is unreliable to the degree that scores are a result of factors other than true scores. Consequently, the more subjectivity there is in the scoring, the more opportunity there is for error factors (such as scorer bias) to distort true scores. Thus, while scoring procedures are important for all tests, they are even

---

[10] In chapter 11 we will discuss the concept of item-difficulty further; you will see that for variability purposes the ideal item has a difficulty index of .50, which means that half of the group gets the item correct and half of the group gets the item incorrect.

more so for nonobjective tests. Every effort must be made to make scoring as objective *as possible* and to eliminate the influence of the scorer on the scores.

Interpretation of validity and reliability coefficients

Certain types of validity and reliability are expressed numerically, usually as a coefficient. A high coefficient indicates high validity or reliability. If a test were perfectly valid and reliable, all coefficients would be 1.00. This would mean that a student's score perfectly reflected her or his true status with respect to the variable being measured. Alas and alack, no test is perfectly valid or reliable. Scores are inevitable affected by systematic errors and errors of measurement resulting from a variety of causes. High validity indicates that systematic errors have been reduced whereas high reliability indicates that random errors have been reduced. Systematic errors affect scores in a systematic way (e.g. lowering them all) whereas random errors of measurement affect scores in a random fashion (i.e., some scores may be increased while others are decreased). Systematic and random errors can be caused by characteristics of the test itself (items may be inappropriate for the group being tested or ambiguous items which some students just happen to interpret correctly), by conditions of administration (directions may not be properly followed), or by the current status of the persons taking the test (some may be tired, others unmotivated), or by a combination of any of the above. High validity and reliability coefficients indicate that these sources of error have been eliminated as much as possible.

A correlation coefficient is the most common way to express degree of validity and reliability, but what a correlation coefficient means is difficult to explain. Some students erroneously (but understandably) think that a correlation coefficient of .50 means that two sets of scores are 50% related. Not true. In measurement talk, a correlation coefficient squared indicates the amount of common variance shared by two sets of scores (WHAT??!!). Now, in English. Each time a test is administered the result will be a range of scores. There will almost always be score variance; that is, everyone will not get the same score. Common variance refers to the variation in one set of scores that is attributable to its tendency to vary with the other set of scores. If two sets of scores are not related (e.g., the test is totally unreliable), then the variability of one set of scores has nothing to do with the variability of the other set. If two sets of scores are perfectly related, then the variability of one set of scores has everything to do with the variability in the other set. Thus, with no relationship between two sets of scores, there is no common variance, but with perfect relationship all variance, or 100% of the variance, is shared, common variance. The percent of common variance is generally less than the numerical value of the correlation coefficient. In fact, to determine common variance you simply square the correlation coefficient. The result is referred to as a *coefficient of determination*. A correlation coefficient of .80 when squared (.80 × .80) yields a value of .64 and indicates 64% common variance. A correlation coefficient of .00 when squared yields .00 and indicates 00% common variance, and a coefficient of 1.00 squared yields 1.00 and indicates 100% common variance. Thus, a coefficient of .50 may not look bad at first but it actually means that the two sets of scores have 25% common variance.

The question remains as to how high a correlation coefficient needs to be to be "good" or "acceptable" or "useful." There are no hard and fast rules that say a coefficient must be at least .70, for example, to be of any value. Interpretation of a correlation coefficient depends upon how it is going to be used. How large it needs to be in order to be useful depends upon the purpose for which it was computed. When correlation coefficients are used to estimate the validity or reliability of measuring instruments, the criterion of acceptability is higher than when they are used for other purposes, such as research studies investigating relationships among variables. A correlation coefficient of .40, for example, would be considered useful in a research study investigating relationship, not useful as an index of predictive validity, and terrible as an index of reliability. A coefficient of .60 would be considered useful in an investigation of possible predictors but would still probably be considered unsatisfactory as an estimate of reliability.

With respect to validity, we most often compute correlation coefficients to determine the predictive validity of instruments, that is, the degree of relationship between scores on a predictor and scores on a criterion. When prediction is involved, we are interested in the value of the coefficient in facilitating accurate predictions. A coefficient of .40, for example, would be of little value for most prediction purposes. Since the relationship is so low—the common variance is only $(.40)^2$, or .16, or 16%—knowing a person's score on one variable would be of little help in predicting his or her score on the other. A correlation coefficient much below .50 is generally useless for either group prediction or individual prediction, although a combination of several variables in this range may yield a reasonably satisfactory prediction. Coefficients in the .60s and .70s are usually considered *adequate* for group prediction purposes, and coefficients in the .80s and above for individual prediction purposes. These figures are, of course, minimums, not standards to shoot for.

What constitutes an acceptable level of reliability is to some degree determined by the type of test although a coefficient over .90 would be acceptable for any test. As with validity, the question is really concerned with what constitutes a minimum level of acceptability. For standardized achievement and aptitude tests, there is generally no good reason for selecting a test whose reliability is not as least .90. A number of achievement and aptitude tests are available which report such reliabilities, and it is therefore not usually necessary to settle for less. Personality measures do not typically report such high reliabilities (although certainly some do) and therefore one would be very satisfied with a reliability in the eighties (e.g. .84) and might even accept a reliability in the seventies. Attitude scale reliabilities, for example, usually fall in the sixties to eighties range, with most being in the seventies. When tests are developed in new areas, one usually has to settle for lower reliability, at least initially. For example, tests which measure curiosity are a relatively recent addition to the testing field. One would not expect high reliabilities for these new tests at this stage of their development. Of course, while such tests may be administered for research or informational purposes, results should not be used for any serious decision making.

If a test is composed of several subtests, then the reliability of each subtest, not just the reliability of the total test, must be assessed. Since reliability is a function of test length, the reliability of a given subtest is typically lower than the total test reliability. Examination of subtest reliability is especially important if one or more of the subtests are going to be administered rather than the total test. You should be a smart consumer when it comes to examining test information. If a test manual states that "the total test reliability is .90 and all subtest reliabilities are satisfactory," you should immediately become suspicious. If subtest reliabilities are "satisfactory" the publisher will certainly want to tell you just how satisfactory they are. Most of the well-established tests do report subtest reliabilities.

Remember, test publishers are in the business of selling tests. If they omit pertinent information, it is your responsibility to be aware of such omissions and to
seek additional data.

At this point we should stop and remind ourselves why we care so much
about all these types of information. The reason is that test results are used to
make all kinds of decisions about people. The decisions are only as valid and reliable as the measurements upon which they are based. Some degree of test invalidity and unreliability is unavoidable, but making bad decisions is not—not if
we select our measurement techniques rationally and interpret results intelligently. The more important the decisions are, that is, the more serious the consequences of the decisions are, the more care must be exercised. And remember, the
most valid decisions are those based on more than one source of data.

Selection of a test

Usually when we speak of selecting a test, we are referring to a norm-referenced,
standardized instrument. In fact, sometimes the decision to use such an instrument or instruments is made a bit too automatically. In a variety of situations, some
other method of measurement may be more appropriate.

Selection of measurement methods

As we have seen, there are a variety of measurement options. These include,
among others, locally-developed instruments such as criterion-referenced
achievement tests, rating scales for assessing procedures and products, and questionnaires. Knowledge of these options tends to reduce overreliance on norm-referenced, standardized tests in evaluation efforts. Which measurement techniques
are selected should depend mainly on the purpose of the testing and the objectives
to be measured. For example, the evaluation plan for an experimental reading curriculum would involve a combination of locally-developed and standardized instruments, mostly the former. The evaluation would probably involve pretesting
and posttesting of the experimental group and a control group, a group learning
under some other reading curriculum. The most important variable to be measured would be reading achievement. Measurement of reading achievement
would probably require both locally-developed, criterion-referenced tests and
standardized, norm-referenced tests. The criterion-referenced tests would be necessary in order to determine whether the experimental curriculum achieved its
own objectives, i.e. whether students did achieve the objectives purported to be
fostered by the curriculum. Observation might also be involved, with students
being rated on their oral reading ability. Attitudinal data would probably also be
collected in order to determine participants' reactions to the experimental program. Other measurement approaches might include interviews with teachers and
other involved personnel, and questionnaires to parents of participants.

The hypothetical situation above is presented to reemphasize that while
this chapter deals with the selection of standardized tests, they represent only one
measurement option; the next chapter deals with instrument development. While
mundane matters such as politics and budget do sometimes influence decisions
concerning measurement techniques to be used, the main considerations should

be what is needed and what is available. Many situations, however, do require standardized tests. Whenever they are used, they must be selected by persons with the necessary knowledge of concepts such as validity and reliability. From a human relations viewpoint, it is a good idea to involve participating staff in the selection process, but at least one person must have sufficient expertise.

One evaluation situation which invariably involves standardized tests is the school testing program. There are a number of "nonmeasurement" factors which influence such a program. The apparent drop in student achievement (discussed in chapter 1) and the increased demand for accountability, for example, have resulted in an increase in state-level testing decisions and a decrease in the autonomy of local school districts. Another trend has been increasing criticism of certain tests and testing procedures by a variety of groups and in some cases court intervention.[11] Some tests which have always been considered essential components of a school testing program are now being seriously questioned. For example, periodic measurement of scholastic aptitude and yearly achievement testing have been the cornerstone of school testing programs at the elementary, junior high, and senior high school levels. Use of scholastic aptitude tests is being challenged, and their fate could have a major impact on testing in general. Tests of character and personality have also been considered highly desirable. These too, although to a lesser degree, have come under fire.

At least for the time being, however, school testing programs typically include the above mentioned tests. At the preschool level individually administered tests requiring psychomotor or verbal responses are usually given. At higher levels tests are generally written and their nature varies from level to level. At the elementary and junior high levels, for example, scholastic aptitude is measured, while at the senior high level differential aptitude is also of interest. And, as discussed previously, standardized readiness and diagnostic tests are desirable at all appropriate levels. While achievement of basic skills has always been of prime concern at the elementary level, recent developments have extended the concern to the junior and senior high levels.

Factors to consider

Whether you are selecting standardized tests for a school testing program, a special program, or classroom use, the same basic factors need to be considered. The first is the availability and completeness of information concerning characteristics of the test. Not surprisingly, there is usually a relationship between the amount of relevant data supplied by a publisher and the quality of the test. Of course the most important information is that concerning validity. Depending upon the alleged purpose of the test, certain kinds of data will be more important than other kinds. If a test is an achievement test, for example, we will be most interested in content validity, and detailed descriptions of content and how it was selected should be available. Regardless of the type of validity involved, we will always be interested in the size, location, and composition of the norm group as well as when the group was tested. Here's an evaluation riddle for you: When is it appropriate to use a test for which there is no validity data? Answer: Never. Strange as this may sound, it is good advice. In certain situations you might *select* a test with

[11] For further discussion of such factors, see Rudman, H. C. The superintendent and testing: Implications for the curriculum. *NCME: Measurement in Education*, 1977, 8(4), 1–8.

no validity data and validate it yourself, but you should never base decisions on the results of an instrument for which no such data are available.

Next, depending upon how the test is to be used, appropriate reliability coefficients should be given as well as the size of the group upon which they are based (if this number is not the same as the size of the norm group). If two forms of the test are to be given, for example, we will be most interested in equivalent-forms reliability. Reliability coefficients should be reported for individual grade and/or age levels and not just, for example, for "primary level" students. Standard error of measurement figures should also be provided, by age and/or grade level at the very least. These data will be of especial interest to us if test results are to be used for making decisions about individuals.

Of course, other types of information should be reported including information related to administration, scoring, and interpretation. A set of standards which indicates the kinds of information which should be reported has been developed by a joint committee of the American Psychological Association, the American Educational Research Association, and the National Council on Measurement in Education.[12] These standards apply primarily to standardized tests which are to be used for practical purposes; they were not developed with basic research uses of instruments in mind.

A word of caution. As noted previously, standardized criterion-referenced tests are a relatively new addition to the testing field. Publishers have begun to grind them out in an attempt to meet a market need. On the whole, such tests have not been too terrific. Typically, domain descriptions are fuzzy and tests do not adequately sample the intended domains. In many cases objectives-based programs are really faced with Hobson's choice—use a questionable standardized criterion-referenced test or use a well established norm-referenced test and attempt to make inferences about the intended behavior domain using the results. The second alternative may seem preferable to the first, but there is evidence to support the contention that standardized NRTs are not appropriate for determining the achievement of local objectives. In 1970 a Virginia state-mandated testing program attempted to measure achievement of 3,365 behavioral objectives, in 23 cognitive subjects, which had been developed by academic specialists and authorities.[13] Achievement of the objectives was assessed by administering well-known standardized tests in grades 4, 7, and 11. Subject specialists determined the tests' content validity with respect to the objectives by making inspectional analyses which compared test items with selected objectives. They found that in none of the subject areas did the tests measure the objectives with sufficient validity to warrant one-to-one assessment comparisons. In fact, percent coverage of given sets of objectives ranged from 0% for secondary work study and library skills to a maximum of 67.3% for reading. They concluded that regional curriculum differences seriously hinder the ability of standardized tests to measure achievement of specific outcomes desired by a school, district, or state. This is not to say that a standardized NRT can never be used to validly measure achievement of a set of local objectives, but the chances are slim. If a test appears on face value to be appropriate, only an item-by-item analysis of it will verify which objectives, if any, it is

[12] American Psychological Association. *Standards for educational and psychological tests.* Washington, D.C.: Author, 1974. To obtain a copy, send $3.50 to: American Psychological Association, 1200 Seventeenth Street, N.W., Washington, D.C. 20036

[13] Woodbury, C. A., Jr., & Jacobson, M. D. Assessment of cognitive behavioral objectives: An essential step in curriculum development and change. Paper presented at the American Educational Research Association Convention, Chicago, 1972.

appropriate for measuring. Thus, in the final analysis it appears that in most cases sets of specific objectives must be assessed by locally-developed instruments since both standardized CRTs and NRTs are not generally valid for this purpose.

Sources of test information

The most important guidelines for test selection are the following related rules: Do not—repeat—do not stop with the first test you find that appears to measure what you want, say, "Eureka, I have found it!" and blithely use it. *Do* identify those tests that are appropriate for your purpose, compare them on relevant factors, and select the best one. If you are knowledgeable about the qualities a test should possess and familiar with the various types of tests that are available (which of course you are by now!), then the selection of an instrument is a very orderly process. Assuming you have defined the purposes of the evaluation, performed a situation analysis, and delineated your objectives, the next steps are: (1) determine precisely what type(s) of test you need; (2) if a standardized instrument is required, identify and locate appropriate tests; and (3) do a comparative analysis of the tests and select the best one. In order to locate appropriate tests, you need to be familiar with sources of test information.

There are many initial sources of test information which you can consult in order to identify the range of possibilities. A good place to start is in a university library. The reference section will have Buros' *Mental Measurement Yearbooks* as well as volumes describing tests in various specialized areas such as early childhood education and physical education. Most libraries also have the ERIC (Educational Resources Information Center) system which contains all sorts of test information. A number of universities also have some type of resource center which contains test manuals and actual tests. Another obvious initial source of information is test publishers who typically disseminate test catalogs upon request. The *Encyclopedia of Educational Evaluation* lists the names and addresses of 37 major publishing companies. Also, measurement texts occasionally present detailed descriptions of major tests in a variety of areas.[14] Once you have determined the type of test you need (e.g. a test of reading comprehension for second graders), however, a logical place to start looking for tests is in Buros' *Mental Measurement Yearbooks*.

The *Yearbooks* have been published for several decades and represent the most comprehensive source of test information available to educators. In addition to a number of curriculum areas such as English, Mathematics, and Reading, major headings in the *Yearbooks* include: Achievement Batteries, Character and Personality, Intelligence and Multi-Aptitude Batteries. Each volume contains information on tests published since the last *Yearbook* as well as additional information on tests which have been substantially revised. To use a *Yearbook*, the following procedure may be utilized:

1 Scan the "Table of Contents" and identify the category which matches the type of test you are seeking, i.e., Achievement Batteries.

2 Go to the back of the volume to the "Classified Index of Tests." The Classi-

---

[14] See, for example, Mehrens, W. A., & Lehmann, I. J. *Measurement and evaluation in education and psychology.* New York: Holt, Rinehart and Winston, 1973.

fied Index is an expanded table of contents which alphabetically lists, by category, all the tests which appear in that volume.

3 Identify promising test titles and record their corresponding entry numbers.

4 Using the entry numbers, locate the test descriptions in the "Tests and Reviews" section of the *Yearbook* (the main body of the volume).

If you are seeking information on a particular test, you can locate its entry number by referring to the "Index of Titles" which is also located in the back of the volume.

Entries for new tests in the "Tests and Reviews" section typically include the following information: title, author, publisher, cost, a brief description, a description of groups for whom the test is intended, validity and reliability data, whether the test is a group or individual test, time requirements, test references, and critical reviews by qualified reviewers. Among other things, the reviews generally cite any special requirements or problems involved in test administration, scoring, and interpretation. A very useful supplement volume to the *Yearbooks* is Buros' *Tests in Print*. This volume is a comprehensive bibliography of all tests which have appeared in preceding *Yearbooks*. The format is basically that of the "Classified Index of Tests" which appears in each volume but gives considerably more information. Both the *Yearbooks* and *Tests in Print* are indispensable reference works for educators.

After reading the descriptions and reviews in the *Yearbooks*, you will quickly eliminate many of the tests whose titles looked promising. Some will not be appropriate for your students (or other participants), some will have inadequate validity and reliability data, and some will have one or more serious problems identified by reviewers. After you have narrowed the list of candidates you will still usually need additional information. A good source of information on a test is the publisher's test manual. Manuals usually include detailed validity and reliability data, a description of the subjects for whom the test is appropriate, conditions for administration, detailed scoring instructions, and requirements for score interpretation. As mentioned previously, however, you must be a smart consumer. The omission of relevant date in the manual probably says something unfavorable about the test. For instance, if information on subscore reliabilities is missing, they probably are not very good. As the Romans used to say, Caveat emptor!

Sometimes you may be aware of a new test which sounds exactly like what you need but on which you can find no information. In this case there are several additional avenues of inquiry. The *Journal of Educational Measurement* is one source that should be checked. The *Journal* contains reviews of recently published tests. *Psychological Abstracts* is also a potential source of information. Using the monthly or annual index, you can quickly determine if the *Abstracts* contain any information on the test. If nothing can be found, or if available information is skimpy, you should be able to obtain additional data by writing to the test developer. Test developers will usually comply with such requests, especially if you offer to supply your results after using the test.

Final selection of a test usually requires examination of the actual tests. A test which appears from all descriptions to be exactly what you need may have some problems detectable only by inspection of the test itself. The test may not be content valid, for example; it may contain items which measure content not covered by your treatment. An initial inspection copy of a test, as well as additional copies if you select that test for your study, should be acquired from the test publisher. For more tests, the publisher's name and address are given in the *Mental Measurement Yearbooks*.

Selecting from alternatives

Eventually a decision must be reached. Once you have narrowed the number of candidates and acquired all relevant information, a comparative analysis of the tests must be made. While there are a number of factors to be considered e.g., validity data and cost, these factors are not of equal importance. (The least expensive test, is not necessarily the best test!) As you should know by now, the most important factor to be considered is validity. Is one of the tests most appropriate for your sample? If you are interested in prediction, does one of the tests have a significantly higher predictive validity coefficient? If content validity is of prime importance, are the items of one test based on the same textbook which will be used in your evaluation? These are typical of the questions which might be raised. If after the validity comparison several tests still seem appropriate, the next factor for consideration is reliability.

Assuming all coefficients were acceptable, you would presumably select the test with the highest reliability, but there are other considerations. A factor to be considered in relation to reliability, for example, is the length of the test and the time it takes to administer it. Shorter tests are generally preferable. A test that can be administered during one class period, for example, would be considerably more convenient than a two-hour test. Shorter tests are also preferable in terms of student fatigue and motivation. However, since reliability is related to length, as you know, a shorter test will tend to be less reliable. Many tests are available in a short form, and the reliability of the short form is invariably lower. If a long form and a short form of a test (or two different tests of different lengths) are both valid for your purpose and your group, the questions to be considered are: How much shorter? How much less reliable? If one test takes half as long to administer and is only slightly less reliable, the shorter test is probably better. For example, suppose Test A (or Form A) has a KR-20 reliability of .94 and takes 90 minutes to administer, and Test B (or Form B) has a KR-20 reliability of .90 and takes 50 minutes to administer; which would you choose? Most likely Test B. If after comparing validity and reliability data, you still have more than one candidate, you should consider administration, scoring, and interpretation requirements.

By the time you get to this point, you have probably already made a decision concerning whether you need an individually administered test. If not, and if there is no essential reason for using an individually administered test, now is the time to eliminate them from contention. Most of the time individually administered tests will not even be a consideration since they are used primarily for certain IQ and personality testing situations. However, when they are, you should keep in mind the potential disadvantages associated with their use: additional cost, additional time, and need for trained administrators, complicated scoring procedures, and the need for trained interpreters. Of course, if the nature of the members of a group to be tested or the variable of interest requires it, by all means use an individually administered test. In either case, you should consider the administration, scoring, and interpretation requirements. In addition to the time, you should consider factors such as unusual administration conditions, difficult scoring procedures, and the need for sophisticated interpretations. Are you qualified to execute the requirements of the test as specified? If not, can you afford to hire the necessary personnel? By this point, the alternatives should be narrowed considerably and format considerations should be examined. While most standardized tests are neatly and clearly printed, some are more attractive than others and factors such as type size do vary somewhat. If after all this soul searching by some miracle you still have more than one test in the running, by all means pick the cheapest one!

There are two additional considerations in test selection which have nothing to do with the psychometric qualities of a test. Both are related to the use of tests in schools. If you are planning to administer tests to school children, as you would in a curriculum evaluation, you should check to see what tests they have already been administered in the recent past. You would not want to administer a test which was familiar to students. Second, you should be sensitive to the fact that some parents or administrators might object to a test which contains items people may be "touchy" about. Certain personality inventories, for example, ask questions related to the sexual behavior of the respondents. If there is any possibility that the test contains potentially objectionable items, either choose another test or acquire appropriate permissions before administering the test. There have been instances where school people have been ordered to destroy (even burn!) test results. As the old saying goes, an ounce of prevention. . . .

Occasionally, though hopefully not very often, you will find yourself in the position of not being able to locate a suitable test. The solution is *not* to use an inadequate test with the rationale "oh well, I'll do the best I can." One solution is to develop your own test. Good test construction requires a variety of skills. As mentioned previously, training at least equivalent to a course in measurement is needed. If you do develop your own test, you must collect validation data. A self-developed test should not be utilized in an evaluation study unless it has been pretested first with a group very similar to the group to be used in the actual study. In addition to collecting validity and reliability data, you will need to try out the administration and scoring procedures. In some cases, the results of pretesting will indicate the need for revisions and further pretesting. This procedure may also sometimes be followed for an existing test. You may find a test which seems very appropriate but for which certain relevant types of validation data are not available. In this case you may decide to try to validate this test with your population rather than develop a test "from scratch."

part four **summary**

7 selection of measuring instruments

Characteristics of a test

1 There are a number of characteristics which are desirable for all tests, but much more likely to be in evidence for standardized tests than for locally-developed tests.
2 Standardized tests are typically developed by experts, and individual test items are analyzed and revised until they meet established standards of quality.
3 Test objectivity, a characteristic of standardized tests, means that an individual's score is the same, or essentially the same, regardless of who is scoring the test.
4 Validity is the most important quality of any test.
5 Validity is concerned with what a test measures and for whom it is appropriate; reliability is concerned with the consistency with which a test measures whatever it measures.
6 Specification of conditions for administering the test is also a very important characteristic of a standardized test.
7 Standardized tests generally include directions for the scoring and interpretation of scores.

Validity

8 Validity is the degree to which a test measures what it is supposed to measure.
9 A test is not valid or invalid per se; it is valid for a particular purpose and for a particular group.
10 It is the "valid for whom" concern that makes the description of the norm group so important.
11 It is the "valid for whom" concern that is at the heart of the test bias issue.
12 If a test is invalid, it is by definition biased.
13 While bias may result from improper test administration, scoring, or interpretation, the major source of bias is the test itself.
14 Low scores do not automatically imply test bias; they do imply that the group tested does not possess a high degree of whatever the test measures—for whatever reason.
15 Validity is a matter of degree, not a characteristic that is present or absent; it is also a somewhat temporal quality in that a test that once had adequate validity may no longer, and a test that currently has adequate validity will not necessarily in the future.

Norm-referenced tests

Content validity

16 *Content validity* is the degree to which a test measures an intended content area; it is of prime importance for achievement tests.

17 *Item validity* is concerned with whether the test items represent measurement in the intended content area.
18 *Sampling validity* is concerned with how well the test samples the total content area.
19 Content validity is determined by expert judgment.
20 When selecting a test for an evaluation, the evaluator assumes the role of "expert" and assesses whether the test is content valid for the situation involved

Construct validity

21 *Construct validity* is the degree to which a test measures an intended hypothetical construct.
22 A construct is a nonobservable trait, such as intelligence, which explains behavior.
23 Validating a test of a construct involves testing hypotheses deduced from a theory concerning the construct.

Concurrent validity

24 *Concurrent validity* is the degree to which the scores on a test are related to the scores on another, already established test administered at the same time or to some other valid criterion available at the same time.
25 The relationship method of estimating concurrent validity involves determining the relationship between scores on the test and scores on some other established test or criterion.
26 Degree of relationship between two variables is expressed as a correlation coefficient; if a relationship exists between two variables, it means that scores within a certain range on one measure are associated with scores within a certain range on another measure.
27 If two variables are highly related, a correlation coefficient near +1.00 (or −1.00) will be obtained; if two variables are not related, a coefficient near .00 will be obtained.
28 The discrimination method of establishing concurrent validity involves determining whether test scores can be used to discriminate between persons who possess a certain characteristic and those who do not, or between those who possess more of it and those who possess less.

Predictive validity

29 *Predictive validity* is the degree to which a test can predict how well an individual will do in a future situation.
30 The predictive validity of a given instrument varies with a number of factors, such as the curriculum involved, textbooks used, and geographic location.
31 Predictions based on a combination of several test scores will invariably be more accurate than predictions based on the scores of any one test.
32 The predictive validity of a test is determined by establishing the relationship between scores on the test and some measure of success in the situation of interest.
33 The test which is used to predict success is referred to as the *predictor*, and the behavior which is predicted is referred to as the *criterion*.
34 Cross-validation involves administering the predictor tests to a different sample from the same population and developing a new equation.

Criterion-referenced tests

35 Since score variability is typically lower for CRTs than for NRTs, traditional approaches may be inappropriate in certain situations involving CRTs.

36 Since CRTs are designed primarily to measure achievement of one or more specific objectives, content validity is the major concern with such measures.

Content validity

37 The content validity of a CRT involves the degree to which the test measures the achievement of the intended objectives.

38 As with NRTs, both item validity and sampling validity, that is, whether the items measure only the intended objectives and how adequately the test samples the objectives, are important.

39 The content validity of CRTs is generally expected to be higher than for NRTs, mainly because the domain of behaviors to be measured, i.e. those described by the objectives, is usually more precisely defined.

40 The content validity of CRTs is determined by expert judgment; for many classroom CRTs, the role of expert is assumed by the teacher.

41 All things being equal (preparation time, for example), a CRT will have higher content validity than an NRT.

Predictive validity

42 As with NRTs, the predictive validity of a CRT involves the ability of the test to predict future performance.

43 Since correlation requires score variability, and since scores on a CRT may or may not involve variability, use of correlational techniques is more or less appropriate depending upon the actual spread of scores involved.

44 One relatively simple way to determine relationship between a predictor and a criterion is to develop an expectancy table; an expectancy table is basically a two-way table that lists predictor scores or categories down the left side and criterion scores or categories across the top.

45 While expectancy tables are often based on norm-referenced scores, they are especially useful for criterion-referenced test scores, especially when low score variability is a factor.

Reliability

46 Reliability is the degree to which a test consistently measures whatever it measures.

47 Any type of measurement involves some kind of error; there are many factors which affect a score besides the degree to which a person possesses the trait being measured.

48 Some sources of error are related to temporary and permanent characteristics of the persons taking the test, such as illness.

49 Other sources of error are related to characteristics of the test itself (e.g. inappropriate items) or to the way in which it is administered, scored, or interpreted.

50 A valid test is always reliable, but a reliable test is not necessarily valid.

51 Classical test theory is based on the assumption that each person's score on a test (X) really represents a combination of two factors—the person's "true" score (T) and errors of measurement (E); that is, $X = T + E$.

52 A person's true score is the score which, theoretically, a person would obtain if there were no errors of measurement and the test were totally reliable.

53 Reliability usually refers to the score consistency of a group; estimates of such consistency typically involve correlation coefficients.

54 When we speak of the accuracy of an individual's score, i.e. how much confidence we can have in any individual's score, then we are interested in the standard error of measurement.

Norm-referenced tests

55 When one test is administered once, estimates of internal consistency reliability are calculated; methods for determining internal consistency reliability include the split-half and rationale equivalence techniques.

56 When one test is administered twice, we are interested in score stability over time, and test-retest reliability is calculated.

57 When two tests are administered once, we are concerned with whether the two tests measure the same behaviors, and equivalent-forms reliability is calculated.

Test-retest reliability

58 *Test-retest reliability* is the degree to which scores are consistent over time.

59 Test-retest reliability indicates score variation that occurs from testing session to testing session as a result of errors of measurement.

60 Test-retest reliability is established by determining the relationship between scores resulting from administering the same test to the same group on two different occasions; the resulting number is called the *coefficient of stability*.

Equivalent-forms reliability

61 *Equivalent forms* of a test are two tests which are identical in every way except for the actual items included.

62 In assessing equivalent-forms reliability, evaluators are interested in whether scores depend upon the particular set of items selected or whether performance on one set of items is generalizable to other sets.

63 Equivalent-forms reliability, also referred to as alternate-forms reliability, indicates score variation that occurs from form to form.

64 Equivalent-forms reliability is established by determining the relationship between scores resulting from administering two different forms of the same test to the same group at the same time; the resulting number is called the *coefficient of equivalence*.

65 If the two forms of the test are administered at two different times, the resulting coefficient is referred to as the *coefficient of stability and equivalence*.

66 Equivalent-forms reliability is the single most acceptable and most commonly used estimate of reliability for most tests used in evaluation and research.

Split-half reliability

67 Split-half reliability is determined by establishing the relationship between the scores on two equivalent halves of a test administered to a total group at one time.

68 Regardless of how the test is organized, an odd-even item split should produce essentially equivalent halves.
69 Since longer tests tend to be more reliable, and since split-half reliability represents the reliability of a test only half as long as the actual test, a correction
   known as the Spearman-Brown prophecy formula must be applied to the
   coefficient.
70 The Spearman-Brown correction formula is

$$r_{\text{total test}} = \frac{2r_{\text{split half}}}{1 + r_{\text{split half}}}$$

Rationale equivalence reliability

71 *Rationale equivalence reliability* is not established through a single correlation
   but rather estimates internal consistency by determining how all items on a
   test relate to all other items and to the total test.
72 Rationale equivalence reliability is determined through application of one of
   the Kuder-Richardson formulas, usually formula 20 or 21 (KR-20 or KR-21).

Scorer/rater reliability

73 There are other situations for which reliability must be investigated, usually
   when the scoring of tests involves subjectivity, such as with essay tests.
74 When test scoring involves subjective judgment, we are concerned with interjudge (interscorer, interrater, interobserver) reliability and/or intrajudge reliability.
75 Interjudge reliability refers to the reliability of two (or more) independent
   scorers; intrajudge reliability refers to the reliability of the scoring of individual scorers.
76 Estimates of interjudge or intrajudge reliability are usually obtained using
   correlational techniques, but can also be expressed simply as percent agreement.

Criterion-referenced tests

77 As with NRTs, the reliability of a CRT refers to the consistency with which a
   test measures whatever it measures.
78 All of the types of reliability which pertain to NRTs are relevant to CRTs.
79 If CRTs are properly constructed, internal consistency should be virtually
   assured.

Nonmastery CRTs

80 For a nonmastery CRT, when sufficient variability is present, traditional measures of computing reliability may be used.
81 In most cases the degree of variability will be lower than for NRTs and the
   reliability coefficient (r) will tend to be lower, that is, will be a conservative
   estimate, or underestimate, of reliability.

Mastery CRTs

82 Livingston's formula for estimating the reliability of a CRT is essentially a
   generalization of classical reliability theory; in essence his formula computes

the reliability of a CRT by first computing a traditional measure of reliability (appropriate for NRTs) then adjusting it based on the criterion, or cut-off, score of the CRT.

83 Livingston's formula is

$$r_{CR} = \frac{r_{NR}(SD^2) + (\overline{X} - C)^2}{(SD^2) + (\overline{X} - C)^2}$$

84 Livingston's estimate of the reliability of a CRT will usually be higher, but in no case lower, than estimates using traditional approaches.

85 One informal approach for getting a rough indication of degree of reliability is to compare the scores of a group on a test on two different occasions and determine the percentage of scores that were different by given percentages.

86 Another informal way to estimate reliability is to compare decisions made on two separate occasions based on test results; we can determine the percentage of students for whom the same decision was made both times, e.g. they were classified as having achieved mastery on both occasions.

Standard error of measurement

87 A small standard error of measurement indicates high reliability, and a large standard error of measurement indicates low reliability.

88 The standard error of measurement allows us to estimate how much difference there probably is between a person's obtained score and true score, the size of the difference being a function of the reliability of the test.

89 We can estimate the standard error of measurement using the following simple formula.

$$SE_m = SD\sqrt{1 - r}$$

90 SE_m estimates are frequently used to construct what are called *confidence intervals*, or bands, around individual scores.

91 We are approximately 68% confident that a person's *true* score falls within the interval $X \pm 1\ SE_m$, where X is the individual's obtained score.

92 Overlapping intervals suggest that the true scores on the test are not really different whereas intervals that do not overlap suggest true score differences.

Factors affecting reliability

93 A number of factors can affect the reliability coefficient of a test; some of these factors are related to the test itself, some to the group taking the test, and some to the environment in which the test is administered, including factors such as test administration and scoring procedures.

94 Knowledge of factors which can affect reliability improves test development procedures, test usage, and analysis of test information.

95 Increasing the reliability *coefficient* is not necessarily the same thing as increasing the reliability of the test.

Test length

96 Other factors being equal, adding items to a test, items that are as good as the items already in the test, increases the reliability.

97 In general, lengthening a test to improve reliability does have reasonable limits.

98 An increase in test length is not accompanied by an equal increase in reliability; if you double the length of a test, for example, you do not double the reliability.

99 To estimate the gain in reliability to be achieved by doubling the length of a test, we use a special case of the Spearman-Brown formula:

$$r_2 = \frac{2r}{1 + r}$$

100 A more general formula can be used to estimate the reliability of a test increased or decreased by any factor; that is, n may equal 3, or 4, or even $\frac{1}{2}$. The generalized Spearman-Brown prophecy formula is

$$r_n = \frac{nr}{1 + (n - 1)r}$$

101 The generalized formula can be rearranged a little bit to solve for n and estimate by what factor a test has to be lengthened in order to achieve a desired reliability coefficient. The formula becomes

$$n = \frac{r_n(1 - r)}{r(1 - r_n)}$$

Score variability

102 If variability is reduced, as may be the case with CRTs, the reliability coefficient is lowered; correspondingly, if variability is increased, the reliability coefficient is increased.

103 Other factors being equal, a test with all average-difficulty items results in more score variability.

104 Other factors being equal, a group in which the persons represent a wide range of ability, from very low to very high, will have a wider spread of scores, that is, more score variability.

105 Separate reliability coefficients should be presented for each age and/or grade level, even if the test is appropriate for several levels.

Score objectivity

106 An objective test is one for which subjectivity in scoring is, at least theoretically, eliminated; anyone scoring a given test should come up with the same score.

107 A test is unreliable to the degree that scores are a result of factors other than true scores, factors such as scorer biases.

Interpretation of validity and reliability coefficients

108 Certain types of validity and reliability are expressed numerically, usually as coefficients; a high coefficient indicates high validity or reliability.

109 High validity indicates that systematic errors have been reduced whereas high reliability indicates that random errors have been reduced.

110 Systematic and random error can be caused by characteristics of the test itself, by conditions of administration, or by the current status of the persons taking the test.

111 To determine the common variance shared by two sets of scores you simply square the correlation coefficient; the result is referred to as the *coefficient of determination*.

112 How large the coefficient needs to be in order to be useful depends upon the purpose for which it was computed.

113 A correlation coefficient much below .50 is generally useless for either group prediction or individual prediction, although a combination of several variables in this range may yield a reasonably satisfactory prediction.

114 Coefficients in the .60s and .70s are usually considered *adequate* for group prediction purposes and coefficients in the .80s and above for individual prediction purposes.

115 What constitutes an acceptable level of reliability is to some degree determined by the type of test although a coefficient over .90 would be acceptable for any test.

116 For standardized achievement and aptitude tests, there is generally no good reason for selecting a test whose reliability is not at least .90.

117 Personality measures do not typically report such high reliabilities (although certainly some do) and therefore one would be very satisfied with a reliability in the eighties (e.g. .84) and might even accept a reliability in the seventies.

118 If a test is composed of several subtests, then the reliability of each subtest, not just the reliability of the total test, must be assessed.

119 Since reliability is a function of test length, the reliability of a given subtest is typically lower than the total test reliability.

120 Some degree of test invalidity and unreliability is unavoidable; but making bad decisions is not—not if we select our measurement techniques rationally and interpret results intelligently.

Selection of a test

Selection of measurement methods

121 There are a variety of measurement options; knowledge of these options tends to reduce overreliance on norm-referenced, standardized tests in evaluation efforts.

122 Which measurement techniques are selected should depend mainly on the purpose of the testing and the objectives to be measured.

123 One evaluation situation which invariably involves standardized tests is the school testing program.

124 Periodic measurement of scholastic aptitude and yearly achievement testing have been the cornerstone of school testing programs at the elementary, junior high, and senior high school levels.

125 Tests of character and personality have been considered highly desirable.

126 At the preschool level individually administered tests requiring psychomotor or verbal responses are usually given.

127 At the senior high level differential aptitude is of interest.

128 Standardized readiness and diagnostic tests are desirable at all appropriate levels.

129 Recent developments have extended the concern for measurement of achievement of basic skills to the junior and senior high levels.

Factors to consider

130 The first factor to consider when selecting a measurement instrument is the availability and completeness of information concerning characteristics of the test.

131 There is usually a relationship between the amount of relevant data supplied by a publisher and the quality of the test.

132 The most important information given about a test is that concerning validity.

133 Regardless of the type of validity involved, we will always be interested in the size, location, and composition of the norm group as well as when the group was tested.

134 Depending upon how the test is to be used, appropriate reliability coefficients should be given as well as the size of the group upon which they are based.

135 Standard error of measurement figures should also be provided, by age and/or grade level at the very least.

136 Other types of information should be reported including information related to administration, scoring, and interpretation.

137 Standardized NRTs are not appropriate for determining the achievement of local objectives.

138 In most cases, sets of specific objectives must be assessed by locally-developed instruments since both standardized CRTs and NRTs are not generally valid for this purpose.

Sources of test information

139 Assuming you have defined the purposes of the evaluation effort, performed a situation analysis, and delineated your objectives, the next steps are to: (1) determine precisely what type(s) of test you need; (2) if a standardized instrument is required, identify and locate appropriate tests; and (3) do a comparative analysis of the tests and select the best one.

140 There are many initial sources of test information which you can consult in order to identify the range of possibilities: these include Buros' *Mental Measurement Yearbooks*, the ERIC system, test publishers and measurement texts.

141 The *Yearbooks* have been published for several decades and represent the most comprehensive source of test information available to educators.

142 After you have narrowed the list of candidates you will still usually need additional information; a good source of information on a test is the publisher's test manual.

143 Final selection of a test usually requires examination of the actual tests.

Selecting from alternatives

144 The most important factor to be considered in test selection is validity.

145 Assuming all coefficients were acceptable, you would presumably select the test with the highest reliability, but there are other considerations such as the length of the test and the time it takes to administer it.

146 You should also consider factors such as unusual administration conditions, difficult scoring procedures, and sophisticated interpretations.
147 Occasionally you will not be able to locate a suitable test. The solution is *not* to use an inadequate test; one logical solution is to develop your own test.

task four **performance criteria**

For each instrument selected, the description should include:

a the name, publisher, and cost
b a description of the instrument
c a description of the norm group
d validity and reliability data
e instrument administration requirements
f training requirements for scoring and interpretation of resulting data
g a synopsis of reviews

All the information required for each test will be found in Buros' *Mental Measurement Yearbooks*.

Following the descriptions of the three tests (for each type of test needed), you should present a comparative analysis of the tests which forms a rationale for your selection of the "most acceptable" test for your purpose. For example, you might indicate that all three tests have similar reliability coefficients but that one of the tests is more content valid for your purpose or objectives.

Communication is the process by which meanings are exchanged between individuals.

part five
development of an instrument

If valid, reliable instruments are available for collecting desired information, they should by all means be used, but an instrument should not be used just "because it is there." If you want the correct answers, you have to ask the correct questions, and that often means developing them yourself.

While hundreds of thousands of standardized tests are administered each year, the number of locally-developed instruments administered is in the millions. A large number of such instruments are developed by persons with little or no training in test development—a pretty frightening fact when you realize that all those tests contribute to decisions which affect the immediate and long-range future of so many individuals. The chances are slim that someone will develop a valid, reliable test without knowing the concepts of test development. Anyone who thinks test development is easy probably does not know much about what is involved. True, developing *a* test is easy, but developing a *good* test requires considerable knowledge, skill, time and, in some cases, money. It is sort of like dancing—anyone can move his feet around and call it dancing, but good dancing requires knowledge of appropriate steps and skill in executing them.

Most tests taken by students are developed by teachers. Consequently, most decisions made concerning students are based on teacher-made instruments. Such tests also have an influence on many decisions made *by* students. Knowing the kinds of tests a teacher usually gives affects how students study, and test results affect how students feel about themselves and their ability, and even their career aspirations. The magnitude of these factors is of course related to the frequency of testing. When good instruments are involved, in diagnostic situations for example, more frequent testing can be very beneficial. Problems can be identified early, feedback provided, and corrective measures taken. This does not mean that testing needs to be a daily event; testing is most meaningful when it follows a meaningful unit of instruction, say a "week's worth." On the other hand, when poor instruments are involved, frequent testing can have cumulative, negative effects on students. The serious consequences of testing make it mandatory that teachers be competent in test development and analysis of results. Strong subject knowledge, though certainly important, is not enough.

All evaluation efforts require tests. In the case of program and project evaluation, as with student evaluation, required instruments almost always have to be developed. The reason is that innovative approaches and materials are invariably involved, and suitably content-valid measures are usually not available. Such instruments have to be developed by program staff, if they possess the necessary competencies, or jointly by program staff and qualified consultants. While having instruments developed by the staff has certain advantages, it is usually more efficient and cost-effective to hire an evaluation consultant than to train inexperienced staff members. Since most evaluation efforts involve assessment of student achievement and/or attitudes, pretests and posttests at a minimum are required and depending upon the situation, tests of entry behavior and retention tests may be appropriate. In formal evaluations developed instruments should be tried out and revised before they are used in the actual evaluation effort. In all cases, the results of developed instruments should be used to assess their quality and effectiveness.

In any given evaluation there are any number of variables that might be measured besides achievement (motivation and creativity, for example). However, it is usually preferable to limit the variables measured to those that are most important. This is especially true when instruments must be developed; it is better to measure just a few things but measure them well. When equivalent forms are involved, as with pretests and posttests, instrument development may be somewhat simplified since the same items may appear on more than one form. If items are developed to measure knowledge objectives, such as the ability to identify and define four types of validity, they may be used on more than one test. Of course when higher-order objectives are involved, such as the ability to interpret validity coefficients, use of parallel but different items is usually more appropriate. In either case, it is imperative that valid, reliable measures result since the "goodness" of decisions is a direct function of the instruments upon which they are based.

While each type of test may involve idiosyncratic development concerns and procedures, many principles of test construction apply to all types of measuring instruments. This part will focus mainly on achievement test development and secondarily on questionnaires, interview guides, and observation forms. Keep in mind that most of the concepts are generalizable to other types of measuring devices.

The goal of part 5 is for you to be able to design, construct, and analyze an instrument for a given set of objectives or content area. After reading part 5, you should be able to do the following task.

task five

a Develop a two-way table of specifications for a test designed to measure achievement of the objectives which you developed for task 2. If your objectives do not involve learning outcomes, a one-way table will be sufficient.

b Develop a test which matches the specifications in the table developed in task a. Develop the test in accordance with the guidelines for item construction.

c Administer the test developed in task b to at least 20 students (or other individuals) *or* generate test results for at least 20 students. Perform item analyses and interpret the results as follows:

  1 Assume the test is norm-referenced and do a traditional item analysis.

2 Assume the test is criterion-referenced and compute and interpret item-achievement percentages and objectives-achievement percentages.

(See Performance Criteria, p. 295.)

8 designing the test

After reading chapter 8, you should be able to:

1 Identify and describe the major components of a table of specifications.
2 Identify and describe the factors which determine the appropriate number of items for a given cell in a table of specifications.

Restriction, definition, and selection of test content

As with most activities, the sooner you begin planning and the more care you take, the more likely it is that you will develop a good test. The more important an event is, the more planning time and effort are required. A large wedding, for example, involves more planning than a tennis date. Testing is important and test development deserves more of your attention than 30 minutes while you watch the Late, Late, Late Show the night before the testing day. Good planning does not guarantee a good product (sometimes the bride or groom just does not show up!), but it definitely increases the odds.

Although the interpretations of results differ, the same basic procedures apply whether the test is designed to be norm-referenced or criterion-referenced, mastery or nonmastery. Given a set of related objectives, the major task is to develop items which measure only behaviors specified in those objectives and which adequately sample the domain of possible behaviors. Depending upon the type of test involved (e.g., norm-referenced or criterion-referenced), desired levels of difficulty will vary as will the standard of comparison for results, but the basic planning process will be very similar regardless.

Initial test design procedures are very logical. The first thing you have to determine is how big a chunk of content will be covered. Then you delineate all the important aspects of that chunk. And finally, you select the aspects which will be included in the test.

Restriction of content

The first step in designing a test is to put boundaries on what is to be covered in the test. Objectives usually form meaningful clusters of topics, and a test should represent a meaningful unit of instruction. A test will normally represent a range from several days to several weeks of instruction, with about a week being a reasonable average. Narrowing test coverage prevents cognitive overload on the part of students and permits a larger, more representative sampling of the behaviors represented by the selected objectives. Of course certain cumulative tests such as final exams require broader coverage and may represent weeks or months of instruction. If individual tests have been carefully designed, however, the task of developing cumulative tests is facilitated since the outcomes measured by such tests (and probably some of the items) represent a sampling of the performances measured on all previous tests.

Definition of content

The next step in designing a test is to make a detailed content outline if such is not already available. If you decided, for example, that a test would cover the topic "The United States Congress," your outline would probably include "The Senate" and "The House of Representatives" as major headings. Such an outline may very well already exist. Even if there are no formal objectives, a teacher will generally have a detailed content outline prior to instruction. This outline may be developed by the teacher or provided in a curriculum guide. The outline needs to be detailed enough to include all knowledge and skill outcomes desired of students. The heading "The Senate," for example, might include such subheadings as "Eligibility Requirements" and "Constitutional Powers and Limitations." While each and every desired outcome may not be measured on the test, they should all at least be candidates for inclusion.

If specific objectives have been formulated, then the desired performances associated with each entry in the outline will already be specified. If not, these behaviors now have to be identified, and we must keep in mind that we are concerned with more than just the possession of knowledge. As discussed in chapter 5, many areas permit assessment of performance at several levels of Bloom's taxonomy. With respect to "Eligibility Requirements," for example, do we want students to be able to list such requirements or be able to read a description of a person's qualifications and determine whether that person is eligible to run for the Senate? Maybe both.

The process described above is analogous to the "domain description" advocated by Popham and others.[1] The intent is to specify all possible items by delineating rules for generating items. A domain description includes an objective, a sample item (including directions) and an amplified objective. An amplified objective includes a description of stimulus elements (the characteristics of the question), response alternatives (the characteristics of the answer choices), and the criterion of correctness (what constitutes an acceptable response). As with writing objectives, the trick is to write domain descriptions that are brief enough to be feasible and usable and yet detailed enough to be objective in the sense that any competent person can judge whether a set of items does or does not conform to the domain requirements. While the concept of using rules to generate items is interesting and worthy of further study, the process is extremely time-consuming, and there are not too many areas besides math and English grammar that lend themselves to the development of item-generating rules.

Selection of test content

The next step in designing a test is to devise a scheme for sampling from the domain of behaviors. With the exception of certain mastery tests, a test invariably represents a sample of behaviors. It is just not possible to measure each and every aspect of each and every outcome. Further, if we carefully select the ones we do measure, we can generalize to the total domain with a reasonable degree of confidence. For example, suppose we want students to be able to identify the capital city of each of the 50 states. We could have one gigantic matching item or 50 short-answer items. We can probably safely assume, however, that a student's ability to identify the capitals of a representative 10 states is highly indicative of that student's ability to do so for all 50. If Lulu correctly identifies the capitals of 5 of 10 states, she probably knows about half of the capitals. The question is how to select

[1] Popham, W. J. Educational Evaluation. Englewood Cliffs, N.J.: Prentice-Hall, 1975.

the 10 states to appear on the test so that they are representative of all 50. Does it matter? It might. Suppose, for example, we choose the following states: Maine, Vermont, New Hampshire, Massachusetts, Connecticut, Rhode Island, New York, New Jersey, Delaware, and Pennsylvania. Notice anything? Do these states have anything in common? Yes, they are all located in the northeast section of the United States. A student from Boston might well be able to name all of the required capitals and yet not know the capital of any state west of the Mississippi. The requirement that the test items constitute a representative sample of desired behaviors is of course synonymous with the requirement that the test be content valid.

The more structured and well defined the content is, the easier this is to accomplish. For example, one way we could select the 10 states to appear on the test would be to select them randomly. When items are selected randomly, each has an equal chance of being selected. The chances of all 10 states being located in the Northeast would be extremely small. Of course, just being aware of the need for representativeness helps immensely. You, at this point, would not put all northeast states on the test. You would know to select some from all areas of the country. Being able to make informed judgments is helpful because few teachers actually randomly select items and in many cases to do so would be very time-consuming. For example, suppose your instructor was going to test you on your ability to interpret a reliability coefficient. If we exclude negative coefficients, there are actually 101 possible coefficients to choose from, ranging from .00 to 1.00. Your instructor *could* randomly select, say, five of the possibilities but would probably use his or her judgment instead. Which of the following sets of coefficients do *you* think would be most representative: (*a*) .02, .04, .07, .09, .10; (*b*) .95, .96, .97, .98, .99; or (*c*) .08, .29, .51, .75, .94? If you picked (c), you understand the concept.

The above examples illustrate another important aspect of selection from the domain of possible behaviors. It is sometimes necessary to stratify the possibilities prior to selection. Basically, stratifying is the act of categorizing all the possibilities and selecting from each category. In the case of the state capitals, we could categorize by geographic region (e.g., Northwest, Southwest) and select at least one state from each region. In the case of the reliability coefficients, we would not want them to be all high or all low; we would want coefficients to represent a range of possibilities. Thus, we might stratify them into the categories .00–.20, .21–.40, .40–.60, .61–.80, and .81–1.00, and select one from each category.

We are just as concerned with adequate sampling and resulting content validity whether we are developing norm-referenced tests or criterion-referenced tests. The same basic principles are applicable to both whether or not we have a set of specific objectives. Adequate sampling is considerably easier to accomplish, however, with criterion-referenced mastery tests. Outcomes are clearly specified and fall within a restricted range. Not only is it easier to select from the possible behaviors, but it is also feasible to select a higher percentage of them. Take spelling. We might have two lists of spelling words. One list may contain 10 very important words for which the goal might be student mastery, and the other list might contain 50 words that are of secondary importance. In both cases we might determine that a score of 90% will indicate that the objective has been achieved, and for the first list that mastery has been attained. We could easily include all 10 words on the first list in one test but probably would not include all 50 words on the second list in one test; we might select 10 or 15 of them. We would probably continue instruction and testing until a given percentage of the students achieved mastery whereas we would probably have lower expectations for the second list.

One systematic approach to test design involves the development of a table of specifications. Once test content has been identified and defined, and all the behavioral outcomes specified, a logical next step is construction of a table of specifications.

Tables of specifications

A table of specifications is essentially a blueprint for a test. As the name implies, it *specifies* the content of the test. Its basic purpose is to insure that all intended outcomes, and only the intended outcomes, are measured and that the test includes the appropriate number of items for each measured outcome. A table of specifications is a two-way table with one axis being essentially a content outline and the other axis indicating the behaviors desired with respect to the content.

Content outline

Along one axis of the table of specifications the major headings and subheadings of the content outline previously discussed are listed. For a test on validity, the major headings might be "Norm-Referenced Tests" and "Criterion-Referenced Tests." Each of these would in turn include a number of subheadings and perhaps "sub-subheadings" (if that's a word!). Our routine might include the following:

> *Validity
>   *Norm-Referenced Tests
>   Content Validity
>   Construct Validity
>   Concurrent Validity
>   Predictive Validity
>   *Criterion-Referenced Tests
>   Content Validity
>   Predictive Validity

The table of specifications might include only those headings that are starred above, or it could include all the topics (see table 8.1). Actually, as we shall see shortly, the more detailed this axis is, the more likely it is that the test will include items for all desired topics. Also, to a great extent, the complexity of the outline is a function of the complexity of the content area being measured.

Behavioral outcomes

Along the other axis of the table the behaviors or performances desired for each topic are given. As table 8.1 illustrates, one way to organize the outcomes is in terms of Bloom's taxonomy. This approach focuses attention on higher-order outcomes and insures that the test will not contain predominantly or totally knowledge-level items. In the example, approximately one-third of the test consists of knowledge-level items and two-thirds, higher-order items. Knowledge items would involve definitions, descriptions, and listings, for example, the ability to

table 8.1
Table of specifications for a test on validity

Content Outline		Behavioral Outcomes			Total
		Knowledge	Comprehension	Application	
Validity		1	2	0	3
NRTs	Content	1	2	0	3
	Construct	1	1	0	2
	Concurrent	1	1	2	4
	Predictive	1	2	2	5
CRTs	Content	1	2	0	3
	Predictive	1	2	2	5
Total		7	12	6	25

list the procedures for determining predictive validity. Comprehension items would involve demonstration of understanding of concepts, for example, the ability to interpret a reliability coefficient. Application items would require demonstration of the ability to apply knowledge in a concrete situation, for example, the ability to describe the basic procedures involved in determining the predictive validity of an algebra aptitude test. Note that only applicable categories from the taxonomy have been included. Synthesis, for example, is not included since no synthesis skills are required or desired.

An alternate but related approach is to be more specific concerning the outcomes. Instead of "Knowledge," for example, we might have categories such as "Knows Definitions" and "Knows Procedures." In its most simplified form this axis may contain only two categories—"Knowledge" and "Higher-Order Outcomes" (or "Use of Knowledge" or "Complex Achievement" or whatever you want to call it). While good arguments could be put forth to justify the use of any one of these approaches over the others, the important thing to remember is that the basic purpose of having a behavioral outcomes axis is to insure that the test is not just a knowledge test; all of the approaches do this. A very formal test development effort would be advised to use a finer breakdown of categories to insure content validity, but for most classroom purposes a smaller number of categories is usually sufficient. One final point. Is it possible to have a test that reflects only one taxonomy category? Sure. A mastery test, for example, might include only knowledge items. In this case, however, it would probably be advisable to break down knowledge into categories such as "Knowledge of Terms" and "Knowledge of Procedures."

It should be evident by now that it is easier to develop a table of specifications for a criterion-referenced test or a norm-referenced test based on objectives because the intended outcomes have already been carefully thought through and delineated. How detailed the table of specifications needs to be, or can reasonably be, depends mainly upon how large a chunk of instruction is represented. For a unit test (on validity, for example), it is advisable to lean toward more detail and to include all desired outcomes. This facilitates interpretation of results; it permits accurate assessment of student achievement, individually and as a group, and provides specific direction to further instructional activities. For a cumulative test (such as a final examination), however, we may use only major headings from preceding tables of specifications. In other words, the behaviors measured on such a test represent a sampling of the behaviors measured on previous unit tests.

Number of items

The intersection of content outline headings and behavioral outcome categories forms cells into which an appropriate number (or percentage) of items is placed. Table 8.1, for example, indicates that one item will be required to measure knowledge of content validity and two items to measure comprehension of content validity. Sometimes, percentages are determined first and then those percentages are translated into numbers of items. For example, we might decide that 30% of the test should be knowledge items and that 15% of the test should be on the content validity of NRTs. In this case we would determine the percentage of items which measure knowledge of content validity by multiplying 30% by 15% and we would get 4.5% (30% × 15% = .30 × .15 = .045 = 4.5%). For a 20-item test, this would translate into 1 item (4.5% × 20 = .045 × 20 = .9, or 1, since you cannot have .9 items). The major problem with this approach is that the size of the test actually determines the number of items for each cell instead of the number of items in each cell determining the size of the test. The number of items should be determined by the objectives—how many items it takes to measure a given behavioral outcome for a given topic. There is nothing that says a test has to have 10 or 20 or 30 items. If the sum of the needed items is 17, so be it. Also, the percentage approach assumes that every cell will be measured. This is not necessarily the case. In table 8.1, for example, the cell for Application of Content Validity contains a 0—no items are required. The more direct approach of judging on an individual basis the number of items needed in each cell is preferable (for the reasons already cited); it is also clearly less time-consuming and eliminates a lot of computation.

The number of items in a given cell is determined primarily by "what it takes" to measure a particular behavioral outcome for a given topic. For knowledge of state capitals, for example, we determined that 10 items would be adequate. For knowledge of content validity, one item measuring knowledge of the definition might be sufficient. Another consideration is the importance of the outcome and the instructional time that was devoted to it. All objectives are not equally important. It is more important for practitioners to understand content validity than construct validity, for example. Therefore, in table 8.1 we have two items for comprehension of content validity and one item for comprehension of construct validity. Two items versus one item may not seem like a big deal, but it does represent twice as many items.

Usually one item per outcome is not sufficient, especially if the test is objective (e.g. multiple-choice). If a student correctly answers, say, three items related to the same outcome we can have more confidence that the student has truly achieved it than if the student answers only one item correctly. A student could easily guess the correct answer to one item on an objective test. For a short-answer test, one item may be sufficient; for example, it is pretty tough to correctly guess the definition of predictive validity. As a general rule, higher-order outcomes usually require more items. A definition is a definition, but one concept may have several different applications. While longer tests tend to be more valid and reliable, a test can be too long, in terms of student fatigue for example. But a test should be as long as it needs to be. If it is judged to be too long, given the age of the students or the length of the class period, it is better to split it into two tests to be administered on two consecutive days than to shorten the test for the sake of convenience. It must be kept in mind that decisions concerning the number of items required to measure given outcomes are basically judgments. There are no formulas for determining the ideal number of items. As with setting the criteria of acceptable performance for objectives, these decisions are tentative and subject to revision based upon experience.

A one-way table of specifications

The major purpose of the behavioral outcome axis in a table of specifications is to insure that higher-order outcomes are measured. There are two situations for which this may not be necessary. The first is the case when the practitioner has had considerable experience in developing two-way tables and tests. Such a person is well aware of the need for higher-order items, and developing them is second nature. The second is when specific objectives have been carefully developed. If all instruction has been objectified, if objectives have been developed at various levels of Bloom's taxonomy, and if test items are to be developed to measure those objectives, then a two-way table may be superfluous. If desired higher-order outcomes have already been thought through, a behavioral outcomes axis probably is not worth the effort. In such cases we can simply develop a one-way table consisting of only the content outline or a listing of objectives and the number of items required for each outline heading or objective. In essence we have a list of topics or objectives and a list of corresponding numbers of items.

Concluding comments

Developing a table of specifications is a planning activity and ideally should be executed during the planning phase of evaluation. The logical time to do it is soon after developing specific objectives. If objectives are laid out for an entire term, a logical next step is to divide them into sets representing manageable units of instruction. In any event, the table of specifications, whether a one-way or two-way table, should be developed as soon as possible. As with objectives, if developed prior to instruction, a table of specifications serves as a guide for instruction since we know what outcomes are intended for what topics and the desired emphases to be placed on each.

Developing a table of specifications is not as time-consuming as it may seem. The first one you do may take some time, but they get easier with practice. Also, if you take the time to develop sound objectives, developing a table of specifications is much easier. Besides, the time spent in planning activities is well worth the valid measurement that results. The more important the test is in terms of subsequent decision making, the more important careful planning is.

It is a good idea, although not always feasible, to have someone else review your objectives and/or your tables of specifications. This "someone" should be a person who is knowledgeable in the content area involved and who preferably has some training in the area of measurement. Of course, unless you have a very good friend, it would probably be an imposition to ask an also-very-busy colleague to review each and every product. For more important tests, however, the feedback is worth the possible inconvenience. Besides, most people would probably be flattered that you sought their opinion.

It is also usually a good idea to share both objectives and tables of specifications with students. What students are expected to learn and demonstrate should not be a secret known only to you. Sharing such information with students is not the same as "teaching to the test." Letting students in on the *kinds* of knowledge and skills they are expected to demonstrate is not the same as telling them what items will be on the test. Such information provides direction to students and influences what and how they study. If they know that you are concerned with demonstration of comprehension, for example, they will not spend all their study time memorizing facts and footnotes.

Before actual test construction begins, the decision must be made concerning the type of test to be developed and the type of items appropriate for each outcome. In most cases a written test will be administered in class without the use of aids, but occasionally an open-book or a take-home exam may be utilized. Such tests may be suitable for certain higher-order outcomes, especially those that involve the use of references in the "real world." An open-book spelling test, for example, does not make much sense, but an open-book statistics test does since we are really interested in whether students can select and apply the appropriate formula for a given situation, not whether they can memorize formulas. Take-home tests usually take the form of a special project rather than a test per se. Preparation for a debate or development of a science project would fall into this category.

Assuming that an in-class written test is to be administered, the next decision is whether it should be an essay test or an objective test, and if an objective test, what kind—short-answer. multiple-choice, true-false, or matching.

9 constructing test items

After reading chapter 9, you should be able to:

1 Identify and briefly describe the general guidelines for item construction.
2 Describe the types of outcomes for which an essay test is most appropriate.
3 State a specific objective and a corresponding essay item, including directions.
4 Briefly describe two approaches to the scoring of essay tests.
5 List the major guidelines for the construction of objective tests, and for each guideline, give an example of an item that violates the guideline and a revised version of the item which does not violate the guideline.
6 State a specific objective of your choice and a corresponding short-answer item, including directions.
7 State a specific objective of your choice and a corresponding multiple-choice item, including directions.
8 State a specific objective of your choice and a corresponding true-false item, including directions.
9 State a specific objective of your choice and a corresponding matching item, including directions.
(Note: The same objective may be used in more than one of items 6–9.)

Overview

There are a number of different types of items and a variety of guidelines for developing items. When students read an item, we want the only factor affecting whether they answer it correctly to be whether they possess the behavior being measured, that is, whether they have achieved the objective. And yet there are a number of characteristics of an item that can either prevent a knowledgeable student from getting it correct or permit an unknowledgeable student to get it correct. The way a question is worded, the nature of the alternatives, and the directions for responding can all affect a student's ability to demonstrate achievement. Some of the potential pitfalls involved with item writing are relatively obvious, others are more subtle. Some are general, and apply to all items, and some are related to a particular type of item.

There are basically two types of test items, essay and objective. Objective items include short-answer, multiple-choice, true-false, and matching items. Test items are also frequently classified as supply or selection items. Essay and short-answer items are referred to as supply items because the answer must be supplied by the student. Multiple-choice, true-false, and matching items are referred to as selection items because the student selects an answer from among provided alternatives. Which item type or types are appropriate for a given test depends mostly upon the nature of the behaviors being measured and the nature of the instruction. A common misconception is that objective tests are only good for measuring facts, or knowledge-level behaviors. Actually any item type can be used to measure any behavioral outcome regardless of its taxonomy level. True, it is difficult to write an analysis-level multiple-choice item, but then it's difficult to write an analysis item of any kind.

Certain kinds of objectives do, however, suggest a particular item type. If an objective involves the ability to solve a quadratic equation, short-answer items would probably be most appropriate although multiple-choice or true-false items could be used. On the other hand, if an objective involves "knowing" the authors of a number of classics, a matching item may be most appropriate. If an objective lends itself to more than one item type, the choice may be based on personal preference. Some teachers, for example, feel more confident with multiple-choice items than with matching items. In general, multiple-choice items are preferable to true-false and matching items because there are systematic procedures for determining the effectiveness of a multiple-choice item and for other reasons to be discussed later in the chapter. A test will not necessarily contain items of more than one type. With tests, there is no virtue in variety for the sake of variety. If all the objectives to be measured suggest short-answer items, then the whole test should be composed of short-answer items. It is also generally a good idea to have as few different item types as possible. Students, especially younger children, may be confused by different sets of directions and the need to "shift gears" several times.

Persons who have never given much thought to item construction and are not aware of all the intricacies involved can consult a number of sources of examples of items. Most school systems have curriculum guides, study guides, and other related materials which contain test items. The various departments in the school of education at most colleges and universities also have a variety of materials which they will share. Some universities also have some type of curriculum lab which contains both instructional materials and specimen tests. The items which appear in such materials are not necessarily models of perfection but they do illustrate the possibilities and are generally reasonably well constructed.

General guidelines

When is the ideal time to develop a test? That's a good question. Certain tests, such a pretests and tests of entry behavior, of course have to be developed before instruction begins. Unit tests, on the other hand, may be developed before, during, or following instruction. Development of posttests of achievement prior to instruction has two major drawbacks. First, it is conducive to unintentional "teaching to the test." Second, it assumes that everything will go exactly according to plan. This is a risky assumption. The essence of the process phase of evaluation is revision based on feedback. The objectives we intended to achieve and the objectives we actually achieve are not necessarily the same. Students may, for example, have more difficulty with a certain set of objectives than we anticipated, and the content covered in a certain test may have to be revised or reduced. This of course requires revision of the table of specifications and the test if it has already been developed.

On the other hand, development of posttests of achievement following instruction also has a major drawback. The test of necessity must be developed in a hurry since you do not want to administer an initial posttest more than a few days following instruction. A test developed in a hurry is not likely to be a good test. Of course, you may wish to administer another similar test at a later date to see how much students have retained (a retention test), but the first test should come as soon after the conclusion of the unit as possible, before subsequent instruction interferes. There are really two basic solutions to the dilemma. You can develop the test ahead of time and revise as necessary, or you can develop the test as you go along. In the latter case, you would develop one or more items each day or every few days as you cover various topics. This approach has another major advantage. Developing a test takes time; spreading the task out over a period of time makes it a little easier, and the last items developed are not as likely to be carelessly constructed. When you are finishing up a test at 2:00 A.M., you have a tendency to lower your standards!

Fortunately, the guidelines for constructing items are essentially the same whether the test is norm-referenced or criterion-referenced, mastery or nonmastery. Recall that you probably cannot tell one from the other by looking at them; the difference is in the intent. As you will quickly see from the discussion to come, one key to good item writing is plain old common sense. Many of the guidelines seem so obvious that you may wonder why they are mentioned at all. Some things, however, are only obvious when you are aware of them (it is pretty obvious the world is round, right?). For example, one guideline is that an item should not be split and appear on two pages because you ran out of room on the first page. This sounds very reasonable and maybe even "obvious," but how may locally-developed tests have you seen in which it was violated? Hmmm?

Objective-item correspondence

Items should directly correspond with the intended behavioral outcome or objective. In other words, the behavior elicited by the item should be precisely the behavior specified in the objective. It should not "sort of" measure the objective, it should exactly measure the objective. Of course if you have no objectives, your definition of intended outcomes may be a little fuzzy, but the basic principle still applies. If an objective stated that a student should be able to compute split-half reliability, then an item asking the student to list the procedures involved in computing split-half reliability would not be appropriate. The only appropriate item would involve presenting students with a set of data and having them actually compute the split-half reliability coefficient. If, indeed, the ability to list the procedures was also believed to be important, then an additional objective (specifying that the student should be able to list the procedures) and of course at least one additional item would be necessary. Relatedly, items calling for demonstration of more than one outcome should definitely be avoided. Examine the following item:

> If you dip litmus paper into an acid solution, what happens to the litmus paper? What happens if you dip it into an alkaline solution?
> a. It turns red in an acid solution and blue in an alkaline solution.
> b. It turns blue in an acid solution and red in an alkaline solution.
> c. In both cases it becomes neutralized.
> d. Nothing happens in either case.

This item really measures two pieces of information, one relating to acid solutions and one relating to alkaline solutions. It would probably be better in this case to have two items, one for each concept.

Item sufficiency

Closely related to the concept of objective-item correspondence is the notion of item sufficiency. Basically *item sufficiency* means that a correct response to an item (or items) constitutes sufficient evidence that the student has demonstrated the intended behavior, or has achieved the objective. Depending upon the nature of the objective, it may not be possible to develop such an item; several items may well be required to meet the sufficiency guideline. It is, however, a goal to work toward.

The concept of item sufficiency can best be explained through an illustrative example. Suppose a high school physical education instructor has the following objective: "Given a bowling score sheet which indicates the number of pins which were knocked down in each of 10 frames, the student will correctly compute and insert the bowler's score in each of the 10 frames." Now examine the following items which could be constructed to measure achievement of that objective:

1. On the score sheet below, compute and insert the bowler's score in each of the 10 frames.

| 4 | 4 | 6 | 3 | – | 8 | 5 | 4 | 9 | – | 5 | 1 | 8 | 1 | F | 7 | 8 | 1 | | 8 | 1 | |

2. On the score sheet below, compute and insert the bowler's score in each of the 10 frames.

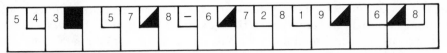

3. On the score sheet below, compute and insert the bowler's score in each of the 10 frames.

Which of the above items do you think does the best job of measuring the objective? Which one does the worst job? I think we would agree that item 2 is a better item than item 1, and item 3 is better than both of them. Why? Because item 3 best represents the range of pin-fall possibilities. A student could correctly fill in all the frames of item 1 and yet not know anything about scoring strikes and spares. Item 2 does include strikes and spares but tells us nothing about a student's ability to score complex combinations of strikes and spares. It may have occurred to you that the probability of producing an item like item 3 could have been greatly increased if the objective had been more carefully stated to better reflect our intentions. Consider the following revision: "Given a bowling score sheet which indicates the number of pins which were knocked down in each of 10 frames, *and which includes examples of open frames, spare frames, strike frames, and combinations of these*, the student will correctly compute and insert the bowler's score in each of the 10 frames." Given this improved version of the objective, items 1 and 2 would clearly not have acceptable objective-item correspondence.

Communication

Communication is generally defined as the process by which meanings are exchanged between individuals. One requirement of an item is that it should clearly communicate to the test takers the meaning intended by the test developer. In other words, the item should be as free from ambiguity as possible. The way the student interprets the item should be the way the test developer intended it to be interpreted. The item should also communicate effectively to any competent scorer, so that any such scorer can correctly determine whether or not a student has answered the item correctly. If an item directed students to write a one-page essay on validity, it would probably not be clear either to students or to scorers (other than the person who wrote the item) whether the student was to discuss the importance of validity, the kinds of validity, or some other unspecified aspect of validity. If, on the other hand, the item directed students to identify and describe the four major types of validity, there would probably be little question as to the correct response.

Item difficulty

Item difficulty is an item characteristic that can be manipulated by the test developer. Appropriate levels of difficulty are a function of both the type of test and the objectives upon which the test is based. Criterion-referenced mastery tests, criterion-referenced nonmastery tests, and norm-referenced tests have different item difficulty requirements. Mastery tests are designed to measure achievement of minimum essentials and are characterized by items of a uniformly low level of difficulty. We are not concerned that such a test may be "too easy"; in fact, we would be deliriously happy if by some chance all students achieved all the objectives and got perfect scores. Criterion-referenced nonmastery tests, on the other hand, normally contain items of varying degrees of difficulty. As with mastery tests, the difficulty of each item is determined by the nature of the objective being measured. We never purposely try to make an item more or less difficult than it needs to be to achieve objective-item correspondence.

The issue of item difficulty gets a little trickier with norm-referenced tests because we are interested in obtaining a spread of scores. The best way to insure a spread is by manipulating the difficulty of the items. As discussed earlier, one way to foster a wide spread of scores is to use items of average difficulty. Average difficulty means basically that half of the students answer the item correctly and half of them answer it incorrectly (this concept will be discussed at greater depth later in the chapter). Items can be developed and revised until they achieve this criterion. When a norm-referenced test is based on a content outline and general behavioral outcomes, there is no problem; item difficulty can be manipulated at will. A complication arises, however, when a norm-referenced test is based on specific objectives. If, as with a criterion-referenced nonmastery test, the difficulty of the item is determined solely by the nature of the objectives, there will of course still be variability in the scores. But maximum variability requires items of average difficulty, and many of the objectives will not lend themselves to such items. Some objectives will reflect knowledge-level outcomes, and the corresponding items will tend to have low levels of difficulty. Other objectives will reflect higher-order outcomes, and the corresponding items will tend to have high levels of difficulty. Thus a compromise must be achieved between desired variability and desired objective-item correspondence. Which way we should lean depends mainly on the purpose for which the test is being administered and the ways in which the results will be used. For a unit test, for example, a teacher may be more interested in how the group is progressing than in individual levels of achievement; in this case objective-item correspondence will take precedence over score variability. For cumulative tests, however, such as a large exam given near the end of a grading period, the teacher will probably be more interested in individual levels of achievement and in rank ordering students for the purpose of assigning letter grades. In this case a degree of objective-item correspondence may be sacrificed for the sake of obtaining a wider range of scores. Easy items that most students would be expected to achieve might even be completely eliminated from the test.

In those situations in which item difficulty is purposely being manipulated, care must be taken to create difficulty in the right ways. The correct way to increase (or decrease) the difficulty of an item is to increase (or decrease) the difficulty of the required responses. We may, for example, develop an application item that requires a deeper understanding of the concept than we might normally expect students to demonstrate. There are a number of "wrong" ways to manipulate item difficulty. We can make the question fuzzy and ambiguous, or we can use high-level vocabulary. We can use words like *loquacious, perturbation,* and *undulation,* for example. Items can also be made less difficult, by including little clues to the correct answer for example. Suppose a multiple-choice item asked who the author of David Copperfield was and the choices were: (*a*) Charles Dickens, (*b*) Mick Jagger, (*c*) Henry Kissinger, and (*d*) O. J. Simpson. Most students could probably figure out the correct answer even if they had never heard of Charles Dickens (*especially* if they had never heard of Charles Dickens!). Manipulating item difficulty in these ways only serves to decrease validity. Item difficulty should be related to the competence of the students who can answer it correctly, not to extraneous variables bearing little or no relationship to knowledge or skill.

Item novelty

Item novelty is a concept that applies primarily to measurement of higher-order outcomes. It refers to the condition where the situation in the item is one that is totally unfamiliar to the student, that is, one that was not previously encountered during instruction. If this condition is not met, an item intended to measure a high-order outcome may in fact be only a knowledge item. For example, suppose our objective is that students be able to analyze test information provided on several tests of the same type and to determine which test is the most acceptable in terms of validity and reliability. Suppose that in class we do this analysis exercise for three IQ tests—The Jeenyus Test, The Eghed Test, and The Graymatter Test— and we conclude that the Eghed Test is the best of the three for a number of reasons. Now if on a subsequent test we provide the same data on these same tests and ask students to perform the comparative analysis, the item would require no more than recall of information and would be a knowledge item. A student only has to have been conscious in class and *remember* the correct answer and reasons. Accurate measurement of the objective would require presentation of information on three different tests not previously discussed.

Domain examples

By now you should have a general, conceptual understanding of what is involved in item writing. Before we discuss individual types of items, we will look at some examples of objectives, one from each of the domains—the cognitive, the affective, and the psychomotor—and an example of an item that corresponds with each. Our general discussion, along with the following examples, should provide a framework for the discussion of specific types of items which follows.

The cognitive domain

Objective: Given a list of reliability coefficients, the student will correctly indicate the type(s) of test (achievement, aptitude or personality), if any, for which each coefficient would represent an acceptable level of reliability.

Sample Item: Below is a list of reliability coefficients. For each coefficient, indicate with an A, B, or C the type of test for which the coefficient would represent an acceptable level of reliability. If the coefficient would be *un*acceptable for

any type of test, indicate this with a D. You may use more
than one letter for each coefficient.

A = achievement test
B = aptitude test
C = personality test
D = none of the above

_____ 1. $r = .59$
_____ 2. $r = .67$
_____ 3. $r = .75$
_____ 4. $r = .84$
_____ 5. $r = .92$

The affective domain

Objective: Given a choice, the student will indicate a preference for foods of greater nutritional value.

Sample Item: For each of the following pairs of foods or beverages, indicate with an X the food or beverage you would rather eat or drink.

1. bran cereal _____ /doughnuts _____
2. cola _____ /orange juice _____
3. potato chips _____ /raisins _____
4. yogurt _____ /chocolate bar _____
5. broiled fish _____ /fried pork _____

The psychomotor domain

Objective: Given two attempts per serve, the student will correctly execute 2 out of 3 of the following tennis serves: American twist, cannon ball, and slice.

Sample Item: (Oral directions) "I am going to call out a type of serve, such as American twist, and you are to execute it. The ball must land in the appropriate service court for you to receive credit. You are allowed two attempts for each serve."

	Correctly Executed		Appropriate Service Court	
Serve	Yes	No	Yes	No
1. American twist	_____	_____	_____	_____
2. Cannon ball	_____	_____	_____	_____
3. Slice	_____	_____	_____	_____

Essay tests

Essay tests are used primarily by teachers for student evaluation. Some standardized tests do contain essay items, and a formal evaluation effort may occasionally utilize such items, but their use is confined mainly to the classroom. An *essay test* is one which contains items which require the student to compose responses, usually lengthy. Essay tests are not really appropriate for knowledge-level outcomes; items typically require both the recall and use of information in the demonstration of a higher-order outcome. Factual information, such as knowledge of terms, can best be measured using objective tests. For certain higher-order outcomes, however, especially those involving synthesis and evaluation, an essay test may be more appropriate. It is difficult to construct objective items which measure certain outcomes. For example, we might have an objective to the effect that the student will be able to develop a weekly budget for a family of four based on a given fixed income. We could develop objective items, but having the students generate the budget items and amounts would be more appropriate and easier. Another example of a measure of higher-order outcomes is an English composition, which is essentially an essay test.

As the above examples illustrate, the scoring of essay tests is somewhat subjective. There is no "one and only one" correct answer or even "two and only two" correct answers. There might be any number of alternative budgets which could be equally acceptable as long as they budgeted appropriately for necessities and emergencies. Because of this variability in correct responses, essay tests normally have to be scored by persons totally knowledgeable concerning both the content area and the objective or behavioral outcome being measured. To a significant degree, the objectivity and accuracy of essay test scoring is a function of the scope of the response elicited by the essay questions. For a more restricted response, such as the response to "List four major characteristics of a standardized test," correct responses can be more clearly defined. The task is more difficult for broader responses such as the response to "Do you think evaluation training should be a required component of every teacher training program? Why?"

Despite the advantages of more restricted response items, less restricted items are usually required for the measurement of higher-order outcomes. A complication that arises with such items is the fact that they involve a number of abilities, such as organization and expression of ideas, which may or may not be specified by the corresponding objective. The major problem of this nature is the difficulty involved in separating quality and accuracy of response from writing ability. As you are probably well aware, some students who know nothing can say it very eloquently while others who do know something have great difficulty expressing what they know. Unless the objective is a writing objective, every effort must be made to ignore variables such as spelling errors, grammatical flaws, and eloquence in the scoring of essay items. This is not to say that a teacher should not provide corrective comments but rather that such factors should not affect a student's score.

Because essay responses are lengthier than those for any objective test, fewer questions can be asked in a given amount of time. Thus, essay tests tend in general to be less content valid and reliable, and scorer reliability is notoriously low. A large part of the problem, however, is due to faulty test development. If you construct an essay test with one or two fuzzy questions such as "Discuss validity" and "Discuss reliability," you are practically guaranteeing a low-quality test. But if you are aware of the potential problems and include a number of clearly stated items (even if testing requires two class periods), you increase your chances of producing a test with at least adequate validity and reliability. If an essay test is based upon one or more well-written, specific objectives, fairly restricted items will in general follow naturally. Again, while essay tests can be used to measure just about any objective, they should be used when they are most appropriate— for higher-order outcomes that do not lend themselves to objective items.

One common misconception is that essay items require recall of information while objective items require recognition only. While it is true that essay items involve recall, objective items do also (with the exception of knowledge-level items). For example, identifying which of four formulas represents the Pythagorean theorem may involve only recognition, but identifying the correct solution to a problem involving the Pythagorean theorem requires recall as well as application of the theorem.

Essay item construction

Objective items are more difficult to construct but are easier to score; essay tests, on the other hand, are tough to score but relatively easy to construct. The general guidelines for item construction—the principles of objective-item correspondence, sufficiency, communication, difficulty and novelty—apply with special emphasis on communication. Since there are no response alternatives to help clarify the question, it is crucial that the desired response be delineated as clearly as possible. Do not tell students to simply "discuss," tell them what to discuss, and use phrases with descriptive terms such as "develop a budget" and "design a lesson plan." Aspects of expected performance should not be left to the student's imagination. If you want students to define terms or give examples, for instance, include those instructions in the item. Further, if scoring is going to be based on factors other than the answers per se (e.g. spelling), make these factors clear. It is also helpful to students to provide them with general guidelines concerning scoring, length, and time. For example, you might say: "Each question is worth 10 points. Four or five sentences should be sufficient for each answer. You have the entire period to complete the test."

An example should make it more clear what is involved in constructing an essay item. We might present students with a hypothesis, a design, and a set of data from a research study (real or hypothetical), followed by one of the items below. Notice how each succeeding item makes the task progressively clearer.

1. Analyze the above set of data.
2. Analyze and interpret the above set of data using descriptive and inferential statistics.
3. Analyze and interpret the above set of data using descriptive and inferential statistics.
   a. Summarize and describe the data using descriptive statistics.
   b. Statistically analyze the data using inferential statistics.
   c. Interpret the results in terms of the research hypothesis.
   d. Present the results of your data analysis in a summary table.

As this example illustrates, one item may be used to measure more than one objective. Item 3 represents at least four different objectives, including the ability to develop a summary table. Item 3 is really a number of items. Parts *a*, *b*, *c* and *d* could be considered as four separate items for scoring purposes, and each part could be further subdivided depending upon the nature of desired behaviors associated with each.

As another example, we might present students with a hypothetical 7-day diet for a 16-year-old male. We could intentionally include undesirable items (such as cakes and cookies) and exclude desirable items (such as leafy green vegetables). The description of the diet would be accompanied by one of the items below. Again, note how each succeeding item makes the task progressively clearer.

1. Discuss the adequacy of the attached diet.
2. State whether you think the attached diet is adequate with respect to nutrition and give reasons for your position.
3. State whether you think the attached diet is more than adequate, adequate, *or* inadequate with respect to nutrition. Defend your position as follows:
   a. Identify any items in the diet which you think should be deleted or limited in quantity. Give reasons for your choices.
   b. Identify any items which you think should be added to the diet or increased in quantity. Give reasons for your choices.
   c. Make as many summary statements as you feel are necessary to describe the overall adequacy of the diet. For example, you might say: "This diet does not include sufficient amounts of leafy green vegetables."

Sometimes students are given a choice of questions on an essay test. They may be instructed, for example, to do any three of five items. This element of choice is an interesting since students are rarely given such options on objective tests. This practice is not a good idea for a number of reasons. If the test is norm-referenced, it is not possible to compare the students' performances if they did not all respond to the same items. If the test is criterion-referenced, it is not possible to determine the degree to which the students have achieved the objectives, only the degree to which *some* students have achieved *some* of the objectives. Further, each student is essentially taking a different test and each of the possible tests has lower content validity because it is based on a smaller sampling of the behaviors than that represented by the total test. The task of estimating reliability will also be greatly complicated, and the reliability of each of the possible tests will of course be lower than if all students answered all items.

Scoring essay tests

As we said earlier, the scoring of essay tests is a difficult and time-consuming process. While it is also *potentially* a very subjective process involving low scorer reliability, the degree of subjectivity can be considerably minimized by careful planning and scoring. Objective tests are easy to score because we can specify *the* right answer. We can objectify essay tests to the degree that we can specify acceptable responses and alternative acceptable responses. If we can clearly spell out what factors should appear in the responses, then any knowledgeable scorer should be able to determine whether or not they are present. There are two basic approaches to the scoring of essay tests, the analytical method and the global method.

The *analytical approach* involves identifying all of the aspects or components of a perfect answer and assigning a point value to each. In our data analysis example, the total item might be worth 100 points, with parts *a*, *b*, *c*, and *d* each worth 25 points. A perfect response for part *a* might require computation of one or more means (X, the average score) and standard deviations (SD, the spread of scores). We could allocate so many points for each correctly computed mean and standard deviation. We could further subdivide the points by allocating so many points for knowing that a mean, for example, should be computed, so many points for applying the correct formula, and so many points for doing it correctly. Answers are then read a second time, points assigned, and the points for the two readings compared. If there are any discrepancies, the item can be reread or the points assigned following the two readings can be averaged. Using this approach scoring can be quite objective. Initial development of a table of specifications facilitates use of the analytic approach. One or more cells related to higher-order outcomes associated with a given topic can be selected to form the basis of an essay item; depending upon the emphases indicated by the table, variable point values can be assigned to the various components of the item or additional components can be developed. If the resulting item does not totally match the table, then either the item can be revised or the table can be revised, depending upon which best reflects the test developer's intent.

The *global approach*, also referred to as the rating method and the holistic approach, results in more subjective, less reliable scoring, but because it takes less time, it is frequently used when a larger number of students is involved. The global approach also involves identifying all of the aspects or components of a perfect answer, but point values are not assigned to each; instead, each response is judged as a whole, as a total unit, and an overall rating is made. Based on the perceived completeness of the response, points are assigned. The item is then reread and rescored and the ratings compared and reconciled. If the item is worth 25 points, for example, then 0–25 points are assigned to the item as a whole.

While both the analytic and global approaches can be used for both CRTs and NRTs, the analytic approach is clearly more appropriate for CRTs (since scores are based on each student's responses considered separately) and the global approach is more appropriate for NRTs. When the global approach is applied to an NRT, a sample of responses is read first to get a feel for the general quality of responses, and then each response is judged to be very good, good, *average*, poor or very poor (or just good, average, or poor), and finally, corresponding points are assigned.

As a general guideline for essay tests, it is a good idea to score each response without knowledge of who wrote it, that is, anonymously. This prevents scores being biased by extraneous factors, such as personal feelings about individual students. Admittedly, this often is not possible. Teachers, for example, become familiar with their students' handwriting and writing styles, and total anonymity of test takers is not possible. But students' anonymity should be preserved as much as possible when scoring. It is also a good idea to score one item at a time (i.e., item 1 for all students and then item 2 for all students, and so forth) rather than to score all the items for one student, and then all the items for another student, and so forth. This promotes consistency of scoring and also reduces scorer biases which can creep in when a total test is scored at one time. If a student responds brilliantly to item 1, for example, the scorer has a tendency to expect a good answer to subsequent items, and it is likely that the student will get a higher score than is warranted by the actual responses. Of course, the reverse is also possible, whereby a poor response to one or more items leads to an expectation of poor performance on remaining items. Thus, objectivity of scoring is promoted by item-by-item scoring.

It is highly recommended that essay responses be read and scored twice, independently, before points are assigned. Ideally, they should be scored by two independent persons, you and another teacher for example. But as with reviewing developed tests, this is rarely feasible. At the very least you should read the essays twice yourself, especially if the test is norm-referenced. A response that did not look so hot when you started scoring may look pretty good the second time around! The easiest way to do this is to score a response and put the point value on the back of the test so that it will not be visible the second time you score the item. You then compare the points assigned at the two readings. If they are essentially the same, you can simply average them. If they are significantly different, you should come back and read the response another time and make your final decision. And of course it is always good practice to provide written feedback on items in the form of both corrections and positive comments. And even if spelling and grammar errors do not affect scores, they should be pointed out to students.

Objective tests

Objective tests are sometimes criticized on the basis that they are appropriate for measuring knowledge-level outcomes only. This is not true, as was pointed out before. While it is true that certain higher-order outcomes can be more easily measured with essay items, objective items can be used to measure outcomes at all levels. With the exception of outcomes such as handwriting ability and organizational skills, objective items can measure most objectives. Further, objective tests should be used whenever they are appropriate for a number of reasons. For one thing, since objective tests can include more items, they tend to sample behavior more adequately and consequently an objective test is invariably more valid and reliable than a comparable essay test. A related big plus for objective tests is accuracy and ease of scoring. Scorer reliability is extremely high; any misscoring is generally a function of carelessness or human error rather than disagreement over the correctness of a given response. On the minus side, objective tests do require considerably more preparation time and skill than essay tests. On balance, however, the advantages of objective tests clearly compensate for this disadvantage, and any time spent in preparation is more than made up for when tests are scored.

The general guidelines for item construction, e.g. communication, of course, apply to objective items. While objective items generally communicate required behaviors to students better than essay tests do, it is still necessary to make a conscious effort to write clear, concise, unambiguous items. In addition, there are a number of pitfalls which can be avoided if you are aware of them.

1 Be careful not to provide *clues* to the correct answer. Such clues may be grammatical or contextual and are very useful to test-wise students. Some students know how to "take a test" better than others and being sensitive to clues is part of their success. The item "A word which is opposite in meaning to another word is called an _____" contains a grammatical clue. The word *an* before the blank indicates that the answer begins with a vowel. The best way to eliminate this particular clue is to use the word "a(n)" which is generally recognized to mean "a or an." The following item contains a contextual clue:

A test which was one-hundred percent reliable would produce a reliability coefficient with a numerical value equal to _____.

The part of a word "one" in the question is a clue to the correct response, +1.00.

2 *Dependent items* should be avoided. Items are dependent if the correct answer to one item is necessary in order to correctly answer another item, or if one item contains a clue to the correct answer of another item. An example of the first case would be the following items:

If $X + 7 = 15$, then

1. X = _____
2. X^2 = _____

If you do not know how to solve for X, you cannot compute X^2 correctly, even if you know how to square a number. An example of the second case would be the following item:

1. Beethoven is best known for his symphonies and sonatas, Bach for his fugues, and Brahms for his lullaby. Strauss is best known for his
   a. concertos.
   b. marches.
   c. symphonies.
   <u>d</u>. waltzes.

2. The name of the composer of the Moonlight Sonata is
   a. Bach.
   <u>b</u>. Beethoven.
   c. Brahms.
   d. Chopin.

3 *Irrelevant difficulty* should not be promoted, either intentionally or unintentionally, by using unnecessarily complex vocabulary or by making the item more complicated than it needs to be. In other words, no tricky stuff. Do not use words like "ambulate" and "altercation" when you mean "walk" and "disagreement." If you want to know if students can compute simple interest, do not give them problems like the following:

If you borrowed $491.22 at 6.83% interest, how much interest would you pay the first year?

Figures such as $500 and 6% will measure the same objective more directly, will avoid irrelevant sources of difficulty and error, and will be more realistic.

4 Avoid *negatives*, especially double negatives. With a little rewording, a negative statement can generally be converted to a positive statement. The item below illustrates the problem:

1. Which of the following is not a requirement for a person desiring to be licensed as a real estate broker in the state of North Carolina?
   <u>a</u>. An age of 21 years or older
   b. No felony convictions
   c. A score of 70% on the ETS Real Estate Brokers' Examination
   d. U.S. citizenship

The answer is *a* because the age requirement is actually 18 years. The question is confusing because of the "not" in the question and the "no" in choice *b*. What does "no felony convictions are *not* a requirement" mean? Depending upon the knowledge being measured, the item could be reworded into one of the following items:

1. The minimum age requirement for a person desiring to be licensed as a real estate broker in the state of North Carolina is
   <u>a</u>. 18.
   b. 19.
   c. 20.
   d. 21.

2. In the state of North Carolina a person may be denied a real estate broker's license for which of the following reasons?
   a. Failure to obtain a police I.D. card
   b. Lack of experience
   c. Lack of a high school diploma
   <u>d</u>. A previous felony conviction

If a negative term is used, it should be emphasized in some way, such as by underlining or by the use of italics. For example:

1. In the state of North Carolina, all of the following are requirements for a person desiring to be licensed as a real estate broker *except*
   a. a minimum age of 18.
   <u>b</u>. one year of experience as a real estate salesperson.
   c. a score of 70% on the ETS Real Estate Brokers' Examination.
   d. U.S. citizenship.

5 *Direct quotes* should be avoided. There is sometimes a tendency, especially when one is in a hurry, to lift sentences from textbooks or other materials and to make items out of them. Besides the fact that this practice encourages meaningless, verbatim memorization, it also results in ambiguous, and sometimes very strange, items. For example:

All evaluation efforts require _____.

Do you know the answer? This happens to be a sentence from the introduction to part 5 and the answer is "tests." As written, however, there are a number of possible correct responses, e.g. "planning." Another example is the following.

The number of items should be determined by _____.

This sentence is from chapter 8, and the intended answer is "the objectives." Out of context, however, the sentence doesn't make too much sense.

6 *Trivia* should not be measured. As with quotes, there is sometimes a tendency to measure knowledge of trivial facts or concepts (even footnotes!). It is a quick way to come up with items, but not good ones. Take the following item:

In a two-way table of specifications, each of the two dimensions is called a(n)
_____ .

The answer is "axis." If your instructor asked this question on a test, you would think it was pretty tacky, even if you knew the correct response. It would be stretching the imagination to think that anyone would have an objective requiring knowledge of the term "axis." If anyone did, it would be a trivial objective.

7 An item should have *one and only one* correct, or best, answer, unless otherwise specified. Usually when more than one answer is correct, it is an inadvertent item flaw; item writers do not purposely write such items. An item such as "Reliability is _____" is almost impossible to get wrong. After all, the response "an 11-letter word" would be a correct response for that item. Another example is the following:

The most serious disease in the United States is
a. cancer.
b. heart disease.
c. mental illness.
d. venereal disease.

The correct answer depends upon what is meant by "serious." Cancer could be the correct answer because it leads to more deaths; mental illness could be the correct answer because it affects more people; and venereal disease could be the answer because it is currently the number one communicable disease in the United States. The question would have to be reworded in order for there to be one correct answer:

The leading cause of death in the United States is
a. cancer
b. heart disease.
c. mental illness.
d. venereal disease.

In some situations, such as when alternative responses are equivalent, more than one answer may be correct. The responses "Alvin," "Dot's brother," and "Mrs. Drone's son" may all refer to the same person and be equally acceptable answers to the question "In the story, who was the main character?" If more than one answer is acceptable, it is important that they all be specified prior to scoring.

That one picture is worth a thousand words is certainly true for test items. You should keep in mind that an item does not have to be totally written. Use of an appropriate picture, diagram, or map, for example, may save a lot of words and make the task at hand clearer to students. Usually when an illustration of some sort is used, it is accompanied by several items. We might present students with a diagram of the human heart and ask a series of questions about its components and functions. When diagrams and the like are used, it is important that they be accurate and legible.

Short-answer items

Basically, a *short-answer item* is a short essay item and the difference between them is often blurred. Short-answer items are best suited for questions requiring a brief response—a word, a phrase, or a sentence. While short-answer items are typically used for knowledge objectives, and essay items are most appropriate for synthesis and evaluation outcomes, short-answer items can easily be used for higher-order outcomes; the item "The area of your math textbook cover is _____ sq. in." is an application item. Also, scoring of short-answer questions is typically less subjective than the scoring of essay tests because of the conciseness of required responses. A short-answer item may take the form of a question, as in "Who was the first president of the United States?", or an incomplete sentence, as in "The name of the first president of the United States is _____." Items of the second type are referred to as completion items. Directions for short-answer items are relatively simple and usually take one of the following forms:

> Answer each of the following questions as briefly as possible. A word, phrase, or sentence will be sufficient.

> Write the word or phrase which best completes each of the statements below.

Occasionally, it may be appropriate to have an item such as the following:

> After each title, write the name of its author.
>
> 1. *Ivanhoe* _____
>
> 2. *Jane Eyre* _____
>
> 3. *Little Women* _____
>
> 4. *Oliver Twist* _____
>
> 5. *Wuthering Heights* _____

This saves repetition in the form of a series of items such as "The name of the author of *Little Women* is _____." The general guidelines for item construction and for objective-item construction, such as avoiding clues, apply to short-answer items. In addition, there are guidelines unique to short-answer items.

Position of blank

As a general rule, there should be only one blank in a completion item and it should come near or at the end of the sentence.
For example:

> One meter is equivalent to _____ inches.

is preferable to

_____ inches is equivalent to one meter.

Some students, especially young ones, tend to get lost in the action and forget the question unless the blank is at the end. Placing the blank at the end also helps to prevent the omission of trivial words. Items such as

Alexander Graham Bell _____ the telephone.

only measure the students' ability to solve a word puzzle. Having one blank, at the end, also eliminates disasters such as the following item (which actually appeared on a high school geometry test):

The _____ of a _____ is found by multiplying _____-_____ the _____ of the _____ times the _____.

Believe it or not, the completed item should read: "The area of a trapezoid is found by multiplying one-half the sum of the bases times the height." Occasionally two blanks, but rarely more than two, may be appropriate. Also, as the above item illustrates, to prevent the size of the blank being a clue to the correct response, all the blanks for all the items should be the same size and should be long enough to accommodate the longest response.

Specification of response units and accuracy

Primarily to simplify scoring, it is a good idea to tell the student the units in which the answer should be expressed. If a math text is 8 inches by 10 inches, then the question, What is the perimeter of your math text? has at least two correct answers—36 inches and 3 feet. One correct answer can be guaranteed by rephrasing the question ("In inches, what is the perimeter. . . .") or by specifying inches at the end of the blank ("_____ inches"). It is also advisable to specify the accuracy required of responses, unless being able to determine the correct accuracy is part of the item. For example, you might say:

If a house which sold for $40,250 in 1979 has appreciated 5.5%, how much could it be sold for today? Express your answer in two decimal places.

The accuracy specified should be consistent with common practice. For example, there is usually no good reason for having students compute interest to five decimal places.

Multiple-choice items

A *multiple-choice item* is composed of a question or incomplete sentence, referred to as the *stem*, and a list of alternative responses. Responses that are not the correct answer are referred to as *distractors*, or foils. Students are instructed to select *the* correct answer or *the best* answer. Directions for multiple-choice items usually take a form such as the following:

> For each of the following items select the correct answer from among the choices presented. Place the letter of your choice in the blank in front of the question.

Instead of "correct answer," they may specify "best answer," and instead of placing a letter in a blank students may be instructed to circle the letter or underline the answer (especially young children). In some cases, they may be instructed to mark the corresponding letter or space on an answer sheet. A variation on the standard multiple-choice item is the analogy item (discussed earlier) which frequently appears on intelligence tests. Since responses do not have to be composed, more items can be included in a given amount of time. Thus, multiple-choice tests tend to be more valid and reliable than the types of tests discussed so far, and scoring reliability is practically perfect. Also, since all students are responding to the same set of alternatives, analysis of wrong choices provides valuable information for item revision and subsequent instruction. If 80% of the class chooses the same wrong response, for example, we know something is wrong.

As with short-answer items, multiple-choice items are sometimes criticized on the basis that they are used to measure knowledge outcomes only. As was pointed out earlier, this is the fault of the test developer, not a characteristic of multiple-choice items. They can be used to measure outcomes at all levels and are especially suited for comprehension and application items. Consider the following example:

> According to the principles of supply and demand, if there is a shortage of cocoa beans what will happen to the price of cocoa? It will
> a. decline.
> b. stay the same.
> c. rise.

Ebel has expressed it best. He points out that the game of chess is essentially a multiple-choice test to a good player; at any point during the game only a few moves are seriously considered out of all possible moves and the player selects the *best* one.[1] The analogy is a good one and the game of chess is certainly not a knowledge-level activity.

The general guidelines for item construction and for objective-item construction, e.g. presenting the stem as clearly as possible for example, apply to multiple-choice tests. In addition, there are guidelines unique to multiple-choice items.

The stem

The stem should contain as much of the problem as possible. In fact, some measurement specialists argue that the stem should be in the form of a question in

[1] Ebel, R. L. Essentials of educational measurement. Englewood Cliffs, N.J., Prentice-Hall, 1979.

order to insure that it contains a complete thought. Stems such as "An arachnid is . . ." usually require lengthy alternatives. The following item illustrates:

An arachnid is
a. an arthropod with three pairs of legs and antennae.
b. an arthropod with three pairs of legs but no antennae.
c. an arthropod with four pairs of legs and antennae.
d. an arthropod with four pairs of legs but no antennae.

The stem should make the nature of the desired response clear, so that students spend their time thinking about the answer, not figuring out the question. Notice how much clearer the following revision is:

An arthropod with four pairs of legs but no antennae is called a(n)
a. annelid.
b. arachnid.
c. insect.
d. mollusk.

As the above item and its revision also illustrate, words should not be repeated in each response. They can usually be included in the stem with very little effort, e.g. "An arthropod *with* . . ." In addition, clues that are provided by using words in the stem which also appear in the responses should be avoided. This guideline also applies to the use of words that are synonymous or sound enough alike to constitute a hint. For example:

An inner seam of a garment is called a(n)
a. dart.
b. hem.
c. inseam.
d. pleat.

Responses

The major guideline for the development of responses is that all distractors should be plausible; that is, they should appear to be reasonable to students who do not really know the correct answer. Examine the following item:

The Mona Lisa was painted by
a. Alexander the Great.
b. da Vinci.
c. Galileo.
d. Napoleon.

To answer this question correctly you do not have to know who painted the Mona Lisa; all you have to know is who of the four choices is an artist and who is not. The following revision contains more reasonable distractors:

The Mona Lisa was painted by
a. da Vinci.
b. Rembrandt.
c. Renoir.
d. van Gogh.

One way to determine plausible distractors is to administer a short-answer test and see what kinds of errors are commonly made. You might ask "The Mona Lisa was painted by what artist?" If a number of students said Rembrandt, you would then use him as a distractor on a subsequent multiple-choice test. In the first example, the chances of anyone saying Napoleon (except perhaps as a ha-ha) would be slim.

Grammatical consistency is especially important for multiple-choice items since responses are supplied. An inadvertent grammatical clue can be a dead giveaway, as in the following item.

> An apparatus for measuring the work performed by a group of muscles is an
> a. dynamometer.
> b. ergometer.
> c. spirometer.
> d. tachometer.

The word "an" in the stem would be enough to make anyone select *b* even if all the choices looked like foreign words! As was pointed out earlier, the obvious way to eliminate this particular grammatical clue is to use "a(n)."

A common error that is committed by unsophisticated item developers is a tendency to make correct answers longer than incorrect ones. This results from a well-intentioned effort to insure that the correct answer is completely correct. For example:

> In order to be elected president of the United States, a presidential candidate must receive at least what proportion of the popular vote?
> a. A plurality, assuming that the votes of the electoral college correspond exactly to the popular vote
> b. Over 50%
> c. At least 66²/₃%
> d. At least 75%

One way to avoid a longer correct answer is to put the qualifier in the stem, as in "Assuming that votes of the electoral college correspond exactly to the popular vote, in order to be elected. . . ."

As all of the previous examples of multiple-choice items illustrate, the responses should be arranged vertically in some logical order. This arrangement makes it easier for students to view the alternatives and locate the correct response, and also naturally varies the position of the correct response; that is, the correct answer is just as likely to be *a* as *b* or *c* or *d*. For many responses the logical order is alphabetical (e.g., dynamometer, ergometer, spirometer, tachometer) or numerical (e.g., 50%, 66 ²/₃%, 75%). For other responses the most logical ordering depends upon the stem, as in the supply-and-demand question, for which the responses in order were "decline," "stay the same," and "rise." If the order of responses really does not matter (which is not very often), then the position of the correct answer should consciously be varied so that *a* is correct just as often as *b* or *c* or *d*.

Relatedly, the number of responses, normally ranging from three to five, should be a function of both the age level of the students and the nature of the items. Three alternatives are about all young children can handle. If you try to have more than five, you usually find yourself hard pressed to come up with enough reasonable distractors. It is much better to have several good distractors than a number of tacky ones. Further, no law says all the items on a test have to have the same number of alternative responses. There is no point in scrounging up a fourth alternative, for example, if there are only three that make sense. The supply-and-demand item had three choices—"decline," "stay the same," and "rise." What other alternative could there possibly be? Those three cover all contingencies.

Often, when someone is trying to dream up an additional alternative, he settles for "all of the above" or "none of the above." Neither of these is generally recommended, mainly because they are rarely appropriate. If there are five alternatives, for example, and a student knows that two of them are true, the student will correctly choose "all of the above" even if she or he knows nothing about the other two alternatives. "None of the above" is not so bad in itself; the problem is that it is usually thrown in for the sake of having an additional alternative and is hardly ever the correct response. Students catch on to this rather quickly and such items end up having one less alternative in essence, anyway. Therefore, if you do use this option, be sure that it is the correct response as often as any of the other responses.

True-false items

The classic *true-false item* is a statement for which a student selects the response "true" or "false." Variations on the basic true-false item include items to which the student responds yes or no, agree or disagree, right or wrong, and so forth. An example of the yes-no variety is the following:

I enjoy the time I spend in school.   Yes   No

Another type of true-false item is the *correction item*. Basically, if a student selects "false," he or she must also write whatever change or correction would make the statement true. For example:

> In each of the items below, one word has been underlined. If you think that the underlined word correctly completes the statement, circle the T. If you believe that the underlined word incorrectly completes the statement, circle the F and write in the blank the word that does correctly complete the statement.
>
> 1. If you mix blue and yellow paint you get *purple*.   T   F   _____

The correct answer would be:

> 1. If you mix blue and yellow paint you get *purple*.   T (F) __green__

As this item illustrates, the word or phrase which is to be corrected should be emphasized in some way, such as by underlining or using italics.

Theoretically, true-false items can be written to measure outcomes at all levels, as the following example illustrates:

$$2X^2 + X^2 + 4 = 3X^4 + 4$$ T $\underline{F}$

For such higher-order outcomes, however, short-answer or multiple-choice items are usually preferred because they provide information concerning errors. Students who choose F for the above item, for example, might do so because they know that $2X^2 + X^2 + 4$ really equals $3X^2 + 4$, or because they believe it equals $2X^4 + 4$, or because of some other reason. You could use a correction item, but with this kind of outcome you are better off selecting a different, more appropriate, item type. Further, since it is difficult to write items that are totally true or totally false, true-false items are best suited for the measurement of attitudes and opinions (e.g., I like to read when I'm home.   T   F), and abilities related to logical argument. Given a series of propositions, for example, students can indicate whether a given conclusion is valid or invalid. Also, we can sometimes "collapse" a number of multiple-choice items into a series of true-false items by presenting one stem followed by a series of responses. This is especially appropriate when a number of multiple-choice items have similar or identical stems. For example:

> In order to become part of the United States Constitution, a proposed amendment must be
> 1. approved by the President.   T   F
> 2. approved by two-thirds of each house of Congress.   T   F
> 3. ratified by two-thirds of the states.   T   F

Like multiple-choice tests, true-false tests permit a broad sampling of behaviors in a limited period of time, tend to be reasonably reliable, and are easy to score. They are not, at least theoretically, generally as reliable as equivalent multiple-choice tests, however, due to reduced variability of scores. Recall that increased variability of scores is related to greater reliability. On a 100-item true-false test, for example, the expected range of scores is 50–100 (a student who guesses on every item is expected to get half of the items right, a score of 50, by chance). On a 100-item, 4-alternative multiple-choice test, however, the expected range of scores is 25–100 (a student who guesses on every item is expected to get one-fourth of the items correct, a score of 25, by chance).

Again, the general guidelines for item construction and for objective-item construction apply to true-false items. It is especially crucial that true-false items be stated as clearly and succinctly as possible since they are especially susceptible to sources of ambiguity. It is also important to avoid the use of negatives since to answer "false" to a negatively worded statement essentially creates a double negative. For example:

> The centaur is not a real creature.   T   F

The choice "false, is not" is rather confusing. In addition, there are also some unique caveats for true-false items.

Irrelevant information

The portion of an item which makes it false should be an important fact or concept. Sometimes we see items which are made false by changing some trivial piece of information. Note the following:

> Hamlet was written by Wilheim Shakespeare.   T   F

The student is going to focus on the basic question, which is, Who wrote Hamlet? and will tend to mark T as soon as he sees the appropriate association—Shakespeare. The problem with items like this is that many students who "know" the answer are likely to miss it. Thus, neither their knowledge nor your instruction is being fairly assessed. Besides, do you really care if they know that Shakespeare's first name is William? In other words, no tricky stuff.

Length and proportion

As with multiple-choice items, there is sometimes a tendency to make items which are true longer than those which are false. A true-false statement *should* be completely true or completely false. If there is *any* situation for which a "true" statement is not true, then the statement is technically false. For example:

Normal body temperature is 98.6.   T   F

Well, that is true, *usually*. There are exceptions, however. Some individuals, for example, have a "normal" body temperature of 98. To be totally true, the item would have to be reworded as follows:

For most people, normal body temperature is 98.6.   T   F

Since it is frequently difficult to develop items which are completely true, lengthy qualifiers are sometimes added to insure that the statement is totally true. For example:

There are 365 days in a calendar year, except leap year which has 366
days in order to account for the fact that there are really 365¼ days in a
year.   T   F

If it is necessary to have a few lengthy "true" items, you should have an approximately equal number of lengthy "false" items. In other words, length of an item should have nothing to do with its truth or falsity.

Relatedly, the proportion of items which are true and the proportion which are false should not be too different. Having a large proportion of false items, for example, may be a clue to the test-wise students; if they are not sure of a certain item they will "go with the odds" (which are no longer 50–50) and select F. Similarly the correct responses for true-false items should not form any type of pattern, such as TFTFTF . . . or TFFTFFTFF . . . . Some students are very quick to catch on to such schemes.

Specific determiners

Specific determiners are words such as "always," "all," "never," "none," "generally," and "usually." Words such as "always" and "none," because they indicate sweeping generalizations, are associated with false items while words such as "generally" and "usually" are associated with true items. For example:

All scorpions have eight legs.   T   F

Theoretically that is true. But there is bound to be at least one little scorpion somewhere with only seven legs, because of a fight with another scorpion perhaps. The

point is that such words should be avoided because they affect the correct response more than the content of the item.

Matching items

While matching items can be used to measure outcomes at all levels, they are
usually used when a number of related facts, such as knowledge of titles and authors, are to be measured. They efficiently permit a relatively large sampling of
behavior. As noted earlier, sometimes when we are developing multiple-choice
items, we notice that there are several items with a similar stem, and we convert
them to a series of true-false items with a common stem. Similarly, we sometimes
notice a number of multiple-choice items with the same, similar, or overlapping
alternatives. In this case we can usually convert the multiple-choice items to a
more efficient matching item. A *matching item* consists of two vertical lists referred
to as the premises and the conclusions, or responses. For each premise there is a
response which "goes with it," or is associated with it. Typical directions for a
matching item read as follows:

> Match each important historical event below with the year in which it occurred. For
> each event, place the letter corresponding to the appropriate date in the blank in
> front of the event.

_____ 1. The Civil War began.	A. 1215
_____ 2. Columbus discovered America.	B. 1492
_____ 3. The Declaration of Independence was signed.	C. 1588
_____ 4. The Magna Carta was signed.	D. 1620
_____ 5. The Pilgrims landed at Plymouth Rock.	E. 1776
_____ 6. The Spanish Armada was defeated by the English.	F. 1787
	G. 1812
	H. 1861

The general guidelines for item construction and objective-item construction, such as avoiding grammatical clues, apply to the construction of matching
items. In addition, there are some suggestions which are unique to matching
items.

Item homogeneity

The premises and conclusions of a matching item should be as homogeneous as possible. In other words, they should have a common theme. In the previous example, all the premises were historical events and the conclusions were
their corresponding dates. When this guideline is violated, we find items that mix
two or more different "things," such as the following:

_____ 1. The cotton gin	A. Alexander Graham Bell
_____ 2. *Idylls of the King*	B. Elizabeth Barrett Browning
_____ 3. "Ode to a Grecian Urn"	C. Thomas Edison
_____ 4. The printing press	D. Johann Gutenberg
_____ 5. *Sonnets from the Portuguese*	E. John Keats
_____ 6. The telephone	F. Percy Bysshe Shelley
	G. Alfred Tennyson
	H. Eli Whitney

It would be difficult for a student to get oriented to this item since it measures knowledge of both inventors and their inventions and poets and their works. Such items usually result from trying to measure more than one objective in one item. The above item could easily be separated to form the nucleus of two items. By adding additional premises and conclusions to each, the result would be two items which would be easier for students to respond to and which would represent a better sampling of the two objectives being measured.

Length and arrangement

In general, the list of premises should be relatively brief: too many premises turns the item into a word search puzzle. How many is too many depends on the age of the students, but 3 to 10 premises is a reasonable range. If there happen to be more than 10 pieces of information which should be included, they may be divided to form two shorter items. There should also be more premises than conclusions, or vice versa; that is, there should not be an equal number of premises and conclusions. The main reason for this guideline is that a student may automatically make a correct match because there is only one conclusion left for the one remaining premise. If the list of conclusions is longer, there will be some conclusions that do not match any premise. These "extras" should be as plausible as the conclusions which actually match premises. If the list of premises is longer, then there will be conclusions which match more than one premise; three titles in a list of premises, for example, may all match the same author in the list of conclusions.

Also, as with multiple-choice items, the premises and conclusions in a matching item should be arranged in some logical order, usually alphabetically or numerically. If you examine the previous examples of matching items, you will see that names and titles are arranged alphabetically (not counting words like "the") and the dates are arranged in numerical order. This makes it easier for students to match conclusions with premises. They do not have to spend extra time searching for the answer in a jumbled list. If a student knows, for example, that the Civil War began in 1861, she or he can quickly locate the appropriate letter.

Directions

While clear directions are always important, they are especially so for matching items. It is not always obvious on what basis matching is to be performed. See if you can do the following item:

_____ 1. Encyclopedia salesperson   A. Mileage
_____ 2. Independent trucker   B. Professional journals
_____ 3. Physician   C. Salary
_____ 4. Law enforcement officer   D. Uniforms
_____ 5. Teacher
_____ 6. Waitress/waiter

Give up? If the directions said, "Match each occupation with the appropriate item in the right-hand column," would that help? Nope. How about these:

For each occupation listed below, select the item in the right-hand column which represents an allowable tax deduction for persons in that occupation. Place the appropriate letter in the blank preceding the matching occupation. Each lettered item may be used more than once or not at all.

Aha! Now the item makes sense. (In case you're interested, the answers are: 1–A, 2–A, 3–B, 4–D, 5–B, and 6–D.) As the above directions also illustrate, the students should be told if a given conclusion can be matched with more than one premise or if a given premise can be matched with more than one conclusion.

10 test construction and reproduction

After reading chapter 10, you should be able to:

1 Describe the major approaches to the organization of test items.
2 Briefly describe the types of directions which should be included in a test.
3 List the major guidelines concerning test format.

Overview

After items have been developed they must be assembled into a test and additional directions must be written. Items must be organized in some logical manner and students must be given general directions concerning the recording and scoring of items and whether guessing is permitted or recommended. Some directions may be oral, especially for small fry, but they are best included in the test, in writing. Finally, the test must be reproduced and readied for distribution to students.

Organization of items

You could take all the items you constructed and put them on a test in no particular order. But this would only make life difficult, for both you and the test takers. Directions would be tough to write since you might, for example, have a multiple-choice item followed by a short-answer question, and similarly scoring would be complicated. From the test takers' viewpoint, the test would be unnerving since they would have to shift gears after every question. The logical organization of test items facilitates efficient use of test taking time. There are several different ways to organize items that make sense. First, if there is more than one type of item, items of the same type (e.g. all the multiple-choice items) should be together. Further, if there is more than one variety of a certain type of item, all items of each variety should be grouped together (e.g., all basic true-false or all correction true-false items). Such arrangements permit the directions for all items of a given type and variety to be presented once and facilitates later scoring of responses. Test takers can organize their thoughts better and make more efficient use of their time.

A second approach to item organization is to arrange items on a continuum from least difficult to most difficult. If there is more than one type of item, items can be clustered by item type and then by difficulty within each cluster. This arrangement has both practical and psychological benefits. If students answer the items in the order given, and if sufficient time is allowed, students will answer all the items they are capable of responding to. They will not get "hung up" on a difficult item and fail to answer easier items which come after the tough one. Thus, a teacher, for example, can get a fairly accurate picture of what each student has achieved. Psychologically, students get a boost because almost all of them can answer at least the first few questions, thus encouraging them to continue. Being hit with a "toughie" at the beginning is demoralizing to less able students and may cause them to mentally give up.

Another logical way to arrange items is by topic; for example, all the items dealing with circles would be put together and all the items dealing with triangles together. At the very least, all the items related to the same objective should be grouped together. They will all have approximately the same level of difficulty and should all be of the same item type. Such an arrangement, therefore, will not interfere with any other organizational arrangements. Having all the items related to the same topic together also helps students since the concepts appear in context.

Clearly, all three of these organizational schemes cannot be applied simultaneously. Frequently, however, one approach is automatically eliminated by the nature of the test. All items in a mastery test, for example, will be of approximately the same low level of difficulty. Thus, if necessary, items can be arranged by type and by topic and objective within each type. Not infrequently, a mastery test may deal with only one objective, in which case organization is greatly simplified. Of course if a test contains both mastery items and nonmastery items, the mastery items should be together and should appear first. Other tests may often be composed of items of all one type (e.g. multiple-choice). In these cases, they can be arranged by topic and objective and by difficulty within each topic. There is no way to specify the ideal choice or combination of organizational schemes. Which approach is most appropriate depends upon the type and content of the test. What is important is to be aware of the alternatives and consciously make the best decision for a given situation.

General directions

As discussed previously, each group of items of a certain type and variety should be grouped together with a common set of directions. In addition, there should be directions for recording responses and information related to scoring. Test directions are basically the same, at least for achievement tests, whether the test is norm-referenced or criterion-referenced. It goes without saying that directions should be as clear as possible, in other words, they should communicate. Clear directions are especially important for young children and students of low ability and certain other groups of students. While it is generally preferable to have written directions included in the tests, for these special groups it may be more effective to give them orally to reduce the effect of reading ability and to insure that all directions are completely understood. In most cases, students will be well aware of the nature of the test and why they are taking it. If the purpose and importance are not self-evident, however, they should be discussed with the students in order to orient them and to motivate them to do their best.

Selection and recording of responses

In addition to directions for selecting (or supplying) answers, students should be instructed as to how to record the answers. Such directions may be presented once at the beginning of the test or prior to presentation of a set of items of one type. If directions are at all complicated or involve procedures unfamiliar to students, an example and a practice item should be presented for each set of directions. Standardized tests nearly always include sample items. If an objective test is at all lengthy and if students are old enough to handle it, it may be more convenient in terms of scoring to have students record responses on a separate answer sheet. If a separate sheet is not used, answer spaces should be placed on the test to facilitate scoring, usually in a vertical column on the right-hand or left-hand margin of each page.

If responses are recorded in an organized manner, whether on a separate sheet or not, some type of scoring key can be developed which does not require the scorer to refer to the items. Many of you have probably seen some type of strip key; such a scoring key has the answers listed in a column so that it can be laid next to an answer column and responses can be compared. For longer tests, preprinted answer sheets, such as those prepared by IBM, may be used. Such sheets are usually appropriate for multiple-choice tests and therefore contain spaces (e.g.

A, B, C, D and E) for blackening in the correct responses for each item. If such sheets are hand scored, a scoring stencil is generally used; such a stencil is laid on top of the answer sheet and contains holes such that the correct answer should show through. For item 1, for example, the hole may correspond to choice C; if a blackened area does not show through, the student selected the incorrect response. When such answer sheets are used, responses can also be machine scored, by the IBM Optical Mark Scoring Reader for example. In such instances students must be instructed to completely blacken each selected answer space (such sheets can obviously not be used for short-answer items) and to avoid, and completely erase, all stray pencil marks.

The main advantage of machine scoring is accuracy; rarely are tests machine-scored incorrectly. Also, in many cases, summary information concerning test results, such as the average score, can be supplied upon request. On the other hand, for many classroom tests machine scoring is not desirable. Machine scoring frequently requires that all students have a no. 2 pencil; therefore the teacher must either provide such pencils or nag students for days before the test to bring them to class. Then you have to worry about students sufficiently blackening the intended spaces and erasing stray marks. You also have the additional inconvenience and delay involved in having tests scored somewhere else. Of course, if the test scoring service can score and return your tests in the same or less time than it would take you to hand score them, the delay will not be a problem. This usually happens, however, only when many students are involved and the test contains many items. Also, depending upon the age and ability of the students, use of separate answer sheets, or even separate answer columns, may be inadvisable. If there is any possibility that some students will be confused by the directions and procedures involved, and thereby suffer a reduced score, then students should be instructed to simply circle or underline (or whatever) the correct response on the test sheet itself. Instructions on such a test sheet might read like this:

> Read each item carefully and decide which of the choices completes the statement correctly. Circle the letter of the answer you choose. Each item has only one correct answer.

Scoring information

Test takers should be informed as to how much the total point value of the test is (e.g. 50 points) and how much each item is worth. If all items are worth 5 points each, tell the students. Further, if an item is composed of subparts to be scored separately (as in an essay test for example), the value of each subpart should be known to students. The easiest way to do this, if all items are of equal value, is to make a statement at the beginning of the test. If item values vary, the points associated with each can be placed in front of its number, usually in parentheses, as shown below:

> (3)   1. A full-grown frog is called a tadpole.   T   F

If is sometimes reasonable to have some items worth more than others. Twenty multiple-choice questions may be worth 5 points each, for example, while two essay questions may be worth 10 points each. It is not a good idea, however, to have items of the same type worth varying amounts, a technique referred to as *weighting*. If some topics are believed to be more important than others, it is better to have more items for these topics (e.g. twice as many) than to assign some items a higher point value (e.g. twice as many points). Of course, if you have objectives, the number of items will also be determined by "what it takes" to measure the intended outcomes. Further, if you score a test with the items weighted, and score it again with the items unweighted, students perform essentially the same, relatively speaking. In other words, the students who do the best do so either way, and likewise the students who do poorly. Thus, there is really no good reason to weight items.

If test taking time is not ample, students should be given some guidelines for using their time effectively. You might tell them that they should not spend more than 20 minutes on part 1, or on the multiple-choice items, and periodically you should post the correct time on the blackboard. Students should also be told whether to attempt all items or whether there will be a penalty for guessing. If there is no penalty for guessing, students should be encouraged to answer every item, even if they are not at all sure of the correct response. If there is a penalty for guessing, students should be instructed to respond only to those items for which they are reasonably sure of the correct answer. Of course, a guessing penalty (referred to as a correction for guessing) is only applicable for items involving selection from given alternatives.

Correction for guessing

Basically, a *correction for guessing* adjusts a score by subtracting that portion of the score believed to be the result of guessing rather than knowledge. The purpose of a correction for guessing is to eliminate any points which may result from blind guessing so that "guessers" have no overall score advantage over "nonguessers," who omit (i.e. do not respond to) items for which they don't know the correct response. To use an extreme example which illustrates the point, suppose we have a 50-item true-false test and a group of students who do not "know" the correct answer to any of them. Some of these students may simply not respond to any of the items and these students' score would be 0. Other students may say, "What the heck, what have I got to lose?" and guess on all 50 items. Since on any one item they have a 50–50 chance of guessing correctly, their expected score is half of the items, or 25 correct. Some will get less than 25 and some will get more than 25, but the odds are that they will all do considerably better than 0. Similarly, if a student totally guesses on an 80-item, 4-alternative multiple-choice test, the expected score is one-fourth of the items, or 20 correct, as opposed to a for-sure 0 for not responding at all.

The correction for guessing formula is

$$\text{C.S.} = R - \frac{W}{N-1}$$

where

C.S. = corrected score
R = the number of correct responses
W = the number of incorrect responses
N = the number of alternatives for each item

Thus, for a multiple-choice test with 4 alternatives for each item, $N - 1 = 4 - 1 = 3$. For a true-false test $N - 1 = 2 - 1 = 1$, and the formula reduces to $R - W$. A student who guessed on all the items on the 80-item multiple-choice test, and got a score of 20, would have a score corrected as follows:

$$\text{C.S.} = R - \frac{W}{N - 1} = 20 - \frac{60}{3} = 20 - 20 = 0$$

A student who guessed on all the items on a 50-item true-false test would similarly have a score corrected as below:

$$\text{C.S.} = R - \frac{W}{N - 1} = R - W = 25 - 25 = 0$$

When such a formula is used, omitted items are ignored, i.e. they do not count as R's or W's. They have been taken into consideration since R will be lower the more items are omitted, but no correction is necessary. As a more realistic example, suppose we administer a 50-item, 5-alternative multiple-choice test. Egor "knows" the answer to 35 of the items and guesses on 15 of them. We would expect his total to be $35 + \frac{1}{5}(15) = 35 + 3 = 38$ (12 wrong). The correction formula subtracts those 3 items Egor got by guessing:

$$\text{C.S.} = R - \frac{W}{N - 1} = 38 - \frac{12}{4} = 38 - 3 = 35$$

Of course the problem with the formula is that it is based on an *expected* score. If Egor really guessed on 15 items he would not necessarily get exactly 3 correct; if he only got 1 correct by guessing we would overcorrect his score, whereas if he got 10 correct by guessing we would uncorrect his score. To look at it another way, if Egor got 38 right and 12 wrong but really knew 38, his score would still be corrected to 35.

The overcorrection/undercorrection problem aside, correcting for guessing is a waste of time for other reasons. For one thing, the chances of getting a decent score on a test by pure guesswork are extremely slim. A student may gain a few points here and there but the odds against getting say a perfect score on a multiple-choice test are astronomical. Also, as with weighting, if all students respond to all items, their relative scores will be essentially the same; that is, the correlation between corrected scores and uncorrected scores will be very high (in the high .90s). Further, the correction formula is based on an assumption of wild guessing which is rarely the case. If students have enough time, they do not blindly mark answers; they read the questions and the alternatives and carefully make a selection. They may be very unsure of some of their responses, but their responses truly reflect their status with respect to the intended outcomes. Wrong choices can be analyzed to determine the sources of confusion and misunderstanding. If a number of students select the same wrong answer, the item may need revision or further instruction may be required. Another argument against corrections for guessing is the fact that some students are going to guess anyway. If everyone is encouraged to answer all questions, scores will not reflect a "willingness-to-take-a-chance" factor. Last, on a practical level, if tests are scored by hand, corrections for guessing only complicate the process and open the door to more sources of scoring error.

One type of test for which a correction for guessing may be appropriate is a speed test. Notice that the above discussion emphasized that the correction for guessing is pointless when all students answer all questions. This is not the case with a speed test on which students are expected to get every item they attempt correct, but are not expected to necessarily complete all items. To illustrate the principle, suppose that on a 40-item, true-false speed test Zack guesses on every item and gets a score of 20. Zeek, on the other hand, carefully answers only the first 20 items and also gets them all correct. If we correct for guessing, Zack's score will be 0 ($R - W = 20 - 20$), whereas Zeek's score will be 20 ($R - W = 20 - 0$) since omitted items are ignored. Since a speed test is a situation where blind guessing is likely to occur, especially as time runs out, a correction for guessing may be a reasonable deterrent. In general, however, it is best to encourage every student to carefully answer every question.

Format considerations

After the directions and items have been written, all must be assembled into a legible, functional whole. There are a number of suggestions which if followed will facilitate both test taking and subsequent scoring. First, items should be numbered consecutively from start to finish, from 1 to 20 for example, and directions should be prominently positioned and separated from the actual items. Putting the word DIRECTIONS in capital letters is one often used attention-getting device. Answer spaces should be of equal size and large enough to accommodate the longest response, especially on short-answer tests; this reduces clues based on size of blank and prevents illegible responses resulting from cramming a long answer into a short space. Answer spaces should be placed in a vertical column in the right-hand or left-hand margin, or a separate answer sheet may be used.

If an item is accompanied by any type of illustration, such as a diagram, it should be accurate and placed adjacent to the item, directly above it if possible or parallel to it on an opposite page if necessary. Further, while it is especially important for illustrated items, it is always highly desirable to have an item start and end on the same page. For example, the stem should not fall on the bottom of one page and the responses on the top of the next; having to flip-flop pages back and forth makes it difficult for students to concentrate.

Last, the test should be typed if at all possible, with extra spacing between items. Typing is not always feasible due to available resources and the nature of the test content; it takes an experienced and willing typist to type an algebra test or a French test. The more important the test is, the more important it is that it be legible and hence typed.

Test reproduction

The final version of the test, typed or not, should be proofread carefully. It is a good practice to read a test twice, once for content and once for accuracy. The first reading may reveal unclear items and inadvertent grammatical errors. A second reading allows you to concentrate on identifying errors such as misspelled words and misnumbered items. When you are satisfied that the test is ready, you must select a method of reproduction. There are several options. Offset printing and xeroxing usually result in high quality copies but are usually too expensive for the average teacher. For most situations the only feasible options are the use of a mimeograph stencil or a ditto master. Both of these can produce good copies. Which method you use really doesn't matter as long as the resulting copies are neat and easy to read. Blurred print or light copies can affect scores as much as ambiguously worded items. Finally, every student should have a copy of the test and it is wise to reproduce a few more copies than are actually needed. There is invariably at least one student who says, "Ms. Hoznoz, I messed up my test, can I have another one?"

11 test revision

After reading chapter 11, you should be able to:

1 Identify and briefly describe the major aspects of test validation.
2 Identify and discuss the major aspects of item analysis appropriate for an NRT, and state the criterion of acceptability for each.
3 Discuss how the results of item analysis for an NRT are interpreted.
4 Identify and discuss the major aspects of item analysis appropriate for a CRT.
5 Discuss how the results of item analysis for a CRT are interpreted.

Rationale

Revision of a test may actually occur prior to its intended use as well as following its formal administration. Instruments developed for a specific, formal evaluation may be administered and revised over and over again until acceptable levels of validity and reliability are achieved and item analysis statistics are satisfactory. This process is loosely referred to as fieldtesting and more specifically as *test validation*. The instruments are validated prior to their use in the intended evaluation. For more informal evaluation, such as student evaluation, test revision is normally based solely on the results of the actual administration to the intended students.

What is the point of analyzing the adequacy of a test *after* it has already been given? Good question, I'm glad you asked. It is true that validity should be a paramount consideration during test construction. But remember, content validity is basically judgmental. Analysis of test results supports or does not support initial validity judgments. Use of techniques such as item analysis helps us to identify specific ways in which the test can be improved. Further, analysis of results can help us to better interpret the scores and to use them more wisely. We would not, for example, make any heavy decisions concerning students based on the results of a test found to have serious defects.

Test validation

Formal evaluation projects are usually staffed by persons competent in the areas to be measured. A project designed to implement and assess the effectiveness of a new reading program, for example, will generally have several reading specialists on the staff. A project may or may not have a full-time evaluation specialist; if not, such services are typically provided by one or more consultants. Together, the content and evaluation personnel are likely to develop valid measures for assessing a program's effectiveness. It is always advisable, however, to have such measures reviewed by a number of other content specialists before the tests are actually administered to students in the program. Such reviewers can make beneficial suggestions regarding factors such as content, wording, and reading level. Test scores should not be influenced by reading ability unless the test is a reading test. The revised version of an instrument, based on input from a review group, will invariably be more valid and reliable than the initial version. But even if the revised version is not significantly better, the time and effort are worth the increased acceptance which results when potential users have an opportunity to contribute to instrument development.

Assessment of reliability usually requires the assistance of the evaluation personnel and involves administration of the instrument to a group very like the group actually involved in the program or project. For example, a group of upper-elementary students who are reading at a first or second grade level might be used as a test group for a reading test. The data from one or more administrations of the test to such a fieldtest group are used to calculate an appropriate estimate of reliability. Depending upon the obtained coefficients, decisions are made concerning the need for further revision. If appropriate, item analysis may also be performed in order to assess such factors as item difficulty. Item analysis will identify bad items which are contributing to low test validity and reliability. Fieldtest administration of a test also permits pretesting of directions, administration procedures, and scoring procedures. For example, some directions may be found to be misleading, time limits may not be sufficient, or scoring procedures may prove to be cumbersome or unreliable. These are all factors which should be determined and corrected to the degree possible *before* the test is used "for real" in the actual evaluation. Remember, inadequate measurement leads to inadequate conclusions and decisions.

Item analysis

Classroom teachers will not normally validate their tests prior to administering them to their students. They may, however, perform item analysis after the test has been administered, especially if some or all of the items will be used again. *Item analysis* basically involves examination of the pattern of responses for each item in order to assess its effectiveness. The results of item analysis permit better interpretation of test results and provide guidance for item revision. If many students miss the same item, for example, it does not necessarily mean that they did not achieve the corresponding objective; the item itself may be defective. Item analysis also indirectly provides feedback to the test developer, concerning factors related to good and poor items, which can be useful in future test development efforts. Usually we associate item analysis with multiple-choice tests. The process may, however, be applied to the results of any test, yes, even an essay test. The two major aspects of item analysis, item difficulty and discriminating power, apply to all types of items. The third aspect of item analysis, analysis of distractors, does apply mainly to multiple-choice items.

    As you read on, item analysis may begin to sound like too much trouble, and in truth, it may take an hour or more. But it does promote better interpretation of results and improved future test development. It also provides a splendid basis for a classroom discussion with students concerning test results. When students complain that item 5 "wasn't fair!", instead of being defensive you can agree with them and show them why. That will catch them off guard! Sharing the results also provides opportunities to clarify misconceptions and points of confusion. You may say, "Some of you selected B, probably because you thought . . ." When these students see that most of the class selected the correct response, they realize that they were in error and that the item was not at fault. Further, while very stringent item analysis procedures are generally applied to standardized tests, a more informal approach is sufficient for most classroom tests. In fact, after one has attained a degree of familiarity and proficiency in performing item analyses, visual inspection of results may be enough to obtain the desired information. Item analysis is not a cure-all that results in subsequently perfect tests. It does not tell a teacher *how* to improve an item. It does, however, identify problem items and provide clues as to the source of the problems. Not only is it worth the time and effort in terms of benefits to be derived, but many teachers actually think that the process is fun!

    Item analysis procedures are different for norm-referenced tests and criterion-referenced tests, mainly because the items in such tests are designed to do different things. Traditional item analysis procedures were designed for norm-referenced tests. Since they are concerned with score variability and how well the test items correctly identify high achievers and low achievers, they are basically inappropriate for criterion-referenced tests. In fact the whole process is designed to maximize the degree to which items discriminate between high and low achievers. Although criterion-referenced tests may result in a degree of score vari-ability, that is not their purpose and we are therefore not interested in statistics which suggest how to increase it.

Norm-referenced tests

The two major aspects of traditional item analysis are determination of degree of item difficulty (the percentage of students who got the item correct) and discrimi-nating power (the degree to which the item discriminates between students who scored high on the total test and those who did poorly). The third aspect of item analysis, which is appropriate for certain types of items, is analysis of distractors. In a multiple-choice test, for example, if no one chooses alternative D of item 4, it is a poor distractor, apparently not a plausible response even for students who do not know the correct response.

The steps and calculations involved in the analysis are really quite simple, even for you nonmathematical types. The first step is to score the test and rank the test scores, i.e. put them in order from highter total score to lowest total score. The next step is to select approximately the top third and bottom third of the scores for analysis. If there are 36 tests, for example, the 12 highest scores will be the top third. The responses of the middle third are not included in the analysis; it is as-sumed that they follow the same pattern as the other thirds. The fraction one-third is used simply because it is a convenient figure. More formal item analyses, such as those performed on the results of standardized tests, are typically based on the upper and lower 27%. For most classroom applications, however, upper and lower thirds are sufficient. If the total number of students is small, say 20 or less, it is probably more appropriate to use the upper half and the lower half. Further, there would be nothing seriously wrong with using the upper and lower fourths if it were more convenient, say, if the total number of students were 40.

After the membership of the upper and lower groups has been deter-mined, we calculate and interpret the difficulty of each item and discriminating power of each item. If appropriate, we then tabulate the number of students *in each group* who chose *each* alternative and assess the effectiveness of each.

Item difficulty

Item difficulty refers to the percentage of students who got the item correct. This probably does not sound right since you would expect difficulty to have something to do with the percentage who got it wrong. Nevertheless, the term difficulty is generally associated with the success figure although it is occasionally based on incorrect responses. The formula for estimating item difficulty is a snap:

$$\text{I.D.} = \frac{R}{T} \times 100$$

where

I.D. = item difficulty
R = the number of students (in the upper and lower groups combined) who got the item correct

$T =$ the total number of students (in the upper and lower groups combined) who responded to the item.

Thus, if the upper and lower groups each contained 10 students, and on item 5, 7 students in the upper group responded correctly and 3 in the lower group, I.D. would be calculated as follows:

$$\text{I.D.} = \frac{R}{T} \times 100 = \frac{(7 + 3)}{20} \times 100 = \frac{10}{20} \times 100 = .5 \times 100 = 50$$

Now the question is, what is "good." Since we are dealing with a norm-referenced test, we do not want items which are too difficult (I.D. near 0) or items which are too easy (I.D. near 100). We want items of average difficulty in order to permit maximum score variability. The ideal value of I.D. varies with the type of item. For short-answer items, an I.D. within the range of 30–70 is usually considered acceptable, but the closer to 50 the better. The 50 figure is ideal in this case because it is entirely possible for all students to miss an item on a short-answer test, and anywhere from 0 to 100% of the students may get it right. As we shall see shortly, the 50 figure permits maximum discrimination between the upper and lower groups.

For other types of objective tests, however, 0 is not a score that is likely to occur, and it is also not likely that there will be any item which no one gets correct. For example, on a 100-item, 4-alternative multiple-choice test, the expected range of scores is 25 to 100 if all students respond to all items. Since guessing occurs, intelligent or not, it is unlikely that there will be an item which everyone in the upper group gets correct and everyone in the lower group misses; some in the lower group will get it right, by chance if nothing else. Thus, it has been suggested that for such tests, the ideal, or average, level of difficulty is really higher than 50, approximately half the difference between the chance score and the maximum score.[1] On the multiple-choice test above, for example, ideal difficulty would be $25 + \frac{1}{2}(75) = 25 + 37.5 = 62.5$, where 25 is the chance score and 75 is the difference between the chance score and the maximum score. Similarly, for a 100-item true-false test, the expected chance score is 50 and the ideal, average difficulty would be $50 + \frac{1}{2}(50) = 50 + 25 = 75$.

Thus the ideal difficulty level ranges from 50 (for a short-answer test) to 75 (for a true-false test). Of course if these figures are used as guidelines, chances are that you will end up with a number of "too-easy" items. The general concept is valid, however—ideal difficulty is 50 or higher depending upon the type of test. Thus, you would be satisfied with an I.D. of 65 for a multiple-choice test with 4 or 5 alternatives per item. In general, items with low or high indices of I.D. must be revised or eliminated from the test. There are items, however, which we expect most students to do well on. Such items may be included for psychological reasons, to get students started, for example, or because they are needed to measure an intended outcome. Eliminating such items simply because they are "too easy" may reduce the content validity of the test. Thus, common sense must be applied in interpreting indices of I.D. and corresponding indices of discriminating power.

---

[1] Adkins, D. C. *Test construction: Development and interpretation of achievement tests.* Columbus: Charles E. Merrill, 1974.

The above discussion, of course, does not apply to criterion-referenced tests. An I.D. of 50 would be disappointing, to say the least. Our goal with CRTs is the highest I.D. possible. This will be discussed further later in the chapter.

Discriminating power

Discriminating power (D.P.) refers to the degree to which an item discriminates between high and low achievers on the test. In other words, if an item has high, positive D.P., then high achievers got it right and low achievers did not. Ideally, we would prefer to validate items by investigating how performance on each relates to some valid measure of achievement in the area being tested, *other than the test itself.* Usually, however, no such independent measure exists, mainly because the test was developed to measure a specific set of objectives or a selected area of content. The best measure of overall achievement that we have is the test itself, and we determine how each item on the test relates to performance on the total test. If the performance pattern on a given item is similar to that on the total test, that is, high scorers get it right and low scorers get it wrong, then the item has good discriminating power. If the test is indeed a valid measure of the intended outcomes, then the process of determining discriminating power does validate the items. Without verification of the total test validity, however, the most we can really say is that a given item does or does not measure *whatever* the total test measures (or, more precisely, that it measures it to a certain degree), which means that we are really looking at an index of internal consistency. For most classroom tests, however, it is fairly safe to assume that they are at least adequately valid and therefore that indices of D.P. are indices of item validity.

Discriminating power is estimated using the following fairly simple formula:[2]

$$\text{D.P.} = \frac{R_U - R_L}{\frac{1}{2}T}$$

where

    D.P. = discriminating power

      R_U = the number of students in the upper group who responded correctly

      R_L = the number of students in the lower group who responded correctly

       T = the total number of students in the item analysis ($\frac{1}{2}T$ is the number of students in each group)

As the formula suggests, there are three basic possibilities: $R_U > R_L$ (more students in the upper group responded correctly), $R_U = R_L$, or $R_L > R_U$. When $R_U > R_L$, the item is behaving the same way as the total test and has positive D.P. When R_U and R_L are essentially the same, or very close, the item has a D.P. near .00, which means that it does not discriminate. Such an item serves no useful purpose since a student's overall achievement level has nothing to do with whether or

---

[2] This formula actually represents a method of estimating *point-biserial correlations.* For many purposes, however, especially when D.P. is calculated by hand, the estimates are adequate.

not she or he can respond correctly to the item. When $R_L > R_U$, the item is behaving in a manner opposite to that of the total test and has a negative D.P.; the "wrong" students, those who did poorly on the total test, are getting the item correct.

What do you suppose is the ideal value of D.P.? Think. If *everyone* in the upper group got the item correct, and *no one* in the lower group got the item correct, what would the D.P. be? Right, +1.00. For example, if $R_U = 15$, $R_L = 0$, and $T = 30$ (there are 15 students in each group):

$$\text{D.P.} = \frac{R_U - R_L}{\frac{1}{2}T} = \frac{15 - 0}{\frac{1}{2}(30)} = \frac{15}{15} = +1.00$$

Note that if the opposite were true, $R_L = 15$ and $R_U = 0$, then D.P. would equal $\frac{0 - 15}{15} = \frac{-15}{15} = -1.00$. Note also that we can only obtain D.P. $= +1.00$ if I.D. $= 50$. In other words, if half of the students in the item analysis get the item correct, I.D. $= 50$; if that half is the upper half, then D.P. $= +1.00$. As was discussed previously, however, average difficulty is in reality usually somewhat higher than 50 for most types of objective tests. To the degree that average difficulty is greater than 50, to that degree the maximum D.P. is less than +1.00. For example, on a 100-item, 4-alternative multiple-choice test, average difficulty is 62.5. Suppose there are 20 students in each group and all 20 in the upper group get a certain item correct. Suppose also that no one in the lower group really knows the correct response but they all respond and by chance alone one-fourth, or 5, of them respond correctly. In this case we have:

$$\text{D.P.} = \frac{R_U - R_L}{\frac{1}{2}T} = \frac{20 - 5}{20} = \frac{15}{20} = .75$$

Thus, .75 represents a realistic ceiling on D.P. for this test.

The question remains as to how high a D.P. is "good enough." A D.P. of .30 is generally accepted as being an adequate value, although the higher the better. A D.P. much less than this makes the item a candidate for revision, especially if the I.D. is too high or too low. Of course, any item with a negative D.P. must either be discarded or undergo major revision.

All of the previous discussion is based on the assumption that the test measures only one type of ability, one type of achievement. If this is so, it makes sense to investigate whether each item is measuring the same type of outcome as the total test. If the test is measuring more than one type of ability, however, then indices of D.P. are likely to be somewhat distorted and in general lower. The reason is that total test scores, in essence, represent a combination of subscores, one for each type of achievement. A student who does well on one type does not necessarily do well on the other type. Therefore, performance on any given item may or may not relate to total test performance. For example, suppose a test is composed primarily of verbal items, such as definitions, but also has a section of items requiring application of formulas. It is quite possible that the D.P. for the formula problems would be very low, possibly even negative. One solution is to divide the test into appropriate subtests and to estimate D.P. for each item in relation to the appropriate subscore, that is, do a separate item analysis for each subtest. At the very least, one should be aware of the potential problem and interpret indices of D.P. appropriately.

As the above discussion suggests, it is not a good idea to label an item as defective just because it has low D.P. If the item is measuring something different from the test as a whole, low D.P. is expected. Eliminating several such items on the basis of their D.P. might actually result in content validity being lowered. Further, as was previously noted, D.P. is related to item difficulty; maximum discrimination is only possible when items are of average difficulty. Since we may intentionally include some very easy items, we know in advance that they will have low D.P. As with I.D., common sense must be used in interpreting indices of D.P.

Distractability

Indices of item difficulty and discriminating power merely indicate whether an item is doing its intended job, not why or why not. If an item is found to be defective, we have to examine possible reasons. The cause might be something as simple as an incorrect scoring key, but that is rare. The problem may be the result of misunderstanding on the part of students, or there may actually be something wrong with the item. If the scoring key checks out, the next logical place to look is at the item itself. Examination of incorrect responses often provides clues concerning the source of the problem. This is not very helpful for true-false tests, but it is for other types of items, especially multiple-choice items. If distractors are not doing their job, that is, they are not all plausible to a student who does not "know" the answer, the result may be an exceptionally easy item and a low index of D.P. There are any number of other undesirable possibilities. Given their purpose, it follows that a good distractor is one which is selected by more students in the lower group than in the upper group. A good distractor has distractability—the ability to distract.[3] If no one selects a given distractor, it has no distractability and is ineffective, useless, and should be replaced. If a distractor is selected by more students in the upper group than the lower group, it has negative distractability. The fault probably lies in the stem (it was ambiguous for example) or in the instruction which preceded the test (*it* was ambiguous!). In this case the stem should be reworded and future instruction should be altered accordingly.

Analysis of distractors does not require application of any formula. Examination of the alternatives selected by each group in the item analysis makes it pretty evident how the distractors worked. If you want to be impressively accurate, however, you can compute D.P. for each alternative. For example, suppose that on a 100-item, 4-alternative multiple-choice test 10 students are in the upper group and 10 in the lower group. Suppose that b is the correct response for item 18 and that the pattern of responses is as follows:

		Upper 10	Lower 10	D.P.
18.	a.	0	0	.00
	b.	4	1	+.30
	c.	4	6	−.20
	d.	2	3	−.10

[3] With apologies to Webster!

Overall, the item is a little too difficult; I.D. = $^5/_{20} \times 100 = 25$. The D.P. of this item is minimally acceptable since the D.P. for the correct response (*b*) is $+.30$. Distractor *a* is not working at all; no one chose it. Distractors *c* and *d* are working in the right direction; they did attract more of the students in the lower group. Distractor *c*, however, attracted as many students from the upper group as the correct answer; this bears looking into. As this example illustrates, the *correct* response should have a positive D.P., whereas the distractors should have a negative D.P. If we wanted to improve this mediocre item, we would first try to determine why alternative *c* was so attractive to both groups. Perhaps the stem needs rewording. We would also replace distractor *a*.

For most classroom purposes, we do not need to actually compute the D.P. of the distractors, since inspection of the choices gives us the information we need. Also, since the number of students in each group is generally small, we are working with general trends anyway. We do have to be careful not to be overly influenced by small differences. We can be satisfied if all of the alternatives are functioning reasonably well in the right direction. Just to be sure you have a basic understanding of the concepts discussed, we will look at two more examples. One item is terrific and one is terrible. See if you can tell which is which.

		Upper 10	Lower 10
4.	a.	1	3
	b.	0	2
	c.	1	3
	d.	8	2

		Upper 10	Lower 10
5.	a.	0	0
	b.	5	2
	c.	3	7
	d.	2	1

$$\text{I.D.} = \frac{(8 + 2)}{20} \times 100 = 50$$

$$\text{D.P.} = \frac{(8 - 2)}{10} = \frac{6}{10} = +.60$$

$$\text{I.D.} = \frac{(3 + 7)}{20} \times 100 = 50$$

$$\text{D.P.} = \frac{3 - 7}{10} = \frac{-4}{10} = -.40$$

If you did not pick item 4 as the good one, go back to page 1! Interestingly, both items have the same index of item difficulty, 50, which is pretty good for a 4-alternative multiple-choice test. The D.P. of each item tells the real story. For item 4, the D.P. of $+.60$ is quite good and all of the distractors are working. If we calculated the D.P. for each distractor, we would get a negative number in each case. All distractors were chosen by members of the lower group and, in fact, the pattern of responses makes it appear that they were equally plausible to members of that group. In item 5, the D.P. of $-.40$ is terrible and the distractors are clearly not working. Distractor *a* was chosen by no one and distractor *d* was chosen by the "wrong" students. The real problem, however, is distractor *b*. For some reason, a number of the high achievers thought that it was the correct choice, whereas the low achievers had little difficulty in identifying *c* as the correct response. Got the idea?

For the record

Everyone has his own little way of storing important materials. Some people keep everything in loose-leaf notebooks and some people prefer manila folders (and some prefer to just throw everything in a drawer!). Whichever your

```
Unit:   Basic Economics

Outcome:   Ability to apply principles of supply and
           demand to given market conditions.

Testing dates:   11/20/80


           According to the principles of supply and demand,
           what will happen to the price of cocoa if there
           is a shortage of cocoa beans?   The price will

                              Upper 10   Lower 10
           a) Decline             2          4        I.D.=55
           b) Stay the same       0          3        D.P.=.50
           c) Rise                8          3

Revisions:   None4
```

figure 11.1
An example of an item record sheet

preference (and let's hope it's not the drawer!), you need to organize and store all the information resulting from your item analysis. You obviously want to keep all the information about a given test together, and all the information concerning a given item should be together. There are two good ways to do this. One way is to put all the information for a particular item on a large index card and file the cards in a file box. This way cards can be redone, replaced, and added to easily. Another good way (and for the same reasons) is to put all the information for a particular item on a sheet of notebook paper and to file all the sheets for a given test in a loose-leaf notebook. If test items are systematically revised, they will get progressively better. Even if they are not used again, a record of the revisions and item analysis data will provide feedback for the future development of items.

The information which should be recorded for a given item is fairly standard. First you will have some identification data, such as the outcome measured (preferably expressed as a specific objective), and the test administration date. The actual item should be recorded, including the stem and all the alternatives, and all item analysis data. How you organize and arrange the data is up to you. Figure 11.1 illustrates one way.

Essay tests

Item analysis can be performed on essay tests without too much difficulty provided that the desired response for each item has been clearly defined and that the analytical method of scoring is used. We can do item analysis on a test with broader, globally scored items, but the information is not nearly as useful. If point

---

[4] How nice!

values are assigned to each subpart of an essay item, then we can treat each subpart as a separate item. The major problem is that by their very nature these "items" tend to be nonindependent since degree of success on one may be related to degree of success on another.

As an example of how such an analysis can be done, suppose essay item 4 has 5 parts and each part is worth 3 points; for our purposes part *d*, for example, would be an item worth 3 points and the results for it could be analyzed as follows:[5]

d.

	Number of Points			
	0	1	2	3
Upper 12	0	3	4	5
Lower 12	4	6	2	0

From this we can determine, for example, that the upper group did get much higher scores than the lower group. In the parentheses, the first number refers to the number of points and the second number refers to the number of students who got that many points:

$$\text{Upper group} = (0 \times 0) + (1 \times 3) + (2 \times 4) + (3 \times 5)$$

$$= 0 + 3 + 8 + 15 = 26.$$

$$\text{Lower group} = (0 \times 4) + (1 \times 6) + (2 \times 2) + (3 \times 0)$$

$$= 0 + 6 + 4 + 0 = 10$$

This shows that the item is performing effectively.

Criterion-referenced tests

The concept of average difficulty has no meaning for a criterion-referenced test as the difficulty is determined mainly by the objective. On a mastery test we expect all the items to be fairly easy as they are based on minimum essential outcomes. On a nonmastery test we expect items to exhibit a range of difficulties reflecting a range of intended outcomes, although we would be delighted if all or most of the students could correctly respond to all or most of the items. What we are really concerned with is a *change* in item difficulty between pretesting and posttesting. If few or none of the students can respond to the item prior to instruction but many of them can do so after instruction, then we have evidence that the item is valid and the instruction was effective. Similarly, indices of discrimination are of no value since we are not the least bit interested in promoting variability, or spreading students' scores out.

What we are interested in is whether or to what degree the students achieved the objectives. To determine that we have to examine the achievement rate for each of the items related to a given objective. Looking at items in isolation or out of context will not give us the information we need. Therefore, if a test mea-

[5] See footnote 1.

sures more than one objective, then all the items that measure a given objective should be analyzed together. The results of the analysis are generally reported to students and parents as percentages, called *item achievement percentages*, that can express both individual and group levels of achievement. We may also report results in terms of mastery or nonmastery, or whether the objectives were achieved (or which ones).[6] For item analysis, however, we are interested in the percentage of students who responded correctly to each item and the pattern of percentages for a given objective.

As an example, suppose we have the following application objective:

> Given accurate drawings of a variety of triangles, each having all needed dimensions shown, the student will correctly compute the area of each, to the nearest whole number, with 80% accuracy.

This objective represents a higher-order outcome and we anticipate that not all students will achieve it. The items written to measure this objective would probably be short-answer items, each consisting of a triangle with necessary dimensions identified and a blank in which to place the computed area; the items would represent different kinds of triangles (e.g., scalene, isosceles). Figure 11.2 presents the hypothetical results for these items. A 1 indicates a correct response and 0 indicates an incorrect response. Now, first question: How many students achieved the objective? The answer is 6, or 60%. The objective stated 80% accuracy and the first 6 students (Lorrie through Debbie) did get 4 out of 5 items (80%) correct. That's not too terrific. Next question: Which items did students have trouble with? Answer: 2 and 4. Only one student missed item 5; it might have presented a right triangle, and apparently the students know how to compute the area of a right triangle. They also did well on item 1 and not too badly on item 3, so apparently they know how to compute the areas of the triangles represented, though a little review probably would not hurt. At least half the class, however, does not know how to compute the area of the triangles reapresented by items 2 and 4. Item 2, for example, might be an isosceles triangle. The first thing we do is to check the items to see if there is anything ambiguous about the drawings—maybe the labeling is misleading. Assuming that the drawings for these items were at least equally as accurate as for the other items, then a logical explanation for the poor performance is that the students do not possess the measured skill. Further instruction and review would be indicated. Of course, it is always possible that the problem lies with the objective, especially the criterion. In our example, if the criterion were 60% (3 out of 5 correct), then 80% of the students would have achieved the objective. Adjusting the criterion, however, is tricky business. There is a fine line between adjusting unrealistically high standards and lowering standards to the level of the students' performance. Thus, you must decide whether an 80% criterion is too high. If you believe that it is not, keep it; if you decide that 60% is sufficient, change it.

If pretest data were available, Figure 11.2 could easily be adapted in order to determine how much was actually learned. Pat, for example, may have transferred from another school and may have known how to compute the area of a triangle *before* instruction took place. In general, however, we would not expect this to be a skill that students would already possess. Figure 11.3 presents this data (column *a* shows pretest results and column *b* posttest results) and indicates that

---

[6] Interpretation and reporting of results will be discussed further in chapters 18 and 19.

Objective 1

	Item Number				
	1	**2**	**3**	**4**	**5**
Lorrie	1	1	1	1	1
Boobie	1	0	1	1	1
Pat	1	0	1	1	1
Namu	1	1	0	1	1
Dot	1	1	1	0	1
Debbie	1	1	1	0	1
Cathy	1	0	0	1	1
Hermie	1	0	1	0	1
Egor	0	0	1	0	1
Ziggy	0	0	0	0	0
% Correct	80	40	70	50	90

figure 11.2
Hypothetical item analysis for a criterion-referenced test showing item achievement percentages

only Lorrie had any previous knowledge of computing the area of a triangle. If others had such knowledge, it was not retained. If the objective were a knowledge item, we might expect more students to get some questions correct on the pretest. As it is, we're happy. We did good!

Objective 1

	Item Number									
	1		**2**		**3**		**4**		**5**	
	a	**b**	**a**	**b**	**a**	**b**	**a**	**b**	**a**	**b**
Lorrie	1	1	0	1	0	1	0	1	1	1
Boobie	0	1	0	0	0	1	0	1	0	1
Pat	0	1	0	0	0	1	0	1	0	1
Namu	0	1	0	1	0	0	0	1	0	1
Dot	0	1	0	1	0	1	0	0	0	1
Debbie	0	1	0	1	0	1	0	0	0	1
Cathy	0	1	0	0	0	0	0	1	0	1
Hermie	0	1	0	0	0	1	0	0	0	1
Egor	0	0	0	0	0	1	0	0	0	1
Ziggy	0	0	0	0	0	0	0	0	0	0
% Correct	10	80	0	40	0	70	0	50	10	90

a = pretest results
b = posttest results

figure 11.3
Hypothetical item analysis for pretest and posttest data for a criterion-referenced test.

Interpretation of results

We have to keep in mind that precision is not a characteristic of item analysis of most locally-developed tests. The number of students is typically small and their traits (e.g. ability) are not necessarily representative of all students who might take the test. If the same test was administered to another class, results would likely be somewhat different. In fact, if several students in the class who were absent had taken the test, the results would have been somewhat different. Item analysis does, however, identify very good items and very poor items and does provide indications of general trends. In large evaluation efforts we are concerned with exact indices of I.D. and D.P. whereas in classroom measurement we are concerned with approximations.

Since we are aware of the imprecise nature of classroom analysis, actual computation may not be necessary for the majority of such tests. Visual inspection of the results may very well give us the information we need. If we see that only two students missed an item and those two students did poorly on the test as a whole, we do not need to calculate I.D. and D.P. to know that the item had a low level of difficulty but discriminates in the right direction. Once you acquire familiarity with these concepts, you will be able to estimate I.D. and D.P. fairly accurately just by looking at the results for the upper group and the lower group. This should be sufficient for all but the most important tests, such as midterms and finals.

We must also keep in mind that our decisions concerning retention, revision, or elimination of items should be based as much on common sense as on item statistics. Our most important concern is validity. If some items measure what we want to measure and are necessary for the content validity of an NRT, for example, we should not eliminate them simply because they are too easy (or too difficult) and do not discriminate. Buros, longtime editor of the *Mental Measurement Yearbooks*, expressed this sentiment strongly in the quote below. His plea applies to all tests but is especially relevant to classroom tests. With regard to the discarding of items based solely on the results of item analysis, he had this to say:

> These techniques have been harmful to the development of the best possible measuring instruments. These statistical methods of item validation confuse differentiation with measurement and exaggerate differences among individuals and between grades. I would like to see their use discontinued. . . . I urge the abandonment of these statistical methods of validating test items as well as the practice of discarding items simply because they were either passed by all or failed by all. I urge that our goal should be measurement, not differentiation.[7]

Well! While Buros does represent the extreme position on the issue, the point is well taken. If he is opposed to item analysis, it is not because of its potential benefits but because of its potential misuse. Instead of throwing out the baby with the bath water, it seems far more reasonable to use item analysis and to interpret the results wisely, taking into consideration all relevant factors.

[7] Buros, O. K. Fifty years in testing: Some reminiscences, criticisms, and suggestions. *Educational Researcher*, 1977, 6(7), 9–15.

12 survey and observation forms

After reading chapter 12, you should be able to:

1 State the dos and don'ts associated with construction of a questionnaire.
2 Briefly describe the purpose of pretesting a survey instrument.
3 Identify the major characteristics of an observation recording form.
4 Describe what is meant by categorization and coding of responses.

Overview

Although they are not generally used in the classroom, questionnaires and interviews and occasionally observation are frequently used in evaluations. Each of
these measurement techniques was discussed in a previous chapter. In this chapter, we will discuss guidelines for the construction and validation of the actual instruments.

Questionnaires

Construction

As a general guideline, the questionnaire should be as attractive and brief and as
easy to respond to as possible. Sloppy-looking questionnaires turn people off,
lengthy questionnaires turn people off, and questionnaires requiring lengthy responses to each question *really* turn people off! Turning people off is not the way
to get them to respond. To meet this guideline you must carefully plan both the
content and the format of the questionnaire. No item should be included which
does not directly relate to the objectives of the evaluation, and structured, or closed-
form, items should be used if at all possible. A *structured item* consists of a question and a list of alternative responses from which the respondent selects. The list
of alternatives should include all possible responses, and each possible response
should be distinctly different from the rest. In some cases, a very short written
response may be required, but generally a structured item is multiple-choice in
nature (yes or no, A, B, C, D, or E). In addition to facilitating response, structured
items also facilitate data analysis; scoring is very objective and efficient. A potential disadvantage is the possibility that a person's true response is not listed
among the alternatives. Therefore, questionnaires should include an "other" category for each item, a space for a person to write in a response not anticipated by
the evaluator. An unstructured item format, in which the respondent has complete
freedom of response (questions are asked and no possible responses indicated), is
sometimes defended on the grounds that it permits greater depth of response and
may permit insight into the reasons for responses. While this may be true, and
unstructured items are simpler to construct, the disadvantages of this approach
generally outweigh the advantages. People often provide information extraneous
to the objectives of the study, responses are difficult to score and analyze, and
people are generally not as happy with an instrument that requires written responses. For certain topics or purposes unstructured items may be necessary and
some questionnaires contain both structured and unstructured items. In general,
however, structured items are to be preferred.

Individual items should also be constructed according to a set of guidelines. The number one rule is that each question should deal with a single concept
and be worded as clearly as possible. Any term or concept which might mean different things to different people should be defined. For example, do not ask, "Do
you spend a lot of time each week preparing for your classes?" One teacher might
consider one hour per day to be "a lot" while another might consider one hour per
week "a lot." Instead, ask, "How many hours per week do you spend preparing

for your classes?" or "How much time do you spend per week preparing for your classes? (*a*) less than 30 minutes, (*b*) 30 minutes to an hour, (*c*) 1 to 3 hours, (*d*) 3 to 5 hours, (*e*) more than 5 hours." Also, when necessary, questions should give a point of reference. For example, do not ask, "How much time do you spend preparing for your classes?" Instead, ask, "How much time do you spend *per day* (or per whatever time period you wish) preparing for your classes?" As another example, if you were interested not only in how many hours were actually spent in preparation but also in teachers' perceptions concerning that time, you would not ask, "Do you think you spend a lot of time preparing for classes?" Instead, you would ask, "Do you think you spend a lot of time *compared to other teachers* (or compared to whatever you wished) preparing for your classes?" As several of the above examples illustrate, underlining (in a typed questionnaire) or italicizing (in a printed one) key phrases may also help to clarify questions.

There are also a number of "don'ts" to keep in mind when constructing items. First, avoid leading questions which suggest that one response may be more appropriate than another. Second, avoid questions which respondents might be touchy about and might not reply to honestly. For example, asking a teacher if he or she sets high standards for achievement is like asking a mother if she loves her children; the answer in both cases is going to be "Of course!" Another major "don't" is not to ask a question that assumes a fact not necessarily in evidence. Such questions present alternatives which are all unacceptable. A typical question of this nature is, "Were you satisfied with the raise in salary you received last year?" The question calls for a simple yes or no response, but how do you respond if you did not receive a raise last year?! If you answer yes, it implies that you were satisfied with no raise; if you answer no, it implies that you received a raise but you weren't happy with it because it wasn't big enough.

Each developed item should be recorded on a separate index card. This facilitates arrangement of the items so that they will be presented in a logical order; it is much easier to reorder index cards than to redo a questionnaire once it is developed. After the items have been developed and their order determined, directions to respondents must be written. Standardized directions promote standardized, comparable responses. Directions should specify how subjects are to respond and where responses should be recorded. When determining how persons should respond, you should consider how the results will be tabulated. If results are to be machine-scored, for example, you might have respondents use separate answer sheets and number two pencils instead of having them circle responses on the questionnaire.

Validation

A too-often-neglected procedure is validation of the questionnaire in order to determine if it measures what it was developed to measure. Validation is probably not done more often because it is not easy and requires much additional time and effort. However, anything worth doing is worth doing well. The appropriate validation procedure for a given questionnaire will depend upon the nature of the instrument. A questionnaire developed to determine the classroom behavior of teachers, for example, might be validated by observing a sample of respondents to determine the degree to which their actual behavior is consistent with their self-reported behavior.

The cover letter

Every mailed questionnaire must be accompanied by a cover letter which explains what is being asked of the recipient and why, and which hopefully motivates the recipient to fulfill the request. The letter should be brief, neat, and addressed specifically to the potential responder ("Dear Dr. Zhivago," not "Dear Sir"). The letter should also explain the purpose of the evaluation, emphasizing its importance and significance, and give the responder a good reason for cooperating. The fact that you need the data for refunding is not a good reason. If at all possible, the letter should state a commitment to share the results. It usually helps if you can get the endorsement of an organization (e.g. a professional organization), institution, group, or administrator with whom the responder is associated, or whom the responder views with respect. If the respondents are too heterogeneous or have no identifiable affiliation in common, a general appeal to professionalism can be made. Sometimes even humor and a little psychology are used. For example, a major car manufacturer sent out a questionnaire concerning one of their models to owners of that model. A quarter was enclosed along with a note indicating that the company was aware that the recipient of the questionnaire was quite busy and that the quarter was a gesture of appreciation for the anticipated cooperation. Besides being mildly amusing, the technique had the effect of making recipients feel like they "owed" the company a response. If possible, having the letter signed by a respected, well-known person also helps.

If the questions to be asked are at all threatening (such as items dealing with sex or attitudes toward the local administration), anonymity or confidentiality of responses must be assured. Complete anonymity probably increases the truthfulness of responses as well as the percentage of returns. On the other hand, anonymity makes follow-up efforts extremely difficult since you do not know who responded and who did not. It also makes subgroup comparisons impossible (for example, secondary teachers versus elementary teachers) unless specific classification items are included in the questionnaire itself (for example, "What grade do you teach?"). If identification is deemed necessary, complete confidentiality of responses must be guaranteed.

A specific deadline date for returning the completed questionnaire should be given. This date should allow ample time to respond but discourage procrastination; two to three weeks will usually be sufficient. Each letter to be sent should be signed individually. When many questionnaires are to be sent, individually signing each letter will admittedly take considerably more time than making copies of one signed letter, but it adds a personal touch which might make a difference in the potential respondent's decision to comply or not comply. Finally, the act of responding should be made as painless as possible. A stamped, addressed, return envelope should be included. If not, your letter and questionnaire will very likely be placed into the circular file, along with the mail addressed to "Occupant"!

Pretesting

The questionnaire should be tried out in a field test. Pretesting the questionnaire yields data concerning instrument deficiencies as well as suggestions for improvement. Having two or three available people complete the questionnaire first will result in the identification of major problems. The subsequently revised instrument and the cover letter should then be sent to a small group from your intended population or a highly similar population. Pretest participants should be encouraged to make comments and suggestions concerning directions, recording procedures, and specific items. If the percentage of returns is very low, then both the letter and the instrument should be carefully reexamined. The feedback from those who do respond should be carefully studied and considered. Last, proposed data tabulation and analysis procedures should be applied to the pretest data. The end product of the pretest will be a revised instrument ready to be mailed.

Interview guides

Construction

The interviewer must have a written guide which indicates what questions are to be asked and in what order, and what additional prompting or probing is permitted. In order to obtain standardized, comparable data from each responder, all interviews must be conducted in essentially the same manner. As with a questionnaire, each question in the interview should relate to a specific objective, and questions may be structured or unstructured. Since an interview is usually used when a questionnaire is not really appropriate, it usually involves unstructured or semistructured questions. Structured questions, which require the interviewee to select from alternatives, are of course easier to analyze but tend to defeat the purpose of an interview. Completely unstructured questions, on the other hand, which allow absolute freedom of response, can yield in-depth responses and provide otherwise unobtainable insights but produce data which are very difficult to quantify and tabulate. Therefore, most interviews use a semistructured approach which involves the asking of structured questions followed by clarifying unstructured, or open-ended, questions. The unstructured questions facilitate explanation and understanding of the responses to the structured questions. Thus, a combination of objectivity and depth can be obtained, and results can be tabulated as well as explained.

Many of the guidelines for constructing questionnaires apply to the construction of interview guides. The interview should be as brief as possible and questions should be worded as clearly as possible. Terms should be defined when necessary and a point of reference given when appropriate. Also, leading questions should be avoided as should questions based on the assumption of a fact not in evidence ("Tell me, were you satisfied with the raise in salary you received last year?")

Pretesting

The interview guide (as well as the interview procedures and analysis procedures, which will be discussed in the next chapter) should be tried out before it is used in the actual evaluation, using a small sample from the same or a very similar group to the one being used in the evaluation. Feedback from a small pretesting effort can be used to revise questions in the guide which are apparently unclear, do not solicit the desired information, or produce negative reactions from respondents. Insights into better ways to handle certain questions can also be acquired. Pretesting will also determine whether the resulting data can be quantified and analyzed in the manner intended. As with the pretesting of a questionnaire, feedback should be sought from the pretest group as well as from the interviewers. As always, pretesting is a worthwhile use of your time.

Observational forms

Definition of observational variables

There is no way that an observer can observe everything that goes on during a session, especially in a natural setting such as a classroom. What will be observed is determined by the objectives of the evaluation. For example, if our project involved determining the effectiveness of training teachers in behavior modification techniques for reducing instances of disruptive behavior, attention would be focused only on "disruptive behavior." The term "disruptive behavior," however, does not have universal meaning. Therefore, once the behavior to be observed is determined, we must clearly define what specific behaviors do and do not match the intended behavior. In the above example, "disruptive behavior" might include talking out of turn, making extraneous noises, throwing things, and getting out of one's seat, but doodling would probably not be considered disruptive.

      Once a behavioral unit is defined, observations must be quantified so that all observers will count the same way. If Hazard screams *and* tips over his chair at the same time, that could be considered as one instance of disruptive behavior or as two instances. We typically divide observation sessions into a number of specific observation periods, that is, we define a time unit. Thus for a one-hour session, a time unit of 30 seconds might be agreed upon resulting in a total of 120 observations per hour. The length of the time unit will usually be a function of the behavior to be observed. If it is simply a matter of observing and recording, the time unit may be 10 seconds. If any judgments or inferences are required on the part of the observer, the time unit is typically longer, perhaps 30 seconds or a minute. The observer then records what occurred during the observation period. If during a 15-second interval a student exhibited disruptive behavior, this would be indicated as one occurrence regardless of how often disruptive behavior occurred in that interval.

Recording observations

One point, which at first reading may seem obvious, is that observers should be observing and recording only one behavior at a time. Even if you are interested in two types of behavior, for example teacher behavior and student behavior, the observer should only have to make one decision at a time. Thus, if two types of behavior are to be observed they should probably be observed alternately. In other words, for the teacher-student observation example, teacher behavior might be observed during the first, third, fifth, and seventh observation periods and student behavior during the second, fourth, sixth, and eighth. Such a procedure would present a fairly accurate picture concerning what occurred in the observed classroom.

      While the point is debatable, as a general rule it is probably best to record observations as the behavior is occurring. Since each observation must be made within a set period of time, say 15 seconds, the recording process should be as simplified as possible. Most observation efforts facilitate recording by using an agreed-upon code, or set of symbols, and a recording instrument. Often the task is not just to determine whether a behavior occurred or not, but to record *what* occurred. The Flanders System, for example, classifies all teacher behavior and all student behavior into one of 10 categories, each of which is represented by a number. Thus, if a teacher praises a student, the observer records that "2" occurred.

There are a number of different types of forms which are used to record observations. Probably the most often used, and the most efficient, is a checklist which lists all behaviors to be observed so that the observer can simply check each behavior as it occurs. This permits the observer to spend his or her time thinking about what is occurring rather than how to record it. Rating scales are also sometimes used. These require the observer to evaluate the behavior and give it a rating from, for instance, one to three. For example, an observer might rate a teacher's explanation as 1 (not very clear), 2 (clear), or 3 (very clear). Although as many as five categories (infrequently more than five) are used, three is probably the ideal number. The more categories, the more difficult it becomes to correctly classify. An observer could probably discriminate between "not very clear" and "clear" fairly easily; deciding between "very unclear" and "not very clear" would not be as simple. Before developing your own observation form, you should check to see if there is a standardized observation form available which is appropriate for your evaluation. Using a standardized observation form has the same advantages as using a standardized test in terms of time saved, validity, and reliability.

Categorizing and coding procedures

While we generally try to avoid open-ended questions, sometimes they are necessary. When they are, we must determine how to categorize and code responses so that they can be tabulated. This requires anticipation of likely responses. For example, suppose we are going to interview principals and one question asks what they feel, in order of priority, are their biggest problems. We could anticipate that responses falling within the categories of budget and absenteeism would be mentioned among others. During the interviews, any response related to money, such as "not enough textbooks," might be recorded as category 1, budget. If we came up with, say, eight categories, we would also include a ninth, labeled "other." When it came time to tabulate responses, we might report that 70% of the principals considered budget concerns one of their top 3 problems, or that the average ranking for "budget" was 1.9 (high priority).

If results are to be computer analyzed, then all information, structured and unstructured, must be coded. Coding involves assigning numerical values to each piece of data. We might code sex as 0 or 1 (male or female) and age as 00–18 (if a student were 15, that would be the code). Scores that are already numerical, such as a posttest score, can be coded as is. But each variable is allotted a certain number of spaces, and all data must fit those spaces. If posttest scores range from 0 to 100, then 3 spaces are required in order to accommodate the largest possible score, 100. Thus, if a student only gets 7 correct, this score is coded as 007. While there are additional steps involved, such as assigning variables to computer card columns and keypunching, such activities are usually supervised by an appropriate evaluation consultant.

part five **summary**

1 The chances are slim that someone will develop a valid, reliable test without knowing the concepts of test development.
2 The serious consequences of testing make it mandatory that teachers be competent in test development and analysis of results.

8 designing the test

Restriction, definition and selection of test content

Restriction of content

3 The first step in designing a test is to put boundaries on what is to be covered.
4 Narrowing test coverage prevents cognitive overload on the part of students and permits a larger, more representative sampling of the behavior represented by the selected objectives.

Definition of content

5 The second step in designing a test is to make a detailed content outline, if such is not already available; the outline needs to be detailed enough to include all knowledge and skill outcomes desired of students.
6 Desired performances associated with each entry in the content outline have to be identified, and we must keep in mind that we are concerned with more than just the possession of knowledge.

Selection of test content

7 The third step in test designing is to devise a scheme for sampling from the domain of behaviors; if we carefully select the ones we measure, we can generalize to the total domain with a reasonable degree of confidence.
8 Behaviors to be measured may be selected randomly or behaviors may be stratified prior to selection; *stratifying* is the act of categorizing all the possible behaviors so that behaviors from each category can be selected.

Tables of specifications

9 The basic purpose of a table of specifications is to insure that all intended outcomes, and only the intended outcomes, are measured and that the test includes the appropriate number of items for each measured outcome.
10 A table of specifications is a two-way table with one axis being essentially a content outline and the other axis indicating the behaviors desired with respect to the content.

Content outline

11 Along one axis of the table of specifications the major headings and subhead-

ings of the content outline are listed; to a great extent, the complexity of the outline is a function of the complexity of the content area being measured.

Behavioral outcomes

12 Along the other axis of the table of specifications the behaviors or perform-ances desired for each topic are given; a very formal test development effort would be advised to use a finer breakdown of categories to insure content va-lidity, but for most classroom purposes a smaller number of categories is usually sufficient.

13 For a unit test, it is advisable to lean toward a more detailed table of specifica-tions which includes all desired outcomes; for a cumulative test, however, only major headings from preceding tables of specifications may be used.

Number of items

14 The intersection of content outline headings and behavioral outcome catego-ries forms cells into which an appropriate number (or percentage) of items are placed.

15 The number of items in a given cell is determined primarily by "what it takes" to measure a particular behavioral outcome for a given topic; such de-cisions are basically judgmental.

A one-way table of specifications

16 If all instruction has been objectified, if objectives have been developed at various levels of Bloom's taxonomy, and if test items are to be developed to measure those objectives, then a two-way table may be superfluous.

17 A one-way table is basically a list of topics or objectives along with the corre-sponding number of items required for each.

9 constructing test items

Overview

18 Which item type or types are appropriate for a given test depends mostly upon the nature of the behavior being measured.

19 It is not true that objective tests are good only for measuring knowledge-level questions; any item type can be used to measure any behavioral outcome.

20 In general, multiple-choice items are preferable to true-false and matching items.

21 A test will not necessarily contain items of more than one type, and it is gen-erally a good idea to have as few different item types as possible.

General guidelines

22 You can develop a test ahead of time and revise as necessary, or you can de-velop a test *as you go along*.

23 The guidelines for constructing items are essentially the same whether the test is norm-referenced or criterion-referenced, mastery or nonmastery.

24 The key to good item writing is plain old common sense.

Objective-item correspondence

25 Items should directly correspond with the intended behavioral outcome or objective; the behavior elicited by the item should be precisely the behavior specified in the objective.

Item sufficiency

26 *Item sufficiency* means that a correct response to the item (or items) constitutes sufficient evidence that the student has demonstrated the intended behavior, or has achieved the objective.

Communication

27 An item should communicate clearly to the test takers (and to the scorers) the meaning intended by the test developer; an item should be as free from ambiguity as possible.

Item difficulty

28 Appropriate levels of difficulty are a function of both the type of test and the objectives upon which the test is based.
29 Mastery tests are designed to measure achievement of minimum essentials and are characterized by items of a uniformly low level of difficulty.
30 Criterion-referenced nonmastery tests normally contain items of varying degrees of difficulty, as determined by the nature of the objectives being measured.
31 With norm-referenced tests we are interested in obtaining a spread of scores; the best way to do this is to use items of average difficulty.
32 For norm-referenced tests based on objectives, a compromise must be achieved between desired variability and desired objective-item correspondence.
33 Item difficulty should be related to the competence of the students who can answer it correctly, not to extraneous variables (such as high-level vocabulary) bearing little or no relationship to knowlege or skill.

Item novelty

34 *Item novelty* is a concept that applies primarily to measurement of higher-order outcomes and refers to the condition where the situation in the item is one that is totally unfamiliar to the student, that is, one that was not previously encountered during instruction.

Essay tests

35 An *essay test* is one which contains items which require the student to compose responses, usually lengthy.
36 Essay tests are not really appropriate for knowledge-level outcomes; they may be more appropriate than objective tests for certain higher-order outcomes, especially those involving synthesis and evaluation.
37 Despite the advantages of more restricted response items, less restricted items are usually required for the measurement of higher-order outcomes.

38 A complication that arises with essay items is the fact that they involve a number of abilities, such as organization and expression of ideas, which may or may not be specified by the corresponding objective.

39 Essay tests tend in general to be less content valid and reliable than objective tests, and scorer reliability is notoriously low.

Essay item construction

40 Since there are no response alternatives to help clarify an essay question, it is crucial that the desired response be delineated as clearly as possible.

41 One essay item may be used to measure more than one objective.

42 Giving students a choice of essay items is not good practice.

Scoring essay tests

43 Essay test scoring tends to be subjective; we can objectify essay tests to the degree that we can specify acceptable responses and alternative acceptable responses.

44 The *analytical approach* to scoring essay tests involves identifying all of the aspects or components of a perfect answer and assigning a point value to each.

45 The *global approach* also involves identifying all of the aspects or components of a perfect answer, but point values are not assigned to each; instead each response is judged as a whole, as a total unit, and an overall rating is made.

46 The analytic approach is clearly more appropriate for CRTs (since scores are based on each student's responses considered separately) and the global approach is more appropriate for NRTs.

47 It is a good idea to score each response without knowledge of who wrote it, that is, anonymously, and to score one item at a time (as opposed to one test at a time).

48 It is highly recommended that essay responses be read and scored twice, independently, before points are assigned.

Objective tests

49 An objective test is invariably more valid and reliable than a comparable essay test, and scorer reliability is extremely high.

50 When constructing objective items, be careful not to provide *clues* to the correct answer; such clues may be grammatical or contextual and are very useful to testwise students.

51 *Dependent items* should be avoided; items are dependent if the correct answer to one item is necessary in order to correctly answer another item, or if one item contains a clue to the correct answer of another item.

52 *Irrelevant difficulty* should not be promoted, either intentionally or unintentionally, by using unnecessarily complex vocabulary or by making the item more complicated than it needs to be.

53 *Negatives*, especially double negatives, should be avoided; with a little rewording, a negative statement can generally be converted to a positive statement.

54 If a negative term is used in an item, it should be emphasized in some way, such as by underlining or using italics.

55 *Direct quotes* (e.g. from texts or other instructional materials) should be avoided.

56 *Trivia* (e.g. the content of footnotes) should not be measured.

57 An item should have *one and only one*, correct, or best, answer unless otherwise specified.

58 If more than one answer is acceptable, it is important that they all be specified prior to scoring.

59 Use of an appropriate picture, diagram, or map may save a lot of words and make the task at hand clearer to students; usually when an illustration is used, it is accompanied by several items.

Short-answer items

60 Basically, *a short-answer item* is a short essay item and the difference between them is often blurred; short-answer items are best suited for questions requiring a brief response—a word, a phrase, or a sentence.

Position of blank

61 As a general rule, there should be only one blank in a completion item and it should come at the end of the sentence.

Specification of response units and accuracy

62 Primarily to simplify scoring, it is a good idea to tell the student the units in which the answer should be expressed.

63 It is also advisable to specify the accuracy required of responses, unless being able to determine the correct accuracy is part of the item.

Multiple-choice items

64 A multiple-choice item is composed of a question or incomplete sentence, referred to as the *stem,* and a list of alternative responses; responses that are not the correct answer are referred to as *distractors.*

65 In multiple-choice items students are instructed to select *the* correct answer or *the best* answer.

The stem

66 The stem should contain as much of the problem as possible.

67 Words should not be repeated in each response; they can usually be included in the stem with very little effort. Clues that are provided by using words in the stem which also appear in the response should be avoided.

Responses

68 The major guideline for the development of responses is that all distractors should be plausible; that is, they should appear to be reasonable to students who do not really know the correct answer.

69 Grammatical consistency is especially important for multiple-choice items since responses are supplied.

70 Correct responses should not have a tendency to be longer than incorrect ones.

71 Responses should be arranged vertically in some logical order.

72 The number of responses, normally ranging from three to five, should be a function of both the age level of the students and the nature of the items.

73 The items on a test do not all need to have the same number of alternative responses.

74 The alternatives "all of the above" and "none of the above" are rarely appropriate and are not recommended.

75 If the option "none of the above" is used, it should be the correct response as often as any of the other responses.

True-false items

76 The classic *true-false item* is a statement for which a student selects the response "true" or "false."

77 Variations on the basic true-false item include items to which the student responds yes or no, agree or disagree, right or wrong, and so forth.

78 Another type of true-false item is the *correction item*; basically, if a student selects "false," he or she must also write whatever change or correction would make the statement true.

79 In a correction item, the word or phrase which is to be corrected should be emphasized in some way, such as by underlining or using italics.

80 Since it is difficult to write items that are totally true or totally false, true-false items are best suited for the measurement of attitudes and opinions and abilities related to logical argument.

81 Like multiple-choice tests, true-false tests permit a broad sampling of behaviors in a limited period of time, tend to be reasonably reliable, and are easy to score.

82 It is especially crucial that true-false items be stated as clearly and succinctly as possible since they are especially susceptible to sources of ambiguity.

83 It is also important to avoid the use of negatives in true-false items since to answer "false" to a negatively worded statement essentially creates a double negative.

Irrelevant information

84 The portion of an item which makes it false should be an important fact or concept, not some trivial piece of information.

Length and proportion

85 If it is necessary to have a few lengthy "true" items, you should have an approximately equal number of lengthy "false" items.

86 The proportion of items which are true and the proportion which are false should not be too different, and the correct responses for true-false items should not form any type of pattern such as TFTFTF.

Specific determiners

87 *Specific determiners* are words such as "always," "all," "never," "none," "generally," and "usually."

88 Words such as "always" and "none," because they indicate sweeping generalizations, are associated with false items while words such as "generally" and "usually" are associated with true items.

Matching items

89 While matching items can be used to measure outcomes at all levels, matching items are usually used when a number of related facts, such as knowledge of titles and authors, are to be measured.

90 A *matching item* consists of two vertical lists referred to as the premises and the conclusions, or responses.

Item homogeneity

91 The premises and conclusions of a matching item should be as homogeneous as possible; that is, they should have a common theme.

Length and arrangement

92 In general, the list of premises should be relatively brief; the right number depends on the age of the students, but 3 to 10 premises is a reasonable range.

93 There should be more premises than conclusions, or vice versa; that is, there should not be an equal number of premises and conclusions.

94 As with multiple-choice items, the premises and conclusions in a matching item should be arranged in some logical order, usually alphabetically or numerically.

Directions

95 While clear directions are always important, they are especially so for matching items since it is not always obvious on what basis matching is to be performed.

10 test construction and reproduction

Organization of items

96 If there is more than one type of item, items of the same type (e.g., all the multiple-choice items) should be together; if there is more than one variety of a certain type of item, all items of each variety should be grouped together, (e.g., all basic true-false or all correction true-false items).

97 A second approach to item organization is to arrange items on a continuum from least difficult to most difficult; if there is more than one type of item, items can be clustered by item type and then by difficulty within each cluster.

98 Another logical way to arrange items is by subject matter topic; at the very least, all the items related to the same objective should be grouped together.

General directions

99 If the purpose and importance of the test are not self-evident, they should be discussed with the students in order to orient them and motivate them to do their best.

Selection and recording of responses

100 In addition to directions for selecting (or supplying) answers, students should be instructed as to how to record the answers.

101 If directions are at all complicated or involve procedures unfamiliar to stu-

dents, an example and a sample item should be presented for each set of directions.

102 If responses are recorded in an organized manner, whether on a separate sheet or not, some type of scoring key can be developed (e.g. a strip key) which does not require the scorer to refer to the items.

103 For longer tests, preprinted answer sheets, such as those prepared by IBM, may be used; if such sheets are hand scored, a scoring stencil is generally used.

104 The main advantage of machine scoring is accuracy; also, in many cases, summary information concerning test results can be supplied upon request.

105 For most classroom tests machine scoring is not worth the trouble.

Scoring information

106 Test takers should be informed as to how much the total test is worth, (e.g. 50 points) and how much each item is worth; the value of each subpart should also be known to students.

107 If some topics are believed to be more important than others, it is better to have more items for these topics than to assign some items a higher value (a technique referred to as "weighting").

108 If test taking time is not ample, students should be given some guidelines for using their time effectively.

109 If there is no penalty for guessing, students should be encouraged to answer every item, even if they are not at all sure of the correct response.

110 If there is a penalty for guessing, students should be instructed to respond only to those items for which they are reasonably sure concerning the correct answer.

Correction for guessing

111 Basically, a *correction for guessing* adjusts a score by subtracting that portion of the score believed to be the result of guessing rather than knowledge.

112 The purpose of a correction for guessing is to eliminate any points which may result from blind guessing so that "guessers" have no overall score advantage over "nonguessers," who omit items for which they don't know the correct response.

113 The problem with the correction for guessing formula is that is is based on an expected score and therefore overcorrects some scores and undercorrects others.

114 Correcting for guessing is a waste of time for the following reasons: (a) the chances of getting a decent score on a test by pure guesswork are extremely slim; (b) the correlation between corrected scores and uncorrected scores will be very high (in the high .90s); (c) the correction formula is based on an assumption of wild guessing which is rarely the case; (d) wrong choices can be analyzed to determine the sources of confusion and misunderstanding; (e) some students are going to guess anyway; and (f) if tests are scored by hand, corrections for guessing only complicate the process and open the door to more sources of scoring error.

115 A correction for guessing may be appropriate when a speed test is involved, since all students do not complete all items.

Format considerations

116 Items should be numbered consecutively, and directions should be prominently positioned and separated from the actual items.

117 Answer spaces should be of equal size and large enough to accommodate the longest response, especially on short-answer tests, and answer spaces should be placed in a vertical column in the right-hand or left-hand margin, or a separate answer sheet may be used.

118 If an item is accompanied by any type of illustration, such as a diagram, it should be accurate and placed adjacent to the item, directly above it if possible or parallel to it on an opposite page if necessary.

119 An entire item should start and end on the same page; for example, the stem should not fall on the bottom of one page and the responses on the top of the next.

120 The test should be typed, if at all possible, with extra spacing between items.

Test reproduction

121 It is a good practice to proofread a test twice, once for content and once for accuracy.

122 Which reproduction method you use really doesn't matter as long as the resulting copies are neat and easy to read.

123 Every student should have a copy of the test and it is wise to reproduce a few more copies of the test than are actually needed.

11 test revision

Rationale

124 Test revision may actually occur prior to its intended use as well as following its formal administration.

125 Instruments developed for a specific, formal evaluation may be administered and revised over and over again until acceptable levels of validity and reliability are achieved and item analysis statistics are satisfactory; this process is loosely referred to as fieldtesting and more specifically as *test validation*.

126 For more informal evaluation, such as student evaluation, test revision is normally based solely on the results of the actual administration to the intended students.

Test validation

127 Together, content and evaluation personnel are likely to develop valid measures for assessing a program's effectiveness.

128 It is always advisable to have such measures reviewed by a number of other content specialists before the tests are actually administered to students in the program.

129 The data from one or more administrations of the test to fieldtest groups are used to calculate an appropriate estimate of reliability.

130 If appropriate, item analysis may also be performed in order to assess such factors as item difficulty.

131 Fieldtest administration of a test also permits pretesting of directions, administration procedures, and scoring procedures.

Item analysis

132 *Item analysis* basically involves examination of the pattern of responses for each item in order to assess its effectiveness.

133 Item analysis procedures are different for norm-referenced tests and criterion-

referenced tests, mainly because the items in such tests are designed to do different things; traditional item analysis procedures were designed for norm-referenced tests.

Norm-referenced tests

134 The first step in item analysis is to score and rank the tests from highest total score to lowest total score; the next step is to select approximately the top third and bottom third (or fourth, or half) of the scores for analysis; using these two groups, we then calculate item difficulty and discriminating power.

Item difficulty

135 *Item difficulty* (I.D.) refers to the percentage of students who got the item correct.

136 I.D. $= \dfrac{R}{T} \times 100$

    where: R = number of students (in the upper and lower groups combined) who got the item correct

                T = total number of students (in the upper and lower groups combined) who responded to the item

137 On a norm-referenced test, items should not be too difficult (I.D. near 0) or too easy (I.D. near 100); items of average difficulty are desired because they permit maximum score variability.

138 For short-answer items, an I.D. within the range of 30-70 is usually considered to be acceptable, but the closer to 50 the better.

139 Ideal item difficulty is 50 or higher depending upon the type of test; for example, an I.D. of 65 for a multiple-choice test with 4 or 5 alternatives per item would be satisfactory.

140 Eliminating items simply because they are "too easy" may reduce the content validity of the test.

Discriminating power

141 *Discriminating power* (D.P.) refers to the degree to which an item discriminates between high and low achievers on the test.

142 If the test is indeed a valid measure of the intended outcomes, then the process of estimating D.P. can be used to validate the items.

143 Without verification of total test validity, the most we can really say is that a given item does or does not measure *whatever* the total test measures (or, more precisely, that it measures it to a certain degree) which means that we are really looking at an index of internal consistency.

144 D.P. $= \dfrac{R_U - R_L}{\frac{1}{2}T}$

    where: R_U = number of students in the upper group who responded correctly

                R_L = number of students in the lower group who responded correctly

                T = total number of students in the item analysis ($\frac{1}{2}T$ is the number of students in each group)

145 When $R_U > R_L$, the item is behaving the same way as the total test and has positive D.P.

146 When R_U and R_L are the same or very close, the item has a D.P. near .00, which means that it does not discriminate; such an item serves no useful purpose.

147 When $R_L > R_U$, the item is behaving in a manner opposite to that of the total test and has a negative D.P.; the "wrong" students, those who did poorly on the total test, are getting the item correct.

148 The ideal value of D.P. is +1.00; this value is only possible when I.D. = 50.

149 Since average difficulty is in reality usually somewhat higher than 50, maximum D.P. is really less than +1.00.

150 A D.P. of .30 is generally accepted as being an adequate value, although the higher the better; a D.P. much less than .30 makes the item a candidate for revision, especially if the I.D. is too high or too low.

151 Any item with a negative D.P. must be discarded or undergo major revision.

152 If the test is measuring more than one type of ability, then indices of D.P. are likely to be somewhat distorted and in general lower; one solution is to divide the test into appropriate subtests and estimate D.P. for each item in relation to the appropriate subtest score; at the very least, one should be aware of the potential problem and interpret indices of D.P. appropriately.

Distractability

153 If an item is found to be defective, we have to examine possible reasons; examination of incorrect responses often provides clues concerning the source of the problem.

154 A good distractor is a response which is selected as the answer by more students in the lower group than in the upper group.

155 If no one selects a given distractor, it has no distractability and is ineffective, useless, and should be replaced.

156 If a distractor is selected by more students in the upper group than the lower group, it has negative distractability; the stem should probably be reworded and future instruction should be altered accordingly.

157 Analysis of distractors does not require application of any formula as inspection of response patterns is usually sufficient; you can, however, compute D.P. for each alternative.

For the record

158 You need to organize and store all the information from your item analysis.

159 One organization and storage method is to put all the information for a given item on a large index card and file the cards in a file box; another method is to put the information for a particular item on a sheet of notebook paper and to file all the sheets for a given test in a loose-leaf notebook.

160 The information which should be recorded for a given item is fairly standard: identification data, the complete item (stem and alternatives), and all the item analysis data.

Essay tests

161 Item analysis can be performed on essay tests without too much difficulty provided that the desired response for each item has been clearly defined and that the analytical method of scoring is used.

162 The major problem with essay test item analysis is that by their very nature

the "items" (the subparts) tend to be nonindependent since degree of success on one may be related to degree of success on another.

Criterion-referenced tests

163 The concept of average difficulty has no meaning for a criterion-referenced test as the difficulty is determined mainly by the objective.

164 What we are really concerned with is a *change* in item difficulty between pre-testing and posttesting.

165 Indices of discrimination are of no value for CRTs since we are not the least bit interested in promoting variability.

166 On a CRT we are interested in whether or to what degree the students achieved the objectives; to determine that we have to examine the achievement rate for each of the items related to a given objective.

167 If a test measures more than one objective, then all the items that measure a given objective should be analyzed together.

168 For item analysis, we are interested in the percentage of students who responded correctly to each item and the pattern of percentages for a given objective.

169 If the item achievement rate is low, there may be something wrong with the item, or the students may not possess the measured knowledge or skill, or there may be something wrong with the objective (especially the criterion).

170 If pretest data are available, you can determine how much students apparently learned by comparing achievement rate on each item on the pretest and the posttest.

Interpretation of results

171 Precision is not a characteristic of item analysis of most locally-developed tests.

172 The number of students is typically small and their traits (e.g. ability) are not necessarily representative of all students who might take the test.

173 Item analysis does, however, identify very good items and very poor items.

174 We must keep in mind that our decisions concerning retention, revision, or elimination of items should be based as much on common sense as on item statistics.

175 If some items measure what we want to measure and are necessary for the content validity of the test, we should not eliminate them simply because they are too easy (or too difficult) and do not discriminate.

12 survey and observation forms

Overview

176 Although they are not generally used in the classroom, questionnaires and interviews and occasionally observation are frequently used in evaluations.

Questionnaires

Construction

177 As a general guideline, the questionnaire should be as attractive and brief and as easy to respond to as possible.

178 No item should be included which does not directly relate to the objectives of the evaluation, and structured, or closed-form, items should be used if at all possible.

179 Each question should deal with a single concept and be worded as clearly as possible; any term or concept which might mean different things to different people should be defined.

180 Avoid leading questions, which suggest that one response may be more appropriate than another, and questions to which the respondent might not reply honestly.

Validation

181 A too-often-neglected procedure is validation of the questionnaire in order to determine if it measures what it was developed to measure.

182 The appropriate validation procedure for a given questionnaire will depend upon the nature of the instrument.

The cover letter

183 Every mailed questionnaire must be accompanied by a cover letter which explains what is being asked of the recipient and why, and which hopefully motivates the recipient to fulfill the request.

184 If the questions to be asked are at all threatening (such as items dealing with sex or attitudes toward the local administration), anonymity or confidentiality of responses must be assured.

185 The act of responding should be made as painless as possible; a stamped, addressed, return envelope should be included.

Pretesting

186 Pretesting the questionnaire yields data concerning instrument deficiencies as well as suggestions for improvement.

187 The instrument and the cover letter should be sent to a small group from the intended population or a highly similar population.

Interview guides

Construction

188 The interviewer must have a written guide which indicates what questions are to be asked and in what order, and what additional prompting or probing is permitted.

189 Most interviews use a semistructured approach which involves the asking of structured questions followed by clarifying unstructured, or open-ended, questions.

Pretesting

190 The interview guide, as well as the interview procedures and analysis procedures, should be tried out before it is used in the actual evaluation, using a small sample from the same or a very similar group to the one being used in the evaluation.

191 As with the pretesting of a questionnaire, feedback should be sought from the pretest group as well as from the interviewers.

Observational forms

Definition of observational variables

192 Once the behavior to be observed is determined, we must clearly define what specific behaviors do and do not match the intended behavior.
193 Once a behavioral unit is defined, observations must be quantified so that all observers will count the same way (e.g. 1 observation every 30 seconds).

Recording of observations

194 Observers should be observing and recording only one behavior at a time.
195 As a general rule it is probably best to record observations as the behavior is occurring.
196 Most observation efforts facilitate recording by using an agreed-upon code, or set of symbols, and a recording instrument.
197 Probably the most often used and most efficient observation form is a checklist which lists all behaviors to be observed so that the observer can simply check each behavior as it occurs; rating scales are also sometimes used.

Categorization and coding procedures

198 While we generally try to avoid open-ended questions, sometimes they are necessary; when they are, we must determine how to categorize and code responses so that they can be tabulated.
199 If results are to be computer analyzed, then all information, structured and unstructured, must be coded; coding involves assigning numerical values to each piece of data.

task five **performance criteria**

a Your table should include a detailed content outline (at least major headings and subheadings). The behavioral outcomes axis should include as many categories as are represented by your objectives. Each cell should indicate the required numbers of items.
b The developed test should be in final form. The items should be organized by type of item, difficulty, topic, objective, or some logical combination of these factors. In addition to directions preceding each item type, there should be general directions related to the selection and recording of answers and the point values of items. The test should be typed and follow general format guidelines.
c If you are not in a position to actually administer the test, the next best thing to do is to make copies of your test and answer the questions for each test as you believe typical respondents (e.g. students) would.

1 The analysis should include indices of difficulty and discrimination, and analysis of distractors if appropriate. Indicate whether each item is adequate "as is," needs revision, or should be replaced, and why. Present the results of your analysis in a manner similar to that depicted in figure 11.1 (page 270) and indicate necessary revisions.
2 The analysis should include computation of item achievement percentages for each item, as well as objective achievement percentages. Indicate which items may need revision and why. Present the results of your analysis in a manner similar to that depicted in figure 11.2. Discuss possible revisions.

While some students are internally motivated, others are not; those who are not must be given some justification for exerting effort in the interest of learning.

part six
evaluation designs and procedures

The process phase of evaluation involves actual implementation of the planned instruction, curriculum, program or project. During this phase strategies, activities, and procedures are executed and decisions are made concerning which are working and which are not. Strategies are judged in terms of their effectiveness in promoting intended outcomes.

For more formal evaluation efforts concerned with determining the effectiveness of a new treatment (e.g. a program, approach, or set of materials), application of an evaluation design is required. With few exceptions, evaluation designs permit us to compare the actual performance of participants at the conclusion of implementation with an estimate of what performance would have been had they not received the treatment under investigation. All designs do not provide equally good estimates, however, and the confidence that we have in the validity of comparisons depends mainly on the adequacy of the design actually applied.

The goal of part 6 is for you to be able to select and apply the best design and strategies from among those that are appropriate and feasible in a given situation. After reading Part 6, you should be able to do the following task.

Task six
For the evaluation situation you described in task 1 and the objectives you developed in task 2, describe the strategy or strategies you would implement during the process phase of evaluation.

a If a unit of instruction is involved (student evaluation), describe (1) how each strategy translates into introductory activities, learning activities, and follow-up activities, and (2) how major instructional variables are dealt with.

b If a formal evaluation effort is involved (e.g. program evaluation), describe (1) the participants and, if appropriate, how they will be selected, and (2) the evaluation design which will be applied.

(See Performance Criteria, p. 378.)

13 instructional strategies and variables

After reading chapter 13, you should be able to:

1 Identify and give examples of the three major types of activities involved in instruction.
2 Identify and describe two instructional variables which are relevant to *each* of the three types of instructional activities, and four which are relevant to *all* three types.

Definition and purpose

The basic evaluation process involves delineation of objectives, implementation of one or more strategies intended to facilitate objective attainment, and measurement of outcomes. Based on results, we reassess our objectives and strategies. As discussed in chapter 3, strategies are general approaches to promoting achievement of one or more objectives, and they generally entail a number of specific activities. We may speak of instructional strategies, curriculum strategies, program strategies, and the like. There are typically a number of strategies from which to choose. One may be designated the most likely to succeed given available information, or there may be two (or more) promising strategies, and the decision may be made to try each of them, at different times with the same students, for example, or at the same time with different students. Or, a combination of several strategies may be called for. If one of the objectives of the Big Brothers–Big Sisters program was "to increase the number of participating adults in Chicago by 10%," to cite a previous example, three major strategies might be broad public exposure (use of mass media), group contact, and individual contact. Each strategy would then entail one or more specific activities. Broad public exposure, for example, could be implemented through placing newspaper ads and 30-second messages on radio and television.

   The process phase of evaluation involves making decisions based upon events which occur during actual implementation of the planned instruction, program, or project. Following initial testing (administration of pretests and/or tests of entry behavior), planned strategies and activities are executed in the predetermined sequence. Data collected during this phase provide feedback concerning whether execution is taking place *as planned* and whether strategies and activities are proving effective. If several strategies are being used simultaneously, then at various points in time decisions will be made as to which ones are working and which are not, and what kinds of changes need to be made. The Big Brothers–Big Sisters program, for example, might conclude after two months that television and radio spots are not bringing in very many new big brothers and big sisters. Since such spots are so expensive, it might be decided to stop them and to concentrate efforts on group contact activities if that strategy does seem to be working.

   When student evaluation is involved, instructional strategies are implemented to facilitate achievement of instructional objectives. In essence, instructional strategies define the nature of the stimuli which will hopefully bring about the desired response—student learning. Objectives address different types of learning, and it has been suggested that different types of learning require different strategies. Gagné, for example, has identified eight types of learning, among them concept learning and rule learning, and has specified conditions which should be considered in instruction for each.[1] Also, certain strategies are more appropriate for specific content areas. The inquiry (or discovery) method, for example, which involves an inductive approach to learning, has been used extensively in social studies instruction. Other more general strategies, however, appear to be applicable across a wide variety of content areas and types of learning. Many of these general strategies, or approaches, have been the focus of considerable research designed to determine their relative effectiveness. Hundreds of studies, for instance, have been conducted to investigate various applications of programmed

[1] Gagné, R. M. *The conditions of learning.* New York: Holt, Rinehart & Winston, 1970.

instruction. The effectiveness of other strategies, especially those "invented" by a particular teacher, is often a matter of personal opinion. In any event, all strategies should deal in one way or another with a number of variables. For example, *feedback* concerning adequacy of performance must be provided to students. Different strategies may involve different approaches and procedures for providing such feedback, but it is an activity which should be systematically conducted regardless of what strategy or strategies are involved.

Instruction involves three major types of activities: introductory activities, learning activities, and follow-up activities. Any instructional strategy should deal with all three types of activities. And, while some instructional variables are of concern for all three types, other variables are more relevant to one type than another. Classroom environment and instructional time, for example, are always relevant, whereas remediation procedures are basically follow-up activities. Introductory activities include: getting students' attention, sharing objectives with students, motivating students, and providing students with advance organizers. While some students are internally motivated, others are not; those who are not motivated must be given some justification for exerting effort in the interest of learning. An instructional device often employed as part of introductory activities is an advance organizer. An *advance organizer* is basically a discourse which relates material which is to be learned to material which has already been learned.[2] Advance organizers provide a general framework into which specific new learnings can be incorporated. An advance organizer for a unit on socialism, for example, might consist of an overview of socialism, comparing and contrasting its major principles with those of democracy. Such organizers are especially appropriate for topics with which students have little or no familiarity. Part 1 of this text, for example, was essentially an advance organizer for the remainder of the book. Relevant variables with respect to learning activities include method of instruction, sequencing (discussed in chapter 3), and feedback. Follow-up activities include review and remediation procedures.

The research data on the effectiveness of a number of instructional strategies and variables are in agreement with what one might expect based on common sense. As pointed out previously with respect to test construction, however, common sense is not necessarily common practice.

Instructional strategies

The number of instructional strategies which could be presented here are numerous. If there were five (or fifteen) most effective teaching methods or curricula, we would build our discussion around them. But there are no such animals. The research evidence overwhelmingly indicates that no curriculum is inherently more effective *in terms of achievement* than any other, although different curricula do produce different outcomes. If two curricula are compared by administering an achievement test to students in each curriculum, the results will favor the curriculum whose content and coverage are best reflected in the test. If content and coverage are very similar for the two curricula, performance of the students will be essentially the same. For example, suppose the Fingers & Toes Math Curriculum emphasizes computation and the Heavy-Duty Math Curriculum emphasizes

---

[2] Ausubel, D. P. *Educational psychology: A cognitive view.* Holt, Rinehart & Winston, 1968.

problem solving. If the selected math achievement test emphasizes calculation, then the Fingers & Toes students will do better. If the test emphasizes problem solving, the Heavy-Duty students will do better. If the test gives equal emphasis to calculation and problem solving, the two curricula will end up looking equally effective since respective advantages will be balanced.[3]

Similar conclusions have been reached concerning the comparative effectiveness of various teaching methods such as lecture versus discussion and small-group versus large-group instruction. These results are rather comforting in a way. They suggest, for example, that more expensive curricula (such as those requiring high-priced equipment or materials) are not inherently more effective. It also suggests that many different curricula have approximately equal potential for fostering student achievement. This is not to say that there is equivalence with respect to all variables, only with respect to group achievement. Some approaches, for example, may result in more positive student attitudes, take less time, or cost less. It is also likely that different approaches are differentially effective for different types of students. Thus, selection of one strategy over another may be based on factors other than achievement, but it is tough to make a bad choice. Also, since variety is the spice of life and tends to sustain student interest, a number of different strategies may be used in a given unit of instruction.

The above discussion brings us back where we started: the number of instructional strategies which could be presented here are many. For the sake of illustration, two general instructional strategies are briefly described below. Both of these have been used extensively and are applicable to a wide range of curriculum areas and types of learning.

Individualized instruction

The term *individualized instruction* is applied to a host of activities designed to personalize instruction in order to meet individual student needs. The one characteristic shared by all alleged individualized instruction efforts is that all students are not performing the same tasks at the same time. Students are different; they have different capabilities, experiences, interests, and motivational levels. Traditional large-group instruction, in essence, ignores these differences and teaches to students in the average range of ability. The result is that bright students get bored and low ability students get lost in the action. One way of dealing with this problem is *grouping*—dividing the class into a number of smaller groups based on some variable, usually ability. While small group instructional activities may be effective for certain situations, this strategy still only attempts to deal with one variable, such as ability. One solution is to further subdivide each small group based on some other variable, such as past achievement. If we carry this process to its logical conclusion, the optimal "group" size is one student.

In its idealized form, individualized instruction is characterized by the following:

   a A different set of specific objectives for each student, depending upon initial entry behavior and subsequent rate of progress
   b Student self-pacing, that is, each student working at his or her own rate

[3] Walker, D. F., & Schaffarzick, J. Comparing curricula. *Review of Educational Research*, 1974, 44, 83–112.

c Availability to students of a wide range of instructional resources such as print and nonprint media

d Individualized testing, that is, each student taking a given test "when ready"

e Constant diagnosis, feedback, and remediation on an individual basis

f Unlimited recycling, that is, each student taking a test for a given objective or set of objectives as many times as is necessary until the objective is achieved.

Thus, individualized instruction is a general strategy which includes a number of specific individualization strategies, such as self-pacing and the availability of a wide range of media. Large-scale individualized instruction programs, such as those implemented by an entire school system, frequently involve development of a large number of modules, or learning packets, each of which contains elements such as a rationale, objectives, a pretest, suggested activities, a list of resources (or the resources themselves), practice tests, and a posttest. The appropriate module is given to a given student at the appropriate time.

Many alleged individualized instruction programs in reality represent only one, or a small subset, of the above characteristics. This is sometimes due to the tremendous amount of clerical record-keeping activities involved. Although ideally implementation of individualized instruction should be accompanied by implementation of an adequate management support system, necessary resources (human and other) are frequently not available to the teacher. In other cases, one or more of the characteristics are intentionally eliminated or modified in the belief that they are not necessary or are inefficient. Some evidence does indeed suggest that self-pacing and unlimited recycling, for example, are undesirable activities. Self-pacing appears to be detrimental to both students and instructors; it has been shown that instructor pacing increases objective achievement rate with no loss in of performance. Unlimited recycling has also been shown to be inefficient and un- and unproductive, even when accompanied by intensive, individualized feedback.[4]

Two well-known types of individualized instruction are mastery learning and programmed instruction. *Mastery learning* (chapter 5), as advocated by Bloom and his associates, is based on the belief that a high percentage of all students can master intended objectives, given appropriate and sufficient instruction.[5] There are a number of alternative strategies for mastery learning which may be implemented, but each must in some way relate instruction to the individual needs of students and deal with factors such as learning time, optimum approaches for each student, communication to students of the nature of required tasks, and student perseverance. *Programmed instruction*, which reached its peak of popularity in the 1960s, is characterized by small-step instruction presented in a linear series of "frames." A frame consists of explanatory material followed by a question. The correct response to the question is typically given in the next frame. Initially responses are strongly cued, making it highly likely that a student will respond correctly. In successive frames, cues (hints) are gradually withdrawn until the student makes the appropriate response to an uncued question.[6] Thus, programmed in-

[4] Gay, L. R. Evolution of an innovation: Development of a competency-based educational research course. *The CEDR Quarterly,* Spring, 1977, *10*(1), 10–12.
[5] Bloom, B. S., Hastings, J. T., & Madaus, G. F. *Handbook on formative and summative evaluation of student learning.* New York: McGraw-Hill, 1971.
[6] For further explanation and illustration, see Markle, S. M. *Good frames and bad: A grammar of frame writing.* New York: John Wiley & Sons, 1964.

struction involves small steps, self-pacing, immediate feedback and reinforcement, practice, and review. Programmed instruction may be presented in printed form, as in an individualized learning packet, or through some type of hardware such as a computer. A variation on basic programmed instruction is *branching*. A branching program directs students to perform different activities depending upon their responses to a given question. Thus, bright students will move on to new concepts quickly while slower students will engage in more practice on fewer concepts. While programmed instruction has not been shown to be more effective (in terms of achievement) than other methods of instruction, it has been shown to be more efficient in that less time is involved in achieving a given set of objectives. Since each programmed unit is self-contained, programmed instruction is especially useful for enrichment and remediation purposes and for students who are unable to attend school for extended periods of time.

Multimedia instruction

The term *media* refers to all modes of communication—human, print, and audiovisual. Although we do not usually think in such terms, the teacher *is* a medium, as is a textbook. Multimedia instruction does not devalue the role of the teacher and text; it simply requires that each be used when it is most appropriate, not all the time. The rationale for multimedia instruction is that instructional objectives involve different types of learning and that certain media are more effective for certain types than for others. Learning to speak a foreign language, for example, can be facilitated by using audio tapes which contain dialogue between native speakers. Further, multimedia instruction is a viable strategy in individualization because different modes of communication are best suited to the individual learning styles of different students. Some students, for example, need the practice provided by programmed texts and workbooks while others need graphic illustrations, such as those provided by filmstrips.[7] Thus, in its idealized form, multimedia instruction involves optimally matching a certain student and a certain objective to a certain medium.

Required media may be selected or developed. It is obviously easier and less expensive if suitable print and audiovisual materials are available and can be acquired as needed. On the other hand, there is no point in using films, audio cassettes, videotapes, or any other media which are not appropriate for intended objectives. Audio cassettes of conversational dialogues are readily available for languages such as French and Spanish. If you are teaching Portuguese, a Spanish cassette will not do; it is not close enough. Thus if Portuguese dialogue audio cassettes are not available but are deemed appropriate and highly desirable, they must be developed if resources permit. The basic media selection process, as presented by Briggs, Campeau, Gagné, and May, involves analyzing each desired outcome in terms of the type of learning involved and the corresponding conditions, and determining the most appropriate medium for each. Analysis of the identified conditions indicates the type of stimuli needed (e.g. printed words or spoken words), and decisions are made concerning the form each will take. Spoken words, for example, may take the form of a lecture, an audio cassette, or a motion picture soundtrack.

[7] Briggs, L. J., Campeau, P. L., Gagné, R. M., & May, M. A. *Instructional media: A procedure for the design of multimedia instruction.* Pittsburgh: American Institutes for Research, 1967.

It is recognized that such an analytical approach to media selection is only feasible for large curriculum development efforts in which appropriate support personnel are available. At the classroom level, a more informal, commonsense approach may be taken to media selection based on a combination of what intuitively seems right and what is realistically available. The basic concept of matching objectives and media, however, is still applicable. The point is that using media just to use media is pointless. Showing a film just to show a film may be a waste of time if the film is of poor quality and the content only tangentially relates to the objectives at hand. When media are utilized, it is imperative that their use be planned carefully in advance to insure availability and to insure that audiovisual media are of high quality and in proper working order. Films, for example, should be screened beforehand. Poor-quality media and malfunctioning equipment can cause student boredom and frustration which effectively counteract any potential beneficial purpose the media may have served.

Instructional variables

All instructional strategies, as we said, must deal in some systematic way with certain variables if learning is to be maximized. These variables can, of course, be essentially ignored; the when and how of their occurrence can be left to chance. But there is sufficient evidence to support the view that there are ways of dealing with them that will result in increased student learning and retention. A number of such variables could be discussed. Logically, we might expect many of them to be quite important to the learning process, but thier effect has yet to be demonstrated. Teacher behavior is one such variable. Research has yet to establish any firm relationship between teacher behavior and student achievement. On the other hand, there are certain variables for which results have been fairly consistent. Review is one such variable. Further, some variables are more critical than others. Effective discipline, for example, is more important to the teaching-learning process than a strict dress code for students. Four variables have been selected for brief discussion—time, discipline, feedback, and review. All four are important variables which are relevant to all curriculum areas and methods of instruction.

Time

Evidence is increasingly piling up to support the not-so-amazing assertion that amount of time spent in learning is more important than the method of instruction. In other words, if more time is spent on reading instruction, reading scores will increase. This finding is very interesting considering that: (1) the number of school days in a year required by state law varies in the United States from 172.6 to 182.7; (2) the length of the average school day varies up to 2 hours; and (3) the number of hours spent on each subject, not to mention the amount of class time spent on actual instruction, also varies.[8] These facts deserve serious consideration. As Wiley and Harnischfeger point out, one implication is that cutbacks in the

[8] Wiley, D. E., & Harnischfeger, A. Explosion of a myth: Quantity of schooling and exposure to instruction, major educational vehicles. *Educational Researcher*, 1974, 3, 7–12.

length of the school year and school day will result in a significant decrease in student achievement. They base this conclusion on the results of several studies, one of which investigated the relationship between verbal, reading, and math achievement, and number of hours of instruction per school year. Based on the results, it was concluded that in schools where students receive 24% more schooling, average gain in reading comprehension will be increased by two-thirds, and gains in math and verbal skills will be increased by more than one-third.

The amount of time spent per day on each subject also has implications for achievement. Typically, the school day is divided equally among subjects resulting in a series of say 55-minute periods. If achievement in the basic skills, for example, is a priority, then perhaps more time should be spent in instruction in these areas and less in others. This statement will of course make some teachers unhappy; most teachers think their subject is the most important one in the curriculum! The intent, however, is not to devalue any particular content area but rather to point out that limited time must be apportioned to various content areas on some rational basis. Further, there are alternatives. One alternative is to extend the length of the school day and to spend the extra time on instruction in priority areas. A second, probably more palatable, alternative is to make decisions on an individual student basis so that, for example, low achievers in math might spend two periods in math instruction and have one less subject than the majority of students.

The foregoing discussion is not meant to suggest that any of the above possibilities be implemented but rather that the issues need to be seriously discussed and resolved, especially in a time when so many are unhappy about declining student test scores on national achievement tests.

Discipline

Another implication of the above discussion is that time wasted in class on off-the-subject activities, such as chitchat and discipline is detrimental to student achievement. Probably more time is wasted on attempts to maintain discipline than on any other activity. Teachers typically identify lack of discipline as their number-one problem. A disruptive classroom is not conducive to learning. Unfortunately, many teachers have never received any training in methods of dealing with student behavior, disruptive or otherwise. And yet there are a number of fairly well-documented techniques which can be easily learned and applied by teachers. Ideally, with proper classroom management, most potential discipline problems can be eliminated before they occur. But even in the best of classrooms crises do arise. The techniques to be discussed can be helpful both in preventing problems and in dealing with them as they arise.[9]

A number of preventive measures which teachers can take in the interest of discipline have been proposed. One suggestion is to maintain an orderly classroom environment by avoiding untimely disruptions and by making smooth transitions from one activity to another. For example, you would not want to make an announcement about an upcoming field trip in the middle of a reading lesson. Another suggestion is to promote and maintain student attention by using a variety of instructional modes and materials and by techniques such as calling on stu-

[9] For further discussion of these and other techniques see: Clarizio, H. F. *Toward positive classroom discipline.* New York: John Wiley & Sons, 1971, *and* Gnagey, W. J. *Maintaining discipline in classroom instruction.* New York: MacMillan, 1975.

dents in an unsystematic manner so that they never know who is "next." A third suggestion, which many teachers would do well to follow, is to start with a few, short, positively-stated rules and to consistently enforce them. It is not a good idea to hand out a list of 99 don'ts on the first day of class such as Don't chew gum, Don't come to class without a pencil, Don't get out of your seat without permission. Etc., etc., etc. Nag, nag, nag. For one thing there is no way such rules can be consistently enforced, and if they could, it would take a large chunk of class time. It is more effective to start with a small, manageable list of rules such as, Ask for permission when you want to leave the room.

Two techniques which have been shown to be effective in dealing with undesirable student behaviors are the use of positive reinforcement and the provision of models.

Positive reinforcement

Positive reinforcement in the form of rewards is a highly effective technique which can be used with virtually all students. Teachers, understandably, have a tendency to ignore students who are behaving and to pay attention to students who are being disruptive or are otherwise exhibiting inappropriate behaviors. A teacher is much more likely to say "Enerjetic, get in your seat!" rather than "How nice, Angelica, you're in your seat!" A basic premise of positive reinforcement is that attention should be given to students who are being "good" and that specific behaviors should be emphasized. Madsen and his colleagues have convincingly demonstrated the soundness of this concept in a number of studies and classroom observations. In one study, for instance, a baseline of frequency of stand-up behavior was established. When teachers were then instructed to increase the frequency of "sit down" commands, stand-ups increased dramatically. When, however, teachers were instructed to reinforce sit-down behavior and to ignore stand-up behavior, stand-up behaviors were progressively reduced to approximately 100 less instances in a 20-minute period.[10]

Rewards may take many forms. They may be tangible (e.g. the old M & M game) or intangible (e.g. verbal praise). Different rewards work better with different kinds of students. In some cases students are given a choice of rewards. You might tell a student that if he or she finishes an assignment before the end of the period, he or she may read, or work on a puzzle, or water the plants, or do something you know will appeal to the student. Students, of course, must learn to behave properly in the absence of rewards; you do not get an M & M *every* time you are good. Thus, rewards are gradually withdrawn. At first a reward is administered immediately for any behavior approximating the desired behavior. Then it is given only for appropriate behavior, immediately, every time it occurs. The reward is then progressively delayed until it is only occasionally given (to maintain the behavior), or more and more is required in order to receive a reward. For example, we might initially reward a child for doing one arithmetic problem; at some later point, we may reward the child only for completing an entire assignment.

Contingency contracts represent an approach based on the principles of positive reinforcement. A *contingency contract* is an agreement jointly developed

[10] Madsen, C. H., Becker, W. C., Thomas, D. R., Koser, L., & Plager, E. An analysis of the reinforcing function of "sitdown" commands. In R. K. Parker (Ed.), *Readings in educational psychology*. Boston: Allyn & Bacon, 1968.

by a student and a teacher. It specifies what task the student will perform and what reward will be received when it is done. A contract might specify that when a student has written the definition of 20 vocabulary words and used each word correctly in a sentence (with no more than say 3 errors), the student will be allowed to go to lunch 15 minutes early (that's a big deal when you're in school!).

Models

Providing models involves exposing students to persons who behave in a desired manner.[11] Models may or may not be "live." Live models include teachers and peers. Appropriate behavior may also be transmitted via media, such as a filmstrip. The powerful influence that students exert on each other is well known. Modeling capitalizes on this influence. The impact of a model is heightened when the model is someone students look up to. If the most popular kid in school smokes marijuana, it is "cool." The strategy of modeling is to get such students "on your side," or to use them as an example. Suppose Randy Rascal, Mr. Popularity, makes wisecracks in class all the time and the other students, who think he is a real riot, follow his example. One strategy is to talk privately to Randy and explain to him that as a leader he has certain responsibilities. If this approach works and Randy stops "mouthing off," the other students will follow suit. If on the other hand, Randy tells you in so many words to buzz off, some other means of stopping his disruptive behavior must be used—a detention, a trip to the office, removal from class, or whatever it takes. If the situation is not too serious, positive reinforcement might be tried, but if the students respect Randy more than they respect you, they will seek his approval, not yours. The point is that students such as Randy are often the key to classroom discipline.

The above example illustrates what is referred to as the *ripple effect,* the effect that teacher interactions with one student have on the behavior of other students.[12] If a student (especially a respected one) is rewarded or punished by a teacher (especially a respected one), the incident has a vicarious effect on the behavior of other students. If Randy Rascal and his teacher have a confrontation and the teacher "wins," the ripple effect will tend to produce improved behavior on the part of other students who witnessed the incident.

Feedback

Feedback, a third important instructional variable, is information concerning the correctness or incorrectness of a response. Learning and retention require feedback. You cannot learn to correctly pronounce words, for example, unless you receive feedback on your attempts. When I first learned to read, I thought the name Charlotte was pronounced *Char-lot-ee,* as in *Charlie.* Then in the fourth grade I gave an oral book report and the main character in the book was named Charlotte. The other kids rolled in the aisles when I said her name. That was getting corrective feedback the hard way! In any event, most instruction involves a phase in which students attempt to demonstrate that they have "learned." This phase is not

[11] See, for example, Bandura, A. *Principles of behavior modification.* New York: Holt, Rinehart & Winston, 1969.
[12] See Kounin, J. *Discipline and group management in classrooms.* New York: Holt, Rinehart & Winston, 1970.

the same as testing but rather involves activities such as filling in a workbook page, doing math problems at the blackboard, writing some sentences, or reading aloud. Feedback which tells a student that an exercise has been done correctly provides positive reinforcement; corrective feedback, which tells a student of an error, increases the probability of a future correct response.

Feedback may be provided by a person such as a teacher, but it can come from other sources too. For some activities, feedback can be self-provided, as a result of information received through the senses. If you get a strike at a bowling alley, you might say to yourself, "If only I could remember what I did right!" If you serve a tennis ball into the net, you know next time to toss the ball higher or to avoid hitting it down. Feedback may also be provided by print or nonprint media —a workbook may give correct answers, a programmed text always gives the correct response, and so on.

For years it was believed, based on a number of animal studies, that corrective feedback should be provided as soon as possible after a performance, immediately if feasible. Then a series of studies conducted by Brackbill and her associates provided evidence that this concept is not necessarily true when human beings are involved.[13] She found that delayed feedback was superior, especially with respect to retention. Subsequent research has confirmed this finding, primarily with respect to test feedback (feedback concerning correct and incorrect responses made on a test), with a delay of one or two days being optimal. On the other hand, there is evidence that fairly immediate feedback may be necessary for initial learning of skills, such as learning to write one's name, which require "shaping," that is, successive approximations of a desired response.

Review

Students forget a great deal of what they learn. A high portion of what has been learned is nonretrievable after even a few months, such as after summer vacation. This loss is especially critical in areas, such as mathematics, in which cumulative learning is involved such that subsequent learnings build on previous learnings. Fortunately, there is considerable research evidence which indicates that systematic review of concepts promotes retention (see chapter 3 for references). Depending upon the type of learning involved, review may take the form of repetitive practice or spaced review. Spaced review, which refers to reviews which occur one or more days after the day of original learning, is generally more appropriate.

Research has repeatedly shown that even one spaced review can significantly increase retention. Further, it does not matter much when the review occurs, although there is a tendency for later reviews to be more effective. In other words, a review one day after original learning is essentially as effective as a review one week after learning. The results concerning the effectiveness of two reviews are even more dramatic—they are definitely worth the time they take in terms of retention. Further, the optimum strategy for such reviews appears to be to have one soon after learning, say after a day, and one after a longer interval, say after a week.[14]

[13] See, for example, Brackbill, Y., & Kappy, M. S. Delay of reinforcement and retention. *Journal of Comparative and Physiological Psychology*, 1962, *55*(1), 14–18.
[14] Gay, L. R. Temporal position of reviews and its effect on the retention of mathematical rules. *Journal of Educational Psychology*, 1973, *61*(2), 171–182.

One type of reactive arrangement occurs when participants feel they are in some way receiving special attention.

14 evaluation designs and procedures

After reading chapter 14, you should be able to:

1 Describe the purpose a control group serves in an evaluation design.
2 Describe what is meant by manipulation of an independent variable and give three specific examples of independent variables which could be manipulated in an evaluation study.
3 Discuss the purpose of control.
4 Identify two major ethical considerations involved in conducting an evaluation study.
5 List the procedures for using a table of random numbers to select a random sample.
6 List the procedures involved in cluster sampling.
7 Define internal validity and external validity.
8 Identify and briefly describe eight major threats to internal validity.
9 Identify and briefly describe four major threats to external validity.
10 Define or describe the concept of experimenter bias.
11 Briefly discuss the purpose of an evaluation design.
12 Identify and briefly describe five ways to control extraneous variables (and you better not leave out randomization!).
13 For each of the research designs which can be used in an evaluation study, draw a diagram, list the steps involved in its application, and identify major sources of invalidity associated with it.
14 Describe each of the Title I evaluation models and the situation for which each is appropriate.
15 Describe the procedures involved in the three types of single-subject designs.
16 Describe the purpose and process of out-of-level testing.

Overview

In the spirit of accountability, most programs and projects must at some point provide evidence concerning their effectiveness. Such evidence usually includes data showing whether and to what degree the program achieved its own objectives. In many cases, comparative data must also be provided which indicate whether program participants are better off in some way (exhibit higher levels of achievement for example) than they would have been if they had not been participants. The Joint Dissemination Review Panel, established by HEW in 1972, reviews the procedures and results of federally funded programs, applies a set of standards, and endorses those efforts considered to be exemplary. While the panel has a number of specific criteria, its overriding theme is that a valid evaluation has two essential ingredients: (1) end results must be assessed using valid and reliable instruments, and (2) there must be some credible estimate of what the results would have been *without* the program intervention. A program is judged to be effective if it can be demonstrated that a significant positive change occurred which would not have occurred in the absence of the program.[1] For example, if a reading program reported that students gained an average of nine months from September to May on a standardized reading test, program effectiveness would not necessarily be supported since a gain that large might normally be expected during a school year. On the other hand, if program participants scored significantly higher in May than an equivalent group of students not in the program, program effectiveness would be demonstrated, assuming that the two groups exhibited essentially equal achievement levels in September.

A major point of disagreement, as noted previously, among evaluators is the issue of whether evaluation studies should be based on research designs, particularly when group comparisons are involved, as in, Does curriculum A lead to higher achievement than curriculum B? Some argue that educational research and educational evaluation have distinctly different purposes—that research seeks control while evaluation assesses what is—and that real-world settings characteristic of evaluation essentially preclude that control. In reality, however, there is often a fine line between research and evaluation, and an evaluation may very easily utilize a research design. Both research and evaluation involve decision making, both are based on the scientific method, and both involve procedures such as instrument selection, delineation and implementation of strategies, and analysis and interpretation of results. Further, many research studies are conducted in real-world settings and are subject to the same control problems which are faced by evaluators. Finally, no alternative can give us the same confidence in our findings that we can have when we apply an experimental research design. While use of a research design is not always appropriate, necessary, or feasible, many evaluation studies could benefit from the application of an experimental or quasi-experimental design to their procedures. Thus, the most reasonable approach is to do the best you can. If it is feasible to use a good experimental design in an evaluation study, do so; if not, do the next best thing that is feasible.

---

[1] Tallmadge, G. K. *Ideabook: The Joint Dissemination Review Panel.* Washington, D.C.: Dept. of Health, Education and Welfare, 1977.

Purpose and process

Effective evaluation of a program frequently requires some type of control group. The behavior of the control group serves as an indication of what the behavior of the program group would have been if participants had not been in the program. The ideal approach is one in which an independent variable is manipulated, all other relevant variables are controlled, and the effect of the independent variable on one or more dependent variables (as measured by posttests) is observed. The independent variable is the conditions to which the groups are exposed and includes *treatment conditions* (the program intervention believed to make a difference) and *control conditions*. Manipulation means that it is determined in advance which subjects, e.g. students, will receive the treatment and which will not. Variables typically manipulated include method of instruction or training, type and arrangement of learning environment, type of learning materials, and alternative instructional staff patterns. The effect of the treatment is assessed in terms of posttest performance of the treatment and control groups. This approach is both the most demanding and the most productive method of evaluation. When well conducted, such evaluation studies produce the soundest evidence concerning hypothesized cause-effect relationships between treatment and performance. The steps involved in such a study are basically the same as for a research study: definition of the problem, selection of participants and measuring instruments, selection of a design, implementation of procedures, analysis of results, and formulation of conclusions. Such a study is ideally guided by at least one hypothesis which states the expected outcome. The actual results either confirm (support) or do not confirm the hypothesis. Everything is planned in advance of implementation, including who the participants will be, who will serve as the control group, the precise nature of the treatment, how extraneous factors will be controlled or controlled for, and how performance will be measured.

An evaluation study typically involves two groups, a treatment group and a control group (although as we shall see later, there may be only one group or there may be more than two groups). The treatment group receives a new, or innovative, treatment, the approach under investigation, while the control group usually either receives a different treatment or is treated as usual. Note that the control group is not "the group that receives *nothing*." If the independent variable was type of reading instruction, the program group might be instructed with a new method while the control group might be instructed with a traditional method. Thus the control group would still receive reading instruction; it would not sit twiddling their thumbs in a closet while the program students received the Individualized Whoopee Reading Program. Otherwise, you would not be evaluating the effectiveness of a new method as compared to a traditional method but rather the effectiveness of a new method as compared to no reading instruction at all! Any method is bound to be more effective than no method at all. The two groups which are to be exposed to the treatment and control conditions are equated on all other variables which might be related to performance on the posttest, reading readiness for example. In other words, every effort is made to insure that the two groups are as equivalent as possible on all variables *except* the independent variable.

After the groups have been exposed to the treatment and control conditions for a sufficient period of time, a posttest of the dependent variable is administered (or the dependent variable is measured some other way), and it is then determined whether there is a significant difference between the groups, whether the treatment made a difference. One problem associated with evaluation and research studies in education is that participants are often not exposed to the treatment for a sufficient period of time. No matter how effective peer counseling is, for example, it is not likely to reduce suspensions if students are exposed to it for only one hour. Thus, to adequately evaluate the effectiveness of peer counseling, the treatment group needs to be exposed to it over a period of time. The treatment should be given a "chance to work."

Another problem associated with comparison studies is that the treatments received by the two groups may not be sufficiently different to make a difference. This situation frequently results when a program is not implemented according to plan or is implemented poorly. A program, for example, may propose to implement an individualized career education curriculum for educable mentally retarded students. But problems may arise; there may be a high degree of staff turnover, for example, and the planned materials may never quite get developed or may be shoddily developed, and many planned activities may not take place. The program students may end up seeing a film on career opportunities and reading a few pamphlets of their choice. It is not then too surprising when program students do not end up with significantly higher aspirations or knowledge concerning career opportunities.

Control

Control refers to efforts to remove, or account for, the effects of any variable, other than the independent variable, which might affect posttest performance. In other words, we want the treatment and control groups to be as similar as possible so that the only major difference between them is the treatment and control conditions. To illustrate the importance of control, suppose you conducted an evaluation of a program intended to assess the effectiveness of student tutors in teaching first graders to read. Student tutors might be older children from higher grade levels. Now suppose that students in both the treatment and control groups received one hour of reading instruction per day with their teachers, and that treatment students received an extra hour of reading instruction each day with their tutors. Would the comparison be fair? Certainly not. The students with the tutors would have received twice as much reading instruction (10 hours per week versus 5 hours per week). Thus, one variable which would need to be controlled would be time. In order for the comparison to be fair, members of both groups would have to receive instruction for the same amount of time. Then the effectiveness of a different kind of instruction, not the effectiveness of *more* instruction, could be assessed.

The above illustration is just one example of the kinds of factors which must be considered in planning an evaluation. Some variables which need controlling may be relatively obvious. In the example above, variables such as reading readiness and intelligence would need to be considered. Other variables in need of control may not be as obvious. In the above evaluation, we would need to insure that both groups used the same reading texts and materials. Thus, we see that there are really two different kinds of variables which need to be controlled: participant variables (such as reading readiness), variables on which participants in the two groups might differ, and environmental variables (such as learning materials), variables which might cause unwanted differences between the groups.

We strive to insure that the characteristics and experiences of the groups are as equal as possible on all important variables except, of course, the independent variable. If at the end of some period of time groups differ in performance on the posttest, the difference can be attributed to the treatment. Control is not easy in educational evaluations which take place in real-world settings such as classrooms. The task is not an impossible one, however, since we can concentrate on identifying and controlling only those variables which might really affect posttest performance. If two groups differ significantly with respect to shoe size, for instance, posttest scores will probably not be affected. Also, as we shall see shortly, a number of techniques can be used to control for unwanted, extraneous variables.

Ethical considerations

While ethical considerations are involved in all areas of evaluation, they are certainly more acute in comparative evaluation studies which by definition "manipulate" and "control" participants. Perhaps the foremost rule of ethics is that participants should not be harmed in any way, physically or mentally. The end does not justify the means. If a treatment involves any risk to participants, they should be completely informed prior to program implementation concerning the nature of the risk, and permission for participation should be acquired in writing from the potential participants themselves or from persons legally responsible for them if they are not of age.

The participant's right to privacy is also an important consideration. Collecting information on participants or observing them without their knowledge or without appropriate permission is unethical. Further, information or data which are collected, either from or about participants, should be strictly confidential, especially if data are at all personal. Individual scores should never be reported, or made public, even for an innocuous measure such as an arithmetic test. It is usually sufficient to present data in terms of group statistics. If individual scores, or raw data, need to be presented, they should not be associated with participants' names or other identifying information. The federal government has become increasingly involved in guaranteeing the individual's right to privacy. The Buckley Amendment of 1974, for example, protects the privacy of the educational records of students. Among other provisions, the act specifies that data may not usually be made available which actually identify the corresponding student unless written permission is acquired from parents. This consent must indicate what data may be disclosed, for what purposes, and to whom.

Above all, the persons involved in an evaluation must have credibility. The reader of an evaluation report must be able to believe that what the report says happened really happened; otherwise the effort is all for nothing. Falsifying data in order to make findings agree with a hypothesis, to "look good," or to get refunded is unprofessional, unethical and unforgivable.[2]

---

[2] For additional guidelines concerning the ethics and legal restrictions of evaluation activities, see Ad Hoc Committee on Ethical Standards in Psychological Research. *Ethical principles in the conducting of research with human subjects.* Washington, D.C.: American Psychological Association, 1973; Michael, J. A., & Weinberger, J. A. Federal restrictions on educational research: Protection for research participants. *Educational Researcher,* 1977, 6(1), 3–7; *and* Weinberger, J. A., & Michael, J. A. Federal restrictions on educational research. *Educational Researcher,* 1976, 5(11), 3–8.

Selection of participants

The first step in selecting participants for an evaluation study is to define the target population. The target population is the group of interest, the group to which we would like the results of the evaluation to be generalizable. The defined population has at least one characteristic which differentiates it from other groups. Examples of target populations include: all secondary-level gifted children in Utah, all primary-level culturally deprived students in the United States, and all middle-school students in Utopia County who are potential dropouts. These examples illustrate two important points about populations. First, populations may be virtually any size and may cover almost any geographical area. Second, the entire group in which we are interested does not always participate in the evaluation.

Selection of participants and members of the control group from the target population is a very important step. The "goodness" of the sample (those selected) determines the validity of the comparison to be made and the generalizability of the results. Since implementation of a program generally requires a great deal of time, energy, and money, invalid comparisons are extremely wasteful. A "good" sample is one that is representative of the population from which it was selected. Selecting such a sample is not a haphazard process, and there are several valid techniques for selecting a sample. While a given technique may be more appropriate for certain situations than for others, each of the techniques does not assure the same degree of representativeness. To illustrate the importance of representativeness, and hence generalizability, suppose a school system authorized the expenditure of funds for the purpose of trying out a proposed strategy for reducing absenteeism. Suppose participating students were all students in six high schools located in an upper-middle-class neighborhood. Even if the program were shown to be effective in these schools, there would be no assurance that the approach would work in other types of schools. In any case, we often have to compromise the ideal for the real, that is, for what is feasible, but we should always do our darnedest to use the best possible selection process.

Regardless of the specific techniques used, the steps in selection are essentially the same: identification of the population, determination of required group sizes, and selection of the sample. The degree to which the treatment and control groups are equivalent is the degree to which performance comparisons are valid. The degree to which those selected represent the entire population is the degree to which results are generalizable. It is important to note that in some cases the entire population participates in the evaluation. A portion of the population may be chosen for the program and the remainder may serve as the control group. In this case it is especially important that the program participants be carefully selected. In other cases, the entire population is involved but participation in the treatment or control group is determined on a random basis. An experimental preschool program, for example, might randomly assign all entering students to either a program class or to a traditional (control) class. In both of these instances, the population is generally not very large. Sometimes the entire population must participate in the program. A number of federally funded programs, for example, require that all eligible students participate. The target population might be defined to be all students who score in the first or second stanine on a standardized reading test, and all such students must participate in a special remedial reading program. In such cases the major evaluation problem is one of identifying a suitable control group. Several designs which deal with this problem will be discussed later in the chapter.

There are four basic sampling techniques or procedures: random sampling, stratified sampling, cluster sampling and systematic sampling. Most evaluation efforts which involve sampling use either random sampling or cluster sampling, especially the latter.

Random sampling

Random sampling is the process of selecting a sample in such a way that all individuals in the defined population have an equal and independent chance of being selected for the sample. In other words, every individual has the same probability of being selected, and selection of one individual in no way affects selection of another individual. You may recall that in physical education class the teacher occasionally formed teams by having the class line up and count off by twos, one-two-one-two and so on. With this method, you could never be on the same team as the person next to you. Selection was not independent. Whether you were on one team or another was determined by where you were in line and the team for which the person next to you was selected. If selection of teams had been random, you would have had a 50-50 chance of being on either team regardless of which team the person next to you was on. Recall that matrix sampling, a technique which is used to select a sample of students to be tested when treatment and control groups are very large, involves random sampling. Matrix sampling basically involves dividing a test into a number of subtests, using random sampling techniques on the items, and administering each subtest to a subgroup of students, also randomly selected from the total group.

Random sampling is the best single way to obtain a representative sample. No technique, not even random sampling, *guarantees* a representative sample, but the probability is higher with this procedure than with any other.

Steps in random sampling

In general, random sampling involves defining the population, identifying each member of the population, and selecting individuals for the sample on a completely chance basis. One way to do this is to write each individual's name on a separate slip of paper, place all the slips in a hat or other container, shake the container, and select slips from the container until the desired number of individuals is selected. This procedure is not really satisfactory, however. For example, if a population had 1,000 members, you would need a very large hat! A much more satisfactory approach is to use a table of random numbers. In essence, a table of random numbers selects the sample for you, each member being selected on a purely random, or chance, basis. Such tables are included in the appendices of most statistics books and some educational research books. They usually consist of columns of five-digit numbers which have been randomly generated by a computer (see table A.1 in the Appendix). Using a table of random numbers to select a sample involves the following specific steps:

1 Identify and define the population.
2 Determine the desired sample size.
3 List all members of the population.

4 Assign all individuals on the list a number in consecutive order from zero to the required number, for example 000–249 or 00–89.

5 Select an arbitrary number in the table of random numbers. (Close your eyes and point!)

6 For the selected number, look only at the appropriate number of digits, counting from the right. For example, if a population has 800 members, you only need to use the last 3 digits of the number in the table; if a population has 90 members, you only need to use the last 2 digits.

7 If the number corresponds to the number assigned to any of the individuals in the population, then that individual is in the sample. For example, if a population had 500 members and the number selected was 375, the individual assigned 375 would be in the sample; if a population had only 300 members then 375 would be ignored.

8 Go on to the next number in the column and repeat step 7.

9 Repeat step 8 until the desired number of individuals has been selected for the sample.

Once the sample has been selected, members may be randomly *assigned* to treatment and control groups (by flipping a coin, for example) if group comparison is involved.

Actually, the random selection process is not as complicated as the above explanation may have made it sound. The following example should make the procedure clear.

An example of random sampling

Suppose a large inner-city school system receives federal funds to implement a special program for potential dropouts at the middle school level. Phase I involves developing and administering a questionnaire to a sample of such students in order to determine the nature of their needs which the school is not meeting. The questionnaire includes questions dealing with interpersonal relationships, attitudes concerning their level of achievement, degree of participation in in-school and out-of-school activities, and the like. The results are to be used to formulate objectives and activities designed to meet the students' needs. The project staff sends each middle school in the system a list of the criteria which are to be used in identifying potential dropouts, such as 40 or more absences during the previous school year. Together, the teachers, guidance counselors and administrators at each school compile a list of names of identified potential dropouts. The staff then combines all the lists and there is a total of 5,000 names. The staff has determined that a random sample of 10%, or in this case 500 students, will be sufficient. We will now apply each of the nine steps described above to show how the sample would be selected:

1 The population is all 5,000 potential dropouts in middle schools in the school system.

2 The desired sample size is 10% of the 5,000 potential dropouts, or 500 students.

3 The staff has compiled a master list of the names of all 5,000 students.

4 Using the master list, the students are each assigned a number from 0000 to 4999.

5 A table of random numbers is entered at an arbitrarily selected number such as the one which is underlined in the partial column below:
88678
16752
44705
89964
09985
42420
91597

6 Since the population has 5,000 members, we are only concerned with the last 4 digits of the number, 4705.

7 There is a student assigned the number 4705, so that student is in the sample.

8 The next number in the column is 89964. The last 4 digits are 9964. Since there are only 5,000 students, there is no student assigned the number 9964. Therefore, that number is skipped.

9 Applying the above steps to the remaining numbers shown in the above column, students 2420 and 1597 are included. This procedure would be applied to members following 91597 in that column and succeeding columns until 500 students were selected.

At the completion of the process the program staff would be likely to have a representative sample of all the potential dropouts. The 500 students could be expected to appropriately represent all relevant subgroups of the population such as seventh graders and females. With random sampling, however, such representation of subgroups is probable but not guaranteed. The probable does not always occur. If you flip a quarter 100 times, the probable outcome is 50 heads and 50 tails. You may get 53 heads and 47 tails, 45 heads and 55 tails, or even 10 heads and 90 tails, but most of the time you can theoretically expect to get close to a 50–50 split. If there were some variable which the staff believed was too important to be left to chance, stratified sampling could be applied. Stratified sampling does guarantee appropriate representation on one or more selected variables. The only difference between stratified random sampling and random sampling is that members of the population are first classified into subgroups and then random selection is made from each subgroup. In the above example, the staff might decide that grade level representation must be guaranteed. In this case, the 5,000 students on the list would be classified as sixth graders, seventh graders, eighth graders, and ninth graders. A proportional number of students would then be randomly selected from each grade-level subgroup; the total number of students would still equal 500.[3]

Cluster sampling

Cluster sampling is sampling in which groups, not individuals, are randomly selected. All the members of selected groups have similar characteristics. Instead of randomly selecting fifth graders, for example, you could randomly select fifth

[3] For further discussion and examples related to this and other topics in the remainder of this chapter, see Gay, L. R. *Educational research: Competencies for analysis and application.* Columbus: Charles E. Merrill, 1976.

grade classrooms and use all the students in each classroom. Cluster sampling is more convenient when the population is very large or spread out over a wide geographic area. Often it is the only feasible method of selecting a sample. It is not always possible, for example, to obtain or compile a list of all members of the population; in such cases, it is not possible to use simple random sampling. Also, frequently program staff and evaluators do not have the control over selection of participants that they would like. For example, if your population was seventh and eighth grade science students, it is very unlikely that you would obtain administrative approval to randomly select seventh and eighth grade science students and to remove a few students from each of a number of classrooms. You would have a much better chance of securing permission to use a number of intact classrooms. Any *intact* group of similar characteristics is a *cluster*. Examples of clusters include: classrooms, schools, city blocks, and hospitals. Cluster sampling usually involves less time and less expense and is generally more convenient than random sampling though not necessarily as good, as we shall see later.

Steps in cluster sampling

The steps in cluster sampling are not very different from those involved in random sampling. The major difference, of course, is that random selection of groups (clusters), not individuals, is involved. Cluster sampling involves the following steps:

1 Identify and define the population.
2 Determine the desired sample size.
3 Identify and define a logical cluster.
4 List all clusters (or obtain a list) which comprise the population.
5 Estimate the average number of population members per cluster.
6 Determine the number of clusters needed by dividing the sample size by the estimated size of a cluster.
7 Randomly select the needed number of clusters (using a table of random numbers).
8 Include in your study all population members in each selected cluster.

Cluster sampling can be done in stages, involving selection of clusters within clusters. This process is called *multistage sampling*. For example, schools can be randomly selected and then classrooms within each selected school can be randomly selected.

One common misconception that seems to exist among novice evaluators is the belief that it is all right to randomly select only one cluster. It is not uncommon, for example, to see an evaluation plan that indicates that the population is all fifth graders in X County, that a cluster is a school, and that *one* school will be randomly selected. Yet the persons who write such plans wouldn't dream of randomly selecting only one student! The principle is the same in both cases. Keeping in mind that a good sample is representative of the population from which it is selected, it is highly unlikely that one randomly selected student could ever be representative of an entire population. Similarly, it is unlikely that one randomly selected school could be representative of all schools in a population. Thus, one would normally have to select a number of clusters in order for the results of the evaluation to be generalizable to the population. The following example should make the procedure involved in cluster sampling clear.

An example of cluster sampling

Suppose students in the Sky Falls School System have been consistently scoring way below the national norm on standardized tests of reading achievement. The decision is made to implement the Stupendous Reading Program on a limited, experimental basis in October with first graders. If subsequent May testing shows that the program is more effective than the currently used approach, it will be implemented throughout the school system the following school year. Since the Stupendous Reading Program involves procedures designed to stimulate reading activities in the home, it is decided that control group students should also be selected, as opposed to selecting treatment students and letting the unselected students serve as the control group. In this way, data can be collected concerning the home reading activities of program and nonprogram students. It is determined that there are approximately 6,000 students currently in the first grade and that a sample of 300 students per group (program and control) will provide an adequate test of the program's effectiveness. We will now apply each of the 8 steps described above to show how the sample would be selected:

1 The population is all 6,000 students currently in the first grade in the school system.
2 The desired sample size is 600 (300 per group).
3 The logical cluster is a first grade class.
4 A list of all the classes is compiled using the teachers' names as identification; there are 200 classes.
5 While there is some variation, there is an average of 30 students per class.
6 The number of clusters (classes) needed equals the desired sample size, 600, divided by the average size of a cluster, 30. Thus, the number of classes needed is $600 \div 30 = 20$.
7 Therefore, 20 of the 200 classes are randomly selected.
8 All of the students in each of the 20 classes will be part of the evaluation (20 classes, with 30 students per class, equals 600 students, the desired sample size).

The 20 selected classes would then be randomly assigned to be either program classes or control classes.

The advantages of cluster sampling are evident, but cluster sampling does have several drawbacks. For one thing, the chances are usually greater of selecting a sample which is not representative in some way of the population. For example, suppose our population were all fifth graders in 10 schools (each school having an average of 120 students in 4 classes of 30 students each), and we wanted a sample of 120 students. There are any number of ways we might select our sample. For example, we could: (a) randomly select one school and use all the fifth graders in that school, (b) randomly select 2 classes from each of 2 schools, or (c) randomly select 120 students from the 10 schools. In any of these ways we would wind up with 120 students, but our sample would probably not be equally "good" in each case. In case a we would have students from only one school. It is very likely that this school would be different from the other nine in some significant way (e.g. socioeconomic level or racial composition). In case *b* we would be doing a little better, but we would still only have 2 of the 10 schools represented. Only in case *c* would we have a chance of selecting a sample containing students from all or most of the schools, and the classes within those schools. If random sampling was not feasible, selecting two classes from each of two schools would be preferable to selecting all the students in one school. Actually, if cluster sampling were used, it would be even better to select one class each from four of the schools. One way we could attempt to compensate for the loss of representativeness associated with cluster sampling would be to select more than four classes. As in most cases, however, the number of classes selected would be not just a matter of desirability but also of feasibility.

Another problem is that commonly used inferential statistics are not appropriate for analyzing data resulting from a study using cluster sampling. Such statistics generally require random sampling. Randomly assigning treatments to existing groups (clusters) is not enough; the groups must be randomly formed. The statistics which are available and appropriate for cluster sampling are generally less sensitive to differences which may exist between groups. Thus, one should carefully weigh the advantages and disadvantages of cluster sampling before choosing this method of sampling.

There is one more type of nonrandom sampling with which you should be familiar: *systematic sampling*. Although systematic sampling is not used very often, it is appropriate in certain situations and is the only feasible way in some instances to select a sample. Basically, systematic sampling is analogous to counting off one-two-one-two in gym class. Given the size of the population, and the desired sample size, a count-off number is determined. For example, suppose you want to send questionnaires to 10% of the teachers in Lackofunion County to see how they feel about the extended school day program which was implemented in the fall. If there are 7,000 teachers listed in a county directory and you want a sample of 700 (10%), all you have to do is to start at some random name near the beginning of the directory and select every 10th name (7,000 ÷ 700 = 10) until you have your sample. That is systematic sampling.

Group size and selection bias

A frequently asked question concerning sampling is, How large should the sample be? The answer is - as large as feasible. While the answer is not very comforting, the question is a difficult one. If the sample is too small, it may not be representative of the population and the results of the evaluation may not be generalizable to the population. The results may hold only for the sample and may not be the same results that would have been obtained if the entire population was used. Another way of looking at it is that if the sample is not large enough, the wrong conclusions may be reached concerning the evaluation question of interest. In general, the *minimum* sample size believed to be acceptable depends upon the nature of the evaluation question. For questionnaires, interviews, and observations, a sample of 10% of the population is considered minimum. For smaller populations, 20% may be required. For evaluations which involve group comparisons, a minimum of 15 persons per group will give *some* degree of confidence that conclusions reached concerning differences between groups are valid. The "minimums" noted above are just that, however, minimums. If it is at all possible for you to select larger samples, you should do so. Using samples larger than the minimums is especially important in certain situations. For example, if treatment effects are small, group differences might not "show up" if the samples are too small.[4]

A large sample size, however, does not guarantee a good, or representative, sample. Even large samples can be biased. If samples are biased, so are results. A major source of bias is the use of volunteers. Volunteers are bound to be different from nonvolunteers. They may be more motivated, for example, or more insecure. Since a population is composed of volunteers and nonvolunteers, the results of an effort using volunteers are not generalizable to the entire population, only to other volunteers. For example, suppose you want to evaluate the effectiveness of a series of human relations workshops with respect to the behavior of teachers in the classroom. You circulate a memo in all the schools indicating that all interested teachers should attend a meeting Monday after school, and that workshops will be held on 10 consecutive Monday afternoons. Sixty teachers show up. You know right off the bat that these 60 are not representative of all the teachers! They may, for example, be the most gung ho, enthusiastic teachers in the system. You then randomly assign the 60 teachers to two groups of 30, one group to participate in the workshops now (the treatment group), and one group to be told that due to the overwhelming response, they will have to wait for the next series of workshops (the control group). The workshop teachers are to meet every Monday for 10 Mondays, for 2 hours per session; the control teachers are to do nothing out of the ordinary. Since they are volunteers, workshop teachers feel free to drop out at any time. Control teachers have no need to drop out since no demands are being made on their time. Workshop teachers, on the other hand, might drop out after one or more sessions, feeling that it is "too much for them." Suppose at the termination of the last workshop, only 15 of the original 30 workshop teachers remain. Observation of the classroom behavior of the 15 workshop teachers and the 30 control teachers indicates that workshop participants as a group are more accepting, warm, and so forth, than control teachers. Could you then conclude that the workshops were effective? Cer-tain-ly not! In essence you would be comparing the behavior of those in the control group with those members of the workshop group who chose to remain. This latter group might well be more motivated, open and enthusiastic as a group than the control group; the less motivated teachers dropped out! It would be very difficult to determine how much of the 15 teachers' behavior was due to the workshops and how much was due to natural personality characteristics. Because of similar problems, nonvolunteers should not be used as controls for a group made up of persons who volunteered to participate in a program or project.

Threats to validity

Any uncontrolled extraneous variables which affect posttest performance are threats to the validity of an evaluation study. Conclusions and decisions are only valid if results obtained are due only to the treatment and control conditions and if

---

[4] There are relatively precise statistical techniques which can be used to estimate required sample sizes for group comparisons. For discussion of these techniques, see: Li, J. C. R. *Statistical inference I.* Ann Arbor, Mich.: Edwards Brothers, 1969.

the results are generalizable. Even if an effort is locally funded and all members of the population participate, generalizability is still an important concern. We want to have some confidence that the results obtained for a current group of students are generalizable, or applicable, to future students with similar characteristics. The two conditions which must be met are referred to as internal validity and external validity.

Internal validity refers to the condition where observed differences between the groups on the dependent variable (different posttest performance) are a direct result of manipulation of the independent variable (treatment and control conditions), not some other variable. In other words, the results are due to the intervention and not something else. If someone can come up with a plausible alternative explanation for your results, your evaluation study was not internally valid. To use a former example, if older student tutors had worked with the participating students for five extra hours per week and if the tutored students outperformed the control students, then amount of instructional time would be a plausible alternate explanation for the results. The degree to which results are attributable to the treatment and control conditions is the degree to which the group comparisons are valid.

External validity refers to the condition where results are generalizable, or applicable, to groups and environments other than those actually involved in the evaluation. In other words, the results, the confirmed cause-effect relationship between the treatment and posttest performance, can be expected to be reconfirmed with other groups in other settings at other times, as long as the conditions are similar to those of the original effort. If a special program for gifted sixth graders is evaluated, the results should be applicable to other groups of gifted sixth graders. If results were not generalizable to any other situation outside of the original setting, then no one could profit from anyone else's evaluation. An evaluation study can only contribute to educational practice if there is some assurance that confirmed effects are replicable and likely to occur at other times and places with other groups.

Unfortunately, there is a "catch-22" which complicates the evaluator's life. Maximization of internal validity requires exercise of very rigid controls over participants and conditions. The more a situation is controlled, however, the less realistic it becomes, the less generalizable. On the other hand, the more natural a setting becomes, the more difficult it becomes to control extraneous variables. It is very difficult, for example, to conduct a well-controlled comparison study in actual classrooms. Thus, one must strive for a balance between control and realism. If a choice is involved, one should err on the side of too much control rather than too little. An evaluation study which is not internally valid is worthless.

In the pages to come many threats to internal and external validity will be discussed. Some extraneous variables are definite threats to internal validity, some are definite threats to external validity, and some may be threats to both. How potential threats are classified, or labeled, is not the important thing. What is important is that you be aware of their existence and make efforts to control for them. As you read, you may begin to feel that there are just too many of them to control all at the same time. The task is not as formidable as it may at first appear, however. As you will see later, there are a number of designs which control many threats for you. All you have to do is select a "good" design and go from there. Also, each of the threats to be discussed is only a potential threat which may not be a problem in a particular evaluation study.

Threats to internal validity

Probably the most authoritative source regarding design and threats to validity is the work of Donald Campbell and Julian Stanley.[5] Campbell and Stanley have identified eight major threats to internal validity, or to put it another way, eight major sources of internal invalidity.

History

History refers to the occurrence of any incidental event which was not planned for but which may affect performance on the posttest. The longer the program is in effect, the more likely it is that history may be a problem. Happenings such as a bomb scare, an epidemic of influenza, or even current events are examples of history. As another example, if you implement a new science program in September, and if at approximately the same time the school board authorizes the hiring of paraprofessional assistants for all science classes, the presence of the new assistants constitutes "history." While you have no control over the occurrence of such events, you can select a design which controls *for* their occurrence.

Maturation

Maturation refers to physical or mental changes which may occur within participants over a period of time, which may affect their performance on a posttest. Especially in programs or projects which last for longer periods of time, participants may become, for example, older, more coordinated, unmotivated, anxious, or just plain bored. Maturation is more of a threat in some efforts than in others. It would be much more likely to be a problem, for example, in the evaluation of the effectiveness of a psychomotor training program than in the evaluation of a new math program, especially if preadolescent students were involved: such students are typically undergoing rapid biological changes. As with history, you cannot control the occurrence of maturation but you can control *for* its occurrence.

Testing

Testing refers to improved scores on a posttest which are a result of participants' having taken a pretest. In other words, taking a pretest may improve performance on a posttest, regardless of whether there is any treatment or instruction in between. Testing is more likely to be a threat when the time between testings is short. A pretest taken in September is not likely to affect performance on a posttest taken in June. This phenomenon is also more likely to occur in some situations than in others. When a pretest measures factual information which can be recalled, posttest performance may be improved. Taking a pretest on algebraic equa-

---

[5] Campbell, D. T., & Stanley, J. C. *Experimental and quasi-experimental designs for research.* Chicago: Rand McNally, 1971.

tions, on the other hand, is much less likely to improve performance on a similar posttest. One obvious way to control for testing is to use a design which does not involve a pretest. Another way to attempt to control for testing is to use alternate forms, one form for the pretest and another for the posttest. Testing is a factor which should at least be considered when selecting both the measuring instrument and the evaluation design.

Instrumentation

Instrumentation refers to unreliability, or inconsistency, in measuring instruments which may result in an invalid assessment of performance. Instrumentation may occur in several different ways. If two different tests are used for pretesting and posttesting and the tests are not of equal difficulty, instrumentation may occur. If the posttest is more difficult, it may fail to show improvement which is actually present; if the posttest is less difficult, it may indicate an improvement which is not present. If data are collected through observation, observers may not be observing or evaluating behavior in the same way at the end of the program as at the beginning. In fact, if they are aware of the nature of the evaluation, they may unconsciously tend to see and record what they know is expected. If data are collected through the use of a mechanical device such as an electroencephalograph, it may be suffering from some malfunction which results in inaccurate measurement. Thus, you must take care in selecting tests, caution observers, and check mechanical devices. In addition, you can select a design which controls for this factor.

Statistical regression

Statistical regression usually occurs when participants are selected on the basis of their extreme scores on some test and refers to the tendency of persons who score highest on a test (e.g. a pretest) to score lower on a retest (e.g. a posttest), and the tendency of those who score lowest on a test to score higher on a retest. The tendency is for scores to regress to, or move toward, the mean (average), or expected, score. The many special programs that are designed for disadvantaged or low-ability students provide us with an example. Suppose you wished to determine the effectiveness of a remedial reading program in improving the reading skills of poor readers. You might administer a 100-item, 4-alternative multiple-choice reading test. You might then select for the remedial program some number of students, those students with the lowest scores. Now suppose a number of the tested students did not know the correct answer to any of the questions and guessed on every single question. With 100 items and 4 choices for each item, a student would be expected to receive a score of 25 just by guessing. Some students, however, just due to rotten guessing, would receive scores much lower than 25, and other students, just by chance, would receive scores much higher than 25. If they were given the test a second time, *without any instruction intervening,* their expected score would still be 25. Thus students who scored very low the first time would be expected to have a second score closer to 25, and students who scored very high the first time would also be expected to score closer to 25 the second time. If students were selected because of their very low initial scores, they would be expected to do better on a posttest, regardless of the program. You might erroneously attribute their improved scores to the remedial program. You must therefore be aware of statistical regression and if at all possible select a design which controls for this phenomenon.

Differential selection

Differential selection occurs when already formed groups are used (as in cluster sampling) and refers to the fact that these groups may be different before the implementation even begins; this initial difference may at least partially account for posttest differences. For example, if you receive permission to use students in a given set of English classes as participants in a new program, you have no guarantee that classes are at all equivalent, or equivalent to the English classes not being used which are serving as controls. If your luck is really bad, all the treatment classes might be honors classes; it would not be too surprising if they did better on the posttest! Thus, using already formed groups should be avoided if possible. If it is the only feasible approach, then treatment and control groups should be selected which are as similar as possible and a pretest should be administered to verify initial equivalence.

Mortality

First, let me make it perfectly clear that mortality does not mean that participants die! *Mortality* is more likely to occur in longer evaluation studies and refers to the fact that persons who drop out of a group may share a characteristic such that their absence has a significant effect on the posttest results. Those who drop out may be less motivated, for example; this is especially a problem when volunteers are used. You cannot assume that persons drop out for random reasons, and if possible, you should select a design which controls for mortality.

Selection-maturation interaction, etc.

The "etc." means that selection may also interact with factors such as history and testing, but *selection-maturation interaction* is most common. What this means is that if already formed groups are used, one group may profit more (or less) from a treatment, or have an initial advantage (or disadvantage), because of maturation, history, or testing factors. Suppose, for example, that you received permission to use eight civics classes which contained average ability students and were apparently equivalent on all relevant variables, and you randomly assigned four of them to be project participants and four of them to be control classes. As luck would have it, however, two of the project classes were taught by Mr. Chips and he had already covered many of the topics included in your materials (remember history?). Unbeknownst to you, the project classes as a group would have a definite advantage to begin with, and it might very well be this initial advantage, rather than your treatment which caused posttest differences. Thus, you must select a design which controls for this potential problem or make every effort to determine if it is operating.

Threats to external validity

There are also several major threats to external validity which potentially limit, or make questionable, generalization of results to other groups and settings.

Pretest-treatment interaction

Pretest-treatment interaction occurs when participants respond or react differently to a treatment because they have been pretested. A pretest may sensitize or alert them to the nature of the treatment. The treatment effect may be different than it would have been had participants not been pretested. Thus results are only generalizable to other pretested groups. The results are not even generalizable to the unpretested population from which the sample was selected. This potential problem is more or less serious depending upon the participants, the nature of the tests, the nature of the treatment, and the duration of the effort. Evaluation studies involving attitude change, for example, are especially susceptible to this problem. Campbell and Stanley have illustrated the effect by pointing out the probable lack of comparability of a group that viewed the film *Gentlemen's Agreement* (which exposes ethnic prejudice) right after taking a lengthy pretest dealing with anti-Semitism, and another group viewing the movie without a pretest.[6] Individuals in the unpretested group could quite conceivably enjoy the movie as a good love story and be unaware that it deals with a social issue. Pretested individuals would be unlikely to miss a connection between the pretest and the message of the film. On the other hand, taking a pretest on algebraic algorithms would probably affect very little (if at all) a group's responsiveness to a new method of teaching algebra. The pretest-treatment interaction would also be expected to be minimized in studies involving very young children, who would probably not see a connection between a pretest and a subsequent treatment, and in studies conducted over relatively long periods of time. Any effects of a pretest taken in September would probably have worn off or been diminished greatly by the time a posttest was given in June. For some studies, however, the potential interactive effect of a pretest is a more serious consideration. In such cases you should select a design which either controls for the effect or allows you to determine the magnitude of the effect.

Selection-treatment interaction

Selection-treatment interaction is similar to the problem of differential selection associated with internal invalidity and also occurs when participants are not randomly selected for treatments. Interaction effects aside, the very fact that participants are not randomly selected from a population severely limits one's ability to generalize since representativeness of the sample is in question. Even if intact groups are randomly selected, the possibility exists that the treatment group is in some important way different from the control group and/or from the larger population.

[6] See footnote 5.

This nonrepresentativeness of groups may also result in a *selection-treatment interaction* whereby the results hold only for the groups involved and are not representative of the treatment effect in the intended population. While the selection-treatment interaction is a definite weakness associated with several of the poorer designs, it is also an uncontrolled variable associated with the designs which involve randomization. One's accessible population is often a far cry from one's target population. The way in which a given population becomes available to an evaluator may make generalizability of findings questionable, no matter how internally valid an experiment may be. As Campbell and Stanley point out, if a project is turned down by nine school systems and accepted by a tenth, the accepting system is bound to be different from the other nine and from the population of schools to which the evaluator would like to generalize.[7] Administrative and instructional personnel in the volunteering school in all probability have "higher morale, less fear of being inspected, and more zeal for improvement" than personnel in an average school. It is therefore recommended that the evaluator report problems involved in acquiring subjects, including the number of times he or she was turned down, so that the reader can judge the seriousness of a possible selection-treatment interaction.

Specificity of variables

Like selection-treatment interaction, specificity is a threat to generalizability *regardless of the design used. Specificity of variables* refers to the fact that a given evaluation study is conducted with a specific kind of participant, using specific measuring instruments, at a specific time, under a specific set of circumstances. For example, student tutors might be found to be effective *when* upper-middle-class second graders are participants and *when* achievement is measured using the Baloney Achievement Test. To deal with this issue, the evaluator must (1) operationally define variables in a way which has meaning outside of the evaluation setting, and (2) be careful in stating conclusions and generalizations. Defining achievement in geometry, for example, solely in terms of memorization of definitions would certainly not help the generalizability of the evaluation since most geometry teachers measure achievement primarily in terms of problem solving. Also, an evaluator would most definitely be overgeneralizing if, based on an evaluation involving fourth-graders, his or her report concluded that a program was effective for elementary-age students.

Reactive arrangements

Reactive arrangements refers to a number of factors associated with the way in which the program or project is executed and the feelings and attitudes of the participants involved. In an effort to maintain a high degree of control, the evaluator may create an environment which is highly artificial and which hinders generalizability of findings to other settings. Another type of reactive arrangement occurs when participants know they are involved in an evaluation or feel they are in some way receiving "special" attention. The effect that such knowledge or feel-

[7] See footnote 5.

ings can have was dramatically demonstrated at the Hawthorne Plant of the West-
ern Electric Company in Chicago years ago. As part of their research on working
conditions, researchers investigated the relationship between light intensity and
worker output. The researchers increased light intensity and production went up.
They increased it some more and production went up some more. The brighter the
place became, the more production rose. As a check, the researchers decreased illumination, and guess what—production went up! The darker it got, the more the
workers produced. The researchers soon realized that it was the attention the
workers were receiving, and not the illumination, that was affecting production.
To this day, the term Hawthorne effect is used to describe any situation in which
behavior is affected not by the treatment per se but by knowledge of participation.

A related effect is known as the John Henry effect. Folk hero John Henry,
you may recall, was a "steeldrivin' man" who worked for a railroad. When he
heard that a steam drill was going to replace him and his fellow steel drivers, he
challenged, and set out to beat, the machine. Through tremendous effort he did
manage to win the ensuing contest, dropping dead at the finish line. This phenomenon has been shown to operate in evaluation and research studies. If for any
reason control groups or their teachers feel threatened or challenged by being in
competition with a new program or approach, they may outdo themselves and
perform way beyond what would normally be expected—even if it "kills" them![8]
When this effect occurs, the treatment under evaluation does not appear to be very
effective since posttest performance of program participants is not much (if at all)
better than that of control participants.

A similar phenomenon in medical research resulted in the placebo effect,
which is in some ways the antidote for the Hawthorne and John Henry effects. In
medical research it was discovered that any "medication" could make subjects feel
better, even sugar and water. To counteract this effect, the placebo approach was
developed in which half of the subjects receive the true medication and half receive a placebo (sugar and water, for example); this fact is of course not known to
the subjects. The application of the placebo effect in evaluation is that all groups
involved should *appear* to be treated the same. Participants should not feel special
if they are in the program group nor should they feel shortchanged if they are in
the control group. Suppose, for example, a number of ninth grade classes are involved in the evaluation of a special vocational career awareness program developed to increase knowledge of vocational career options and to promote positive
attitudes toward a vocational career. If half of the classes are to be excused periodically from their classes in order to view a series of films dealing with various vocational careers, then the control classes also should be excused and shown some
other films whose content is unrelated to vocational careers (*Great Moments in
Sports* would do!). As an added control, you might have all the classes told that
there are a number of movies and that eventually all of them will see all of the
movies. In other words, it should *appear* as if *all* students are doing the same
thing.

Another related type of reactive arrangement is the novelty effect. The
novelty effect refers to increased interest, motivation, or involvement on the part
of participants simply because they are doing something different. In other words,
a treatment may be effective because it is different not better. To counteract the

---

[8] See, for example, Saretsky, G. The OEO P.C. experiment and the John Henry Effect. *Phi Delta Kappan*,
1972, *53*, 579–581.

novelty effect, the treatment should be conducted over a period of time sufficient to allow the "newness" to wear off. This is especially true if the treatment involves activities very different from the participants' usual routine.

Contamination and bias

Contamination occurs when the outcome of the evaluation is affected because the program staff, teachers, or evaluators are familiar with the participants. These people may unintentionally influence participants' behavior or be subjective in evaluating their behavior. The contamination is similar to that associated with the halo effect in that knowledge of a person's behavior in one situation may color judgment concerning his or her behavior in another. If you know Ronnie Shining-star is a good student, you may tend to rate his group leadership ability a little higher than it actually is. Further, expectations concerning outcomes may actually contribute to producing those outcomes. Knowing which participants are in which group may cause one to be unintentionally biased in evaluating their performance. Rosenthal has demonstrated the bias effect in a number of interesting studies. In one study, two groups of graduate students were each given rats and instructions to train the rats to perform a discrimination-learning task.[9] One group of graduate students was told that due to selective breeding their rats were "maze-bright" and would learn quickly and well. The other graduate students were told that their rats were "maze-dull." In reality both sets of rats were just average, run-of-the-mill rats which had been randomly assigned to the two groups of graduate students. But lo and behold, the "smart" rats significantly outperformed the "dumb" rats! As Tallmadge points out, the analogy to educational evaluation is clear.[10] If the same teachers establish the objectives, design the curriculum or program, teach the students, know which students are treatment students and which are control students, develop the tests, and administer the posttests, then the treatment students are bound to do better. Factors such as unconscious (or conscious) teaching to the test and tester bias are very likely to have an influence on results. The warning is clear. As a general rule, anyone with a vested interest of any kind in the program under evaluation should not be directly involved in its implementation or assessment of its effectiveness. Further, program staff and/or evaluation personnel should avoid communicating outcome expectations to anyone who is involved in implementation or data collection.

Evaluation designs

The validity of an evaluation, as we said, is a function of the degree to which extraneous variables are controlled. If such variables are not controlled, it is difficult to evaluate the effectiveness of a treatment and the generalizability of effects. The term *confounding* is sometimes used to refer to the fact that the effects of the treatment may be interfered with, or "confounded," by extraneous variables so that it

[9] Rosenthal, R., & Fode, K. L. The effect of experimenter bias on the performance of the albino rat. *Behavioral Science*, 1963, *8*, 183–189.
[10] See footnote 1.

is difficult to separate the effects of the treatment variable from those of the extraneous variables. This is what design is all about—control of extraneous variables. Good designs control many sources of invalidity, poor designs control few. Two types of extraneous variables in need of control were previously identified: participant variables and environmental variables. Participant variables include organismic variables and intervening variables. *Organismic variables*, as the term implies, are characteristics of the participants or organism (e.g. sex), which cannot be directly controlled but which can be controlled *for*. *Intervening variables*, as the term suggests, are variables which intervene between the treatment and the posttest (such as anxiety or boredom), which cannot be directly observed or controlled but which can also be controlled *for*.

Control of extraneous variables

Randomization is the best single way to attempt to control for many extraneous variables all at the same time. The logical implication of the above statement is that randomization should be used whenever possible: participants should be randomly selected from a population whenever possible, participants should be randomly assigned to groups whenever possible, treatments should be randomly assigned to groups whenever possible, and anything else you can think of should be randomly assigned if possible! Recall that random selection means selection by pure chance and is usually accomplished using a table of random numbers. Random assignment means assignment by pure chance and is usually accomplished by flipping a coin if two groups are involved, (heads you are in the treatment group, tails you are in the control group) or by rolling a die if more than two groups are involved.

Randomization is effective in creating equivalent representative groups which are essentially the same on all relevant variables thought of, and probably even a few not thought of. The rationale is that if participants are assigned at random to groups, there is no reason to believe that the groups are greatly different in any systematic way. Thus, the groups would be expected to perform essentially the same on the posttest *if* the independent variable makes no difference; therefore, if the groups perform differently at the end of the study, the difference can be attributed to the treatment, or independent variable. The larger the groups, the more confidence we can have in the effectiveness of randomization. In addition to equating groups on variables such as intelligence, randomization also equalizes groups on environmental variables. Teachers, for example, can be randomly assigned to groups so that the treatment groups will not have all the "Carmel Kandee" teachers or all the "Hester Hartless" teachers (and likewise the control groups). Clearly, you should use as much randomization as possible. If participants cannot be randomly selected, those available should at least be randomly assigned. If participants cannot be randomly assigned to groups, then at least treatment condition should be randomly assigned to the existing groups.

In addition to randomization, there are other ways to control for extraneous variables. Certain environmental variables, for example, can be controlled by holding them constant for all groups. Recall the student tutor example. Instructional time was an important variable that had to be held constant, or be kept the same, for the two groups. Other such variables which might need to be held constant include learning materials, meeting place and time (students might be more alert in the morning than in the afternoon), and years of experience of participating teachers. Controlling participant variables is critical. If the groups are not the same to start with, you have not even given yourself a fighting chance. Regardless of whether groups can be randomly formed, there are a number of techniques at your disposal which can be used to try to equalize groups.

Matching

Matching is a technique for equating groups on one or more variables which have been identified as being highly related to posttest performance. One approach to matching involves random assignment of pair members, one member to the treatment group and one member to the control group. In other words, for each of the available participants we attempt to find another participant with the same or a similar score on the control variable (the variable on which participants are being matched). If we are matching on sex, obviously the "match" must be of the same sex, not a similar sex. If we are matching on variables such as pretest scores or IQ, however, the "similar score" concept makes sense. For example, if we matched on IQ, then a participant in one group with an IQ of 130 would have a match in the other group, a person with an IQ at or near 130. Unless the available number of participants is very large, it is unreasonable to try to make exact matches. Thus, we might decide that IQ scores within 10 points of each other constitute an acceptable match. As each matched pair is identified, one member of the pair is randomly assigned to one group and the other member to the other group. If a person does not have a suitable match, she or he is excluded from the evaluation. Such a person may become a member of one of the groups, but his or her posttest score will not be included in the analysis of results. The resulting matched groups are identical or very similar with respect to the identified variable. If randomization is not possible, as when existing groups are involved (remember cluster sampling?), matching is done in a slightly different way. For each participant in one group you identify a participant in the second group with the same or a similar score on the control variable. Again, if a participant in either group does not have a suitable match, he or she is excluded from analysis of results.

A major problem with matching is that there are invariably persons who do not have a match. This fact may cost the program many participants, especially if matching is attempted on two or more variables (imagine trying to find a match for a male student with an IQ near 140 and a GPA between 1.00 and 1.5!). One way to combat loss of participants is to match less closely. We might decide that two students with IQ scores within 20 points of each other constitute an acceptable match. This procedure may increase participants but it tends to defeat the purpose of matching. A related procedure, which can be used when randomization is feasible, is to rank all of the participants from highest to lowest based on their scores on the control variable. The first two participants (those with the highest and the next highest scores) are the first pair, no matter how far apart their scores are. One member is randomly assigned to one group and one member to the other group. The next two participants (those with the third and fourth highest scores) are the next pair, and so on. The major advantage of this approach is that no participants are lost; the major disadvantage is that it is a lot less precise than matching by pairs. Advanced statistical procedures, such as analysis of covariance (to be discussed shortly), and the availability of computer programs to compute such statistics have greatly reduced the use of matching.

Comparing homogeneous groups and subgroups

Another way of controlling an extraneous variable is to compare groups which are homogeneous with respect to that variable. For example, if IQ was an identified extraneous variable and if randomization was possible, you might select a group of students with IQs between 85 and 115 (the average IQ range). You would then randomly assign half of the selected students to the treatment group and half to the control group. If randomization was not possible, you might select only groups containing students of average IQ. Of course, this procedure also lowers the number of participants and additionally restricts the generalizability of the findings. Further, if random assignment is possible, using only a homogeneous subgroup really only makes sense if you want an additional guarantee concerning group equality on the control variable.

A similar but more satisfactory approach is to form subgroups within each group which represent all levels of the control variable. For example, available participants might be divided into high (116 and above), average (85–115), and low (84 and below) IQ subgroups. Half of the selected participants from each of the subgroups would then be randomly assigned to the treatment group and half to the control group. Incidentally, the procedure just described illustrates stratified sampling. If randomization was not possible and existing groups were being used, and if the groups were large enough, each existing group might be divided into high, average, and low IQ subgroups. The comparable subgroups in each group could be compared, high IQ with high IQ and so on. In addition to controlling for an extraneous variable, this technique has the added advantage of permitting us to see if the treatment affects performance differently at different levels of the control variable. If this question is of interest, however, the best approach is not to do several separate analyses but instead to build the control variable right into the design and analyze the results with a statistical technique called factorial analysis of variance.[11]

Analysis of covariance

The analysis of covariance is a statistical method for equating groups on one or more variables. In essence, analysis of covariance adjusts scores on a posttest for initial differences on some other variable, such as pretest scores, IQ, readiness, or aptitude (assuming that performance on the "other variable" is related to performance on the posttest). Although analysis of covariance is useful, and can be used when groups are not randomly formed, its use is most appropriate when randomization is used. Despite randomization, for example, it might be found that two groups differ significantly in terms of pretest scores. Analysis of covariance can be used to "correct," or adjust, posttest scores for initial pretest differences. Unfortunately, the situation for which covariance is least appropriate is the situation for which it is most often used—when nonrandomly formed groups are involved. Calculation of an analysis of covariance is quite a complex and lengthy procedure, and you would not want to do one by hand. Fortunately, com-

---

[11] Discussion of factorial designs and factorial analysis of variance is beyond the scope of this text. Most educational research texts contain descriptions of factorial designs and most statistics texts present the procedures for conducting a factorial analysis.

puter programs are readily available which can do the work for you if you know how to use them (or know somebody who knows!).

Types of designs

A selected design dictates to a great extent the specific procedures of an evaluation study. Selection of a given design dictates such factors as whether there will be a control group, whether participants will be randomly assigned to groups, whether each group will be pretested, and how resulting data will be analyzed. Depending upon the particular combination of such factors represented, different designs are appropriate for answering different kinds of questions and testing different types of hypotheses. Also, designs vary widely in the degree to which they control the various threats to internal and external validity. In selecting a design, you must first determine which designs are appropriate for your study, for answering your evaluation question or testing your hypothesis. You then determine which of those that are appropriate are also *feasible* given any constraints under which you may be operating. If, for example, you must use existing groups, a number of designs will automatically be eliminated. From the designs which are appropriate and feasible, you select the one which controls the most sources of internal and external invalidity. In other words, you select the best design you possibly can which will yield the data you need to answer your question or test your hypothesis.

As noted previously, there is considerable disagreement concerning whether evaluation studies should be based on research designs. The "con" argument is that research and evaluation have different purposes and that the real-world settings characteristic of evaluation essentially preclude the control required by good research designs. The "pro" argument is that there is often a fine line between research and evaluation, especially when group comparisons for the purpose of establishing cause-effect relationships are involved. Further, many research studies are also conducted in real-world settings and are subject to the same control problems faced by evaluators. The question really is not *whether* to use a research design but rather *when* to use a research design, and the answer is: whenever it is possible and feasible to do so.

There are many evaluation situations which could, with a little effort, utilize a good experimental research design. For other situations, in which randomization is out of the question, there are several quasi-experimental designs which can be applied, designs which provide controls not possible with a nonresearch design. There are, however, many situations which preclude use of any respectable research design. A number of programs, for example, require (legally or ethically) that any student who meets a given set of criteria *must* participate in program activities. In these instances the entire population is the treatment group, and the evaluator's problem is to find a suitable control group. For such evaluation situations, special models have been developed which use inventive means to estimate what posttest performance would have been without the treatment. One requirement that is common to all control groups, however, is that the dates of their pretesting and posttesting must coincide, exactly or approximately, with the dates of pretesting and posttesting of the treatment group; otherwise, performance comparisons are not fair. For example, if both groups are pretested in mid-September, but the control group is posttested the first week in April and the treatment group the first week in May, the treatment group has an advantage—

an extra month of instruction. Different testing dates for the groups may result in overestimates or underestimates of treatment effects.

In the pages to follow we will discuss both research designs and special evaluation models. The major concept to keep in mind is that you should select and apply the best design or model that is feasible in your situation. If you can use a true experimental design, do so. If that is not possible but application of a quasi-experimental design is, use one of them. If neither is possible, then do the best you can; of the designs and models that are feasible, select the best one. In this world, all we can do is our best! Some of the designs to be discussed are really awful. They are presented here only so that you will know what *not* to do, and why.

Research designs

Two types of research designs will be discussed: experimental designs and ex post facto designs. *Experimental research designs,* which involve manipulation of the independent variable, include true experimental designs, quasi-experimental designs, and pre-experimental designs. There are many more experimental designs than those which will be presented here. Only those which have a likelihood of being used (rightly or wrongly) in an evaluation have been selected for discussion. Ex post facto designs, as the name implies, are designs which involve after-the-fact comparisons, i.e. trying to establish the cause, or reason, for an observed effect.

True experimental designs

No design controls for *all* sources of invalidity, but true experimental designs do the best job. As figure 14.1 indicates, all true experimental designs have one characteristic in common which none of the other designs has—random assignment of participants to groups. Ideally, participants should be randomly selected and randomly assigned. However, to qualify as a true experimental design, at least random assignment must be involved.

The pretest-posttest control group design. This design involves at least two groups formed by random assignment (R). Both groups are pretested (O), one group receives a new, or unusual, treatment (X), and both groups are posttested (O).[12] Depending upon the size of the groups, each group may be subdivided, to form a number of classrooms for example. Posttest scores are compared to determine the effectiveness of the treatment. This design may be symbolized as shown in figure 14.1 or as follows (each line represents a group):

$$R \quad O \quad X_1 \quad O$$
$$R \quad O \quad X_2 \quad O$$

---

[12] Although a number of measures may be administered before a program begins (for stratified sampling purposes, for example), the term "pretest" usually refers to a test of the dependent variable (which is also measured by the posttest).

This representation makes it clear that both groups are being exposed to some form or some level of the independent variable; one group is receiving the new, or unusual treatment (the program group), and one group is receiving the usual, or traditional (the control group). Expressing the design this way makes many people feel more comfortable since the other way it looks as if the control group is doing nothing. The pretest-posttest control group design may be expanded to include any number of groups, but this is rarely necessary in evaluation studies.

The combination of random assignment and the presence of a pretest and a control group serve to control for all sources of internal invalidity. Random assignment controls for regression and selection factors; the pretest controls for mortality; randomization and the control group control for maturation; and the control group controls for history, testing, and instrumentation. Testing, for example, is controlled because if pretesting leads to higher posttest scores, the advantage should be equal for both the treatment and control groups. The only definite weakness with this design is a possible interaction between the pretest and the treatment which may make the results generalizable only to other pretested groups. As discussed before, the seriousness of this potential weakness depends upon factors such as the nature of the pretest, the nature of the treatment, and the length of the study. It is more likely to occur with reactive measures such as attitude scales and in short studies. When this design is used, you should assess and report the likelihood of pretest-treatment interaction. You might indicate, for example, that possible pretest interaction was believed to be minimized by the nonreactive nature of the pretest (chemical equations) and by the length of the program (nine months). Of course the existence of a control group (in this and other designs) permits the occurrence of events which are group-specific, events such as a power failure or a violent storm. These events, referred to as within-group, or intrasession, history, are more likely to occur when groups are "treated" at different times.

There are three basic ways in which scores can be analyzed in order to determine the effectiveness of the treatment and to answer the evaluation question or test the evaluation hypothesis; one of them is clearly inappropriate, one is not very appropriate, and one is clearly the most appropriate. One approach to analyzing scores is to compare the pretest to the posttest scores within each group. If the treatment group improves significantly but not the control group, it is concluded that the treatment was effective. This approach is inappropriate because the real question is whether the treatment group performs better than the control group. Thus the appropriate comparison is of the posttest scores of each group. If we find that both groups have improved significantly (for example, each group's average posttest reading score is significantly higher than its pretest reading score after nine months of different instruction) this still does not indicate whether one group is significantly better than the other. We would expect both groups to improve their reading in nine months, so the question involves whether the treatment has done a better job. A second approach to analyzing scores is to compute gain, or difference, scores for each participant (posttest score minus pretest score) and then to compare the average gain of the treatment group with the average gain of the control group. There are problems with gain scores, however. For one thing, all students do not have the same "room" to gain. On a 100-item test, who has really achieved more, a student who goes from a pretest score of 80 to a posttest score of 99 (a gain of 19) or a student who goes from a pretest score of 20 to a posttest score of 70 (a gain of 50)? The third approach, and the one usually recommended, is to simply compare the posttest scores of the two groups. The pretest is

Designs	Sources of Invalidity								
	Internal								External[13]
	History	Maturation	Testing	Instrumentation	Statistical Regression	Selection	Mortality	Selection Interactions	Pretest-Treatment Interactions
True Experimental Designs									
Pretest-Posttest Control Group Design R O X O R O O	+	+	+	+	+	+	+	+	−
Posttest-Only Control Group Design R X O R O	+	+	(+)	(+)	(+)	+	−	+	(+)
Quasi-experimental Designs									
Nonequivalent Control Group Design O X O $\overline{O$ $O}$	+	+	+	+	−	+	+	−	−
Time Series Design O O O O X O O O O	−	+	+	−	+	(+)	+	(+)	−
Pre-experimental Designs									
One-shot Case Study X O	−	−	(+)	(+)	(+)	(+)	−	(+)	(+)
One-group Pretest-posttest Design O X O	−	−	−	−	−	(+)	−	(+)	−
Static Group Comparison X O $\overline{ O}$	+	−	(+)	(+)	(+)	−	−	−	(+)

Symbols: R = random assignment of students to groups   Each line represents a group
 X = unusual treatment   + = factor controlled for
 O = test, pretest, or posttest   (+) = factor controlled for
 − − − = groups are not randomly formed   because not relevant
     − = factor not controlled for

Note: Figure 14.1 basically follows the format used by Campbell and Stanley and is presented with a note of caution: The figure is intended to be a supplement to, not a substitute for, textual discussions. You should not totally accept or reject designs because of their +'s and −'s. Also you should be aware that which design is most appropriate for a given evaluation is determined not only by the controls provided by the design but also by the nature of the evaluation and the setting in which it is to be conducted.

 While the symbols used in this figure, and their placement, vary somewhat from Campbell and Stanley's format, the intent, interpretations, and textual discussions of the two presentations are in agreement (Donald T. Campbell, April 22, 1975: personal communication).

figure 14.1
Sources of invalidity for experimental designs.

used to see if the groups are essentially the same on the dependent variable. If they are, posttest scores can be directly compared using a *t* test. If they are not (random assignment does not *guarantee* equality), posttest scores can be analyzed using analysis of covariance. Recall that covariance adjusts posttest scores for initial differences on any variable, including pretest scores.

A variation of the pretest-posttest control group design involves random assignment of members of matched pairs to the groups, one member to each group, in order to more closely control for one or more extraneous variables. There is really no advantage to this technique, however, since any variable that can be controlled through matching can be controlled better using other procedures such as analysis of covariance.

The posttest-only control group design. This design is exactly the same as the pretest-posttest control group design *except* that there is no pretest. Participants are randomly assigned to groups, exposed to the independent variable, and posttested. Posttest scores are then compared to determine the effectiveness of the treatment. This design may be represented as in figure 14.1 or as follows:

$$R \quad X_1 \quad O$$
$$R \quad X_2 \quad O$$

This representation indicates that both groups are being exposed to the independent variable: one group is receiving the new, or unusual, treatment and one group is receiving the usual, or traditional approach. As with the pretest-posttest control group design, the posttest-only control group design can be expanded to include more than two groups.

The combination of random assignment and the presence of a control group serve to control for all sources of internal invalidity except mortality. Mortality is not controlled for because of the absence of pretest data on participants. However, mortality may or may not be a problem. If the program is relatively short in duration, for example, no participants may be lost. In this case we may report that while mortality is a potential threat to validity with this design, it did not prove to be a threat in our particular evaluation since the group sizes remained constant throughout the duration of the program. Thus, if the probability of differential mortality is low, the posttest-only design can be a very effective design. Of course if there is any chance that the groups may be different with respect to initial knowledge related to the dependent variable (despite random assignment), the pretest-posttest control group design should be used. Which design is "best" depends upon the study. If the study is to be short and if it can be assumed that neither group has any knowledge related to the dependent variable, then the posttest-only design may be the "best." If the study is to be lengthy (good chance of mortality), or if there is a chance that the two groups differ on initial knowledge related to the dependent variable, then the pretest-posttest control group design may be the best.

A variation of the posttest-only control group design involves random assignment of members of matched pairs to the groups, one member to each group, in order to more closely control for one or more extraneous variables. As with the pretest-posttest control group design, however, there is really no advantage to this

---

[13] Recall that other sources of external invalidity are potential problems regardless of the design used.

technique; any variable that can be controlled through matching can be controlled better using other procedures.

Quasi-experimental designs

Sometimes, as we said, it is just not feasible to randomly assign participants to groups. In order to receive permission to use school children in an evaluation, for example, we often have to agree to use existing classrooms. When this occurs, however, there are still designs available which provide adequate control of sources of invalidity; these designs are referred to as *quasi-experimental designs*. Keep in mind that designs such as these should be your second choice, to be used only when it is not feasible to use a true experimental design.

The nonequivalent control group design. This design should be familiar to you since it looks very much like the pretest-posttest control group design. The only difference is that the nonequivalent control group design does not involve random assignment of participants to groups (although treatment should be randomly assigned to groups if possible). Two existing groups are pretested, given a treatment, and posttested. Again, each group may comprise any number of classrooms. Thus we might take 10 classrooms and randomly assign 5 of them to be treatment classes and 5 of them to be control classes. The lack of random assignment adds sources of invalidity not associated with the pretest-posttest control group design—possible regression and interaction between selection and variables such as maturation, history, and testing. The more similar the groups are, the better. We should make every effort to use groups that are as equivalent as possible. Comparing advanced algebra classes with remedial algebra classes, for example, would not do. If differences between the groups on any major extraneous variable are identified, analysis of covariance can be used to statistically equate the groups. An advantage of this design is that since classes are used "as is," possible effects from reactive arrangements are minimized. Participants may not even be aware that they are involved in an evaluation. As with the pretest-posttest control group design, the nonequivalent control group design may be represented as X_1 versus X_2 rather than X versus no X and may also be extended to include more than two groups.

The time-series design. This design is actually an elaboration of the one-group pretest-posttest design to be discussed shortly (see figure 14.1). One group is repeatedly pretested, exposed to a treatment, and then repeatedly posttested. If a group scores essentially the same on a number of pretests and then significantly improves following a treatment, we have some degree of confidence in the effectiveness of the treatment.

History is a problem with this design, however, since something might happen between the last pretest and the first posttest, the effect of which might be confused with the treatment effect. Instrumentation may also be a problem but not an expected problem unless for some reason the measuring instruments are changed during the study. Pretest-treatment interaction can also be a source of invalidity. It should be clear that if one pretest can interact with a treatment, more than one pretest can only make matters worse!

While statistical analyses appropriate for this design are rather advanced, determining the effectiveness of the treatment basically involves analysis of the pattern of the test scores. Figure 14.2 illustrates several possible patterns which might be found. Campbell and Stanley discuss a number of other possibilities.[14] In figure 14.2 the vertical line falling between O_4 and O_5 indicates the point at which the treatment was introduced. Pattern A does not indicate a treatment effect; performance was increasing before the treatment was introduced, and continued to increase at the same rate following introduction of the treatment. Patterns B and C both do indicate a treatment effect; the effect appears to be more permanent in pattern C than in pattern B. Pattern D does not indicate a treatment effect even though student scores are higher on O_5 than O_4. The pattern is too erratic. Scores appear to be fluctuating up and down, so the O_4 to O_5 fluctuation cannot be attributed to the treatment. The four patterns shown illustrate that just comparing O_4 and O_5 is not sufficient. In all four cases O_5 indicates a higher score than O_4, but only in two of the patterns does the difference appear to be due to a treatment effect.

A variation of the time-series design, which is referred to as the *multiple time-series design*, involves the addition of a control group to the basic design as follows:

$$O \quad O \quad O \quad O \quad X \quad O \quad O \quad O \quad O$$
$$O \quad O \quad O \quad O \qquad O \quad O \quad O \quad O$$

This variation eliminates history and instrumentation as threats to validity and thus represents a design with no probable sources of internal invalidity. This design can be more effectively used in situations where testing is a naturally occurring event not likely to be regarded as unusual, as in evaluations involving school classrooms.

Pre-experimental designs

As figure 14.1 illustrates, none of the pre-experimental designs does a very good job of controlling extraneous variables which jeopardize validity. With slight modification, two of the three pre-experimental designs to be discussed could be greatly improved; as is, they leave much to be desired. They are presented here only as examples of what not to do.

The one-shot case study. This design involves one group which is exposed to a treatment and then posttested. Not all of the sources of invalidity are relevant; testing, for example, is not a concern since there is no pretest. As figure 14.1 indicates, however, none of the threats to validity which are relevant is controlled. Even if the participants score high on the posttest, you cannot attribute their performance to the treatment since you do not even know what they knew before you administered the treatment. So, if you have a choice between using this design and not implementing a program, do not bother!

[14] See footnote 5.

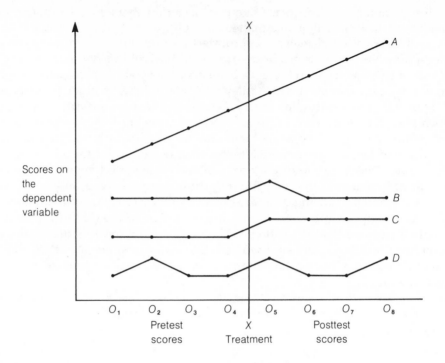

figure 14.2
Possible patterns for the results of an evaluation based on a time-series design.

The one-group pretest-posttest design. This design involves one group which is pretested, exposed to a treatment, and post-tested. The success of the treatment is determined by comparing pretest and posttest scores. However, although this design controls invalidity not controlled by the one-shot case study, a number of additional factors are relevant to this design which are not controlled. If participants do significantly better on the posttest, it cannot be assumed that the improvement is due to the treatment. History and maturation are not controlled. Something may happen *to* the participants or *inside* the participants to make them perform better the second time. The longer the program is, the more likely this becomes. Testing and instrumentation are not controlled. The participants may learn something on the first test which helps them on the second test, or unreliability of the measures may be responsible for the apparent improvement. Statistical regression is also not controlled for. Even if participants are not selected on the basis of extreme scores (high or low), it is possible that a group may do very poorly on the pretest just by bad luck. For example, they may guess badly just by chance on a multiple-choice pretest and improve on a posttest simply because their score based on guessing is more in line with an expected score. Pretest-treatment interaction, the external validity factor, is also not controlled. Pretest-treatment interaction may cause participants to react differently to the treatment than they would have if they had not been pretested.

To illustrate the problems associated with this design, let's examine a hypothetical situation. Suppose the administration and staff of a soon-to-be-integrated junior high school anticipate conflict and hostility among students. In an attempt to deal with the potential problem, they spend a month developing a packet of materials to give to students on the first day of school. The materials are designed to foster positive attitudes toward members of the various races, and contain items such as short biographies and autobiographies of persons of different races who have made major cultural and scientific contributions. On the first day of school an appropriate attitude scale is administered to all students, and they are then given a packet and instructions to read the materials as soon as possible. As the weeks go by, the situation seems to get better and better; incidents of conflict and hostility occur less and less frequently. At the end of a two-month period the staff again administers the attitude scale and, sure enough, the students indicate more positive attitudes than they did on the first day of school. The staff members are well satisfied with their materials and their effectiveness in improving attitudes. However, their satisfaction is not well founded. If you think about it, you will see that there are a number of alternative factors that could explain the improved attitudes. For example, students would be more likely to be anxious and hostile on the first day of school because of not knowing what to expect (fear of the unknown). As they got to know each other as individuals and began to form friendships, their fears would naturally subside. Another problem with estimating effectiveness is that the staff would not even know whether the students read the materials!

The problems associated with this design are even more serious when other types of measures are involved, as attitudes tend to be more stable and resistant to change than most other variables. Of course the above evaluation could have been greatly improved by the addition of a few additional pretests and posttests. If the staff, for example, measured attitudes on several occasions *before* handing out the materials, they would be able to see if attitudes were improving naturally. In this situation the time-series design could easily be applied and would provide much more valid evidence concerning the effectiveness of the materials.

The static-group comparison design. This design involves at least two groups. One group receives a new or unusual treatment, the other, the control group, receives the usual or traditional treatment, and both groups are posttested. The design can be written as follows:

$$\frac{X_1O}{X_2O}$$

The broken line separating the groups indicates that the groups are not randomly formed. The degree to which the groups are equivalent is the degree to which their comparison is reasonable. But since participants are not randomly assigned to groups and since there are no pretest data, it is difficult to determine just how equivalent they are. It is always possible that posttest differences are due to group differences, not just treatment effects (maturation, selection, and selection interactions). Mortality is also a problem since if you lose participants you have no information concerning what you have lost (no pretest data). On the positive side, the presence of a control group controls for history since it is assumed that events which occur outside of the experimental setting will equally affect both groups. In most situations in which the static-group comparison design is used, however, a pretest could have easily been administered to both groups. Now think. If you did add a pretest to the static-group comparison design, what would you have? Right!

The nonequivalent control group design, a much improved design in terms of controlling sources of invalidity.

Ex post facto designs

It is understandable that ex post facto designs, also called *causal-comparative designs,* and experimental designs are at first difficult to distinguish. Both are used in an attempt to establish cause-effect relationships and both involve group comparisons. With experimental designs, however, the independent variable is manipulated; that is, it is determined *in advance* who is going to get what. Then the effect of the treatment is established by comparing the posttest performance of the treatment and control groups. In contrast, with ex post facto designs, the independent variable is not manipulated; the "treatment" has already occurred, and no control was exercised in selecting participants. A comparison is made of the posttest performance of two groups, one of which received the treatment and one which did not (see figure 14.3). For example, in an attempt to evaluate the effectiveness of a preschool program, we might measure the first grade achievement of two groups of students—a group of students who *were* in the program and a group of students who *were not.* We would have nothing to do with who did or did not participate, we would simply identify program students. As another example, we might wish to investigate what long-range effect our social promotion policy has on the self-concept of beginning junior high school students so promoted. At the end of a school year we would identify a group of seventh graders who had been socially promoted to the seventh grade the year before, and a group of sixth graders who had been held back the year before and made to repeat the sixth grade. The measured self-concepts of the two groups would then be compared. We might also wish to compare their achievement on a standardized achievement battery.

As the above examples illustrate, in evaluations such designs usually involve "treatments" which *could be* manipulated or "treatments" which ethically *should not be* manipulated. As an example of a "could be" situation, suppose a su-

	Group	Independent Variable	Dependent Variable
Case A	(T)	(X)	O
	(C)		O
Case B	(T)	(X₁)	O
	(C)	(X₂)	O

Symbols:
　　T = treatment group
　　C = control group
　　X = independent variable
　　O = dependent variable
　　( ) indicates no manipulation

figure 14.3
The basic causal-comparative design.

perintendent was considering the adoption of systems reading in his or her school system. The superintendent might consider trying it out on an experimental basis for a year in a number of schools or classrooms before implementing it throughout the system. However, even such limited adoption would be costly in terms of materials and teacher training. Thus, as a preliminary step, to aid decision making, the superintendent might conduct an ex post facto study and compare the reading achievement of students in school districts currently using systems reading with students in school districts not currently using systems reading. Since most districts have yearly testing programs which assess the status of students in areas such as reading, acquisition of the necessary data would not be difficult. If the results indicated that the students learning through systems reading were achieving higher, the superintendent would probably decide to go ahead with an experimental tryout of systems reading in her or his own districts. If no differences were found, the superintendent would probably not go ahead with the experimental tryout and would thus not waste unnecessary time, money, and effort. As an example of a "should not" situation, it would not be ethical to select some students to participate in a visual screening program, and not others. Any manipulation which might cause physical or mental harm to participants (in this case the control group) is definitely unethical and may in some instances be illegal. In such cases use of an ex post facto design may be the only feasible way to evaluate a program.

As figure 14.3 illustrates, two groups of participants are selected; they are loosely referred to as treatment and control groups although it is probably more accurate to refer to them as comparison groups. As with experimental designs, the groups may differ in that one group has had an experience which the other has not (Case A), *or* the groups may differ in degree, and may have had different kinds of experiences (Case B). An example of Case A would be two groups, one which had received preschool training and one which did not. An example of Case B would be two groups, one which had learned algebra via programmed instruction and one which had learned algebra via traditional instruction. In both cases, the groups are compared on some dependent variable. As with experimental designs, we may administer a test of the dependent variable or collect already available data, such as the results of standardized testing conducted by a school. If samples are to be selected, random selection is generally the preferred method of selection, that is, random selection of a group from the population of participants and a group from the population of nonparticipants. It is important to select samples that are representative of their respective populations and similar with respect to all relevant variables except the "treatment" variable.

Since the random assignment, manipulation, and control which characterize experimental designs are missing in an ex post facto design, extreme caution must be applied in interpreting results. The apparent cause of an observed effect (posttest difference) may not be in fact the real cause. One possibility is that the groups are different on some other variable besides the identified "treatment" variable, and it is this variable which is the real cause of the observed difference between the groups. For example, if we simply compared a group of students who had received a preschool program with a group who had not, the conclusion might be drawn that participation if the preschool program resulted in better reading achievement in first grade. But suppose that in the region in which the evaluation was conducted, all preschool programs were private and required high tuitions. In this case we would really be evaluating the effects not just of the preschool program but also the effects of membership in a well-to-do family. It might very well be that parents in such families provide early informal reading instruction for their children. It would be very difficult to evaluate only the effect of the preschool program. If we were aware of the situation, however, we could control for this variable by selecting only children of well-to-do parents for both groups. Thus, the two groups to be compared, one which had attended the preschool program and one which had not, would be equated with respect to income level of their parents, an extraneous variable. Thus, every attempt must be made to determine the equivalence of the comparison groups. Information on a number of background and participant variables may be collected. In order to promote equality, or to correct for identified inequalities, any of the control procedures previously described (e.g. matching) can be used.

Only a good experimental design can truly establish cause-effect relationships between treatments and posttest performance. Any relationships established with ex post facto designs are tentative and tenuous at best. Ex post facto designs do, however, permit evaluation of variables which cannot or should not be investigated with an experimental design; they also provide preliminary data for possible experimental efforts and are less costly on all dimensions.

Title I models

Title I projects are federally funded programs designed to meet the academic needs of disadvantaged students. The Title I evaluation system recommended by the United States Office of Education (USOE) was developed by the RMC Research Corporation and involves three basic alternative models: Model A —the Norm-Referenced Design, Model B—the Control Group Design, and Model C—the Special Regression Design. The primary purpose of the evaluation system is to provide evidence as to whether the achievement of Title I students is higher than it would have been if they had not participated in the program. In other words, the aim of the evaluation system is to determine the effectiveness of Title I programs. All three models involve comparing *actual* posttest performance with the expected no-treatment performance, that is, an estimate of what posttest performance would have been had students not participated in a Title I program. The models differ in the method used to estimate expected posttest performance.

While Title I evaluations are conducted on a local basis, they are intended to produce results which are standard and comparable on a national basis. While local education agencies (LEAs) may generally use the model of their choice, they must provide standardized data which can be expressed in terms of a common metric, namely normal curve equivalents (NCEs). NCEs are normalized standard scores which range from 1 to 99, with a mean, or average, score of 50.[15] If, for example, the actual mean score corresponds to an NCE of 30 and the expected mean score corresponds to an NCE of 20, then the Title I impact is said to be 10 NCEs (30 − 20 = 10). Thus, while a locally-developed test may be sufficiently valid and reliable to provide evidence concerning the effectiveness of a Title I program, the resulting data do not meet the requirement that results be reported on a common standard of measurement. This requirement can only be fulfilled through the administration of a nationally normed standardized test. Fortunately, local districts have considerable latitude in selecting the standardized test which will be used. This permits each LEA to select the test which best measures the student outcomes reflected in the local program's objectives. While USOE states that all three models

[15] Standard scores will be discussed further in chapter 17.

result in unbiased, comparable data regarding the effectiveness of Title I programs, data which can be interpreted collectively in determining the effectiveness of Title I efforts nationally, there is little evidence to support this claim. In fact, the results of investigations conducted to date indicate that in general, and especially under certain circumstances, the models are not equal in terms of their ability to provide unbiased estimates of program effectiveness.

Because the Title I evaluation models can handle a number of situations for which there is no legitimate or readily identifiable control group (e.g. when the entire target population is in the program), their popularity has been growing with state and local education agencies. The Title I models are applicable in the evaluation of a variety of programs and projects, not just in the evaluation of Title I programs. In many cases one of the Title I models may be much easier to implement than a traditional research design. In other cases, application of a Title I model may really be the only feasible approach to evaluation of a given program. It must be kept in mind that while there are often serious problems associated with application of a Title I model, these models were developed to meet a need, and they do fill that need. Each of the models will be briefly discussed. As with the research designs, they are presented in order of "goodness." If further information is desired on any of the models, the RMC *User's Guide* should be consulted.[16]

Model B—the control group design

Model B is typically "the road not taken" when a Title I model is selected since it encompasses traditional experimental designs. In its ideal form, Model B is the pretest-posttest control group design which involves random assignment of students to groups. The nonequivalent control group design is also permitted if it can be verified that the groups are essentially equivalent on all relevant variables. Aside from the fact that Model B is frequently opposed on practical grounds, because it is more difficult to implement, it is also often opposed on philosophical or feasibility grounds. Withholding students with a demonstrated need from a potentially beneficial program may be opposed or actually prohibited (as in the case of Title I programs). Thus, while the pretest-posttest control group design is clearly superior from a design standpoint, it is not always viewed with much enthusiasm in real-world settings due to legal, ethical, and practical considerations.

Model C—the special regression design

Of the remaining two models to be discussed, Model C is generally considered to be the more valid model, although Model A is quite popular due to its ease of application. Model C deals very nicely with those situations in which all members of an identified target population must participate in program activities, as with many remediation programs. Specifically, the special regression model is applicable in situations in which participants are selected based on their scores on a given test (or on some composite scores which are based on a combination of criteria). Scores for all potential participants are compared to some cut-off score.

[16] Tallmadge, G. K., & Wood, C. T. *User's guide: ESEA Title I evaluation and reporting system.* Mountain View, Calif.: RMC Research Corporation, 1976.

Any student whose score falls below the cut-off score *must* participate in the program, and any student whose score is above the cut-off score *cannot* participate. The two resulting groups are referred to as the treatment and control groups. The control group participates in normal classroom activities, the activities the treatment group would have participated in if they had not been selected for the program. At the appropriate time both groups are posttested.

The process of estimating program effectiveness involves a statistical procedure called regression (which should not be confused with statistical regression, a threat to internal validity). While a full discussion of regression is beyond the scope of this text, the basic process is not too difficult to understand and can be explained briefly. It involves the same concept that is applied when we predict achievement in an algebra course based on algebra aptitude test scores, or when we predict college GPA or posttest scores using high school GPA. For example, suppose we selected participants for a program based on high school GPA so that all students with GPAs less than 2.0 were selected. If nonprogram students with GPAs of 4.0, 3.0, and 2.0 had posttest scores on an achievement test of 40, 30, and 20, respectively, we would *predict* that program students with a GPA of 1.0 would have a posttest score of 10—if they did not participate in the program (see figure 14.4). In essence, points such as those shown in figure 14.4 produce a regression line from which *expected* posttest scores (scores we would expect in the absence of program participation) are predicted. When Model C is used, expected posttest scores are predicted based on pretest scores. Program effectiveness is determined by comparing *predicted* posttest scores with *actual* posttest scores. If, for instance, we predict an average posttest score of 10 for the program group and the actual

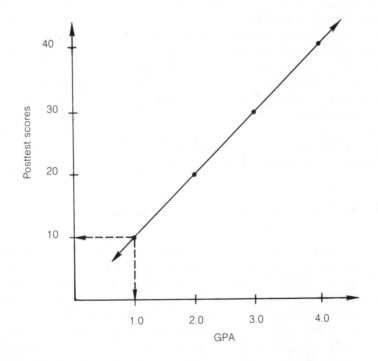

figure 14.4
Hypothetical, simplified regression line for predicted posttest scores based on GPA.

group average is 15, we conclude that the program caused the 5 point difference.[17] Of course the relationship between pretest scores and posttest scores is never as perfect as the relationship depected in figure 14.4, but this figure does illustrate the basic concept.

Model A—the norm-referenced design

Model A, as we said, is quite popular with state and local education agencies because of its ease of application. It is also appropriate for situations in which formation of a reasonably equivalent control group is not feasible. Basically, Model A involves pretesting and posttesting of the program students and determining whether and to what degree their percentile position changed (with respect to the norms on some valid and reliable standardized test) presumably as a result of the program. Percentile position is determined by averaging standard scores and converting the average standard score to a percentile. The assumption is that without the program students would be at the same percentile at the end of the program period as at the beginning. In other words, if the pretest performance of a group of students corresponded to the 17th percentile, we would expect that they would remain in the same relative position with respect to the performance of their peers (the national norm group) *if* they did not participate in the program. If their percentile position increases (say from the 17th percentile to the 32nd percentile on the posttest), the effectiveness of the program has presumably been demonstrated. The norm group, in essence, serves as the control group. In order to make this comparison of the program group with test norms, dates of pretesting and posttesting must coincide rather closely with norming dates. In other words, if test norms are based on a May 15 testing date, then the program students should be posttested on or near May 15 (within a week or two before or after May 15).[18]

It is also generally agreed that a valid comparison requires that: (1) a different test be used for pretesting than for selecting participants; (2) the same test be used for pretesting and posttesting; and (3) only the scores of students who take both the pretest and the posttest be considered in analysis of results. The validity of the comparison is a function of how similar the program students are to students in the norm group. Thus, tests which provide special norms for disadvantaged students are appropriate in many situations. The equi-percentile assumption, the assumption that the group's percentile would remain stable over time without program intervention, is reasonable only if the norm group is similar to the program group on relevant characteristics. Recent efforts have been directed at supporting or refuting some of these generally held principles.

As with the other Title I models, results are reported in terms of normal curve equivalents (NCEs). Using appropriate tables, NCEs can be converted to percentiles, and vice versa. Model A procedures entail: (1) establishing the average standard score for the group at the time of testing; (2) converting the average standard score to a percentile; and (3) converting the percentile to an NCE (using a table). The NCE determined at the time of pretesting serves as the no-treatment

[17] For a relatively straightforward presentation of the procedures involved, see Mandeville, G. K. An evaluation of Title I Model C_1: The Special Regression Model. Paper presented at the American Educational Research Association Convention, Toronto, 1978. Mandeville is at the University of South Carolina.

[18] Recall the previous discussion concerning the importance of pretesting and posttesting treatment and control students at the same time.

expectation at the time of posttesting. In other words, we assume that the NCE would be the same for pretest scores and for posttest scores *if* students did not participate in the program. Therefore, we assume that the NCE will be the same (or lower) if the program is ineffective. If there is essentially no difference between the expected NCE and the actual NCE at the time of posttesting, the program is judged to have been ineffective since students performed as we would assume they would perform without the program. If there is a significant difference, the program is judged to have been effective. For example, suppose we administer a pretest in September and a posttest in May, and the pretest NCE is 37.1, the 27th percentile. If the program is ineffective, students will presumably maintain their position from September to May and in May will have a posttest NCE of 37.1 (or close to it). If the actual posttest NCE is 46, the program was effective—students performed significantly beyond normal expectations.

Although both Model A and Model C involve sources of bias in estimating treatment effects, Model C does appear to be more accurate in its assessments. The fact that bias does exist, and is serious in some cases, casts some doubt on the advisability of collective interpretations regarding the effectiveness of the Title I program on a national basis. The major conclusions to be reached is that with respect to design validity Model C is definitely to be preferred; with respect to feasibility Model A is clearly the people's choice.

Single-subject designs

In some cases programs are required to determine the effectiveness of their efforts on an individual participant basis. Federally funded programs for handicapped students typically have this requirement. In single-subject designs each participant serves as his or her own control in variations on a time-series design. Basically, the student is alternately exposed to a treatment and nontreatment condition, and performance is repeatedly measured during each phase. In research design symbolism, the basic design looks something like this:

Student 1   *O   O   O   X   O   X   O   X   O   O   O*

Thus, a student's performance is first measured (tested or observed) under a control, no-treatment condition on several occasions. Then treatment is introduced and the student's performance is measured on several occasions. Finally, the treatment is withdrawn and several additional measurements are taken. If performance is significantly higher during the treatment condition phase than during either control phase, then the treatment is judged to be effective. This basic design can of course be modified in a number of ways. For example, the treatment phase can be repeated following the second control phase, producing a stronger case for the impact of the treatment. The major problem with such designs is that the effects of many treatments do not disappear when treatment is removed (see figure 14.2, patterns B and C). Actually, it is highly desirable if they do not. Reinforcement techniques, for example, are designed to produce improved behavior which will be maintained when external reinforcements are withdrawn.

A second type of single-subject design is the *treatment reversal design*. This design is very similar to the basic design described above except that the treatment phase is not followed by a control phase but rather by a treatment reversal phase. In other words, a condition which is essentially the opposite of the treatment condition is implemented. To use a former example, we could apply the treatment reversal design to demonstrate the effectiveness of positive reinforcement in reducing stand-up behavior. We would first collect baseline data using observation on stand-up behavior. Then we would initiate positive reinforcement for in-seat behavior and record instances (hopefully reduced in number) of stand-up behavior. Then we would initiate treatment reversal in the form of reinforcement for stand-up behavior and record instances (probably dramatically increased in number) of stand-up behavior. The major problem with this design is that its application is not very often feasible or desirable. If we were trying to reduce violent outbursts of behavior, for example, encouraging them for the sake of treatment reversal would not be advisable for obvious reasons.

A third, more satisfactory type of single-subject design is the *multiple baseline design*. Instead of collecting initial baseline (control) data for one student and one behavior, we collect data either on one behavior for several students or several behaviors for one student. We then systematically, over a period of time, apply the treatment to each student (or to each behavior) one at a time until all students (or behaviors) are under treatment. Application of this design might look something like the following:

Student 1   O O O X O X O X O O O
Student 2   O O O O O X O X O O O
Student 3   O O O O O O O X O O O

In this case, student 1 received treatment first and then student 2 and then student 3, until all 3 students were under treatment. If measured performance increases in each case only after treatment is introduced, then the treatment is judged to be effective. The advantages of this design are clear as it handles nicely a number of the problems involved with the other designs.

The major problem with all single-subject designs is the lack of generalizability of findings. We can verify treatment effects for a given student, but results based on the performance of one or even several students do not provide convincing evidence. Of course if the treatment effect is repeatedly demonstrated with a relatively large group of students, say 15, our confidence in the findings increases. Further, a limited range of treatments lend themselves to such designs. On the plus side, they do provide a systematic approach to determining the effectiveness of a given treatment or program approach on a student by student basis, as opposed to examining group results only.

Functional-level testing[19]

Standardized tests and their accompanying norms represent a relatively limited range of achievement in the area being tested. A sixth-grade math test, for example, does not contain simple addition problems nor does it contain solid geometry concepts. A test for a given grade level represents a range of coverage designed to accommodate the competence of *most* students. But the range of ability and achievement within a given grade level is invariably greater than a given test can provide for. As a consequence, such a test will be too difficult for some students

[19] This topic could have been discussed earlier, in chapter 7 under "Selection of a test." It is included here because functional-level testing is often used when a Title I design is applied.

and too easy for others. If a test is too difficult for a given group, we have what is called a *floor effect*. Such a test is characterized by many low scores, resulting mainly from guessing. If a test is too easy for a given group, we have a *ceiling effect*. In this case many students achieve relatively high scores. If either the floor effect or the ceiling effect is operating in an evaluation, the result will probably be an overestimate or underestimate of achievement gains. Since many special programs are designed for low achievers, the floor effect is more often a problem. If, for example, a group of selected program students knows essentially none of the measured concepts on a 4-alternative multiple-choice test, their scores should be essentially zero. Due to the guessing or chance factor, however, they may well get an average of 25% of the items correct. Thus, the difference between pretest scores and posttest scores may not be as great as the actual difference in achievement in many situations.

   To counteract this problem, and to more accurately estimate a program's effect on achievement, a number of evaluation efforts utilize a strategy called functional-level testing. *Functional-level testing* refers to the practice of testing students at their actual level of competence, at whatever test level is necessary to accurately assess their achievement. Thus functional-level testing includes in-level testing and out-of-level testing. If you administer a test recommended *for* fourth graders *to* fourth graders, you are conducting in-level testing. Out-of-level testing, on the other hand, involves selection and administration of a test recommended for a *different* age or grade based on the student's actual level of achievement. This might mean that a group of low achieving fourth graders would be given a test designed for second graders. Since most types of tests are available for a number of levels (e.g. Level I for first graders, Level 2 for second graders, and so forth), out-of-level testing involves administration of a test at a level higher or lower than the one suggested by the students' age or grade. Out-of-level testing reduces ceiling and floor effects by giving students a better chance to show what they know and can do. If a fourth grade test is too difficult for a given group of fourth graders, their score will likely reflect mainly guessing behavior. If these same students are given, say, a second grade test, they are more likely to seriously consider each question, and their performance will more closely reflect their actual level of competence.

   Functional-level testing may be done on a group basis, on a subgroup basis, or on an individual basis. If a group is fairly homogeneous with respect to achievement level, then the same test (in-level or out-of-level) may be appropriate for the entire group. A group of gifted students, for example, might all be given a test one level above that generally recommended for their grade. If a group has distinct subgroups, say average and below-average ability students, then two different levels of a test may be required. And of course if we take the process to its logical conclusion, we can attempt to give each student the test at the level most appropriate for each as an individual. The finer we differentiate the testing, however, the more involved it becomes. It is more complicated than the individualized testing which characterizes individualized instruction since in this case the tests being administered are standardized. You cannot simply hand a student a standardized test and send her or him off to a corner to take it. The written and oral directions specified by the test must be followed exactly. Thus, functional-level testing rarely involves more than two or three different levels.

   The tricky part of out-of-level testing is interpretation of results. If fourth graders take a second grade test, it does not make sense to compare their raw scores to those of fourth graders who took a fourth grade test. Nor is it reasonable to compare their raw scores to those of the second graders who took the second grade test. The performance of the fourth graders, however, must be interpreted in terms of fourth grade norms, no matter what level test was actually taken. Fortunately, many publishers have facilitated this process by providing tables and/or expanded standard scores which permit us to transform a score at one level to a corresponding score at another level (higher or lower). In other words, based on a student's raw score at one level, we can determine what that student's raw score probably would have been if the student had taken a higher or lower level test, thereby reducing the guessing or chance factor. Once we determine the equivalent score at the student's actual grade (or age) level, we can interpret it in terms of the norms for that level.

15 data collection procedures

After reading chapter 15, you should be able to:

1 List the major activities which are involved in the data collection stage of formal evaluations.
2 Discuss the problems associated with nonresponse and ways to deal with it.

General considerations

Usually we tend to associate data collection with the administration of an achievement test, standardized or locally-developed. In addition to everything that has already been said on the subject of data collection, it is important to note that maximization of test scores requires that test takers be prepared. They should know in advance when a test is going to be administered and for what purpose, and the nature of the test. If the test is standardized, it may be helpful to have a practice session for students on activities such as marking a machine-scorable answer sheet. Another consideration is the level of test-taker anxiety. The more important a test is, the more anxiety it is likely to arouse. Excessive levels of anxiety have been shown to interfere with performance. Saying things like "Do your best because your whole future depends upon how well you do" is not a good idea! On the other hand, a complete absence of anxiety is also counterproductive since test takers are not motivated to do their best. Saying things like "This is a stupid, meaningless test and nobody cares how you do on it" is not a good idea either. Some reasonable middle ground is required so that the test takers realize that while the test may be important, their lives do not depend on how well they do, and that they will probably do better if they relax and take each question as it comes.

Methods of data collection other than achievement tests have been discussed in previous chapters. While all data collection methods have certain characteristics in common, such as formulation of objectives and instrument development procedures, each method is also associated with its own set of unique considerations. Since this chapter deals with the process phase of evaluation, we will shortly discuss implementation procedures and strategies associated with three major data collection techniques—questionnaires, interviews, and observation.

Collecting any kind of data requires planning and organization. In addition to determining *what* will be done, it must also be decided *who* will do it. Responsibilities for instrument development, sample selection, and data collection must be clearly defined. In the classroom the situation is simplified since the teacher is responsible for everything (how well you know, right?!). In a special program or project, however, there may be a number of activities which must be assigned to appropriate staff members and coordinated by the director. Depending upon the size of the staff, outside help may be required. Faculty and students from neighboring colleges and universities, as well as persons from the community, may be hired from time to time to perform various tasks, especially those related to data collection such as interviewing and observation. The characteristics which are required or desired of temporary assistants will vary depending upon the task. Interviewers would, of course, have to know how to read and write, for example, whereas it might also be highly desirable for them to have had some type of training or experience in evaluation or research methodology (such as a university course). If those hired will be interacting with people, then consideration should be given to personality variables such as disposition and tact, since these may be related to their ability to obtain required data.

Regardless of their intended functions, temporary or part-time assistants should participate in some type of orientation activities presenting the nature of the program or project and the part they will play in it. Also, they should receive training related to their assigned task and be given opportunities for supervised practice. Simulations, in which they go through the entire task (e.g. conducting an interview) with each other or with staff members, are an especially effective training strategy. They should also be given clear instructions concerning to whom they are to report, how often, and when; for example, "Report to Helen Honcho, Mondays and Thursdays at 10:00 A.M."

Before any data are actually collected, anyone involved in any way with data collection procedures should become thoroughly familiar with all relevant restrictions, legal or otherwise, related to the collection, storing, and sharing of obtained information. All necessary permissions from participants, school administrators, federal agencies, and the like should be obtained *in writing*. And finally, all data collection activities should be carefully and systematically monitored to insure that correct procedures are being followed.

Murphy's Law states approximately that "if anything can go wrong, it will." Gay's Law states that "if anything can go wrong, it will—unless you make sure that it doesn't!" Most of the minor tragedies that occur during evaluation efforts could have been avoided with proper planning, good coordination, and careful monitoring. Part of good planning is anticipation. Do not wait until something happens before you figure out how to deal with it. Try to anticipate potential problems which might arise and then do what you can to prevent them. Plan your strategies for dealing with them if they do occur. For example, you might anticipate resistance on the part of some principals to giving you permission to use their students as participants in your program. To deal with this contingency you should work up the best sales pitch possible. Do not ask, "Hey, can I use your kids for my program?" Instead, tell them how wonderful the program is and how it will benefit their students or their schools. If there is still opposition, you might tell them how enthusiastic the biggies in central administration are about the program and how they assured you that you would receive full cooperation. Got the idea?

You cannot guarantee that a given program will be effective, but you can guarantee that things go as smoothly as possible, that the program is executed as planned, that changes are made as needed, and that the program gets a fair trial. Finally, you may tend to get frustrated at times because you cannot do everything the way you might like to due to real or bureaucratic constraints. Don't let such obstacles exasperate you. Just relax and do your best.

Questionnaires

In previous chapters we discussed construction of a questionnaire, construction of a cover letter, and guidelines for mailing a questionnaire (e.g. responding should be made as painless as possible). Additional considerations include selection of the persons to whom the questionnaire will be sent (recipients), follow-up activities, and ways of dealing with nonresponse.

Selection of recipients

Recipients should be selected using an appropriate sampling technique (an entire population may also be used), and identified recipients must be persons who (1) have the desired information and (2) are likely to be willing to give it. Individuals who possess the desired information but are not sufficiently interested, or for whom the topic under study has little meaning, are not likely to respond. It is sometimes worth the effort to do a preliminary check of potential respondents to determine their receptivity. In some cases it is more productive to send the questionnaire to a person of authority rather than directly to the person with the desired information. If a person's boss passes along a questionnaire and asks that person to complete and return it, that person is more likely to do so than if *you* ask him or her directly!

Follow-up activities

Not everyone to whom you send a questionnaire is going to return it (what an understatement!). Some recipients have no intention of completing it, and others mean to but put it off so long that they either forget about it or lose it. It is primarily for this latter group that follow-up activities are conducted. The higher your percentage of returns, the better. Although you should not expect 100%, you should not be satisfied with whatever you get after your first mailing. If your percentage of returns is not at least 70%, the validity of your conclusions will be weak. Given all the work you have already done, it makes no sense to end up with shaky findings of limited value when some additional effort on your part can make a big difference.

An initial follow-up strategy is to simply send out a reminder postcard. This will prompt those who intended to fill the forms out, but have put it off, and to return their questionnaires (assuming they have not yet lost them!). If responses are not anonymous, you will be able to mail a card only to those who have not responded. If responses are anonymous, and you cannot tell who has and who has not responded, simply send a card to everyone. Include a statement like the ones used by finance companies: "If you have already responded, please disregard this reminder. Thank you for your cooperation." Full-scale follow-up activities are usually begun shortly after the deadline for responding has passed. A second set of questionnaires is sent but with a new cover letter, and of course another stamped envelope. The new letter should suggest that you know they *meant* to respond but that they may have misplaced the questionnaire or perhaps they never even received it. In other words, do not scold them. Proivde them with an acceptable reason for their nonresponse. The significance and purpose of the evaluation should be reemphasized and the importance of *their* input should be stressed again. The letter should suggest subtly that many others are responding. This implies that their peers have found the evaluation to be important and so should they.

If the second mailing does not result in an overall acceptable percentage of return, be creative. Magazine subscription agencies have developed follow-up procedures to a science and have become very creative. I once let a subscription to a popular weekly magazine lapse and received several gentle reminders and some "sensational one-time-only offers." One afternoon I received a long-distance call from several thousand miles away, and the sweet voice at the other end suggested that my mail was apparently not getting through and asked wouldn't I like to renew my subscription. I bit! The point is that phone calls, if feasible, may be used, or any other method of written, verbal, or personal communication which might induce additional persons to respond. People may grow to admire your persistence!

If your questionnaire is well constructed and your cover letter well written, you should get at least an adequate response rate. First mailings will typically produce at least a 40% return. A second mailing should bring your percentage up to at least 70%. Mailings beyond a second are generally not too effective. After a second mailing, use other approaches until an acceptable percentage of returns is achieved.

Dealing with nonresponse

Despite all your initial and follow-up efforts, you may find yourself with an unacceptably low response percentage, say 60%. This raises the problem of nongeneralizability of results since you do not know if the 60% represents the population from which the sample was originally selected as well as the total original sample. If you knew that those responding were essentially a random sample of the total sample, there would be no problem; but you don't know that. The recipients who responded may be different in some systematic way from nonrespondents (the old volunteer syndrome). They may be better educated, feel more strongly about the issue (positively or negatively), or be more successful. In follow-up studies of program graduates, for example, successful graduates might tend to respond more than unemployed graduates or those in low-paying jobs. Generalizations based on information provided by respondents only would suggest a rosier picture than if all graduates responded.

The usual approach to dealing with excessive nonresponse is to try to determine if nonrespondents are different from responders in some systematic way by randomly selecting a small subsample of nonrespondents and interviewing them, either in person or by phone. Through an interview, we not only can obtain responses to questionnaire items but can also try to determine any distinguishing characteristics. If responses are essentially the same for those interviewed as for the original respondents, it may be assumed that the response group is representative and the results generalizable. If they are significantly different, such differences as well as resulting limitations to generalizability must be discussed in the evaluation report. For example, instead of concluding that generally program graduates express satisfaction with their training, you might conclude that *successful* program graduates express satisfaction (naturally!).

Interviews

The steps involved in collecting data with interviews are essentially the same as for questionnaires. A sample (or population) of persons who posses the desired information, for example, is selected in the usual manner except that the sample is typically smaller. An effort must be made to get a promise of cooperation from those selected. Persons who do not attend interviews present the same problems as recipients who do not return questionnaires. The problem is more serious for interviews, however, since the sample size is smaller to begin with. The major differences between interview and questionnaire procedures are: the nature of the instrument involved (an interview guide versus a questionnaire), the need for human relations and communication skills, methods for recording responses, and the nature of pretest activities. The first and last of these have already been discussed in previous chapters.

Communication during the interview

Effective communication during the interview is critical and interviewers should be well trained before the interviews begin. Since first impressions can make a big difference, getting the interview "off on the right foot" is important. Before the first formal question is asked, some time should be spent in building rapport and putting the interviewee at ease. The purpose of the interview should be explained and strict confidentiality of responses should be assured. As the interview proceeds, the interviewer should make full use of the advantages of the interview situation. The interviewer can, for example, explain the purpose of any question whose relevance to the purpose of the evaluation is unclear to the interviewee. The interviewer should also be sensitive to reactions and proceed accordingly. If a person appears to be threatened by a particular line of questioning, for example, the interviewer should move on to other questions and return to the "threatening" questions later, when the interviewee is likely to be more relaxed. Or, if the interviewee gets carried away with a question and strays off the subject, the interviewer can gently get him or her back on the track. Above all, the interviewer should avoid words or actions which may make a person feel unhappy or threatened. Frowns and disapproving looks have no place in an interview!

Recording responses

Responses made during an interview can be recorded manually by the interviewer or mechanically by a recording device. When the interviewer records the responses, space is provided after each question in the interview guide, and responses are recorded either during the interview as it progresses or shortly after the interview is completed. If responses are recorded during the interview, the interview may be slowed down somewhat, especially if responses are at all lengthy. Also, some interviewees may become nervous if they know someone is writing down every word they say. If responses are recorded after the interview, the interviewer is not likely to recall every response exactly as given, especially if many questions are asked. On the other hand, when a recording device such as a cassette recorder is used, the interview moves more quickly and responses are recorded exactly as given. If responses need clarifying, several persons can listen to the recordings independently and classifications can be compared. A recorder, of course, may also initially make interviewees nervous, but they usually tend to forget its presence as the interview progresses, whereas they are constantly aware when someone is writing down their responses. In general, mechanical recording is more objective and efficient.

Observation

The procedures involved in observation are essentially the same as for questionnaires and interviews. Like the interview technique, observation is time-consuming and typically involves smaller samples. Concepts related to the defining of observational variables and the selection or development of recording forms have already been discussed (chapter 12). At this point we will discuss factors related to insuring accurate observations.

Promoting observer reliability

Unreliable observations are as useless as data based on an unreliable test. Determining observer reliability generally requires that at least two observers independently make observations. Their recorded judgments as to what occurred can then be compared to see how well they agree. Sometimes it is not possible to have several observers observe the same situation at the same time. One solution is to record the to-be-observed situation, with a videotape or audiotape recorder for example. This allows each observer to play back tapes at a time convenient for her or him. Another advantage to recording a situation is that you can replay it as often as you like. If behaviors to be observed are at all complex or occur at a fairly rapid rate, for example, it may be difficult to obtain reliable observations. If you record the behavior, you can play it back to your heart's content, as can other observers. This is especially useful if judgment and evaluation are required on the part of the observer. Regardless of whether observations are recorded as they occur or while viewing or listening to a tape—and assuming that a valid, reliable observation system is being used—the best way to increase observer reliability is to thoroughly train observers.

Training observers

In order to determine agreement among observers, at least two observers are required. That means that there will be at least one other person besides yourself (or two, if you are not going to personally observe) who needs to be familiar with the observational procedures. Additional observers need to be trained so that you have some assurance that all observers are observing and recording the same behaviors in the same way. Thus, they must be instructed as to what behaviors are to be observed, how behaviors are to be coded, how behaviors are to be recorded, and how often (time unit). Observers should participate in numerous practice sessions at which they observe situations similar to those to be involved in the evaluation and compare their recordings. Each point of disagreement should be discussed so that the observer who is incorrect understands why. Practice sessions using recordings of behavior are very effective since segments with which observers have difficulty can be replayed for discussion and feedback purposes. Estimates of observer reliability should be calculated periodically to determine the effectiveness of the training and practice. Observer reliability should increase with each session. Training may be terminated when a satisfactory level of reliability is achieved, say .75.

part six **summary**

13 instructional strategies and variables

Definition and purpose

1 Strategies are general approaches to promoting achievement of one or more objectives, and they generally entail a number of specific activities.

2 We may speak of instructional strategies, curriculum strategies, program strategies, and the like.

3 There are typically a number of strategies from which to choose. One may be designated the most likely to succeed; or there may be two (or more) promising strategies and the decision may be made to try each of them; or a combination of several strategies may be called for.

4 Following initial testing (administration of pretest and/or tests of entry behavior), planned strategies and activities are executed in the predetermined sequence.

5 If several strategies are being used simultaneously, then at various points in time decisions will be made as to which ones are working and which are not, and what kinds of changes need to be made.

6 When student evaluation is involved, instructional strategies are implemented; in essense, instructional strategies define the nature of the stimuli which will hopefully bring about the desired outcomes, or objectives.

7 Different types of learning require different strategies, and certain strategies are more appropriate for specific content areas. Other general strategies, however, appear to be applicable across a wide variety of content areas and types of learning.

8 All strategies must deal in one way or another with a number of variables such as feedback and review.

9 Any instructional strategy should deal with the three major types of activities involved in instruction: introductory activities, learning activities, and follow-up activities.

10 Introductory activities include getting students' attention, sharing objectives with students, motivating students, and providing students with advance organizers; relevant variables with respect to learning activities include method of instruction, sequencing and feedback; follow-up activities include review and remediation procedures.

Instructional strategies

11 The research evidence overwhelmingly indicates that no curriculum is more effective *in terms of achievement* than any other, although different curricula do produce different outcomes; similar conclusions have been reached concerning the comparative effectiveness of various teaching methods.

12 Different instructional approaches are not equivalent with respect to all variables, only with respect to group achievement; thus, selection of one strategy over another may be based on other factors, such as cost and time.

Individualized instruction

13 The term *individualized instruction* is applied to a host of activities designed to personalize instruction in order to meet individual student needs.

14 The one characteristic shared by all alleged individualized instruction efforts is that all students are not performing the same tasks at the same time.

15 In its idealized form, individualized instruction is characterized by the following: (a) different objectives for different students, (b) student self-pacing, (c) availability of a wide variety of instructional resources, (d) individualized testing, (3) constant diagnosis, feedback and remediation on an individual basis, and (f) unlimited recycling.

Multimedia instruction

16 The term *media* refers to all modes of communication—human, print and audiovisual.

17 The basic media selection process involves analyzing each desired outcome in terms of the type of learning involved and the corresponding conditions, and determining the most appropriate medium for each.

Instructional variables

18 There is sufficient evidence to support the view that there are ways of dealing with certain instructional variables that will result in increased student learning and retention.

Time

19 Evidence is increasingly piling up to support the not-so-amazing assertion that amount of time spent in learning is more important than the method of instruction.

20 The implication is that serious consideration should be given to the amount of time spent per day on each subject and to the amount of class time actually spent on instruction.

Discipline

21 Probably more time is wasted on attempts to maintain discipline than on any other activity; teachers typically identify lack of discipline as their number one problem.

22 Measures to prevent a lack of discipline include: maintaining an orderly classroom environment by avoiding disruptions and making smooth transitions; promoting student attention by using a variety of instructional modes and materials; and starting with a few, short, positively stated rules and consistently enforcing them.

Positive reinforcement

23 Positive reinforcement in the form of rewards is a highly effective technique which can be used with virtually all students.

24 A basic premise of positive reinforcement is that attention should be given to students who are being "good" and that specific behaviors should be emphasized.

25 Rewards may take many forms; they may be tangible (e.g. M & Ms) or intangible (e.g. verbal praise).
26 Students, of course, must learn to behave properly in the absence of rewards; therefore, rewards are gradually withdrawn.
27 A contingency contract is an agreement jointly developed by a student and a teacher; it specifies what task the student will perform and what reward will be received when it is done.

Models

28 Providing models involves exposing students to persons who behave in a desired manner; the impact of a model is heightened when the model is someone students look up to.
29 The ripple effect refers to the effect that teacher interactions with one student have on the behavior of other students; if a student is rewarded or punished by a teacher, the incident has a vicarious effect on the behavior of others.

Feedback

30 Feedback is information concerning the correctness or incorrectness of a response; learning and retention require feedback.
31 Feedback which tells a student that an exercise has been done correctly provides positive reinforcement; corrective feedback, which tells a student of an error, increases the probability of a future correct response.
32 Fairly immediate feedback may be necessary for initial learning of skills such as learning to write one's name which require "shaping," that is, successive approximations to a desired response. Delayed feedback appears to be superior with respect to retention, especially for test feedback.

Review

33 Considerable research evidence indicates that systematic review of concepts promotes retention.
34 Depending upon the type of learning involved, review may take the form of repetitive practice or spaced review; spaced review, which refers to reviews which occur one or more days after the day of original learning, is generally more appropriate.
35 Research has repeatedly shown that even one spaced review can significantly increase retention, regardless of when it occurs; two reviews increase retention even more dramatically.

14 evaluation designs and procedures

Overview

36 A valid evaluation has two essential ingredients: (1) end results must be assessed using valid and reliable instruments, and (2) there must be some credible estimate of what the results would have been *without* the program intervention.

37 A program is judged to be effective if it can be demonstrated that a significant positive change occurred which would not have occurred in the absence of the program.

38 No alternative can give us the same confidence in our findings that we can have when we apply an experimental research design.

Purpose and process

39 Effective evaluation of a program frequently requires some type of control group; the behavior of the control group serves as an indication of what the behavior of the program group would have been if participants had not been in the program.

40 The ideal approach is one in which an independent variable is manipulated, all other relevant variables are controlled, and the effect on one or more dependent variables (as measured by posttests) is observed.

41 The independent variable is the conditions to which the groups are exposed, and includes treatment conditions (the program intervention believed to make a difference) and control conditions.

42 Manipulation means that it is determined in advance which subjects (e.g., students) will receive the treatment and which will not.

43 The effect of the treatment is assessed in terms of posttest performance of the treatment and control groups.

44 Everything is planned in advance, including who the participants will be, who will serve as the control group, the precise nature of the treatment, how extraneous factors will be controlled or controlled for, and how performance will be measured.

45 The treatment group receives a new, or innovative, treatment, the approach under investigation, while the control group usually either receives a different treatment or is treated as usual.

46 The treatment group needs to be exposed to the treatment for a sufficient period of time; the treatment should be given a "chance to work."

47 The conditions to which the treatment and control groups are exposed must be different enough to make a difference.

Control

48 *Control* refers to efforts to remove or account for the effects of any variable, other than the independent variable, which might affect posttest performance.

49 There are two different kinds of variables which need to be controlled: participant variables (such as reading readiness), variables on which participants in the two groups might differ, and environmental variables (such as learning materials), variables which might cause unwanted differences between the groups.

50 When such variables are controlled, then at the end of some period of time, if groups differ in performance on the posttest, the difference can be attributed to the treatment.

Ethical considerations

51 Perhaps the foremost rule of ethics is that participants should not be harmed in any way, physically or mentally.

52 The participant's right to privacy is also an important consideration; it is usually sufficient to present data in terms of group statistics; if individual scores need to be presented, they should not be associated with participants' names or other identifying information.

53 Falsifying data in order to make findings agree with a hypothesis, to "look good," or to get refunded, is unprofessional, unethical and unforgivable.

Selection of participants

54 The first step in selecting participants for an evaluation study is to define the target population, that is, the group of interest, the group to which we would like the results of the evaluation to be generalizable.

55 A defined population has at least one characteristic which differentiates it from other groups; an example is all middle school students in Utopia County who are potential dropouts.

56 Populations may be virtually any size and may cover almost any geographical area; the entire group in which we are interested does not always participate in the evaluation.

57 A "good" sample is one that is representative of the population from which it was selected; selecting such a sample is not a haphazard process.

58 Regardless of the specific sampling techniques used, the steps in selection are essentially the same: identification of the population, determination of required group sizes, and selection of the sample.

59 The degree to which the treatment and control groups are equivalent is the degree to which performance comparisons are valid; the degree to which those selected represent the entire population is the degree to which results are generalizable.

60 In some cases the entire population participates in the evaluation; a portion of the population may be in the program and the remainder may be chosen for the control group, or participation in the treatment or control group is determined on a random basis.

61 Sometimes the entire population must participate in the program; in such cases the major evaluation problem is one of identifying a suitable control group.

Random sampling

62 *Random sampling* is the process of selecting a sample in such a way that all individuals in the defined population have an equal and independent chance of being selected for the sample.

63 Random sampling is the best single way to obtain a representative sample.

64 In general, random sampling involves defining the population, identifying each member of the population, and selecting individuals for the sample on a completely chance basis.

65 A random sample is generally selected using a table of random numbers.

66 Once the sample has been selected, members may be randomly *assigned* to treatment and control groups (by flipping a coin, for example) if group comparison is involved.

67 Stratified sampling does guarantee appropriate representation on one or more selected variables; the only difference between stratified random sampling

and random sampling is that members of the population are first classified into subgroups and then random selection is made from each subgroup.

Cluster sampling

68 *Cluster sampling* is sampling in which groups, not individuals, are randomly selected.

69 All the members of selected groups have similar characteristics; any intact group of similar characteristics is a *cluster*.

70 The steps in cluster sampling are similar to those in random sampling except that the random selection of groups (clusters), not individuals, is involved.

71 Cluster sampling can be done in stages, involving selection of clusters within clusters (*multistage sampling*); for example, schools can be randomly selected and then classrooms within each selected school can be randomly selected.

72 Basically, systematic sampling is analogous to counting off one-two-one-two in gym class. Given the size of the population and the desired sample size, a count-off number is determined; then you start at some random name near the beginning of a given list and count off every so many names (e.g. every fifth name) until the desired sample is selected.

Group size and selection bias

73 A sample should be as large as feasible; if it is too small, it may not be representative of the population and the results of the evaluation may not be generalizable to the population.

74 For questionnaires, interviews, and observation, a sample of 10% of the population is considered minimum; for evaluations which involve group comparisons, a minimum of 15 persons per group will give some degree of confidence that conclusions reached concerning differences between groups are valid.

75 A large sample size, however, does not guarantee a good, or representative, sample; even large samples can be biased and if samples are biased, so are results.

76 A major source of bias is the use of volunteers; since a population is composed of volunteers and nonvolunteers, the results of an effort using volunteers are not generalizable to the entire population, only to other volunteers.

Threats to validity

77 Any uncontrolled extraneous variables which affect posttest performance are threats to the validity of an evaluation study.

78 *Internal validity* refers to the condition where observed differences between the groups on the dependent variable (different posttest performance) are a direct result of manipulation of the independent variable (treatment and control conditions), not some other variable.

79 *External validity* refers to the condition where results are generalizable, or applicable, to groups and environments other than those actually involved in the evaluation.

80 Where validity is concerned, one must strive for a balance between control and realism. If a choice is involved, one should err on the side of too much control rather than too little; an evaluation study which is not internally valid is worthless.

Threats to internal validity

History

81 *History* refers to the occurrence of an incidental event which was not planned for but which may affect performance on the posttest.

Maturation

82 *Maturation* refers to physical or mental changes which may occur within participants over a period of time, which may affect their performance on a posttest.

Testing

83 *Testing* refers to improved scores on a posttest which are a result of participants' having taken a pretest.

Instrumentation

84 *Instrumentation* refers to unreliability, or inconsistency, in measuring instruments which may result in invalid assessment of performance.

Statistical regression

85 *Statistical regression* usually occurs when participants are selected on the basis of their extreme scores on some test and refers to the tendency of persons who score highest on a test (e.g. a pretest) to score lower on a retest (e.g. a posttest), and the tendency of those who score lowest on a test to score higher on a retest.

Differential selection

86 *Differential selection* occurs when already formed groups are used (as in cluster sampling) and refers to the fact that these groups may be different before the implementation even begins; this initial difference may at least partially account for posttest differences.

Mortality

87 *Mortality* is more likely to occur in longer evaluation studies and refers to the fact that persons who drop out of a group may share a characteristic such that their absence has a significant effect on the posttest results.

Selection-maturation interaction, etc.

88 The "etc." means that selection may also interact with factors such as history and testing, but *selection-maturation interaction* is more common. What this means is that if already formed groups are used, one group may profit more (or less) from a treatment, or have an initial advantage (or disadvantage), because of maturation, history, or testing factors.

Threats to external validity

Pretest-treatment interaction

89 *Pretest-treatment interaction* occurs when participants respond or react differently to a treatment because they have been pretested; the treatment effect

may be different than it would have been had participants not been pretested.

Selection-treatment interaction

90 Selection-treatment interaction is similar to the problem of differential selec-
    tion associated with internal invalidity and also occurs when participants are
    not randomly selected.
91 Interaction effects aside, the very fact that participants are not randomly se-
    lected from a population severely limits one's ability to generalize since rep-
    resentativeness of the sample is in question.
92 This nonrepresentativeness of groups may also result in a *selection-treatment
    interaction* whereby results hold only for the groups involved and are not rep-
    resentative of the treatment effect in the intended population.

Specificity of variables

93 Like selection-treatment interaction, specificity is a threat to generalizability
    regardless of the design used.
94 *Specificity of variables* refers to the fact that a given evaluation study is con-
    ducted with a specific kind of participant, using specific measuring instru-
    ments, at a specific time, under a specific set of circumstances.
95 To deal with the specificity issue, the evaluator must (1) operationally define
    variables in a way which has meaning outside of the evaluation setting, and
    (2) be careful in stating conclusions and generalizations.

Reactive arrangements

96 *Reactive arrangements* refers to a number of factors associated with the way in
    which the program or project is executed and the feelings and attitudes of the
    participants involved.
97 The evaluator may create an environment which is highly artificial and which
    hinders generalizability of findings to other settings.
98 The term Hawthorne effect is used to describe any situation in which partici-
    pants' behavior is affected not by the treatment per se but by their knowledge
    that they are participating in an evaluation or their feeling that they are in
    some way receiving special attention.
99 The John Henry effect refers to the phenomenon in which control groups (or
    their teachers) feel threatened or challenged by being in competition with a
    new program or approach and therefore outdo themselves, performing way
    beyond what would normally be expected.
100 When the John Henry effect occurs, the treatment under evaluation does not
    appear to be very effective since posttest performance of program participants
    is not much (if at all) better than that of control participants.
101 The placebo effect is in some ways an antidote for the Hawthorne effect and
    the John Henry effect. Its application in evaluation is that all groups involved
    should *appear* to be treated the same.
102 The novelty effect refers to increased interest, motivation, or involvement on
    the part of participants simply because they are doing something different.

Contamination and bias

103 *Contamination* occurs when the outcome of the evaluation is affected because
    the program staff, teachers, or evaluators are familiar with the participants;

these people may unintentionally influence participants' behavior or be subjective in evaluating their behavior.

104 Expectations concerning outcomes may actually contribute to producing those outcomes (experimenter bias).

105 As a general rule, anyone with a vested interest of any kind in the program under evaluation should not be directly involved in its implementation or assessment of its effectiveness. Further, program staff and/or evaluation personnel should avoid communicating outcome expectations to anyone who is involved in implementation or data collection.

Evaluation designs

106 The validity of an evaluation is a function of the degree to which extraneous variables are controlled; if they are not controlled, it is difficult to evaluate the effectiveness of a treatment and the generalizability of effects.

107 Control of extraneous variables is what design is all about; good designs control many sources of invalidity, poor designs control few.

108 Two types of extraneous variables in need of control are *participant variables* and *environmental variables;* participant variables include organismic variables and intervening variables.

109 *Organismic variables* are characteristics of the participants or organism (e.g. sex), which cannot be directly controlled but which can be controlled *for.*

110 Intervening variables, as the term implies, are variables which intervene between the treatment and the posttest (e.g. anxiety, boredom), which cannot be directly observed or controlled but which also can be controlled *for.*

Control of extraneous variables

111 Randomization is the best single way to control for many extraneous variables all at the same time.

112 Randomization should be used whenever possible: participants should be randomly selected from a population whenever possible, participants should be randomly assigned to groups whenever possible, treatments should be randomly assigned to groups whenever possible, and anything else you can think of should be randomly assigned if possible!

113 Randomization is effective in creating equivalent representative groups which are essentially the same on all relevant variables thought of, and probably even a few not thought of.

114 In addition to equating groups on variables such as intelligence, randomization also equalizes groups on environmental variables; certain environmental variables can be controlled by holding them constant for both groups.

115 Controlling participant variables is critical.

Matching

116 Matching is a technique for equating groups on one or more variables which have been identified as being highly related to posttest performance.

117 One approach to matching involves random assignment of pair members, one member to the treatment group and one member to the control group. For each of the available participants we attempt to find another participant with the same or a similar score on a measure of the variable to be controlled.

118 If randomization is not possible, as when existing groups are involved, then

for each participant in one group you identify a participant in the second group with the same or a similar score on a measure of the variable to be controlled.

119 A major problem with matching is that there are invariably persons who do not have a match; this fact may cost the program many participants, especially if matching is attempted on two or more variables.

120 One way to combat loss of participants is to match less closely; this procedure may increase participants, but it tends to defeat the purpose of matching.

121 A related procedure, which can be used when randomization is feasible, is to rank all of the participants from highest to lowest based on their scores on the control variable; each two participants with adjacent scores constitute a pair.

Comparing homogeneous groups and subgroups

122 Another way of controlling an extraneous variable is to compare groups which are homogeneous with respect to that variable.

123 A similar but more satisfactory approach is to form subgroups within each group which represent all levels of the control variable.

Analysis of covariance

124 The analysis of covariance is a statistical method for equating groups on one or more variables.

125 In essence, analysis of covariance adjusts scores on a posttest for initial differences on some other variable, such as pretest scores, IQ, readiness, or aptitude (assuming that performance on the "other variable" is related to performance on the posttest).

Types of designs

126 A selected design dictates to a great extent the specific procedures of an evaluation study, such as whether there will be a control group, whether participants will be randomly assigned to groups, whether each group will be pretested and how resulting data will be analyzed.

127 Depending upon the particular combination of such factors represented, different designs are appropriate for answering different kinds of questions and testing different types of hypotheses; also, designs vary widely in the degree to which they control the various threats to internal and external validity.

128 From the designs which are appropriate and feasible, you select the one which controls the most sources of internal and external invalidity.

129 The question really is not *whether* to use a research design but rather *when* to use a research design, and the answer is: whenever it is possible and feasible to do so.

130 In those instances in which the entire population is the treatment group, the evaluator's problem is to find a suitable control group.

131 One requirement that is common to all control groups is that the dates of their pretesting and posttesting must coincide, exactly or approximately, with the dates of pretesting and posttesting of the treatment group; otherwise, performance comparisons are not fair.

132 The major concept to keep in mind is that you should select and apply the best design or model that is feasible in your situation.

Research designs

True experimental designs

133 No design controls for *all* sources of invalidity, but true experimental designs do the best job.

134 Ideally, participants should be randomly selected and randomly assigned; however, to qualify as a true experimental design, at least random assignment must be involved.

The pretest-posttest control group design

135 The *pretest-posttest control group design* involves at least two groups formed by random assignment (R); both groups are pretested (O), one group receives a new, or unusual treatment (X), and both groups are posttested (O).

136 The combination of random assignment and the presence of a pretest and a control group serve to control for all sources of internal invalidity.

137 The only definite weakness with this design is a possible interaction between the pretest and the treatment which may make the results generalizable only to other pretested groups.

138 The best approach to data analysis is simply to compare the posttest scores of the two groups. The pretest is used to see if the groups are essentially the same on the dependent variable. If they are, posttest scores can be directly compared using a *t* test; if they are not (random assignment does not *guarantee* equality), posttest scores can be analyzed using analysis of covariance.

The posttest-only control group design

139 The *posttest-only control group design* is exactly the same as the pretest-posttest control group design *except* there is no pretest; participants are randomly assigned to groups, exposed to the independent variable, and posttested.

140 Posttest scores are compared to determine the effectiveness of the treatment.

141 The combination of random assignment and the presence of a control group serve to control for all sources of internal invalidity except mortality.

Quasi-experimental designs

142 Quasi-experimental designs provide adequate control of sources of invalidity when it is not feasible to randomly assign participants to groups.

The nonequivalent control group design

143 The *nonequivalent control group design* looks very much like the pretest-posttest control group design; the only difference is that the nonequivalent control group design does not involve random assignment of participants to groups (although treatment should be randomly assigned to groups if possible).

144 The lack of random assignment adds sources of invalidity not associated with the pretest-posttest control group design.

145 We should make every effort to use groups that are as equivalent as possible; if differences between the groups on any major extraneous variables are identified, analysis covariance can be used to statistically equate the groups.

146 An advantage of this design is that since classes are used "as is," possible effects from reactive arrangements are minimized.

The time-series design

147 The *time-series design* is actually an elaboration of the one-group pretest-post-test design; one group is repeatedly pretested, exposed to a treatment, and then repeatedly posttested.

148 If a group scores essentially the same on a number of pretests and then significantly improves following a treatment, we have some degree of confidence in the effectiveness of the treatment.

149 History is a problem with this design since something might happen between the last pretest and the first posttest, the effect of which might be confused with the treatment effect.

150 While statistical analyses appropriate for this design are rather advanced, determining the effectiveness of the treatment basically involves analysis of the pattern of the test scores.

151 A variation of the time-series design, which is referred to as the *multiple time-series design*, involves the addition of a control group to the basic design.

Pre-experimental designs

The one-shot case study

152 The *one-shot case study* involves one group which is exposed to a treatment and then posttested; none of the threats to validity which are relevant is controlled.

The one-group pretest-posttest design

153 The *one-group pretest-posttest design* involves one group which is pretested, exposed to a treatment, and posttested.

154 The success of the treatment is determined by comparing pretest and posttest scores.

155 Although this design controls invalidity not controlled by the one-shot case study, a number of additional factors are relevant to this design which are not controlled.

The static-group comparison design

156 The *static-group comparison design* involves at least two groups; one receives a new, or unusual treatment, the other, the control group, receives the usual or traditional treatment, and both groups are posttested.

157 Since participants are not randomly assigned to groups and since there is no pretest data, it is difficult to determine just how equivalent the groups are.

158 It is always possible that posttest differences are due to group differences, not just treatment effects.

Ex post facto designs

159 With ex post facto (causal-comparative) designs, the independent variable is not manipulated; the treatment has already occurred and no control was exercised in terms of selection of participants.

160 In evaluations such designs usually involve "treatments" which *could be* manipulated or "treatments" which ethically *should not be* manipulated.

161 As with experimental designs, the groups may differ in that one group has

had an experience which the other has not *or* the groups may differ in degree, and may have had different kinds of experiences.

162 It is important to select samples that are representative of their respective populations and similar with respect to all relevant variables except the "treatment" variable.

163 Since the random assignment, manipulation, and control which characterize experimental designs are missing in an ex post facto design, extreme caution must be applied in interpreting results.

164 Every attempt must be made to determine the equivalence of the comparison groups; information on a number of background and participant variables may be collected.

165 In order to promote equality, or to correct for identified inequalities, any of the control procedures (e.g. matching) can be used.

166 Although relationships established with these designs are tenuous, ex post facto designs do permit evaluation of variables which cannot or should not be investigated with an experimental design.

Title I models

167 Title I projects are federally funded programs designed to meet the academic needs of disadvantaged students.

168 The primary purpose of the Title I evaluation system is to provide evidence as to whether the achievement of Title I students is higher than it would have been if they had not participated in the program; that is, its aim is to determine the effectiveness of Title I programs.

169 All three models used in Title I evaluations involve comparing *actual* posttest performance with the *expected* no-treatment performance, that is, with an estimate of what posttest performance would have been had students not participated in a Title I program.

170 Because Title I evaluation models can handle a number of situations for which there is no legitimate or readily identifiable control group (e.g. when the entire target population is in the program), their popularity has been growing with state and local education agencies.

171 The Title I models are applicable in the evaluation of a variety of programs and projects, not just in the evaluation of Title I programs. In many cases one of the Title I models may be much easier to implement than a traditional research design or it may be the only feasible approach to evaluation of a given program.

Model B—the control group design

172 Model B encompasses traditional experimental designs, and in its ideal form Model B is the pretest-posttest control group design; the nonequivalent control group design is also permitted if it can be verified that the groups are essentially equivalent on all relevant variables.

173 Model B is frequently opposed on practical grounds because it is more difficult to implement, and on philosophical and/or feasibility grounds; withholding students with a demonstrated need from a potentially beneficial program may be opposed or actually prohibited (as in the case of Title I programs).

Model C—the special regression design

174 Model C deals very nicely with those situations in which all members of an

identified target population must participate in program activities, as with many remediation programs.

175 Specifically, the special regression model is applicable in situations in which participants are selected based on their scores on a given test (or on some composite scores); those who score below a given cut-off score participate, and those who score above the cut-off score do not.

176 Expected posttest scores are predicted based on pretest scores; program effectiveness is determined by comparing predicted posttest scores with actual posttest scores.

Model A—the norm-referenced design

177 Model A is also appropriate for situations in which formation of a reasonably equivalent control group is not feasible.

178 Model A involves pretesting and posttesting of the program students and determining whether and to what degree their percentile position changed (with respect to the norms on some valid and reliable standardized test), presumably as a result of the program.

179 The assumption is that without the program students would be at the same percentile at the end of the program period as at the beginning; if their percentile position increases (say from the 17th percentile on the pretest to the 32nd percentile on the posttest), the effectiveness of the program has presumably been demonstrated.

180 The norm group, in essence, serves as the control group; in order to make this comparison of group performance with test norms, dates of pretesting and posttesting must coincide rather closely with norming dates.

181 It is also generally agreed that a valid comparison also generally requires that: (1) a different test be used for pretesting than for selecting participants; (2) the same test be used for pretesting and posttesting; and (3) only the scores of students who take both the pretest and the posttest be considered in analysis of results.

182 The validity of the comparison is a function of how similar the program students are to students in the norm group.

183 The major conclusion to be reached is that with respect to design validity Model C is definitely to be perferred; with respect to feasibility Model A is clearly the people's choice.

Single-subject designs

184 In single-subject designs each participant serves as his or her own control in variations on a time-series design.

185 Basically, the student is alternately exposed to treatment and nontreatment conditions and performance is repeatedly measured during each phase.

186 If performance is significantly higher during the treatment condition phase than during either control phase, then the treatment is judged to be effective.

187 The *treatment reversal design* is very similar to the basic design except that the treatment phase is not followed by a control phase but rather by a treatment reversal phase; that is, a condition which is essentially the opposite of the treatment condition is implemented.

188 A more satisfactory type of single-subject design is the *multiple-baseline design*. Instead of collecting initial baseline (control) data for one student and one behavior, we collect data either on one behavior for several students or

several behaviors for one student. We then systematically, over a period of time, apply the treatment to each student (or to each behavior) one at a time until all students (or behaviors) are under treatment.

189 In a multiple-baseline design, if measured performance increases in each case only after treatment is introduced, then the treatment is judged to be effective.

Functional-level testing

190 If a test is too difficult for a given group, we have what is called a *floor effect*; such a test is characterized by many low scores, resulting mainly from guessing.

191 If a test is too easy for a given group, we have a *ceiling effect*; in this case many students achieve relatively high scores.

192 If either the floor effect or the ceiling effect is operating in an evaluation, the result will probably be an overestimate or underestimate of achievement gains.

193 Functional-level testing refers to the practice of testing students at their actual level of competence, at whatever test level is necessary to accurately assess their achievement.

194 Functional-level testing includes in-level testing and out-of-level testing. If you administer a test recommended *for* fourth graders *to* fourth graders, you are conducting in-level testing.

195 Out-of-level testing involves selection and administration of a test recommended for a *different* age or grade based on the students' actual level of achievement. Since most types of tests are available for a number of levels, out-of-level testing involves administration of a test at a level higher or lower than the one suggested by the students' age or grade level.

15 data collection procedures

General considerations

196 Maximization of test scores requires that test takers be prepared. They should know in advance when a test is going to be administered and for what purpose, and the nature of the test.

197 Excessive levels of anxiety have been shown to interfere with performance; a complete absence of anxiety, however, is also counterproductive since test takers are not motivated to do their best.

198 Collecting any kind of data requires planning and organization; in addition to determining *what* will be done, it must also be decided *who* will do it.

199 In a special program or project, there may be activities which must be assigned to appropriate staff members and coordinated by the director.

200 The characteristics which are required or desired of temporary assistants will vary depending upon the task.

201 Regardless of their intended functions, temporary or part-time assistants should (1) participate in some type of orientation to the program, (2) receive training related to their assigned task, and (3) be given opportunities for supervised practice.

202 Before any data are actually collected, anyone involved in any way with data collection procedures should become thoroughly familiar with all relevant re-

strictions, legal or otherwise, related to the collection, storing, and sharing of obtained information; also, all necessary permissions from participants, school administrators, federal agencies, and the like should be obtained *in writing*.

203 All data collection activities should be carefully and systematically monitored to insure that correct procedures are being followed.

Questionnaires

Selection of recipients

204 Recipients should be selected using an appropriate sampling technique (an entire population may also be used), and identified recipients must be persons who (1) have the desired information and (2) are likely to be willing to give it.

Follow-up activities

205 An initial follow-up activity is to simply send out a reminder postcard.
206 Full-scale follow-up activities are usually begun shortly after the deadline for responding has passed. A second set of questionnaires is sent but with a new cover letter, and of course another stamped envelope.

Dealing with nonresponse

207 A response rate of less than 70% raises the problem of nongeneralizability of results since you do not know if the persons who did respond represent the population from which the sample was originally selected as well as the original sample.
208 The usual approach to dealing with excessive nonresponse is to try to determine if nonrespondents are different from responders in some systematic manner by randomly selecting a small subsample of nonrespondents and interviewing them, either in person or by phone.

Interviews

209 Persons who do not attend interviews present the same problems as recipients who do not return questionnaires, but the problem is more serious for interviews since the sample size is smaller to begin with.

Communication during the interview

210 Before the first formal question is asked, some time should be spent in building rapport and putting the interviewee at ease.
211 The interviewer should make full use of the advantages of the interview situation, and should be sensitive to the reactions of the interviewee and proceed accordingly.

Recording responses

212 Responses made during an interview can be recorded manually by the interviewer or mechanically by a recording device.
213 In general, mechanical recording is more objective and efficient.

Observation

214 The procedures involved in observation are essentially the same as for questionnaires and interviews; like the interview technique, observation is time-consuming and typically involves smaller samples.

Promoting observer reliability

215 Determining observer reliability generally requires that at least two observers independently make observations; their recorded judgments as to what occurred can then be compared to see how well they agree.
216 Recording situations to be observed allows each observer to play back tapes at a time convenient for him or her, and to play them back as often as needed.

Training observers

217 Observers need to be trained so that you have some assurance that all observers are observing and recording the same behaviors in the same way.
218 Observers must be instructed as to what behaviors are to be observed, how behaviors are to be coded, how behaviors are to be recorded, and how often.
219 Practice sessions using recordings of behaviors are very effective since segments with which observers have difficulty can be replayed for discussion and feedback purposes.
220 Training may be terminated when a satisfactory level of reliability is achieved, say .75.

task 6 **performance criteria**

a If a unit of instruction is involved, describe the major characteristics of the selected instructional strategy (or strategies) e.g. multimedia instruction. Describe how introductory activities, learning activities, and follow-up activities will be implemented (even if hypothetically) within the framework of the selected strategy, e.g. using a film to motivate students. Describe also how major instructional variables will be dealt with, e.g. every class will begin with a review of the previous day's work.
b If a formal evaluation effort is involved, describe the size and major characteristics of the participant population and how participants will be selected (even if hypothetically). If appropriate, describe how comparison groups will be formed. For the selected evaluation design, indicate why it was selected, potential threats to validity associated with the design, and aspects of the implementation which might minimize them. If a research design is involved, a figure should be included which illustrates the selected design. For example, you might say:

> Since random assignment of participants to groups is possible and since a verification of initial group equivalence is desired, the pretest-posttest control group design has been selected (see Figure 1).

Group	Assignment	N	Pretest	Independent Variable	Posttest
1	Random	120	RRRT*	Structured Preschool Program	RRRT
2	Random	120	RRRT	Unstructured Preschool Program	RRRT

* Rah-Rah Readiness Test

figure 1
Evaluation design

The description of procedures should describe in detail all the steps which will be executed, including: (1) how and when pretest data will be collected; (2) the ways in which the groups will be different (the independent variable); (3) environmental variables which will be the same for both groups (control procedures); and (4) how and when posttest data will be collected.

Does it look bad? Is it? What will it turn into?

part seven
analysis and interpretation of results

Every type of evaluation involves analysis and interpretation of results. Teachers, for example, must continually analyze test scores and interpret the results of both classroom tests and standardized tests. Since raw scores by themselves tell us very little, they must generally be compared with the scores of some defined group or with some defined criterion, depending upon whether the test is norm-referenced or criterion-referenced. Appropriate interpretation of norm-referenced test scores invariably requires application of a number of statistics. Application of most statistical methods to criterion-referenced test scores, on the other hand, is frequently inappropriate because these methods require score variance. Therefore, analysis and interpretation of criterion-referenced test scores is greatly simplified.

Analysis and interpretation of results is a critical process because it leads directly to the formulation of conclusions and the making of decisions. Anyone involved should be knowledgeable of relevant procedures. Even if you are not directly involved in calculating necessary statistics, interpreting the results properly requires familiarity with the applied statistical techniques. Statistics is not a foreign language. It's simply a set of procedures for describing, synthesizing, and interpreting quantitative data. One-thousand scores, for example, can be represented by a single number. Choice of appropriate statistical techniques is determined by factors such as the type of evaluation, the evaluation questions of interest, and if applicable, the type of evaluation design involved. Like other components of the evaluation process, statistical procedures and techniques are identified during the planning phase. Analysis and interpretation of results is as important as any other component of the evaluation process; regardless of how well the evaluation is conducted, inappropriate analyses can lead to inappropriate conclusions.

This part describes and explains only those statistics most commonly used in educational evaluation. For our purposes, it is important that you be able to apply and interpret these statistics, *not* necessarily that you understand their theoretical rationale and mathematical derivation. Despite what you may have heard, statistics is easy. In order to calculate the statistics we'll be using, you only need to know how to add, subtract, multiply, and divide. That's all there is. All formulas, no matter how gross they may look, turn into arithmetic problems when applied to a set of scores. The arithmetic problems involve only the operations of addition, subtraction, multiplication, and division; the formulas tell you how often, and in what order, to perform those operations. Now, if you are a smarty, you're probably thinking, What about square roots? While many of the formulas do involve square roots, you do not have to know how to find the square root of anything. All the "square rootin'" has been done for you, and the square root of any reasonable number (six trillion is not a reasonable number) can be found in a table (see table A.2 in the Appendix).

Even if you have a hangup about math and haven't had a math course since junior high school, you'll be able to calculate statistics; no calculus is required. The very hardest formula still requires only arithmetic, maybe sixth grade arithmetic if you have to divide by a big number, but arithmetic just the same. In fact, you don't even have to divide big numbers if you do not want to—you're allowed to use a calculator! So if you follow the steps as they're presented, you can't go wrong. You're going to be pleasantly surprised to see just how easy statistics is. Trust me.

The goal of part 7 is for you to be able to correctly analyze and interpret test scores, applying statistical methods when appropriate. After reading part 7, you should be able to do the following task.

task seven
Using the test scores obtained in task 5, perform the following:
a Construct a frequency polygon.
b Compute the mean and standard deviation.
c Compute and interpret the split-half reliability.
d Apply the Spearman-Brown prophecy formula to the reliability coefficient obtained in **c** and interpret the resulting value.
e Compute and interpret the standard error of measurement (SE_m).
f Convert each score to a T score.
g Assume the distribution is normal and use the normal curve equivalency figure to convert each T score to a percentile and a stanine.
h Assume the test is norm-referenced and make a statement concerning each student's performance (score) relative to the rest of the group.
i Assume the test is criterion-referenced, state your criterion (or criteria), and make a statement concerning each student's performance (score) relative to the objectives measured by the test.
(See Performance Criteria, p. 473.)

16 pre-analysis procedures

After reading chapter 16, you should be able to:

1 List the steps involved in scoring locally-developed tests.
2 Identify and describe the four scales of measurement.
3 List three examples of each of the four scales of measurement.

Overview

The process of evaluation, especially the product phase, involves considerable raw data resulting from the administration of one or more standardized or locally-developed instruments, or from the collection of naturally available data (such as grade point averages). Collected data must be accurately scored, if appropriate, and systematically tabulated and organized in a manner which facilitates analysis. As with the other aspects of evaluation, scoring and tabulation procedures should be planned prior to implementation; depending upon the format of the instrument selected or developed, different scoring and tabulation routines will be optimally efficient. Of course, the more participants involved, the more complex are the procedures, but even a classroom of 25 students generates a fair amount of data which must be treated in some organized fashion.

In large-scale evaluation efforts data may be collected at a number of sites (e.g. schools) and forwarded to a central location. Such data should be carefully checked at each individual location prior to forwarding as a precautionary measure. Any problems, such as incomplete data or improperly completed tests and forms, can be more easily identified and efficiently handled at the point of origin. All data should be checked twice for completeness and accuracy, once at the individual sites and again at the central collection point, or twice at the same location if only one site is involved. Every time data changes hands, a new source of error arises. Students may incorrectly complete answer sheets, teachers may misplace answer sheets, temporary assistants may miscode responses which are to be computer analyzed, and so forth. And while it is not likely, it is possible that a computer, or other mechanical device, may incorrectly score and/or analyze data. Thus, data must be carefully checked both before and after analysis. As suggested previously, specific activities related to scoring, tabulation, and analysis should be assigned to specific persons. And regardless of how many people are actually involved in data collection, there should be one person at each site with overall responsibility for the compilation, checking, and forwarding of data.

Scoring procedures

All instruments administered should be scored accurately and consistently. Each person's test should be scored using the same procedures and criteria. When a standardized instrument is used, the scoring process is greatly facilitated. The test manual usually spells out the steps to be followed in scoring each test (or answer sheet) and a scoring key is often provided. If the manual is followed conscientiously and each test is scored carefully, scoring errors are minimized. As an extra check, it is usually a good idea to recheck all hand-scored tests, or at least some percentage of them, say 25% (every fourth test).

Scoring locally developed instruments is more complex, especially if open-ended, free response items are involved. There is no manual to follow and there are no directions for categorizing responses, and scoring procedures have to be developed and refined. Steps for scoring each item and for arriving at a total score must be delineated and carefully followed. If nonobjective items are to be scored it is highly advisable also to have at least one other person score the tests as a reliability check. Even if objective items are involved, it is usually a good idea to recheck all or some percentage of the tests. Tentative scoring procedures should always be tried out beforehand by administering the instrument to a group from the same or a similar population as the one from which participants will be selected for the actual evaluation study. Problems with the instrument or with scoring procedures can be identified and corrected before it is too late to do anything about them. The procedure ultimately used to score evaluation instruments should be described in detail in the final evaluation report.

Again, if answer sheets are to be machine scored, as they are likely to be in a large-scale evaluation effort, they should be checked carefully for stray pencil marks and a percentage of them should be scored by hand just to make sure that the key is correct and that the machine is scoring properly. The fact that responses are being scored by a machine does not relieve you of the responsibility of carefully checking your data before and after processing.

Tabulation procedures

After instruments have been scored, the results are transferred to summary data sheets and/or data cards. Recording of the scores in a systematic manner facilitates examination of the data as well as data analysis. Whether analysis involves the scores of a group of eighth graders on a midterm exam or pre- and posttest scores of a treatment group and a control group, data are generally placed in columns, one for each group, in ascending or descending order. If pretest (or other) scores are involved, similar, additional columns are formed, as shown in table 16.1. Even this simple ordering of data reveals information not readily discernible when scores are in random order. In table 16.1 for example, we can see that the pretest scores of the two groups appear to be very similar. If planned analyses involve subgroup comparisons, scores or responses should be tabulated separately for each subgroup. To use a former example, a special program might be developed to better meet the needs of potential dropouts at the middle school level. Results might be tabulated separately for each grade level, (i.e. grades six, seven, eight, and nine). Or, a superintendent might be interested in comparing the attitudes toward unions of elementary level teachers with those of secondary teachers. Thus, for a question such as "Would you join a union if given the opportunity?" the superintendent would tally the number of "yes," "no," and "undecided" responses separately for elementary and secondary teachers.

When a number of different kinds of data are collected for each participant, such as several test scores and biographical information, data are frequently recorded on data cards, one card for each participant. The card for each participant follows the same format, and both the variable names and the actual data are frequently coded. The variable "pretest reading comprehension scores," for example, may be coded as PRC, and sex of student may be recorded as "1" or "2" (male or female). When a number of different analyses are to be performed, data cards facilitate analysis since they can be easily sorted and re-sorted to form the piles, or subgroups, required for each analysis.

If complex or multiple analyses are to be performed, or if a large number of participants are involved, evaluators frequently let computers do the calculations. If a computer is to be used, data must be presented in a machine-readable form, usually on punched cards. Using a procedure called keypunching, which is similar to typing, data can be transferred from data sheets or data cards onto special cards which are "fed into" the computer. In essence, a keypunch machine translates numbers into a series of punched holes in a card which the computer can "read," or understand. Since keypunching represents an extra step and thus one more point where mistakes can be made, it is vital that data be recorded systematically

table 16.1
Hypothetical summary data sheet for the results in an evaluation based on a pretest-posttest control group design

	Treatment	Control
Pretest	50	51
	58	57
	60	60
	62	62
	64	63
	64	64
	65	65
	65	65
	66	67
	67	69
	70	71
	72	72
	72	73
	75	77
	78	78
Posttest	68	55
	72	60
	76	65
	78	70
	80	72
	84	74
	84	74
	85	75
	86	75
	86	76
	88	76
	90	76
	91	78
	92	82
	96	87

and consistently on data sheets or cards so that keypunch errors are minimized. Of course keypunched data cards should always be checked against original data sheets or cards before analysis.[1]

Once the data have been prepared for analysis, the choice of statistical procedures to be applied is determined not only by the evaluation questions, hypotheses and/or design but also by the type of measurement scale represented by the data.

Types of measurement scales

Data for analysis result from the measurement of one or more variables. Depending upon the variables, and the way in which they are measured, different

[1] More will be said concerning the use of the computer in data analysis later in this chapter.

kinds of data result, representing different scales of measurement. There are four types of measurement scales: nominal, ordinal, interval, and ratio. It is important to know which type of scale is represented by your data since different statistics are appropriate for different scales of measurement.

Nominal scales

A *nominal scale* represents the lowest level of measurement. Such a scale classifies persons (or objects) into two or more categories. Whatever the basis for classification, a person can only be in one category, and members of a given category have a common set of characteristics. Classifying students as tall versus short, male versus female, or introverted versus extroverted, are all examples of nominal scales. When a nominal scale is used, the data simply indicate how many persons are in each category. For 100 first graders, for example, it might be determined that 40 attended kindergarten and 60 did not.

For identification purposes, categories are sometimes numbered from 1 to however many categories there are, say 4. It is important to realize, however, that the category labeled 4 is only different from the category labeled 3; 4 is not more, or higher, than 3, only different from 3. To avoid confusion, it is sometimes a good idea to label categories with letters instead of numbers—A, B, C, D instead of 1, 2, 3, 4. While nominal scales are not very precise, occasionally their use is necessary.

Ordinal scales

An *ordinal scale* not only classifies persons (or objects) but also ranks them in terms of the degree to which they possess a characteristic of interest. In other words, an ordinal scale puts people in order from highest to lowest, from most to least. With respect to height, for example, 50 students might be ranked from 1 to 50; the student with rank 1 would be the tallest and the student with rank 50 would be the shortest. It would be possible to say that one student was taller or shorter than another student. A student's rank in a graduating class and the expression of a test score as a percentile rank are measures of relative standing which represent ordinal scales.

While ordinal scales do indicate that some persons are higher, or possess more of a trait, than others, they do not indicate how much higher or how much more. In other words, intervals between ranks are not equal. The difference between rank 1 and rank 2 is not necessarily the same as the difference between rank 2 and rank 3, as the example below illustrates:

Rank	Height
1	6'2"
2	6'1"
3	5'11"
4	5'7"
5	5'6"
6	5'5"
7	5'4"
8	5'3"
9	5'2"
10	5'0"

The difference in height between the person with rank 1 and the person with rank 2 is 1 inch; the difference between rank 2 and rank 3 is 2 inches. In the example given, differences in height represented by differences in rank range from one inch to four inches. Similarly, differences in achievement represented by differences in rank may vary greatly. Thus, while an ordinal scale results in more precise measurement than a nominal scale, it still does not allow the level of precision usually desired for evaluation purposes.

Interval scales

An *interval scale* has all the characteristics of a nominal scale and an ordinal scale, but in addition it is based upon predetermined equal intervals. Most of the tests used in educational evaluation, such as achievement tests, aptitude tests, and intelligence tests, represent interval scales. Therefore, you will most often be working with statistics appropriate for interval data. For example, when scores have equal intervals, it is assumed that the difference between a score of 30 and a score of 40 is essentially the same as the difference between a score of 50 and a score of 60. Similarly, the difference between 81 and 82 is approximately the same as the difference between 82 and 83. If height is considered as an interval scale, then clearly the difference between a height of 5'6" and 5'5" (1 inch) is the same as the difference between 5'4" and 5'3". Thus, with an interval scale we can say not just that Egor is taller than Ziggie, but also that Egor is seven feet tall and Ziggie is five feet tall. Interval scales, however, do not have a true zero point. Such scales typically have an arbitrary maximum score and an arbitrary minimum score, or zero point. If an IQ test produces scores ranging from 0 to 200, a score of 0 does not indicate the absence of intelligence nor does a score of 200 indicate possession of the ultimate intelligence. A score of 0 only indicates the lowest level of performance possible on that particular test and a score of 200 represents the highest level. Thus, scores resulting from administration of an interval scale can be added and subtracted, but not multiplied or divided. We can say that an achievement test score of 90 is 45 points higher than a score of 45 but we cannot say that a person scoring 90 knows twice as much as a person scoring 45. Similarly, a person with a measured IQ of 140 is not necessarily twice as smart, or twice as intelligent, as a person with a measured IQ of 70. For most educational measurement, however, such generalizations are not needed.

Ratio scales

A *ratio scale* represents the highest, most precise, level of measurement. A ratio scale has all the advantages of the other types of scales and in addition it has a meaningful, true zero point. Height, weight, and time are examples of ratio scales. The concept of "no time," for example, is a meaningful one. Because of the true zero point, we can say not only that the difference between a height of 3'2" and a height of 4'2" is the same as the difference between 5'4" and 6'4", but also that a man 6'4" is twice as tall as a child 3'2". Similarly, 60 minutes is 3 times as long as 20 minutes, and 40 pounds is 4 times as heavy as 10 pounds. Thus, with a ratio scale we can say that Egor is tall and Ziggie is short (nominal scale), Egor is taller than Ziggie (ordinal scale), Egor is seven feet tall and Ziggie is five feet tall (interval scale), *and* that Egor is seven-fifths as tall as Ziggie. Since most physical measures represent ratio scales, but psychological measures do not, ratio scales are not used very often in educational evaluation.

A statistic appropriate for a lower level of measurement may be applied to data representing a higher level of measurement. A statistic appropriate for ordinal data, for example, may be used with interval data, since interval data possess all the characteristics of ordinal data and more. The reverse, however, is not true. A statistic appropriate for interval data cannot be applied to ordinal data since such a statistic requires equal intervals.

17 data analysis

After reading chapter 17, you should be able to

1 List the steps involved in constructing a frequency polygon.
2 Define or describe three measures of central tendency.
3 Define or describe three measures of variability.
4 List four characteristics of normal distributions.
5 Define or describe each of the following measures of relative position: percentile ranks, Z scores, T scores, stanines, deviation IQ.
6 Define or describe grade equivalents and age equivalents.
7 Describe how a correlation coefficient is interpreted, using a hypothetical coefficient (e.g. .62).
8 Define or describe two methods of computing a correlation coefficient.
9 Generate a column of 10 numbers in which each number falls between 1 and 10 (in other words, make them up). You may use a number more than once. Assume these numbers are scores on a test. Using these "scores," give the formula and compute each of the following (show your work):
   a mean
   b standard deviation
   c z scores
   d T scores
   e the Spearman rho
   f the Pearson r
   (For e and f, divide your column in half to make two columns of five scores each.)
10 Define or describe the null hypothesis and give an example.
11 State the purpose of a test of significance.
12 State the purpose of the t test.
13 Define or describe independent and nonindependent samples.
14 Describe one major problem associated with the use of gain scores.
15 List the major steps involved in using the computer for data analysis.

Descriptive statistics

The first step in data analysis is to describe, or summarize, the data using descriptive statistics. In some evaluation efforts the analysis procedure may consist solely of calculating and interpreting descriptive statistics. A teacher, for example, may be interested only in describing the performance of the class and the achievement level of each individual in relation to average class performance. Descriptive statistics permit us to meaningfully describe many, many scores with a small number of indices by providing answers to questions such as: What was the average score on the test? Were most of the scores close to the average score or were they considerably spread out? Was the test reliable? And so forth. Descriptive statistics also permit us to make interpretive statements (both norm-referenced and criterion-referenced, but mainly the former) about individual scores by providing answers to questions such as: Is this particular score above the average score or below it? How much higher or lower? What percentage of the scores was lower than this score? And so forth. Whether locally-developed or standardized instruments are administered, descriptive statistics are invariably involved in interpretation of results.

Types

The major types of descriptive statistics are measures of central tendency, measures of variability, measures of relative position, and measures of relationship. *Measures of central tendency* are used to determine the typical or average score of a group of scores; *measures of variability* indicate how spread out a group of scores are; *measures of relative position* describe a person's performance compared to the performance of all other persons in a defined group who took the same test; and *measures of relationship* indicate to what degree two sets of scores are related. Before actually calculating any of these measures, it is often useful to present the data in graphic form.

Graphing data

As discussed previously, data are often recorded on summary sheets, in columns, and placed in ascending order. Data in this form are easily graphed. Graphing data permits us to see what the distribution of scores looks like. The shape of the distribution may not be self-evident, especially if a large number of scores are involved, and, as we shall see later, the shape of the distribution may influence our choice of certain descriptive statistics. Also, some people who cannot relate to numbers can relate to graphs. Depicting a set of scores graphically helps these people to better understand the nature of the distribution of scores and each score's position within that distribution.

The most common method of graphing data is to construct a frequency polygon. A *frequency polygon* basically shows how many persons attained each score. The first step in constructing a frequency polygon is to list all scores and to tabulate how many persons received each score. If 85 tenth-grade students were

table 17.1
Frequency distribution based on 85 hypothetical achievement test scores

Score	Frequency of Score
78	1
79	4
80	5
81	7
82	7
83	9
84	9
85	12
86	10
87	7
88	6
89	3
90	4
91	1
	Total: 85 students

given an achievement test, the results might be as shown in table 17.1. Once the scores are tallied, the steps are as follows:

1 Place all the scores on a horizontal axis, at equal intervals, from lowest score to highest.
2 Place the frequencies of scores at equal intervals on the vertical axis, starting with zero.
3 For each score, find the point where the score intersects with its frequency of occurrence and make a dot.
4 Connect all the dots with straight lines.

From figure 17.1 we can see that most of the tenth graders in our example scored at or near 85, with progressively fewer students achieving higher or lower scores. In other words, the scores appear to form a relatively normal distribution, a concept to be discussed a little later. This knowledge would be helpful in selecting an appropriate measure of central tendency.

If the range of scores is great, say more than 20, it is usually more appropriate to tally and graph the frequencies of scores within given intervals. If the scores in figure 17.1, for example, ranged from 17 to 91 instead of 78 to 91, it would be impractical to place every individual score (i.e. 17, 18, 19, 20 . . . 88, 89, 90, 91) on the horizontal axis. In such cases we apply the following, or a similar, procedure:

1 Compute the range of scores by subtracting the lowest score (L) from the highest score (H) and adding one, i.e. $H - L + 1$.
2 Divide the range by the desired number of intervals, say 15, and round to the nearest whole number. The resulting number is the number of scores in each interval.
3 Make the lowest score actually earned the lowest score in the first interval.

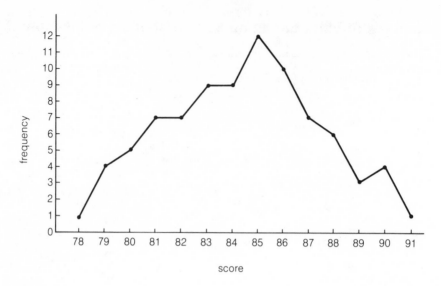

figure 17.1
Frequency polygon based on 85 hypothetical achievement test scores.

It really makes very little difference whether we define the range to be $H - L + 1$ or $H - L$, but $H - L + 1$ is more accurate. If, for example, the highest score was 10 and the lowest score was 5, $H - L$ would equal 5 whereas $H - L + 1$ would equal 6, which is the actual number of scores in the range (i.e. 5, 6, 7, 8, 9, 10). If we applied the above three steps to the scores in table 17.1, we would get the following results:

1 The range is $H - L + 1 = 91 - 78 + 1 = 13 + 1 = 14$.
2 The range, 14, divided by 15 (usually a good number) = .93. The nearest whole number is 1. Thus, each interval contains only one score.
3 The first interval is the score 78, the second is 79, and so forth, as shown in figure 17.1.

If, on the other hand, the lowest score was 17 and the highest 91, we would get the following results:

1 The range is $H - L + 1 = 91 - 17 + 1 = 74 + 1 = 75$.
2 The range, 75, divided by 15 = 5. Thus, each interval contains five scores.
3 The lowest score is 17 so the first interval will be 17–21 and will contain the 5 scores 17, 18, 19, 20, 21. The second interval will be 22–26, and so forth. Thus, the scores represented on the horizontal axis of a frequency polygon will be 17, 22, 27, 32, 37, 42, 47, 52, 57, 62, 67, 72, 77, 82, 87, 92.

For many classroom tests an interval of one, as shown in table 17.1 and figure 17.1, will be reasonable. For larger classroom tests and many standardized tests, grouping scores into intervals is more appropriate.

Measures of central tendency

Measures of central tendency provide a convenient way of describing a set of data with a single number. The number which results from computation of a measure of central tendency represents the average or typical score attained by a group. The three most frequently encountered indices of central tendency are the mode, the median, and the mean. Each of these indices is appropriate for a different scale of measurement. The mode is appropriate for nominal data, the median for ordinal data, and the mean for interval or ratio data. Since most measurement in educational evaluation represents an interval scale, the mean is the most frequently used measure of central tendency.

The mode

The *mode* is the score which is attained by more people than any other score. For the data presented in figure 17.1, for example, the mode is 85 since 12 students achieved that score. The mode is not established through calculation; it is determined by looking at a set of scores or at a graph of scores to see which score occurs most frequently. There are several problems associated with the mode, and it is therefore of limited value and seldom used. For one thing, a set of scores may have two (or more) modes, in which case it is referred to as bimodal. Another problem with the mode is that it is an unstable measure of central tendency. Equal-sized samples randomly selected from the same accessible population are likely to have different modes. When nominal data are involved, however, the mode is the only appropriate measure of central tendency.

The median

The *median* is the point in a distribution above and below which are an equal number of scores. In other words, the median is the midpoint. If there are an odd number of scores, the median is the middle score (assuming the scores are arranged in order). For example, for the scores 75, 80, 82, 83, 87, the median is 82, the middle score. If there are an even number of scores, the median is the point halfway between the two middle scores. For example, for the scores 21, 23, 24, 25, 26, 30, the median is 24.5; for the scores 50, 52, 55, 57, 59, 61, the median is 56. Thus, the median is not necessarily the same as one of the scores.

The median is only the midpoint of the scores and does not take into account each and every score. It ignores, for example, extremely high scores and extremely low scores. Two quite different sets of scores may have the same median. For example, for the scores 60, 62, 65, 67, 72, the median is 65; for the scores 60, 62, 65, 67, 89, the median is also 65. As we shall see shortly, this apparent lack of precision may be advantageous at times.

The median is the appropriate measure of central tendency when the data represent an ordinal scale. For certain distributions, the median may be selected as the most appropriate measure of central tendency even though the data represent an interval or ratio scale. While the median appears to be a rather simple index to determine, it cannot always be arrived at by simply looking at the scores;

it does not always neatly fall between two different scores. For example, determining the median for the scores 80, 82, 84, 84, 84, 88 would require application of a relatively complex formula.[1] This situation does not arise very often with classroom results. When it does, an estimate of the median is usually sufficient. If we consider the median of 80, 82, 84, 84, 84, 88 to be 84, for example, subsequent analyses and interpretations will be very close to what they would have been had the exact value of the median been determined.

The mean

The *mean* is the arithmetic average of the scores and is the most frequently used measure of central tendency. It is calculated by adding up all of the scores and dividing that total by the number of scores. By the very nature of the way in which it is computed, the mean takes into account, or is based on, each and every score. Unlike the median, the mean is definitely affected by extreme scores. Thus, in certain cases, the median may actually give a more accurate estimate of the typical score.

In general, however, the mean is the preferred measure of central tendency. It is appropriate when the data represent either an interval or a ratio scale and is a more precise, stable index than both the median and the mode. If equal-sized samples are randomly selected from the same population, the means of those samples will be more similar to each other than either the medians or the modes. While the mode is almost never the most appropriate measure of central tendency when the data represent an interval or ratio scale, the median may be. In the situation described previously, in which there are one or more extreme scores, the median will not be the most accurate representation of the performance of the total group, but it will be the best index of typical performance. As an example of this concept, suppose you had the following IQ scores: 96, 97, 97, 98, 99, 100, 101, 102, 103, 104, 149. For these scores, the measures of central tendency are:

Mode = 97 (most frequent score)
Median = 100 (middle score)
Mean = 104.18 (arithmetic average)

In this case, the median clearly best represents the typical score. The mode is too low, and the mean is higher than all of the scores except one. The mean is "pulled up" in the direction of the 149 score whereas the median essentially ignores it. The different pictures presented by the different measures are part of the reason for the phrase "lying with statistics." And in fact, by selecting one index of central tendency over another one may present a particular point of view in a stronger light. In a debate concerning federal income taxes, for example, very different estimates of typical tax amounts paid can be obtained depending upon which index of central tendency is used. Let us say that the following are typical of taxes paid in 1979 by individuals in a given company: $250, $500, $500, $600, $700, $800, $3,000. For these tax amounts, the measures of central tendency are:

Mode = $500
Median = $600
Mean = $907.14

[1] For an explanation of the procedure used to determine the median, see Downie, N. M., & Heath, R. W. *Basic statistical methods* (4th ed.). New York: Harper & Row, 1974.

Both IRS representatives and tax revolt advocates could overstate their case, IRS representatives by using the mode and tax revolt advocates by using the mean. The mean is higher than every tax amount except one, $3,000, which in all likelihood would be the taxes paid by a company executive. Thus, in this case, the most appropriate, and most accurate, index of typical taxes paid would be the median.

In evaluation, we are not interested in "making cases" but rather in describing the data in the most accurate way. For the majority of sets of data the mean is the appropriate measure of central tendency.

Measures of variability

Although measures of central tendency are very useful statistics for describing a set of data, they do not tell us enough. Two sets of data which are very different can have identical means or medians. As an example, consider the following sets of data:

Set A	59	59	59	60	61	61	61
Set B	30	40	50	60	70	80	90

The mean of both sets of scores is 60 and the median of both is 60, but set A is very different from set B. In set A the scores are all very close together and clustered around the mean. In set B the scores are much more spread out; that is, there is much more variation, or variability, in set B. Thus, there is a need for a measure which indicates how spread out the scores are, how much variability there is. There are a number of descriptive statistics which serve this purpose, and they are referred to as *measures of variability*. The three most frequently encountered are the range, the quartile deviation, and the standard deviation. While the standard deviation is by far the most often used, the range is the appropriate measure of variability for nominal data, and the quartile deviation is the appropriate index of variability for ordinal data. As with measures of central tendency, measures of variability appropriate for nominal and ordinal data may be used with interval or ratio data even though the standard deviation is generally the preferred index for such data.

The range

As discussed previously, the *range* is defined either as the difference between the highest score and the lowest score ($R = H - L$), or as the difference plus one ($R = H - L + 1$), the latter being more accurate. For example, the range for the scores 59, 59, 59, 60, 61, 61, 61 is 3, whereas the range for the scores 30, 40, 50, 60, 70, 80, 90 is 61. Thus, if the range is small, the scores are close together whereas if the range is large, the scores are more spread out. Like the mode, the range is not a very stable measure of variability, and its chief advantage is that it gives a quick, rough estimate of variability.

The quartile deviation

In "statistics talk," the *quartile deviation* (also referred to as the semi-interquartile range) is one-half of the difference between the upper quartile and the lower quartile in a distribution. In English, the upper quartile is the 75th percentile, that point below which are 75% of the scores; the lower quartile, correspondingly, is the 25th percentile, that point below which are 25% of the scores. By subtracting the lower quartile from the upper quartile and then dividing the result by two, we get a measure of variability:

$$QD = \frac{Q_3 - Q_1}{2}$$

As an example, if there are 60 scores, Q_1 is the point below which are 15 of the scores (15 = 25% of 60), and Q_3 is the point below which are 45 of the scores (45 = 75% of 60). If the quartile deviation is small, the scores are close together whereas if the quartile deviation is large, the scores are more spread out. The quartile deviation is a more stable measure of variability than the range and is appropriate whenever the median is appropriate. Calculation of the quartile deviation involves a process very similar to that used to calculate the median, which just happens to be the second quartile, Q_2.[2]

The standard deviation

The *standard deviation* is appropriate when the data represent an interval or ratio scale and is by far the most frequently used index of variability. Like the mean, the measure of central tendency which is its counterpart, the standard deviation is the most stable measure of variability and takes into account each and every score. In fact, the first step in calculating the standard deviation involves finding out how far each score is from the mean, that is, subtracting the mean from each score. Then (concentrate!) if we square each difference, add up all the squares, and divide by the number of scores, we have a measure of variability called *variance*. If the variance is small, the scores are close together; if the variance is large, the scores are more spread out. The square root of the variance is called the standard deviation and, like variance, a small standard deviation indicates that scores are close together and a large standard deviation indicates that the scores are more spread out.

If you know the mean and the standard deviation of a set of scores, you have a pretty good picture of what the distribution looks like. An interesting fact associated with the standard deviation is that if the distribution is relatively normal (about which we will have more to say shortly), then the mean plus 3 standard deviations and the mean minus 3 standard deviations encompasses just about all the scores, over 99% of them. In other words, each distribution has its own mean and its own standard deviation which are calculated based on the scores. Once they are computed, three times the standard deviation added to the mean, and three times the standard deviation subtracted from the mean, gives you a range which includes just about all the scores in the distribution.[3] The symbol for the

---

[2] For an explanation of the procedures used to determine the quartile deviation, see Downie & Heath (footnote 1).

[3] The number 3 is a constant. In other words, for any normal distribution of scores, the standard deviation multiplied by 3 and then added to the mean and subtracted from the mean will include almost all the scores in the distribution.

mean is $\overline{X}$ and the standard deviation is usually abbreviated as SD. Thus, the above described concept can be expressed as follows:

$$\overline{X} \pm 3SD = 99+\% \text{ of the scores}$$

For example, suppose that for a set of scores the mean $(\overline{X})$ is calculated to be 60 and the standard deviation (SD) to be 1. In this case the mean plus three standard deviations, $\overline{X} + 3SD$, is equal to $60 + 3(1) = 60 + 3 = 63$. The mean minus three standard deviations, $\overline{X} - 3SD$, is equal to $60 - 3(1) = 60 - 3 = 57$. Thus, almost all the scores fall between 57 and 63. This makes sense since a small standard deviation (in this case SD = 1) indicates that the scores are close together, or not very spread out.

As another example, suppose that for another set of scores the mean $(\overline{X})$ is again calculated to be 60, but this time the standard deviation (SD) is calculated to be 5. In this case the mean plus three standard deviations, $\overline{X} + 3SD$, is equal to $60 + 3(5) = 60 + 15 = 75$. In case you still do not see, 60 plus 1SD = $60 + 5 = 65$; 60 plus 2SD = $60 + 5 + 5 = 70$; 60 plus 3SD = $60 + 5 + 5 + 5 = 75$. Or, to explain it another way, $60 + 1SD = 60 + 5 = 65$, plus another SD = $65 + 5 = 70$, plus one more (the third) SD = $70 + 5 = 75$. Now, the mean minus three standard deviations, $\overline{X} - 3SD$ is equal to $60 - 3(5) = 60 - 15 = 45$. In other words, 60 minus 1SD = $60 - 5 = 55$; 60 minus 2SD = $60 - 5 - 5 = 50$; 60 minus 3SD = $60 - 5 - 5 - 5 = 45$. Thus, almost all the scores fall between 55 and 75. This also makes sense since a larger standard deviation (in this case SD = 5) indicates that the scores are more spread out.

Clearly, if you know the mean and standard deviation of a set of scores you have a pretty good idea of what the scores look like. You know the average score and you know how spread out, or how variable, the scores are. Thus, together they describe a set of data quite well. Most formal evaluation reports describe the performance of each group involved by providing the appropriate means and standard deviations and the number (N) of students upon which each is based. For example:

	$\overline{X}$	SD	N
Louzee Curriculum	61.22	11.02	191
Grate Curriculum	82.45	12.50	202

The normal curve

The ± 3 concept is valid only when the scores are normally distributed, that is, form a normal, or bell-shaped, curve. Most of you are probably familiar with the concept of grading "on the normal curve." In its extreme form, this practice means that a certain percentage of students receive a grade of C, a smaller percentage receive B's and D's and an even smaller percentage receive A's and E's, or F's. Such grading is based on the assumption (which may or may not be true in a given case) that the students' scores do indeed form a normal curve. Many, many variables, such as height, weight, IQ scores, and achievement scores, do yield a normal curve if a sufficient number of people are measured.

Normal distributions

A *normal curve* is essentially a frequency polygon constructed for a set of normally distributed scores. Thus, figure 17.2 is based on a vertical axis labeled "frequency" and a horizontal axis labeled "scores." If a variable is normally distributed, that is, does form a normal curve, then several things are true. First, the area under the curve represents all (100%) of the scores, and 50% of the scores are above the mean and 50% of the scores are below the mean. Second, the mean, the median, and the mode are the same. Third, most scores are near the mean and the farther from the mean a score is, the fewer the number of persons who attained

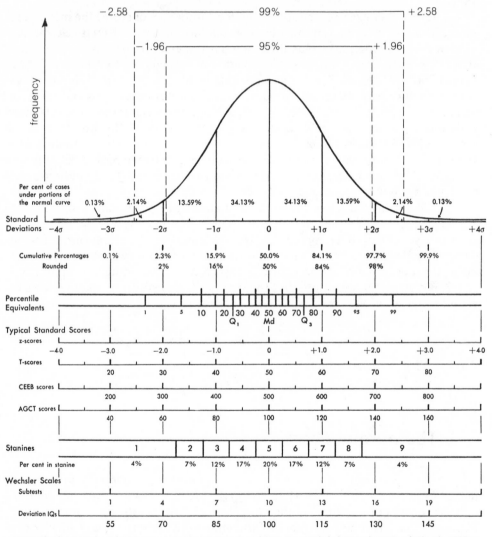

NOTE: *This chart cannot be used to equate scores on one test to scores on another test. For example, both 600 on the CEEB and 120 on the AGCT are one standard deviation above their respective means, but they do not represent "equal" standings because the scores were obtained from different groups.*

figure 17.2
Characteristics of the normal curve

Note. Based on a figure appearing in *Test Service Bulletin* No. 48, January, 1955 of The Psychological Corporation.

that score. Fourth, the same number, or percentage, of scores is between the mean and plus-one standard deviation ($\overline{X}$ + 1SD) as between the mean minus one standard deviation ($\overline{X}$ − 1SD), and likewise for $\overline{X}$ ± 2SD and $\overline{X}$ ± 3SD (see figure 17.2). As figure 17.2 indicates, the symbol σ (the Greek letter sigma) is frequently used to represent the standard deviation, that is, 1σ = 1SD, and the mean ($\overline{X}$) is designated as 0. The vertical lines at each of the SD (σ) points delineate a certain percentage of the total area under the curve. As figure 17.2 illustrates, if a set of scores forms a normal distribution, then the $\overline{X}$ + 1SD includes 34.13% of the scores and the $\overline{X}$ − 1SD includes 34.13% of the scores. Each succeeding standard deviation encompasses a constant percentage of the cases. Since the $\overline{X}$ ± 2.58SD (approximately 2½SD's) includes 99% of the cases, we see that $\overline{X}$ ± 3SD includes almost all the scores, as pointed out previously.

Below the row of SD's is a row of percentages. As you move from left to right, from point to point, the cumulative percentage of scores which fall below each point is indicated. Thus, at the point which corresponds to −3SD, we see that only .1% of the scores fall below this point. The numerical value which corresponds to +1SD, on the other hand, is a figure higher than 84.1% (rounded to 84% on the next row) of the scores. Relatedly, the next row, percentile equivalents, also involves cumulative percentages. The figure 20 in this row, for example, indicates that 20% of the scores fall below this point. While we will discuss percentiles and the remaining rows further as we proceed through this chapter, we will look at one more row at this time. Near the bottom of figure 17.2, under Wechsler Scales, is a row labeled Deviation IQs. This row indicates that the mean IQ for the Wechsler Scale is 100 and the standard deviation is 15 (115 is in the column corresponding to +1SD (+1σ) and since the mean is 100, 115 represents $\overline{X}$ + 1SD = 100 + 15 = 115). An IQ of 145 represents a score 3SD's above the mean (average) IQ. If your IQ is in this neighborhood you are certainly a candidate for MENSA! An IQ of 145 corresponds to a percentile of 99.9. On the other side of the curve we see that an IQ of 85 corresponds to a score one standard deviation below the mean ($\overline{X}$ − 1SD = 100 − 15 = 85) and to the 16th percentile. Note that the mean always corresponds to the 50th percentile. In other words, the average score is always that point above which are 50% of the cases and below which are 50% of the cases. Thus, if scores are normally distributed the following statements are true:

$\overline{X}$ ± 1.0SD = approximately 68% of the scores
$\overline{X}$ ± 2.0SD = approximately 95% of the scores
                    (1.96SD is exactly 95%)
$\overline{X}$ ± 2.5SD = approximately 99% of the scores
                    (2.58SD is exactly 99%)
$\overline{X}$ ± 3.0SD = approximately 99+% of the scores

And similarly, the following statements are always true:

$\overline{X}$ − 3.0SD = approximately the .1 percentile
$\overline{X}$ − 2.0SD = approximately the 2nd percentile
$\overline{X}$ − 1.0SD = approximately the 16th percentile
        $\overline{X}$ = the 50th percentile
$\overline{X}$ + 1.0SD = approximately the 84th percentile
$\overline{X}$ + 2.0SD = approximately the 98th percentile
$\overline{X}$ + 3.0SD = approximately the 99th+ percentile

These equivalents are generalizable to the scores of any group on any measure to the degree that the scores approximate a normal curve.

You may have noticed that the ends of the curve never touch the baseline and that there is no definite number of standard deviations which corresponds to 100%. This is because the curve allows for the existence of unexpected extremes at either end and because each additional standard deviation includes only a tiny fraction of a percent of the scores. As an example, for the IQ test the mean plus 5 standard deviations would be $100 + 5(15) = 100 + 75 = 175$. Surely 5SD's would include everyone. Wrong! There has been a very small number of persons who have scored near 200, which corresponds to +6.67SD's. Thus, while ±3SD's includes just about everyone, the exact number of standard deviations required to include every score varies from variable to variable.

As mentioned earlier, many variables form a normal distribution including physical measures, such as height and weight, and psychological measures, such as intelligence and aptitude. In fact, most variables measured in education form normal distributions *if* enough persons are tested. In other words, a variable which is normally distributed in a large population may not be normally distributed in a small group. Depending upon the size and nature of a particular group, the assumption of a normal curve may or may not be a valid one. Since classroom evaluation, for example, deals with a finite number of students, and often not a very large number, test data only more or less approximate a normal curve.[4] Likewise, all of the equivalencies (e.g. standard deviation, percentiles) are also only approximations. This is an important point since many statistics used in educational evaluation are based on the assumption that the variable is normally distributed. If this assumption is seriously violated in a given sample group, then certain statistics should not be used.

In general, however, the fact that most variables are normally distributed allows us quickly to determine many useful pieces of information concerning a set of data.

Skewed distributions

When a distribution is not normal, it is said to be *skewed*. A normal distribution is symmetrical and the value of the mean, the median, and the mode are the same. A distribution which is skewed is not symmetrical, and the values of the mean, the median, and the mode are different. In a symmetrical distribution, there are approximately the same number of extreme scores (very high and very low) at each end of the distribution. In a skewed distribution there are more extreme scores at one end than the other. If the extreme scores are at the lower end of the distribution, the distribution is said to be negatively skewed. If the extreme scores are at the upper, or higher, end of the distribution, the distribution is said to be positively skewed (see figure 17.3).

As we can see by looking at the negatively skewed distribution, most of the students did well but a few did very poorly. Conversely, with the positively skewed distribution, most of the students did poorly but a few did very well. Since the mean is affected by extreme scores and the median is not, the mean is always closer to the extreme scores than the median. Thus, for a negatively skewed

---

[4] Thus, we see the fallacy of some normal curve grading, which assumes that each class forms a normal distribution of ability and effort, a highly improbable event.

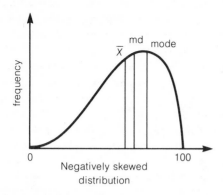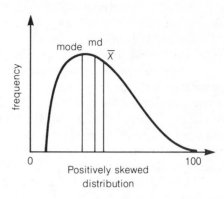

figure 17.3
A positively skewed distribution and a negatively skewed distribution, each
resulting from the administration of a 100-item test.

distribution the mean ($\overline{X}$) is always lower (smaller) than the median (md). For a
positively skewed distribution the mean is always higher (greater) than the median. Since the mode is not affected by extreme scores, no "always" statements
can be made concerning its relationship to the mean and the median in a skewed
distribution. Usually, however, as figure 17.3 indicates, in a negatively skewed
distribution the mean and median are lower, or smaller, than the mode, whereas
in a positively skewed distribution the mean and the median are higher, or
greater, than the mode. To summarize:

> Negatively skewed: mean < median < mode
> Positively skewed: mean > median > mode

Since the relationship between the mean and the median is a constant, the skew-
ness of a distribution can be determined without constructing a frequency polygon. If the mean is less than the median, the distribution is negatively skewed. If
the mean and the median are the same, or very close, the distribution is symmetrical; if the mean is greater than the median, the distribution is positively skewed.
The farther apart the mean and the median are, the more skewed the distribution
is. If the distribution is very skewed, then the assumption of normality required
for many statistics is violated.

Measures of relative position

A numerical value which summarizes the responses actually made on a
test by an individual is called a *raw score*. This value is usually the total number of
correct answers but may be some other index, total number of typographical errors
for example. Raw scores have essentially no meaning in and of themselves.
Knowing that Linus scored 35 on a test tells you practically nothing about how
well he did on the test, in relation to either a criterion score or the performance of
others who took the same test. If you also know the highest score on the test, you
can convert the raw scores to a percent. For a 50-item test, for example, a score of

35 would equal 70%. This information may be helpful for a criterion-referenced test, but it still tells us nothing about performance in relation to that of others who took the test. Clearly there is a need for methods of transforming raw scores into values which facilitate the interpretation of scores on both an individual and group basis. Measures of relative position fill this need.

Measures of relative position indicate where a score is in relation to all other scores in the distribution. In other words, measures of relative position permit you to express how well an individual has performed as compared to all other individuals in some group who have been given the same test. An individual's performance may be compared to the performance of a norm group or to the performance of the group of which he or she is actually a member. A major advantage of such measures is that they make it possible to compare the performance of an individual on two or more different tests (or subtests). For example, if Ziggy's raw score in reading is 40 and his raw score in math is 35, it does not follow that he did better in reading; 40 may have been the lowest score on the reading test and 35 the highest score on the math test! By the same token, the same raw score on two different tests does not necessarily indicate equal levels of performance. A raw score of 40 on one test may correspond to the 30th percentile whereas a raw score of 40 on another test may correspond to the 80th percentile. Measures of relative position express different scores on a common scale, a common frame of reference, thus permitting valid comparisons of scores on different tests.

Raw scores that have been transformed systematically into equivalent values which indicate relative position are referred to as *derived scores*. Standardized test manuals almost always provide norms tables which contain raw scores and one or more equivalent derived scores. The most common type of derived scores are percentile ranks, standard scores, and grade equivalents. The most frequently reported and used standard scores are z scores, T scores, and stanines. A good manual is quite comprehensive. In addition to complete information related to test development and validation, directions for administering and scoring the test, and a description of the norm group, it provides detailed instructions for interpretation of given scores. These instructions usually take the form of one or more norms tables and accompanying explanatory material. A number of manuals provide separate tables for each of a number of levels of a given test. The term "level" refers to the grade or age range for which the test is supposedly appropriate. The Stanford Achievement Test, for example, has six level tests, each appropriate for a given grade range (indicated in parentheses):

Primary Level I (1.5–2.4)	Intermediate Level I (4.5–5.4)
Primary Level II (2.5–3.4)	Intermediate Level II (5.5–6.9)
Primary Level III (3.5–4.4)	Advanced Level (7.0–9.5)

Separate tables are also frequently provided for each of a number of subtests.

Occasionally, although fortunately not very often, a norms table does not provide derived scores for each and every raw score. Some systematic portion of the raw scores and their equivalents are presented, such as every other or every third raw score. In such cases it is necessary to extrapolate, i.e. estimate, missing values. In other words, if a particular raw score of interest is not included in the table, then desired derived scores must be extrapolated using values which *are* given. As an example, suppose a table indicates that a raw score of 20 corresponds to a percentile rank of 46 and a raw score of 22 corresponds to a percentile rank of 50. If a student scores 21 correct, the percentile rank has to be extrapolated. In this case the best estimate would be a value half way between 46 and 50, i.e. 48. While estimating missing values does not represent the ideal situation, it is necessary at times and it does not alter subsequent interpretations to any significant degree.

All of the types of derived scores to be discussed are included in figure 17.2. Keep in mind that the equivalencies between derived scores indicated on the normal curve figure—for example, a T score of 60 corresponds to the 84th percentile—are accurate to the degree that the distribution upon which they are based is normally distributed. While it is not likely that classroom distributions will be normal, it is also true that teachers are not likely to need all of those derived scores anyway. Further, the norms tables for major standardized tests are invariably based on a large sample, thus insuring a relatively normal distribution. Therefore, the problem of normal distribution/not normal distribution is really not much of a problem after all in practice.

Percentile ranks

Because percentile ranks are virtually always reported, it is important for anyone involved with interpretation of standardized test results to be familiar with their symbolism and meaning. Although local evaluation efforts (such as classroom evaluation) are not likely to involve actual computation of percentile ranks, they may, especially if a locally-developed test is administered to a large number of students. While the percentile rank concept is a fairly simple one, there are a number of misconceptions associated with interpretation of percentiles and percentile ranks. For one thing, percentile ranks tell us essentially nothing about percentages of correct answers. *Percentile ranks* indicate the percentage of persons who scored as well as or lower than a given score, not the percentage of items answered correctly. Also, while the terms percentile and percentile ranks are often used as if they are synonymous, there is a distinction between them. A percentile is a point in a distribution whereas a percentile rank indicates the relative position of a score in a distribution.

A *percentile* is a *point* which cuts off a given percentage of a distribution. There are 99 percentiles and thus a distribution is divided into 100 equal parts. The first percentile, symbolized as P_1, is the point below which are one percent of the scores. Similarly, P_{50} is the point below which are 50% of the scores, and P_{90} is the point below which are 90% of the scores.

A percentile rank (PR) indicates the percentage of scores which are equal to or less than a given score. Thus, if a raw score of 48 corresponds to a percentile rank of 80 (symbolized PR 80), this means that 80% of the scores are equal to or less than 48. In other words, if Betty Bright had a percentile rank of 98, this would mean that she did as well or better than 98% of the members of some group which took the same test. Conversely, if Vera Verislow had a percentile rank of 2, this would mean that Vera only did as well as or better than 2% of the members of the comparison group. Percentiles and percentile ranks are appropriate for data representing an ordinal scale, although they are frequently computed for interval data. The median of a set of scores corresponds to the 50th percentile which makes sense since the median is the middle point and therefore the point below which are 50% of the scores. Thus, percentile ranks basically allow us to determine how well an individual did in relative terms, as compared to others who took the same test. If percentile ranks are given for a number of subtests, they also provide a rough means of comparing an individual's relative performance in a number of different areas.

One point to keep in mind when interpreting percentile ranks is that they are ordinal not interval measures. Therefore, we do not have equal intervals between percentile points. An increase of a given number of percentile points corresponds to a different number of raw score points depending upon where we are in the distribution. The difference between the 45th and 50th percentiles, for example, does not represent the same increase in raw scores as the difference between the 90th and 95th percentiles. As figure 17.2 indicates, the percentiles are much closer together at the middle of the distribution, near the mean, than at the ends of the distribution. An increase in 5 raw score points, for example, will increase the corresponding percentile much more if the score is near the middle of the distribution than if it is at either end. The reason, as figure 17.2 illustrates, is that there are more people near the middle than at the extremes. Therefore, an increase of a given number of raw score points results in more people "being passed," that is, more scores being surpassed. To put it another way, if you increase your raw score a few points, you overtake, or do better than, a lot of people if your score is near the middle but very few people if your score is at either end, simply because there are more people near the middle, or average, score.

Another alleged drawback associated with percentile ranks is that theoretically you cannot perform arithmetic operations on them. You might wish, for example, to average a student's percentile ranks on a number of subtests to produce an average percentile rank. Mathematically speaking, you cannot do this and have an interpretable result. In reality, however, averaging percentile ranks often provides a fairly reasonable estimate of typical performance. However, since the practice is questionable, and since there are derived scores which permit such manipulations, it is probably wise to avoid tampering with percentile ranks.

While percentiles are 99 points which divide a distribution into 100 parts, quartiles (discussed previously under Measures of Variability) are three points which divide a distribution into four equal parts. Figure 17.2 shows the relationship between percentiles and quartiles. The first quartile (symbolized as Q_1) corresponds to the 25th percentile, the second quartile (Q_2) corresponds to the 50th percentile (the median), and the third quartile (Q_3) corresponds to the 75th percentile. Quartiles are not used very often. Functions which they once served, such as providing a basis for grouping, have largely been taken over by stanines (to be discussed shortly). Similarly, deciles, nine points which divide a distribution into ten equal parts, are infrequently reported or used.

Standard scores

Figure 17.2 depicts a number of standard scores. Basically, a *standard score* is a derived score which expresses how far a given raw score is from some reference point, typically the mean, in terms of standard deviation units. A standard score is a measure of relative position which is appropriate when the test data represent an interval or ratio scale of measurement. The most commonly reported and used standard scores are z scores, T scores (or Z scores), and stanines. Standard scores allow scores from different tests to be compared on a common scale and, unlike percentiles, we can validly perform mathematical operations on them in order to average them, for example. Averaging scores on a series of classroom tests in order to arrive at a final grade is like averaging apples and oranges and getting an "orapple." Such tests are likely to vary in level of difficulty and variability of scores. By converting test scores to standard scores, however, a teacher can average them and arrive at a valid final grade.

As noted previously, the normal curve equivalencies indicated in figure 17.2 for the various standard scores are accurate only to the degree to which the distribution is normal. Further, standard score equivalencies hold only if all the derived scores are based on the raw scores of the same group. A CEEB (College Entrance Examination Board) score of 700, for example, is not equivalent to a Wechsler IQ of 130 because the tests were normed on different groups. If a set of raw scores is normally distributed then so are the standard score equivalents. But all distributions are not normal, even if the variable being measured is. Height, for example, is normally distributed, but the measured heights of the girls in a seventh grade gym class may not be for a variety of reasons. There is a procedure for transforming a set of raw scores which insures that the distribution of standard scores will be normal. Raw scores thus transformed are referred to as *normalized scores*. All resulting standard scores are normally distributed and the normal curve equivalencies are accurate.

z scores. A *z score* is the most basic standard score. It expresses how far a score is from the mean in terms of standard deviation units. A score which is exactly "on" the mean corresponds to a z of 0; a score which is exactly 1 standard deviation above the mean (such as an IQ of 115) corresponds to a z of +1.00; a z score which is exactly 2 standard deviations below the mean (such as an IQ of 70) corresponds to a z of −2.00. Get it? As figure 17.2 indicates, if a set of scores is transformed into a set of z scores (each score is expressed as a z score), the new distribution has a mean of 0 and a standard deviation of 1.

The major advantage of z scores is that they allow scores from different tests or subtests to be compared. As an example, suppose Bobby Bonker's mother, a woman who is really on top of things, comes in and asks his teacher, "How is Bobby doing in the basic skills areas?" If the teacher tells her that Bobby's reading score was 50 and his math score was 40, she still does not know how well Bobby is doing. In fact, she might get the false impression that he is better in reading when in fact 50 might be a very low score on the reading test and 40 may be a very good score on the math test. Now suppose Bobby's teacher also tells his mother that the average score (the mean, $\overline{X}$) on the reading test was 60, and the average score on the math test was 30. Aha! Now it looks as if Bobby is better in math than in reading. Further, if the standard deviation (SD) on both tests was 10, Bobby's true status becomes even more evident. Since his score in reading is exactly 1SD below the mean (60 − 10 = 50), his z score is −1.00. On the other hand, his score in math is 1SD above the mean (30 + 10 = 40) and his z score is +1.00. Converting z scores to percentiles shows that Bobby is clearly better in math than in reading:

	Raw Score	$\overline{X}$	SD	z	Percentile
Reading	50	60	10	−1.00	16th
Math	40	30	10	+1.00	84th

Of course, scores do not always happen to be exactly 1SD (or 2SD, or 3SD) above or below the mean. Usually we have to apply the following formula to convert a raw score to a z score:

$$z = \frac{X - \overline{X}}{SD}, \qquad \text{where } X = \text{the raw score}$$

The only problem with z scores is that they involve negative numbers and decimals. It would be pretty hard to explain to Mrs. Bonker that her son was a −1.00. How do you tell a mother her son is a negative?! A simple solution is to transform z scores into T (or Z) scores. As Figure 17.2 indicates, z scores are actually the building blocks for a number of standard scores. Other standard scores represent transformations of z scores which communicate the same information in a more generally understandable form by eliminating negatives and/or decimals.

T scores. A *T score* is nothing more than a z score expressed in a different form. To transform a z score to a T score, you simply multiply the z score by 10 and add 50. In other words, $T = 10z + 50$. Thus a z score of 0 (the mean score) becomes a T score of 50 [$T = 10(0) + 50 = 0 + 50 = 50$]. A z score of +1.00 becomes a T score of 60 [$T = 10(1.00) + 50 = 10 + 50 = 60$], and a z score of −1.00 becomes a T score of 40 [$T = 10(-1.00) + 50 = -10 + 50 = 40$]. Thus, when scores are transformed to T scores, the new distribution has a mean of 50 and a standard deviation of 10 (see figure 17.2). It would clearly be much easier to communicate to Mrs. Bonker that Bobby is a 40 in reading and a 60 in math and that the average score is 50 than to tell her that he is a +1.00 and a −1.00 and the average score is .00.

Recall that if the raw score distribution is normal, then so is the z score distribution. If this is the case, then the transformation $10z + 50$ produces a T distribution. If, on the other hand, the original distribution is not normal (such as when a small sample group is involved), then neither is the z score distribution. In such cases the distribution resulting from the $10z + 50$ transformation is more accurately referred to as a z distribution. Of course even with a set of raw scores that are not normally distributed, we can produce a set of normalized z scores. In either case, we can use the normal curve equivalencies to convert such scores into corresponding percentiles, or vice versa. As figure 17.2 indicates, for example, at T of $50 = P_{50}$. Similarly, the second percentile corresponds to a T of 30 and a T of 60 corresponds to the 84th percentile. The same is true for the other standard score transformations illustrated in figure 17.2. The CEEB distribution is formed by multiplying T scores by 10 in order to eliminate decimals; it is calculated directly using $CEEB = 100z + 500$. The AGCT (Army General Classification Test) distribution is formed by multiplying T scores by 2, and is formed directly using $AGCT = 200z + 100$. In both cases, given values can be converted to percentiles (and vice versa) using normal curve equivalencies. Thus, a CEEB score of 400 corresponds to the 16th percentile and the 98th percentile corresponds to an AGCT score of 140.

Stanines. *Stanines* are standard scores that divide a distribution into nine parts. Stanine (short for "standard nine") equivalencies are derived using the formula $2z + 5$ and rounding resulting values to the nearest whole number. Stanines 2 through 8 each represent ½SD of the distribution; stanines 1 and 9 include the remainder. In other words, stanine 5 includes ½SD around the mean ($\overline{X}$); that is, it equals $\overline{X} \pm$ ¼SD. Stanine 6 goes from +¼SD to +¾SD (¼SD + ½SD = ¾SD), and so forth. Stanine 1 includes any score that is less than −1¾SD (−1.75SD) below the mean, and stanine 9 includes any score that is greater than +1¾SD

(+1.75SD) above the mean. As figure 17.2 indicates (see the row of figures directly beneath the stanines), stanine 5 includes 20% of the scores, stanines 4 and 6 each contain 17%, stanines 3 and 7 each contain 12%, 2 and 8 each contain 7%, and 1 and 9 each contain 4% of the scores (percentages approximate).

Using the theoretical percentages anyone, a teacher for example, can translate a set of scores into stanines. To do this, first you simply arrange the scores in ascending order and identify the median (midpoint). Then you assign the 10% of the scores just above the median and the 10% just below the median to stanine 5 (stanine 5 contains 20% of the scores). Then you assign the next 17% (on both sides) of the scores to stanines 4 and 6 respectively, and so forth. Of course unless the raw score distribution is normal, which is not likely in many local situations, the percentages in each category will only more or less approximate the identified percentages. For most purposes, however, this is not a serious problem and the resulting stanines are useful. The only thing you have to guarantee is that all persons with the same score end up in the same stanine. If, for example, four students have the same score, the percentages may indicate that two of the students should be in stanine 6 and two of them should be in stanine 7. Logically, however, this does not make any sense; students with the same raw score cannot have different score equivalents. All four students must be assigned to the same stanine, 6 or 7, and the necessary adjustments made.

Like percentiles, stanines are very frequently reported in norms tables for standardized tests. They are very popular with school systems because they are so easy to understand and to explain to others. While they are not as exact as other standard scores, they are useful for a variety of purposes. As mentioned earlier they are frequently used as a basis for grouping. They are also used as a criterion for selecting students for special programs. A remediation program, for example, may select students who scored in the 1st and 2nd (and perhaps the 3rd) stanine on a standardized reading test.

Deviation IQ. At one time IQ (scholastic aptitude, mental ability) was estimated using the following formula:

$$IQ = \frac{MA}{CA} \times 100, \qquad \text{where MA = mental age}$$
$$\text{CA = chronological age}$$

The MA value was determined by administering of a mental ability test. Thus, if a person's MA was estimated to be 12 and that person was 12 years of age, the IQ estimate would be $^{12}/_{12} \times 100 = 100$. The problem with this approach is that MA scores do not increase evenly from year to year; intellectual growth is more rapid among younger children and slows down with age. An alternate approach to estimating IQ involves computation of what is referred to as a deviation IQ (DIQ). Evolution of this concept began with the work of Arther Otis and today it is generally regarded as being the most acceptable index of IQ. A DIQ is a standard score which is based on how far a person's score (on a given IQ test) is from the average score of persons in the same age group. The WAIS (Wechsler Adult Intelligence Scale), for example, has separate norms for each of seven age groups: 16–17, 18–19, 20–24, 25–34, 35–44, 45–54, and 55–64. The score for a person 29 years of age, for example, is compared to the scores of persons in the 25–34 age group.

Computation of DIQ's basically involves calculating of z scores for each age group and transforming the z scores to form a distribution with a mean of 100 and a standard deviation of 15 (or 16); that is $DIQ = 15z + 100$. The Wechsler scales, which are currently the most accepted and used IQ tests, report results in terms of DIQ's. The WAIS, for example, has six subtests which are used to produce a verbal IQ, and five subtests related to a performance score. Raw scores for each subtest are converted to a set of standard scores having a mean of 10 and a standard deviation of 3 (see figure 17.2). For example, if Instine gets 29 of the 29 questions correct on the Information subtest, this corresponds to a standard (scaled) score of 19; his score is 3SD's above the mean because $\overline{X} = 10$ and $SD = 3$ on each subtest. These standard score equivalents are presented in tables and simply have to be looked up. The standard scores for the verbal subtests are summed and converted to a verbal IQ, also using a table of equivalents. Likewise the standard scores for the performance subtests are summed and converted to a performance IQ. The total of the standard scores for all 11 subtests is similarly converted to an overall, or full-scale, IQ.

In interpreting IQ scores you have to be careful when comparing the IQ scores of two individuals who took two different tests, or comparing two scores for the same person if they are based on two different tests. IQ scores are only comparable if they are based on the same version of the same test. Different tests are normed on different groups and standard deviations vary from test to test, and therefore derived standard scores and IQ equivalents also vary. A lower IQ score may actually represent a greater standard score. Thus, Ziggy's IQ score may *appear* to have dropped somewhat when in reality it is essentially the same but has been measured using a different test.

Scaled scores. Scaled scores are standard scores which are comparable across levels of the *same* test or subtest from grade to grade, battery to battery, and form to form. They are not comparable for different tests or subtests. In other words, the range of scaled scores is different for each test and subtest. A scaled score of 140 on a vocabulary subtest cannot be compared to a scaled score of 130 on a spelling subtest; it can, however, be compared to the scaled score for the vocabulary subtest of a different *level* test. A scaled score for vocabulary, based on the administration of the Stanford Achievement Test, Primary II Level, can be compared to the scaled score for vocabulary based on the administration of the Stanford Achievement Test, Intermediate I Level. Because they are comparable across levels, they are used for analyzing pupil growth and for interpreting the results of out-of-level testing.

The process for deriving scaled scores is somewhat complex and is based on a procedure developed by Thurstone over fifty years ago.[5] Basically, however, it involves two major steps. First, raw scores at successive levels of a test are equated by administering more than one level test to the same students. A large group of fifth graders, for example, might be given the level 5 test, which is designed for fifth graders, and the level 4 test. Another group of fifth graders might be administered the level 5 test and the level 6 test. Then, using Thurstone's scaling procedure, raw scores at each level are transformed into standard scores which are comparable across levels.

As mentioned, scaled scores are used to analyze the results of out-of-level testing. To illustrate how they are used, let us suppose that a test has five levels. Suppose we administer the level 3 test to a group of fifth graders, even though the level 5 test is the one designed for fifth graders. In order to interpret the results in

[5] Thurstone, L. L. The unit of measurement in educational scales. *Journal of Educational Psychology*, 1927, *28*, 505–524.

terms of level 5 norms, we have to translate the level 3 raw scores into level 5 raw scores. We can do this using scaled scores. For a given level 3 raw score, we determine the corresponding scaled score. A raw score of 25, for example, might correspond to a scaled score of 130. We then go to the level 4 tables, locate the scaled score of 130, and identify the corresponding level 5 raw score. We can then convert that raw score to any derived score of our choice (e.g. a percentile).

Grade and age equivalents

A *grade equivalent* (or grade score) of a given raw score is the grade level of students whose typical (mean or median) score is the same as the given raw score. For example, if the median raw score on a reading comprehension test is 29 for a norm group of students beginning the fourth grade, then any student who scores 29 will have a grade equivalent of 4.0, regardless of what grade the student is actually in. A grade equivalent expresses both the grade and the month in the grade. Thus, 4.0 indicates the beginning of the fourth grade, 4.5 indicates the fifth month of the fourth grade, and 4.8 indicates the eighth month of the fourth grade. The year is typically divided into 10 parts such that the first 9 parts (4.0–4.8) correspond to the months of the school year and the tenth part corresponds to summer vacation.

Interpretation of grade equivalents is tricky, mainly because so many values are based on extrapolation (estimation). Typically, a test being normed is administered to large groups of students in each of several successive grade levels at the beginning of a school year and at the end. For example, a test may be administered in September and May to third, fourth, fifth, and sixth grade students. Intermediate values within each grade level (e.g. the score corresponding to 4.4) and sometimes values for grade levels above and below those actually tested (e.g. the seventh grade) are extrapolated. Such extrapolations, especially those which extend beyond the grade levels actually tested, are not very sound and are a source of much misinterpretation. If Cal Culator, currently completing the fourth grade, earns grade equivalents of 7.4, 7.2, and 7.6, respectively, on the Arithmetic Computation, Arithmetic Concepts, and Arithmetic Applications Subtests of the Stanford Achievement Test, does this mean that we should schedule Cal into seventh grade math classes in September? No. All these grade equivalents tell us is that Cal is very advanced for a fourth grader. It is extremely unlikely that he actually has achieved all of the arithmetic competencies taught in the fifth and sixth grades, and that he would do well on a test designed for a higher grade level. Further, grade equivalent extrapolations are based on the assumption that scores increase evenly, or by the same amount, from month to month and from year to year. This may be essentially true in lower grades in which instruction in certain content areas (e.g. reading) is continuous from grade to grade, but it becomes a progressively less valid assumption at higher grade levels.

Another interpretation problem associated with grade equivalents arises from the fact that the same grade equivalent on two different tests or subtests does not necessarily indicate the same relative position (i.e. percentile rank). In fact, it is entirely possible for a student to have a higher grade equivalent on one subtest than on another and yet have a lower percentile for that subtest. The reason is that the distribution of scores is different for each test or subtest; some have greater variability than others. It is easier, for example, to score very highly in verbal areas than in mathematical areas; achievement in math is more dependent on instruction. A related concept is that of modal age norms. When *modal age norms* are involved, grade equivalents are based upon the performance of only those students who are in a normal age range for a particular grade. Scores of atypically young or old students are not included in computation of the grade norms, thus eliminating bias in the estimation of typical performance.

All in all, grade equivalents leave much to be desired. Their popularity persists, however, because they are considered to be fairly easy for most people to understand. While we could probably do without them very easily, given the variety of alternative equivalents which are available to us, they will probably continue to be reported for some time to come. Thus, one may either ignore them or interpret them intelligently, realizing that they are rough indicators at best.

Age equivalents are just like grade equivalents except that they are based on the average score of students of a particular age instead of a particular grade level. In other words, an *age equivalent* of a given raw score is the chronological age of students whose typical (mean or median) score is the same as the given raw score. Age equivalents express age in terms of both years and months, and are used primarily for mental ability tests. Age equivalents are reported less often than grade equivalents but when they are, they are subject to the same problems and should be interpreted with the same caution.

Measures of relationship

Correlation involves collecting data in order to determine whether, and to what degree, a relationship exists between two or more quantifiable variables— not a causal relationship, just a relationship. Degree of relationship is expressed as a correlation coefficient which is computed based on the two sets of scores. The correlation coefficient provides an estimate of just how related two variables are. As discussed previously, correlational techniques have a number of applications in educational evaluation. First, correlation is used to establish degree of certain types of validity and reliability. Second, it is used to answer questions concerning the degree of relationship between variables of interest, such as "Is there a significant relationship between the number of 'significant others' in a student's life and school attendance?" And third, correlation is used to determine if a relationship is strong enough to permit valid predictions. A managerial training program, for example, might wish to establish which of a number of candidate variables (e.g. years of experience, years of schooling) are most highly related to some measure of success as a manager. Having established, say, the three most highly related variables, the program would use those variables as a basis for selecting program participants from among applicants.

For results to be valid, coefficients must be based on a sufficient number of persons, and 30 is generally considered to be *minimally* acceptable. It is also important to select or develop valid, reliable measures of the variables being studied (unless of course the purpose of the effort is to establish degree of validity and reliability). If inadequate data are collected, the resulting coefficients will represent inaccurate estimates of degree of relationship. The basic correlational procedure is not too complicated. Two (or more) scores are obtained for each member of a selected group, one score for each variable of interest, and the paired scores are then correlated. The resulting correlation coefficient indicates the degree of relationship between the two variables. Different efforts investigate different numbers of variables, and some utilize complex statistical procedures, but the basic process is similar whenever degree of relationship is investigated.

Interpretation

When two variables are correlated, the result is a correlation coefficient. A *correlation coefficient* is a decimal number, between .00 and +1.00, or .00 and −1.00, which indicates the degree to which two variables are related. If the coefficient is near +1.00, the variables are positively correlated. This means that a person with a high score on one variable is likely to have a high score on the other variable, and a person with a low score on one is likely to have a low score on the other. An increase on one variable is associated with an increase on the other variable. If the coefficient is near .00, the variables are not related. This means that a person's score on one variable is no indication of what the person's score is on the other variable. If the coefficient is near −1.00, the variables are inversely related. This means that a person with a high score on one variable is likely to have a low score on the other variable, and a person with a low score on one is likely to have a high score on the other. An increase in one variable is associated with a decrease on the other variable, and vice versa (see table 17.2). Table 17.2 presents four scores for each of eight twelfth-grade students: IQ, GPA, weight, and errors on a 20-item final exam. As table 17.2 illustrates, IQ is positively related to achievement, not related to weight, and negatively, or inversely, related to errors. The students with progressively higher IQ's have progressively higher GPA's. On the other hand, students with higher IQ's tend to make fewer errors (makes sense!). The relationships are not perfect and it would be very strange if they were. One's GPA, for example, is related to other variables besides intelligence, such as motivation. The data do indicate, however, that IQ is one major variable related to both GPA and examination errors. The data also illustrate an important concept often misunderstood: namely, that a high negative relationship is just as strong as a high positive relationship. The coefficients −1.00 and +1.00 indicate equally perfect relationships. A coefficient near .00 indicates no relationship. The farther

table 17.2
Hypothetical sets of data illustrating a high positive relationship between two variables, no relationship, and a high negative relationship

	High Positive Relationship		No Relationship		High Negative Relationship	
	IQ	GPA	IQ	Weight	IQ	Errors
1. Iggie	85	1.0	85	156	85	16
2. Hermie	90	1.2	90	140	90	10
3. Fifi	100	2.4	100	120	100	8
4. Teenie	110	2.2	110	116	110	5
5. Tiny	120	2.8	120	160	120	9
6. Tillie	130	3.4	130	110	130	3
7. Millie	135	3.2	135	140	135	2
8. Jane	140	3.8	140	166	140	1

away from .00 the coefficient is, in either direction (toward -1.00 or $+1.00$), the stronger the relationship. Both high positive and high negative relationships are equally useful for making predictions. Knowing that Iggie has a low IQ score would enable you to predict both a low GPA and a high number of errors.

Interpretation of a correlation coefficient depends upon how it is to be used. In other words, how large it needs to be in order to be useful depends upon the purpose for which it was computed. In establishing validity and reliability, satisfactory coefficients range from the seventies on up, depending upon the type of test. When relationships are being investigated, lower values are useful (the thirties on up), and a coefficient is interpreted in terms of its statistical significance (a concept to be discussed later in the chapter). When prediction is the objective, statistical significance is secondary to the value of the coefficient in facilitating accurate predictions. When interpreting a correlation coefficient you must also keep in mind that you are talking about a relationship only, not a cause-effect relationship. A high (significant) correlation coefficient may suggest a cause-effect relationship but does not establish one. The only way to establish a cause-effect relationship is through the application of a true experimental design. When one finds a high relationship between two variables, it is often very tempting to conclude that one "causes" the other. In reality, it may be that neither is the cause of the other; there may be a third variable which "causes" both of them. For example, the existence of a positive relationship between self-concept and achievement could mean one of three things: a higher self-concept leads to higher achievement, higher achievement tends to increase self-concept, or there is a variable which results in both higher self-concept and higher achievement. It might be, for example, that parental behavior is a major factor in both self-concept and achievement; parents who praise their children may also encourage them to do well in school. Which of the alternatives is in fact the true explanation cannot be determined through correlation.

Linearity assumption

Most correlational techniques are based on the assumption that the relationship being investigated is a linear one. If a relationship is linear, then plotting the scores on the two variables will result in something which resembles a straight line. If a relationship is perfect ($+1.00$ or -1.00), the line will be perfectly straight. If there is no relationship, the points will form no pattern but will instead be scattered in a random fashion. Figure 17.4, which plots the data presented in table 17.2, illustrates the concept of a linear relationship. Not all relationships, however, are linear; some are curvilinear. If a relationship is curvilinear, an increase in one variable is associated with a corresponding increase in another variable *up to a point*, and at that point further increase in the first variable results in a corresponding decrease in the other variable (or the reverse may be true—first decrease, then increase). The relationship between age and agility, for example, is a curvilinear one. If a relationship is suspected of being curvilinear, then a correlational technique which results in something called an eta ratio is required. If you try to use a correlational technique which assumes a linear relationship when the relationship is in fact curvilinear, your estimate of the degree of relationship will be way off base. Since it will in no way resemble a straight line, the coefficient will generally indicate little or no relationship. The positive relationship and negative relationship which combine to form a high curvilinear relationship will in a sense cancel

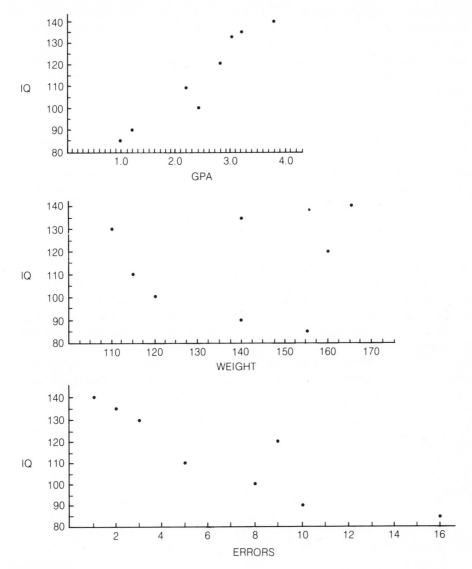

figure 17.4
Data points for scores presented in Table 17.2 illustrating a high positive relationship (IQ and GPA), no relationship (IQ and weight), and a high negative relationship (IQ and errors).

each other out if a technique which assumes linearity (totally positive or totally negative) is applied.[6]

In addition to computing correlation coefficients for a total sample group, it is sometimes profitable to examine relationships separately for certain defined subgroups. The relationship between two variables may be different, for example, for females and males, college graduates and non-college graduates, or high ability

[6] For further discussion concerning eta, as well as other advanced correlational procedures such as factor analysis and partial correlation, see: Nunnally, J. C. *Psychometric theory*. New York: McGraw-Hill, 1967.

students and low ability students. When the subgroups are lumped together, such differential relationships may be obscured. There are also other factors which may contribute to an inaccurate estimate of relationship. Attenuation, for example, refers to the tendency of correlation coefficients to be lowered due to the fact that less-than-perfectly-reliable measures are utilized. In establishing relationship a correction for attenuation can be applied which provides an estimate of what the coefficient would be if both measures were perfectly reliable. If such a correction is used, it must be kept in mind that the resulting coefficient does not represent what was actually found. Such a correction is not used in prediction studies since predictions must be made based on existing measures, not hypothetical, perfectly reliable instruments. Another factor which may lead to a coefficient which represents an underestimate of the true relationship between two variables is a restricted range of scores. The more variability there is in each set of scores, the higher the coefficient is likely to be. The correlation coefficient for IQ and grades, for example, tends to decrease as these variables are measured at higher educational levels. Thus, the relationship will not be found to be as high for college seniors as for high school seniors. The reason is that not many low IQ individuals are college seniors; low IQ individuals either do not enter college or drop out long before their senior year. In other words, the range of IQ scores is much smaller, or more restricted, for college seniors, and a correlation coefficient based on such scores will tend to be reduced. There is also a correction for restriction in range which may be applied to obtain an estimate of what the coefficient would be if the range of scores were not restricted. It should be interpreted with the same caution as the correction for attenuation since it does not represent what was actually found.

Methods of computing coefficients

There are a number of different methods of computing a correlation coefficient. Which one is appropriate depends upon the scale of measurement (i.e. nominal, ordinal, interval, or ratio) represented by each variable. The two most frequently used correlational analyses are the rank difference correlation coefficient, usually referred to as the Spearman rho, and the product moment correlation coefficient, usually referred to as the Pearson r.

The Spearman rho. If the data for one or both of the variables are expressed as ranks instead of scores, the *Spearman rho*[7] is the appropriate measure of correlation. Rank data are involved when, instead of using a score for each person, persons are arranged in order of score and each person is assigned a rank from one to however many persons there are. For a group of 30 people, for example, the person with the highest score would be assigned a rank of 1, the person with the second highest score a rank of 2, and the person with the lowest score a rank of 30. The Spearman rho is thus appropriate when the data represent an ordinal scale (although it may be used with interval data) and is used when the median and quartile deviation are used.

If only one of the variables to be correlated is in rank order, say class standing at the time of graduation, then the other variables to be correlated with it must also be expressed in terms of ranks in order to use the Spearman rho tech-

[7] Rho is a Greek letter and is pronounced like *roe* as in Marilyn Mon*roe*.

nique. Thus, if intelligence were to be correlated with class standing, students would have to be ranked in terms of intelligence, and IQ scores per se would not be involved in actual computation of the correlation coefficient. The Spearman rho is interpreted in the same way as the Pearson r and produces a coefficient somewhere between -1.00 and $+1.00$ (if a group of people achieve identical ranks on two variables the coefficient will be $+1.00$), but there is one difference between the techniques which should be mentioned. The Pearson r permits several persons to have the same score on a given variable, but the Spearman rho does not permit several persons to have the same rank. If more than one person receives the same score, their ranks are averaged. For example, if two persons have the same highest score they are each assigned the average of rank 1 and rank 2, namely rank 1.5. Similarly, the 24th and 25th highest scores, if identical, would each be assigned the rank 24.5.

Although the Pearson r is more precise, with a small number of people (less than 30) the Spearman rho is much easier to compute. Further, the Spearman rho results in a coefficient which is close to the one which would have been obtained had a Pearson r been computed. Thus, for most classroom purposes the Spearman rho provides an adequate estimate of degree of relationship and is fairly simple to compute. When the number of students is large, however, the process of ranking becomes more time consuming and the Spearman rho loses its only advantage over the Pearson r.[8]

The Pearson r. The most commonly used technique is the Pearson r, which is the most appropriate measure of correlation when the sets of data to be correlated represent either interval or ratio scales. Since most instruments used in education, such as achievement measures and personality measures, are expressed in the form of interval data, the Pearson r is usually the appropriate coefficient for determining relationship. Like the mean and the standard deviation, the Pearson r takes into account each and every score in both distributions. It is the most stable, reliable estimate of correlation and its use if preferable in many situations, even when other methods may be applied. An assumption associated with the application of the Pearson r is that the relationship between the variables being correlated is a linear one. If this is not the case, the Pearson r will not yield a valid indication of relationship. If there is any question concerning the linearity of the relationship, the two sets of data should be plotted as previously shown in figure 17.4.

Two concepts associated with the use of correlation to estimate reliability were discussed in chapter 7—the standard error of measurement (SE_m) and the Spearman-Brown prophecy formula. The SE_m provides an estimate of how often you can expect errors of a given size, errors in estimating a person's true score, errors resulting from the fact that no test is perfectly reliable. The Spearman-Brown prophecy formula is used to estimate the reliability of the total test when split-half reliability is computed. More generally, the Spearman-Brown formula is used to estimate the reliability of a test increased or decreased in length by any factor.

Other methods. There are also a number of other correlational techniques which are encountered less often but which should be used when appropriate.

---

[8] Pearson and Spearman are the two people credited with the development of their respective techniques for computing correlation coefficients.

Some variables, for example, can only be expressed in terms of a dichotomy. Since an individual is usually either male or female, the variable of sex cannot be expressed on a scale from 1 to 30. Thus sex is typically expressed as a 1 or 0 (female or male) or as a 1 or 2 (female or male). A 2, however, does not mean more of something than a 1, and 1 does not mean more than 0. These numbers indicate difference only, not difference in amount. Other variables which may be expressed as a dichotomy include political affiliation (democrat or republican), smoking status (smoker or nonsmoker), and educational status (high school graduate or high school dropout). The above examples illustrate "true" dichotomies in that a person is or is not a female, a democrat, a smoker, or a high school graduate. Artificial dichotomies may also be created by operationally defining a midpoint and categorizing subjects as falling above it or below it. Students with IQ scores of 100 or above might be classified as "high IQ students," for example, and students with IQ scores of 99 or below might be classified as "low IQ students." Such classifications are also typically translated into a "score" of 1 or 0.[9]

Multiple regression. When prediction is an intent of an evaluation, a predictor variable is correlated with a criterion variable. Since a combination of variables usually results in a more accurate prediction than any one variable, prediction efforts typically involve a number of predictor variables. In this situation we do not compute a series of correlation coefficients, one for each predictor variable. Instead we formulate an equation referred to as a *multiple regression equation*. A multiple regression equation uses all variables which individually predict the criterion to make a prediction which is more accurate. College admissions personnel, for example, use prediction equations which include a number of variables in order to predict college GPA. Since relationships are rarely perfect, predictions made by a multiple regression equation are not perfect. Thus, predicted scores are generally placed in a confidence interval. For example, a predicted college GPA of 1.20 might be placed in an interval of .80 to 1.60. In other words, students with a predicted GPA of 1.20 would be predicted to earn a GPA somewhere in the range between .80 and 1.60. A college which does not accept all applicants will probably as a general rule fail to accept any applicants with such a projected GPA range, even though it is very likely that some of those students would be successful if admitted. While the predictions for any given individual might be way off (either too high or too low), predictions for the total group of applicants are quite accurate on the whole; most applicants predicted to succeed do so. As with relationship studies, and for similar reasons, prediction equations may be formulated for each of a number of subgroups as well as for a total group.

An interesting phenomenon characteristic of multiple regression equations is referred to as shrinkage. *Shrinkage* is the tendency of a prediction equation to become less accurate when used with a different group, a group other than the one on which the equation was originally formulated. The reason for shrinkage is that an initial equation may be the result of chance relationships which will not be found again with another group. Thus, any prediction equation should be validated with at least one other group, and variables which are no longer found to be related to the criterion measure should be taken out of the equation. This procedure is referred to as *cross-validation*.

[9] For additional discussion concerning alternative techniques for calculating correlation coefficients see Glass, G. V., & Stanley., J. C. *Statistical methods in education and psychology.* Englewood Cliffs, N.J.: Prentice-Hall, 1970.

Calculation for interval data

Since most data in educational evaluation represent interval scales, we will calculate measures of central tendency, variability, relative position, and relationship appropriate for interval data. Also, because of its ease of application we will also compute the Spearman rho. Since most standard scores are transformations of z scores, we will compute z scores and illustrate one such transformation, T scores. There are several different formulas available for computing each of the measures; in each case, however, we will use the easiest formula, the raw score formula. At first glance some of the formulas may look intimidating, but they are really easy. The only reason they look bad is because they involve symbols with which you are unfamiliar. As promised, however, each formula transforms "magically" into an arithmetic problem in one easy step. All you have to do is substitute the correct numbers for the correct symbols. Believe it or not, after you have calculated these measures a number of times, you will be able to look at a set of data and estimate the various values fairly accurately.

Symbols

Before we start calculating, you should get acquainted with a few basic symbols. First, X is usually used to symbolize a raw score, any score. If you see a column of numbers, and at the top of that column is an X, you know that the column represents a set of scores. If there are two sets of scores, they may be labeled X_1 and X_2 or X and Y—it does not matter which.

Another symbol used frequently is the Greek letter Σ (sigma) which is used to indicate addition. It means "the sum of" or "add them up." Thus ΣX means "add up all the X's," and ΣY means "add up all the Y's." Isn't this easy?

Now, if any symbol has a bar over it, such as $\bar{X}$, that indicates the mean, or arithmetic average, of the scores. Thus $\bar{X}$ refers to the mean of the X scores and $\bar{Y}$ refers to the mean of the Y scores.

A capital N refers to the number of students (or other participants). $N = 20$ means that there are 20 students (N for number of students makes sense, doesn't it?). If one analysis involves several groups, the number of students in each group is frequently indicated with a lowercase letter n and a subscript indicating the group. If there are two groups, and the first group has 74 students and the second group has 70 students, this is symbolized as $n_1 = 74$ and $n_2 = 70$. The total number of students is represented as $N = 144$ ($74 + 70 = 144$).

A squiggly or script X, written as x, indicates a deviation score. A deviation score represents how far a given score is from the mean. In other words, $x = X - \bar{X}$, which reads "the deviation score equals the score minus the mean." Every score in a distribution can be expressed as a deviation score.

Finally, you must get straight the difference between ΣX^2 and $(\Sigma X)^2$; they do not mean the same thing. Different formulas may include one or the other or both and it is very important to interpret each correctly. A formula tells you what to do and you must do exactly what it tells you. Now let's look at ΣX^2. What does it tell you? The Σ tells you that you are supposed to add something up. What you are supposed to add up are X^2's. What do you suppose X^2 means? Right. It means the square of the score. If $X = 4$, then $X^2 = 4^2 = 4 \times 4 = 16$. Thus, ΣX^2 says to square each score and *then* add up all the squares. Now let's look at $(\Sigma X)^2$. Since whatever is in the parentheses is always done first, the first thing we do is ΣX. You already know what that means, it means "add up all the scores." And then what? Right. You add up all the scores and *then* you square the total. Do you see the difference between ΣX^2 (square each number and then add up all the squares) and $(\Sigma X)^2$ (add up all the scores and then square the total)? Good.

To summarize, symbols commonly used in statistical formulas are as follows:

X = any score
Σ = the sum of; add them up
ΣX = the sum of all the scores
$\overline{X}$ = the mean, or arithmetic average, of the scores
N = total number of students
n = number of students in a particular group
x = deviation score; $x = X - \overline{X}$
ΣX^2 = the sum of all the squares (square each score and add up all the squares)
$(\Sigma X)^2$ = the square of the sum (add up all the scores and square the sum, or total)

The mean

Although a sample size of 5 is hardly ever considered to be acceptable, we will work with this number for the sake of illustration. In other words, all of our calculations will be based on the test scores for 5 students so that you can concentrate on how the calculation is being done and will not get lost in the numbers. For the same reason we will also use very small numbers. Now let us assume we have the following scores for some old friends of ours and we want to compute the mean, or arithmetic average.

	X
Egor	2
Ziggy	4
Hermie	6
Hornrim	8
Instine	10

Remember that a column labeled X means "here come the scores!"

The formula for the mean is:

$$\overline{X} = \frac{\Sigma X}{N}$$

You are now looking at a statistic. Looks awful, right? But let's see what it really *says*. It reads "the mean ($\overline{X}$) is equal to the sum of the scores (ΣX) divided by the number of students (N). So, in order to find $\overline{X}$ we need ΣX and N.

X
2
4
6
8
10

$\Sigma X = 30$

Clearly, $\Sigma X = 2 + 4 + 6 + 8 + 10 = 30$
$N = 5$ (There are 5 students, right?)

Now we have everything we need to find the mean, and all we have to do is substitute the correct number for each symbol.

$$\overline{X} = \frac{\Sigma X}{N} = \frac{30}{5}$$

Now what do we have? Right! An arithmetic problem. A hard arithmetic problem? No! An elementary school arithmetic problem? Yes! And all we did was to substitute each symbol with the appropriate number. Thus,

$$\overline{X} = \frac{\Sigma X}{N} = \frac{30}{5} = 6$$

so the mean is equal to 6. If you just *look* at the scores, you can see that 6 is clearly the average score. Was that hard? Cer-tain-ly not! It was a cinch. And guess what —you just learned how to do a statistic! Are they all going to be that easy? Of course!

The standard deviation

Earlier we discussed the fact that the standard deviation is the square root of the variance which is based on the distance of each score from the mean. To calculate the standard deviation (SD), however, we do not have to calculate deviation scores; we can use a raw score formula which gives us the same answer with less grief. Now, before you look at the formula remember that no matter how bad it looks it is going to turn into an easy arithmetic problem. Ready?

$$SD = \sqrt{\frac{\Sigma X^2 - \frac{(\Sigma X)^2}{N}}{N}}$$

Now just relax and look at each piece of the formula. You already know what each piece means. Starting with the easy one, N refers to what? Right—the number of students. How about (ΣX)? Right—the sum of the scores. And $(\Sigma X)^2$? Right—square of the sum of the scores. That leaves ΣX^2, which means the sum of what? Fantastic—the sum of the squares. Okay, let's use the same scores we used to calculate the mean. The first thing we need to do is to square each score and then add those squares up, and while we're at it, we can also go ahead and add up all the scores.

	X	X^2
Egor	2	4
Ziggy	4	16
Hermie	6	36
Hornrim	8	64
Instine	10	100
	$\Sigma X = 30$	$\Sigma X^2 = 220$

$\Sigma X = 30,$
$\Sigma X^2 = 220,$ and
$N = 5$

Do we have everything we need? Does the formula ask for anything else? We are in business. Substituting each symbol with its numerical equivalent we get:

$$SD = \sqrt{\frac{\Sigma X^2 - \frac{(\Sigma X)^2}{N}}{N}} - \sqrt{\frac{220 - \frac{(30)^2}{5}}{5}}$$

Now what do we have? A statistic? No! An arithmetic problem? Yes! A hard arithmetic problem? No. Okay, it *is* harder than $30/5$, but it is not *hard*. If we just do what the formula tells us to do, we'll have no problem at all. The first thing it tells us to do is to square 30:

$$SD = \sqrt{\frac{220 - \frac{(30)^2}{5}}{5}} = \sqrt{\frac{220 - \frac{900}{5}}{5}}$$

So far so good? Now, just in case you are not too good at squaring ($30 \times 30 = 900$), many numbers have been squared for you in table A.2 in the Appendix. The next thing the formula tells you to do is to divide 900 by 5:

$$SD = \sqrt{\frac{220 - \frac{900}{5}}{5}} = \sqrt{\frac{220 - 180}{5}}$$

You have to admit "it" looks a lot better. Now it really *is* an easy arithmetic problem. Okay, the next step is to subtract 180 from 220:

$$SD = \sqrt{\frac{220 - 180}{5}} = \sqrt{\frac{40}{5}}$$

Mere child's play. Think you can figure out the next step? Terrific!

$$SD = \sqrt{\frac{40}{5}} = \sqrt{8}$$

Almost done. Hmmm, you say you're not very good at "square rootin'"? As luck would have it, and as you may have already noticed, table A.2 also includes square roots for many numbers, including 8.[10] Thus:

$$SD = \sqrt{8} = 2.83$$

and the standard deviation is 2.83. If we had calculated the standard deviation for the IQ distribution shown in figure 17.2, what do you think we would have gotten? Right—15. Now you know how to do *two* statistics.

Standard scores

The z score is the basic standard score and it is even easier to calculate than the standard deviation. A z score expresses a deviation score in standard deviation

[10] Remember, it's perfectly all right to use a calculator. In fact, it's a good idea! Some calculators will compute square roots for you.

units. Recall that a score exactly 1SD above the $\overline{X}$ translates into $z = +1.00$, and a score 1SD below the mean to $z = -1.00$. But few scores are exactly 1SD (or 2SD, or 3SD) above or below the mean. Thus, we need a formula to calculate other values. Since a deviation score x is equal to the score minus the mean $(X - \overline{X})$, the formula for a z score is:

$$z = \frac{x}{SD} = \frac{X - \overline{X}}{SD}$$

To convert scores to z scores we simply apply that formula to each score. Therefore, the first thing we need to do is to transform each raw score into a deviation score:

	X	$\overline{X}$	$X - \overline{X}$
Egor	2	6	−4
Ziggy	4	6	−2
Hermie	6	6	0
Hornrim	8	6	2
Instine	10	6	4

We previously computed the mean $(\overline{X})$ to be 6.

Now all we have to do is to divide each score by the standard deviation which we have already calculated to be 2.83. Let's see how Egor's score works out:

$$\text{Egor} \qquad z = \frac{X - \overline{X}}{SD} = \frac{-4}{2.83} = -1.41$$

In other words, Egor is almost 1½SD's below the mean. Not too good.

In case you have forgotten, if the signs of the terms in a multiplication or division problem are the same (two positives or two negatives), the answer is a positive number; if the signs are different, the answer is a negative number, as in Egor's case. For the rest of our friends, the results are:

$$\text{Ziggy} \qquad z = \frac{X - \overline{X}}{SD} = \frac{-2}{2.83} = -.71$$

$$\text{Hermie} \qquad z = \frac{X - \overline{X}}{SD} = \frac{0}{2.83} = .00$$

$$\text{Hornrim} \qquad z = \frac{X - \overline{X}}{SD} = \frac{2}{2.83} = +.71$$

$$\text{Instine} \qquad z = \frac{X - \overline{X}}{SD} = \frac{4}{2.83} = +1.41$$

Notice that since Hermie's score was the same as the mean score, his z is .00; his score is *no* distance from the mean.

If we want to eliminate the negatives, we convert each z score to a T score (or Z score, depending upon the distribution). To do that we simply multiply each z score by 10 and add 50:

$$T = 10z + 50$$

If we apply this formula to our z scores, we get the following results:

Egor $\qquad T = 10z + 50 = 10(-1.41) + 50$
$$= +14.1 + 50$$
$$= 50 - 14.1$$
$$= 35.9$$

Ziggy $\qquad T = 10z + 50 = 10(-.71) + 50$
$$= -7.1 + 50$$
$$= 50 - 7.1$$
$$= 42.9$$

Hermie $\qquad T = 10z + 50 = 10(.00) + 50$
$$= .00 + 50$$
$$= 50.0$$

Hornrim $\qquad T = 10z + 50 = 10(+.71) + 50$
$$= 7.1 + 50$$
$$= 50 + 7.1$$
$$= 57.1$$

Instine $\qquad T = 10z + 50 = 10(+1.41) + 50$
$$= 14.1 + 50$$
$$= 50 + 14.1$$
$$= 64.1$$

Isn't this fun!

The Spearman rho

Suppose we wanted to determine if there is a relationship between the scores that we have been working with and the scores on some other test. Technically, the Pearson r would be the appropriate correlational method. We might decide that for our purposes the Spearman rho will provide an adequate estimate of relationship. To use the Spearman rho we have to convert the scores to ranks. We will refer to the scores on the first test as X and to the scores on the second test as Y:

	X	Y
Egor	2	3
Ziggy	4	5
Hermie	6	8
Hornrim	8	7
Instine	10	10

Translating these scores into ranks, we get:

	X	rank$_x$	Y	rank$_y$
Egor	2	5	3	5
Ziggy	4	4	5	4
Hermie	6	3	8	2
Hornrim	8	2	7	3
Instine	10	1	10	1

The question is, Are these two sets of ranks related? Positively? Negatively? Not at all?

Instine is ranked #1 on both tests because he had the highest score, and Egor is ranked fifth because he had the lowest score. To determine the relationship between the ranks we use the following formula:

$$\text{rho} = 1 - \frac{6\Sigma d^2}{N(N^2 - 1)}$$

You already know what Σ and N stand for so the only question is, what in the world is a d? Take a wild guess. Right! The d stands for difference. You're so clever. The difference between what? Right, d is the difference between the ranks for each student. Thus, $d = \text{rank}_x - \text{rank}_y$. Got it? Okay, let's find the d for each pair of ranks. While we're at it, we might as well get the squares (d^2) and the sum of the squares (Σd^2).

	rank$_x$	rank$_y$	d	d^2
Egor	5	5	0	0
Ziggy	4	4	0	0
Hermie	3	2	1	1
Hornrim	2	3	-1	1
Instine	1	1	0	0
			Σd^2	= 2

Now we have everything we need and all we have to do is substitute the correct number for the correct symbol in the formula:

$$\text{rho} = 1 - \frac{6\Sigma d^2}{N(N^2 - 1)} = 1 - \frac{6(2)}{5(25 - 1)}$$

If you were tempted to use $N = 10$, remember that $N = $ the number of students, not the number of scores. Now what do we have? Cor-rect! An easy arithmetic problem. The first thing we do is to reduce the bottom term in parentheses:

$$\text{rho} = 1 - \frac{6(2)}{5(25 - 1)} = 1 - \frac{6(2)}{5(24)}$$

Next, we multiply the terms in the numerator and denominator of the fraction (for you nonmathetical types, that's the top and the bottom):

$$\text{rho} = 1 - \frac{6(2)}{5(24)} = 1 - \frac{12}{120}$$

Now we divide 12 by 120. We could reduce $^{12}/_{120}$ to $^1/_{10}$ first, but we would get the same answer:

$$\text{rho} = 1 - \frac{12}{120} = 1 - .10$$

Just in case you forgot:

$$120\overline{)12.0}^{.1}$$
$$\underline{12.0}$$

One more step. We have to subtract .10 from 1. To refresh your memory, the main thing to remember is to line up your decimal points:

$$rho = 1 - .10 = .90$$

Put another way: 1.00
                   $-$ .10
                   ———
                     .90

Are those two sets of ranks related? A lot? Of course. You knew that just by *looking* at the scores. What if our answer had been rho = 1.20? Wow! That would mean that the ranks are *really* related, right? Wrong! That would mean that we are lousy in arithmetic—the highest a correlation coefficient can be is 1.00.

Were any of the statistics we have done so far hard? Is anybody out there suffering brain-strain? No. Now just keep remembering that when you look at the next formula. No matter how bad it *looks*, it is really just an arithmetic problem.

The Pearson *r*

The formula for the Pearson *r looks* very, very complicated, but it is not (have I lied to you so far?). It looks bad because it has a lot of pieces, but each piece is quite simple to calculate. Now, to calculate a Pearson *r* we need two sets of scores. Just to make things interesting, let's use the same sets of scores we used for the Spearman rho:

	X	Y
Egor	2	3
Ziggy	4	5
Hermie	6	8
Hornrim	8	7
Instine	10	10

The question is Are these two sets of scores related? Positively? Negatively? Not at all?

Now take a deep breath. Here goes!

$$r = \frac{N\Sigma XY - \Sigma X \Sigma Y}{\sqrt{[N\Sigma X^2 - (\Sigma X)^2][N\Sigma Y^2 - (\Sigma Y)^2]}}$$

Does it look bad? Is it? What will it turn into?[11] Now, if you look at each piece you will see that you already know how to calculate all of them except one. You should have no problem with ΣX, ΣY, ΣX^2, or ΣY^2. And even though there are 10 scores, there are only 5 students, so $N = 5$. What is left? The only new symbol in the formula is ΣXY. What could that mean? Well, you know that it is the sum of something, namely the XY's, whatever they are. An XY is just what you would guess it is—the product of an X score and its corresponding Y score. Thus, Egor's XY score is $2 \times 3 = 6$, and Hornrim's XY score is $8 \times 7 = 56$. Okay, let's get all the pieces we need:

---

[11] The answers are: Yes! No! An arithmetic problem.

	X	Y	X²	Y²	XY
Egor	2	3	4	9	6
Ziggy	4	5	16	25	20
Hermie	6	8	36	64	48
Hornrim	8	7	64	49	56
Instine	10	10	100	100	100
	$\Sigma X = 30$	$\Sigma Y = 33$	$\Sigma X^2 = 220$	$\Sigma Y^2 = 247$	$\Sigma XY = 230$

Now guess what we are going to do. Right. We are going to turn that horrible-looking statistic into a horrible-looking arithmetic problem! Just kidding. It will really be an easy arithmetic problem if we do it one step at a time.

$$r = \frac{N\Sigma XY - \Sigma X \Sigma Y}{\sqrt{[N\Sigma X^2 - (\Sigma X)^2][N\Sigma Y^2 - (\Sigma Y)^2]}} = \frac{5(230) - (30)(33)}{\sqrt{[5(220) - (30)^2][5(247) - (33)^2]}}$$

Granted, it still doesn't look very good, but you have to admit it looks better! Let's start with the numerator (the top part). First, we multiply 5 by 230:

$$r = \frac{5(230) - (30)(33)}{\sqrt{[5(220) - (30)^2][5(247) - (33)^2]}} = \frac{1150 - (30)(33)}{\sqrt{[5(220) - (30)^2][5(247) - (33)^2]}}$$

Next, we multiply 30 by 33:

$$r = \frac{1150 - (30)(33)}{\sqrt{[5(220) - (30)^2][5(247) - (33)^2]}} = \frac{1150 - 990}{\sqrt{[5(220) - (30)^2][5(247) - (33)^2]}}$$

The next step is a real snap. All we have to do is subtract 990 from 1150:

$$r = \frac{1150 - 990}{\sqrt{[5(220) - (30)^2][5(247) - (33)^2]}} = \frac{160}{\sqrt{[5(220) - (30)^2][5(247) - (33)^2]}}$$

So much for the numerator. Was that hard? No! Au contraire, it was very easy. Right? Right. Now for the denominator (the bottom part). The first thing the formula says to do is to multiply 5 by 220:

$$r = \frac{160}{\sqrt{[5(220) - (30)^2][5(247) - (33)^2]}} = \frac{160}{\sqrt{[1100 - (30)^2][5(247) - (33)^2]}}$$

Now we square 30; we multiply 30 by 30 or look up the square of 30 in table A.2:

$$r = \frac{160}{\sqrt{[1100 - (30)^2][5(247) - (33)^2]}} = \frac{160}{\sqrt{[1100 - 900][5(247) - (33)^2]}}$$

Can you figure out the next step? Good. We subtract 900 from 1100:

$$r = \frac{160}{\sqrt{[1100 - 900][5(247) - (33)^2]}} = \frac{160}{\sqrt{[200][5(247) - (33)^2]}}$$

It is looking a lot better, isn't it? Okay, moving right along, now we need to multiply 5 by 247:

$$r = \frac{160}{\sqrt{[200][5(247) - (33)^2]}} = \frac{160}{\sqrt{[200][1235 - (33)^2]}}$$

Now, we square 33:

$$r = \frac{160}{\sqrt{[200][1235 - (33)^2]}} = \frac{160}{\sqrt{[200][1235 - 1089]}}$$

Hang in there, it won't be long now. Next we subtract 1089 from 1235:

$$r = \frac{160}{\sqrt{[200][1235 - 1089]}} = \frac{160}{\sqrt{[200][146]}}$$

Can you figure out what to do next? If you can, you're smarter than you thought, you little shining star. Next, we multiply 200 by 146:

$$r = \frac{160}{\sqrt{[200][146]}} = \frac{160}{\sqrt{29200}}$$

Now we need the square root of 29200. Rats! We seem to have a problem. Table A.2 only goes up to 1000. How are we going to find the square root of 29200? Actually there are several courses of action available. If you are a math whiz you can directly calculate the square root. If not, you can either find a math whiz to do it for you, consult a larger table, or use a calculator with a square root button. If the answer does not have to be exactly correct, down to the last decimal place, there is a way that we can use table A.2. Now concentrate. We want the square root of 29200, and the table only goes up to 1000. But even though the number 29200 is not in the table, the *square root* of 29200 *is* in the table because it is surely not larger than 1000. Thus, there is a number in the table for which the *square* is 29200, or close to it. So, we look down the square column until we find the closest number to 29200; the closest number is 29241 and it is the square of 171. Therefore, 171 is the square root of 29241 and is close to the square root of 29200. In reality, the precise square root of 29200 is 170.88. Pretty close, huh? In case you are not following this, suppose we wanted the square root of 49, but 49 wasn't in the table. We would look down the square column until we found the number closest to 49. As it is, 49 is in the square column; it is the *square* of 7 and therefore, 7 is the *square root* of 49. Got it? Let's finish the *r* calculations with the estimated square root of 29200 as 171:

$$r = \frac{160}{\sqrt{29200}} = \frac{160}{171}$$

Dividing 160 by 171 we have:

$$r = \frac{160}{171} = .935 = .94$$

If we use the precise value of the square root, we have:

$$r = \frac{160}{\sqrt{29200}} = \frac{160}{170.88} = .936 = .94$$

In this case our estimates of r are practically identical. Thus, for most situations, our little "trick" works very well. I promised you that you wouldn't *have* to calculate any square roots!

Whew! We finally finished it. In case you got lost in the action, .94 is the correlation coefficient, the Pearson r. In other words, $r = .94$. When we estimated the relationship using the Spearman rho, we got rho = .90. Pretty close. The r of .94 is the most accurate estimate, but .90 is not a bad estimate and for most classroom inquiries it would be close enough.

Now the question is, Is .94 good? Well, in general, it depends. The real question is, Is it "significant"? A coefficient's significance depends upon two factors, its *statistical* significance and its *practical* significance. If it is statistically significant, then it is probably different from zero and probably indicates a true relationship, not a chance one. If it is practically significant, then the coefficient is large enough to be of some value. If enough students are measured, for example, a coefficient of .19 may be statistically significant, indicating a small, but real, relationship. But such a relationship is too small to be of any real use. The statistical significance of a coefficient is determined mathematically whereas practical significance is a judgmental matter which depends to some degree on the purpose for which it is to be used. A coefficient of $r = .65$, for example, is usually considered to be adequate for group prediction purposes, but not for individual prediction.

To determine whether a given coefficient is statistically significant, we consult a table (see table A.3 in the Appendix). This table indicates how large our r needs to be in order to be significant given the number of students (or other participants) we have and the probability level (level of significance) we have selected. The number of students affects the degrees of freedom (df) which for the Pearson r are always computed by the formula $N - 2$. Thus, for our example, $df = N - 2 = 5 - 2 = 3$. The probability level (p) we select indicates how likely it is that we are making the wrong decision concerning the existence of a true relationship. In other words, based on one group of a given size, we cannot determine positively whether there is or is not a true relationship between the variables, but we can say there *probably* is or is not such a relationship. Moreover, a hypothesis concerning relationship or lack of it can be supported or not supported. Due mainly to tradition, we usually select a probability level, p, of .05 or .01. If a coefficient is significant at $p = .05$, this means that we would expect to find a coefficient as large (or larger) as we have found *by chance* only 5 times out of 100, or 5% of the time. If a coefficient is significant at $p = .01$, we would expect to find a coefficient that large only 1% of the time. In other words, there *probably* is a relationship.[12]

For our example, $r = .94$, let us select $p = .05$. We already have determined that $df = 3$. We are now ready to use table A.3. Look at table A.3, find the column labeled df, and run your left index finger down the column until you hit 3, the df associated with our r. Keep your left finger right there for the time being. Now run your right index finger across the top of the table, until you come to .05,

---

[13] In depth discussion of the terms degrees of freedom, significance level, and other related terms is beyond the scope of this text. Although they will be touched on again later in the chapter, a research or statistics text should be consulted for full treatment of these topics.

the significance level we have selected. Now run your left finger straight across the table and your right finger straight down the table until they meet. If you follow directions well, you should have ended up at .8783 which rounds off to .88. Now we compare our coefficient to the table value. Is .94 ≥ .88? Yes, .94 is greater than or equal to .88. Therefore, our coefficient does indicate a true relationship between the X scores and the Y scores. We are not positive that there is a relationship, but the odds favor it. Note (see table A.2) that if we had had just one less student (N = 4), our df would have been 2 (N − 2 = 4 − 2 = 2) and our coefficient would not have indicated a significant relationship (.94 is not ≥ .95). Note too that the same table would have been used if r had been a negative number, − .94. The table does not know or care whether the r is positive or negative. It only tells you how large r must be numerically in order to indicate a relationship is significantly different from .00, is a true relationship.

   As the above example illustrates, for the same probability level, or significance level, a larger coefficient is required when smaller samples are involved. We can generally have a lot more confidence in a coefficient based on 100 students than one based on 10 students. Thus, for p = .05 and 10 students (df = 8), for example, you would need a coefficient of at least .6319 in order to conclude the existence of a relationship. On the other hand, with 102 students (df = 100) you would need a coefficient of only .1946. This concept makes sense if you consider the case where data on every member of a population, not just a sample group, is collected. In such a case, no inference would be involved, and regardless of how small the actual correlation coefficient was, it would represent the true degree of relationship between the variables for that population. Even if the coefficient was only .11, for example, it would still indicate the existence of a relationship, a low one, but a relationship just the same. The larger the sample, the more closely it approximates the population and therefore the more probable it is that a given coefficient represents a true relationship.

   You may also have noticed another related concept. For a given group size, the value of the correlation coefficient needed for significance increases as the p value decreases, gets smaller. Thus, for 10 students (df = 8) and p = .05, a coefficient of .6319 is required; for 10 students and p = .01, however, a coefficient of .7646 is required. In other words, the more confident you wish to be that your decision concerning significance is the correct one, the larger the coefficient must be. Beware, however, of confusing significance with strength. No matter how significant a coefficient is, a low coefficient represents a low relationship. The level of significance only indicates the probability that a given relationship is a true one, regardless of whether it is a weak relationship or a strong relationship. Also, do not forget that even if a correlation coefficient is statistically significant, it does not necessarily mean that the coefficient has any practical significance. Whether the coefficient is useful depends upon the use to which it will be put. A coefficient to be used in a prediction study needs to be much higher than a coefficient to be used in a relationship study.

   As the above discussion suggests, when we are concerned with the statistical significance of a correlation coefficient, r is really an inferential statistic, not just a descriptive statistic. We are interested not just in describing the degree of relationship but also in determining whether a relationship found for a sample group really represents a relationship present in the population from which the sample group was selected. There are actually a variety of inferential statistics; they are usually used only in more formal evaluation efforts.

Inferential statistics

Inferential statistics deal with (of all things!) inferences. Inferences about what? Inferences about populations based on the behavior of sample groups. Many educational evaluation efforts involve sample groups. Recall that the "goodness" of the various sampling techniques is a function of their effectiveness in producing representative sample groups. The more representative a sample is, the more generalizable the results will be to the population from which the sample was selected. Results which hold only for the sample upon which they are based are of limited value. Consequently, random samples are preferred since they seem to do the job best. Inferential statistics are concerned with determining how likely it is that results based on a sample or samples are the same results which would have been obtained for the entire population.

If a posttest difference between means is found for two groups (a treatment group and a control group), the question of interest is whether a similar difference exists in the population from which the samples were selected. It could be that no real difference exists in the population and that the difference found for the samples was a chance one. If two different samples had been used, it is likely that no difference would have been found. And now we get to the heart of inferential statistics, the concept of "how likely is it." If I find a difference between two sample means and conclude that the difference is large enough to infer that a true difference exists in the population, how likely is it that I am wrong? In other words, inferences concerning populations are only probability statements. The evaluator is only probably correct when he or she makes an inference and concludes that there is a true difference, or true relationship, in the population.

Concepts underlying application

While in-depth discussion of the concepts underlying application of inferential statistics is beyond the scope of this text, there are a few basic concepts with which you should have at least a nodding acquaintance.

Hypotheses

Whether they are actually stated or not, most formal evaluation efforts are based on one or more hypotheses. Hypotheses state expected outcomes and should be made explicit. For example, implied in the evaluation question "Is the Warm Fuzzy Preschool Program more effective than the Cold Shoulder Preschool Program?" is the hypothesis "The Warm Fuzzy Preschool Program *is* more effective than the Cold Shoulder Preschool Program." Typically, we use a statistic to test what is called a null hypothesis, to determine whether a difference between two groups occurred by chance. When we talk about the difference between two sample means being a true difference, we mean that the difference was caused by the treatment (the independent variable) and not by chance. In other words, the difference is either caused by the treatment, or is the result of chance, i.e. random sampling error. The chance explanation for the difference is called the null hypothesis. The *null hypothesis* says in essence that there is no true difference or relationship in the populations and that any difference or relationship found for the samples is the result of sampling error. A null hypothesis might state:

> There is no significant difference between the mean reading achievement of preschool children who participate in the Warm Fuzzy Preschool Program and preschool children who participate in the Cold Shoulder Preschool Program.

This hypothesis says that there really is not any difference between the two programs and if you find one it is not a true difference but a chance difference resulting from sampling error.

In order to test a null hypothesis, we need a test of significance and we need to select a probability level which indicates how much risk we are willing to take that the decision we make is wrong.

Tests of significance

After we administer a posttest, we typically have two (or more) group means. We do not expect these means to be *exactly* the same, even if the treatment is equally as effective as the control condition; these means are very likely to be at least a little different. We must then decide whether the means are significantly different, different *enough* to conclude that they represent a true difference. In other words, we must make the decision whether or not to reject the null hypothesis, i.e. conclude that it is false. We do not make the decision based on our own best guess. Instead, we select and apply an appropriate test of significance. The test of significance helps us to decide whether we can reject the null hypothesis and infer that the difference is a true one, a population difference, not a chance one resulting from sampling error. Based on sample data, the test of significance determines whether the difference is significantly greater than a chance difference. If the difference is too large to attribute to chance, we reject the null hypothesis; if not, we do not reject it.

The test of significance is made at a preselected probability level and allows us to state that we have rejected the null hypothesis because we would expect by chance to find a difference as large as we have found only 5 times out of 100 ($p = .05$), or only 1 time in 100 ($p = .01$), or whatever. Therefore, we conclude that the null hypothesis is *probably* false and reject it. Obviously, if we can say we would expect such a difference by chance only 1 time in 100, we are more confident in our decision that if we say we would expect such a chance difference 5 times in 100. How confident we are depends upon the level of significance, or probability level, at which we perform our test of significance.

Types of significance tests

There are a number of different tests of significance which can be applied in evaluation studies, one of which is more appropriate in a given situation. Factors such as the scale of measurement represented by the data, the method of participant selection, the number of groups, and the number of independent variables determine which test of significance should be selected for a given evaluation. It is important that an appropriate test be selected. An incorrect test can lead to incorrect conclusions. We will briefly discuss only a few of the most commonly used tests of significance.

The *t* test

The *t* test is a statistic which is frequently used in evaluation studies. The *t* *test* is used to determine whether two means (usually the treatment mean and the control mean) are significantly different at a selected probability level. In other words, for a given sample size the *t* indicates how often a difference $(\bar{X}_1 - \bar{X}_2)$ as large or larger would be found when there is no true population difference.

The *t* test for independent samples

Independent samples are samples which are randomly formed, that is, formed without any type of matching. The members of one group are not related to the members of the other group in any systematic way other than that they are selected from the same population. If two groups are randomly formed, the expectation is that they are essentially the same prior to implementation with respect to performance on the dependent variable. Therefore, if they are essentially the same at the time of posttesting, the null hypothesis is probably true. If they are significantly different at the time of posttesting, the null hypothesis is probably false; that is, the treatment does make a difference. The key word, remember, is *essentially*. We do not expect the two groups to be identical at the end; they are bound to be somewhat different. The question is whether they are significantly different. Thus, the *t* test for independent samples is used to determine whether there is probably a significant difference between the means of two independent samples.

The *t* test for nonindependent samples

Nonindependent samples are samples formed by some type of matching. The ultimate matching, of course, is when the two samples are really the same sample group at two different times, as when one group receives two different treatments at two different times or when one group is pretested before a treatment and then posttested. When samples are not independent, the members of one group are systematically related to the members of a second group (especially if it is the same group at two different times). Thus, the *t* test for nonindependent samples is used to determine whether there is probably a significant difference between the means of two matched, or nonindependent, samples or between the means for one sample at two different times.

When Model B is used to assess program effectiveness, the *t* test is usually the appropriate statistic. Pretest and posttest scores are transformed into standard scores, and pretest scores are compared. If pretest scores are essentially the same, then posttest scores are compared using the *t* test. If pretest scores are significantly different, then posttest scores are compared using analysis of covariance.

When a t test is used to analyze results, the evaluation report should present the group means, standard deviations, and n's for both the treatment group and the control group. The t value and the significance level (e.g. .05) should also be reported. Depending upon the evaluation, the above information may be presented for a number of groups. Analyses may be performed and reported by grade level, for example.

Analysis of gain scores

When two groups are pretested, given a treatment, and then posttested, the t test may or may not be the appropriate analysis technique. It is sometimes assumed that the logical procedure is to: (1) subtract each person's pretest score from his or her posttest score (which results in a gain, or difference, score); (2) compute the mean gain, or difference, score for each group; and (3) calculate a t value for the difference between the two average mean differences. The reliability of gain scores is typically lower than the reliability of the scores themselves, and there are a number of problems associated with this approach, the major one being lack of equal opportunity to grow. Every person does not have the same room to grow. A person who scores very low on a pretest has a lot of room, and a person who scores very high has a little room. Who has improved, or gained, more—someone who goes from 20 to 70 (a gain of 50) or someone who goes from 85 to 100 (a gain of only 15 but perhaps a perfect score)?

The correct analysis of posttest scores for two groups depends upon the performance of the two groups on the pretest. If both groups are essentially the same on the pretest, say neither group knows anything, then posttest scores can be directly compared using a t test. If, on the other hand, there is a difference between the groups on the pretest, the preferred posttest analysis is analysis of covariance. Recall that analysis of covariance adjusts posttest scores for initial differences on some variable (in this case the pretest) related to performance on the dependent variable. Thus, in order to determine whether analysis of covariance is necessary, a Pearson r can be calculated to determine if there is a significant relationship between pretest scores and posttest scores. If not, a simple t test can be computed on posttest scores.

Simple analysis of variance

Simple, or one-way, *analysis of variance* (ANOVA) is used to determine whether there is a significant difference between two or more means at a selected probability level. In an evaluation involving three groups, for example, the ANOVA is the appropriate analysis technique. Three (or more) posttest means are bound to be different. The question is whether the differences represent true differences or chance differences resulting from sampling error. To answer this question at a given probability level, the ANOVA is applied to the data and an F ratio is computed. You may be wondering why you cannot just compute a lot of t tests, one for each pair of means. Aside from some statistical problems concerning resulting distortion of your probability level, it is more convenient to perform one ANOVA than several t's. For four means, for example, six separate t tests would be required $(\overline{X}_1 - \overline{X}_2, \overline{X}_1 - \overline{X}_3, \overline{X}_1 - \overline{X}_4, \overline{X}_2 - \overline{X}_3, \overline{X}_2 - \overline{X}_4,$ and $\overline{X}_3 - \overline{X}_4)$.

Multiple comparisons

If the F ratio is determined to be nonsignificant, the party is over. But what if it is significant? What do you know? All you know is that there is at least one significant difference somewhere; you do not know where that difference is. You do not know which means are significantly different from which other means. It might be, for example, that three means are equal but all greater than a fourth mean, that is, $\overline{X}_1 = \overline{X}_2 = \overline{X}_3$, and each mean is greater than $\overline{X}_4$ ($\overline{X}_1$, $\overline{X}_2$, and $\overline{X}_3$ might represent three treatments and $\overline{X}_4$ might represent a control group). Or it might be that $\overline{X}_1 = \overline{X}_2$, and $\overline{X}_3 = \overline{X}_4$, but $\overline{X}_1$ and $\overline{X}_2$ are each greater than $\overline{X}_3$ and $\overline{X}_4$. When the F ratio is significant, and more than two means are involved, *multiple comparison procedures* are used to determine which means are significantly different from which other means. There are a number of different multiple comparison techniques available to the evaluator, of which the Scheffé test is probably the most generally acceptable.

Analysis of covariance

The *analysis of covariance* is a statistical method for equating groups on one or more variables. In essence, analysis of variance adjusts scores on a dependent variable for initial differences on some other variable(s) such as pretest performance, IQ, or reading readiness (assuming that performance on the "other variable" is related to performance on the dependent variable). Analysis of covariance is a control technique which is useful for ex post facto designs in which already formed, not necessarily equal, groups are used and for experimental designs in which existing groups or randomly formed groups are used. Randomization does not guarantee that groups will be equated on all variables.

Any variable which is correlated with the dependent variable can be controlled for using analysis of covariance. Essentially, this technique adjusts posttest scores for initial differences on some variable and compares adjusted means. In other words, the groups are equalized with respect to the control variable(s) and then compared.

Chi square

Chi square, symbolized as χ^2, is a test of significance appropriate when the data are in the form of frequency counts occurring in two or more mutually exclusive categories.[13] Chi square is not appropriate when the data are in the form of test scores. A chi square test compares proportions actually observed with proportions expected, to see if they are significantly different. Expected proportions are usually the frequencies which would be expected if the groups were equal, although they may be based on past data. The chi square value increases as the difference between observed and expected frequencies increases.

The chi square is usually used in evaluations to compare the frequencies of certain behaviors occurring in two or more groups. As an example, you might

---

[13] Chi is pronounced with a k sound and rhymes with *high*.

wish to compare the effectiveness of two different types of reinforcement, social and token, to see which is more effective in reducing instances of classroom misbehavior. At the end of a six-month period you might have observers observe each group for a week. Tabulation might reveal that the social reinforcement group exhibited a total of 100 instances of misbehavior and the token reinforcement group 80 instances. Would this represent a true difference or a chance difference? In this case, the total number of instances of misbehavior was 180 (100 + 80); if the groups were essentially the same you would expect each group to exhibit the same number of instances of misbehavior, namely, 180 ÷ 2 = 90. In order to determine whether the groups were significantly different, you would compare the observed frequencies (100, 80) with the expected frequencies (90, 90) using a chi square test of significance.

Using the computer

The computer can save the evaluator many hours of computation time and re-checking time. The computer, however, is not magic, nor is it a gigantic toy.

When to use the computer

Some people seem to think that all they have to do is turn over their data to the computer and "Poof!" out will come the analyses. These people also have a tendency to want to analyze everything in sight. After all they don't have to do the work; the computer will. The decision to use the computer, however, should not be an automatic one. Preparing data for computer analysis takes time and the actual processing costs money. For many evaluations we may actually save time and money by not using the computer. If group sizes are not large, if a limited number of variables are involved, and if relatively simple statistical analyses are to be performed, using a calculator may be the most efficient approach to data analysis. Of course if the opposite is true, the computer is a logical choice of an analysis tool. Some statistical analyses, such as analysis of covariance, are rarely done by hand by experienced evaluators.

A good guideline for beginners, however, is that you should not use the computer to perform an analysis which you have never done yourself by hand. After you have performed several t tests on various sets of data, for example, you will have the knowledge and comprehension necessary to effectively use the computer for subsequent analyses. Instructions for preparing data for computer processing will make sense to you and you will know what the resulting output sheets should look like. After you have acquired first-hand experience with a variety of statistics, you will be in a position to judge whether the data for a given study can more efficiently be handled by computer analysis. If you do not have the necessary statistical experience, then there should be someone on the project staff who does, either a full-time staff member or a part-time consultant. Normally such a person will be experienced in using the computer for data analysis.

If you will be involved in using the computer, you should acquaint yourself with the computer center which will be utilized. You should become familiar with the facilities, services and equipment available and should sign up for the related instruction which is usually available. To draw an analogy, you do not just hand your money to a bank officer, tell him or her to take care of it, and hope everything turns out all right. Before you put your money in a bank, you try to find out as much about the bank as possible. Before you open an account, you want to know the bank's hours, services available, and charges associated with each service. When you receive your monthly statement you check it very carefully for errors, and you make sure you understand every number on the printout. The same care should be taken in using a computer center. Before you start processing data you should learn as much as you can, and when you get your output sheet, it should be as understandable to you as a bank statement. You should know where all the numbers come from and what they mean.

Costs associated with computer use

Computer services are generally budgeted for in funded evaluation efforts, and some school systems provide these services to administrators and teachers free of charge. In any case, such costs are typically quite reasonable. The major costs associated with computer analysis are for programming, keypunching, and computer time. Programming costs for statistical analyses are usually nil or very minimal. This is because programs for many standard analyses have already been written and are available for use. Occasionally an existing program may require some modification, but usually you will be able to locate one that does exactly what you need done. Keypunching costs usually involve paying a keypuncher so much an hour to transform your data from data sheets to the punched cards which are fed into the computer. Keypunching is a relatively simple process, however, which is worth your while to learn. Doing your own keypunching not only saves you money but also may reduce keypunching errors since you can read your data sheets better than anyone else. The third major cost, charges for computer time, is usually very reasonable (if not free). While the costs per hour for computer processing time are high, the analyses typically required for an evaluation usually use no more than a few minutes. Thus, if you use an existing program, keypunch your own data, and are given free processing time, the entire operation may cost you nothing but time.

Steps in using the computer

The first step in using the computer is to select an appropriate program. The program selected will indicate how the data may be keypunched and what instruction cards need to be punched. Instruction cards tell the computer all about your data and include such information as group sizes, number of variables, and how the data are arranged on the data cards. Then the data and the instructions are keypunched onto 80-column cards. All resulting cards must be checked for accuracy. In fact, many computer centers have a machine which will print out on a sheet the information punched on your cards. When you are through, you are ready to turn in your program deck for processing. It is always a good idea to make a second set of cards just in case something happens to the first deck. Most computer centers also have a machine that will make a duplicate deck for you. Turnaround time, or how long it takes to get your output after you have submitted your cards, depends usually on how busy the center is at the time. You may have to wait only a few minutes or you may be advised to come back after some specified period of time. When you pick up your output, the first things you look for are error messages. They tell you that the analyses were not performed because you did something wrong, anything from not following program instructions to putting a card in the wrong place. If your program has run successfully, you then examine the output figures to see if they make sense. If you read your data in wrong, the program may be executed correctly, but you may have "wrong" answers. For example, if your data are IQ scores, and the output tells you that the mean IQ was 10.4, you probably misplaced a decimal point somewhere!

18 post-analysis procedures

After reading chapter 18, you should be able to

1 List one major guideline to be followed in verifying data and one to be followed in storing data.
2 Define or describe an individual profile based on the results of a norm-referenced test, and explain how it is used by school personnel.
3 List four ways in which a group summary chart, based on the results of a norm-referenced test, can be used by a teacher.
4 Describe how an item achievement chart, based on the results of a criterion-referenced test, is used to interpret (*a*) individual performance and (*b*) group performance.
5 Describe the difference between statistical significance and practical significance.

Verification and storage of data

After you have completed all the statistical analyses necessary to describe your data and answer your evaluation questions or test your hypotheses, you do not say "Hooray! I'm done!" and happily throw away all your data and your worksheets. The data must be thoroughly checked and stored in an organized manner.

Verification

The very first thing you should do when you think you are done is to recheck all your work. You should have double-checked test scores before you started data analysis. Make sure all scores were correctly recorded onto data sheets or cards if you have not already done so. Then carefully check all your calculations. You may have noticed that we applied each statistic step by step, leaving no steps to the imagination. This was probably helpful to some and annoying to others. Math superstar types seem to derive great satisfaction from doing several steps in a row "in their heads" and writing down the results instead of separately recording the result of each step. This may save time in the short run but not necessarily in the long run. If you end up with a result that just does not look right, it is a lot easier to spot an error if every step is on the page in front of you. Make sure you are using the correct formula and that you have substituted the correct numbers. The results should make sense. If your scores range from 25 to 95 and you get a standard deviation of 1.07, you have probably made a mistake because 1.07 does not look reasonable. Similarly, if you end up with a Pearson r of 1.22, you'd better check everything ve-ry carefully.

   The above discussion applies equally well regardless of whether your analyses are done by hand, with the aid of a calculator, or with the aid of a computer. There is really no need for anyone to do any analysis by hand when calculators are so readily available. In fact, an inexpensive one (they sell for under $10) which performs only addition, subtraction, multiplication, and division is an excellent investment. Besides making life easier for you, they also reduce the likelihood of computational errors. If you punch the correct numbers in, they almost always give you the correct answer. Some of the more sophisticated desk models also provide a record of your work on a tape. Most campuses have at least one such machine somewhere.

   As discussed previously, if you use the computer you should double-check both your input and your output. Make sure you are giving the correct data and the correct directions concerning what to do with the data. Also, although you can usually be pretty safe in assuming that the computer will accurately execute each analysis, it is a good idea to spot-check. The computer only does what it has been programmed to do, and programming errors do occur. Thus, if the computer gives you six means and six standard deviations, you should calculate at least one of each yourself. If they agree with the ones the computer gave you, the rest are probably correct.

Storage

When you are convinced that your work is accurate, all data sheets or cards, worksheets, and records of calculations should be labeled, organized, and filed in a safe place. You never know when you might need your data again. Sometimes further analysis is desired or required at a later date. For example, an external evaluator or auditor sent from a funding source may request an additional analysis. Also, data from one evaluation may be used in a subsequent evaluation. Therefore, all of the data should be carefully labeled with as many identifications as necessary. Labels may indicate, for example, the inclusive dates of the evaluation, the nature of the various treatment and control groups, and whether data are pretest data, posttest data, or data for a control variable (such as reading readiness). All worksheets should also be clearly labeled to indicate the identity of the group(s), the analysis, and the scores; for example, you might have "Warm Fuzzy Group/standard deviation/posttest." If the same analysis covers more than one page, fully label each page and indicate "page 1 of 4," "2 of 4," and so on. A convenient, practical way to store data is in loose-leaf ring binders, or notebooks. Notebooks can be labeled on the spine, for example, "Title I, 1979–80," and pages are not likely to slip out and become lost as when manila folders are used. Lastly, find a safe place for all and guard it very carefully.

Interpretation of results

There are certain kinds of tests, especially nonachievement measures such as some personality measures, which require interpretation by persons with special training. Most test results, however, are interpretable by any person who has had a reasonably comprehensive measurement course. Unfortunately, apparently many educators have not had such a course. The attitudes and behaviors of people who are not knowledgeable concerning measurement concepts and principles seem to be on opposite ends of a continuum. At one extreme are those who treat the whole business of testing too lightly. They do not attach much importance to test results, and in some cases may actually have hostile feelings toward them. In either case they make little use of them, in the classroom for example. At the other extreme are those who treat the results entirely too seriously. They interpret test scores as if they represent the truth, as if each score is a "true" score. Proper interpretation requires recognition of the fact that while many tests do provide very accurate estimates, they do not measure with the same precision that yardsticks do. Intelligent interpretation also requires knowledge of the test in question. What a given score *means* depends upon such factors as what the test actually measures as well as its indices of validity and reliability. For example its estimated standard error of measurement needs to be considered.

The results of the application of tests of significance to group data also require intelligent interpretation. Application of a test of significance produces a number and only a number, a value which is or is not statistically significant. What it actually *means* requires interpretation. It must be interpreted in terms of the purpose of the evaluation, that is, the original question or hypothesis.

Norm-referenced tests

Standardized test results are reported in terms of the raw score equivalents discussed earlier. While any number of equivalents may be available in norms tables, one (or several) of these are generally selected for presentation on individual or group profile sheets; these permit easy comparison of relative performance on a number of subtests. Such profiles of equivalents may also be constructed at the local level if county, or district, norms are developed for a locally-developed test. At the classroom level, of course, the whole procedure is greatly simplified. The teacher is quite familiar with the "norm" group (his or her class), and most tests do not typically contain subtests. Thus, while one or more raw score equivalents may well be calculated, profile sheets are rarely (if ever) constructed.

Individual profiles

The meaning of an individual's raw score depends upon what was measured, the composition of the norm group, and the values of the individual's derived scores. Standardized test publishers are assuming more and more responsibility for providing all the information necessary for making valid interpretations of test scores. Manuals have become increasingly comprehensive, and a number of the major publishers provide separate manuals for the various phases involved in the use of a standardized test, such as administration and scoring, interpretation, and so forth. Interpretation materials typically include norms tables as well as considerable explanatory information and guidelines for usage. Some manuals also provide tables for more than one norm group, or for subgroups within a norm group, and in such cases it is important that the most appropriate tables be selected for interpretation purposes. Further, while it is usually a safe assumption, you should check to make sure that derived scores for different subtests are based on the same norm group, or else relative performance across subject areas cannot be validly interpreted. Finally, it must be reemphasized that perhaps the greatest source of misinterpretation comes from thinking of the average score of a norm group as being a goal for all students. By definition this notion is absurd. In the first place, norms represent scores actually obtained, not idealized standards. Second, "average" means that half of a group scored higher and half lower. Being concerned because half of the students in your class are "below the national average" on an achievement test is like being upset because half of them are too short, i.e. below average in height!

An individual profile presents raw scores and/or one or more derived scores, for each of a number of subtests, in a graphic or tabular manner. Such a profile permits us to identify a student's relative strengths and weaknesses at a glance; we use the term *relative* because a student's highest score may represent a performance well below average. The derived scores most often presented on a profile sheet are percentile ranks, stanines, and grade equivalents. In addition, profile sheets include appropriate identification information such as the name, form, and level of the test, the date of testing, and the student's name and sex.

Profile sheets of most major tests also provide an explanation of the contents of the profile and directions for interpretation. Such directions typically mention the fact that every score reflects some measurement error and should be thought of as being the midpoint in some range or band of scores (usually those which fall between $\pm 1SE_m$). This band is often actually depicted on the profile, especially when percentile ranks are presented. As the directions typically indicate, such bands facilitate interpretation of scores on the various subtests. Usually the overlapping bands concept is employed so that a true difference in performance on any two subtests is indicated only if the bands for those subtests do not overlap at all. For stanines, the directions typically suggest that in comparing performance on any two subtests, a difference of only one stanine (e.g. 6 versus 7) probably does not reflect a true difference in performance; a difference of two or more stanines probably does. At the risk of being boring and repetitious (it hasn't stopped me so far has it?), it must be remembered that comparison of scores made on different tests are meaningful only if the tests were normed on the same group. If not, the validity of comparisons is a direct function of the comparability of the norm groups.

The concepts just discussed are illustrated in figures 18.1, 18.2, 18.3 and 18.4, reproductions of profiles of the Stanford Achievement Test and the Differential Aptitude Tests. The Stanford Achievement Test, which provides a *Teacher's Guide for Interpreting*, presents results for each student in terms of percentile ranks (PR) and stanines (S). In addition to being listed, stanines are graphically depicted in categories which indicate below average, average, or above average performance. Percentile ranks and stanines are presented for each subtest, for area totals (e.g. Total Reading), for the complete battery, and for the Otis-Lennon Mental Ability Test (when such results are available). The profile indicates the national or local norms on which the percentile ranks and stanines are based, the date of testing, and the student's name and grade. Figure 18.1, Charlie Brown's profile, indicates that Charlie's percentile ranks range from 16 in Social Science to 92 in Math Concepts and Spelling. His stanines range from 3 in Social Science to 8 in Math Concepts, Spelling, and Listening Comprehension. The stanine chart indicates that Charlie is average to above average in all areas except Social Science. This pattern is reflected in the Battery Total stanine of 6. Charlie seems to be achieving at an acceptable level, given that his mental ability stanine, 5, is in the average category.

The Stanford Achievement Test also provides an individual record form for each student (see figure 18.2). This form is essentially an expansion of the pupil profile. In addition to the information included on the pupil profile, the individual record form presents results in terms of raw scores (number right), scaled scores, and grade equivalents. This form also gives a more specific description of the tests administered and the norms used. Thus we see that in Vocabulary Charlie's grade equivalent is 3.2, which reads the second school month of the third grade. Since the test was administered in October, it appears that Charlie is achieving at grade level in vocabulary, in terms of national norms. Overall, Charlie's grade equivalents range from a low of 2.1 in Social Science to a high of 5.3 in Spelling. Recall that this does not mean that Charlie is ready for fifth grade spelling words. Note that the norms used were those for grade 3.2 for the Stanford Achievement Test and the beginning of the third grade for the Otis-Lennon Mental Ability Test. This is appropriate given that Charlie is in the second month of the third grade. Given the nature of the information included in the individual record form (i.e. scaled scores and grade equivalents), it is clearly more appropriate for student record purposes, i.e. inclusion in a student's cumulative folder, than for dissemination to parents and students. The pupil profile is best suited for reporting purposes.

The Differential Aptitude Test (DAT) present results for individuals in terms of percentiles (see figure 18.3). Across the top of each profile the raw scores and corresponding percentile ranks are given for each of the subtests. Directly beneath each raw score and percentile rank is a column for graphing percentile ranks and placing them in bands. Directions for doing so accompany the profile sheet, and each column has a parallel column which marks off the various percentiles. At the fiftieth percentile there is a heavy horizontal line; this line makes it easy to identify above and below average abilities. Thus, we see that Jane scored well in all areas except Clerical Speed and Accuracy. Her scores in Numerical Ability and

STANFORD Achievement Test				PUPIL PROFILE				

School
SOUTH ELEMENTARY
Compared To
NATIONAL NORMS

for Charlie Brown

Date of Testing
10/73

Grade
3

HBJ
Scoring
Service

STANINES

TESTS	PR	S	1	2	3	4	5	6	7	8	9
Vocabulary	50	5				–5–					
Reading - Part A	80	7							–7–		
Reading - Part B	84	7							–7–		
Reading Comprehension	84	7							–7–		
Word Study Skills	40	5				–5–					
Math Concepts	92	8								–8–	
Math Computation	72	6						–6–			
Math Applications	68	6						–6–			
Spelling	92	8								–8–	
Language											
Social Science	16	3			–3–						
Science	54	5				–5–					
Listening Comprehension	90	8								–8–	
AREA TOTALS											
Total Reading	60	6						–6–			
Total Math	82	7							–7–		
Total Auditory	74	6						–6–			
BATTERY TOTAL											
COMPLETE BATTERY	72	6						–6–			
OTIS-LENNON MAT	57	5					–5–				

1	2	3	4	5	6	7	8	9
	Below Average			Average			Above Average	

HOW TO INTERPRET THESE SCORES

The report above shows the scores this pupil obtained on the *STANFORD ACHIEVEMENT TEST*. The test results are presented in terms of Percentile Rank (PR) and Stanine (S) scores.

Stanine scores range from a low of 1 to a high of 9 with 5 being average. Stanines are used to plot the test results in the Profile thus providing a graphic presentation of the pupil's achievement level in the various subjects.

A Percentile Rank is a score which can range from a low of 1 to a high of 99 with 50 being average. A Percentile Rank reflects a pupil's standing in some particular group. For example, if a pupil obtained a Percentile Rank of 42, this means that 42% of the comparison group obtained the same score or lower scores.

Continued on back.

000–0000–000

figure 18.1
Sample Stanford Achievement Test individual pupil profile
Note. Reproduced from the Stanford Achievement Test. Copyright 1973 by Harcourt Brace Jovanovich, Inc. Reproduced by special permission from the publisher.

Abstract Reasoning suggest that she has an aptitude for areas requiring mathematical ability. Notice that at the bottom of the chart there is a space for indicating the norms upon which the percentile ranks are based, and a key indicating F or S (first semester or second semester testing and percentiles). This key is for the figure presented to the right of the student's name at the top of the profile under

STANFORD Achievement Test
1973 Edition

INDIVIDUAL RECORD

for   Brown Charlie

Teacher

School

System

Date of Testing

Grade

HBJ
Scoring
Service

SCORE DETAIL						NATIONAL STANINE PROFILE			
Number Right / Number Possible	Scaled Score	%ile Rank Local / Nat'l.	Grade Equiv.		TESTS	1 2 3 Below Average	4 5 6 Average	7 8 9 Above Average	
26/37	133	50	3.2		Vocabulary		−5−	
43/45	148	80	4.2		Reading - Part A			−7−
44/48	151	84	4.4		Reading - Part B			−7−
87/93	148	84	4.4		Reading Comprehension			−7−
43/65	121	40	2.5		Word Study Skills		−5−	
32/35	155	92	5.0		Math Concepts			−8−
28/37	141	72	3.5		Math Computation		−6−	
21/28	142	68	3.7		Math Applications		−6−	
40/43	158	92	5.3		Spelling			−8−
					Language			
15/27	118	16	2.1		Social Science	−3−		
20/27	130	54	3.3		Science		−5−	
43/50	151	90	4.9		Listening Comprehension			−8−
					AREA TOTALS			
130/158	138	60	3.5		Total Reading		−6−	
81/100	143	82	4.0		Total Mathematics			−7−
69/87	139	74	4.0		Total Auditory		−6−	
					BATTERY TOTAL			
355/442	139	72	3.8		COMPLETE BATTERY		−6−	

SCORE DETAIL									
Mental Age Yrs. / Mos.	Raw Score	Grade Norms PR / S	Age Norms %ile Rank Local / Nat'l.	Dev. I.Q.	OTIS - LENNON MENTAL ABILITY TEST	1 2 3 Below Average	4 5 6 Average	7 8 9 Above Average	
08 10	52	46 5	57	103	AGE NORM STANINE −−−		−5−	

OTHER PUPIL DATA: **TEACHER NOTES:**

Age   08   yrs.   10   mos.

Other Information

Pupil Number

TEST INFORMATION:

	Level	Form	Norms Used
Stanford	PRIMARY 2	A	GRADE 3.2
Otis-Lennon	ELEMENT 1	J	GR 3 BEG

Local Norms based on   pupils.   Process No. 000−0000−000

See back for aids
for interpretation.

figure 18.2
Sample Stanford Achievement Test individual record form

Note. Reproduced from the Stanford Achievement Test. Copyright 1973 by Harcourt Brace Jovanovich, Inc. Reproduced by special permission from the publisher.

Year. Thus, for Jane, 73S means second semester, 1973. The DAT also provides a computer-produced profile (see figure 18.4). This profile provides the same information as the vertical profile but in horizontal form. Instead of providing instructions for constructing percentile bars, which are already given in the form of a row of X's, instructions for interpreting each row of X's are given.

A profile gives us an indication of each student's performance or ability compared to a given norm group. It provides information concerning the student's

INDIVIDUAL REPORT FORM

VERTICAL PROFILE
(FOR HAND PLOTTING)

DIFFERENTIAL APTITUDE TESTS

G. K. Bennett, H. G. Seashore, and A. G. Wesman

FORMS **S** AND **T**

Ψ

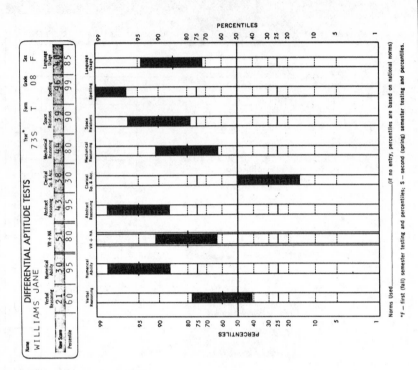

PROFILING YOUR DAT SCORES

The numbers that tell how you did on each test are in the row marked "Percentile." Your percentile tells where you rank on a test in comparison with boys or girls in your grade in numerous schools across the country. If your percentile is 50, you are just in the middle—that is, one-half of the students in the national group did better than you and one-half did less well.

If your percentile on one test is 80, you are at the top of 80 percent of the group—only 20 percent made higher scores than yours. If you scored in the 25th percentile, this means about 75 percent of the group did better than you on the test. These percentiles indicate your relative standing among students of your sex and grade. They do NOT tell you how many questions (or what percent of them) you answered correctly.

Using the information printed in the "Percentile" row, you can now draw your aptitude profile on the chart provided. There are nine columns to be marked; in each of these make a *heavy short line* across the column at the level corresponding to your percentile on that test. (In some cases, the line you draw will coincide with a dotted or solid line already printed on the chart.) Then blacken each column for a distance of one-half inch above and one-half inch below the short line you have drawn, so that you end up with a solid black bar in each column. (For extremely high or low percentiles, you will not be able to blacken one-half inch in both directions without running off the chart.)

HOW BIG A DIFFERENCE IS IMPORTANT?

Since tests cannot be perfectly accurate, you should not overestimate the importance of small differences between two percentiles in comparing your aptitudes. The bars on your profile help by indicating the more important differences.

Look at the bars for any *two* tests and notice whether or not the ends of the bars overlap. If they do not, chances are that you really are better in the kind of ability represented by the bar that is *higher* on the profile chart. If the bars overlap, but not by more than half their length, consider whether other things you know about yourself agree with this indication; the difference may or may not be important. If they overlap by more than half their length, the difference may be disregarded; so small a difference is probably not meaningful. This method of looking at the overlap of bars works for any two abilities you want to compare, whether they are listed next to each other or several columns apart on the chart.

figure 18.3
Sample Differential Aptitude Tests vertical profile (for hand plotting)

Note. Reproduced from the Differential Aptitude Tests. Copyright 1972 by The Psychological Corporation. Reproduced by special permission from the publisher.

DIFFERENTIAL APTITUDE TESTS

G. K. Bennett, H. G. Seashore, and A. G. Wesman

FORMS **S** AND **T**

INDIVIDUAL REPORT FORM

COMPUTER-PRODUCED PROFILE

Name		School	Year*		Form	Grade	Sex
CLARK LARRY		HALL	1972	F	S	10	M

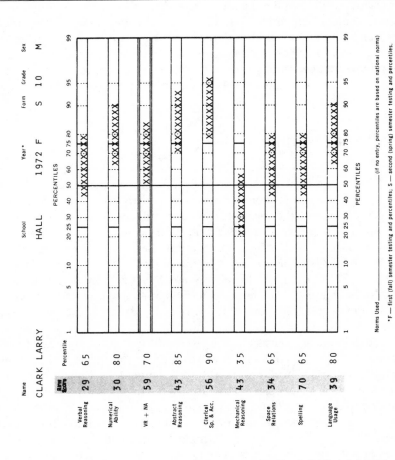

YOUR PROFILE OF DAT SCORES

The numbers that tell how you did on each test are in the column marked "Percentile." Your percentile tells where you rank on a test in comparison with boys or girls in your grade in numerous schools across the country. If your percentile is 50, you are just in the middle—that is, one-half of the students in the national group did better than you and one-half did less well.

If your percentile on one test is 80, you are at the top of 80 percent of the group—only 20 percent made higher scores than yours. If you scored in the 25th percentile, this means about 75 percent of the group did better than you on the test. These percentiles indicate your relative standing among students of your sex and grade. They do NOT tell you how many questions (or what percent of them) you answered correctly.

On your profile, a bar of X's has been printed in the row for each test you took. The percentile you earned is at the middle of the bar, except when the bar has been shortened in the case of an extremely high or low percentile so as not to run off the chart. (The reason for the bar instead of a single X is that a test is not a perfect measure of your ability; however, you can be reasonably sure that you stand somewhere within the area covered by the bar.)

HOW BIG A DIFFERENCE IS IMPORTANT?

Since tests cannot be perfectly accurate, you should not overestimate the importance of small differences between two percentiles in comparing your aptitudes. The bars of X's help by indicating the more important differences.

Look at the bars for any two tests and notice whether or not the ends of the bars overlap. If they do not, chances are that you really are better in the kind of ability represented by the bar farther to the right. If they overlap but not by more than half their length, consider whether other things you know about yourself agree with this indication; the difference may or may not be important. If they overlap by more than half their length, the difference may be disregarded; so small a difference is probably not meaningful. This method of looking at the overlap of bars works for any two abilities you want to compare, whether they are listed next to each other or several rows apart on the chart.

figure 18.4
Sample Differential Aptitude Tests computer-produced profile

Note: Reproduced from the Differential Aptitude Tests. Copyright 1972 by The Psychological Corporation. Reproduced by special permission from the publisher.

strengths and weaknesses among the profiled scores also. Further interpretation requires additional knowledge concerning the individual, an index of mental ability for example. If Hermie has a measured IQ of 101, and his stanines on the Stanford Achievement Test are all 5 or above, he is doing well. On the other hand, if Instine has an IQ of 130 and his stanines are all 5 and below, there seems to be a problem somewhere. Further data, such as that available in Instine's cumulative record folder, are needed before we can determine an appropriate course of action. Thus, each student's results must be interpreted in terms of what we know about him or her as an individual.

Group results

Unless the instructional program is individualized, a teacher is also interested in analyzing the performance of her or his students as a group. This requires compilation of the individual results into some sort of summary form. Of course, such a summary sheet may also be used for interpretation of individual results if it contains all necessary information. Some test companies provide forms for this purpose. The Stanford Achievement Test, for example, provides a Class Record form. This form is simply a summary sheet with spaces for student names, derived scores (grade equivalents, percentile ranks, stanines) for each student on each test, total scores (e.g. Total Battery, Total Reading) for each student, and other optional information such as IQ scores.

Such summary forms allow us to easily spot students who are exceptional in some way. If all of Egor's scores correspond to stanines 1 and 2, he might well be a candidate for a special program; he may even have a physical problem (poor vision for example) or a learning disability. Conversely, if all of Instine's scores correspond to stanines 8 and 9, he probably should be in a program for the gifted or some other type of accelerated program, if such is available. If students such as Egor and Instine remain in the class, they require special activities and attention. Another possibility is that Hornrim may have scores corresponding to stanine 5 or above in all areas except one, in which his score is in stanine 2. Depending upon the area of deficiency, this situation may suggest a problem with Hornrim, or a need for special instruction. If the area of deficiency is Listening Comprehension, for example, he may have an auditory problem. And so forth. Of course such information could be obtained from individual profile sheets, but a summary sheet permits us to identify all such "exceptional" individuals easily. Such forms are very useful and if they are not provided for a particular test, something similar can easily be constructed.

Many publishers also provide some type of group profile which summarizes results for a class as a whole. The Stanford Achievement Test, for example, provides a Class Summary which summarizes in descriptive terms the data presented on the individual record forms (see figure 18.5). Thus we see that in Miss Jones's class the mean (average) raw score (number right) on the Vocabulary subtest was 25. The Stanine Summary portion of the Class Summary is especially useful. For each subtest, the Stanine Summary indicates the number and percent of students who scored in each stanine category: below average (stanines 1-3), average (stanines 4-6), and above average (stanines 7-9). The last column, No. Tested, indicates that 27 students in Miss Jones's class took the test. On the Vocabulary subtest, 10 students (37%) scored in stanine 1, 2 or 3; 9 students (33%) scored in stanine 4, 5 or 6; and 8 students (30%) scored in stanine 7, 8 or 9. Since we expect approximately one-fourth (23%) of the students to be in each of the stanine catego-

STANFORD Achievement Test
1973 Edition

INDIVIDUAL RECORD for CLASS SUMMARY

Teacher
School
System
Date of Testing
Grade

HBJ Scoring Service

SCORE DETAIL: Number Right / Number Possible	Scaled Score	%ile Rank Local	%ile Rank Nat'l.	Grade Equiv.	TESTS	NATIONAL STANINE PROFILE 1 2 3 Below Average N	%	4 5 6 Average N	%	7 8 9 Above Average N	%	NO. TEST-ED
MEAN SCORES						STANINE SUMMARY						
25	132			3.0	Vocabulary	10	37	9	33	8	30	27
41	139			3.7	Reading - Part A	6	22	11	41	10	37	27
40	138			3.5	Reading - Part B	7	26	10	37	10	37	27
80	138			3.6	Reading Comprehension	6	22	10	37	11	41	27
52	133			3.4	Word Study Skills	9	33	10	37	8	30	27
25	137			3.4	Math Concepts	8	30	9	33	10	37	27
27	139			3.4	Math Computation	10	37	6	22	11	41	27
20	138			3.5	Math Applications	9	33	10	37	8	30	27
36	142			3.9	Spelling	2	8	16	59	9	33	27
					Language							
19	130			3.3	Social Science	8	30	11	41	8	30	27
21	133			3.5	Science	5	19	13	48	9	33	27
37	132			3.4	Listening Comprehension	7	26	8	30	12	44	27
					AREA TOTALS							
133	139			3.5	Total Reading	7	26	11	41	9	33	27
73	137			3.4	Total Mathematics	6	22	12	44	9	33	27
62	131			3.1	Total Auditory	5	19	13	48	9	33	27
					BATTERY TOTAL							
343	136			3.6	COMPLETE BATTERY	7	26	11	41	9	33	27

SCORE DETAIL: Mental Age Yrs.	Mental Age Mos.	Raw Score	Grade Norms PR	Grade Norms S	Age Norms %ile Rank Local	Age Norms %ile Rank Nat'l.	Dev. I.Q.	OTIS - LENNON MENTAL ABILITY TEST	1 2 3 Below Average		4 5 6 Average		7 8 9 Above Average		NO TEST-ED
		47					100	AGE NORM STANINE ---	6	22	16	59	5	19	27

OTHER PUPIL DATA:

Age yrs. mos.

Other Information

Pupil Number

TEACHER NOTES:

TEST INFORMATION:

	Level	Form	Norms Used
Stanford	PRIMARY 2	A	GRADE 3.2
Otis-Lennon	ELEMENT 1	J	GR 3 BEG

Local Norms based on pupils. Process No. 000-0000-000

See back for aids for interpretation.

figure 18.5

Sample Stanford Achievement Test class summary

Note. Reproduced from the Stanford Achievement Test. Copyright 1973 by Harcourt Brace Jovanovich, Inc. Reproduced by special permission from the publisher.

ries 1–3 and 7–9, and about half (54%) of them to be in stanine category 4–6, these summary figures permit us to compare a class *as a whole* with the norm group. This comparison will give a rough estimate of where the class is with respect to achievement, e.g. below average.

There are a number of ways such a chart can be used in planning future instructional objectives and strategies. We can, for example, examine the stanine pattern for each subtest. If a majority of the students scored below average in a particular area, they may not have received sufficient instruction in that area, especially if other measures indicate that the class has average scholastic aptitude.[1] Miss Jones's class does not appear to have any outstanding deficiencies although achievement is lower in some areas (e.g. Vocabulary and Math Computation) than in others. The Otis-Lennon data indicate that her class as a whole has essentially average ability. We can also make comparisons across subtests. If the students are clustered in the higher stanines in some areas and the lower stanines in others, a change in emphasis may be called for so that more time is devoted to the areas of deficiency. Miss Jones, for example, might wish to spend less time on spelling and more time on vocabulary. Results may also suggest areas in which grouping would be appropriate. If most of the students are clustered in a given stanine category (e.g. average), no grouping is called for. If, on the other hand, there are two or three obvious clusters, such that there are a number of students in two or three stanine categories, grouping might be a reasonable strategy. Miss Jones could use the Stanine Summary to group her students for instruction in any of the test areas.

Group results can be interpreted on many levels, such as classroom, school, district, and county. Procedures similar to those in the classroom are applied, and similar decisions are made. At the district level, results may suggest, for example, that more resources should be directed toward the science program. One problem frequently associated with analysis of group results arises when comparisons are made between and among groups (e.g. schools). Such comparisons made frequently (by the media for example) are based solely on test results and do not take into consideration other relevant factors such as other characteristics of the students in the schools being compared. Thus, one school may have higher scores overall than another but may also have correspondingly higher scholastic aptitude scores. Such comparisons, whether at the classroom level or the district level, are only valid to the degree that students are comparable on other variables such as ability and socio-economic status. The principle is the same as that involved in determining whether a norm group is appropriate.

Ex post facto results

Ex post facto designs nearly always involve a norm-referenced test. As repeatedly pointed out, interpretation of findings in an ex post facto effort requires considerable caution. Due to lack of randomization, manipulation, and other types of control characteristic of experimental designs, it is difficult to establish cause-effect relationships with any great degree of confidence. The cause-effect relationship may in fact be the reverse of the one hypothesized (the alleged cause may actually be the effect), or there may be a third factor which is the "real" cause of both the alleged cause (independent variable) and effect (dependent variable). In some cases, reversed causality is not a reasonable alternative and need not be considered. For example, preschool training may "cause" increased reading achievement in first grade, but reading achievement in first grade cannot "cause" preschool training. Similarly, one's sex may affect one's achievement in mathematics, but one's achievement in mathematics certainly does not affect one's sex!

[1] If the necessary information is available, an informal item analysis may be useful. For example, if many students in the class did poorly on a mathematics application subtest, a review of the items might be made to determine if specific areas of difficulty, say graph reading and interpretation, can be identified.

In other cases, however, reversed causality is more plausible and should be investigated. For example, it is equally plausible that achievement affects self-concept and that self-concept affects achievement. It is also equally plausible that excessive absenteeism causes, or leads to, involvement in criminal activities as that involvement in criminal activities causes, or leads to, excessive absenteeism. The way to determine the correct order of causality, which variable caused which, is to determine which one occurred first. If, in the above example, it could be demonstrated that periods of excessive absenteeism were frequently followed by students' getting in trouble with the law, then it could more reasonably be concluded that excessive absenteeism leads to involvement in criminal activities. On the other hand, if it was determined that prior to a student's first involvement in criminal activities his or her attendance was good, but following it poor, then the hypothesis that involvement in criminal activities leads to excessive absenteeism would be more reasonable.

The possibility of a third, common cause is plausible in many situations. Recall the example that parental attitude may affect both self-concept and achievement. One way to control for a potential common cause is to equate groups on the suspected variable. In the above example, students in both the high self-concept group and low self-concept group could be selected from students whose parents had similar attitudes. It is clear that in order to investigate or control for alternative hypotheses, we must be aware of them when they are plausible and must present evidence that they are not in fact the true explanation for the behavioral differences being investigated.

Criterion-referenced tests

Interpretation of results is considerably more straightforward for a criterion-referenced test. For one thing, such tests are almost always locally-developed, and therefore all the cautions and problems associated with norm groups are not applicable. The most efficient way to approach interpretation is to construct item achievement charts for all objectives as previously shown in figures 11.2 and 11.3. Based on such charts, we can determine for each student whichever of the following are appropriate: (1) the percentage of items correct for each objective; (2) which objectives were achieved; (3) the total percentage of items correct; (4) the percentage of objectives achieved; and (5) whether mastery was attained. Similar information can easily be compiled on a group basis: (1) the percentage of students who answered each item correctly; (2) the average percentage of items correct per objective; (3) the percentage of students who achieved each objective; (4) the average total number (or percentage) of items correct; (5) the average percentage of the objectives achieved; and (6) the percentage of students achieving mastery.

Thus, we can easily pinpoint the strengths and weaknesses of each individual as well as those of the group with respect to very specific behaviors. Using the results to plan future objectives and strategies is a simple process compared to that involved in using standardized test results since we know precisely what everyone knows and can do and what he does not know and cannot do. Instead of finding that "many students are *weak* in arithmetic computation," we can say that "70% of the students have difficulty adding improper fractions." At a very specific level we can determine whether a given deficiency is an individual problem or a group problem. Further, the percentage of students with a given deficiency determines how much additional class time will be devoted to the objectives in question and how much revision of instructional strategy is required.

We may occasionally, on a major test for example, wish to derive norm-referenced interpretations for criterion-referenced test results. If there are a sufficient number of students and if there is sufficient score variability, the raw scores of a nonmastery criterion-referenced test can be transformed into percentiles, or stanines, or whatever equivalent is appropriate.

Questionnaires

When presenting the results of a questionnaire, the response rate for each item should be given as well as the total sample size and the overall percentage of returns, since all respondents may not answer all questions. The simplest way to present the results is to indicate the percentage of respondents who selected each alternative for each item. For example, you might say, "On item 4 dealing with possession of a master's degree, 50% said 'yes,' 30% said 'no,' and 20% said they were working on one." In addition to simply determining choices, relationships between variables can be investigated by comparing responses on one item with responses on other items. For example, it might be determined that 80% of those reporting possession of a master's degree expressed favorable attitudes toward individualized instruction while only 40% of those reporting lack of a master's degree expressed a favorable attitude. Thus, possible explanations for certain attitudes and behaviors can be explored by identifying factors which seem to be related to certain responses. This type of relationship analysis can also be used to test hypotheses. For example, it might be hypothesized that teachers with advanced degrees are more receptive to nontraditional methods of instruction. The above finding concerning master's degrees and attitudes toward individualized instruction would be data in support of the hypothesis. Establishment of a direct cause-effect relationship between training and attitudes would not, however, be warranted. Due to lack of manipulation of variables it would not be possible to determine whether increased training actually results in increased receptivity to new ideas or whether receptive teachers seek out additional education. Resolution of such issues would require conduction of an investigation based on a research design.

Hypothesized versus unhypothesized results

The evaluation reports of special programs and projects should include a discussion concerning whether the results were or were not those hypothesized. If the results are those anticipated, the results provide support for the effectiveness of the program, but they do not *prove* anything. They only show that in one situation the program was effective. Further, it is not necessarily the case that the program would "work" with different populations, different materials, and different dependent variables (other measures of posttest performance). For example, if peer tutoring is found to be effective with respect to the reading comprehension of elementary students, this does not mean that peer tutoring will necessarily be effective in improving math achievement at the junior high school level. In other words, do not overgeneralize.

If, on the other hand, the results do not turn out as anticipated, you do not apologize. The natural reaction in this situation for many people is to be very disappointed. In the first place, nonsignificant results do not necessarily mean that the program is ineffective in general, and even if it is, it is just as important to know what does not work as what does. Of course, if there were some serious validity problems involved you should describe them in detail. Also, if for some reason you lost a number of participants you should discuss why and explain how the results may have been affected. But do not rationalize. If your evaluation was well planned and well conducted, and no unforeseen mishaps occurred, do not try to come up with some reason why things did not "come out right."

Any totally unexpected outcomes should be reported but should be interpreted with great care. Often as an evaluation is being carried out, an apparent relationship will be noticed which was not hypothesized. You might notice, for example, that the attendance rate of the students in the treatment group has progressively increased, an unanticipated outcome. You do not go change the original objectives of the program or "slip in" a new one. You can, however, collect and analyze data on these unforeseen outcomes and present your results as such. These findings may form the basis for a later investigation, conducted by yourself or someone else.

Statistical versus practical significance

As discussed previously, the fact that results are statistically significant does not automatically mean that they are of any educational value. Statistical significance only means that your results would be likely to occur by chance a certain percentage of the time, say 5%. This only means that the observed relationship or difference is probably a real one, not necessarily an important one. The fact that method A is significantly more effective than method B *statistically* does not mean that the whole world should immediately adopt method A! There are several factors which affect the *educational* significance of a finding. One factor is the actual magnitude of the difference. A mean difference of 10 points is more impressive than a 3 point difference, especially since a very small difference (or relationship) can be statistically significant if enough participants are involved (recall the discussion of correlation coefficients). A second factor is the current priority of the area in which the difference occurred. A modest difference in reading achievement would be considered to be more important than a modest difference in some other areas. A third factor is cost. To put it simply, the more expensive a new program is, the larger the resulting difference has to be. A very expensive program which produces small, but statistically significant, results would not be considered educationally significant because it would not represent an economically viable alternative; it would not be cost-effective.

Replication of results

To be convincing, results have to be either based on a large number of participants, or replicated. Replication of results is probably the strongest evidence for the effectiveness of a program. *Replication* means that the entire effort, from pretesting to posttesting, is done again using different participants. In certain cases, the significance of a relationship or difference may be enhanced if it is replicated in a more natural setting. A highly controlled evaluation, for example, might find that curriculum A is more effective than curriculum B *in a laboratory-like environment*. Interpretation and discussion of the results in terms of practical significance and implications for classroom practice would have to be stated with caution. If the same results could then be obtained in a natural classroom situation, however, the report could be less tentative concerning their generalizability.

The need for replication is especially great when the treatment involved (or relationship investigated) is highly unusual, or when the results have practical significance and the treatment investigated might really make a difference. Interpretation and discussion of a replicated result will invariably be less "hedgey" than a first-time-ever finding, and rightly so.

part seven **summary**

16 pre-analysis procedures

Scoring procedures

1 All instruments administered should be scored accurately and consistently; each person's test should be scored using the same procedures and criteria.
2 When a standardized instrument is used, the scoring process is greatly facilitated; the test manual usually spells out the steps to be followed in scoring each test (or answer sheet) and a scoring key is often provided.
3 Since there is no manual to follow, scoring locally-developed instruments is more complex, especially if open-ended, free response items are involved; steps for scoring each item and for arriving at a total score must be delineated and carefully followed, scorer reliability must be checked, and tentative procedures should be tried out prior to actual implementation.
4 The fact that responses are being scored by a machine does not relieve you of the responsibility of carefully checking your data before and after processing.

Tabulation procedures

5 After instruments have been scored, the results are transferred to summary data sheets and/or data cards.
6 Data are generally placed in columns, one for each group, in ascending or descending order.
7 If planned analyses involve subgroup comparisons, scores or responses should be tabulated separately for each subgroup.
8 When a number of different kinds of data are collected for each participant, such as several test scores and biographical information, data are frequently recorded on data cards, one card for each participant.
9 The card for each participant follows the same format, and both the variable names and actual data are frequently coded.
10 If a computer is to be used for analysis, data must be presented in a machine-readable form, usually on punched cards.
11 Once the data have been prepared for analysis, the choice of statistical procedures to be applied is determined not only by the evaluation questions, hypotheses and/or design, but also by the type of measurement scale represented by the data.

Types of measurement scales

12 Depending upon the variables, and the way in which they are measured, different kinds of data result, representing different scales of measurement.

Nominal scales

13 A *nominal scale* represents the lowest level of measurement.
14 A nominal scale classifies persons (or objects) into two or more categories.

15 Whatever the basis for classification, a person can only be in one category, and members of a given category have a common set of characteristics.

Ordinal scales

16 An *ordinal scale* not only classifies persons (or objects) but also ranks them in terms of the degree to which they possess a characteristic of interest; that is, an ordinal scale puts people in order from highest to lowest, from most to least.

17 Intervals between ranks in an ordinal scale are not equal; the difference between rank 1 and rank 2 is not necessarily the same as the difference between rank 2 and rank 3.

Interval scales

18 An *interval scale* has all the characteristics of a nominal scale and an ordinal scale, but in addition it is based upon predetermined equal intervals.

19 Most of the tests used in educational evaluation such as achievement tests, aptitude tests, and intelligence tests, represent interval scales; you will most often be working with statistics appropriate for interval data.

20 Interval scales typically have an arbitrary maximum score and an arbitrary minimum score, or zero point; they do not have a true zero point.

Ratio scales

21 A *ratio scale* represents the highest, most precise, level of measurement.

22 A ratio scale has all the advantages of the other types of scales and in addition it has a meaningful, true zero point.

23 Because of the true zero point, we can say not only that the difference between a height of 3'2'' and a height of 4'2'' is the same as the difference between 5'4'' and 6'4'', but also that a man 6'4'' is twice as tall as a child 3'2''.

24 Since most physical measures represent ratio scales, but psychological measures do not, ratio scales are not used very often in educational evaluation.

25 A statistic appropriate for a lower level of measurement may be applied to data representing a higher level of measurement; the reverse, however, is not true.

17 data analysis

Descriptive statistics

26 The first step in data analysis is to describe, or summarize, the data using descriptive statistics.

27 Descriptive statistics permit us to meaningfully describe many, many scores with a small number of indices, which provide answers to questions such as, What was the average score on the test?

28 Descriptive statistics also permit us to make interpretive statements (both norm-referenced and criterion-referenced, but mainly the former) about individual scores by providing answers to questions such as, Is this particular score above the average score or below it?

Types

Graphing data

29 Graphing data permits us to see what the distribution of scores looks like.

30 The most common method of graphing data is to construct a *frequency polygon* which basically shows how many persons attained each score.

31 The first step in constructing a frequency polygon is to list all scores and to tabulate how many persons received each score. Once the scores are tallied, the steps are as follows: (1) place all the scores on a horizontal axis, at equal intervals from lowest score to highest; (2) place the frequencies of scores at equal intervals on the vertical axis, starting with zero; (3) for each score, find the point where the score intersects with its frequency of occurrence and make a dot; and (4) connect all the dots with straight lines.

32 If the range of scores is great, say more than 20, it is usually more appropriate to tally and graph the frequencies of scores within given intervals.

Measures of central tendency

33 Measures of central tendency provide a convenient way of describing a set of data with a single number.

34 The number which results from computation of a measure of central tendency represents the average or typical score attained by a group.

35 Each index of central tendency is appropriate for a different scale of measurement: the mode is appropriate for nominal data, the median for ordinal data, and the mean for interval or ratio data.

The mode

36 The mode is the score which is attained by more people than any other score.

37 The mode is not established through calculation; it is determined by looking at a set of scores or at a graph of scores to see which score occurs most frequently.

38 There are several problems associated with the mode, and it is therefore of limited value and seldom used.

The median

39 The median is the point in a distribution above and below which are an equal number of scores; that is, the median is the midpoint.

40 The median is only the midpoint of the scores and does not take into account each and every score; it ignores, for example, extremely high scores and extremely low scores.

The mean

41 The mean is the arithmetic average of the scores and is the most frequently used measure of central tendency.

42 By the very nature of the way in which it is computed, the mean takes into account, or is based on, each and every score.

43 The mean is appropriate when the data represent either an interval or a ratio scale and is a more precise, stable index than both the median and the mode.

44 For a distribution in which there are one or more extreme scores, the median

will not be the most accurate representation of the performance of the total group but it will be the best index of typical performance.

Measures of variability

45 Two sets of data which are very different can have identical means or medians; thus, there is a need for a measure which indicates how spread out the scores are, how much variability there is.

46 While the standard deviation is by far the most often used measure of variability, the range is the appropriate measure of variability for nominal data, and the quartile deviation is the appropriate index of variability for ordinal data.

47 As with measures of central tendency, measures of variability appropriate for nominal and ordinal data may be used with interval or ratio data even though the standard deviation is generally the preferred index for such data.

The range

48 The *range* is defined either as the difference between the highest score and lowest score ($R = H-L$), or the difference plus one ($R = H-L+1$), the latter being more accurate.

49 Like the mode, the range is not a very stable measure of variability, and its chief advantage is that it gives a quick, rough estimate of variability.

The quartile deviation

50 The *quartile deviation* (also referred to as the semi-interquartile range) is one-half of the difference between the upper quartile (the 75th percentile) and the lower quartile (the 25th percentile) in a distribution.

51 The quartile deviation is a more stable measure of variability than the range and is appropriate whenever the median is appropriate.

The standard deviation

52 The *standard deviation* is appropriate when the data represent an interval or ratio scale and is by far the most frequently used index of variability.

53 Like the mean, the measure of central tendency which is its counterpart, the standard deviation is the most stable measure of variability and takes into account each and every score.

54 If you know the mean and the standard deviation of a set of scores, you have a pretty good picture of what the distribution looks like.

55 If the distribution is relatively normal, then the mean plus 3 standard deviations and the mean minus 3 standard deviations encompasses just about all the scores, over 99% of them; that is, $\overline{X} \pm 3\,SD = 99+\%$ of the scores.

The normal curve

Normal distributions

56 A *normal curve* is essentially a frequency polygon constructed for a set of normally distributed scores.

57 If a variable is normally distributed, that is, does form a normal curve, then several things are true: (1) the area under the curve represents all (100%) of the scores, and 50% of the scores are above the mean and 50% of the scores

are below the mean; (2) the mean, the median, and the mode are the same; (3) most scores are near the mean and the further from the mean a score is, the fewer the number of persons who attained that score; and (4) the same number, or percentage, of scores is between the mean and plus one standard deviation ($\overline{X}$ + 1SD) as is between the mean and minus one standard deviation ($\overline{X}$ − 1SD), and likewise for $\overline{X}$ ± 2SD and $\overline{X}$ ± 3SD.

58 If scores are normally distributed, the following statements are true:

$\overline{X}$ ± 1.0SD = approximately 68% of the scores
$\overline{X}$ ± 2.0SD = approximately 95% of the scores
               (1.96 SD is exactly 95%)
$\overline{X}$ ± 2.5SD = approximately 99% of the scores
               (2.58 SD is exactly 99%)
$\overline{X}$ ± 3.0SD = approximately 99+% of the scores

And similarly, the following statements are always true:

$\overline{X}$ − 3.0SD = approximately the .1 percentile
$\overline{X}$ − 2.0SD = approximately the 2nd percentile
$\overline{X}$ − 1.0SD = approximately the 16th percentile
       $\overline{X}$ = the 50th percentile
$\overline{X}$ + 1.0SD = approximately the 84th percentile
$\overline{X}$ + 2.0SD = approximately the 98th percentile
$\overline{X}$ + 3.0SD = approximately the 99th+ percentile

These equivalents are generalizable to the scores of any group on any measure to the degree that the scores approximate a normal curve.

59 Many variables form a normal distribution including physical measures, such as height and weight, and psychological measures, such as intelligence and aptitude; in fact, most variables measured in education form a normal distribution *if* enough persons are tested.

60 Since classroom evaluation deals with a finite number of students, and often not a very large number, test data only more or less approximate a normal curve; likewise, all of the equivalencies (e.g. standard deviation, percentiles) are also only approximations.

Skewed distributions

61 When a distribution is not normal, it is said to be *skewed*.

62 A distribution which is skewed is not symmetrical, and the values of the mean, the median, and the mode are different.

63 In a skewed distribution there are more extreme scores at one end than the other. If the extreme scores are at the lower end of the distribution, the distribution is said to be negatively skewed; if the extreme scores are at the upper, or higher, end of the distribution, the distribution is said to be positively skewed.

64 The mean is "pulled" in the direction of the extreme scores; it is always closer to the extreme scores than the median.

65 In a negatively skewed distribution the mean ($\overline{X}$) is always lower (smaller) than the median (md) whereas in a positively skewed distribution the mean is always higher (greater) than the median; also, in a negatively skewed distribution the mean and median are usually lower (smaller) than the mode whereas in a positively skewed distribution the mean and the median are usually higher (greater) than the mode.

Measures of relative position

66 A numerical value which summarizes the responses actually made on a test by an individual is called a *raw score;* a raw score is usually the total number of correct answers, and has essentially no meaning in and of itself.

67 There is a need for methods of transforming raw scores into values which facilitate the interpretation of scores on both an individual and group basis; measures of relative position fill this need.

68 Measures of relative position indicate where a score is in relation to all other scores in the distribution.

69 Measures of relative position permit you to express how well an individual has performed as compared to all other individuals in some group who have been given the same test; an individual's performance may be compared to the performance of a norm group or to the performance of the group of which he or she is actually a member.

70 A major advantage of such measures is that they make it possible to compare the performance of an individual on two or more different tests (or subtests); measures of relative position express different scores on a common scale, a common frame of reference, thus permitting valid comparisons of scores on different tests.

71 Raw scores that have been transformed systematically into equivalent values which indicate relative position are referred to as *derived scores.*

72 Standardized test manuals almost always provide norms tables which contain raw scores and one or more equivalent derived scores.

73 A number of manuals provide separate tables for each of a number of levels of a given test; the term "level" refers to the grade or age range for which the test is supposedly appropriate.

74 Occasionally, a norms table does not provide derived scores for each and every raw score; in such cases it is necessary to extrapolate, i.e. estimate, missing values.

75 The equivalencies between derived scores indicated on the normal curve figure (e.g. a T score of 60 corresponds to the 84th percentile) are accurate to the degree that the distribution upon which they are based is normally distributed.

Percentile ranks

76 *Percentile ranks* indicate the percentage of *persons* who scored as well as or lower than a given score, not the percentage of items answered correctly.

77 Percentiles and percentile ranks are appropriate for data representing an ordinal scale, although they are frequently computed for interval data.

78 The median of a set of scores corresponds to the 50th percentile, which makes sense since the median is the middle point and therefore the point below which are 50% of the scores.

79 One point to keep in mind when interpreting percentile ranks is that they are ordinal not interval measures; therefore, we do not have equal intervals between percentile points. An increase in a given number of percentile points corresponds to a different number of raw score points depending upon where we are in the distribution.

80 While percentiles are 99 points which divide a distribution into 100 parts, quartiles are three points which divide a distribution into four equal parts.

Standard scores

81 Basically, a *standard score* is a derived score which expresses how far a given raw score is from some reference point, typically the mean, in terms of standard deviation units.

82 A standard score is a measure of relative position which is appropriate when the test data represent an interval or ratio scale of measurement.

83 Standard scores allow scores from different tests to be compared on a common scale, and, unlike percentiles, we can validly perform mathematical operations on them in order to average them, for example.

84 Standard score equivalencies hold only if all the derived scores are based on the raw scores of the same group.

85 There is a procedure for transforming a set of raw scores which insures that the distribution of standard scores will be normal; raw scores thus transformed are referred to as *normalized scores*.

z scores

86 A *z score* is the most basic standard score and it expresses how far a score is from the mean in terms of standard deviation units.

87 If a set of scores is transformed into a set of z scores (each score is expressed as a z score), the new distribution has a mean of 0 and a standard deviation of 1.

88 The major advantage of z scores is that they allow scores from different tests or subtests to be compared.

89 Other standard scores represent transformations of z scores which communicate the same information in a more generally understandable form by eliminating negatives and/or decimals.

T scores

90 To transform a z score to a T score, you simply multiply the z score by 10 and add 50; that is, $T = 10z + 50$.

91 When scores are transformed to T scores, the new distribution has a mean of 50 and a standard deviation of 10.

92 If the original distribution is not normal (such as when a small sample group is involved), then neither is the z distribution; in such cases the distribution resulting from the $10z + 50$ transformation is more accurately referred to as a Z distribution.

Stanines

93 *Stanines* are standard scores that divide a distribution into nine parts.

94 Stanine (short for "standard nine") equivalencies are derived using the formula $2z + 5$, and rounding resulting values to the nearest whole number.

95 Stanines 2 through 8 each represent ½SD of the distribution; stanines 1 and 9 include the remainder.

96 Stanine 5 includes 20% of the scores, stanines 4 and 6 each contain 17%, stanines 3 and 7 each contain 12%, 2 and 8 each contain 7%, and 1 and 9 each contain 4% of the scores (percentages approximate).

97 Using the theoretical percentages anyone, a teacher for example, can translate a set of scores into stanines by (1) arranging the scores in ascending order, (2) identifying the median (midpoint), and (3) assigning the 10% of the scores right above the median and the 10% right below the median to stanine 5

(stanine 5 contains 20% of the scores), the next 17% (on both sides) of the scores to stanines 4 and 6 respectively, and so forth.

98 While stanines are not as exact as other standard scores, they are useful for a variety of purposes such as grouping and selection of students for special programs.

Deviation IQ

99 A *deviation IQ* (DIQ) is a standard score which is based on how far a person's score (on a given IQ test) is from the average score of persons in the same age group.

100 Computation of DIQ's basically involves calculating z scores for each age group and transforming the z scores to form a distribution with a mean of 100 and a standard deviation of 15 (or 16); that is, $DIQ = 15z + 100$.

101 IQ scores are only comparable if they are based on the same version of the same test.

Scaled scores

102 Scaled scores are standard scores which are comparable across levels of the *same test or subtest* from grade to grade, battery to battery, and form to form; they are not comparable for different tests or subtests.

103 Because scaled scores are comparable across levels, they are used for analyzing pupil growth and for interpreting the results of out-of-level testing.

104 Deriving scaled scores involves equating raw scores at successive levels of a test and transforming the raw scores into standard scores which are comparable across levels.

105 Scaled scores permit us to transform a raw score based on a given level test to a corresponding raw score on a different level test.

Grade and age equivalents

106 A *grade equivalent* (or grade score) of a given raw score is the grade level of students whose typical (i.e. mean or median score) score is the same as the given raw score.

107 A grade equivalent expresses both the grade and the month in the grade; for example, 4.0 indicates the beginning of the fourth grade and 4.5 indicates the fifth month of the fourth grade.

108 Typically, a test being normed is administered to large groups of students in each of several successive grade levels at the beginning of a school year and at the end; intermediate values within each grade level, and sometimes values for grade levels above and below those actually tested, are extrapolated.

109 Grade equivalent extrapolations are based on the questionable assumption that scores increase evenly, or by the same amount, from month to month and from year to year.

110 The same grade equivalents on two different tests or subtests does not necessarily indicate the same relative position (i.e. percentile rank).

111 When *modal age norms* are involved, grade equivalents are based upon the performance of only those students who are in a normal age range for a particular grade.

112 All in all, grade equivalents leave much to be desired; their popularity persists, however, because they are considered to be fairly easy for most people to understand.

113 Age equivalents are just like grade equivalents except that they are based on the average score of students of a particular age instead of a particular grade level.

Measures of relationship

114 *Correlation* involves collecting data in order to determine whether, and to what degree, a relationship exists between two or more quantifiable variables—not a causal relationship, just a relationship.

115 Degree of relationship is expressed as a correlation coefficient which is computed based on the two sets of scores.

116 Correlational techniques have a number of applications in educationsl evaluations: estimating validity and reliability, establishing degree of relationship between variables of interest, and determining if relationships are strong enough to permit valid predictions.

117 For results to be valid, coefficients must be based on a sufficient number of persons, and 30 is generally considered to be minimally acceptable.

118 It is important to select or develop valid, reliable measures of the variables being studied (unless of course the purpose of the effort is to establish degree of validity and reliability).

119 The basic correlational procedure is not too complicated: two (or more) scores are obtained for each member of a selected group, one score for each variable of interest, and the paired scores are then correlated.

Interpretation

120 When two variables are correlated, the result is a correlation coefficient. A *correlation coefficient* is a decimal number, between .00 and + 1.00, or .00 and − 1.00, which indicates the degree to which two variables are related. If the coefficient is near + 1.00, the variables are positively related; if the coefficient is near .00, the variables are not related; if the coefficient is near − 1.00, the variables are inversely related.

121 Interpretation of a correlation coefficient depends upon how it is to be used; that is, how large it needs to be in order to be useful depends upon the purpose for which it was computed.

122 A high (significant) correlation coefficient may suggest a cause-effect relationship but does not establish one.

Linearity assumption

123 Most correlational techniques are based on the assumption that the relationship being investigated is a linear one; if a relationship is linear, then plotting the scores on the two variables will result in something which resembles a straight line.

124 If a relationship is curvilinear, an increase in one variable is associated with a corresponding increase in another variable *up to a point,* and at that point further increase in the first variable results in a corresponding decrease in the other variable (or the reverse may be true—first decrease, then increase).

125 If a relationship is suspected of being curvilinear, then a correlational technique which results in something called an eta ratio is required.

126 Attentuation refers to the tendency of correlation coefficients to be lowered due to the fact that less-than-perfectly-reliable measures are utilized.

127 A correction for attenuation can be applied which provides an estimate of what the coefficient would be if both measures were perfectly reliable.

128 Another factor which may lead to a coefficient which represents an underestimate of the true relationship between two variables is a restricted range of scores.

129 A correction for restriction in range may be applied to obtain an estimate of what the coefficient would be if the range of scores were not restricted.

Methods of computing coefficients

The Spearman rho

130 If the data for one of the variables are expressed as ranks instead of scores, the Spearman rho is the appropriate measure of correlation.

131 Rank data are involved when instead of using a score for each person, persons are arranged in order of score and each person is assigned a rank from one to however many persons there are (e.g. 1 to 30).

132 The Spearman rho is appropriate when the data represent an ordinal scale (although it may be used with interval data) and is used when the median and quartile deviation are used.

133 If only one of the variables to be correlated is in rank order, then the other variables to be correlated with it must also be expressed in terms of ranks in order to use the Spearman rho technique.

134 The Spearman rho is interpreted in the same way as the Pearson r and produces a coefficient somewhere between -1.00 and $+1.00$ (if a group of people achieve identical ranks on two variables the coefficient will be $+1.00$).

135 If more than one person received the same score, their ranks are averaged; for example, if two persons have the same, highest score they are each assigned the average of rank 1 and rank 2, namely rank 1.5.

136 For most classroom purposes the Spearman rho provides an adequate estimate of degree of relationship and is fairly simple to compute.

The Pearson r

137 The most commonly used technique is the Pearson r, which is the most appropriate measure of correlation when the sets of data to be correlated represent either interval or ratio scales.

138 Since most instruments used in education, such as achievement measures and personality measures, are expressed in the form of interval data, the Pearson r is usually the appropriate coefficient for determining relationship.

139 Like the mean and the standard deviation, the Pearson r takes into account each and every score in both distributions, and it is the most stable, reliable estimate of correlation.

Multiple regression

140 When prediction is an intent of an evaluation, a predictor variable is correlated with a criterion variable.

141 Since a combination of variables usually results in a more accurate prediction than any one variable, prediction efforts typically involve a number of predictor variables; in such situations we formulate an equation referred to as a multiple regression equation.

142 A multiple regression equation uses all variables which individually predict the criterion to make a prediction which is more accurate.

143 Since relationships are rarely perfect, predictions made by a multiple regression equation are not perfect; thus, predicted scores are generally placed in a confidence interval.

144 *Shrinkage* is the tendency of a prediction equation to be less accurate when used with a different group, a group other than the one on which the equation was originally formulated.

145 Because of shrinkage, any prediction equation should be validated with at least one other group, and variables which are no longer found to be related to the criterion measure should be taken out of the equation; this procedure is referred to as *cross validation*.

Calculation for interval data

Symbols

146 Symbols commonly used in statistical formulas are as follows:

X = any score
Σ = the sum of; add them up
ΣX = the sum of all the scores
$\overline{X}$ = the mean, or arithmetic average, of the scores
N = total number of students
n = number of students in a particular group
x = deviation score; $x = X - \overline{X}$
ΣX^2 = the sum of all the squares (square each score and add up all the squares)
$(\Sigma X)^2$ = the square of the sum (add up all the scores and square the sum, or total)

The mean

147 The formula for the mean is:

$$\overline{X} = \frac{\Sigma X}{N}$$

The standard deviation

148 The formula for the standard deviation is:

$$SD = \sqrt{\frac{\Sigma X^2 - \frac{(\Sigma X)^2}{N}}{N}}$$

Standard scores

149 The formula for a z score is:

$$z = \frac{x}{SD} = \frac{X - \overline{X}}{SD}.$$

150 The formula for a T score is: $T = 10z + 50$.

The Spearman rho

151 The formula for the Spearman rho is:

$$\text{rho} = 1 - \frac{6\Sigma d^2}{N(N^2 - 1)}$$

The Pearson r

152 The formula for the Pearson r is:

$$r = \frac{N\Sigma XY - \Sigma X\Sigma Y}{\sqrt{[N\Sigma X^2 - (\Sigma X)^2][N\Sigma Y^2 - (\Sigma Y)^2]}}$$

153 A coefficient's significance depends upon two factors, its *statistical* significance and its *practical* significance.

154 To determine whether a given coefficient is statistically significant, we consult a table which indicates how large our r needs to be in order to be significant given the number of students (or other participants) we have and the probability level (level of significance) we have selected.

155 Degrees of freedom (*df*) for the Pearson r are always computed by the formula $df = N - 2$.

156 The probability level (*p*) we select (usually .05 or .01) indicates how likely it is that we are making the wrong decision concerning the existence of a true relationship.

157 For the same probability level, or significance level, a larger coefficient is required when smaller samples are involved.

158 For a given group size, the value of the correlation coefficient needed for significance increases as the *p* value decreases, or gets smaller.

Inferential statistics

159 Inferential statistics deal with inferences about populations based on the behavior of sample groups.

160 If a posttest difference between means is found for two groups (a treatment group and a control group), the question of interest is whether a similar difference exists in the population from which the samples were selected.

Concepts underlying application

Hypotheses

161 Whether they are formally stated or not, most formal evaluation efforts are based on one or more hypotheses, hypotheses state expected outcomes and should be made explicit.

162 Typically, we use a statistic to test what is called a null hypothesis, to determine whether a difference between two groups occurred by chance.

163 When we talk about the difference between two sample means being a true difference, we mean that the difference was caused by the treatment and not by chance; the explanation that the difference occurred by chance is called the null hypothesis.

164 The *null hypothesis* says in essence that there is no true difference or relation-

ship in the population and that any difference or relationship found for the samples is the result of sampling error.

165 In order to test a null hypothesis, we need a test of significance and we need to select a probability level which indicates how much risk we are willing to take that the decision we make is wrong.

Tests of significance

166 After we administer a posttest, we typically have two (or more) group means. We do not expect these means to be *exactly* the same, even if the treatment is equally as effective as the control condition; these means are very likely to be at least a little different.

167 The test of significance helps us to decide whether we can reject the null hypothesis and infer that the difference is a true one, a population difference, not a chance one resulting from sampling error.

168 The test of significance is made at a preselected probability level and allows us to state that we have rejected the null hypothesis because we would expect to find a difference as large as we have found by chance, say only 5 times out of 100 ($p = .05$) or only 1 time in 100 ($p = .01$); therefore, we conclude that the null hypothesis is *probably* false and reject it.

Tests of significance: types

169 Factors such as the scale of measurement represented by the data, the method of participant selection, the number of groups, and the number of independent variables determine which test of significance should be selected for a given evaluation.

170 It is important that an appropriate test be selected; an incorrect test can lead to incorrect conclusions.

The *t* test

171 The *t test* is used to determine whether two means (usually the treatment mean and the control mean) are significantly different at a selected probability level.

The t test for independent samples

172 *Independent samples* are samples which are randomly formed, that is, formed without any type of matching; the members of one group are not related to the members of the other group in any systematic way other than that they are selected from the same population.

173 Thus, the *t* test for independent samples is used to determine whether there is probably a significant difference between the means of two independent samples.

The t test for nonindependent samples

174 *Nonindependent samples* are samples formed by some type of matching; when samples are not independent, the members of one group are systematically related to the members of the second group (especially if it is the same group at two different times).

175 Thus, the *t* test for nonindependent samples is used to determine whether

there is probably a significant difference between the means of two matched, or nonindependent, samples or between the means for one sample at two different times.

176 When a *t* test is used to analyze results, the evaluation report should present the group means, standard deviations, and *n*'s for both the treatment group and the control group, as well as the *t* value and the significance level (e.g. .05).

Analysis of gain scores

177 Analyzing gain scores involves: (1) subtracting each person's pretest score from his or her posttest score (which results in a gain, or difference, score); (2) computing the mean gain, or difference, score for each group; and (3) calculating a *t* value for the difference between the two average mean differences.

178 The reliability of gain scores is typically lower than the reliability of the scores themselves.

179 There are a number of problems associated with this approach, the major one being lack of opportunity to grow; every person does not have the same room to gain.

180 The correct analysis of posttest scores for two groups depends upon the performance of the two groups on the pretest.

181 If both groups are essentially the same on the pretest, then posttest scores can be directly compared using a *t* test; if, on the other hand, there is a difference between the groups on the pretest, the preferred posttest analysis is analysis of covariance.

Simple analysis of variance

182 *Simple*, or one-way, *analysis of variance* (ANOVA) is used to determine whether there is a significant difference between two or more means at a selected probability level.

183 When ANOVA is applied to the data, the result is an *F* ratio.

Multiple comparisons

184 When the *F* ratio is significant, and more than two means are involved, *multiple comparison procedures* are used to determine which means are significantly different from which other means.

185 There are a number of different multiple comparison techniques available to the evaluator, of which the Scheffé test is probably the most generally acceptable and useful.

Analysis of covariance

186 The *analysis of covariance* is a statistical method for equating groups on one or more variables.

187 In essence, analysis of covariance adjusts scores on a dependent variable for initial differences on some other variable(s) such as pretest performance, IQ, or reading readiness (assuming that performance on the "other variable" is related to performance on the dependent variable).

188 Essentially, this technique adjusts posttest scores for initial differences on some variable and compares adjusted means; that is, the groups are equalized with respect to the control variable(s) and then compared.

Chi square

189 *Chi square*, symbolized as χ^2, is a test of significance appropriate when the data are in the form of frequency counts occurring in two or more mutually exclusive categories.

190 A chi square test compares proportions actually observed with proportions expected, to see if they are significantly different.

191 Expected proportions are usually the frequencies which would be expected if the groups were equal, although they may be based on past data.

192 The chi square is usually used in evaluations to compare the frequencies of certain behaviors occurring in two or more groups.

Using the computer for data analysis

When to use the computer

193 If group sizes are not large, if a limited number of variables is involved, and if relatively simple statistical analyses are to be performed, using a calculator may be the most efficient approach to data analysis.

194 A good guideline for beginners is that you should not use the computer to perform an analysis which you have never done yourself by hand.

195 If you will be involved in using the computer, you should acquaint yourself with the computer center which will be utilized; you should become familiar with the facilities, services and equipment.

Costs associated with computer use

196 Costs for computer services are typically quite reasonable; the major costs associated with computer analysis are for programming, keypunching, and computer time.

197 Programs for many standard analyses have already been written and are available for use.

198 Doing your own keypunching not only saves you money but also may reduce keypunching errors since you can read your data sheets better than anyone else.

199 While the costs per hour for computer processing time are high, the analyses typically required for an evaluation usually use no more than a few minutes.

200 If you use an existing program, keypunch your own data, and are given free processing time, the entire operation may cost you nothing but time.

Steps in using the computer

201 The first step in using the computer is to select an appropriate program; the program selected will indicate how the data may be keypunched and what instruction cards need to be punched.

202 Instruction cards tell the computer all about your data and include such information as group sizes, number of variables, and how the data are arranged on the data cards.

203 All keypunched cards must be checked for accuracy.

204 When you pick up your output, the first thing you look for is error messages.

18 post-analysis procedures

Verification and storage of data

Verification

205 The very first thing you should do when you think you are done is to recheck all your work, including all your calculations.

206 The results of your analyses should make logical sense.

207 If you use the computer, you should double-check both your input and your output for accuracy.

Storage

208 When you are convinced that your work is accurate, all data sheets or cards, worksheets, and records of calculations should be labeled, organized, and filed in a safe place.

209 All of the data should be carefully labeled with as many identification labels as necessary; labels may give information such as the inclusive dates of the evaluation, the nature of the various treatment and control groups, and whether data are pretest data, posttest data, or data for a control variable (such as reading readiness).

210 All worksheets should also be labeled to indicate the identity of the group(s), the analysis, and the scores, (e.g. "Warm Fuzzy Group/standard deviation/posttest").

211 A convenient, practical way to store data is in loose leaf ring binders, or notebooks.

Interpretation of results

212 Proper interpretation of test results requires recognition of the fact that while many tests do provide very accurate estimates, they do not measure with the same precision that yardsticks do.

213 Intelligent interpretation also requires knowledge of the test in question; what a given score *means* depends upon such factors as what the test actually measures as well as its indices of validity and reliability, for example, its estimated standard error of measurement.

214 Application of a test of significance produces a number, a value which is or is not statistically significant; it must be interpreted in terms of the purpose of the evaluation, that is, the original question or hypothesis.

Norm-referenced tests

215 While any number of raw score equivalents may be available in norms tables, one (or several) of these are generally selected for presentation on individual or group profile sheets; these permit easy comparison of relative performance on a number of subtests.

Individual profiles

216 The *meaning* of an individual raw score depends upon what was measured, the composition of the norm group, and the values of the individual's derived scores.

217 Some test manuals provide tables for more than one norm group, or for sub-

groups within a norm group; and in such cases it is important that the most appropriate tables be selected for interpretation purposes.

218 While it is usually a safe assumption, you should check to make sure that derived scores for different subtests are based on the same norm group, or else relative performance across subject areas cannot be validly interpreted.

219 Perhaps the greatest source of score misinterpretation comes from thinking of the average score of a norm group as being a goal for all students.

220 An individual profile presents raw scores and/or one or more derived scores for each of a number of subtests in a graphic or tabular manner.

221 An individual profile permits us to identify a student's relative strengths and weaknesses at a glance.

222 The derived scores most often presented on a profile sheet are percentile ranks, stanines, and grade equivalents.

223 Profile sheets of most major tests provide an explanation of the contents of the profile and directions for interpretation.

224 Directions on profile sheets typically include reference to the fact that every score reflects some measurement error and should be thought of as being the midpoint in some range or band of scores (usually those scores which fall between $\pm 1SE_m$).

225 Usually the overlapping bands concept is employed so that a true difference in performance on any two subtests is indicated only if the bands for those subtests do not overlap at all.

226 For stanines, the directions typically suggest that in comparing performance on any two subtests, a difference of only one stanine (e.g. 6 versus 7) probably does not reflect a true difference in performance; a difference of two or more stanines probably does.

227 The profile gives us an indication of each student's performance or ability compared to a given norm group; it also provides information concerning the student's relative strengths and weaknesses.

228 Further interpretation requires additional knowledge concerning the individual, an index of mental ability for example.

Group results

229 A teacher is also interested in analyzing the performance of her or his students as a group; this requires compilation of the individual results into some sort of summary form.

230 A basic class summary sheet has spaces for student names, derived scores (grade equivalents, percentile ranks, stanines) for each student on each test, total scores for each student, and other information such as IQ scores.

231 Such summary forms allow us to easily spot students who are exceptional in some way, e.g. students who are candidates for special programs (remedial or advanced).

232 Many publishers also provide some type of group profile which summarizes results for a class as a whole.

233 Stanine summary figures permit us to compare a class *as a whole* with the norm group; this comparison will give a rough estimate of where the class is with respect to achievement.

234 There are a number of ways such a summary chart can be used in planning future instructional objectives and strategies. We can, for example, examine the stanine pattern for each subtest and can make comparisons across subtests; results may also suggest areas in which grouping would be appropriate.

235 Group results can be interpreted on many levels - classroom, school, district, county, and so forth.

236 One problem frequently associated with analysis of group results arises when comparisons between and among groups (e.g. schools) are based solely on test results and do not take into consideration other relevant factors such as the characteristics of the students.

237 Group comparisons, whether at the classroom level or the district level, are only valid to the degree that students in the groups are comparable on other variables such as ability and socio-economic status.

Ex post facto results

238 Due to lack of randomization, manipulation, and other types of control characteristic of experimental designs, it is difficult to establish cause-effect relationships in ex post facto designs with any great degree of confidence.

239 The cause-effect relationship may in fact be the reverse of the one hypothesized (the alleged cause may actually be the effect), or there may be a third factor which is the "real" cause of both the alleged cause and effect.

Criterion-referenced tests

240 The most efficient way to approach interpretation of criterion-referenced tests is to construct item achievement charts for all objectives.

241 Based on such charts, we can determine for each student information such as which objectives were achieved and the total percentage of items correct.

242 Similar information can easily be compiled on a group basis, information such as the percentage of students who achieved each objective and the average percentage of the objectives achieved.

243 We can easily pinpoint the strengths and weaknesses of the individual as well as those of the group with respect to very specific behaviors.

244 At a very specific level we can determine whether a given deficiency is an individual problem or a group problem; the percentage of students with a given deficiency determines how much additional class time will be devoted to the objectives in question and how much revision of instructional strategy is required.

245 We may occasionally, on a major test for example, wish to derive norm-referenced interpretations for criterion-referenced test results; if there are a sufficient number of students and if there is sufficient score variability, the raw scores of a nonmastery criterion-referenced test can be transformed to percentiles, or stanines, or whatever equivalent is appropriate.

Questionnaires

246 When presenting the results of a questionnaire, the response rate for each item should be given as well as the total sample size and the overall percentage of returns, since all respondents may not answer all questions.

247 The simplest way to present the results is to indicate the percentage of responders who selected each alternative (e.g. yes, no, undecided) for each item.

Hypothesized versus unhypothesized results

248 The evaluation reports of special programs and projects should include a discussion concerning whether the results were or were not those hypothesized.

249 If the results are those anticipated, the results provide support for the effectiveness of the program, but they do not *prove* anything.
250 If results do not turn out as anticipated, you do not apologize; nonsignificant results do not necessarily mean that the program is ineffective in general, and even if it is, it is just as important to know what does not work as what does.
251 If for some reason you lost a number of participants, you should discuss why and explain how the results may have been affected.
252 Any totally unexpected outcomes should be analyzed and reported but should be interpreted with great care.

Statistical versus practical significance

253 The fact that results are statistically significant does not automatically mean that they are of any educational value.
254 Statistical significance only means that your results would be likely to occur by chance a certain percentage of the time, say 5%.
255 There are several factors which affect the *educational* significance of a finding—the actual magnitude of the difference, the current priority of the area in which the difference occurred, and cost.

Replication of results

256 Replication of results is probably the strongest evidence for the effectiveness of a program.
257 *Replication* means that the entire effort, from pretesting to posttesting, is done again using different participants.
258 In certain cases, the significance of a relationship or difference may be enhanced if it is replicated in a more natural setting, such as a natural classroom environment.
259 The need for replication is especially great when the treatment involved (or relationship investigated) is highly unusual, or when the results have practical significance and the treatment investigated might really make a difference.

task seven **performance criteria**

Your work in task 7 should be based on the scores you obtained (or generated) for task 5. For most of you a score interval of one will be feasible in constructing a frequency polygon. For each required computation you should give the formula and show your work. The norm-referenced interpretations you make for each student will depend somewhat on the variable measured by the test. For an achievement test, for example, your statements might be similar to the following:

> Student 4 performed as well or better than 98% of the students who took the test and is in the top stanine group.

Criterion-referenced interpretations will depend on whether the test was a mastery or nonmastery test, and on how many objectives were measured. These factors were determined in task 5. Your statements might resemble one of the following:

> Student 1 scored 90% and achieved mastery.

> Student 1 scored 70% and achieved 4 of the 5 objectives.

All evaluation activities should be described, including collection of data in the field.

part eight
analyzing results

The results of tests administered to students are reported to and used by a number of diverse groups within the school system and community. A major use of teacher-developed test results is in deriving and assigning grades. Regardless of the system used, grading should be based on a sufficient amount of valid data systematically collected over a period of time. While there are a number of problems associated with grades, the need to communicate student achievement makes them a necessity.

While grades and test results for individuals are reported only to students and parents, standardized test results for groups (e.g. schools) are also reported to school boards, administrators, teachers, community members, the media, and various other audiences. The two foremost principles of reporting are that results should be communicated in a form and manner which are understandable to the intended group, and that recipients should be given instruction and guidance concerning the proper interpretation and use of results.

The goal of part 8 is for you to be able to transform scores into percent, norm-referenced, and criterion-referenced grades, and to properly report grades and the results of standardized tests to parents and other interested groups. After reading part 8, you should be able to do the following task.

task eight
Based on the results from task 5 and the analyses performed in task 7, perform the following for student evaluation:

a Assign each student a percent grade, a norm-referenced grade, and a criterion-referenced grade; explain how each type of grade was derived.

b Briefly discuss how you would report

each of the three types of grades to parents.

c Select the highest score, the average score, and the lowest score. Assume that all three students who achieved these scores also scored at the 50th percentile on a standardized aptitude test in the area measured by the test (e.g. math). Describe how your discussion with parents concerning each student's achievement would differ.

d Write a brief report which summarizes the performance of the group.

For other types of evaluation, write a brief, formal report which summarizes the major aspects of the evaluation.

(See Performance Criteria, p. 520.)

19 using and reporting results

After reading chapter 19, you should be able to:

1 Briefly state the overall major use of test results.

2 Briefly describe the kinds of information concerning each student a counselor should have access to.

3 Briefly describe how the results of testing are used to improve curricula and classroom instruction.

4 Give at least three arguments to support or refute the position "Grades should be abolished."

5 Give at least three arguments to support or refute the position "Grades should be based on achievement only and ability should not be a factor."

6 Briefly describe the three major methods of grading and the corresponding procedure(s) for transforming test scores into grades.

7 Rank order the three major methods of grading in terms of the degree to which they fulfill the three major purposes of grades, and give reasons for your ranking.

8 State *which* approach to assigning letter grades to criterion-referenced results you think is most acceptable and *why*.

9 State four general principles of reporting.

10 List the major types of comparisons of group results which are typically made and reported (e.g. system performance versus norm group performance).

11 Make a list of ten questions which parents might ask concerning individual and/or group test results and give a brief response to each.

12 Identify and briefly describe the major components of a formal evaluation report.

Utilization of results

Evaluation is the systematic process of collecting and analyzing data in order to make decisions. Thus, the results of data analysis are used for decision making. The types of decisions range from deciding whether an individual student is making satisfactory progress to determining whether the American educational system is achieving its objectives. While standardized tests are by no means the only source of required input, they do provide a large portion of the data. Further, standardized tests have certain advantages over locally-developed tests and permit decisions not otherwise possible. One major advantage is the wealth of information, in the form of various computer-printout presentations of results, which are provided by test publishers and which can be made readily available to all involved persons. They provide norms tables and summary profiles of derived scores which permit achievement comparisons to be made between and among students, classes, schools, districts and norm groups. They also allow us to interpret the achievement of individuals and groups in relation to their general and specific aptitudes. An achievement score can only be labeled as satisfactory or unsatisfactory when aptitude is taken into consideration.

A number of groups, both inside and outside of the school system, are interested in the results of testing, including legislators, school boards, administrators, teachers, students, and parents. Each group, however, views the data from a different perspective and uses the results to make different kinds of decisions. School boards are concerned with the performance of the system as a whole and with whether resources are being allocated and used effectively. Based on all relevant information, they make budget decisions which have considerable impact on all aspects of the system's operation. Principals, quite naturally, are more interested in the performance of the students in their own schools and in appraising the effectiveness of the various instructional programs and projects. Based on all available input, they make decisions regarding ways in which resources will be expended in the future. Teachers, on the other hand, make very few fiscal decisions; they use results to make instructional decisions related to group objectives and activities and procedures for meeting individual student needs. Students also use results to make both short-term and long-term decisions. Based on a combination of classroom and standardized test results, students make decisions regarding a range of factors, from course selections to future career goals.

The major nonschool-based group interested in results is parents. Their concerns are partly fiscal and partly personal. Like all taxpayers, they want to know whether the schools are using funds efficiently and effectively. As parents, however, their main concern is whether the school system is providing their sons and daughters with an adequate education, one that will permit their children to compete equitably with students from other systems. Based on information at their disposal, parents make fiscal decisions, such as whether or not to vote for a school bond issue, and personal decisions, such as whether to remove their children from the public school system and place them in a private school. Parents have every right to be concerned with the effectiveness of their children's education since factors such as standardized test scores can play a big part in determining a student's whole future. Both admissions people at institutions of higher education and employers are concerned not only with the courses that students have had and the grades they earned, but also with how well they have scored on standardized tests of interest, such as the CEEB.

Thus, the results of testing are used by a variety of groups for making decisions concerning the effectiveness and efficiency of the total system and each component in it, and for taking future actions. The results of testing at any given point in time, however, are never considered in isolation from previous results and from other types of data. The most current results indicate where students are *now*, compared to other students. Results from previous testings provide a point of reference for determining trends in achievement, especially if the various results have been interpreted with respect to the same (or a similar) norm group. On both an individual and a group basis we can determine whether level of achievement is increasing or decreasing in various areas. Both gradual changes and dramatic shifts are of interest. If a school system, for example, made an all-out effort to improve reading skills, a significant increase in measured reading achievement might be anticipated. By examining trends in performance we can make projections concerning future performance and make appropriate decisions. Objectively, for example, a student's math achievement may compare favorably with national norms and may represent only a slight decrease in achievement in relation to the previous year's scores. The pattern for several years, however, might reveal a gradual but steady decline from year to year, representing a significant decrease in achievement over a three-year period. Thus, in anticipation of further achievement losses, we might attempt to determine their cause and to take action to reverse the trend.

How useful results are obviously depends to a great extent on how they are utilized. If they are treated lightly or misused, they will have either no impact on the educational experiences of students or a negative one. If, on the other hand, they are viewed as being valuable sources of input and are studied carefully, they can lead to improved decision making at all levels of the educational community. As the above discussion suggests, regardless of the level at which decisions are made, they ultimately have an effect on each and every student. The decisions which have the greatest impact on students, however, are probably those made by guidance and instructional personnel since they affect students as individuals.

Guidance

It is critical that results be used very judiciously in counseling as the consequences of poor guidance can be serious and far-reaching. Telling a student there is absolutely no way she or he could make it successfully through medical school because test scores indicate only average aptitude and achievement in science is not good practice. On the other hand, it is equally unwise to tell students that they can be anything they want to be if they work hard enough. Appraisals of a student's capabilities and potential should be realistic, not overly pessimistic or overly optimistic, and should be based on an array of data. It is the counselor's responsibility to use whatever information is necessary to help each student make wise curriculum decisions and long-term career decisions. The counselor also has a measure of responsibility for helping students to cope with emotional problems. The results of personality inventories as well as achievement and aptitude measures will often provide insights into the reasons for a student's difficulty. A student, for example, may exhibit an excessive amount of anxiety resulting from failure to attain desired levels of achievement, levels which appear to be unrealistic in light of the results of aptitude measures. Depending upon the nature of the problem and available information, a counselor may recommend further testing or professional help (from a psychologist for example), or may attempt to deal personally with the problem, in frequent individual and group counseling sessions.

The more a counselor knows about a student, both academically and personally, the better position he or she is in to advise students. The results of valid, reliable standardized tests of achievement, aptitude, personality, and interest are all relevant, as well as grades, classroom effort and conduct, teacher comments, and home environment. With all relevant data at their disposal, counselors assess students' strengths and weaknesses and make realistic recommendations for future pursuits. A counselor, however, should not make definite statements but should talk in probabilistic terms. No data available to the counselor result from totally valid and reliable instruments or procedures, and therefore no conclusions based on such data can be viewed as totally valid or reliable. Thus, a student may be told that it is not *likely* that she or he could successfully complete medical school, but a student shouldn't be told that she or he doesn't have a "cold chance in Hades" of doing so. A more productive approach is to indicate that becoming a doctor would be very difficult and to suggest reasonable, related alternatives more in line with the student's abilities. A counselor might, for example, suggest that a student consider a career as a paramedic or a nurse's aide.

It is not sufficient for the counselor to have only current information on students. Proper interpretation and analysis require the availability of cumulative information based on the periodic and systematic collection of data. Thus, the student's cumulative folder is not something to be grudgingly kept up to date but rather is a valuable tool which should be as complete and well organized as possible. A cumulative folder is most useful when results are recorded in the same form from year to year. A cumulative stanine chart, for example, showing a student's achievement in the various areas from year to year can be very informative. Of course, adequately maintained cumulative folders are also invaluable sources of information for teachers. The conscientious teacher will review such records at the beginning of each school year and will consult them as necessary.

Instruction

The results of testing, both standardized and local, are used to made periodic decisions regarding the school curriculum and classroom instruction. Such decisions may affect all students in the school, some students, or just one student. An end-of-year review of data, for example, might result in decisions to (1) require a writing lab for all students, (2) expand the range of vocational courses, and (3) recommend that in September Ziggy be placed in a class for educable mentally retarded students. As mentioned previously, when necessary data are available, an item analysis of standardized test results in terms of item difficulty can provide necessary information for needed changes in curriculum and instruction. Such analyses can be performed on both a total school and individual classroom basis. Deficiencies which are evident across classrooms can be dealt with at the program level whereas classroom-specific areas of difficulties can be handled by the teacher. A shift in emphasis may be called for rather than any drastic change. If students are scoring very well in general on items dealing with fractions but relatively poorly on decimal problems, for example, a reallocation of time and resources is indicated. Such analyses are facilitated by the tables of item difficulty for the norm groups which are provided by most major test publishers. Thus, we will be more concerned when students exhibit low indices of item difficulty (many students answered the item incorrectly) when items are of average difficulty for the norm group.

How a teacher reports results to students is as important as how they are used. When discussing results with the class as a whole, individual scores should not be referred to. Statements such as "Instine did the best—way to go, Instine, and Ziggy did the worst—I don't know what I'm going to do with *him*" are clearly inappropriate. Instead, a class profile should be presented with a discussion of areas of strength and weakness. The same guidelines hold for teacher developed tests, and for such tests specific items can be discussed to give students feedback on their performance. Above all, the teacher should project a positive attitude about the test itself and about the general performance of the class on the test. If appropriate, the teacher should share with students ways in which test results will be used. A number of such uses have already been discussed. Student performance data are used in planning instruction—in selecting appropriate objectives and activities, during instruction—in determining degrees of progress, identifying areas of specific difficulty, and adapting instruction accordingly (on both an individual and group basis), and at the conclusion of some phase of instruction (e.g. a unit)—in assessing level of achievement, in determining the degree to which objectives have been achieved, and in estimating degree of improvement of performance. And, like the counselor, the teacher uses test results to determine individual patterns of ability and to identify exceptional students with special needs.

Should the results of standardized tests be used in the evaluation of teachers? By now it should be clear to you that the answer is yes and no, but mostly no. There are so many factors which affect student achievement, such as characteristics of the students and the appropriateness of the norm group, that it is very difficult to separate out the effects of teaching, good or bad. On the other hand, if there are a number of classes with very similar characteristics (scholastic aptitude, socio-economic status, resources, and so forth), and one class achieves significantly lower scores, it is highly probable that the teaching is at least partially responsible. Thus, the achievement of students should be one of many factors considered in teacher evaluation.

Similarly, standardized test results should be but one factor of many considered in making promotion decisions for individual students. Grades, on the other hand, are based almost entirely on the results of teacher-developed tests, although mental ability may be a consideration.

Grading

Have you ever received a grade you thought was totally unfair? Probably, and probably more than once. There are lots of reasons why you felt highly indignant. Perhaps you thought the standards were too tough, or perhaps the requirements were never made clear to you. In any event, you probably uttered a few choice expletives in connection with your instructor. If you have subsequently entered a profession which requires you to evaluate students or employees, no doubt you have acquired a new perspective on the whole process of grading. Grading is tough and represents a tremendous responsibility. Grades assigned to students have both an immediate and a long-term effect on their lives. Students are painfully aware of this, as are their parents, and the pressure to do well makes the whole process of assigning and receiving grades an emotional one. To make matters worse, whether or not a grade satisfies a student depends on the individual. Instine may be just as upset with a B as Ziggy is with an F. Grading, however, like testing, is a necessary procedure. The progress and achievement of students must be reported to parents and others, and grading serves this purpose. Given the seriousness of the consequences, however, it is imperative that grading be done in a serious, conscientious, and systematic manner and that the bases for grades be made clear to students.

It is difficult to discuss grading because it is far from being a cut-and-dry area. There is great difference of opinion among educators concerning grading, and selection of a certain grading procedure is mainly a matter of personal or institutional philosophy. Here we will attempt to discuss various alternatives objectively and to present, when applicable, the most widely accepted position on a given issue. A few personal biases, however, are likely to creep into such a discussion; such biases should be easily distinguishable from majority opinions.

Definition and purpose

A *grade* is an alphabetical or numerical symbol, or mark, that indicates the degree to which intended outcomes have been achieved. The major purpose of grades is to communicate how well a student is doing in the various subject areas. Grades are issued periodically to keep the student and his or her parents and counselor informed of the student's progress. Grades are recorded in cumulative folders and communicate level of achievement at various points in time to interested persons at a later date. If a student changes schools, for example, the cumulative folder will communicate past achievement to staff members in the new school. In the long run, grades communicate to admissions personnel and employers the student's pattern of achievement. Another purpose often attributed to grades is that they serve as a motivator for student performance. To some extent they represent a reward for effort on the part of the student. True, hard work may not get a low-ability student an A, but effort may make the difference between a failing grade and a passing grade. This does not mean that a student is graded on effort; it simply means that a student who studies more is likely to learn more and subsequently achieve better grades. Grades also serve as an indication of achievement to be expected in the future. Past performance is the best single predictor of future performance. As with any prediction, the relationship between past and future achievement is not perfect, but it is fairly good. Knowledge of this relationship helps guidance personnel to advise students on the realism of their long-range goals.

Grading has many critics and not all of them are students! For various reasons, grades are viewed by many as being unnecessary, meaningless or even harmful. Some go so far as to recommend that grades be done away with. While this position is a bit extreme, critics do make some valid points which should be considered. The most rational approach to dealing with these criticisms, however, would seem to be to improve grading practices rather than to eliminate them.[1]

The major objection to grades is that there is considerable variability associated with the meaning of a given grade. Grading criteria vary from teacher to teacher, school to school, town to town, and so forth, and there are no generally agreed upon definitions of what each grade should mean. Further, there are so

---

[1] For further discussion of the criticisms discussed in this chapter and responses to them, see Ebel, R. L. Shall we get rid of grades? *NCME: Measurement in Education*, 1974, 5(4), 1–5.

many different methods of grading and such a diversity of symbols that it is difficult to interpret exactly what a given set of grades means. But in spite of this variability—which does exist—there is surprisingly a great deal of consistency in students' grades. Students who get "good" grades tend to do so wherever they are. Rarely does a student go from being a B student to being a D student just because of a change of teachers or change of school. There is also a high degree of agreement between a student's grades and her or his scores on standardized tests. Students with high stanines tend to get high grades and students with low stanines tend to get low grades. Further, the fact that current grades do predict future grades rather well supports the contention that there is considerably more consistency across grading practices than critics allege.

A second serious charge made by opponents of grading is that it is basically an inhumane process with many negative effects. They point out that some parents punish their children for grades that do not meet their expectations and that some teachers use grades as a form of punishment for misbehavior ("If you don't behave I'll give you an F for the day!"). Further, they maintain that the pressures are great and lead to negative consequences such as cutthroat competitive behaviors, cheating, resignation to failure, anxiety, depression, and even suicide. Again, negative consequences do occur. But the misuse of grades by parents and teachers and the undesirable behaviors of students are not problems inherent in grading—they are people problems. Parents who are punitive with respect to grading probably exhibit similar behaviors in other areas; in other words, their attitude with respect to grades is probably symptomatic of their basic personality structure. The solution is not to abolish grades, but to better educate teachers and parents regarding the proper use of grades. As for the pressure which they place on students, it can be argued that a reasonable amount of pressure leads to increased achievement. Anxiety research supports this view. Further, life is full of pressures and students must at some point learn to cope with them in positive ways. And yes, they must also learn to deal with failure. No one succeeds at *everything* she or he attempts. In real life people get fired, get divorced, and so forth. As with misuse of grades, bizarre responses to grading pressures on the part of students are frequently symptomatic of a basic personal-social adjustment problem. Students who exhibit such behaviors need counseling and help in dealing with life in general. As Ebel points out, low grades do not cause low achievement, they report it.[2] Similarly, low grades do not cause adjustment problems, they reflect them. Finally, if a program is properly designed to meet the needs of all students, no one is doomed to failure since students are assigned tasks which they are capable of performing.

There are any number of less serious criticisms of grades. For example, it is frequently claimed that some teachers are too casual about grading, that they do not base them on sufficient, valid data and do not assign them on any rational, justifiable basis. As with the "variability of standards" objection, however, the observed consistency of grades tends to indicate that at least on the average teachers do a pretty good job of grading. Proponents of mastery learning argue that if all students attain mastery, there is no need for grades per se since all students have exhibited the same level of achievement. In one sense this is true since all students do exhibit the same behavior. On the other hand, students definitely differ with respect to the time they take to achieve mastery and the number of attempts they require. Grading can be based on these differences.

[2] See footnote 1.

All in all, it is easier to defend the need for grades than to defend the premise that they should be abolished. They serve a number of purposes and most of the criticisms of grades are really criticisms of unsatisfactory ways in which they are used or dealt with. Like testing, grading is not always a pleasant duty; but it is a necessary one and one that should be done in the most rational, conscientious manner possible.

General principles of grading

By now you should be reasonably convinced that grading is serious business. Even if you do not personally believe in grades, you must accept the fact that other people take them seriously and use them to make a variety of decisions about students. Thus, for their sake you should plan for grading just as conscientiously as you plan for instruction. A student's grade in a course should not be based on subjective impressions concerning achievement or on one hastily developed test given at the end of the term. Grades should be based on a sufficient amount of valid data systematically collected over a period of time. The assertion that grades should not be based on personal feelings, or subjective impressions, needs little explanation. Personal feelings are subject to all sorts of biases (e.g. the halo effect), and although a teacher probably has a fairly accurate general idea of the level at which each student is performing, the importance of grades demands a level of precision only obtainable through the systematic collection of valid data.

When we discussed sampling, it was pointed out that there is no way that one randomly selected student can adequately represent an entire population; the more students are selected, the more representative a sample group is likely to be. Any given test represents a sampling of behavior. Thus, a grade based on a combination of a number of test scores is more likely to accurately reflect a student's achievement level than a grade based on a single test score. Also, recall that a longer test tends to be more reliable because it better represents the domain of all possible items. Similarly a grade based on a number of scores will tend to be more reliable; the combination of the scores on all the tests, in essence, represents the score on a "longer", more inclusive test.

On the other hand, grading should not be overdone. Some teachers become obsessed with grading and grade everything in sight, including classwork sheets, responses to oral questions, and homework. This is not good practice. Students should have numerous nonthreatening opportunities to try new skills or otherwise demonstrate new learnings. Practice and feedback are necessary conditions for most types of learning. There is nothing wrong with grading everything and providing corrective comments for the sake of feedback, but all such grades should not be included in computation of the final course grade. Moreover, students should know *in advance* which grades "count" and which do not, and should be informed concerning how final grades will be determined and on what basis. Requirements should not be made up as the course progresses so that students never know from one moment to the next what is expected of them. This is especially important for older students who may have a number of out-of-class assignments and who must plan how they will allocate their time to the various projects. It is simply not fair to announce one week before the end of the term that you want a biology notebook from everyone. The requirement for such a notebook should be announced at the beginning of the term and detailed instructions should be given concerning its purpose and contents. Further, if weekly tests will constitute one-third of the student's grade, the midterm one-third, and the final one-third, students should know this from day one.

There is general consensus that a final grade may be based on a combination of any number of factors such as written tests and various procedures and products, such as science projects or oral reports. There is some difference of opinion, however, concerning whether grades should be based on actual achievement only or also on such factors as effort and conduct. And if grading is done on the basis of achievement only, should level of achievement be assessed in relation to a student's ability or should it be evaluated in terms of the achievement of other students? These are tough questions. The general consensus, however, is that since the major purpose of grades is to communicate level of achievement, grades should report achievement only. This is not to say that factors such as effort and conduct should not be reported, only that they should not affect the course grade. Many systems use a three-symbol grading system which allows effort and conduct to be reported independently. Thus, an A-2-C might indicate an achievement grade of A, an effort level of 2 (with 1 being maximum) and a conduct level of C. There are many variations on this basic scheme which are utilized in various school systems.

A corollary to the "achievement only" position is that every grade that contributes to the final grade should also be based on achievement only. Thus, if a science project represents a component of the final grade, it should be graded on factors such as knowledge of scientific concepts demonstrated, not on effort. This principle becomes increasingly more important for older students as they get closer and closer to participation in the real world. At the elementary level it can easily be argued that affective objectives such as fostering positive attitudes towards school are just as important as cognitive objectives. At the high school level, however, students are preparing to enter society in one capacity or another, and the real world evaluates actual performance not effort. Effort only counts if it produces desired results. Employers, for example, do not look favorably upon typists who make 10 errors per page, regardless of how hard they *try*. This is not to say that effort does not count. But as pointed out earlier, increased effort usually results in increased achievement scores. Few students get good grades without effort, and those who do should not be penalized for being bright.

If we accept the premise that grades should be based solely on achievement, the next issue is the context within which a certain level of achievement should be evaluated. Should it be compared to previous levels of achievement? Should it be assessed in relation to a student's ability? Should it be compared to the achievement of other students? Of course there is another option, and that is to compare achievement to prespecified standards of performance as in mastery systems. In such systems, however, grading is greatly simplified; it basically involves no more than reporting mastery or nonmastery of various objectives. Grading on the basis of amount of improvement involves the same problems as analyzing gain scores. Students with the lowest initial levels of achievement, for example, are in a position to exhibit the greatest amount of improvement.

Grading in terms of ability is a related but more complex issue. On the one hand, it can be argued that since the major purpose of grading is to communicate achievement, ability (or aptitude) should not be considered. This position is supported by parents who cannot understand why their children failed a competency test or scored poorly on a standardized test when they have been bringing home average or above average grades. On the other hand, it can be argued that failure to take ability into consideration ignores individual differences and literally dooms some students to an endless series of D and F grades; if ability is not a factor, then there is nothing some students can do to ever get a good grade. Both positions are clearly defensible. The position here taken, however, is that like effort, ability should be less and less of a factor as a student moves from elementary school to junior high school to senior high school, and for the same reasons. At the high school level it becomes increasingly more important to communicate achievement objectively. At lower levels, however, giving students a grade higher than they objectively deserve probably does more good than harm. True, the real world involves failure and students must learn to cope with it, but it is also true that it is in the best interest of a democratic society to have citizens with as much education as possible. A student with a history of failure is quite likely to drop out of school as soon as it is legal to do so. Giving such students higher grades than they objectively "deserve" would seem to be preferable since it would give them a reason for staying in school. It could even be argued that it is in everyone's best interest to "pass" such students through all 12 years of school and award them a diploma (or certificate of completion), and then let their grades speak for themselves.

Implicit in the above discussion is the fact that grading is usually done on a relative basis; that is, achievement is labeled as "good" or "poor" in relation to the performance of the total group. The highest performance level is an A and the lowest performance level is an F; if ability is taken into consideration, an F may become a D, and so forth. This raises another issue. Should Ziggy be awarded an A if he is the best student in a remedial English class? Should Instine be awarded an F if he is achieving the least in an honors English class? If you think not, then should all the students in the remedial class get low grades and all the students in the honors class get high grades? Hmmm. While there is clearly no entirely satisfactory answer, the best solution would seem to be to treat each class as a norm group and to award grades accordingly, assuming that permanent records clearly indicate the context within which grades were assigned. In other words, if Ziggy is clearly the best student in his class you can give him an A *if* the record will show that the A was achieved in a remedial class. Of course, reason and good judgment have to be exercised in all grading. If all students in an honors class do outstanding work, there is no justification for awarding low grades based on fine distinctions between levels of achievement. If the lowest grade on the final exam is 88, it is just plain crazy to equate that with a failing grade just because it is the lowest grade.

Thus, grades represent a complex combination of achievement and effort. Achievement is assessed partly in relation to objective standards and partly in relation to the performance of other students. There is no scientific formula for arriving at grades, and they are typically based on both actual scores and common sense. Given the observed consistency of grades discussed previously, however, the process is apparently not as nebulous as one might think.

Methods of grading

The search for the perfect grading system is ongoing. An amazing array of grading systems have been tried over the years. Interestingly, "new" grading systems are rarely new. Pass-fail grading, for example, has come and gone a number of times in the history of education. While users of grades, such as admissions personnel and employers, invariably prefer norm-referenced, relative grading systems, educators hold more diverse views on the subject. Although there are many alternative grading systems, most of them are variations on one of three basic approaches: percent grading, norm-referenced grading, and criterion-referenced grading.

Percent grading

Percent grading involves just what it sounds like it involves; scores are averaged and converted to a percent. The percent itself may be reported as the grade (e.g. History, 84%), or the percent may be translated into a letter grade equivalent (e.g. A = 94–100%). Percent grading is not viewed with much favor mainly because the meaning of such grades is so obscure. In a criterion-referenced system, a given percent may have real meaning (e.g. mastery or nonmastery), but in other contexts it could mean any number of things. A grade of 75%, for example, could mean nothing more than that the student answered 75% of all test items correctly. Such a grade tells us nothing about how much the student learned, either in relation to intended outcomes or in relation to what other students achieved. It is often very difficult to determine whether such grades represent a low level of achievement, average achievement, or high achievement. A grade of 98% is probably good, but what about 75%? It looks OK but it might be the lowest grade in the class. Percent grading is sometimes referred to as absolute grading. The term "absolute," however, is clearly a misnomer; a grade of 98% does not mean that the student knows 98% of the material.

Townsend and Burke have suggested a rational procedure for assigning percent grades when such are a required procedure.[3] It involves equating the lowest acceptable score with the percent that represents a passing grade and adjusting the rest of the scores accordingly. To use their example, suppose 65% represents "passing" in a given school and your scores range from 23 to 42. You might decide that 27 should be the lowest passing score; 27 would then become 65%. The highest score of 42 might be equated with 100% or you might decide that it deserves no more than a 95%. The percentage range would then be 30 (from 65% to 95%), and the raw score range would be 15 (27 to 42). Each raw score point would then be equal to 2 percentage points (30 ÷ 15 = 2). Thus, a score of 28 would equal 65% + 2% = 67%, a score of 29 would equal 67% + 2% = 69%, and so forth. And score below 27 would be converted to a percent in a similar fashion; thus, a score of 26 would equal 65% − 2% = 63%.

Percent grading is not used as much as it once was. The two major systems in competition today are norm-referenced grading and criterion-referenced grading.

Norm-referenced grading

Norm-referenced grading is the traditional favorite. It involves rank ordering students and expressing a given student's achievement in relation to the achievement of the rest of the class; in essence, the class serves as the norm group. You will recall that in norm-referenced measurement an attempt is made to develop items of average difficulty in order to produce maximum variability of scores. The intent is to produce a wide range of scores. In such a system most stu-

---

[3] Townsend, E. A., & Burke, P. J. *Using statistics in classroom instruction.* New York: Macmillan, 1975.

dents receive a grade which indicates average achievement, e.g. a C, a few students fail and a few students receive A's, and so forth. A norm-referenced grade does not communicate what a student has actually achieved but rather how a student's achievement compared to the achievement of others in the class. Sometimes, especially at the elementary level, an achievement grade is accompanied by a ranking on a number of affective variables. Thus, a student might be rated as above average, average, or below average on factors such as initiative, attention, neatness, and so forth. Such ratings are of course subjective, and biases such as the halo effect are possible.

Normal curve grading

As discussed previously, in its extreme form norm-referenced grading is based on an assumption of a normal distribution, and a fixed percentage of students receive each grade. It might be determined, for example, that the top 2–3% of the scores will be equated with an A, the next 15% with a B, the middle 65% with a C, and so forth. A commonly used percentage scheme assigns the top 5% an A, the next 23% a B, the middle 40% a C, the next 23% a D, and the bottom 7% a failing grade (E or F). Thus, if there are 33 scores, the top 2 scores receive an A (7% of 33 = .07 × 33 = 2.31). Clearly, some students must receive failing grades regardless of their actual level of achievement. Such a system essentially ignores the actual distribution and often makes trivial distinctions between the various levels of achievement. If scores range from 80 to 100, for example, giving out D's and F's does not seem to make much sense. As another example, if all but one of the scores are between 70 and 100 and there is one score of 50, it does not seem reasonable to award the score of 50 and the score of 70 the same grade, even if they are the bottom two scores.

A related problem is that the same grade does not necessarily indicate the same level of achievement. Depending upon the composition of the particular class of which a student happens to be a member, the same score may become a B or a C or a D. If the student was in a different class, her or his grade might well be different.

Pass-fail grading

Another form of norm-referenced grading is pass-fail grading. Usually when we think of pass-fail grading we think of criterion-referenced measurement, i.e. everyone who achieves the criterion of acceptable performance passes, and those who do not fail. But pass-fail grading, which is most often used at the college level and occasionally at the high school level, is frequently norm-referenced. Students are typically given an option to take a certain number of courses on a pass-fail basis. Students who choose this option are usually in a class with students who are working for letter grades. If a pass-fail student achieves a level of performance which is no lower than the level which will be awarded a D or C grade (depending upon policy), the student passes. As the graduate level. B-level performance may be required for a "pass."

The basic rationale behind the use of the pass-fail option is that such a system takes some of the pressure off students and allows them to take courses they might ordinarily avoid because of fear of receiving a low grade. While this sounds very reasonable, available evidence indicates that such a system usually results in a reduction of achievement levels. Quite naturally, students are less motivated to do well in such courses and devote most of their energies to those courses in which they will receive a letter grade. In other words, if a student's "pass" is translated into a letter grade, it is usually lower than the student's typical grade.[4] Thus, pass-fail grading does not fulfill any of the purposes of grades— communication, motivation, and prediction. A grade of "pass" communicates nothing except that the student achieved some minimum level of performance. If all students received nothing but pass-fail grades, it would be very difficult for college admissions personnel, for example, to select from among applicants since all applicants would have the same grades. As for motivation, the evidence clearly indicates that pass-fail grading decreases rather than increases motivation. And since a restricted range of scores depresses a correlation coefficient, grades of pass and fail are of little value for predictive purposes.

All in all, pass-fail grading does not have much going for it. While its use may be justifiable on a very limited basis, for electives for example, in general its use should be discouraged.

Standard score grading

A more satisfactory approach to norm-referenced grading involves conversion of scores on each test (or other measure) to standard scores such as z scores or Z scores, averaging the Z scores, and assigning grades based on the average Z score value. Thus, any student with an average Z score of 65 or greater might receive an A, a student with a Z score between 55 and 65 a B, a student with a Z score between 45 and 55 a C, and so forth. The major advantage of Z scores is that we can perform arithmetic operations on them (e.g. averaging). Thus, we can meaningfully combine scores in a way that adjusts appropriately for the fact that the various contributing tests had different degrees of variability.

Another advantage of standard score grading is that it permits us to assign differential weights to scores.[5] Rarely are all tests and assignments in a course of equal importance. If they were, then a student who failed a quiz but got an A on the final exam would get the same grade as a student who got an A on the quiz and failed the final exam. Standard score grading allows us to assign each score a desired weight. We might decide, for example, that the midterm and final should each count twice as much as each of four unit tests. Suppose Hornrim scored Z's of 55, 50, 58, and 52, respectively, on the four unit tests, 60 on the midterm and 58 on the final. We would compute his average Z as follows:

Test 1	$Z = 55 \times 1 = 55$
Test 2	$Z = 50 \times 1 = 50$
Test 3	$Z = 58 \times 1 = 58$
Test 4	$Z = 52 \times 1 = 52$
Midterm	$Z = 60 \times 2 = 120$
Final	$Z = 58 \times \underline{2} = \underline{116}$
	$8 \qquad 451$

---

[4] See, for example, Karlins, M., Kaplan, M., & Stuart, W. Academic attitudes and performance as a function of differential grading systems: An evaluation of Princeton's pass-fail system. *The Journal of Experimental Education*, 1969, 37(3), 38–50.

[5] See footnote 3.

We multiplied the last 2 scores by 2 because they were judged to be worth twice as much as each test score. The average Z would be $451 \div 8 = 56.38$. If B $= 55 - 65$, then Hornrim would receive a B. Of course as Townsend and Burke point out, following strict Z score–letter grade equivalencies (e.g. a Z of 45 to 55 $=$ C) is just as unwise as strictly following normal curve equivalencies.[6] Good judgment has to enter into the grading process. If all the students performed quite well, you might decide that all average Z's of 50 and above $=$ A and all below 50 $=$ B, or A $= 55$ and above, B $= 45$–54, and C $= 44$ and below. The point to keep in mind is that norm-referenced grading simply rank orders the students; it indicates nothing about actual level of achievement. Final grades have to be based on a combination of scores and good judgment.

In some cases, weighting is built into the scores. If quizzes, for example, are worth 10 points, tests 25 points, and the final 50 points, for a total of 200 points, then summing the raw scores will result in a value in which each score is proportionally represented. A low score on a quiz will affect such a total very little whereas a high score on the final will affect the total a great deal.

Criterion-referenced grading

Criterion-referenced grading is currently the major challenger to the supremacy of norm-referenced grading. Criterion-referenced grading involves expressing a student's achievement in relation to prespecified criteria rather than in relation to the achievement of others in the class. The standards are absolute, not relative, and all students who achieve the same standards achieve the same grade. No student is failed simply because he or she achieved lower than other students provided the student achieves the criterion. Grading is considerably simplified in the ideal criterion-referenced system. Students who reach criterion on every required task "pass," or receive "credit," and those who do not "fail," or receive "no credit." Unlike a norm-referenced grade, a criterion-referenced grade provides very specific information concerning what the student has actually achieved, what he or she knows and can do.

Also, in the ideal criterion-referenced system very few students do not pass. Criterion-referenced tests make it very easy for the teacher to identify problem areas and to act accordingly. Thus, deficiencies are quickly corrected and students do not get farther and farther behind. Students are allowed to progress at their own individual rates and are also usually given multiple opportunities to achieve criterion. Thus, at the end of a given period of time most students have reached criterion on all required objectives. Of course criterion-referenced pass-fail grading is subject to the same problems associated with norm-referenced pass-fail grading. Students tend to do just enough to reach criterion and to pass; there is little motivation to do more.

In some cases, especially at the elementary level, grades of pass or fail are not awarded, but rather achievement of each objective is reported on a percent basis. For mastery objectives, a student's report card will list various objectives, give a percentage score for each, and indicate whether the score is high enough for mastery. For example:

[6] See footnote 3.

Instine Eyeque

Objective	Percent Correct	Mastery Level	Mastery
1. Can reduce proper fractions to lowest terms	90%	80%	Yes
2. Can reduce improper fractions to lowest terms	75%	80%	No

A report listing objectives communicates to parents areas in which students are achieving, areas in which they are having minor difficulties (as in objective 2 above), and areas in which they are having major difficulties. Such reports make it easy for concerned parents to help their children at home with problem areas. A similar report card is used for nonmastery objectives. For nonmastery objectives, however, we may also wish to provide some measure of relative position. Such an index may be simply a rank based on score level, where the top score equals a rank of 1. For example:

Ziggie Zealot

Objective	Percent Correct	Acceptable Performance	Rank (1 to 25)
1. Can multiply two proper fractions	70%	80%	19
2. Can multiply two improper fractions	60%	75%	23

Another way in which an index of relative position can be presented is to state the number of objectives achieved by the student and his or her corresponding class rank; the student achieving the most objectives is assigned a rank of 1. Of course if rank (or some other index) is to be reported, its meaning must be carefully explained somewhere on the report card.[7]

For both mastery objectives and nonmastery objectives, the most difficult task is setting the criterion for mastery or acceptable performance. It is difficult to defend such standards to parents, even if they have been set by curriculum experts in a curriculum guide, because they are based primarily on judgment. If parents question the fairness of the standards, the best approach is to show them the test papers so that they can see exactly what their children missed. They should be able to see that any student who has "mastered" a concept or skill should be able to respond correctly to items which their children missed. Standards can also be defended by showing them the distribution of scores. The teacher can point out that the majority of students scored at the level of acceptable performance. Such information lends credibility to the validity of the standards.

---

[7] For further discussion and examples of this type of grading, see Gronlund, N. E. *Preparing criterion-referenced tests for classroom instruction.* New York: Macmillan, 1973.

Norm-referenced versus criterion-referenced grading

Which grading system is "best" is largely a matter of personal or institutional philosophy since each system serves different functions. Also, each system has its own advantages and disadvantages. One way to approach a comparison is to consider the basic purposes of grades. The major purpose of grades is the communication of level of achievement. Both norm-referenced and criterion-referenced systems communicate achievement but in different ways. Norm-referenced grades report the achievement of an individual in relation to the achievement of the group. Criterion-referenced grades report achievement in relation to fixed standards; that is , they report what a student knows and can do. As with several other issues discussed previously, the position taken here is that it is less important to report relative achievement at the elementary level and becomes progressively more important at the junior and senior high school levels. Also, it would seem to be more important to continually identify specific deficiencies and to remedy them at the elementary level since learnings at this level form the foundation for all subsequent learnings. Further, content at the elementary level tends to be more hierarchial in that current learning is very much dependent on previous learning. At the high school level this is not the case. Successful achievement in geometry, for example, is not dependent on successful achievement in algebra. Also, at the high school level it is necessary to provide indices of relative position since students will soon be in competition with respect to admission to institutions of higher education and employment.[8] Thus, if we view each system in its "ideal" form, norm-referenced grading would seem to be preferable in terms of the communication function at the junior and senior high levels and criterion-referenced grading at the elementary level.

With respect to the second purpose of grades, student motivation, the evidence indicates that criterion-referenced grading results in decreased motivation, at least at the higher grade levels. Logically, the problem would increase at the higher grade levels because pressures associated with grades tend to increase as students get progressively closer to graduation. It can be argued that if all grading were pass-fail, there would be no need for students to devote most of their energy to the traditionally graded courses at the expense of the pass-fail courses. It can also be argued, however, that if all courses were pass-fail, student motivation (and subsequent achievement) would decrease across the board. In any event, the evidence does support the position that criterion-referenced grading may be more appropriate at the elementary level.

With respect to the third purpose of grading, prediction of future achievement, norm-referenced grading clearly has the edge. As pointed out previously, a restricted range of scores (i.e. pass or fail, 1 or 0) results in a depressed correlation coefficient which is not very useful for prediction purposes. The results of criterion-referenced measurement *can* be used for prediction if a variable other than achievement is used. We might, for example, use number of attempts required to reach criterion, or time required to reach criterion, as a predictor. Such indices, however, are more norm-referenced than criterion-referenced.

---

[8] Although against the purist philosophy of criterion-referenced measurement, we have seen that it is possible to assign norm-referenced interpretations to criterion-referenced results. There are also ways to assign traditional letter grades to such scores. These will be discussed shortly.

No grading system can serve all purposes of grading equally well. With the except of communication of objectives achieved, however, norm-referenced grading seems to do the best job, at least at higher grade levels. Further, while pass-fail criterion-referenced grading can be defended on philosophical grounds, in practice most institutions which have tried such systems have eventually reverted to some type of norm-referenced system, mainly for practical reasons.

Types and precision of grading symbols

The most commonly used alphabetical norm-referenced symbols are the letter grades A, B, C, D, and E (or F) and P and F (for pass and fail). The most commonly used numerical symbols are percents (e.g. 80%, 90%, 100%). There are many other symbols which are used in various schools, such as E, G, S, U and V (*excellent, good, satisfactory, unsatisfactory, and very unsatisfactory*) and 5, 4, 3, 2 and 1 (5 being the highest grade). Using alternatives to traditional symbols, however, is not good practice. Most people have a pretty good idea what A, B, C, D and E mean, for example, and using symbols like E, G, S, U and V only confuses those to whom the grades are communicated. Alternative symbol systems are usually defended on the basis that they are less obvious and less threatening to students. Kids, however, are a lot smarter than we sometimes give them credit for being. They know that a U is really a D just like they know that the "bluebirds" read better than the "robins"!

Criterion-referenced grading systems typically use P and F or CR and NCR (credit and no credit) although some systems also include an HP (high pass or honors pass) or an HCR (high credit or honors credit). In some situations, instructors are required to assign letter grades (i.e. A, B, C, D and E) even though measurement has been criterion-referenced. Theoretically, such grading is counter to the basic philosophy of criterion-referenced measurement. In reality, however, there are a number of ways to do it. Some of the approaches to assigning letter grades to criterion-referenced results require norm-referenced interpretations, but it is possible to assign letter grades using strictly criterion-referenced standards. One approach is to assign grades based on the number of attempts required to reach criterion. If a student reaches criterion on a test the first time it is taken, for example, the grade is A; if two attempts are necessary, the grade is B; and so forth. Another approach is to base grades on the number of objectives achieved during a given period of time. This can be done on a norm-referenced basis (e.g. the students who achieve the most objectives get A's) or on a criterion-referenced basis (e.g. any student who achieves 40 objectives gets an A, any student who achieves 30 objectives get a B, and so forth). If aptitude is taken into consideration, the number and nature of the objectives required for a given grade may be agreed upon in advance, on an individual basis, by the teacher and each student. This practice is referred to as performance contracting.

There is another approach which can be used which combines the advantages of criterion-referenced and norm-referenced measurement. Each test or task is worth a certain number of points which combine for a certain total, say 150. Predetermined standards are set for each letter grade. For a total of 150 points, for example, a grade of A might require at least 140 points, B might require 130 points, and so forth. Required point values for each letter grade are determined based on acceptable performance for each test. Thus, on a 20-item test, a score of 18 might represent acceptable performance. If a student scores at the acceptable level on each test, her or his total score will equal the number of points required for a C (or B at the graduate level). Thus, a grade of C communicates that the student averaged acceptable performance, achieved most of the objectives. The student may have scored higher or lower than the acceptable level on the various tests, but *on the average* performance was acceptable. A grade of A communicates higher performance than the minimally acceptable level on most if not all tests. And so forth. Theoretically, using such a system we might have a class of students all of whom achieved a grade of A, for example. In reality, however, students' grades tend to be spread out so that while most students achieve a grade of C, some students get A's, some get B's, and a few get D's. Due to the nature of a criterion-referenced system, we expect fewer low grades than in a norm-referenced system, and this is usually the case.

A number of educators believe that when grades are used it is better to have a smaller number of categories, such as honors, pass, and fail rather than A, B, C, D, E or A+, A, A−, B+, and so on. Their position is that it is difficult to make finer distinctions between levels of achievement in a reliable manner. This is not the case. It has been demonstrated mathematically that the fewer the number of categories, the less reliable grades tend to be. It may be easier to use fewer categories (the decisions are not as tough), but such a practice cannot be defended in the name of reliability.[9] In general, five categories seem to represent a reasonable compromise between the desire for reliability and practicality. Schools that have tried grading systems with more or fewer categories have usually eventually reverted to a five-point grading scale. Credit−no credit grading systems, for example, become honors credit−credit−no credit grading systems, which in turn become A−B−C−D−no credit systems, and finally A−B−C−D−E systems.

An interesting problem has arisen in recent years. Traditionally, a grade of C has denoted average, or satisfactory, performance. Students' grades, however, have been progressively "improving" to the point where the average grade in many places has become B. Unfortunately, these higher grades do not reflect higher achievement. The trend is probably a result of increased students' rights (as evidenced by grievance and appeals procedures) and the current practice of having students rate instructors. While student rating of instructors was once a practice confined mainly to institutions of higher learning, it has been increasingly adopted by public school systems. Giving students inflated grades only serves to defeat the major purpose of grades—to communicate level of achievement. In some instances the opposite problem occurs; an instructor makes it almost impossible to get a good grade. The *nobody*-in-my-class-gets-an-A-approach, however, is just as pointless as the *everybody*-in-my-class-gets-an-A-approach.

Alternatives to grading

Grades are sometimes supplemented with or supplanted by checklists, rankings, and reports of objectives achieved. There are a number of additional approaches which have been proposed as more acceptable alternatives to symbols. Some edu-

[9] Ebel, R. L. *Essentials of educational measurement.* Englewood Cliffs, N.J.: Prentice-Hall, 1979.

cators believe that there is a great deal of information which should be communicated concerning a child and that symbols are simply inadequate vehicles. The two most frequently suggested substitutes are letters, or written reports, and parent-teacher conferences. The intended content of both is essentially the same and they are both subject to the same problems. Ideally, they both are used to communicate detailed information concerning achievement, in both a norm-referenced and criterion-referenced context, and for discussion of the character and personality traits of the student. They are very time-consuming procedures, however, and they are rarely actualized as intended. Written reports tend to be short and vague, and actually less informative than a grade. Parent-teacher conferences, which are often held during school hours, are very difficult to schedule and take away from instructional time.

Most criticisms which can be directed at grading symbols can be more convincingly applied to the alternatives. The content of written reports and conferences is apt to be less standard from teacher to teacher and location to location than symbols, and they are certainly no less threatening. Also, they are highly impractical from the standpoint of record keeping. A cumulative folder full of letters or summaries of parent-teacher conferences (if such even exist) are much more difficult to review and summarize than records of grades. While a parent-teacher conference should always be arranged if requested by a parent, letters and conferences are probably best used to report special problems of individual students and the results of standardized testing. If a student's achievement suddenly starts dropping for no apparent reason, for example, or inappropriate behavior increases, a letter or conference is in order. As systematic, periodic reporting procedures, however, they are too time-consuming to be practical substitutes for grades.

Promotion

A student's grades represent the major input for decisions concerning promotion. Should a student who has not achieved to a satisfactory degree (has failing grades or has not achieved minimum objectives) be promoted to the next grade anyway? This is obviously a philosophical question with no single right answer. One can argue that social promotions are harmful to the student in that he or she enters the next grade inadequately prepared for the work and consequently gets farther and farther behind and experiences unnecessary frustration. Also, a policy of social promotion means that a number of students who are functionally illiterate are awarded meaningless diplomas. On the other hand, one can argue that holding students back often results in serious emotional damage (e.g. lowered self-concept) and causes students great embarassment. Further, holding students back seems to do little good since they do not achieve significantly better the second time around. Both positions on the issue have validity.

Probably the best solution to the promotion dilemma is to make promotion decisions on an individual basis, rather than to uniformly promote or not promote all questionable students. The best policy is to require that all such decisions be made jointly by a number of persons (e.g. the student's teacher, counselor, and parents) based on a number of agreed-upon variables such as grades, standardized test scores, and behavior patterns. In most cases, however, it is probably better to promote than not to promote. It is easier to remedy achievement deficiencies than to erase emotional scars. Each grade, especially at the elementary level, should have systematic remedial procedures built into the curriculum. Skill deficiencies should be corrected as soon as they are identified.

Reporting procedures

All data collected and analyzed concerning the performance of students, including the results of locally-developed and standardized tests, are reported to parents. The results of data collection, from whatever sources, must also be reported to funding sources. The results of standardized tests, however, are reported to a number of audiences, including: school boards, school administrators, teachers, students, parents, community members and the media. The accountability movement has resulted in increased pressure on school systems to release detailed information concerning the achievement of students, especially in the basic skills areas. The community wants to know how students are presently performing and how current achievement compares to previous achievement. It is the superintendent, with the assistance of a variety of staff members, who has ultimate responsibility for analyzing, organizing, and disseminating results to the various audiences. Generally, the superintendent's staff reports results to the various school administrators who in turn report to both teachers and community members, usually on a face-to-face basis. Also, the superintendent, or a designated spokesperson generally reports directly to representatives of the media.

The foremost principle of reporting is that results must be communicated in a form and manner which are understandable to the intended group. Technical and statistical terms should be avoided or carefully defined, and extensive use should be made of graphs and charts. Results for subtests of achievement batteries and scholastic aptitude tests should all be presented using the same, easy-to-understand type of derived score so that comparisons across year and across subject area, and comparisons of achievement and aptitude can easily be made. Stanines are especially well suited for this purpose. A second, related principle is that recipients of results should be given instruction and guidance on the proper use of results. Principals should know that the results of standardized testing should not form the basis for teacher evaluation. Teachers should know that class grades should not be influenced by standardized test results (e.g. IQ scores). Parents and other community members should know that standardized achievement test results should not be the only factor considered in determining whether one school is more effective than another, and so forth. Thus, anyone involved with or concerned about test results should be informed of both appropriate and inappropriate uses of results.

Another general principle of reporting, mentioned earlier, is that results for individual students should be kept confidential and reported only to students, their parents, and appropriate school personnel. Reports of results to community groups and representatives of the media should always be given in terms of groups. Usually only achievement and aptitude results are released. Occasionally other results may be reported. If students in a given system exhibit exceptionally low self-concepts, for example, this fact may be released and discussed since self-concept is a variable related to achievement.

Finally, we must always keep in mind that the various concerned groups have a right to know the results of testing. It is not our place to decide, for example, what information a parent can handle. It is our responsibility to report the results and to help recipients to understand what they mean.

Reporting within the school system

Results are reported to school board members, administrators, counselors, curriculum specialists, teachers and students. Each group has different responsibilities and uses the data in different ways. The results must be communicated to each group in the manner which best meets their individual needs.[10]

The school board

One of the major responsibilities of a school board is to allocate funds within the school system. Typically, the superintendent annually submits a proposed budget to the board. Hearings are held and individual budget items are discussed. Any funds not allocated in the approved budget are placed into a contingency fund. At various points in time, the board requires accountings, to verify that funds are being spent as intended and evidence that funds are being used effectively. Standardized test results provide a major source of data for the latter. The results help the board to assess the current effectiveness of various components of the system and to make informed decisions concerning future allocations and operating policies.

School board members are typically respected members of the community but are not necessarily familiar with testing jargon and statistical terms. Thus, results must be presented in the simplest manner possible which conveys the required information. Stanine charts or percentile band graphs, accompanied by appropriate interpretive information, are usually sufficient. Since a number of different comparisons are usually desired, results may be presented in various ways—for the system as a whole by grade level, for each school by grade level, and so forth. Results for the previous year are also generally discussed, especially in larger systems where local norms have been developed. In addition to achievement and aptitude test results, information concerning other variables thought to be related to achievement are generally reported, such as attendance rates and the appropriateness of the national norm group. Finally, any actions which have already been taken based on the results are reported and recommendations are made concerning actions to be taken by the board.

Administrators

Test information typically flows from the top down. In other words, the superintendent's staff (generally) reports to administrators, who in turn report to school staff members, who in turn report to students. Thus, it is important that administrators be given enough information and explanation to give them a

[10] Many of the concepts presented here are discussed in greater detail in manuals furnished by major standardized test publishers. See, for example, Prescott, G. A. *Metropolitan Achievement Tests: Manual for Interpreting.* New York: Harcourt Brace Jovanovich, 1972.

reasonably complete understanding of the results and what they mean. In many cases, meetings or workshops for administrators are held prior to testing in order to explain the nature and purposes of the tests to be given, uses to be made of the results, and procedures for administering the tests. As soon as possible following testing, meetings or workshops are held in order to report and interpret the results. The majority of participants are typically school principals, who quite naturally are most interested in how the results for their schools, by grade and by class, compare with the results for the total system. Curriculum specialists will be concerned mainly with scores for their area, e.g. reading, in the various schools, by grade. Thus, subtest results should be available for the total system by grade, for each school by grade, and for individual classes within schools. Depending upon the comparisons to be made, stanine charts, percentile band graphs, or even quartile graphs may be the most appropriate presentation mode.

Of course when scores are summarized, descriptive statistics are involved. Usually the median is used to depict the typical score; for example, the median percentile rank for second graders in the system on each of the subtests might be given. If an index of variability is desired, Q_1 and Q_3 (the 25th and 75th percentiles) are usually presented. While such summary statistics are usually disseminated and discussed in detail in a lengthy report, they should also be presented graphically for ease of interpretation. Such graphs should be handed out to each participant for information and discussion purposes. Finally, it must be reemphasized that achievement results should be discussed and interpreted in relation to other characteristics of the students involved. Whether a given level of achievement is viewed as acceptable, gratifying, or disappointing is very much dependent on the status of students with respect to factors such as scholastic aptitude and socio-economic status.

Teachers

Like administrators, teachers frequently participate in meetings or workshops prior to and following testing, and for similar reasons. As soon as possible following their meetings, principals schedule meetings in their individual schools. The content and procedures of these meetings are very similar to those held for administrators. In addition, there should be extensive discussion of appropriate and inappropriate uses of the results. For the benefit of those teachers who have not had evaluation training, individual and class profile sheets should be explained, as well as the various types of information which can be extracted from them. Concepts such as the relationship between achievement and factors such as scholastic aptitude should be carefully explained. If available, item analysis data should also be presented and explained. Such discussions are critical; teachers cannot make use of the results if they do not know how to, and if they are going to use them, every effort should be made to insure that they do so in ways that are appropriate.

Teachers will be very interested in seeing how their classes compared with other classes in the same school and within the system. *The Metropolitan Achievement Tests: Manual for Interpreting* suggests that teachers receive a summary profile sheet which depicts the 25th, 50th and 75th percentiles (in terms of national percentile ranks) for the total system and for the school. Each teacher can then plot the results for his or her classroom on the same profile sheet, thus permitting all comparisons of interest. Since such a graph can get rather crowded, it is also suggested that the points for the system, school and class each be connected using a different color. Since such a chart may be somewhat confusing at first, it may be helpful to first distribute a similar graph showing only median points (50th percentile), and to let teachers plot the medians for their classes. The more complicated graph will then be easier to understand. Again, teachers should be made aware of legitimate reasons why their classes may have achieved at lower levels than other classes of the same type.

Students

How technical and detailed reports to students are depends mainly on the age of the students. The discussion early in the chapter (under Guidance) concerning the interpretation of results to students was concerned mainly with older students. High school students are especially interested in knowing the purpose of the test, how they did in relation to other students, and what implications their scores have for their goals. Group results are of no concern to students; providing them with their individual profiles is sufficient. While discussion of the test itself and how to interpret profiles may be done on a group basis in the classroom, individual conferences should be held with each student if at all possible. Such conferences are generally the responsibility of the guidance staff.

Reporting to younger students is a more simplified process. They probably do not even need to be told about the concept of a norm group; the idea of an external comparison group may be too abstract for young children. Thus, results concerning the performance of the class and individuals can be reported in more general terms. The teacher generally reviews the purpose and nature of the test, and makes broad statements about the strengths and weaknesses of the class, always in positive terms. For example:

Well, all in all, you did quite well, especially in arithmetic. We need to spend a little more time in reading so you will be just as good in reading as you are in arithmetic. I'm very proud of all of you.

While individual results are not usually presented to students, they may be in certain situations. A teacher may have a talk with a student who scored in stanine 9 on all subtests, for example, to see if she or he would be interested in pursuing more advanced work. Or, if a good student did surprisingly poorly on the test, the teacher may try to determine possible causes such as illness on the day of testing or a crisis at home. The important principle is that the results should never be presented in a threatening or punitive manner. They should be viewed by students as a means of showing what they know and of finding out what they need to work on.

Reporting to the community

The push for accountability and the great number of media reports covering the level of achievement of the American student have created a community which is very much interested in the results of standardized testing. Further, community

members are not satisfied with verbal generalities concerning the performance of
the system, they want to see the data and to draw their own conclusions. Thus
more and more systems have become involved in developing systematic presentations, complete with visual aids and handouts, to insure that results are presented
accurately and accompanied by appropriate interpretations. Results are reported
to groups, either in person (e.g. at PTA meetings) or through the media, and to
individual parents via the mail or at parent-teacher conferences.

Communication with the public should not be a once-a-year event, occurring after spring testing. The community should be constantly kept informed,
through the media and memoranda for example, concerning activities of the
schools. Testing time should not come as a surprise to them. They should know in
advance when testing will take place, what will be measured and why, and how
results will be reported and used, and by whom. Results should then be reported
as soon as possible following testing. Announcements should be made through
the local media, and notices should be sent to each parent as to when public meetings will be held to discuss results. Any reputable community group which requests a presentation should be obliged.

As with the school board, community members are not generally familiar
with testing jargon and statistical terms. Results must be presented in the simplest
manner possible which accurately conveys the information of interest. Stanine
charts or percentile band graphs, accompanied by appropriate interpretive information, are usually sufficient. Presentations should involve considerable visual
material such as handouts, slides, and transparencies, and data should be provided in summary form.

While it is important to speak in terms which can be readily understood, it
is equally important to avoid being condescending or seeming to be condescending. Parents are not dumb, they are just not familiar with some terminology. Any
concept can be explained in plain English without resorting to two-letter words.
Below are some examples of folksy definitions which convey the meaning of the
terms in nontechnical language:

> Median: Average score; typical score.
> Stanines: All the scores are placed in order from highest to lowest
>   and then divided into nine categories called stanines; the
>   lowest scores are in stanine 1 and the highest scores are in
>   stanine 9. Stanines 1, 2, and 3 represent below average
>   achievement, stanines 4, 5 and 6 represent average
>   achievement, and stanines 7, 8 and 9 represent above av-
>   erage achievement.
> Percentiles: A percentile rank tells you how many students had lower
>   scores. Percentile ranks range from 1 to 99 and a percentile
>   rank of 50 indicates average achievement—half of the stu-
>   dents had higher scores and half had lower scores.

It should be explained that the reason we change raw scores into other forms such
as stanines is so that we can compare performance on different tests. It should also
be explained that which stanine a given score corresponds to depends upon how
well other students in the system (for local norms) or country performed. It should
also be pointed out that the use of score equivalents such as stanines allow us to
see how achievement has changed from testing to testing, for example, whether
we have made any improvements in previous areas of weakness. And, as always,

the relationship between scholastic aptitude scores and achievement scores should be made clear. They should understand, for example, that it is unreasonable to expect a school with a median IQ stanine of 3 to have above average achievement stanines.

If reporting is done well, community members will come to view themselves as allies of the school system, not opponents. They will be aware of which problems are mostly beyond the system's control (e.g. high absenteeism) and which are not, and of efforts the system is making to deal with its problems, both academic and nonacademic. Thus it is critical that school personnel be well informed, so that they can converse intelligently with community members, and that presentations be carefully planned and organized.

Local groups

In a group setting results are generally presented for the school system as a whole and for individual schools within the system. Reports may be made at some type of regular community meeting, such as a town meeting, or at special meetings held in the individual schools. At the school level, the principal generally assumes responsibility for presenting the results. By the time such meetings are held, parents have generally received some type of written report on their children's scores and are at least familiar with what areas were tested. They can relate discussion of how the school's performance compared to the system's to how their children's performance compares to the average for the school.

A number of suggestions for making presentations to local groups are offered by Badal and Larsen in their discussion of the Oakland Public Schools guidelines.[11] The Oakland model, entitled *Tentative Guidelines for Interpretation of Test Scores*, outlines test interpretation procedures, and involves a one-hour presentation utilizing a number of transparencies. They were developed specifically for principals and suggest specific steps to be followed and ways of explaining important concepts in simple terms. Part 1 of the guidelines involves a description of the testing program itself and uses of the results. Part 2 concerns understanding test scores, including key questions involved in interpreting test results (what skills were measured, with whom are students being compared [norms], and what type of score equivalents are being used [e.g. stanines]), the answers to those questions, and a discussion of summary statistics (e.g. the median and quartiles). Part III, "Suggested Data for Presentation," discusses various data comparisons that are made—national, state, district, and school performance, year to year changes, grade by grade comparisons, achievement versus scholastic aptitude, and subject by subject comparisons—and possible reasons for varying levels of achievement of the compared groups.

Presentations should be followed by a discussion of factors believed to be having an adverse effect on achievement, actions that are being taken in an attempt to deal with these factors, and ways in which the community can help. Negative factors cited might include student-related problems such as an excessively high absenteeism rate or an identified drug problem, or budget-related problems such as overcrowding or the low morale among underpaid teachers. Responsive

[11] Badal, A. W., & Larsen, E. P. On reporting test results to community groups. *NCME: Measurement in Education*, 1970, *1*(4), 1–12.

and appropriate action by the schools might include a peer counseling program or a required course in drug education. Suggestions for community assistance may involve a request related to the provision of additional funds, but not necessarily. Parents and others, for example, may be encouraged to serve as volunteer teachers' aides so that poor readers can be given more opportunities to read aloud. Requests such as this serve to make the parents realize that the schools are not interested in more money per se but rather in the growth and achievement of their children.

Finally, sufficient time should be allowed for members of the audience to ask questions. Most questions can be, and should be, anticipated in advance so that presenters will be prepared with knowledgeable responses. Some typical questions are listed below. By now *you* should be able to answer most, if not all, of them. See if you can:

> Don't tests do more harm than good?
> Do students from better neighborhoods do better?
> Aren't tests biased against disadvantaged students?
> Why do the scores have to go into students' cumulative folders? Won't this information bias future teachers?
> Why are the scores so much better in arithmetic than in language arts?

At the conclusion of the session, interested persons should be informed of ways in which they can acquire additional information or discuss results further. Information on how to obtain a complete report of results may be provided, for example, and parents given the details on how to arrange a parent-teacher conference.

Parents

Most parents, in their role *as parents* (as opposed to their role as taxpayers) are genuinely interested in their children's achievement and ways in which they can help. Their prime concern is how well their children are doing compared to other children. This concern, however, leads to a desire to know specific skill deficiency areas and to receive suggestions as to how they can work with their children at home. While a report of scores accompanied by a brief explanation may be mailed to parents, such information is certainly insufficient for a meaningful understanding. Despite the problems associated with their use, parent-teacher conferences represent the best approach to the discussion of individual results. While communications may take place during some type of open house, individual conferences specifically scheduled for the purpose of discussing an individual student's achievement are definitely more appropriate; the teacher can insure that communications are totally private and that each parent is allotted sufficient time.

Conferences should not be totally extemporaneous happenings. The teacher should prepare for them by collecting and organizing all pertinent information about each student, and by reviewing it prior to the conferences. The teacher should be prepared to discuss not just test results but also class performance with respect to variables such as achievement, class participation and behavior. Perhaps the most important factor in the success of a conference is the teacher's demeanor. A parent who perceives the teacher as being a warm, caring person will be much more receptive to a frank discussion of the student's capabilities and potential. The key is for the teacher to be both diplomatic and realistic, and to tell the parents whatever they want to know in a positive but truthful manner.

Following the usual exchange of pleasantries, a good way to start the conference proper is with a description of past and present class activities. The teacher should share specific objectives, if available, and discuss how the student has been achieving in relation to those objectives and in relation to other students in the class. If the conference follows standardized testing, testing is the logical next item for discussion. The components of such a discussion will be very similar to those included in group presentations, but the emphasis will be on the performance of the individual student. The purpose and nature of the test should be explained, as well as the ways in which results are used (e.g. for grouping). Thus, the student's profile sheet should be interpreted, beginning with the definition and purpose of score equivalents and the concept of a norm group. The derived score that was used on the profile is the only derived score which needs to be explained, say stanines or percentiles. If stanines were used, broad interpretative statements are appropriate to the effect that stanines 1–3 are labeled "below average," 4–6 "average," and 7–9 "above average." If percentiles were used, band interpretations should be explained. If a profile contains more than one type of derived score and one of them is grade equivalents, ignore them if possible; they are subject to too many sources of misinterpretation. If a parent insists on knowing what they mean, they can be briefly explained and the relative advantages of other derived scores pointed out. As always, the simpler the terms used the better. There is really no reason to use the term "norm group," for example. A statement to the effect that "Egor's scores were compared to the scores of . . ." is sufficient.

As much as possible, numerical data should be translated into verbal statements. As the teacher and the parent examine the profile together, statements such as the following are appropriate:

> As you can see, Egor is very close to average in all areas except those involving arithmetic.
> Instine is very interested in science and, as you can see, he did well on both the math and science tests. We do, however, need to try to get him to read more.
> Well, as his scores indicate, Ziggy is not very schoolwork oriented. His aptitude scores, however, suggest that he would be successful in a vocational program, perhaps auto mechanics.

As the above example illustrates, areas of weakness can usually be discussed within a positive context. A teacher can take this strategy one step further in some cases by indicating that a number of students share the same weaknesses. For example:

> Difficulty with arithmetic computation is not uncommon.
> I'm going to place all the students who scored poorly in this area together for an hour a day and have them. . . .

Thus, the teacher can indicate what steps are being taken to remedy a deficiency. At this point a discussion of ways in which the parent can help is appropriate.

After achievement data have been presented, they should be related to other performances and characteristics of the student. If a student is performing at a lower level than would be expected based on IQ scores, for example, possible reasons should be explored. If a student is working at or above expectations, this fact should be strongly applauded. If a parent appears to have unrealistic goals for the student, it is the teacher's responsibility (with the assistance of the counselor if necessary) to convey this fact, for the sake of the student, in the most diplomatic manner possible. For example:

> I understand that Ziggy comes from a long line of doctors. His abilities, however, seem to be in other areas. He's very interested in cars and Mr. Piston, his auto mechanics teacher, tells me he has the makings of a top-notch mechanic. Goodness knows we need more of them:

Above all, a teacher should make every effort to find something nice to say; for example, Ziggy is so (1) polite, (2) well behaved, (3) well liked, (4) cooperative, (5) neat (pick one!). Any teacher who can't find anything positive to say about a student isn't looking hard enough.

While conferences can be very productive, they do have their drawbacks. One problem inherent in conferences is that they take so much time. If scheduled during the day, they take away from instructional time. If scheduled at night they may consume as much as a week's worth of the teacher's "free" time. Thus it is not practical to schedule them frequently on a regular basis, such as at the end of each grading period. More than likely, they are held once (or maybe twice) a year following spring testing (and sometimes at the beginning of the school year). While such annual conferences do serve the purpose of informing parents of their children's progress, they are not too useful for working with parents to improve student achievement or behavior. Other problems related to conferences are people problems, not inherent characteristics of conferences. In too many cases, teachers do not prepare adequately; they do not have all the information of interest to parents readily available and often give the impression that they really do not know the students very well. Also, as with interviews, parents do not always show up for scheduled conferences. Despite their shortcomings, however, conferences probably represent the most effective method of communication between the school and parents.

The media

It has become increasingly common for the local media, (newspapers, radio stations, and television stations) to report on the results of standardized testing. If left to their own devices, media people are likely to make reports which contain inaccuracies or misinterpretations. Therefore, it is in the school system's best interest to hold press conferences to present and discuss the data and to answer questions. As with the community, communication should be in the simplest terms possible and should be an ongoing activity, not a once-a-year event. A presentation to media representatives should be planned just as carefully as a presentation to a community group. Further, since newspapers will want to publish graphs, charts and/or tabular presentations of results by school, the wise superintendent will see to it that such visuals are prepared in advance and distributed at the press conference.

Errors in reporting are rarely intentional. They result when data are solicited from unofficial sources and when news people who know little about the subject of standardized testing try to write and report on it. If they are given sufficient time to get all the information they want and to ask all of their questions, not only will their reports be more accurate but also they will probably project a more positive attitude toward the school system. Good public relations can only help. Instead of being viewed as a threat or an adversary, the media should be considered potential vehicles for generating support among community members, especially those who will never attend a presentation or conference.

Funding sources: the evaluation report

Funding sources—local, state, national and private—invariably require a formal, written evaluation report at the end of each funding period, in addition to a number of informal, periodic progress reports. Such formal reports are typically audited, and evaluation staff members are required to explain and document various entries in the report. Since initial funding is almost always based on the submission of an evaluation plan, or proposal, writing the final report basically involves revising and refining the original document and adding the results and conclusions. The evaluation may not be executed exactly as planned, but the procedures should not diverge drastically from the original plan. While the evaluation plan may have been written in the future tense ("Participants *will be* randomly selected . . ."), the evaluation report will of course be in the past tense ("Participants *were* randomly selected . . ."). The funding source generally spells out in detail format and style requirements for the report and these must be conscientiously followed. There are also several general rules of good report writing which the report writer should be aware of and follow.

Probably the foremost rule of report writing is that the writer should be as objective as possible in reporting the evaluation. The report should not contain subjective statements ("*Clearly* the presently used curriculum is no good"), overstatements ("Wow, what fantastic results!"), or emotional statements ("We owe it to our long-deprived children to implement the Warm Fuzzy Curriculum"). Further, the report should not be written as if it were a legal brief intended to present arguments in favor of a position ("The purpose of this evaluation was to prove . . ."). The report should contain an objective, factual description of the entire evaluation. Consistent with the goal of objective reporting, personal pronouns such as "I," "my," "we," and "our" should be avoided. Instead, impersonal pronouns and the passive voice should be used. Phrases such as "subjects *were* randomly selected" should be used instead of "*we* randomly selected subjects."

The report should be written in a clear, simple, straightforward style but you do not have to be boring, just concise. In other words, say what you have to say in the fewest number of words and using the simplest language. The report should also reflect scholarship; correct spelling, grammatical construction, and punctuation are not too much to ask. And don't excuse yourself by saying that you are the world's worst speller; everyone has access to a dictionary, and a host of other reference books for that matter. The same standards of scholarship apply to the typing of the report as to the writing of the report. When you read a report full of typos, you cannot help but wonder if the evaluation was conducted in the same careless manner as the report was proofread. The final typed report should be carefully proofread at least twice, once for typographical errors and once for errors in content. The format and style requirements for the report, as spelled out by the funding source, should be carefully followed. While specific formats may vary in terms of specific headings required, most evaluation reports include at least an introduction, a methods section, a presentation of results, conclusions and recommendations, and a summary.

Introduction

The introduction typically includes the following: the purpose of the evaluation (including a description of relevant legislation); the evaluation questions or hypothesis of interest; an operational definition of terms used in the report which do not have a commonly known meaning (e.g. "warm," "fuzzy"); and an explanation of any constraints which were imposed upon the evaluation.

Method

The method section generally includes a description of the participants, the measuring instruments used, the evaluation design employed, specific procedures which were followed, and limitations involved in any of the above. The description of participants includes a definition and description of the population from which the participants were selected, the method used to select participants, and if appropriate, the way in which the treatment and control groups were formed. The description of the population should indicate its size and major characteristics such as age, grade level, ability level, and socio-economic status. Information should be provided on any variable which might be related to performance on the posttest. A good description should permit the reader to determine how similar participants were to members of the population from which they were selected. Final group sizes should be given and if the sampling plan was at all complicated, a figure should be used to show the configuration of the final sample group (e.g. the number of schools, the number of classrooms per school, and the number of treatment and control students in each). Finally, any problems or possible sources of bias should be openly discussed.

The description of instruments should identify and describe all instruments used to collect data pertinent to the evaluation, whether tests, questionnaires, interview forms, or observation forms. The description of each instrument should include the function of the instrument (e.g. to select participants or to measure the dependent variable), what the instrument is intended to measure, and data related to reliability and validity. If an instrument was developed specifically for the evaluation, the description needs to be more detailed and should also relate the manner in which it was developed, a description of pretesting efforts and subsequent instrument revisions, steps involved in scoring, and guidelines for interpretation. A copy of the instrument itself, accompanying scoring keys, and other pertinent data related to a newly developed test are generally placed in an appendix.

The description of the design is especially important. The description of the basic design (or variation of a basic design) applied in the evaluation should include a rationale for selection, a discussion of sources of invalidity associated with the design, and reasons why they may have been minimized in the evaluation being reported. Use of figure to illustrate the design is often appropriate. The procedures section should describe each step followed in conducting the evaluation, in chronological order and in great detail. If not done so earlier, the method of participant selection should be described in detail. It should be clear exactly how participants were assigned to groups and how treatments were assigned to groups. Time and conditions of pretest administration (if appropriate) should be described, followed by a detailed explanation of the evaluation itself. If applicable, the ways in which groups were different (treatment) should be clearly delineated as well as ways in which they were similar (control procedures). All evaluation activities should be described, including data collection in the field (interviews of parents, for example), contacts with community agencies, and the like. Any unforeseen events which occurred which might have affected the results should be discussed in terms of their seriousness and probable consequences. Also, any insights on ways to improve procedures should be shared so that others may benefit.

Results

The results section describes the statistical techniques which were applied to the data, a rationale for their selection, and the results of each analysis, including the number of persons on whom each analysis was based. For each evaluation question or hypothesis, the statistical techniques selected and applied to the data are described followed by a discussion of the answer to the question or whether the hypothesis was supported. Data should be presented for every instrument which was administered.

Tables and figures are used to present findings in summary or graph form and add clarity to the presentation. Tables present numerical data in rows and columns and usually include descriptive statistics, such as means and standard deviations, and the results of tests of significance, such as t ratios. While a figure may be any nontabular presentation of information (such as a diagram or chart), figures in the results section are usually graphical presentations of data, such as frequency distributions. Care should be taken that tables and figures agree with the textual discussion upon which they are based.

Conclusions and recommendations

Every evaluation report has a section which discusses and interprets the results, draws conclusions and makes recommendations. If only one evaluation question or hypothesis is involved or if the discussion is brief, it may be included in the results section. Recommendations in an evaluation report usually take the form of suggestions concerning ways to improve the program or project which was evaluated.

Administrative activities

Many evaluation reports contain a section which reports administrative activities. This section may include items such as the project director's log of significant events, a time schedule of program activities, staff assignments, and a record of staff meetings (including those held with part-time data collectors). The exact nature of items to be included in this section is specified by the funding source.

Summary

All evaluation reports include some form of summary which provides an overview of the evaluation. Since the summary may be the only part of the report which is read by some people, it should describe the most important aspects of the evaluation, including: the evaluation questions or hypotheses, the number and type of participants involved, the major instruments which were administered and when, the design, the procedures, the major results and the major conclusions.

Appendices

The summary may be followed by one or more appendices which include information and data pertinent to the evaluation which are not important enough or which are too lengthy to be included in the main body of the report. Appendices contain such entries as materials especially developed for the evaluation (e.g. tests, questionnaires, and cover letters), raw data, and data analysis sheets. Also, some funding sources request that vitae of major evaluation staff members be included. A vita is a short autobiography which describes professionally related activities and experiences of the author. Information typically included in a vita describes educational training and degrees earned, professional work experience, memberships in professional organizations, and publications, if any.

Funding sources also frequently provide special reporting forms which are placed at the beginning or at the end of the report. These forms ask for information such as project costs by category (e.g. salaries and travel) and the number of participants in each of a number of categories, for example the number of public school versus private school participants, the number of males versus females, and so forth.

part eight **summary**

19 Using and reporting results

Utilization of results

1 The results of standardized testing are used by a variety of groups for making decisions concerning the effectiveness and efficiency of the total system and each component in it, and for taking future actions.
2 The results of standardized testing at any given point in time are never considered in isolation from previous results and from other types of data.

Guidance

3 Appraisals of a student's capabilities and potential should be realistic, not overly pessimistic or overly optimistic, and should be based on an array of data.
4 It is the counselor's responsibility to use whatever information is necessary to help each student make wise curriculum decisions and long-term career decisions; the counselor also has a measure of responsibility for helping students to cope with emotional problems.
5 The results of valid, reliable standardized tests of achievement, aptitude, personality, and interest are all relevant to counseling, as well as grades, classroom effort and conduct, teacher comments, and home environment.
6 Proper interpretation and analysis require the availability of cumulative information based on the periodic and systematic collection of data.

Instruction

7 When necessary data are available, an item analysis of standardized test results in terms of item difficulty can provide necessary information for needed changes in curriculum and instruction.
8 Deficiencies which are evident across classrooms can be dealt with at the program level whereas classroom-specific areas of difficulty can be handled by the teacher.
9 When discussing results with the class as a whole, individual scores should not be referred to; a class profile should be presented with a discussion of areas of strength and weakness.
10 Student performance data are used in planning instruction, in determining degree of progress, and in assessing final level of achievement at the conclusion of some phase of instruction.
11 Like the counselor, the teacher uses test results to determine individual patterns of ability and to identify exceptional students with special needs.
12 The achievement of students should be but one of many factors considered in teacher evaluation.

Grading

13 Grading, like testing, is a necessary procedure; the progress and achievement of students must be reported to parents and others, and grading serves this purpose.

Definition and purpose

14 A *grade* is an alphabetical or numerical symbol, or mark, that indicates the degree to which intended outcomes have been achieved.

15 The major purpose of grades is to communicate how well a student is doing in the various subject areas.

16 Another purpose often attributed to grades is that they serve as a motivator for student performance.

17 Grades also serve as an indication of achievement to be expected in the future; past performance is the best single predictor of future performance.

18 The major objection to grades is that there is considerable variability in the meaning of a given grade; further, there are so many different methods of grading and such diversity of symbols that it is difficult to interpret exactly what a given set of grades means.

19 There is, however, a surprising degree of consistency among students' grades and a high degree of agreement between a student's grades and his or her scores on standardized tests.

20 The fact that current grades do predict future grades rather well supports the contention that there is considerably more consistency across grading practices than critics allege.

21 A second serious charge made by opponents of grading is that it is basically an inhumane process with many negative effects; some parents and teachers use them punitively and the pressures on students can produce negative behaviors as a result.

22 The misuse of grades by parents and teachers and the undesirable behaviors of students are not problems inherent in grading—they are people problems.

23 As for the pressure grades place on students, it can be argued that a reasonable amount of pressure leads to increased achievement.

24 Life is full of pressures and students must at some point learn to cope with them in positive ways; students who exhibit bizarre behaviors need counseling and help in dealing with life in general.

25 Low grades do not cause low achievement, they report it; similarly, low grades do not cause adjustment problems, they reflect them.

26 Grades serve a number of purposes and most of the criticisms of grades are really criticisms of unsatisfactory ways in which they are used or dealt with.

General principles of grading

27 Grades should be based on a sufficient amount of valid data systematically collected over a period of time.

28 Any given test represents a sampling of behavior; thus, a grade based on a combination of a number of test scores is more likely to accurately reflect a student's achievement level than a grade based on a single test score.

29 There is nothing wrong with grading everything and providing corrective comments for the sake of feedback, but all such grades should not be included in computation of the final course grade.

30 Students should know *in advance* which grades "count" and which do not, and should be informed concerning how final grades will be determined and on what basis.

31 A final grade may be based on a combination of any number of factors such as written tests and various procedures and products.

32 The general consensus is that since the major purpose of grades is to commu-

nicate level of achievement, grades should report achievement only; this is not to say that factors such as effort and conduct should not be reported, only that they should not affect the course grade.

33 Every grade that contributes to the final grade should also be based on achievement only.

34 Grading on the basis of amount of improvement involves the same problems as analyzing gain scores; students with the lowest initial levels of achievement, for example, are in a position to exhibit the greatest amount of improvement.

35 Like effort, ability should be less and less of a factor as a student moves from elementary school to junior high school to senior high school.

36 Grading is usually done on a relative basis; that is, achievement is labeled as "good" or "poor" in relation to the performance of the total group.

37 Grades represent a complex combination of achievement and effort; achievement is assessed partly in relation to objective standards and partly in relation to the performance of other students.

Methods of grading

38 Users of grades, such as admissions personnel and employers, invariably prefer norm-referenced, relative grading systems.

Percent grading

39 *Percent grading* involves averaging scores and converting them to a percent.

40 The percent itself may be reported as the grade, e.g. History, 84%, or the percent may be translated into a letter grade equivalent (e.g. A = 94–100%).

41 Percent grading is not viewed with much favor mainly because the meaning of such grades is so obscure; such a grade tells us nothing about how much the student achieved, either in relation to intended outcomes or in relation to what other students achieved.

42 One procedure for assigning percent grades, when such are required, involves equating the lowest acceptable score with the percent that represents a passing grade and adjusting the rest of the scores accordingly.

Norm-referenced grading

43 Norm-referenced grading involves rank ordering students and expressing a given student's achievement in relation to the achievement of the rest of the class; in essence, the rest of the class serves as the norm group.

44 A norm-referenced grade does not communicate what a student has actually achieved but rather how a student's achievement compared to the achievement of others in the class.

45 Sometimes, especially at the elementary level, an achievement grade is accompanied by a ranking on a number of affective variables such as initiative.

Normal curve grading

46 In its extreme form norm-referenced grading is based on an assumption of a normal distribution, and a fixed percentage of students receive each grade; some students must receive failing grades regardless of their actual level of achievement.

47 A normal curve grading system essentially ignores the actual distribution and often makes trivial distinctions between the various levels of achievement.

48 A related problem with normal curve grading is that the same grade does not necessarily indicate the same level of achievement.

Pass-fail grading

49 Available evidence indicates that a pass-fail system usually results in a reduction of achievement levels; quite naturally, students are less motivated to do well in such courses and devote most of their energies to those courses in which they will receive a letter grade.

50 Pass-fail grading does not fulfill any of the purposes of grades—communication, motivation, and prediction.

Standard score grading

51 A more satisfactory approach to norm-referenced grading involves conversion of scores on each test (or other measure) to standard scores such as z scores or Z scores, averaging the Z scores, and assigning grades based on the average Z score value.

52 The major advantage of Z scores is that we can perform arithmetic operations on them (e.g. averaging).

53 Another advantage of standard score grading is that it permits us to assign differential weights to scores.

54 Following strict Z score–letter grade equivalencies, (e.g. a Z of 45 to 55 = C) is just as unwise as strictly following normal curve equivalencies.

55 Norm-referenced grading simply rank orders the students; it indicates nothing about actual level of achievement.

Criterion-referenced grading

56 Criterion-referenced grading involves expressing a student's achievement in relation to prespecified criteria rather than the achievement of others in the class.

57 The standards in criterion-referenced grading are absolute, not relative, and all students who achieve the same standards achieve the same grade; students who reach criterion on every required task "pass," or receive "credit," and those who do not "fail," or receive "no credit."

58 Unlike a norm-referenced grade, a criterion-referenced grade provides very specific information concerning what the student has actually achieved, what he or she knows and can do.

59 In the ideal criterion-referenced system very few students do not pass.

60 Criterion-referenced pass-fail grading is subject to the same problems associated with norm-referenced pass-fail grading; students tend to do just enough to reach criterion and to pass because there is little motivation to do more.

61 In some cases, especially at the elementary level, grades of pass or fail are not awarded, but rather achievement of each objective is reported on a percent basis; a student's report card lists various objectives, gives a percentage score for each, and indicates whether the score for each objective is high enough to represent mastery or acceptable performance.

62 For nonmastery objectives we may also wish to provide some measure of rela-

tive position; such an index may be simply a rank based on score level, where the top score equals a rank of 1.

63 Another way in which an index of relative position can be presented is to state the number of objectives achieved by the student and his or her corresponding class rank; in this case, the student achieving the most objectives is assigned a rank of 1.

64 For both mastery objectives and nonmastery objectives, the most difficult task is setting the criterion for mastery or acceptable performance.

Norm-referenced versus criterion-referenced grading

65 Which grading system is "best" is largely a matter of personal or institutional philosophy since each system serves different functions. Also, each system has its own advantages and disadvantages.

66 Both systems communicate achievement (the major purpose of grades) but in a different manner. Norm-referenced grades report the achievement of an individual in relation to the achievement of the group; criterion-referenced grades report achievement in relation to fixed standards; that is, they report what a student knows and can do.

67 It is less important to report relative achievement at the elementary level and becomes more important at the junior and senior high school levels.

68 With respect to student motivation (the second purpose of grades), the evidence indicates that criterion-referenced grading results in decreased motivation, at least at the higher grade levels.

69 With respect to prediction of future achievement (the third purpose of grading), norm-referenced grading clearly has the edge because of the greater variability of scores.

70 No grading system can serve all purposes of grading equally well; with the exception of communication of objectives achieved, however, norm-referenced grading seems to do the best job, at least at higher grade levels.

71 While pass-fail criterion-referenced grading can be defended on philosophical grounds, in practice most institutions which have tried such systems have eventually reverted to some type of norm-referenced system, mainly for practical reasons.

Types and precision of grading symbols

72 The most commonly used alphabetical norm-referenced symbols are the letter grades A, B, C, D and E (or F) and P and F (for pass and fail); the most commonly used numerical symbols are percents (e.g. 80%, 90%, 100%).

73 Using alternatives to traditional symbols is not good practice; most people are familiar with the traditional symbols and using alternatives only confuses those to whom the grades are communicated.

74 Criterion-referenced grading systems typically use P and F or CR and NCR (credit and no credit) although some systems also include an HP (high pass or honors pass) or an HCR (high credit or honors credit).

75 Some of the approaches to assigning letter grades to criterion-referenced results require norm-referenced interpretations, but it is possible to assign letter grades using strictly criterion-referenced standards.

76 One approach to criterion-referenced grading is to assign grades based on the number of attempts required to reach criterion (e.g. one attempt = A).

77 Another approach to criterion-referenced grading is to base grades on the

number of objectives achieved during a given period of time; the students who achieve the most objectives get A's *or* any student who achieves X objectives (e.g. 40) gets an A, and so forth.

78 If aptitude is taken into consideration, the number and nature of the objectives required for a given grade may be agreed upon in advance, on an individual basis, by the teacher and each student (performance contracti g).

79 Another approach to criterion-referenced grading is to make each test or task worth a certain number of points which combine for a certain total; predetermined standards are set for each letter grade (e.g. 140 out of a total 150 points = A). Required point values for each grade are determined based on acceptable performance for each test.

80 It has been demonstrated mathematically that the fewer the number of categories, the less reliable grades tend to be.

81 In general, five categories seem to represent a reasonable compromise between the desire for reliability and practicality; schools that have tried grading systems with more or fewer categories have usually eventually reverted to a five-point grading scale.

82 Students' grades have been progressively "improving" to the point where the average grade in many places has become B; unfortunately, these higher grades do not reflect higher achievement.

83 Giving students inflated grades only serves to defeat the major purpose of grades—to communicate level of achievement.

Alternatives to grading

84 Grades are sometimes supplemented or supplanted by checklists, rankings, and reports of objectives achieved.

85 The two most frequently suggested substitutes for grades are letters, or written reports, and parent-teacher conferences.

86 Ideally, both reports and conferences are used to communicate detailed information concerning achievement, in both a norm-referenced and criterion-referenced context, and for discussion of the character and personality traits of the student.

87 Conferences and reports are very time-consuming procedures and they are rarely actualized as intended; most criticisms which can be directed at grading symbols can be more convincingly applied to the alternatives.

88 As systematic, periodic reporting procedures, both reports and conferences are too time-consuming to be practical substitutes for grades.

Promotion

89 A student's grades represent the major input for decisions concerning promotion.

90 Probably the best solution to the promotion dilemma is to make promotion decisions on an individual basis, rather than to uniformly promote or not promote all questionable students.

91 The best policy is to require that all promotion decisions be made jointly by a number of persons (e.g. the student's teacher, counselor, and parents) based on a number of agreed-upon variables such as grades, standardized test scores, and behavior patterns.

92 In most cases, it is probably better to promote than not to promote; it is easier to remedy achievement deficiencies than to erase emotional scars.

Reporting procedures

93 The accountability movement has resulted in increased pressure on school systems to release detailed information concerning the achievement of students, especially in the basic skills areas.

94 Generally, the superintendent's staff reports standardized test results to the various school administrators who in turn report to both teachers and community members, usually on a face-to-face basis.

95 The foremost principle of reporting is that results must be communicated in a form and manner which are understandable to the intended group; technical and statistical terms should be avoided or carefully defined, and extensive use should be made of graphs and charts.

96 Results for subtests of achievement batteries and scholastic aptitude tests should all be presented using the same, easy to understand type of derived score so that comparisons across year and across subject area, and comparisons of achievement and aptitude can easily be made; stanines are especially well suited for this purpose.

97 A second principle of reporting is that recipients of results should be given information on appropriate and inappropriate uses of results.

98 Another general principle of reporting is that results for individual students should be kept confidential and reported only to students, their parents, and appropriate school personnel.

99 We must always keep in mind that the various concerned groups have a right to know the results of testing; it is not our place to decide what information a given group can or cannot handle.

Reporting within the school system

The school board

100 One of the major responsibilities of a school board is to allocate funds within the school system.

101 At various points in time, the board requires accountings, to verify that funds are being spent as intended, and evidence that funds are being used effectively; standardized test results provide a major source of data for the latter.

102 The results of standardized testing help the board to assess the effectiveness of various components of the system and to make informed decisions concerning future allocations and operating policies.

103 Since a number of different comparisons are usually desired, results may be presented in various ways—for the system as a whole by grade level, for each school by grade, level, and so forth.

Administrators

104 Test information typically flows from the top down; reports are made to administrators, who in turn report to school staff members, who in turn report to students; thus, it is important that administrators be given enough information and explanation to give them a reasonably complete understanding of the results and what they mean.

105 When scores are summarized, descriptive statistics are involved. Usually the median is used to depict the typical score, for example, the median percentile rank for second graders in the system on each of the subtests might be given.

If an index of variability is desired, Q_1 and Q_3 (the 25th and 75th percentiles) are usually presented.

106 Achievement results should be discussed and interpreted in relation to other characteristics of the students involved, such as scholastic aptitude and socio-economic status.

Teachers

107 At school meetings held after testing, there should be extensive discussion of appropriate and inappropriate uses of the results.

108 For the benefit of those teachers who have not had evaluation training, individual and class profiles should be explained, as well as the various types of information which can be extracted from them.

109 Concepts such as the relationship between achievement and factors such as scholastic aptitude should be carefully explained; if available, item analysis data should also be presented and explained.

110 Teachers will be very interested in seeing how their classes compared with other classes in the same school and within the system; one approach is the dissemination to teachers of a summary profile sheet which depicts the 25th, 50th, and 75th percentiles (in terms of national percentile ranks) for the total system and for the system; each teacher can then plot the results for his or her classroom on the same profile sheet, thus permitting all comparisons of interest.

Students

111 How technical and detailed reports to students are depends mainly on the age of the students.

112 High school students are especially interested in knowing the purpose of the test, how they did in relation to other students, and what implications their scores have for their goals.

113 Reporting to younger students is a more simplified process; results concerning the performance of the class and individuals can be reported in more general terms.

114 With younger children, the teacher generally reviews the purpose and nature of the test, and makes broad statements about the strengths and weaknesses of the class, always in positive terms.

Reporting to the community

115 More and more systems have become involved in developing systematic presentations, complete with visual aids and handouts, to insure that results are presented accurately and accompanied by appropriate interpretations.

116 Results are reported to groups, either in person (e.g. at PTA meetings) or through the media, and to individual parents via the mail or at parent-teacher conferences.

117 The community should be constantly kept informed, through the media and memoranda for example, concerning activities of the schools.

118 Results must be presented in the simplest manner possible which accurately conveys the information of interest; stanine charts or percentile band graphs, accompanied by appropriate interpretive information, are usually sufficient.

Presentations should involve considerable visual material such as handouts, slides, and transparencies, and data should be provided in summary form.

119 If reporting is well done, community members will come to view themselves as allies of the school system, not opponents.

Local groups

120 In a group setting, results are generally presented for the school system as a whole and for individual schools within the system.

121 Presentations typically begin with a description of the testing program itself and uses of the results, followed by a discussion of concepts involved in interpreting test results (e.g. norms and score equivalents, and summary statistics).

122 The presentation describes data comparisons which have been made—national, state, district and school performance, year to year changes, grade by grade comparisons, achievement versus scholastic aptitude, and subject by subject comparisons—and possible reasons for varying levels of achievement of the compared groups.

123 Presentations should be followed by a discussion of factors believed to be having an adverse effect on achievement, actions that are being taken in an attempt to deal with these factors, and ways in which the community can help.

124 Sufficient time should be allowed for members of the audience to ask questions; most questions can be, and should be, anticipated in advance so that presenters will be prepared with knowledgeable responses.

125 At the conclusion of the session, interested persons should be informed of ways in which they can acquire additional information or discuss results further.

Parents

126 Despite the problems associated with their use, individual parent-teacher conferences represent the best approach to the discussion of individual results.

127 Conferences should not be totally extemporaneous happenings; the teacher should prepare for them by collecting and organizing all pertinent information about each student, and by reviewing it prior to the conferences.

128 The key to a successful conference is for the teacher to be both diplomatic and realistic, and to tell to parents whatever they want to know in a positive but truthful manner.

129 The conference includes a discussion of class activities, the student's achievement in class, and the results of standardized testing; the components of such a discussion will be very similar to those included in group presentations, but the emphasis will be on the performance of the individual student.

130 The student's profile sheet should be interpreted, beginning with the definition and purpose of score equivalents and the concept of a norm group.

131 The derived score that was used on the profile is the only derived score which needs to be explained; if stanines were used, they should be described in broad categories (e.g. 4–6 represents average), and if percentiles are used, band interpretations should be explained.

132 As much as possible, numerical data should be translated into verbal statements.

133 After achievement data have been presented, they should be related to other performances and characteristics of the student, such as scholastic aptitude.

134 While conferences can be very productive, they do have their drawbacks. One problem inherent in conferences is that they take so much time. Other problems related to conferences are people problems, not inherent characteristics of conferences; some teachers may not prepare adequately for the conferences and some parents do not show up for scheduled conferences.

The media

135 If left to their own devices, media people are likely to make reports which contain inaccuracies or misinterpretations.

136 It is in the school system's best interest to hold press conferences to present and discuss the data and to answer questions.

137 As with the community, communication should be in the simplest terms possible and should be an ongoing activity, not a once-a-year event.

138 The media should be considered potential vehicles for generating support among community members, especially those who will never attend a presentation.

Funding sources: the evaluation report

139 Funding sources—local, state, national and private—invariably require a formal, written evaluation report at the end of each funding period, in addition to a number of informal, periodic progress reports.

140 Since initial funding is almost always based on the submission of an evaluation plan, or proposal, writing the final report basically involves revising and refining the original document and adding the results and conclusions.

141 Probably the foremost rule of report writing is that the writer should be as objective as possible in reporting the evaluation; the report should not contain subjective statements, overstatements, or emotional statements.

142 The report should be written in a clear, simple, straightforward style, and should reflect scholarship in the form of correct spelling, grammatical construction, and punctuation.

Introduction

143 The introduction of an evaluation report typically includes the purpose of the evaluation, the evaluation questions or hypotheses of interest, an operational definition of terms, and an explanation of any constraints which were imposed upon the evaluation.

Method

144 The method section of an evaluation report generally includes a description of the participants, the measuring instruments used, the evaluation design employed, specific procedures which were followed, and limitations involved in any of the above.

145 The description of participants includes a definition and description of the population from which the participants were selected, the method used to select participants, and if appropriate, the way in which the treatment and control groups were formed; possible sources of bias should also be discussed.

146 The description of instruments should identify and describe all instruments used to collect data pertinent to the evaluation, be they tests, questionnaires, interview forms, or observation forms.

147 The description of each instrument should include the function of the instrument (e.g. to select participants or to measure the dependent variable), what the instrument is intended to measure, and data related to reliability and validity.

148 The description of the basic design (or variation of a basic design) applied in the evaluation should include a rationale for selection, a discussion of sources of invalidity associated with the design, and reasons why they may have been minimized in the evaluation being reported.

149 The procedures section should describe each step followed in conducting the evaluation, in chronological order and in great detail.

150 If applicable, the ways in which groups were different (treatment) should be clearly delineated as well as ways in which they were similar (control procedures).

151 Any unforeseen events which occurred which might have affected the results should be discussed in terms of their seriousness and probable consequences.

Results

152 The results section describes the statistical techniques which were applied to the data, a rationale for their selection, and the results of each analysis, including the number of persons on whom each analysis was based.

153 Data should be presented for every instrument which was administered.

Conclusions and recommendations

154 Recommendations in an evaluation report usually take the form of suggestions concerning ways to improve the program or project which was evaluated.

Administrative activities

155 Many evaluation reports contain a section which reports administrative activities such as a time schedule of program activities and a record of staff meetings.

Summary

155 All evaluation reports include some form of summary which provides an overview of the evaluation; since the summary may be the only part of the report which is read by some people, it should describe the most important aspects of the evaluation.

Appendices

156 The summary may be followed by one or more appendices which include information and data pertinent to the evaluation which are not important enough or which are too lengthy to be included in the main body of the report.

157 Funding sources frequently provide special reporting forms which are placed
at the beginning or at the end of the report; these forms ask for information
such as project costs by category (e.g. salaries and travel) and participant information.

task eight **performance criteria**

For student evaluation:

a After you have assigned the required grades, you will have a list of 20 scores
and three grades for each. Explain how each type of grade was derived. For the
norm-referenced grades, for example, you might list Z scores and corresponding letter grades and explain the basis on which the letter grades were assigned
(e.g. A = 65 and above).

b In discussing how you would report the various grades to parents, you should
include an explanation of how the grades were derived (using plain English)
and an explanation of what the grades *mean* in terms of student achievement,
either in relative or absolute terms. For example, you might say:

> A grade of C indicates that Egor eventually achieved an acceptable level of
> performance for all required objectives.

c In discussing achievement in relation to aptitude, factors such as expected performance versus actual performance and reasons for discrepancies should be
considered.

d Your summary report should include: (1) a heading which indicates to whom
the report is addressed (e.g. "Report to Parents"); (2) presentation and interpretation of appropriate descriptive statistics; and (3) at least one table or graph.

For other types of evaluation:

Your report should include the following headings: Introduction, Method,
Results, Conclusions and Recommendations, Summary, and Appendix (if needed).
The Results section should include presentation and interpretation of appropriate
descriptive statistics and at least one table or graph.

appendix

reference tables

Table A.1
Ten thousand random numbers

	00–04	05–09	10–14	15–19	20–24	25–29	30–34	35–39	40–44	45–49
00	54463	22662	65905	70639	79365	67382	29085	69831	47058	08186
01	15389	85205	18850	39226	42249	90669	96325	23248	60933	26927
02	85941	40756	82414	02015	13858	78030	16269	65978	01385	15345
03	61149	69440	11268	88218	58925	03638	52862	62733	33451	77455
04	05219	81619	81619	10651	67079	92511	59888	72095	83463	75577
05	41417	98326	87719	92294	46614	50948	64886	20002	97365	30976
06	28357	94070	20652	35774	16249	75019	21145	15217	47286	76305
07	17783	00015	10806	83091	91530	36466	39981	62481	49177	75779
08	40950	84820	29881	85966	62800	70326	84740	62660	77379	90279
09	82995	64157	66164	41180	10089	41757	78258	96488	88629	37231
10	96754	17676	55659	44105	47361	34833	86679	23930	53249	27083
11	34357	88040	53364	71726	45690	66334	60332	22554	90600	71113
12	06318	37403	49927	57715	50423	67372	63116	48888	21505	80182
13	62111	52820	07243	79931	89292	84767	85693	73947	22278	11551
14	47534	09243	67879	00544	23410	12740	02540	54440	32949	13491
15	98614	75993	84460	62846	59844	14922	49730	73443	48167	34770
16	24856	03648	44898	09351	98795	18644	39765	71058	90368	44104
17	96887	12479	80621	66223	86085	78285	02432	53342	42846	94771
18	90801	21472	42815	77408	37390	76766	52615	32141	30268	18106
19	55165	77312	83666	36028	28420	70219	81369	41943	47366	41067
20	75884	12952	84318	95108	72305	64620	91318	89872	45375	85436
21	16777	37116	58550	42958	21460	43910	01175	87894	81378	10620
22	46230	43877	80207	88877	89380	32992	91380	03164	98656	59337
23	42902	66892	46134	01432	94710	23474	20523	60137	60609	13119
24	81007	00333	39693	28039	10154	95425	39220	19774	31782	49037
25	68089	01122	51111	72373	06902	74373	96199	97017	41273	21546
26	20411	67081	89950	16944	93054	87687	96693	87236	77054	33848
27	58212	13160	06468	15718	82627	76999	05999	58680	96739	63700
28	70577	42866	24969	61210	76046	67699	42054	12696	93758	03283
29	94522	74358	71659	62038	79643	79169	44741	05437	39038	13163
30	42626	86819	85651	88678	17401	03252	99547	32404	17918	62880
31	16051	33763	57194	16752	54450	19031	58580	47629	54132	60631
32	08244	27647	33851	44705	94211	46716	11738	55784	95374	72655
33	59497	04392	09419	89964	51211	04894	72882	17805	21896	83864
34	97155	13428	40293	09985	58434	01412	69124	82171	59058	82859
35	98409	66162	95763	47420	20792	61527	20441	39435	11859	41567
36	45476	84882	65109	96597	25930	66790	65706	61203	53634	22557
37	89300	69700	50741	30329	11658	23166	05400	66669	48708	03887
38	50051	95137	91631	66315	91428	12275	24816	68091	71710	33258
39	31753	85178	31310	89642	98364	02306	24617	09609	83942	22716
40	79152	53829	77250	20190	56535	18760	69942	77448	33278	48805
41	44560	38750	83635	56540	64900	42912	13953	79149	18710	68618
42	68328	83378	63369	71381	39564	05615	42451	64559	97501	65747
43	46939	38689	58625	08342	30459	85863	20781	09284	26333	91777
44	83544	86141	15707	96256	23068	13782	08467	89469	93842	55349
45	91621	00881	04900	54224	46177	55309	17852	27491	89415	23466
46	91896	67126	04151	03795	59077	11848	12630	98375	53068	60142
47	55751	62515	22108	80830	02263	29303	37204	96926	30506	09808
48	85156	87689	95493	88842	00664	55017	55539	17771	69448	87530
49	07521	56898	12236	60277	39102	62315	12239	07105	11844	01117

Reprinted by permission from *Statistical Methods* by George W. Snedecor and William G. Cochran, Sixth Edition © 1967 by The Iowa State University Press, Ames, Iowa.

Table A.1 (continued)

	50–54	55–59	60–64	65–69	70–74	75–79	80–84	85–89	90–94	95–99
00	59391	58030	52098	82718	87024	82848	04190	96574	90464	29065
01	99567	76364	77204	04615	27062	96621	43918	01896	83991	51141
02	10363	97518	51400	25670	98342	61891	27101	37855	06235	33316
03	96859	19558	64432	16706	99612	59798	32803	67708	15297	28612
04	11258	24591	36863	55368	31721	94335	34936	02566	80972	08188
05	95068	88628	35911	14530	33020	80428	33936	31855	34334	64865
06	54463	47237	73800	91017	36239	71824	83671	39892	60518	37092
07	16874	62677	57412	13215	31389	62233	80827	73917	82802	84420
08	92494	63157	76593	91316	03505	72389	96363	52887	01087	66091
09	15669	56689	35682	40844	53256	81872	35213	09840	34471	74441
10	99116	75486	84989	23476	52967	67104	39495	39100	17217	74073
11	15696	10703	65178	90637	63110	17622	53988	71087	84148	11670
12	97720	15369	51269	69620	03388	13699	33423	67453	43269	56720
13	11666	13841	71681	98000	35979	39719	81899	07449	47985	46967
14	71628	73130	78783	75691	41632	09847	61547	18707	85489	69944
15	40501	51089	99943	91843	41995	88931	73631	69361	05375	15417
16	22518	55576	98215	82068	10798	86211	36584	67466	69373	40054
17	75112	30485	62173	02132	14878	92879	22281	16783	86352	00077
18	80327	02671	98191	84342	90813	49268	94551	15496	20168	09271
19	60251	45548	02146	05597	48228	81366	34598	72856	66762	17002
20	57430	82270	10421	00540	43648	75888	66049	21511	47676	33444
21	73528	39559	34434	88586	54086	71693	43132	14414	79949	85193
22	25991	65959	70769	64721	86413	33475	42740	06175	82758	66248
23	78388	16638	09134	59980	63806	48472	39318	35434	24057	74739
24	12477	09965	96657	57994	59439	76330	24596	77515	09577	91871
25	83266	32883	42451	15579	38155	29793	40914	65990	16255	17777
26	76970	80876	10237	39515	79152	74798	39357	09054	73579	92359
27	37074	65198	44785	68624	98336	84481	97610	78735	46703	98265
28	83712	06514	30101	78295	54656	85417	43189	60048	72781	72606
29	20287	56862	69727	94443	64936	08366	27227	05158	50326	59566
30	74261	32592	86538	27041	65172	85532	07571	80609	39285	65340
31	64081	49863	08478	96001	18888	14810	70545	89755	59064	07210
32	05617	75818	47750	67814	29575	10526	66192	44464	27058	40467
33	26793	74951	95466	74307	13330	42664	85515	20632	05497	33625
34	65988	72850	48737	54719	52056	01596	03845	35067	03134	70322
35	27366	42271	44300	73399	21105	03280	73457	43093	05192	48657
36	56760	10909	98147	34736	33863	95256	12731	66598	50771	83665
37	72880	43338	93643	58904	59543	23943	11231	83268	65938	81581
38	77888	38100	03062	58103	47961	83841	25878	23746	55903	44115
39	28440	07819	21580	51459	47971	29882	13990	29226	23608	15873
40	63525	94441	77033	12147	51054	49955	58312	76923	96071	05813
41	47606	93410	16359	89033	89696	47231	64498	31776	05383	39902
42	52669	45030	96279	14709	52372	87832	02735	50803	72744	88208
43	16738	60159	07425	62369	07515	82721	37875	71153	21315	00132
44	59348	11695	45751	15865	74739	05572	32688	20271	65128	14551
45	12900	71775	29845	60774	94924	21810	38636	33717	67598	82521
46	75086	23537	49939	33595	13484	97588	28617	17979	70749	35234
47	99495	51534	29181	09993	38190	42553	68922	52125	91077	40197
48	26075	31671	45386	36583	93459	48599	52022	41330	60651	91321
49	13636	93596	23377	51133	95126	61496	42474	45141	46660	42338

Table A.1 (continued)

	00–04	05–09	10–14	15–19	20–24	25–29	30–34	35–39	40–44	44–49
50	64249	63664	39652	40646	97306	31741	07294	84149	46797	82487
51	26538	44249	04050	48174	65570	44072	40192	51153	11397	58212
52	05845	00512	78630	55328	18116	69296	91705	86224	29503	57071
53	74897	68373	67359	51014	33510	83048	17056	72506	82949	54600
54	20872	54570	35017	88132	25730	22626	86723	91691	13191	77212
55	31432	96156	89177	75541	81355	24480	77243	76690	42507	84362
56	66890	61505	01240	00660	05873	13568	76082	79172	57913	93448
57	41894	57790	79970	33106	86904	48119	52503	24130	72824	21627
58	11303	87118	81471	52936	08555	28420	49416	44448	04269	27029
59	54374	57325	16947	45356	78371	10563	97191	53798	12693	27928
60	64852	34421	61046	90849	13966	39810	42699	21753	76192	10508
61	16309	20384	09491	91588	97720	89846	30376	76970	23063	35894
62	42587	37065	24526	72602	57589	98131	37292	05967	26002	51945
63	40177	98590	97161	41682	84533	67588	62036	49967	01990	72308
64	82309	76128	93965	26743	24141	04838	40254	26065	07938	76236
65	79788	68243	59732	04257	27084	14743	17520	94501	55811	76099
66	40538	79000	89559	25026	42274	23489	34502	75508	06059	86682
67	64016	73598	18609	73150	62463	33102	45205	87440	96767	67042
68	49767	12691	17903	93871	99721	79109	09425	26904	07419	76013
69	76794	55108	29795	08404	82684	00497	51126	79935	57450	55671
70	23854	08480	85983	96025	50117	64610	99425	62291	86943	21541
71	68973	70551	25098	78033	98573	79848	31778	29555	61446	23037
72	36444	93600	65350	14971	25325	00427	52073	64280	18847	24768
73	03003	87800	07391	11594	21196	00781	32550	57158	58887	73041
74	17540	26188	36647	78386	04558	61463	57842	90382	77019	24210
75	38916	55809	47982	41968	69760	79422	80154	91486	19180	15100
76	64288	19843	69122	42502	48508	28820	59933	72998	99942	10515
77	86809	51564	38040	39418	49915	19000	58050	16899	79952	57849
78	99800	99566	14742	05028	30033	94889	55381	23656	75787	59223
79	92345	31890	95712	08279	91794	94068	49337	88674	35355	12267
80	90363	65162	32245	82279	79256	80834	06088	99462	56705	06118
81	64437	32242	48431	04835	39070	59702	31508	60935	22390	52246
82	91714	53662	28373	34333	55791	74758	51144	18827	10704	76803
83	20902	17646	31391	31459	33315	03444	55743	74701	58851	27427
84	12217	86007	70371	52281	14510	76094	96579	54853	78339	20839
85	45177	02863	42307	53571	22532	74921	17735	42201	80540	54721
86	28325	90814	08804	52746	47913	54577	47525	77705	95330	21866
87	29019	28776	56116	54791	64604	08815	46049	71186	34650	14994
88	84979	81353	56219	67062	26146	82567	33122	14124	46240	92973
89	50371	26347	48513	63915	11158	25563	91915	18431	92978	11591
90	53422	06825	69711	67950	64716	18003	49581	45378	99878	61130
91	67453	35651	89316	41620	32048	70225	47597	33137	31443	51445
92	07294	85353	74819	23445	68237	07202	99515	62282	53809	26685
93	79544	00302	45338	16015	66613	88968	14595	63836	77716	79596
94	64144	85442	82060	46471	24162	39500	87351	36637	42833	71875
95	90919	11883	58318	00042	52402	28210	34075	33272	00840	73268
96	06670	57353	86275	92276	77591	46924	60839	55437	03183	13191
97	36634	93976	52062	83678	41256	60948	18685	48992	19462	96062
98	75101	72891	85745	67106	26010	62107	60885	37503	55461	71213
99	05112	71222	72654	51583	05228	62056	57390	42746	39272	96659

Table A.1 (continued)

	50–54	55–59	60–64	65–69	70–74	75–79	80–84	85–89	90–94	95–99
50	32847	31282	03345	89593	69214	70381	78285	20054	91018	16742
51	16916	00041	30236	55023	14253	76582	12092	86533	92426	37655
52	66176	34037	21005	27137	03193	48970	64625	22394	39622	79085
53	46299	13335	12180	16861	38043	59292	62675	63631	37020	78195
54	22847	47839	45385	23289	47526	54098	45683	55849	51575	64689
55	41851	54160	92320	69936	34803	92479	33399	71160	64777	83378
56	28444	59497	91586	95917	68553	28639	06455	34174	11130	91994
57	47520	62378	98855	83174	13088	16561	68559	26679	06238	51254
58	34978	63271	13142	82681	05271	08822	06490	44984	49307	61617
59	37404	80416	69035	92980	49486	74378	75610	74976	70056	15478
60	32400	65482	52099	53676	74648	94148	65095	69597	52771	71551
61	89262	86332	51718	70663	11623	29834	79820	73002	84886	03591
62	86866	09127	98021	03871	27789	58444	44832	36505	40672	30180
63	90814	14833	08759	74645	05046	94056	99094	65091	32663	73040
64	19192	82756	20553	58446	55376	88914	75096	26119	83898	43816
65	77585	52593	56612	95766	10019	29531	73064	20953	53523	58136
66	23757	16364	05096	03192	62386	45389	85332	18877	55710	96459
67	45989	96257	23850	26216	23309	21526	07425	50254	19455	29315
68	92970	94243	07316	41467	64837	52406	25225	51553	31220	14032
69	74346	59596	40088	98176	17896	86900	20249	77753	19099	48885
70	87646	41309	27636	45153	29988	94770	07255	70908	05340	99751
71	50099	71038	45146	06146	55211	99429	43169	66259	99786	59180
72	10127	46900	64984	75348	04115	33624	68774	60013	35515	62556
73	67995	81977	18984	64091	02785	27762	42529	97144	80407	64524
74	26304	80217	84934	82657	69291	35397	98714	35104	08187	48109
75	81994	41070	56642	64091	31229	02595	13513	45148	78722	30144
76	59337	34662	79631	89403	65212	09975	06118	86197	58208	16162
77	51228	10937	62396	81460	47331	91403	95007	06047	16846	64809
78	31089	37995	29577	07828	42272	54016	21950	86192	99046	84864
79	38207	97938	93459	75174	79460	55436	57206	87644	21296	43393
80	88666	31142	09474	89712	63153	62333	42212	06140	42594	43671
81	53365	56134	67582	92557	89520	33452	05134	70628	27612	33738
82	89807	74530	38004	90102	11693	90257	05500	79920	62700	43325
83	18682	81038	85662	90915	91631	22223	91588	80774	07716	12548
84	63571	32579	63942	25371	09234	94592	98475	76884	37635	33608
85	68927	56492	67799	95398	77642	54913	91583	08421	81450	76229
86	56401	63186	39389	88798	31356	89235	97036	32341	33292	73757
87	24333	95603	02359	72942	46287	95382	08452	62862	97869	71775
88	17025	84202	95199	62272	06366	16175	97577	99304	41587	03686
89	02804	08253	52133	20224	68034	50865	57868	22343	55111	03607
90	08298	03879	20995	19850	73090	13191	18963	82244	78479	99121
91	59883	01785	82403	96062	03785	03488	12970	64896	38336	30030
92	46982	06682	62864	91837	74021	89094	39952	64158	79614	78235
93	31121	47266	07661	02051	67599	24471	69843	83696	71402	76287
94	97867	56641	63416	17577	30161	87320	37752	73276	48969	41915
95	57364	86746	08415	14621	49430	22311	15836	72492	49372	44103
96	09559	26263	69511	28064	75999	44540	13337	10918	79846	54809
97	53873	55571	00608	42661	91332	63956	74087	59008	47493	99581
98	35531	19162	86406	05299	77511	24311	57257	22826	77555	05941
99	28229	88629	25694	94932	30721	16197	78742	34974	97528	45447

Table A.2
Squares and square roots

NUMBER	SQUARE	SQUARE ROOT	NUMBER	SQUARE	SQUARE ROOT
1	1	1.000	51	26 01	7.141
2	4	1.414	52	27 04	7.211
3	9	1.732	53	28 09	7.280
4	16	2.000	54	29 16	7.348
5	25	2.236	55	30 25	7.416
6	36	2.449	56	31 36	7.483
7	49	2.646	57	32 49	7.550
8	64	2.828	58	33 64	7.616
9	81	3.000	59	34 81	7.681
10	1 00	3.162	60	36 00	7.746
11	1 21	3.317	61	37 21	7.810
12	1 44	3.464	62	38 44	7.874
13	1 69	3.606	63	39 69	7.937
14	1 96	3.742	64	40 96	8.000
15	2 25	3.873	65	42 25	8.062
16	2 56	4.000	66	43 56	8.124
17	2 89	4.123	67	44 89	8.185
18	3 24	4.243	68	46 24	8.246
19	3 61	4.359	69	47 61	8.307
20	4 00	4.472	70	49 00	8.367
21	4 41	4.583	71	50 41	8.426
22	4 84	4.690	72	51 84	8.485
23	5 29	4.796	73	53 29	8.544
24	5 76	4.899	74	54 76	8.602
25	6 25	5.000	75	56 25	8.660
26	6 76	5.099	76	57 76	8.718
27	7 29	5.196	77	59 29	8.775
28	7 84	5.292	78	60 84	8.832
29	8 41	5.385	79	62 41	8.888
30	9 00	5.477	80	64 00	8.944
31	9 61	5.568	81	65 61	9.000
32	10 24	5.657	82	67 24	9.055
33	10 89	5.745	83	68 89	9.110
34	11 56	5.831	84	70 56	9.165
35	12 25	5.916	85	72 25	9.220
36	12 96	6.000	86	73 96	9.274
37	13 69	6.083	87	75 69	9.327
38	14 44	6.164	88	77 44	9.381
39	15 21	6.245	89	79 21	9.434
40	16 00	6.325	90	81 00	9.487
41	16 81	6.403	91	82 81	9.539
42	17 64	6.481	92	84 64	9.592
43	18 49	6.557	93	86 49	9.644
44	19 36	6.633	94	88 36	9.695
45	20 25	6.708	95	90 25	9.747
46	21 16	6.782	96	92 16	9.798
47	22 09	6.856	97	94 09	9.849
48	23 04	6.928	98	96 04	9.899
49	24 01	7.000	99	98 01	9.950
50	25 00	7.071	100	1 00 00	10.000

Reprinted from *Statistics for Students of Psychology and Education,* by Herbert Sorenson (New York: McGraw-Hill, 1936), by permission of the author.

Table A.2 (continued)

Number	Square	Square Root	Number	Square	Square Root
101	1 02 01	10.050	151	2 28 01	12.288
102	1 04 04	10.100	152	2 31 04	12.329
103	1 06 09	10.149	153	2 34 09	12.369
104	1 08 16	10.198	154	2 37 16	12.410
105	1 10 25	10.247	155	2 40 25	12.450
106	1 12 36	10.296	156	2 43 36	12.490
107	1 14 49	10.344	157	2 46 49	12.530
108	1 16 64	10.392	158	2 49 64	12.570
109	1 18 81	10.440	159	2 52 81	12.610
110	1 21 00	10.488	160	2 56 00	12.649
111	1 23 21	10.536	161	2 59 21	12.689
112	1 25 44	10.583	162	2 62 44	12.728
113	1 27 69	10.630	163	2 65 69	12.767
114	1 29 96	10.677	164	2 68 96	12.806
115	1 32 25	10.724	165	2 72 25	12.845
116	1 34 56	10.770	166	2 75 56	12.884
117	1 36 89	10.817	167	2 78 89	12.923
118	1 39 24	10.863	168	2 82 24	12.961
119	1 41 61	10.909	169	2 85 61	13.000
120	1 44 00	10.954	170	2 89 00	13.038
121	1 46 41	11.000	171	2 92 41	13.077
122	1 48 84	11.045	172	2 95 84	13.115
123	1 51 29	11.091	173	2 99 29	13.153
124	1 53 76	11.136	174	3 02 76	13.191
125	1 56 25	11.180	175	3 06 25	13.229
126	1 58 76	11.225	176	3 09 76	13.266
127	1 61 29	11.269	177	3 13 29	13.304
128	1 63 84	11.314	178	3 16 84	13.342
129	1 66 41	11.358	179	3 20 41	13.379
130	1 69 00	11.402	180	3 24 00	13.416
131	1 71 61	11.446	181	3 27 61	13.454
132	1 74 24	11.489	182	3 31 24	13.491
133	1 76 89	11.533	183	3 34 89	13.528
134	1 79 56	11.576	184	3 38 56	13.565
135	1 82 25	11.619	185	3 42 25	13.601
136	1 84 96	11.662	186	3 45 96	13.638
137	1 87 69	11.705	187	3 49 69	13.675
138	1 90 44	11.747	188	3 53 44	13.711
139	1 93 21	11.790	189	3 57 21	13.748
140	1 96 00	11.832	190	3 61 00	13.784
141	1 98 81	11.874	191	3 64 81	13.820
142	2 01 64	11.916	192	3 68 64	13.856
143	2 04 49	11.958	193	3 72 49	13.892
144	2 07 36	12.000	194	3 76 36	13.928
145	2 10 25	12.042	195	3 80 25	13.964
146	2 13 16	12.083	196	3 84 16	14.000
147	2 16 09	12.124	197	3 88 09	14.036
148	2 19 04	12.166	198	3 92 04	14.071
149	2 22 01	12.207	199	3 96 01	14.107
150	2 25 00	12.247	200	4 00 00	14.142

Table A.2 (continued)

Number	Square	Square Root	Number	Square	Square Root
201	4 04 01	14.177	251	6 30 01	15.843
202	4 08 04	14.213	252	6 35 04	15.875
203	4 12 09	14.248	253	6 40 09	15.906
204	4 16 16	14.283	554	6 45 16	15.937
205	4 20 25	14.318	255	6 50 25	15.969
206	4 24 36	14.353	256	6 55 36	16.000
207	4 28 49	14.387	257	6 60 49	16.031
208	4 32 64	14.422	258	6 65 64	16.062
209	4 36 81	14.457	259	6 70 81	16.093
210	4 41 00	14.491	260	6 76 00	16.125
211	4 45 21	14.526	261	6 81 21	16.155
212	4 49 44	14.560	262	6 86 44	16.186
213	4 53 69	14.595	263	6 91 69	16.217
214	4 57 96	14.629	264	6 96 96	16.248
215	4 62 25	14.663	265	7 02 25	16.279
216	4 66 56	14.697	266	7 07 56	16.310
217	4 70 89	14.731	267	7 12 89	16.340
218	4 75 24	14.765	268	7 18 24	16.371
219	4 79 61	14.799	269	7 23 61	16.401
220	4 84 00	14.832	270	7 29 00	16.432
221	4 88 41	14.866	271	7 34 41	16.462
222	4 92 84	14.900	272	7 39 84	16.492
223	4 97 29	14.933	273	7 45 29	16.523
224	5 01 76	14.967	274	7 50 76	16.553
225	5 06 25	15.000	275	7 56 25	16.583
226	5 10 76	15.033	276	7 61 76	16.613
227	5 15 29	15.067	277	7 67 29	16.643
228	5 19 84	15.100	278	7 72 84	16.673
229	5 24 41	15.133	279	7 78 41	16.703
230	5 29 00	15.166	280	7 84 00	16.733
231	5 33 61	15.199	281	7 89 61	16.763
232	5 38 24	15.232	282	7 95 24	16.793
233	5 42 89	15.264	283	8 00 89	16.823
234	5 47 56	15.297	284	8 06 56	16.852
235	5 52 25	15.330	285	8 12 25	16.882
236	5 56 96	15.362	286	8 17 96	16.912
237	5 61 69	15.395	287	8 23 69	16.941
238	5 66 44	15.427	288	8 29 44	16.971
239	5 71 21	15.460	289	8 35 21	17.000
240	5 76 00	15.492	290	8 41 00	17.029
241	5 80 81	15.524	291	8 46 81	17.059
242	5 85 64	15.556	292	8 52 64	17.088
243	5 90 49	15.588	293	8 58 49	17.117
244	5 95 36	15.620	294	8 64 36	17.146
245	6 00 25	15.652	295	8 70 25	17.176
246	6 05 16	15.684	296	8 76 16	17.205
247	6 10 09	15.716	297	8 82 09	17.234
248	6 15 04	15.748	298	8 88 04	17.263
249	6 20 01	15.780	299	8 94 01	17.292
250	6 25 00	15.811	300	9 00 00	17.321

Table A.2 (continued)

NUMBER	SQUARE	SQUARE ROOT	NUMBER	SQUARE	SQUARE ROOT
301	9 06 01	17.349	351	12 32 01	18.735
302	9 12 04	17.378	352	12 39 04	18.762
303	9 18 09	17.407	353	12 46 09	18.788
304	9 24 16	17.436	354	12 53 16	18.815
305	9 30 25	17.464	355	12 60 25	18.841
306	9 36 36	17.493	356	12 67 36	18.868
307	9 42 49	17.521	357	12 74 49	18.894
308	9 48 64	17.550	358	12 81 64	18.921
309	9 54 81	17.578	359	12 88 81	18.947
310	9 61 00	17.607	360	12 96 00	18.974
311	9 67 21	17.635	361	13 03 21	19.000
312	9 73 44	17.664	362	13 10 44	19.026
313	9 79 69	17.692	363	13 17 69	19.053
314	9 85 96	17.720	364	13 24 96	19.079
315	9 92 25	17.748	365	13 32 25	19.105
316	9 98 56	17.776	366	13 39 56	19.131
317	10 04 89	17.804	367	13 46 89	19.157
318	10 11 24	17.833	368	13 54 24	19.183
319	10 17 61	17.861	369	13 61 61	19.209
320	10 24 00	17.889	370	13 69 00	19.235
321	10 30 41	17.916	371	13 76 41	19.261
322	10 36 84	17.944	372	13 83 84	19.287
323	10 43 29	17.972	373	13 91 29	19.313
324	10 49 76	18.000	374	13 98 76	19.339
325	10 56 25	18.028	375	14 06 25	19.365
326	10 62 76	18.055	376	14 13 76	19.391
327	10 69 29	18.083	377	14 21 29	19.416
328	10 75 84	18.111	378	14 28 84	19.442
329	10 82 41	18.138	379	14 36 41	19.468
330	10 89 00	18.166	380	14 44 00	19.494
331	10 95 61	18.193	381	14 51 61	19.519
332	11 02 24	18.221	382	14 59 24	19.545
333	11 08 89	18.248	383	14 66 89	19.570
334	11 15 56	18.276	384	14 74 56	19.596
335	11 22 25	18.303	385	14 82 25	19.621
336	11 28 96	18.330	386	14 89 96	19.647
337	11 35 69	18.358	387	14 97 69	19.672
338	11 42 44	18.385	388	15 05 44	19.698
339	11 49 21	18.412	389	15 13 21	19.723
340	11 56 00	18.439	390	15 21 00	19.748
341	11 62 81	18.466	391	15 28 81	19.774
342	11 69 64	18.493	392	15 36 64	19.799
343	11 76 49	18.520	393	15 44 49	19.824
344	11 83 36	18.547	394	15 52 36	19.849
345	11 90 25	18.574	395	15 60 25	19.875
346	11 97 16	18.601	396	15 68 16	19.900
347	12 04 09	18.628	397	15 76 09	19.925
348	12 11 04	18.655	398	15 84 04	19.950
349	12 18 01	18.682	399	15 92 01	19.975
350	12 25 00	18.708	400	16 00 00	20.000

Table A.2 (continued)

NUMBER	SQUARE	SQUARE ROOT	NUMBER	SQUARE	SQUARE ROOT
401	16 08 01	20.025	451	20 34 01	21.237
402	16 16 04	20.050	452	20 43 04	21.260
403	16 24 09	20.075	453	20 52 09	21.284
404	16 32 16	20.100	454	20 61 16	21.307
405	16 40 25	20.125	455	20 70 25	21.331
406	16 48 36	20.149	456	20 79 36	21.354
407	16 56 49	20.174	457	20 88 49	21.378
408	16 64 64	20.199	458	20 97 64	21.401
409	16 72 81	20.224	459	21 06 81	21.424
410	16 81 00	20.248	460	21 16 00	21.448
411	16 89 21	20.273	461	21 25 21	21.471
412	16 97 44	20.298	462	21 34 44	21.494
413	17 05 69	20.322	463	21 43 69	21.517
414	17 13 96	20.347	464	21 52 96	21.541
415	17 22 25	20.372	465	21 62 25	21.564
416	17 30 56	20.396	466	21 71 56	21.587
417	17 38 89	20.421	467	21 80 89	21.610
418	17 47 24	20.445	468	21 90 24	21.633
419	17 55 61	20.469	469	21 99 61	21.656
420	17 64 00	20.494	470	22 09 00	21.679
421	17 72 41	20.518	471	22 18 41	21.703
422	17 80 84	20.543	472	22 27 84	21.726
423	17 89 29	20.567	473	22 37 29	21.749
424	17 97 76	20.591	474	22 46 76	21.772
425	18 06 25	20.616	475	22 56 25	21.794
426	18 14 76	20.640	476	22 65 76	21.817
427	18 23 29	20.664	477	22 75 29	21.840
428	18 31 84	20.688	478	22 84 84	21.863
429	18 40 41	20.712	479	22 94 41	21.886
430	18 49 00	20.736	480	23 04 00	21.909
431	18 57 61	20.761	481	23 13 61	21.932
432	18 66 24	20.785	482	23 23 24	21.954
433	18 74 89	20.809	483	23 32 89	21.977
434	18 83 56	20.833	484	23 42 56	22.000
435	18 92 25	20.857	485	23 52 25	22.023
436	19 00 96	20.881	486	23 61 96	22.045
437	19 09 69	20.905	487	23 71 69	22.068
438	19 18 44	20.928	488	23 81 44	22.091
439	19 27 21	20.952	489	23 91 21	22.113
440	19 36 00	20.976	490	24 01 00	22.136
441	19 44 81	21.000	491	24 10 81	22.159
442	19 53 64	21.024	492	24 20 64	22.181
443	19 62 49	21.048	493	24 30 49	22.204
444	19 71 36	21.071	494	24 40 36	22.226
445	19 80 25	21.095	495	24 50 25	22.249
446	19 89 16	21.119	496	24 60 16	22.271
447	19 98 09	21.142	497	24 70 09	22.293
448	20 07 04	21.166	498	24 80 04	22.316
449	20 16 01	21.190	499	24 90 01	22.338
450	20 25 00	21.213	500	25 00 00	22.361

Table A.2 (continued)

Number	Square	Square Root	Number	Square	Square Root
501	25 10 01	22.383	551	30 36 01	23.473
502	25 20 04	22.405	552	30 47 04	23.495
503	25 30 09	22.428	553	30 58 09	23.516
504	25 40 16	22.450	554	30 69 16	23.537
505	25 50 25	22.472	555	30 80 25	23.558
506	25 60 36	22.494	556	30 91 36	23.580
507	25 70 49	22.517	557	31 02 49	23.601
508	25 80 64	22.539	558	31 13 64	23.622
509	25 90 81	22.561	559	31 24 81	23.643
510	26 01 00	22.583	560	31 36 00	23.664
511	26 11 21	22.605	561	31 47 21	23.685
512	26 21 44	22.627	562	31 58 44	23.707
513	26 31 69	22.650	563	31 69 69	23.728
514	26 41 96	22.672	564	31 80 96	23.749
515	26 52 25	22.694	565	31 92 25	23.770
516	26 62 56	22.716	566	32 03 56	23.791
517	26 72 89	22.738	567	32 14 89	23.812
518	26 83 24	22.760	568	32 26 24	23.833
519	26 93 61	22.782	569	32 37 61	23.854
520	27 04 00	22.804	570	32 49 00	23.875
521	27 14 41	22.825	571	32 60 41	23.896
522	27 24 84	22.847	572	32 71 84	23.917
523	27 35 29	22.869	573	32 83 29	23.937
524	27 45 76	22.891	574	32 94 76	23.958
525	27 56 25	22.913	575	33 06 25	23.979
526	27 66 76	22.935	576	33 17 76	24.000
527	27 77 29	22.956	577	33 29 29	24.021
528	27 87 84	22.978	578	33 40 84	24.042
529	27 98 41	23.000	579	33 52 41	24.062
530	28 09 00	23.022	580	33 64 00	24.083
531	28 19 61	23.043	581	33 75 61	24.104
532	28 30 24	23.065	582	33 87 24	24.125
533	28 40 89	23.087	583	33 98 89	24.145
534	28 51 56	23.108	584	34 10 56	24.166
535	28 62 25	23.130	585	34 22 25	24.187
536	28 72 96	23.152	586	34 33 96	24.207
537	28 83 69	23.173	587	34 45 69	24.228
538	28 94 44	23.195	588	34 57 44	24.249
539	29 05 21	23.216	589	34 69 21	24.269
540	29 16 00	23.238	590	34 81 00	24.290
541	29 26 81	23.259	591	34 92 81	24.310
542	29 37 64	23.281	592	35 04 64	24.331
543	29 48 49	23.302	593	35 16 49	24.352
544	29 59 36	23.324	594	35 28 36	24.372
545	29 70 25	23.345	595	35 40 25	24.393
546	29 81 16	23.367	596	35 52 16	24.413
547	29 92 09	23.388	597	35 64 09	24.434
548	30 03 04	23.409	598	35 76 04	24.454
549	30 14 01	23.431	599	35 88 01	24.474
550	30 25 00	23.452	600	36 00 00	24.495

Table A.2 (continued)

Number	Square	Square Root	Number	Square	Square Root
601	36 12 01	24.515	651	42 38 01	25.515
602	36 24 04	24.536	652	42 51 04	25.534
603	36 36 09	24.556	653	42 64 09	25.554
604	36 48 16	24.576	654	42 77 16	25.573
605	36 60 25	24.597	655	42 90 25	25.593
606	36 72 36	24.617	656	43 03 36	25.612
607	36 84 49	24.637	657	43 16 49	25.632
608	36 96 64	24.658	658	43 29 64	25.652
609	37 08 81	24.678	659	43 42 81	25.671
610	37 21 00	24.698	660	43 56 00	25.690
611	37 33 21	24.718	661	43 69 21	25.710
612	37 45 44	24.739	662	43 82 44	25.729
613	37 57 69	24.759	663	43 95 69	25.749
614	37 69 96	24.779	664	44 08 96	25.768
615	37 82 25	24.799	665	44 22 25	25.788
616	37 94 56	24.819	666	44 35 56	25.807
617	38 06 89	24.839	667	44 48 89	25.826
618	38 19 24	24.860	668	44 62 24	25.846
619	38 31 61	24.880	669	44 75 61	25.865
620	38 44 00	24.900	670	44 89 00	25.884
621	38 56 41	24.920	671	45 02 41	25.904
622	38 68 84	24.940	672	45 15 84	25.923
623	38 81 29	24.960	673	45 29 29	25.942
624	38 93 76	24.980	674	45 42 76	25.962
625	39 06 25	25.000	675	45 56 25	25.981
626	39 18 76	25.020	676	45 69 76	26.000
627	39 31 29	25.040	677	45 83 29	26.019
628	39 43 84	25.060	678	45 96 84	26.038
629	39 56 41	25.080	679	46 10 41	26.058
630	39 69 00	25.100	680	46 24 00	26.077
631	39 81 61	25.120	681	46 37 61	26.096
632	39 94 24	25.140	682	46 51 24	26.115
633	40 06 89	25.159	683	46 64 89	26.134
634	40 19 56	25.179	684	46 78 56	26.153
635	40 32 25	25.199	685	46 92 25	26.173
636	40 44 96	25.219	686	47 05 96	26.192
637	40 57 69	25.239	687	47 19 69	26.211
638	40 70 44	25.259	688	47 33 44	26.230
639	40 83 21	25.278	689	47 47 21	26.249
640	40 96 00	25.298	690	47 61 00	26.268
641	41 08 81	25.318	691	47 74 81	26.287
642	41 21 64	25.338	692	47 88 64	26.306
643	41 34 49	25.357	693	48 02 49	26.325
644	41 47 36	25.377	694	48 16 36	26.344
645	41 60 25	25.397	695	48 30 25	26.363
646	41 73 16	25.417	696	48 44 16	26.382
647	41 86 09	25.436	697	48 58 09	26.401
648	41 99 04	25.456	698	48 72 04	26.420
649	42 12 01	25.475	699	48 86 01	26.439
650	42 25 00	25.495	700	49 00 00	26.458

Table A.2 (continued)

Number	Square	Square Root	Number	Square	Square Root
701	49 14 01	26.476	751	56 40 01	27.404
702	49 28 04	26.495	752	56 55 04	27.423
703	49 42 09	26.514	753	56 70 09	27.441
704	49 56 16	26.533	754	56 85 16	27.459
705	49 70 25	26.552	755	57 00 25	27.477
706	49 84 36	26.571	756	57 15 36	27.495
707	49 98 49	26.589	757	57 30 49	27.514
708	50 12 64	26.608	758	57 45 64	27.532
709	50 26 81	26.627	759	57 60 81	27.550
710	50 41 00	26.646	760	57 76 00	27.568
711	50 55 21	26.665	761	57 91 21	27.586
712	50 69 44	26.683	762	58 06 44	27.604
713	50 83 69	26.702	763	58 21 69	27.622
714	50 97 96	26.721	764	58 36 96	27.641
715	51 12 25	26.739	765	58 52 25	27.659
716	51 26 56	26.758	766	58 67 56	27.677
717	51 40 89	26.777	767	58 82 89	27.695
718	51 55 24	26.796	768	58 98 24	27.713
719	51 69 61	26.814	769	59 13 61	27.731
720	51 84 00	26.833	770	59 29 00	27.749
721	51 98 41	26.851	771	59 44 41	27.767
722	52 12 84	26.870	772	59 59 84	27.785
723	52 27 29	26.889	773	59 75 29	27.803
724	52 41 76	26.907	774	59 90 76	27.821
725	52 56 25	26.926	775	60 06 25	27.839
726	52 70 76	26.944	776	60 21 76	27.857
727	52 85 29	26.963	777	60 37 29	27.875
728	52 99 84	26.981	778	60 52 84	27.893
729	53 14 41	27.000	779	60 68 41	27.911
730	53 29 00	27.019	780	60 84 00	27.928
731	53 43 61	27.037	781	60 99 61	27.946
732	53 58 24	27.055	782	61 15 24	27.964
733	53 72 89	27.074	783	61 30 89	27.982
734	53 87 56	27.092	784	61 46 56	28.000
735	54 02 25	27.111	785	61 62 25	28.018
736	54 16 96	27.129	786	61 77 96	28.036
737	54 31 69	27.148	787	61 93 69	28.054
738	54 46 14	27.166	788	62 09 44	28.071
739	54 61 21	27.185	789	62 25 21	28.089
740	54 76 00	27.203	790	62 41 00	28.107
741	54 90 81	27.221	791	62 56 81	28.125
742	55 05 64	27.240	792	62 72 64	28.142
743	55 20 49	27.258	793	62 88 49	28.160
744	55 35 36	27.276	794	63 04 36	28.178
745	55 50 25	27.295	795	63 20 25	28.196
746	55 65 16	27.313	796	63 36 16	28.213
747	55 80 09	27.331	797	63 52 09	28.231
748	55 95 04	27.350	798	63 68 04	28.249
749	56 10 01	27.368	799	73 84 01	28.267
750	56 25 00	27.386	800	64 00 00	28.284

Table A.2 (continued)

Number	Square	Square Root	Number	Square	Square Root
801	64 16 01	28.302	851	72 42 01	29.172
802	64 32 04	28.320	852	72 59 04	29.189
803	64 48 09	28.337	853	72 76 09	29.206
804	64 64 16	28.355	854	72 93 16	29.223
805	64 80 25	28.373	855	73 10 25	29.240
806	64 96 36	28.390	856	73 27 36	29.257
807	65 12 49	28.408	857	73 44 49	29.275
808	65 28 64	28.425	858	73 61 64	29.292
809	65 44 81	28.443	859	73 78 81	29.309
810	65 61 00	28.460	860	73 96 00	29.326
811	65 77 21	28.478	861	74 13 21	29.343
812	65 93 44	28.496	862	74 30 44	29.360
813	66 09 69	28.513	863	74 47 69	29.377
814	66 25 96	28.531	864	74 64 96	29.394
815	66 42 25	28.548	865	74 82 25	29.411
816	66 58 56	28.566	866	74 99 56	29.428
817	66 74 89	28.583	867	75 16 89	29.445
818	66 91 24	28.601	868	75 34 24	29.462
819	67 07 61	28.618	869	75 51 61	29.479
820	67 24 00	28.636	870	75 69 00	29.496
821	67 40 41	28.653	871	75 86 41	29.513
822	67 56 84	28.671	872	76 03 84	29.530
823	67 73 29	28.688	873	76 21 29	29.547
824	67 89 76	28.705	874	76 38 76	29.563
825	68 06 25	28.723	875	76 56 25	29.580
826	68 22 76	28.740	876	76 73 76	29.597
827	68 39 29	28.758	877	76 91 29	29.614
828	68 55 84	28.775	878	77 08 84	29.631
829	68 72 41	28.792	879	77 26 41	29.648
830	68 89 00	28.810	880	77 44 00	29.665
831	69 05 61	28.827	881	77 61 61	29.682
832	69 22 24	28.844	882	77 79 24	29.698
833	69 38 89	28.862	883	77 96 89	29.715
834	69 55 56	28.879	884	78 14 56	29.732
835	69 72 25	28.896	885	78 32 25	29.749
836	69 88 96	28.914	886	78 49 96	29.766
837	70 05 69	28.931	887	78 67 69	29.783
838	70 22 44	28.948	888	78 85 44	29.799
839	70 39 21	28.965	889	79 03 21	29.816
840	70 56 00	28.983	890	79 21 00	29.833
841	70 72 81	29.000	891	79 38 81	29.850
842	70 89 64	29.017	892	79 56 64	29.866
843	71 06 49	29.034	893	79 74 49	29.883
844	71 23 36	29.052	894	79 92 36	29.900
845	71 40 25	29.069	895	80 10 25	29.917
846	71 57 16	29.086	896	80 28 16	29.933
847	71 74 09	29.103	897	80 46 09	29.950
848	71 91 04	29.120	898	80 64 04	29.967
849	72 08 01	29.138	899	80 82 01	29.983
850	72 25 00	29.155	900	81 00 00	30.000

Table A.2 (continued)

Number	Square	Square Root	Number	Square	Square Root
901	81 18 01	30.017	951	90 44 01	30.838
902	81 36 04	30.033	952	90 63 04	30.854
903	81 54 09	30.050	953	90 82 09	30.871
904	81 72 16	30.067	954	91 01 16	30.887
905	81 90 25	30.083	955	91 20 25	30.903
906	82 08 36	30.100	956	91 39 36	30.919
907	82 26 49	30.116	957	91 58 49	30.935
908	82 44 64	30.133	958	91 77 64	30.952
909	82 62 81	30.150	959	91 96 81	30.968
910	82 81 00	30.166	960	92 16 00	30.984
911	82 99 21	30.183	961	92 35 21	31.000
912	83 17 44	30.199	962	92 54 44	31.016
913	83 35 69	30.216	963	92 73 69	31.032
914	83 53 96	30.232	964	92 92 96	31.048
915	83 72 25	30.249	965	93 12 25	31.064
916	83 90 56	30.265	966	93 31 56	31.081
917	84 08 89	30.282	967	93 50 89	31.097
918	84 27 24	30.299	968	93 70 24	31.113
919	84 45 61	30.315	969	93 89 61	31.129
920	84 64 00	30.332	970	94 09 00	31.145
921	84 82 41	30.348	971	94 28 41	31.161
922	85 00 84	30.364	972	94 47 84	31.177
923	85 19 29	30.381	973	94 67 29	31.193
924	85 37 76	30.397	974	94 86 76	31.209
925	85 56 25	30.414	975	95 06 25	31.225
926	85 74 76	30.430	976	95 25 76	31.241
927	85 93 29	30.447	977	95 45 29	31.257
928	86 11 84	30.463	978	95 64 84	31.273
929	86 30 41	30.480	979	95 84 41	31.289
930	86 49 00	30.496	980	96 04 00	31.305
931	86 67 61	30.512	981	96 23 61	31.321
932	86 86 24	30.529	982	96 43 24	31.337
933	87 04 89	30.545	983	96 62 89	31.353
934	87 23 56	30.561	984	96 82 56	31.369
935	87 42 25	30.578	985	97 02 25	31.385
936	87 60 96	30.594	986	97 21 96	31.401
937	87 79 69	30.610	987	97 41 69	31.417
938	87 98 44	30.627	988	97 61 44	31.432
939	88 17 21	30.643	989	97 81 21	31.448
940	88 36 00	30.659	990	98 01 00	31.464
941	88 54 81	30.676	991	98 20 81	31.480
942	88 73 64	30.692	992	98 40 64	31.496
943	88 92 49	30.708	993	98 60 49	31.512
944	89 11 36	30.725	994	98 80 36	31.528
945	89 30 25	30.741	995	99 00 25	31.544
946	89 49 16	30.757	996	99 20 16	31.559
947	89 68 09	30.773	997	99 40 09	31.575
948	89 87 04	30.790	998	99 60 04	31.591
949	90 06 01	30.806	999	99 80 01	31.607
950	90 25 00	30.822	1000	100 00 00	31.623

Table A.3

Values of the correlation coefficient for different levels
of significance (p)

df	p			
	.10	.05	.01	.001
1	.98769	.99692	.99988	.99999
2	.90000	.95000	.99000	.99900
3	.8054	.8783	.95873	.99116
4	.7293	.8114	.91720	.97406
5	.6694	.7545	.8745	.95074
6	.6215	.7067	.8343	.92493
7	.5822	.6664	.7977	.8982
8	.5494	.6319	.7646	.8721
9	.5214	.6021	.7348	.8471
10	.4973	.5760	.7079	.8233
11	.4762	.5529	.6835	.8010
12	.4575	.5324	.6614	.7800
13	.4409	.5139	.6411	.7603
14	.4259	.4973	.6226	.7420
15	.4124	.4821	.6055	.7246
16	.4000	.4683	.5897	.7084
17	.3887	.4555	.5751	.6932
18	.3783	.4438	.5614	.6787
19	.3687	.4329	.5487	.6652
20	.3598	.4227	.5368	.6524
25	.3233	.3809	.4869	.5974
30	.2960	.3494	.4487	.5541
35	.2746	.3246	.4182	.5189
40	.2573	.3044	.3932	.4896
45	.2428	.2875	.3721	.4648
50	.2306	.2732	.3541	.4433
60	.2108	.2500	.3248	.4078
70	.1954	.2319	.3017	.3799
80	.1829	.2172	.2830	.3568
90	.1726	.2050	.2673	.3375
100	.1638	.1946	.2540	.3211

Table A.3 is taken from Table VII of Fisher and Yates: *Statistical Tables for Biological, Agricultural and Medical Research,* published by Longman Group Ltd., London (previously published by Oliver and Boyd, Edinburgh), and by permission of the authors and publishers.

Author index

Subject Index